RENOVATION 3RD EDITION

RENOVATION 3RD EDITION

Michael W. Litchfield

Chip Harley, Technical Editor

The Taunton Press

The Taunton Press
Inspiration for hands-on living®

The Taunton Press, Inc., 63 South Main Street, PO Box 5506, Newtown, CT 06470-5506

e-mail: tp@taunton.com

Editor:	Neil Soderstrom
Technical editor:	Chip Harley
Jacket/Cover design:	Alexander Isley, Inc.
Interior design:	Carol Petro
Layout:	Carol Petro
Illustrator:	Vincent Babak
Photographers:	Michael W. Litchfield and Ken Gutmaker, except where noted
Cover Photographer:	Randy O'Rourke

Library of Congress Cataloging-in-Publication Data

Litchfield, Michael W.
    Renovation / Michael Litchfield ; Chip Harley, technical editor.-- 3rd ed., completely rev. and updated.
        p. cm.
    ISBN-13: 978-1-56158-588-5
    ISBN-10: 1-56158-588-2
    1. Dwellings--Remodeling. 2. Dwellings--Conservation and restoration. 3. Dwellings--Maintenance and repair. I. Title.
    TH4816.L57 2005
    643'.7--dc22
                            2005000110
Printed in the United States of America
10 9 8 7 6 5 4 3 2

"Many hands make work light."

This book is dedicated to the many
hands that helped mine.

Acknowledgments

I MUST BE ONE OF THE LUCKIEST PEOPLE ON EARTH. In the course of writing seven books on building and having the privilege of launching *Fine Homebuilding* magazine, I've visited hundreds and hundreds of building sites around North America. And on every site, I've learned something interesting or met people who, busy though they were, were willing to take time to explain what they were doing, answer my questions, and allow me to photograph them at work. Granted, I waited till the saws stopped whining or the torches were shut off. And I stood some folks lunch. But good timing and turkey sandwiches don't begin to explain my good luck. A more likely explanation is that most people are generous souls and take pride in what they do. Their generosity made this big, complicated book possible, so I have a lot of people to thank.

Glenn Jarvis, John Larson and their colleagues at Glenn Jarvis Associates gave me entrée to jobs, contacts, and clients in the earliest days of this book. Sandor Nagyszalanczy, Scott Fitzgerrell, Tom Andreoni, Bill Jetton, Keir Lenihan, Bill Hinkamp, David Peterson, Barry Schultz, Gary Earl Parsons, Peter Singelstadt, and Ken Holland also opened many doors for me. Thanks to Julie and Roland Weinstein. Bernard and Valery Sadoulet. Thanks to my friend Rob Thallon for his inspiring designs and thoughtful books. Thanks, Paddy Morrissey. And heartfelt thanks to George and Sally Kiskaddon of Builders Booksource, who have championed all three editions of *Renovation*.

These people contributed significantly to individual chapters: **Inspecting a House:** Roger Robinson of the Star Inspection Group, my partner on *HouseCheck: Finding and Fixing Common House Problems* (Taunton Press), let me cherry-pick his extensive photo collection once again. **Planning:** Stephen Rynerson extensively renovated this chapter, and he and his wife, Juanita, allowed photos in their home. And thanks to Dean and Martha (Marty) Rutherford for repainting the downstairs in time. **Tools and Building Materials:** Thanks to Dave Yungert at Truitt & White Lumber for loaning many of the new tools shown here and for allowing me to roam the lumberyard, snapping pix. **Roofs:** John Dalzell of Westco Roofing shared his extensive knowledge of roofing and human nature, roofside and elsewhere; also helpful were Steve Roland, Brian Wade, Brian Billock. **Doors, Windows, and Skylights:** Addison Thomas shared his old-school ways of installing doors and windows.

The chapter also shows the solid craft of Jesus Beltran, Augustin Cerda, Leo Garcia, Carlos Martinez, Juan Escobar, Roberto Martinez, and Daniel Garcia. And Gary Schroeder is at the top of his game in the book's skylight installation. **Exteriors:** Les Williams, an artist with copper, is shown installing solid copper gutters; Oliver Govers answered a steady stream of questions without missing a shingle. Thanks, too, to Patrick Griffin, Ray Costello, and Grateful Gutters. **Structural Carpentry:** Doug Carver; Chuck Plitsch; John Michael Davis; and thanks again to Jesus, Augustin, and the rest of the Holland & Harley crew. **Masonry:** Sally McKnight and Enzo Palaco of Irish Sweep repaired chimneys high and low; Robert Darley is the skilled mason of the whimsical wall. **Foundations and Concrete:** Special thanks to Mike Massoumi for explaining foundation fine points. **Electrical Wiring:** Four electricians contributed to this important chapter: Rafael Maldonado and Douglas Hanson fielded scores of questions; Redwood Kardon gave it the most rigorous reading I've ever encountered; Kevin McCarthy allowed me to photograph his jobs for roughly a year; thanks also to Mike Zelinka of Laner Electric. Special thanks to Elliot Josephson. **Plumbing:** Marc Brenner reviewed the chapter and even allowed me to call him on site (!) whenever I needed; Albert Nahman graciously made his crews available to me. Old neighbor and good friend Ron Kyle of Moran Plumbing Supply loaned me a small truckload of tools and fittings; and Leigh Marymor lent a hand once again. **Kitchens and Baths:** Architect John Malick, whose handsome kitchen opens the chapter, has been a fountain of contacts and sparkling wit since Day One; thanks, too, to his wife, Susan; Tom Sullivan and James Guido of Sullivan Countertops; Les Baker of Baker Granite & Marble; Steve Kirby and Ben Johnson patiently explained the fine points of installing cabinets. And big thanks to David Edrington for sharing a cozy Oregon kitchen. **Energy Conservation and Air Quality:** Jim Dulley; Joel Janeiro and Coleman Munch of Ceridono Heating & Cooling; All-Seasons Insulation; Synergy Environmental; special thanks to Kevin Ramirez and Scott Anderson of the Insulation Works. **Finish Surfaces:** John Gullak, Robert Horton, Shane Reynolds, and Armando Marquez. **Tiling:** Tiling had a star-studded cast: Nick Razzo, Dan Blume, Wayne Brasher, Anthony Sueuga, and Jessica Remkiewicz. And especially Riley Doty—a genius if ever I've met one and a generous source of leads and ingenious solutions.

Finish Carpentry: It would take a chapter to thank restoration carpenter Jim Spaulding for all his help; Thomas Clark's capable hands are busy throughout this book; thanks to Randall Evans, and to Mike McClintock for lightening my load during a particularly exhausting stretch of road. Thanks also to Marvin Escobar, Carlos Gomez, and Jose Cervacio. **Painting:** Though I hit Greg Scillitani with scores of questions, I didn't scratch the surface of his knowledge; Bruce Nelson and Dean Pearson showed incredible sophistication in mixing colors and restoring woodwork; and thanks to Paul D'Orleans for sharing his craft. **Wallpapering:** Peter Bridgman is widely considered the finest installer of wall coverings in the San Francisco area, and he introduced me to craftspeople and to a level of craft I couldn't imagine. Thanks also to his associate, Steffen Richards; and to Kasey Lippi of Paper Dolls. **Flooring:** Janka White and Julie Jacobson of Floor Dimensions gave me free run of their showroom and access to two capable artisans, Mark Clarine and Jeff Molina, shown installing resilient flooring and carpeting, respectively. Thanks to Or Dobrin and Amber Flooring for the refinishing sequence; and to Russell Smith of Floor Show.

Thanks to the many gifted people at The Taunton Press who supplied leads, answered questions, or will—in the course of things—help make this book a reality. At *Fine Homebuilding*, Kevin Ireton, Chuck Miller, Roe Osborn, Tom O'Brien, Charles Bickford, Mike Guertin, and others whose insights or photos I drew on. Thanks to Tim Hupfer for posing in a freezing house for the cover shot. On the book side, thanks to Carolyn Mandarano, Paula Schlosser, Wendi Mijal, Carol Petro, Kathleen Williams, Candace Levy; and to Jennifer Peters, who moved a mountain of pages and photos, and attended to a million and one requests—and slightly fewer complaints—capably and equably. A huge thanks to Vincent Babak for his excellent illustrations. Finally, thanks to Executive Editor Helen Albert, whose hand on the tiller brought this great ship safely to port.

And so to the last lap: Dean Rutherford is an encyclopedia on construction, a master tiler, a builder of bridges, and a huge soul. He and his wife, Marty, will always have a room in my heart. Chip Harley, my technical editor, may be the calmest contractor I know. Countless times, I could hear subs or saws screaming in the background, yet he always answered my questions calmly and concisely. And after 12-hour days, he somehow found the energy to read this manuscript. I couldn't have done it without him. I could say the same of manuscript editor Neil Soderstrom, whose steady hand, wit, and good sense got me to the summit of Everest and safely back. He is a true friend. Finally, much love and thanks to Judith, Chloe, and Tyler, who gave me the space, support, and love I needed to complete so long and difficult a journey.

—Mike Litchfield
Berkeley, California

And thanks to Allyson, Veronica and Lucia; Victor Argueta, Francisco Barrera, David Bass, Michele Bender, Butch Bernhardt, Eric Brasher, Blair Buchanan, Richard Cano, Ricardo Carreño, Norberto Coronado, Carol & Bill Cathell, Arleta Chang , Michael Clawson, Tim Cisneros, Oden Connolly, Thomas Conover, Mercedes Corbel, Martin Coyle, Todd Dado, Leonard Davis, Mark Doss, Jay Duffy, Sven Eberlein, Roy Ellis, Mike Emerson, Victor Estrada, Craig Falchi, Seth Fitzgibbon, Barry Foster, Scott Gamble, Brian Garrett, John Gill, Vic Goeriz, Miguel Gomez, Carlos Gonzalez, Jorge Gonzalez, José Gonzalez, Andrew Hamilton, Jose Hassett, Will Hasson, Rosmarie Hausherr, Taz Haynes, John Herbert, Mario Hernandez, Rafael Hernandez, Raul Hernandez, Greg Hester, Arielle Hoffman, Terry Holland, Greg Hopkins, Ken Hoyer, Sam Hoyer, Men Huynhn, Maryann Hymer, Patrick Jacla, Bob Jones, Gabriel Kalmon, Deborah Kay, John Lancaster, Natalie Langdon, Eric Lau, Richard Lear, Zack Lodato, Brian Lucchesi, Ron Lugton, Jacob Lyman, Rich Maltsberger, Richard Martinez, Joe McFadden, Roger Murray, Jose Najera, Ronald Nattress, Katherine Newcomb, Henry Nguyen, Ken O'Brien, José Olivares, Byron Osinko, Sergio Perez, Karen and Tenold Peterson, William Peterson, Tim Pfalzer, Robin Pennell, Scott Rector, Natalie Rejefsk, Hipolito Robles, Javier Ronguillo, Michael Rubovits, Gabriel Saloma, Javier Sanchez, Joe Scollard, Dena Sicard, David Silverstein, Tim Smith, Daniel Soares, Cuauhtemoc Torres, Jorge Unefro, Alberto Urino, Carolyn Van Lang, Jacques Watteyne, Steven West, Gary Whitehead, Paul and Nina Winans, Ken Winfield, Marcie Zellner.

Introduction

I HAVE BEEN WRITING AND UPDATING one edition or another of this book for nearly three decades. I started the first edition in 1978, when Jimmy Carter was president and most computers were the size of closets. Since publication of the second edition in 1990, building materials and tools have changed so dramatically that I decided to rewrite the book completely this time around, adding new chapters. All told, *Renovation* represents thousands of conversations with carpenters, electricians, engineers, plumbers, painters, masons, architects, and other building professionals. And its nearly 700 new photos were winnowed from more than 9,000 shots taken on job sites across North America.

That last point—"on job sites"—is what distinguishes this book and is what should prove most useful to you when you're in the thick of your renovation: It tells which sawblade to use. What nail size and spacing. When to tear out and when to make do. How to lay out and prep a job so it goes smoothly. Because this book contains thousands of tips and techniques from contractors who had schedules and budgets to meet, it will also save you time and money. In other words, the methods in this book have proven themselves. So, supported with lifetimes of practical experience, you can proceed confidently.

This book is as much concerned with *what* and *why* as it is with *how to*. Thus, for every topic—from foundations to finish flooring—you'll find the tools and materials you'll need, the problems you may encounter, and workable solutions to see you through. Because the information in each chapter follows the sequence of an actual renovation, you'll know what to anticipate at every stage. Equally important, *R 3*'s often-ingenious solutions will help you deal with the unexpected situations that are a part of every renovation.

PLAY IT Safe

Please heed all safety warnings: They are there for your protection. The publisher and I have made every effort to describe safe construction procedures in a clear and straightforward manner. But because of the differences in skill and experience of each reader and because of variations in materials, site conditions and the like, neither I nor the publisher can assume responsibility for results with particular projects.

How to Use This Book

Read the opening remarks in a chapter before reviewing guidance for specific tasks. That is, each chapter's information tends to be somewhat cumulative. The first few paragraphs often introduce vital terms and concepts. Thereafter, you'll find tools and techniques presented more or less chronologically, in the manner you'd need them in a renovation.

Although new terms are defined early in each chapter and later in context, you may come across terms whose definitions you skipped over earlier. If you need a definition, consult the glossary or the index.

An in-depth review of tools and materials is beyond the scope of this book. If you want more information on either, consider browsing the Web. Although I do mention specific brand names and occasional Internet addresses, please consider them reference points for research and not product endorsements. Most of the brand names are those I encountered on job sites or were praised by a builder whose opinions I value.

Maybe it's always been so, but research has become a big part of renovation. So supplement your reading and Web searches by talking to neighbors, local contractors, and building-material suppliers. Experience is always the best teacher—even if it's someone else's experience. A friend or neighbor who's been through a renovation may be able to recommend reliable builders and suppliers and may also be a calm voice when you need one most. So go to it. As Aristotle once said (though not to me directly), "Courage is first among human virtues, for without it, we're unlikely to practice many of the others."

Table of Contents

1 Inspecting a House

With a little practice, you can train your eye to see both a house's potential and its pitfalls.

Every house has stories to tell. If you know where to look, you can see how skillfully the house was built or remodeled, how well it has weathered the elements, and how carefully the owners took care of it.

This chapter explains how to read a house's history from sometimes subtle symptoms and then systematically figure out what caused them. So when inspecting houses, you need to observe closely and search for patterns, whether you're a homeowner, a house shopper, or a renovation contractor.

▶ **Inspecting your own home, you may be surprised to discover how many areas need attention, whether for safety, repair, updating, appearance, or preventive maintenance. Thus this inspection may guide your renovation.**

▶ **If you're house shopping, your inspection may reveal conditions bad enough to dissuade you from buying. Or, if you decide to buy, those problems may give you leverage when negotiating price. Remember, most aspects of purchase agreements are negotiable.**

▶ **If you're a remodeling contractor, this chapter will likely prove helpful in assessing systems you may be less familiar with, and subsequent chapters will specify techniques and materials that can make your renovation projects more time and cost effective.**

Finally, think of this chapter as gateway to solutions throughout the book. Consequently, many of the house problems in this chapter are followed by page numbers or chapter numbers that direct you to further explanations or possible solutions. *Note:* Within this chapter and others, if you don't find specific cross-references to topics you'd like to learn more about, consult the book's index.

TRAINING YOUR EYE

The house shown on the facing page says much to a trained eye. Though nicely crafted, it's showing its age. Despite the gleaming paint on the parts that can be easily reached, this house's upper floors haven't been painted in 20 years or 30 years, suggesting that the parts you can't see probably weren't maintained either. The fretwork above the porch is splintering, and the green shingle demi-roof over the living room window has worn through to the wood shingles underneath. Chances are this small roof isn't flashed where it abuts the siding, so water may have gotten behind and soaked the framing.

Still, it's a charmer, and it's got great bones. Skilled carpenters were needed to frame such a complex roof, so there's probably good workmanship throughout the house, which is old enough that its 2×4s are probably full-size 2×4s. The walls are plumb; the roof ridge doesn't sag; and despite its weathered appearance, the siding is largely intact.

However, if you're house shopping, you'd want to get a bid for replacing the roof. Because the old shingles are tired, reroofing would likely be expensive, given the complexity of the roof structure and the likelihood of rot up there. Also, from the street, there's no sign of gutters, so it would be crucial to inspect the joists, the mudsills, and the foundation itself.

Given the age of this house, the foundation probably isn't reinforced with steel; and that, coupled with poor drainage, could mean big-ticket repairs—possibly a new foundation.

All in all, though, this old house would be an exciting prospect and is certainly worth a closer look.

GATHERING INFORMATION

If you feel strongly about a house, start by asking the real estate agent or owner for a recent termite report and a disclosure statement, and read them closely. Most states require such disclosures from owners; if you are working with an agent, such statements are probably mandatory. Disclosure statements describe (1) things not originally built with a permit or not built according to code, (2) code violations recently observed by an inspector, and (3) other conditions that the homeowner knows need fixing. Armed with this information, you can begin looking for unreported problems, which always exist.

For Nesters: Keeping Emotions in Check

When shopping for a house, it's hard to keep emotions in check. Unless you're buying a property solely as an investment, you're probably looking for a nest. If you're like most of us, you'll imagine yourself living there, surrounded by friends and family. Those warm feelings are all understandable human stuff but probably not the best frame of mind for making one of the biggest financial decisions of your life. By all means, listen to your feelings; just don't lead with them.

Look at a lot of houses. Read this chapter to get an overview of house systems and learn building lingo. Then scrutinize every house you enter—whether it's for sale or not. Be cold eyed: Look beyond the lace curtains and the fresh paint. Look for problems and try to figure out what's causing them. Then when you begin shopping "for real" and find that certain place that wins your heart, you won't lose your head.

Also, if you like a house, check out the neighborhood, and talk to neighbors to see what they are like. Ask about traffic, schools, shopping, city services, and crime. This will help you imagine what living there will be like.

Building Terms

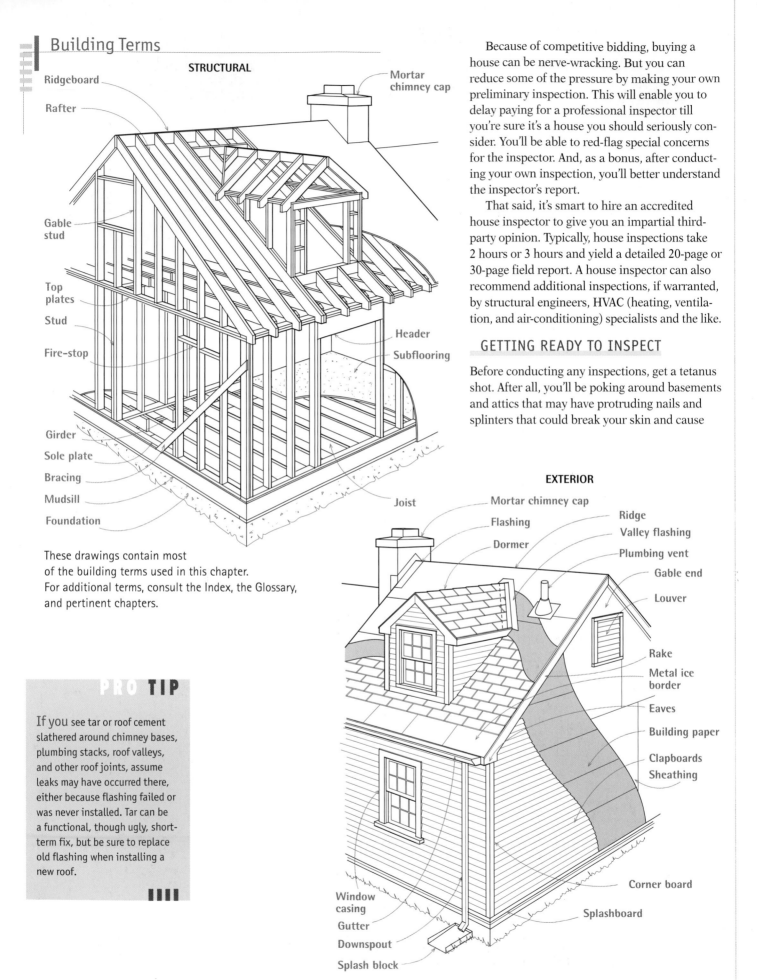

STRUCTURAL

Ridgeboard

Rafter

Gable stud

Top plates

Stud

Fire-stop

Girder

Sole plate

Bracing

Mudsill

Foundation

Mortar chimney cap

Header

Subflooring

Joist

These drawings contain most of the building terms used in this chapter. For additional terms, consult the Index, the Glossary, and pertinent chapters.

Because of competitive bidding, buying a house can be nerve-wracking. But you can reduce some of the pressure by making your own preliminary inspection. This will enable you to delay paying for a professional inspector till you're sure it's a house you should seriously consider. You'll be able to red-flag special concerns for the inspector. And, as a bonus, after conducting your own inspection, you'll better understand the inspector's report.

That said, it's smart to hire an accredited house inspector to give you an impartial third-party opinion. Typically, house inspections take 2 hours or 3 hours and yield a detailed 20-page or 30-page field report. A house inspector can also recommend additional inspections, if warranted, by structural engineers, HVAC (heating, ventilation, and air-conditioning) specialists and the like.

GETTING READY TO INSPECT

Before conducting any inspections, get a tetanus shot. After all, you'll be poking around basements and attics that may have protruding nails and splinters that could break your skin and cause

EXTERIOR

Mortar chimney cap

Flashing

Dormer

Ridge

Valley flashing

Plumbing vent

Gable end

Louver

Rake

Metal ice border

Eaves

Building paper

Clapboards

Sheathing

Corner board

Splashboard

Window casing

Gutter

Downspout

Splash block

PRO TIP

If you see tar or roof cement slathered around chimney bases, plumbing stacks, roof valleys, and other roof joints, assume leaks may have occurred there, either because flashing failed or was never installed. Tar can be a functional, though ugly, short-term fix, but be sure to replace old flashing when installing a new roof.

infections. Dress the part. Wear sneakers or crepe-soled shoes if you'll be on ladders or roofs; if you're crawling around basements and the like, wear heavy-soled boots, and old clothes. Carry a pad of graph paper and a pencil, a flashlight, a pocketknife, a spirit level, and binoculars.

Conduct your inspection alone. You're after facts, not the opinions of an owner or real estate agent who's eager to sell. Nor are you now courting the opinions of your partner, who may be eager to buy. If your agent or partner must be present, ask him or her to bring along something to read so you can concentrate on your inspection.

Begin outside, scrutinizing the house methodically, top to bottom. As you see flaws and suspect areas, record them on a sketch of the building. Then go inside and repeat the process, as suggested in this chapter. Finally, as you inspect, look for patterns in what you observe: If there's water damage at the top of an interior wall or near a window, look outside for worn roofing, missing flashing, and the like. Water will be the cause of many, if not most, problems.

The Roof

Because water is usually a house's main enemy, spend time examining the roof—the first line of defense against rain, snow, and ice. Few homeowners would allow a prospective buyer on a sloped roof, whether fearing roof damage or your falling off. Yet even if you're sure-footed and could obtain permission, it's probably wiser to stay off. Use your binoculars to take a closer look, unless of course you'll be inspecting a flat roof.

ROOF CHECKPOINTS

Sight along the ridge to see if it's straight. If the ridge sags in the middle, suspect too many layers of roofing or undersize rafters. If the roof sags between rafters, the roof sheathing may be too thin and should be replaced during the next reroofing.

Next, look for flashing at the bases of chimney and plumbing vents. These projections can dam water and allow it to leak through the roof. If flashing is absent, rusty, or otherwise deteriorated, there's a good chance of water damage.

The valleys between roof sections should be flashed because they carry a lot of water. Thus, where roof planes converge, you'll see either metal flashing down the valley (an open valley) or interwoven shingles (a closed valley).

Drip-edge is specialized flashing that should protrude from beneath the lowest courses of roofing. It allows water to drip clear of the roof. Older homes lacking drip-edges often suffer water damage because water soaks backward

under sheathing onto the tops of walls (see "Eaves Flashing," on p. 9).

Wherever roofs adjoin walls or dormer walls, look for roof-to-wall and step flashings, as shown in "Flashing a Shed Roof," on p. 75. At brick chimneys, consider whether saddle and step flashings are properly counterflashed, as shown in "Chimney Flashing," on p. 74.

ASPHALT SHINGLES

If the granular surface of asphalt shingles is worn and if shingles are cupped and dog-eared, it's time for a new roof. Ditto if gutters contain a significant amount of gravel washed off the surface of the shingles.

If the roofing is lumpy and uneven, it probably has two or more layers of shingles that weren't well installed and so need to be stripped to the sheathing before reroofing.

Do you see odd-colored shingles? If so, they are probably patches over old leaks. Or if the roof is relatively new and shingles are worn in only one area, perhaps one bundle of shingles was defective.

A roof less than 5 years old with a large number of loose or missing shingles indicates that the installer's power nailer was set too deep and drove the nails too far through the shingles. In this case, that roofing needs to be replaced.

TWO'S THE LIMIT

If there are two or more layers of roofing, strip the roof to its sheathing before reroofing. The best place to count layers is along the edges. But, as you count, keep in mind that roofers often double the shingles along the edges, to stiffen the shingle overhang so water drips freely off its edge.

FLAT Roofs AREN'T FLAT

Flat roof is a misnomer: Even relatively flat roofs need some slope so water can exit down a drain or gutter. (After all, a cubic yard of water weighs 1,684 lb.) Still, water tends to pool on such low-slope roofs, so their roofing membranes must be intact to keep water out.

WOOD SHINGLES AND SHAKES

Shingle wear will almost always be greater on a south-facing roof because that side gets the most sun. If shingle ends are cupping and splitting, plan to reroof soon.

Mossy shingles or shakes are common in wet climates and on shady roof sections. Although moss-covered shingles can be relatively sound, the condition will induce rot because moss retains water.

If the house is in a fire-risk area, insurers may refuse to give a policy on a wood-shingle or wood-shake roof. In this case, replace it with noncombustible roofing.

SLATE SHINGLES

Do not attempt to walk on slate roofs. Even when dry, they're slippery. They're also brittle and so break easily.

Off-color areas may indicate replacement shingles for those that suffered damage from a tree branch. Later, when you are in the attic, check for water stains on supporting lumber.

If you see rust-colored streaks or cockeyed slates, the installer may have used nails that weren't galvanized, which by now have rusted through. Although it's possible to remove and renail slate, the job requires a costly specialist. However, if many nails have rusted through, the roof is dangerous, and the slate should be removed.

ROOF TILES

Stay off tile roofs. Even when the roof slope isn't steep, your weight could damage the tiles. Inspect them from an extension ladder and with binoculars.

Look for odd-colored tiles from earlier repairs. Obviously cracked or broken tiles can be replaced, but the job is costly. In the attic, check for water stains.

Look closely at the ridge. Sagging ridge and rafters suggest too much weight on the framing. It's a big expense to remove the tile, bolster or replace sagging rafters, replace sheathing, and then replace tiles.

METAL ROOFING

Stay off metal roofs. They are slippery, whether wet or dry.

Even though a rusty roof may not look great, it could be watertight with a lot of years left. Roofs with superficial rust can be sanded and repainted. In the attic, check for evidence of leaks.

Note: Roofing panels should be nailed at the high point of metal folds. If you see many nails in the roofing channels themselves—where the water runs—the installation was inept, and you'll need a new roof.

BUILT-UP ROOFING

On older built-up roofs, there were alternating layers of heavy building paper and hot tar, covered with light-colored gravel to reflect sunlight and protect the layers from ultraviolet (UV) damage. More recently, modified bitumin (MB) has largely replaced hot building paper. MB roofs typically have cap membranes "torched on" (heated with a propane flame) to fuse them to fiberglass-reinforced interplies, or base coats.

Blisters in built-up roofs are usually caused by water trapped beneath layers of roofing. Individual blisters can be patched with three-course patches (see Chapter 5), but if blisters are widespread, it's time to reroof.

Foot traffic, furniture, and such can abrade and puncture flat roofs. If you find no evidence of water damage below, you can spot-patch abused areas, lay down new gravel, lock the door to the roof, and consider yourself very lucky.

Most leaks occur at *turn-ups*, where the flat roof joins walls, parapets, and other vertical surfaces. If the turn-up surfaces are cracked, split, sagging, or unpainted, water may have gotten in and done damage. A large amount of tar at the base of walls may indicate inadequate flashing.

Cracking or blistering around downspout outlets and internal drains indicates inadequate maintenance. Are there wire baskets in the openings? Are openings free of debris? If you have doubts, flush the outlets with a hose to see how well they drain.

Is the flashing around plumbing vents sound? This is not a major repair, but it can indicate general neglect.

CHIMNEYS

Although the homeowner probably won't let you on the roof, chimneys need closer inspection than binoculars allow. Even if the chimney looks good through binoculars, make the purchase agreement contingent on a professional chimney inspection. Here's what a pro will look for:

This old brick chimney has four strikes against it: crumbling mortar, failed base flashing, no flue lining, and a wind-buffeted TV antenna that stresses mortar joints.

▶ Are mortar joints solid or crumbly? Repointing mortar isn't a big job unless it's badly eroded—in which case, the chimney may be unsound and so may need to be partially torn down near the top or removed all the way down to the roof ridge.

▶ Is there a sloping mortar chimney cap or crown at the top of the chimney, to shed water? A mortar cap is easy enough to repair, but a cracked or missing cap suggests a lack of general maintenance and, possibly, water and ice damage inside the chimney. Concrete-based caps in snow country should overhang bricks at least 1 in. (see "Overhanging Chimney Crown," on p. 194).

▶ If there is a prefabricated metal or concrete cap elevated above the chimney top to keep precipitation out, it too must be crack free and well attached. Elevated caps interfere with fireplace draft, so look for smoke marks above the fireplace opening.

▶ Is chimney flashing at the roof intact? Tired flashing can be replaced when it's time to reroof, but missing or degraded flashing may mean rotted framing in the attic.

▶ To be safe, chimneys must have an intact liner (usually flue tile in older houses). If the flue is only brick and mortar instead of flue tile or if there's creosote running down the outside of the chimney, the chimney is unsafe.

Any cracks in a flue—or no flue at all—can allow superheated gases to escape and ignite the adjacent framing.

House Exterior

After inspecting the roof, examine the gutters and eaves. The overhanging eaves are actually a transition from roof to wall and are composed of several building materials.

GUTTERS AND DOWNSPOUTS

Eyeball the eaves trim. Is it intact or splitting? Do you see stains or discoloration? Water damage along eaves is usually caused by clogged gutters or missing drip-edge flashing on the roof and, less often, by roof leaks.

You'll need to replace metal gutters that have rusted through or that leak widely. But this a moderate expense, unless you replace them with copper gutters.

If the deteriorated gutters are wood, they will usually be nailed directly to fascia trim or, less often, built into a cornice. By the time they fail, they may have allowed a lot of rot behind them. Probe to see how much. Wood gutters are the most expensive to replace, so consider alternatives.

Stained siding behind downspouts may have been caused by gutter seams that rusted through. Or if the downspouts and gutters are new, upper downspout sections may have been mistakenly slipped *over* lower ones, rather than into them.

Eaves Flashing

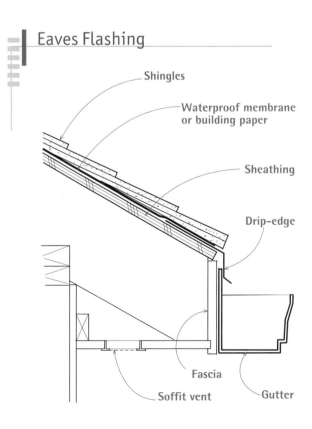

Shingles

Waterproof membrane or building paper

Sheathing

Drip-edge

Fascia

Soffit vent

Gutter

Leaking pipes and vegetation too close to the house were factors in causing this siding to rot.

If rainwater gushes over the gutter, either the downspout screen, the downspout itself, or the ground drainpipe is clogged. Aboveground clogs are easy to fix. Belowground clogs require either reaming tools or digging, still only moderate expenses. But if the drainpipe is clogged with tree roots, you'll need to replace the underground pipe and seal its joints to prevent tree-root penetration.

SIDING

Wood siding will deteriorate if it's not well maintained, especially along south-facing walls, which get the most sun. A certain amount of weathering is normal.

Cracked and worn shingles or clapboards can be replaced, but if the deterioration is widespread, you'll need to re-side the whole wall.

If you see widespread vertical black-brown stains on siding that's otherwise in good shape, installers likely failed to use galvanized or corrosion-resistant nails. Fixing the problem may mean sinking, filling, and priming the nail heads—a tedious undertaking.

Siding that's discolored along the base could be caused by any of several factors: (1) bottom siding that's too close to the ground, (2) nearby plants keeping the siding surface damp, (3) splashback from roof runoff, or (4) a badly positioned lawn sprinkler. All are easy fixes themselves, but moisture may already have caused the underlying framing to rot.

Imitation wood siding that delaminates or sprouts fungus is probably an exterior hardboard that's been discontinued because of class-action lawsuits. Replace the siding.

Chronically peeling paint on the exterior walls of bathrooms and kitchens is usually caused by excessive room moisture migrating outdoors. The remedy is usually to improve room ventilation—a moderate expense.

Stucco is strong and relatively maintenance free, but it will crack if the building shifts. (See "Tattletale Cracks," on the facing page.)

Loose or bulging stucco has separated from the lath behind. This is a modest repair, unless the problem is widespread. If you see extensive patching, be suspicious.

Loose, crumbling stucco is common if the base of a wall is close to the soil or in contact with it. This is usually a modest repair cost.

Newer homes with rot in the walls may have incorrectly installed "synthetic stucco," or EIFS; this is especially a problem in the Southeast. Have an EIFS specialist certify that the house is sound; this is a headache you don't need.

Brick is strong but its joints may crack if the foundation moves, whether from settling, frost heave, or earth tremor.

If a brick veneer half-wall is pulling away from an exterior wall or if a full-story brick facade is bowing outward, the metal ties holding the brick to the wall sheathing may have rusted out. Repairs will be expensive. This condition may also signal water damage and foundation problems. Eroded mortar joints can be repointed with mortar if the bricks are sound.

Mortar joints that have step cracks above doors and windows are usually caused by rusting steel lintels. Support the bricks above the opening before replacing the lintel.

Vinyl or metal siding doesn't require much maintenance and protects the structure if it's properly installed. However, if there are gaps between sections or where siding abuts trim, suspect a sloppy installation and probe for rot behind.

WINDOWS AND DOORS

Is there flashing over doors and windows? If not, suspect water damage behind.

Examine windows and doors very carefully. Are frames solid? Deteriorated window sashes should be replaced, creating costs that quickly add up. Also inspect doorsills and windowsills, which are rot prone if water collects there. Before replacing them, you'll first need to improve drainage.

Carefully inspect doors for fit and function. Look for signs of warping, sagging, or separation between rails and stiles. Examine the jambs of exterior doors for damage from abuse, changing the hardware, or even forced entry.

Doors and windows badly out of square suggest a house that has shifted and may still be shifting. This can result from poor drainage and an inadequately sized foundation.

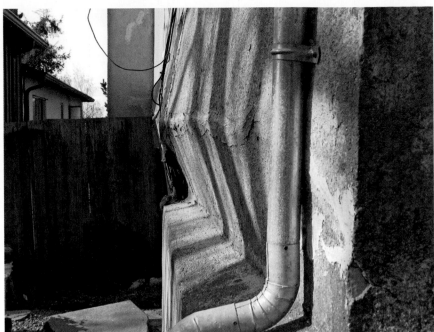

The base of this wall was kicked out by a rotating foundation.

Tattletale CRACKS

Diagonal cracks running out from the upper corners of windows or doors may telegraph big trouble. Building loads often concentrate on a header—a load-bearing member over a door or window opening—and diagonal cracking may be a sign that the header is not adequately supported. That is, the house's framing or foundation may be shifting. Get a structural engineer's opinion on this.

Swollen or rotted basement windows will need to be replaced with durable all-vinyl units. But first you'll need to attend to drainage problems that have allowed water to collect.

AROUND THE HOUSE

Walk around the house. Although you will be able to see more of the foundation inside, damp basements and cracked foundations are often caused by faulty drainage outside.

Does the ground slope away from the base of the house? Or would runoff from the roof collect next to the building? Is the soil damp or compacted next to the house? Although drainage may seem a minor factor, faulty drainage can cause wet basements and even foundation failure.

Where do downspouts empty? Is runoff carried away from the house by drainpipes or, at very least, are there splash blocks beneath downspouts to direct water from the foundation?

Mark the positions of foundation cracks on your graph paper, especially cracks greater than ¼ in. Also look for signs of foundation settling or leaning around downspouts, water sources, and areas on the uphill side of the house.

Inspect chimney bases closely, both where additions join the main house and where loads concentrate on foundation bearing points. If there's cracking where the chimney base joins the main house foundation or if the chimney base is tilting, it may be undersize and need replacing.

Do bushes or dirt touch the siding? If so, prod the siding and splashboard with your pocketknife. If soft, that area is retaining a lot of moisture. Dirt can also be an avenue for termites, so look for the telltale dirt tubes that termites construct, further discussed on p. 170.

Interiors

Armed with your outdoor observations, go inside. Start with attics and basements. Most vulnerable to the elements, they are prime places for serious house problems.

IN THE ATTIC

Review the notations you made about the roof, chimney, and eaves. Now look for outdoor–indoor relationships such as missing flashing and stains on the underside of roof sheathing.

Structural condition is the first thing to consider. Are the rafters and ridge sagging? If so, you should hire a structural engineer to see how serious the damage is. This damage likely resulted from too many layers of roofing. Deformed framing may need replacing or additional support, as shown in "Reinforcing a Roof," on p. 12.

PRO TIP

In the attic, walk on the ceiling joists or use plank walkways across them. It's unsafe to step anywhere else. Wear a hard hat so roofing nails above don't stab your head—another a good reason for that tetanus shot. You'll likely get dirty crawling around, so you'll be glad you've dressed the part.

Reinforcing a Roof

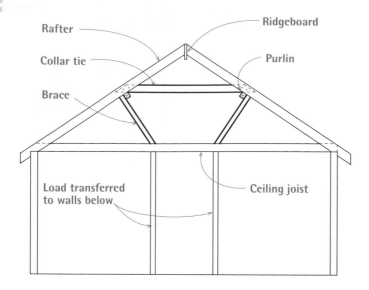

Tired roof framing sometimes needs additional support to keep rafters from sagging or spreading.

Here, rafter rot, mildewed ceilings, and delaminating roof sheathing were caused by inadequate ventilation.

And excessive layers of roofing may need to be stripped off to lighten the load. *Caution:* Truss-type floor or rafter systems will be weakened if cut into.

If the roof sheathing is bellying (sagging) between the rafters, it's probably too thin and should be replaced with thicker plywood when you replace the roofing.

Water damage is one of the most common problems. Dark brown stains around the chimney that smell of creosote are probably caused by cracked flue tile, which allowed caustic creosote compounds to work their way through mortar joints. Such a chimney is unsafe to use and must be either relined or replaced.

Cracks in the chimney's mortar joints may be caused by an undersize or shifting chimney footing—another major cause of flue failure.

Water stains around plumbing vents, dormers, and chimneys are more likely caused by failed or absent flashing. If the wood is damp after a rain, the leaks are active.

Ventilation and insulation are crucially important but often misunderstood. Attics that lack adequate ventilation are excessively hot in the summer. In winter in cold climates, unventilated attics allow rising water vapor from the living area to collect as frost on the underside of roof sheathing. The frost eventually melts, soaks the sheathing, drips onto the attic floor, and perhaps soaks through top-floor ceilings. Also in winter, unventilated attics trap warm air from below, which warms the roof, causing snow to melt and run into unwarmed overhangs where it refreezes, resulting in ice dams that can damage roofing and leak behind the siding. Adding soffit, gable, and ridge vents sometimes alleviates these types of problems.

Discolored rafters along the roof–wall joint and delaminated roof sheathing, coupled with stains at the top of interior walls below, are caused by warm, moist air from living spaces. To mitigate the problem, add insulation to the attic floor, improve ventilation, and/or add bath and kitchen vent fans.

Types of attic insulation and standards for their installation are addressed in Chapter 14.

Attic floors and attic insulation may also show roof leaks clearly. And if moisture is migrating up from the living spaces, the insulation's underside may be moldy. Pull up affected sections and see if water has collected there and caused damage.

WALLS

Most home buyers repaint or repaper walls to suit their tastes anyway. So instead of concerning yourself with paint colors or wallpaper patterns themselves, focus on surfaces that suggest underlying problems that may require remedies. Also, after consulting the notes you recorded outside, study wall–ceiling joints, which also can tell stories.

Water stains on interior outside walls, especially above windows, may have multiple causes: missing outside flashing, gaps between siding and exterior trim, and leaks in the gutters or roof.

Crumbling drywall or plaster and extensive mold at the top of walls may be caused by exterior leaks or, just as likely, by excessive moisture in the living areas. If the problems are severe, rot-inducing mold may be growing on framing inside the walls. After correcting the sources of moisture, you may need to tear out drywall or plaster and replace studs and plates.

Large diagonal cracks in drywall or plaster at the corners of doors and windows may correspond with cracks on the house exterior. Such cracks suggest structural shifting and foundation distress.

Door and window trim that tilts toward a common low point suggests failure in the substructure (girder, post, or pad) or in the foundation itself.

FLOORS AND STAIRS

Squeaky floors may take 2 minutes to repair or 2 days, when the cause is elusive. If you can live with some squeaks, they're rarely a sign of anything serious.

Excessively springy floors suggest subflooring or underlayment that's not strong enough to span the joists. Additional layers of subflooring or flooring should firm things up.

Deteriorating flooring near an exterior doorsill suggests that rain or snow has soaked the sill and subflooring. You'll need to replace damaged materials and install an all-weather doorsill.

Widespread cracking in tile floors may result from insufficient adhesive between tile and subflooring or an underlayment that's too thin and thus not rigid enough. Repairing it may mean tearing out the tile and perhaps the underlayment before replacing both.

Cracked stair treads may be worn, undersize, or inadequately supported by the carriages

The water damage and rot beneath this toilet could have been avoided by replacing a $2 wax gasket.

underneath. If the problem is widespread, remove the treads and examine the substructure.

Stairs sloping badly to one side, with cracked walls along the stair suggest a stair carriage that is pulling loose from wall mountings or other framing members. If the underside of the stairs is not accessible, repairing the problem can be complex and costly.

Handrails and newel posts that wobble more than ½ in. should be resecured. If balusters are missing, it can be costly to have replacements hand-turned to match. As a cost-saving alternative, you might be able to find replacements at a salvage yard.

KITCHENS AND BATHROOMS

If there are stained, springy floors around the base of a toilet, the subfloor and the joists below may be water damaged. The cause of the leak may be simple—just a worn-out wax ring gasket under the toilet. But if damage is significant, you may need to pull up flooring and replace it.

Damaged linoleum or vinyl around cabinets, shower stalls, or tubs often foretells water damage below. If there's an unfinished basement beneath those fixtures, inspect there for damage. Otherwise, look for water damage in finished ceilings below.

If tiled tub enclosures are in poor repair, test the firmness of the substrate behind by pushing with the heel of your hand. If the walls flex, the tile may be installed over ordinary drywall, which deteriorates if it absorbs water. One remedy is tearing out the tile and drywall and installing a cement-based backer board before retiling.

Check tub–wall joints closely. They must be well caulked to forestall leaks.

Use your pocketknife to prod for damage under lavatory and kitchen sink cabinets. Rusted-out drainpipes or leaking supply-pipe connections are easily replaced, but extensive water damage can be costly to remedy.

PRO TIP

To test whether a toilet is securely mounted, bend over the toilet, grab the edges of the bowl (while wearing work gloves) and try to rock it from side to side. If the bowl moves slightly, tighten the toilet nuts at the base—but don't overtighten or you'll crack the porcelain—and then try again. If it still rocks, the subfloor may be spongy and need replacing.

If supply pipes are galvanized steel, their useful life is about 25 years. Copper supply pipes installed before 1990 may contain lead in solder joints, which can leach into drinking water. So before making an offer, get the water tested for lead and other toxins. If the pipes appear to be otherwise in good condition, an in-line filtration system with replaceable filters may be a cost-effective solution to this problem.

If bathrooms or kitchens smell musty or are mildewed, especially at the top of walls, there's inadequate ventilation. Scrubbing walls and adding vent fans will probably cure the problem, unless the drywall is crumbling (see Chapter 14 for repair information).

IN THE BASEMENT

Safety note: Stay out of basements or crawl spaces if there's standing water, wet soil, or substandard electrical wiring! Metal pipes or ductwork could become energized by a short circuit.

Dampness can be mitigated by gutters and downspouts, as well as a ground surface that slopes away from the house. Musty smells and mild mold can usually be reduced by improving ventilation. Beyond that, fixes get more complex and more expensive.

Wetness is often caused by surface water and may respond to the remedies mentioned in the preceding paragraph. Stronger remedies include sump pumps, perimeter drains, and engineered solutions. For example, water seeping through an uphill foundation wall may need to be intercepted and rerouted by drainpipes or swale drains farther uphill. Solutions can become expensive.

Insects: Hungry for a Home

If you'd like to buy a house, make your offer contingent on a licensed pest-control inspector's report. You probably won't see insects, but you might see any of these signs:

▶ Sandy brown tubes, ¼ in. in diameter, that run up a foundation wall and wood burrows that run parallel with the grain indicate the presence of subterranean termites.

▶ Pellets outside insect entry holes and burrowing in all directions of wood grain, with no tubes on the foundation, indicate non-subterranean termites.

▶ Holes that may range from pin size to BB size and light-colored powdery debris indicate powderpost beetles.

▶ Coarse sawdust beneath damp wood with galleries excavated parallel with the wood grain indicates carpenter ants. Simply spraying carpenter ant nests usually does the trick.

Cracks range from cosmetic surface lines that you can ignore to larger, deeper fissures caused by water pressure, soil movement, foundation failure, or a combination of those causes.

In general, a serious crack is any gap that runs through the foundation or is at least ¼ in. wide, combined with foundation rotation. Have a structural engineer assess the cause.

Vertical cracks through a foundation that are wider at the top may be caused by differential settlement. For example, a corner of the house may be sinking because of drainage problems or a second-story addition that's too heavy for the original foundation.

Horizontal cracks through the foundation wall, just below ground level, may be caused by *adfreezing*, in which damp soil freezes to the top of a foundation and lifts it. This condition most often occurs in unheated buildings.

The foundation's bowing-in along horizontal cracks is extremely serious; it's caused by soil movement and strong hydrostatic pressure. Given the magnitude of the problem, the engineered solution will be very expensive.

Older foundations of unreinforced concrete or brick may be adequate beneath single-story houses on flat lots. But long term, you should plan to replace them. Unreinforced foundations are often poor quality (crumbling) and may have cracks that go all the way through the concrete.

Wood structure is most often damaged from sustained moisture below grade, insect damage, settling of the foundation, or unwise sawcuts into the structure during earlier remodeling.

Use your pocketknife to examine the perimeter of the mudsill—and the studs atop it—for rot or insect damage. To prevent recurrence of rot, replace damaged sections with treated lumber, install drainage systems, and slope soil away from the house.

If you encounter sagging girders or joists, posts supporting them will likely have sunk. In

Any crack that runs through a foundation is serious.

this case, upsize the concrete pads beneath the posts or replace posts. In some cases, shorten joist spans by adding girders and posts beneath.

Wooden posts rotting at the bottoms suggest that moisture is wicking up from the ground through the concrete pad. Replace the posts, putting a metal or plastic moisture barrier between their bottoms and the concrete.

Joists and girders may have been seriously weakened by cutting to accommodate ducts and drainpipes. See "Maximum Sizes for Holes and Notches," on p. 287, for information about how much and where you can safely cut and drill structural members.

Mechanical Systems

Mechanical systems include electrical, plumbing, and HVAC. Your comfort and safety depend on up-to-date and adequately sized *mechanicals*, as they are called.

ELECTRICAL SYSTEM

Only a licensed electrician should assess the capacity and condition of your electrical service. In particular, do *not* remove the covers of service panels. 🚫 Before examining receptacles, switches and other devices, always *turn off the electricity* and make sure it's off by using a voltage tester before handling any electrical device.

If you see scorch marks, rust stains, or condensation on the service panel or damp conditions around it, that service is unsafe. Dampness

Knob-and-tube wiring is outdated but often serviceable.

is particularly unsafe, and many electricians will refuse to work on a panel till surrounding dampness is remedied.

In older homes, electrical service is often undersize. If your house has only two cables running from the utility pole, it has only 120-volt service. After purchasing the house, have your power company upgrade to three-wire, 240-volt service.

A 100-amp, circuit-breaker service panel is considered minimal today. If an older home has a fuse panel, it will typically be only 60 amps, which you'll need to upgrade.

Any electrical cable with cracked or frayed sheathing should be replaced. Such deteriorated cable is usually visible as it approaches the service panel and as it runs along joists in attics and unfinished basements. Visible wire splices or cable that sags from joists is unsafe and substandard. Don't handle such wiring. Just note its condition.

Use a voltage tester to ensure that power to an outlet is off.

KNOB-AND-TUBE Wiring

If you see individual wiring secured to ceramic insulators in the basement or attic, that's knob-and-tube wiring. Although outdated, such wiring is generally acceptable if it's in good condition and used only for lighting. To be safe, check with your local code officials or your electrician—and then with your prospective insurance company.

PRO TIP

If cleanout traps show fresh wrench marks, suspect recent clogging; if traps are badly scarred, they have been opened many times. This may mean nothing more than children dropping things down the sink or it may indicate an inadequately sized pipe that needs replacing. See "Minimum Drain, Trap, and Vent Sizes," on p. 281.

Using a voltage tester, you can safely see if house receptacles are operable. If the cover plates of any receptacles are warm, if tester lights flicker, or if there's an odd smell, there may be aluminum circuit wiring in the walls, which tends to overheat and cause fires. Have your electrician check for this too.

To prevent electrical shocks in high-moisture areas, all bathroom receptacles, kitchen receptacles within 4 ft. of a sink, outdoor outlets, and some garage outlets must be GFCIs. Your local building code will have the final say on GFCIs.

PLUMBING

Questions suggested under "Kitchen and Bathrooms," earlier in this chapter, should be addressed here, too—particularly if you noted water damage around tubs or toilets. By the way, if the house has only a crawl space, replacing the plumbing will take longer and be more costly than if it has a basement.

Drainage, waste and vent (DWV) pipes should be replaced if they're rusted, corroded, or leaking. Waste pipes past their prime often show powdery green or white deposits along their horizontal runs, where wastes accumulate. Also, if joists around the closet bend are discolored, probe for rot. If rotted, they'll need to be replaced.

Supply pipes. If water pressure is poor and plumbing is old, it's likely that the pipes are galvanized iron. With a typical life span of about 25 years, the fittings rust out first.

Copper pipe will last indefinitely unless the water is acidic, in which case you'll see blue-green deposits on fixtures and pinhole leaks in the pipe. But if copper pipes aren't too far gone, an acid-neutralizing filter on supply lines may cure the problem.

Septic TIPS

If the house has a septic tank, ask when it was last emptied. Most tanks are sized according to the number of users and should normally be emptied every few years. Also inquire how the owner determines the exact location of the tank's clean-out lid, which will usually be buried under more than 1 ft. of soil.

Then walk the area. If the ground is damp and smelly, the most recent servicing wasn't soon enough. Besides tardy servicing, this could indicate that the tank or the drainage field may be undersize, clogged, or incorrectly installed. A new septic system is a significant expense.

Copper and galvanized pipe joined together will corrode, owing to a process called *galvanic action*. To join these metals, you need to install a dielectric union between them.

A water test by the health department should be part of the purchase agreement; this is especially important if the house has its own well.

Water heaters. Water heaters 10 years to 12 years old should be replaced. A manufacturer's plate on the heater will tell its age and capacity. As a rule of thumb, a 40-gal. gas-fired water heater is about right for a family of four. Electric water heaters should be 50-gal. capacity because they recover a little slower.

There should be a temperature-pressure relief (TPR) valve on or near the top of the water heater. Without TPR protection, a water heater can explode and level the house. If the TPR valve drips, you'll need to replace it. If you own the home, make sure you have a TPR valve.

If a cast-iron waste pipe is this rusty, it needs replacing.

Corroded galvanized-steel pipe atop a water heater tells you it's time to replace both the heater and the supply pipes.

Gas lines that smell and corroded gas pipes are unsafe: Call the gas utility immediately. (Most provide a free inspection.) Gas lines are typically "black iron" pipe with threaded fittings or copper joined by flared fittings. Gas lines should *never* include PVC plastic pipe, sweated (soldered) copper joints, or compression fittings such as those used for water supply.

HEATING, VENTILATION, AND AIR-CONDITIONING

Heating and cooling systems are varied and complex, so make your house purchase contingent on a professional inspection by an HVAC contractor. In your walk-through, look for the following:

▶ **If the bottom of the heating unit is rusted out or if it's 15 years to 20 years old, it probably should be replaced. It's certainly not efficient and probably not safe.**

▶ **Soot around heat registers or exhaust smells in living areas mean that the furnace is dirty and poorly maintained or that the furnace heat exchanger is cracked, allowing exhaust gases to escape. If an HVAC specialist can see flame through the heat exchanger, it's definitely time to replace the unit. It may be a fire safety and health hazard.**

▶ **If your house has forced hot-air heat, your family could develop respiratory problems if the furnace has one of the older, reservoir-type humidifiers, which are notorious for breeding harmful organisms in the always-wet drum. An HVAC specialist can suggest alternatives.**

▶ **If certain rooms are always cold, an HVAC specialist may be able to balance heat distribution or add registers. That failing, you'll need to upsize the furnace or boiler.**

▶ **If ducts, pipes, or the central heating unit are wrapped with white or gray paper-tape, your older heating system may be insulated with asbestos. Do not disturb it—an HVAC specialist can assess its condition and recommend an asbestos-abatement expert.**

▶ **Air-conditioning (AC) systems that run constantly but don't cool may need the coolant to be recharged. An AC system that cycles too rapidly and makes the house too cold may simply be too large for the house. Both problems just need adjustments by an HVAC contractor.**

FIREPLACE OR WOODSTOVE

Loose bricks in the fireplace firebox or smoke stains between the wall and the fireplace mantel (or surround) could allow flames or superheated

gases to ignite wood framing around the fireplace. A mason or chimney specialist can usually make necessary repairs.

If there are gaps between the hearth (firebox floor) and the hearth extension, stray coals could fall into the gaps and start a fire, so repoint gaps with mortar (if there's brick) or grout (tile floors).

Local building codes usually specify minimum distances woodstoves and stovepipes must be from flammable surfaces. Ask to see a certificate of occupancy (C.O.) issued for the existing installation. If the owner can't produce one, make the C.O. part of your purchase agreement.

Estimating Project Difficulty and Costs

It's hard to generalize how difficult a job will be for individual do-it-yourselfers because skills vary greatly. Still, it's possible to suggest relative difficulties of various tasks, giving you some reference at least. Chapters or sections of this book greatly expand on the following topics.

BEGINNER TO INTERMEDIATE

Demolishing. Make sure your tetanus shot is up to date. Before you begin work, wear full safety gear, including hard hat, eye protection, and boots that nails can't puncture. If you will generate dust, wear a dust mask. Also, prevent dust from migrating to other rooms by shutting or sealing door openings and air ducts with plastic. Always shut off power to an area you're demolishing. During demolition, make sure you're not compromising either the electrical system or the support structures. Be methodical, removing debris as you generate it, and sweep up the work site at the end of each day.

Interior painting. Preparing the walls and being fastidious are keys to success.

Exterior painting. Rent scaffolding if it's a two-story house. Homeowners often run planks between ladder brackets on extension ladders,

A temperature–and–pressure relief (TPR) valve can prevent water-heater explosions caused by excess pressure. The discharge pipe running from the valve should end 4 in. above the floor.

but the job will be far safer and many times faster if you work from scaffolding. Again, surface preparation is crucial to a lasting job.

Stripping paint, inside or out. This isn't as difficult as it is messy. Before you begin, buy a lead-paint testing kit from a building supplier. Lead paint dust and shavings are hazardous wastes and should be dealt with accordingly. Avoid open-flame paint stripping; the fire hazard is too great. Use a respirator mask with replaceable cartridges

Wallpapering. Practice on a small, out-of-the way area to get the hang of it. Wall prep is crucial. Use only the paste recommended by the wallcovering manufacturer.

Hanging drywall. This isn't difficult if you've got help. Measuring carefully and getting the edges of the first sheets plumb (or level) are keys to success.

Patch repairing walls. This is generally quite easy. Sand or cut back the damaged parts to ensure a solid surface for the patch.

Insulating. Stuff or spray insulation into every nook and cranny to stop air infiltration. However, there should be air space over insulation between rafters, so that heated air under the roof can escape. Gloves, a long-sleeved shirt, a hat, and a face mask are imperative.

Weatherstripping. It's easy but exacting work to fit the stripping snugly against doors, windows, and frames. You may be surprised how long this job takes.

INTERMEDIATE TO DIFFICULT

Framing and sheathing. These tasks are enjoyable if you can swing a hammer accurately and work with someone more experienced to explain how to raise walls. If you use a power nailer to speed up the job, read the operation manual carefully. Hard hats and eye protection are a must.

Hanging windows and doors. A well-framed rough opening (RO) makes the job a lot easier. You'll need patience to plumb, level, and center the pre-cased unit in the RO, adjusting and readjusting shims till everything's perfect.

Installing flooring. To get a good floor, make sure underlayment is level and solidly attached, measure and cut flooring carefully, and use appropriate fasteners or adhesives.

Plastering. This is difficult for the novice. Plaster consistency and technique and the room's temperature are all crucial. The skill of plastering takes time to master.

Refinishing floors. Take your time doing this, especially with power sanders. Be conscientious about vacuuming and sanding lightly between finish coats. Use a respirator mask with filters.

Installing pre-built cabinets. Like hanging doors, this job takes careful planning, accurate measurement, and lots of patience. Shimming the bottoms of base cabinets is the key to leveling cabinets and aligning them with one another.

Installing interior trim. This takes patience, careful measurements, and a quality miter saw.

Installing exterior trim and siding. You need patience and a good miter saw. Be sure to caulk and weatherize carefully.

Stripping a roof. This is miserable work and dangerous. Don't do it. Instead, hire an insured tear-off crew.

Reroofing. Hire pros if the roof pitch is steep. Keys to a good job: correctly flashing and aligning the shingle courses. This work is inherently unsafe, however, because you're high up on a sloping surface without a net to catch you.

Running ductwork. Cutting and running ducts isn't difficult, but balancing the heat output to all rooms takes skill. Consider hiring a pro.

Plumbing and electrical wiring. You could learn a lot by working with a licensed pro for a day or two, but local codes may prohibit you from doing your own work. The work is enjoyable, steady, and logical—and requires close attention to detail. Don't do it if you're not fastidious. Either trade requires specialized tools.

JUST PLAIN TOUGH

Framing stairs and complex roofs. Many angles need to be reckoned with to do these jobs.

Masonry. Each masonry unit—whether brick or block—must be placed exactly. This takes strength, dexterity, patience, and a sure eye.

Changing bearing walls. Be sure to obtain the guidance of a structural engineer or a seasoned contractor.

Adjusting the furnace. Other than basic maintenance tasks, leave this to an HVAC pro.

Tiling in fresh mortar. It takes years to learn how to prep the surface correctly, mix the "mud" to the right consistency, trowel it on, and then screed it off until the plane is flat. Hire a pro to create the mud bed. Then you can concentrate on tiling.

Planning

Planning is one of the most satisfying aspects of renovation. On paper, you can live imperially—fruit trees beneath the windows, Italian marble in the bathrooms. When you tire of that, you can remove the tiles and replant the trees...with an eraser. Of course, your finished plans will be a trade-off between what you'd prefer and what you can afford. Yet, during early stages of planning, feel free to let your imagination run wild.

Creating a Home That Suits You

Your house should fit you. In the words of building contractor Dean Rutherford, whose own home is featured near the end of this chapter, "For me, building is about creating a sense of who you are. A place of pause and reflection.

A place where you can be comfortable with yourself." Indeed, a house should be an expression of who you are, your lifestyle, your loved ones, your dreams. So it's helpful to begin planning by getting in touch with who you are, which isn't always easy.

Few homeowners are good at conceptualizing spatially. Still fewer can draw well enough to convey their concepts to an architect. Thus one savvy architect asks his clients to write up a scenario for a happy day in a perfect house. He says it's surprising how quickly the writing helps people move beyond physical trappings to describing the experiences that make them happy in a home. For example, some people prefer to wake up slowly while reading in bed or having breakfast on the patio. They may want to putter in a secluded garden or host lavish candlelight dinners. Whatever you wish for.

Place a tissue-paper overlay on a measured floor plan to make a quick, accurate sketch.

If you plan to own a home for a long time, making it comfortable should be your prime objective. With this goal, you can plan remodeling projects long-term and schedule them as time and money are available. Moreover, living in a house for a while is the best way to learn its strengths and shortcomings.

Quick turn-arounds are trickier. During real estate booms you can make money by doing little more than refinishing floors and applying a fresh coat of paint. But timing the market is everything—and impossible to predict. Houses can also be illiquid (hard to sell) when interest rates rise and the economy slows. So even if you're speculating, buy a house you wouldn't mind living in, just in case you have to.

Whatever you enjoy most, home is the place where you get to do it.

KEEP A RENOVATION NOTEBOOK

Much as you'd create a shopping list, jot down house-related thoughts as they occur and file them in a renovation notebook. A notebook is also a convenient place to stash ideas clipped from magazines and newspapers, along with photos you may have shot. If you have kids, encourage their contributions too. At some point, consolidate the notebook ideas and begin creating a wish list of the features you'd like in your renovated home. This list will come in handy when you begin weighing design options.

Architects call items on the wish list *program requirements* and consider them an essential first step for planning because they establish written criteria against which you can later compare proposed improvements. The list should contain both objective, tangible requirements (such as the number of bedrooms and baths) and subjective, intangible requirements (such as how the house should eventually *feel*). If you're presently living in the house you'll renovate, you'll have strong opinions about what inconveniences you're willing to tolerate and what you're not. Here are questions to help you get started.

Comfort. Start with your gut feelings. Are the rooms big enough? Ceilings high enough? Do you have enough bedrooms and storage? Enough room to do the things you like? How's the traffic flow? Do some rooms have two approaches/exits? Or do most feel like dead ends? Must you walk through one bedroom to get to another?

Is the house too drafty? Warm enough? Do rooms receive enough sunlight? Does window screening take advantage of prevailing winds? Can you shut out street noise? Do you feel safe? Can you see who's on the porch without opening the door? Is the house easy to keep clean? Will your furniture suit your design plans?

Cooking and dining. Do you cook a little or a lot? Do you entertain often? Do you have enough counter space? Are the sink and appliances ideally suited to your cooking preferences? Are counters the right height? Does your kitchen have useful continuous counter space or are the counters interrupted by doors, windows, and foot traffic? Can you reach all shelves? Is storage space sufficient? The refrigerator large enough?

Can you easily transport food to and from dining areas? Can people hang out while you cook? While cooking, do you like to talk on the phone or watch TV? If you recycle cans and bottles, do you have a place to put them?

For recommended minimum cabinet and counter dimensions and common kitchen configurations, see pp. 302 and 303.

Being social. If you plan to entertain, will it be formal or informal? Small card parties with friends or 40-chair club meetings? Is the living room cozy? How about accommodations for overnight guests? Can you escape hubbub when you prefer solitude? That is, when the kids have friends over, do they drive you crazy? (Of course, this may have nothing to do with the house.)

Bathrooms. Do you have enough bathrooms, or do jam-ups occur during rush hours? When everyone showers in the morning, do you have enough hot water? Is there a linen closet nearby? Enough cabinet space for sundries?

Do you have tubs and showers where needed? In the tub, can you relax and soak in peace? Is the tub big enough for two? Can you shower without leaving pools of water outside the tub or stall? Is your bathroom presentable for entertaining?

Family doings. If you have small children, are surfaces easy to keep clean? Do you have places to store toys? Are other cabinets childproof? Is there an enclosed, outdoor, safe play area? A room where kids can play on a rainy day? Do you have rooms conducive to reading and homework? Do your kids have enough privacy? And room for their possessions? Will the rooms meet their needs in 5 years? When the kids move out, will your empty nest be too big?

Working at home. If you bring work home or simply work at home, do you have a room that's adequate for it? Are the walls soundproofed so you can work in peace or work late without disturbing others? Are there enough electrical outlets? How about adequate lighting? Can you shut a door, making your workspace safe from pets and toddlers?

Outer spaces. Do porches protect you from the rain while you're searching for house keys? Does the yard receive enough sun for a garden? Do you need an outbuilding for lawn equipment and tools? A garage that can double as vehicle shelter and workshop? A spigot near the driveway for car washing? Do you cook out often? Need a fence for privacy or to screen off the neighbors? Need a deck or patio for entertaining outdoors?

Documenting What's There

This section explains how to measure rooms and record the location and condition of the structure and mechanical systems (plumbing, electrical, heating/cooling) as well as how to explore building elements that affect design. Here, too, you learn how to map the site and consider how well exterior renovations will suit the neighborhood.

MEASURING ROOMS

Start by drawing a basic plan of each floor. Using a 25-ft. retractable tape measure, record the overall dimensions of each room, noting the position of existing doors, windows, closets, fireplaces—anything that affects space. Take the time to record this information accurately. Be consistent in your measurements, always measuring to window and door jambs, not just to casings. (You are really measuring finished openings in walls.) Also note header and sill heights as well as ceiling heights and plane changes. Determine interior and exterior wall thicknesses by measuring door jambs.

Room Rater

Rating YOUR ROOMS

As you work up your wish list (program requirements), systematically rate how well each room works. Is the bedroom away, or at least screened, from a noisy street? Is the nursery or small child's bedroom near a bathroom? Is the home office inside of or detached from the main house? Does each room receive sunlight at optimal times? Are the rooms big enough for your furniture? Especially note conflicts within or between rooms, because such conflicts often generate useful design changes. Your room rating sheet might look something like the one shown here.

Room	Jake's bedroom (he's 15)
Where	2nd floor, SE corner
Size	9 ft. 2 in. x 10 ft.
Also used for	Homework, phone booth
Sunlight	Most of day, but he keeps the shades down (for computer)
Privacy	Door shut most of time
Noise level	Headphones help, but he's a night owl; can hear him through wall
Nearby rooms	Master BR, full bath, MJ's BR
Storage/closets	Okay, but clothes on floor, mostly
Traffic issues	Bathroom jam in a.m., last one gets cold shower
Gut reaction	Growing pains, needs his space
Possible solutions	Move J to room off kitchen? (NE corner)
Pluses	Jake next to kitchen, near laundry; linoleum floor indestructible; more privacy for him, more sleep for us; lots of shelves.
Minuses	Not much sun, but he won't care; only half-bath near kitchen now (maybe bust through pantry wall to add shower)
Definites	Need bigger water heater

To create accurate floor plans, transfer your recorded measurements to graph paper. Graph paper is handy because it helps you draw square corners and maintain scale without needing fancy drafting equipment. As to scale, most people find that ¼ in. = 1 ft. is large enough for detail and thus doesn't require graph paper larger than 8½ in. × 11 in.

MAPPING THE BUILDING SITE

Once you've created floor plans, use a 100-ft. tape to measure the overall exterior dimensions. Using graph paper with a smaller scale than you used for the interior drawings (say, ⅛ in. = 1 ft.), position the house as accurately as you can on the lot. If you don't know exact lot dimensions, check the closing documents you obtained upon purchasing the house or consult public records.

Also sketch locations of major site features, such as fences, trees, driveways, walks, ponds, streams, gardens, dog runs, and outbuildings. In the margins of the sketch or on separate sheets, draw in or note structures and features on adjacent properties that affect your property or its use—such as a tree you enjoy seeing or a garage you don't. As you gather information, think about how your proposed renovation might affect your neighbors. If a house addition blocks a neighbor's view, you might have trouble getting it approved. Likewise, there's no point in adding a window if it would overlook something ugly.

Most communities have *setback requirements*, minimum distances from structures to property lines; and seeking variances from setbacks is often a long, frustrating process. Finally, don't assume that existing fences accurately represent property lines. Verify property lines early on.

MAPPING STRUCTURE AND UTILITIES

Renovations beyond cosmetic changes will probably require some alteration of the structure as well as of plumbing, electrical, and heating/cooling systems. As with many other aspects of renovation, it's usually best to disturb as little as possible. Until you demolish walls you won't know the exact location of every last pipe and wire, but by mapping what you can see, you'll get a sense of where larger, more problematic ducts and pipes are, and thus save time and money by not proceeding with an obviously impractical design.

Now, using the floor plans you drew earlier as templates, create a map for each house system. For each system, use a tracing-paper overlay or mark up a photocopy of the basic floor plan, whichever is more convenient. While you're examining each room, it's also smart to note water stains, tired windows, outdated fixtures, ungrounded outlets, sagging floors, and so on. Use the various house assessment lists in Chapter 1 to guide you.

Structural elements should be assessed by a licensed structural engineer, who should also review any design plans that require altering or removing structure. Usually, the big question is whether the walls to be removed are load bearing, and that answer is not always obvious. In addition, in high-wind or earthquake regions, walls may be *shear walls,* which help a building resist lateral (sideways) forces. Don't cut or drill into, run pipes through, or remove shear walls until a structural engineer has okayed it.

For the best understanding of your house's structure, start in the basement, where joists and girders are visible, or in an unfinished attic, where rafters and floor joists are frequently exposed. In finished living spaces, wood floors are usually installed perpendicular to joists, so look at flooring-nail patterns. Common sense can be reliable: If the floor slopes down to the base of a wall, there's a good chance that wall is bearing a load—and may be insufficiently supported.

In most wood-frame houses, bearing walls run perpendicularly to the joists they support, in effect, shortening the distance those joists must span. Bearing walls are usually supported by bearing walls below, on down to the basement, where they will be supported by a girder and posts. However, there are framing eccentricities, especially for additions.

In apartments and row houses, interior walls often aren't bearing because most apartments are framed with steel girders, and the floors consist

Creating Floor Plans

Using a 25 ft. measuring tape, record the dimensions of each room. Graph paper makes the task easier.

Bearing and Nonbearing Walls

BEFORE

AFTER

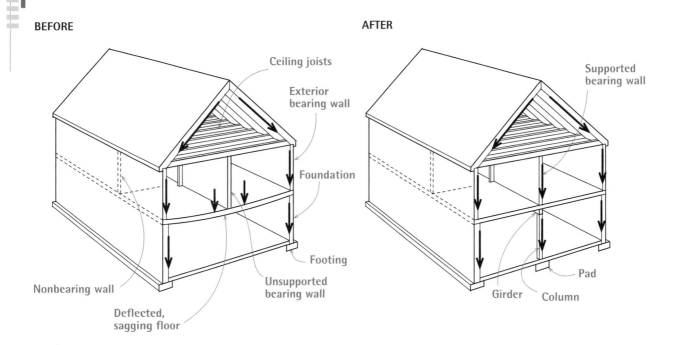

Ceiling joists

Exterior bearing wall

Foundation

Footing

Unsupported bearing wall

Nonbearing wall

Deflected, sagging floor

Supported bearing wall

Pad

Girder   Column

of reinforced concrete slabs. In row houses, joists and rafters customarily run the width of the house, between exterior walls. Thus interior walls running parallel to joists or rafters are rarely bearing. Partitions running perpendicularly to framing members were *probably* not bearing walls originally, but they may have become so if joists were undersize to begin with or if their effective spans were reduced by "remuddlers" cutting into them. In such instances partitions may become bearing walls, and floors may slope toward them.

If a wall is nonbearing, removing it may not cause problems. But if it is bearing, you must first transfer the loads it bears to temporary supports, called *shoring*, before you can alter it. Similarly, avoid removing any structural buttresses with impunity, such as braces and rafter collar ties. Otherwise unsupported structural elements may sag.

Plumbing fixtures and pipes are usually grouped around a 3-in. or 4-in. soil stack located in a wall near the toilet. Drainpipes are often routed between nearby joists. If the DWV (drainage-waste-vest) system is in decent shape, try not to disturb larger pipes because rerouting them is expensive. Draw fixtures on your plumbing map, and note where main drains emerge in the basement and where vent stacks protrude from the roof.

Supply pipes are rarely a design constraint. That is, because supply pipes are smaller and their water is under pressure, they don't need to

be pitched, as do waste and drainpipes. In many houses, large vents are concealed within "wet walls" framed out with 2×6s that provide plenty of room for even the biggest pipe. Moreover, drains should slope downward at least ¼ in. per foot. Thus a 3-in. drain would need almost an 8 in. height for a 12-ft. horizontal run (3½ in. for the exterior diameter of pipe, 3 in. for slope, 1 in. of clearance) and, therefore, would need 2×10 joists, as a minimum. Because cutting 4-in. holes *through* joists would seriously weaken them, it's

Plumbing Map

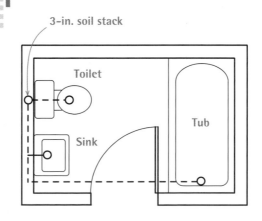

3-in. soil stack

Toilet

Tub

Sink

Plumbing fixtures are often grouped around a 3-in. or 4-in. soil stack. Because of their size, the soil stack and the main drain it feeds are the most problematic to relocate.

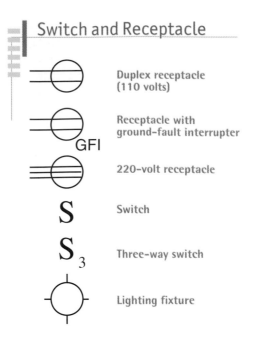

Switch and Receptacle

Duplex receptacle
(110 volts)

Receptacle with
ground-fault interrupter

220-volt receptacle

Switch

Three-way switch

Lighting fixture

Use these symbols to map your home's electrical system. Use different-color felt-tip markers to denote different circuits. See p. 234 for more electrical symbols.

easy to see why large drainpipes almost always need to be routed between joists, rather than through them. If the existing joists don't provide the height needed to run 3-in. or 4-in. drains, it's possible to build up a platform over an existing floor or to frame out false ceilings below. Yet if such complications present themselves, consider a simpler design.

Heating and cooling systems can also affect design plans, depending on the type of system. The renovator's primary concern in placing heating and cooling systems is to make sure that pipes and ductwork do not encounter joists, fire-stops, bridging, or other impediments. Modern hydronic (hot-water) heating systems are typically fed by ¾-in. pipe and so can usually be relocated easily; whereas steam heat, supplied by 1½-in. to 2-in. pipe, will require planning. By far, forced hot air (FHA) is the most difficult heating system to plan around because the ducts are so bulky. In this case, where space is tight, false walls, floors, and ceilings are commonly employed. But because the hot air is pushed by a fan, ducts do not need to be sloped upward (although this is desirable) to function well. When renovations require the gutting of wall surfaces, vertical duct runs can easily fit between standard 2×4 studs. Flexible insulated duct greatly expands routing options.

Ventilators for bathrooms and appliances are rarely problematic, since exhaust fans draw air from relatively small, isolated areas. By placing ovens, cooktops, or stoves near exterior walls or beneath a venting bonnet, you can easily route cooking exhaust to the outside.

When mapping a FHA system, note the locations of registers and the furnace. Then intuit the locations of ductwork, using dotted lines to suggest duct runs. In most cases, ducts or hydronic piping will be visible in the basement. For upper-story heat outlets, delivery ducts and pipes generally travel straight up between studs. In general, avoid running ducts within structural walls, because that would require the cutting of wall plates.

Electrical wiring rarely affects design phases unless you intend to move a service panel. Small and flexible, electrical cable is easily routed through walls, floors, and ceilings. Where you don't want to cut into existing surfaces, or can't— as with masonry floors—run rigid conduit or track wiring along the surface.

Mapping the electrical system is best done by two people: one standing at the service panel flipping the circuit breakers off and on (or removing fuses from a fused panel), while the other inserts a voltage tester into electrical outlets, as shown in "Using a Voltage Tester," on p. 235. When the light goes out, you've identified the circuit controlling it. (Using cell phones to communicate with each other will save a lot of yelling between floors.) It's difficult to know exactly where cables are, but by noting where cables enter the panel from floors above and using your map of electrical circuits, you can make an educated guess.

Finally, map electrical safety as best you can (see Chapter 11). In your survey, did you find ungrounded, two-hole receptacles or grounded, three-hole outlets? Is lighting adequate in bathrooms and kitchens? Light switches at the top and bottom of stairs? How about shock protection? Kitchen receptacles within 4 ft. of a sink and all bathroom receptacles must be protected by *ground-fault circuit interrupters* (GFCIs), which cut off power within ¼₀ second when they detect even a slight leak (4 milliamps to 6 milliamps). Local codes may also specify *arc-fault circuit interrupters* (AFCIs), which can prevent fires caused by loose or corroded electrical connections, nails puncturing wires, and the like. For more about GFCI and AFCI protection, see Chapter 11.

Design Constraints

Information you've gathered thus far will be useful whether you're hiring a general contractor and an architect or trying to tackle various parts of the job yourself. But before you begin exploring design solutions, consider realities that will have an impact on your plans.

BUDGET CONSTRAINTS

Consult a licensed general contractor (GC) about construction costs, especially before asking an architect to generate a lot of design options, called *schematic drawings*. An experienced contractor can cite construction costs per square foot in your region but may be reluctant to do so without qualifying those estimates. Such qualifiers will be well founded because every renovation is different, and there's no way of knowing what surprises a job holds till you open up walls and floors. Most contractors won't charge for a brief exploratory meeting, they're courting a client, after all; but if consultations drag on, be prepared to pay consulting time. Fair's fair.

In this initial meeting, you're trying to get ballpark figures so you can see if your plans are realistic. Typically a contractor will offer costs per square foot for "vanilla" space such as bedrooms or living rooms as well as for more complicated spaces such as kitchens and bathrooms. Armed with those preliminary numbers, be prepared to modify and trim the scope of your project so you can stay within your budget when you proceed with detailed designs. Try not to proceed with plans you can't presently afford, unless you are prepared to complete the work in phases, which could mean living with an unfinished renovation, perhaps for years.

CONSTRAINTS FROM PLANNING DEPARTMENTS

Once you've mapped the house, but before you sketch any proposed solutions, visit the planning department in your community to learn the ground rules for remodeling. Additions or other expansions of the physical envelope of your house need to be checked against regulations governing setbacks, lot coverage, height limits, parking requirements, and so on. An addition may also be subject to a design review, and you may need to apply for a *variance*, depending on the scope of the project. A variance may require that you obtain the approval of neighbors. Thus an early visit to local authorities could prevent your falling too deeply in love with a design you won't be allowed to build.

STYLISTIC CONSTRAINTS

As you renovate, respect what's already there. Design is tricky stuff to articulate, but a building's integrity comes from the proportion of its windows to walls, the width and contour of its trim, the slope of its roof—in short, from its parts, just as we humans are distinctive by the color of our hair, the set of our eyes, and the shape of our nose.

Each historical period has its distinctive architectural elements, and generally you're better off not mixing them. When you must change something, be guided by what's there. If your house has been modified by earlier owners and you question their judgment, walk around the neighborhood with your camera looking for other houses of the same period. Often, nearby houses will have been built from similar plans or even by the same builder. Here, digital photographs are useful because, once you load them into your computer, you can readily modify them with a software program, such as PhotoShop™.

From Preliminary Designs to Working Drawings

The easiest way to envision change is to draw it. For this, tape tracing paper over the floor plans you drew earlier and start rearranging rooms. Because you drew your floor plans to scale, your overlay drawings will likely be reasonably accurate. If you're unsure about the dimensions of a room, a fixture, or a piece of furniture, measure again. Also measure the space you'll need to open and pass through doors, pull chairs away from a

Confusion Is Costly: A Primer for Owner–Builders

There are many ways you could save renovation money by doing jobs yourself: obtaining permits, ordering materials, hiring and scheduling subcontractors, demolishing walls, hauling rubble, and completing finish work. But such work isn't for everyone. And because homeowner skills and experience vary, there are no easy rules for deciding what to attempt yourself. Yet there are times when even scarce money is well spent for a skilled professional, and there are times when regulations require it.

Hire a pro whenever these situations apply:

▶ You're confused and don't know how or where to start a renovation task.

▶ You lack the technical skills to do a job—in which case, learning by working with a pro makes sense.

▶ You're rushed for time and can probably earn more elsewhere (to pay for the work) than you could save by doing it yourself.

▶ Tasks require special or hard-to-find tools.

▶ The job is inherently dangerous: For example, an amateur should not install an electric service panel.

▶ Building codes, bank agreements, insurance policies, or other legally binding documents require that work be done by a licensed professional.

Last, poorly organized projects and confusing drawings can idle workers, costing you big-time. If you're not well organized, patient, and willing to field phone calls at all hours, hire a GC who is. Likewise, if you're not construction savvy and a capable draftsperson, hire a pro to generate final working drawings. It's far cheaper to resolve construction issues on paper, especially if a project is complicated.

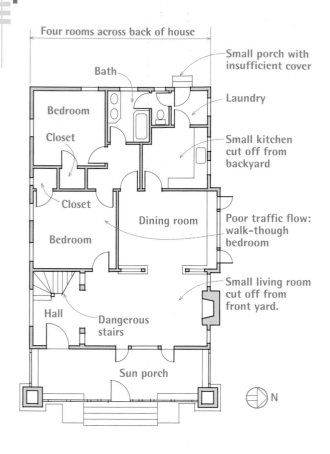

Four rooms across back of house

Bath

Bedroom

Closet

Closet

Bedroom

Dining room

Hall

Dangerous stairs

Sun porch

Small porch with insufficient cover

Laundry

Small kitchen cut off from backyard

Poor traffic flow: walk-though bedroom

Small living room cut off from front yard.

N

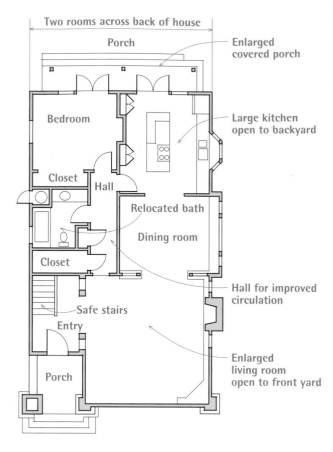

Two rooms across back of house

Porch

Bedroom

Closet

Hall

Closet

Safe stairs

Entry

Porch

Enlarged covered porch

Large kitchen open to backyard

Relocated bath

Dining room

Hall for improved circulation

Enlarged living room open to front yard

FLOOR PLAN: BEFORE

The original floor plan presented a pleasant face to the street, but the back of the house was a hodge-podge of doors, dead spaces, and tiny rooms.

FLOOR PLAN: AFTER

After weighing a number of floor plans, the architect settled on the design that solved the most problems.

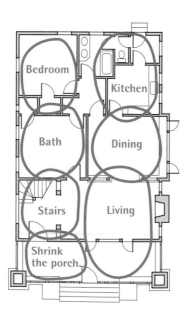

Bedroom

Kitchen

Bath

Dining

Stairs

Living

Shrink the porch.

Bubble diagrams like this allow you to consider layout alternatives quickly.

table, or remove food from the oven. Have fun, but be realistic: Don't try to fit too much into a small space.

Whether you draw "bubble diagrams" to indicate room usage or arrows to show traffic flow between areas, create optional arrangements, including some you at first might not think you'll like, for they might suggest possibilities you otherwise might not have considered. Think creatively, "outside the box," as they say. On paper, it's easy to move rooms to different locations. Analyze the trade-offs between one floor plan and another. In general, the more problems a design solves, the better. Feel free to borrow features from one plan and graft them onto another. Considering different designs also helps you decide your priorities.

Some layouts will dictate themselves—such as dining rooms next to kitchens with lavatory nearby—but most are fluid and all should be based on common sense. Put bedrooms away from noisy rooms and busy streets, if possible.

When visiting the bathroom in the middle of the night, you shouldn't need to pass through another bedroom or a public room. Don't forget to include closets in or near each bedroom, and a closet by the front door.

Design with nature. If your kitchen faces east, you can enjoy morning sun with breakfast. A living room on a westerly wall gives a view of the sunset. North-facing bedrooms will be cooler at night.

Glazing along a south wall can provide a substantial amount of free solar heat in colder months but may require awnings or heat-reducing window films in warmer months. If you live in the Sun Belt, where heat gain is less desirable, try to exploit prevailing breezes and to provide sufficient overhangs along south-facing walls. In this regard, many states regulate the energy budget for houses and additions by controlling the amount and type of glazing allowed and by requiring energy-performance standards for other building components.

Other ways to look at things. In order to see how your floor plan will translate into a three-dimensional structure, either draw elevations or build a model of the existing house with the proposed changes. Until you have drawn elevations or built a model, you can't be sure your design will work, especially if you are expanding the envelope of the house.

If you're dexterous, make a model of cardboard; most art-supply stores stock the necessary materials. Using a scale of ½ in. = 1 ft., draw floor plans and an elevation for each face onto the cardboard, cut them out with a utility knife, tape them together, and install a roof.

DOUBLE-CHECK YOUR DESIGN

Design is a process of continuing revision that doesn't stop until you have finished architectural drawings, if then. The closer you get to a design that works, the more information you need. Once you have a floor plan that satisfies most of your program requirements, double-check the assumptions underlying your design. Then revisit your local planning department with your proposed floor plan superimposed on your lot and with elevations or a model. Make sure you ask detailed questions about anything that seems unclear.

Remember, the more specific information you bring to the planner, the better feedback you'll get. You can save yourself a lot of backtracking if you confirm that officials will allow you to do the renovations as designed and that you can afford to continue. Make sure you understand the approval process. Many communities require design review or other approvals before you can even apply for a building permit. If you will be living in the house while working on it, get a temporary certificate of occupancy (C.O.).

The same principle applies when discussing construction costs with a contractor. Though you may not yet have the working drawings required for a detailed estimate, you'll have enough to confirm ballpark costs with a reputable contractor. If you have floor plans and elevations or a model, you are about one-third of the way through the design process.

WORKING DRAWINGS

Once you've reconsidered layouts in light of the constraints noted above, proceed to *working drawings,* which should include accurately drawn floor plans and elevations. Details required for these drawings depend on several variables, the most important being how big the job is and who's doing the work. A conscientious, experienced builder who practices sound construction and knows code requirements can usually intuit what needs doing even if drawings lack occasional details.

Elevation Plan

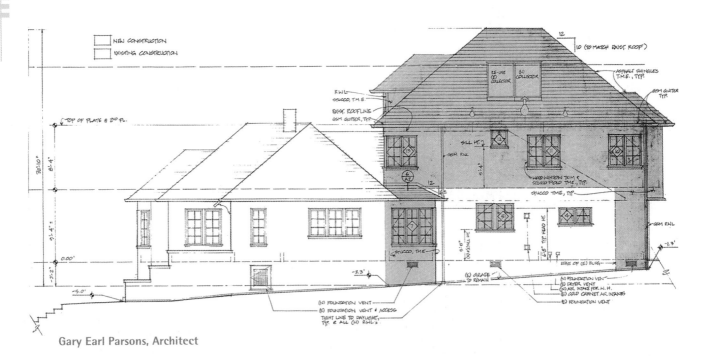

Gary Earl Parsons, Architect

Working drawings include a complete set of detailed elevations. Shaded areas are new construction.

In addition, final drawings are essential because (1) the contractor needs them to give you a solid estimate; (2) they help the contractor anticipate problems and suggest changes before scheduling subcontractors; (3) lenders require them; and (4) many municipalities require tight drawings before issuing work permits—that is, in most communities, both planning and building departments review plans.

How detailed should finished drawings be?
As a minimum, building departments require a cross section from foundation to roof so they can see how the building is framed, insulated, sheathed, and finished. Thus if the job is complex—say, a major kitchen remodeling or more than one room—hire an architect to create a set of working drawings. Because construction documents are usually 40 percent to 50 percent of an architect's total fee, and that fee is customarily 10 percent to 15 percent of total costs, figure that working drawings with floor plans, elevations, and cross sections will be roughly 5 percent of your total budget.

An Overview of Renovation

For handy reference, here's a step-by-step review of important planning considerations. It begins by reiterating planning steps and then presents a typical sequence for construction.

A PLANNING OVERVIEW

1. Make wish lists, and analyze what works and what doesn't in the existing house. Keep a renovation notebook. Then consider how well your designs will satisfy your wish list.

2. Measure rooms, noting the location and condition of the structure and utility systems. Map the site, and consider how well exterior design changes fit the neighborhood.

3. Consider physical and financial constraints. Talk to a contractor about renovation costs. Get preliminary approval on financing. Visit your local planning department.

4. Generate design variations. As favorites emerge, compare them to your wish list and to any constraints. Rework designs until you settle on one.

5. Double-check your design. Revisit the planning department with floor plans and either elevation drawings or a cardboard model.

6. Prepare permit plans and obtain permits. In most communities, the permit process consists of two steps (planning permits and building permits). If you will be living in the house while working on it, get a temporary C.O.

7. Prepare working drawings. List in detail all building components, assemblies, materials, and finishes.

8. Obtain bids from contractors, and select one. The more detail you give bidders, the more realistic and accurate the bids will be.

A RENOVATION SEQUENCE

Be prepared to continue making design decisions as work proceeds. No matter how detailed your plans, you'll need to make adjustments as you renovate. The order in which you complete tasks also depends on the coordination of subcontractors. Here's a typical sequence, if such a thing exists.

1. Clean up. Clean out debris and add rough weather-proofing to gaping holes. Organize the site for efficient work flow.

2. Secure the building so you can store materials and, if necessary, live there.

3. Install temporary facilities such as electrical field receptacles and chemical toilets; hook up temporary utilities.

4. Handle major structural work in the basement or crawl space, repairing damage and flaws that could cause further settling. Correct water problems that could threaten the structure.

5. Replace or replumb posts, columns, girders, and joists that have deteriorated.

6. Demolish walls, ceilings, and floors, and remove debris as it accumulates. If you're not living in the house, install temporary facilities before you start demolition.

7. Do necessary structural carpentry, such as altering load-bearing walls, joists, headers, and collar ties.

8. Attend to the roof as soon as practical. (But make structural changes first, because they could undermine the integrity of a finished roof.)

9. Install windows, doors, and exteriors.

10. Erect interior partitions, the nonbearing walls not framed earlier.

11. Rough out heating, plumbing, gas, and electrical systems (no fixtures yet). Install insulation.

12. Hang wall and ceiling surfaces such as drywall.

13. Install underlayment for finish floors; apply tile floors.

14. Set plumbing fixtures and radiators for baseboard heat, wire electrical receptacles, and so on.

15. Finish taping drywall.

16. Install cabinetwork and countertops.

17. Paint and wallpaper. (Some renovators do this after trim is in place.)

18. Repair and replace trim around windows and doors. Hang doors, and finish all interior woodwork.

19. Finish floors.

20. Install final details, such as baseboard trim, interior doors, electrical outlet plates, hardware, and floor registers.

Case Histories

Renovation is rarely an easy road. Even the happy endings can take more time and money than owners thought they had. Renovation also requires the courage to start and then the stamina to stay with it.

RUTHERFORD HOUSE

The renovators: Martha Rutherford, an educator, loved traveling and collecting indigenous art. Her husband, Dean, a contractor, had lived for six years in Latin America before deciding that the priesthood was not for him.

The house: Two-story, owner-built box was erected in 1929. The builder's widow finally moved on in 1992, after spending most of the previous decade in the living room with four Dobermans, a goat, and a duck. The animals rarely went outside. Dean and Marty stepped carefully into the gloomy interior (the ceiling was painted black), looked at the living room, looked at each other, looked at their real estate agent, and said, "We'll take it."

What worked: Location, location, location. Marty is a city gal, Dean a country boy. The wooded site in the Berkeley hills allowed them to live near a major metropolitan area and yet be in the country. But the decision to buy was more mystical than rational.

The Rutherford house, shortly after it was purchased in 1992. Owner-built in 1929, it was long overdue for some tender loving care.

What didn't work: The widow had abandoned the bottom floor because it had a year-round stream running through it. The northwest corner of the house was completely gone. The kitchen floor joists were so sodden they were spongy, and the bathroom had rotted out. Between every pair of rafters was a rat's nest. A beehive blocked the furnace flue. Dean: "I guess the house brought out my seminarian training—you know, salvation and all."

Constraints:

▶ Dean had just 3 months to get the house habitable before resuming his construction business full-time.

▶ The Rutherfords were determined to live within their means, so the renovation would need to stretch over several years.

▶ Although neighbors were delighted that the property would finally be fixed up, they were wary of the job's scope and impact.

The plan:

▶ Stabilize the structure.

▶ Add a third story to gain views of the setting and give the house street appeal.

▶ Open it up: "We wanted a house totally open to the outdoors, with a deck off almost every room."

The Rutherford house in 2003. The third story includes a master bedroom suite, balconies, and forested views to the east.

The living room, looking southeast: As the sun travels throughout the day, it alters the effects of the saturated room colors.

The living room as seen from the study: Because rooms are painted vividly different colors, doorways frame the space you're about to enter much as a velvet curtain frames a stage.

Compromises: Initially, color was a source of conflict. Because her mother had been a painter, Marty grew up surrounded with vibrant colors. Having spent years in monastic settings, Dean had grown up, as he terms it, "in a white world" and feared that Marty's saturated colors would absorb light and darken the interior, but agreed to them anyway.

Surprises: Because Marty and Dean entered no farther than the living room when they committed to buying the house, the structural problems were a shock. Yet, for Dean the biggest pleasant surprise may have been the colors Marty felt so passionate about. As the two added skylights, opened walls, and installed French doors, they

Schneider House

Stained concrete floors glow in the afternoon sun.

Shoring stabilizes a crumbling foundation.

The exterior is ready for landscaping.

The house abounds with tile, often used to case windows and doors. South and Central American objects collected over the years socialize in odd nooks and crannies. A hand-wrought snake handrail slithers up the wall to the left of the stairs.

could see the light shifting throughout the day, the saturated colors softening and glowing.

All in all: It's one of the happiest houses you can imagine. Said one guest, "It's so sensuous. The textures, the colors, the fireplace shape—it's all so unexpected. It beckons you to explore every nook and cranny." See the kitchen on p. 323 and the main bath on p. 377.

Shared thoughts: Marty, on the renovation: "We didn't rush. We just did things as we could afford them. And in the end, if you take more time, it just doesn't matter. We do a lot of intuitive things. And every time you go by heart, it works out."

This big steel I-beam will help underpin the old structure.

Workers are disguising an I-beam with wood box beams.

Rebirth of a Basement

The Albert Schneider house, built in 1907, was designed by the internationally famous architect Bernard Maybeck. Largely made of redwood, the house weathered well. But by the end of the century, its unreinforced concrete foundation was so weak it could be shattered with a claw hammer. A new design turned a funky, dirt-floored basement into a redwood-trimmed suite of rooms that Maybeck would have loved. It features lots of south- and west-facing windows, so the space is light and airy. Capping the design are concrete floors that glow like polished stone and three runs of I-beams nicely housed within box beams. (The longest I-beam was a W8x58, 20 ft. long.)

RYNERSON HOUSE

The renovators: Juanita and Steve Rynerson had lived in the original house 14 years while raising two sons. According to Juanita, a teacher, and Steve, an architect, "we no sooner had an empty nest than we demolished it." To make an ambitious renovation affordable, they house-sat various houses for a year, which required that they move from house to house, while working full-time jobs and overseeing the renovation.

The house: This two-bedroom Craftsman cottage was built in 1915. In the mid-1960s, according to Steve, "the previous owners stuck their heads in the attic and said, 'Oh, we can put two more bedrooms up here.'"

What worked: Great schools, nice neighborhood, large pleasant backyard. Being an old-house person, Steve loved the architectural elements that had evolved over a long time and gave the house integrity—the formal dining and living rooms toward the front of the house, the wide trim and high ceilings, the graceful overhangs.

What didn't work: From the start, Juanita found the house dark and depressing. Both agreed that, given the scant light, poor traffic flow on the first floor, and serious structural problems on the second, only major remodeling would set things right. Together, they created a detailed list of the cottage's shortcomings (see the drawings on p. 26).

▶ The layout along the back of the house was "a mess," with four rooms—a small bedroom, a laundry, a kitchen, and a bathroom with a shower and tub—crammed into the building's 30-ft. width. The kitchen was little more than a closet with a water heater.

▶ The house was uninsulated, with a single floor-furnace for heat.

▶ The second floor was not worth saving. The rafters were skimpy 2×4s, spaced a too-wide 32 in. on center, with 3 ft. 6 in. overhangs—"more like a tent than a roof," Steve noted. The original attic floor joists were 2×4s, and when the previous owners converted the attic into bedrooms, the increased loads sagged the ceiling (and floor) of the dining room below.

Constraints: To avoid the hassle and delay of seeking a zoning variance (or knocking down the house and starting over) the Rynersons decided not to increase the existing house footprint. Also, they didn't want to encroach on the backyard.

Previous owners converted the attic space into two bedrooms but largely ignored structural issues. The attic stairs, at right, were also minimal.

Though it needed structural reinforcement, the classic Craftsman dining room was the least changed in appearance.

A view from the living room, looking southeast, shows how extensive the renovation was. At right are the original front door and entry trim.

After renovation: Although the remodeling raised the ridge 6½ ft. and added 750 sq. ft. of living space, from the street, the house looks smaller than it is.

Before renovation: This two-bedroom Craftsman cottage was built in 1915.

And they wanted the new design to respect the scale of the houses around it.

The plan: Build up. Add a second story, but maintain the intimate cottage feeling. (One of their interior designers referred to the new design as "a Craftsman on steroids.") Improve first-floor traffic flow, move the master bedroom upstairs so it will have more natural light and long views, upgrade and add bathrooms, and tie the house to the backyard.

Compromises: Steve noted, "Renovation is kind of a slippery slope, so we ended up replacing more of the house than we anticipated. A lot of it was structural stuff we had to do. So the project took longer and cost more. You deal with it."

Surprises: House-sitting was an adventure. A year of living simply—living *on* houses rather than *in* them—forever changed the way the Rynersons live. Their renovated house is spare and uncluttered. Combining the roles of architect/ client and husband/wife was also a challenge, but the constant communication required by the remodel brought them closer and reminded them, over and over, of the traits they cherished in each other.

All in all: The workmanship is exquisite, relying more on the subtle beauty of natural materials than on fancy edges or shiny finishes. Simple shapes; honest forms. In one bathroom, as shown on p. 323, we see fine-grained black granite counters, luminous cherry cabinets, and nautilus-shaped fossils swimming in limestone that was a seabed in Jurassic times.

Shared thoughts: Juanita mused: "The painter ran late, and the house reeked of fresh paint the day we were to move back in. Sometimes, you just have to let things go. So we pitched a tent under the redwood in the backyard, ran an extension cord to the house so we could watch TV, and camped out for a few days. It was good to be home."

A still life of Craftsman elements: Dining-room trim frames a view of the living room.

Creating a light-filled living room required some work—namely, demolishing a dark porch, moving the wall out, raising the ceiling, and expanding the bank of windows.

Once you enter the front door, the space opens dramatically as the stairwell soars two stories. As Craftsman-inspired as the renovation is, this entry leaves historicity behind. The squiggly railing, the floating ceiling fixtures, and the wall colors are light-hearted and new.

The new floor plan improved traffic circulation dramatically. Beyond the dining room, a gourmet kitchen opens to a lush backyard.

3 Tools

The tools in this chapter are a subjective collection. Yours should be too. Choose tools that are right for the scope of your renovation, your experience, your storage space, your budget, and your physical strength. Because tools become an extension of your hands, shop for tools that are comfortable to use. Other specialized tools are presented in pertinent chapters.

Tool Safety

Few things will slow a job more than an injury, to say nothing of the pain and expense involved. Don't be afraid of tools, but respect their power and heed their dangers. The following suggestions come from professional builders and tool manufacturer owner's manuals, so read and heed them. Always comply with safety tips provided in tool-operating manuals. Some may pertain to features or hazards unique to particular makes and models.

Wearing appropriate eye and hearing protection will reduce fatigue, increase productivity, and prevent injury. This protection is especially important when you are operating power equipment or using any tool at eye level.

Disconnect electricity. Be sure to cut off the electricity to the areas you'll disturb. Then use a voltage tester to double-check that current is off in affected outlets. Also avoid cutting or puncturing wires hidden behind wall surfaces.

Plan the job and pace yourself. The job will go more safely and smoothly if you assemble your tools and materials beforehand. Take regular breaks, and you'll stay sharp longer.

Don't work when sick. Take the day off when you're excessively tired, preoccupied, or taking any substance that impairs your judgment.

Operate tools safely. Study, and comply with, tool manufacturer owner's manuals. Never remove safety devices. Avoid electrical tools whose wires are frayed, cut, or exposed. Never force tools—saws can kick back and high-torque drills can knock you off a ladder.

Don't work alone. When you're on a steep roof or a tall ladder, make sure someone is close by. He or she needn't be working with you, but should be within earshot if you need help. If you need to work alone, have a cell phone handy.

Keep work areas well lit. Don't work where the light's poor. If you disconnect the power to a work area, run an extension cord and droplight to it.

Miscellany. Keep kids away from work sites. If you store equipment at home, lock up power tools, dangerous solvents, and the like.

Tools to Own

Consider buying most of the safety equipment listed here.

SAFETY EQUIPMENT

Hearing protectors will prevent permanent ear damage and reduce fatigue while using power tools. There are a number of styles, from reusable foam plugs to earmuffs; properly fitted, they should reduce noise 15 decibels to 30 decibels (db). Look for models that meet American National Standards Institute (ANSI) S3.19-1974 specifications.

Eye protection is a must when you're using power tools or striking nails or chisels with a hammer. Safety glasses or goggles that meet ANSI Z87.1-1989 specs are strong enough to stop a chunk of metal, masonry, or wood without shattering the lens. (Most lenses are polycarbonate plastic.) Get eyewear that has vents to prevent fogging; you can also get combination safety glasses/sunglasses with UV 400 protection.

A hard hat won't protect you if you don't wear it, so find one that fits well. There are basically two types: Type I protects the top of your head,

Safety equipment. From left to right, top: hard hat, work gloves, and knee pads; center: ear plugs, safety glasses, safety sunglasses, and hearing protection; bottom: head lamp and respirator mask.

whereas type II (ANSI Z89.1-1997) offers some additional protection if a blow to the head is somewhat off-center. Both are invaluable when you're handling objects overhead or someone is working above you.

Work gloves are essential when handling caustic, abrasive, or sharp materials. Some rubber-coated work gloves will let you work with concrete without suffering skin burns, yet are flexible enough to pick up a dime. Auto-supply stores carry latex-free nitrile plastic gloves that are cheap, durable, and quite flexible.

A respirator mask with changeable cartridges can prevent inhalation of toxic fumes, such as those from epoxy resins and paint solvents. Such respirators are discussed further in Chapter 19. A disposable paper dust mask is okay when working around nontoxic materials like sawdust.

Knee pads with hard-plastic kneecaps and substantial padding allow you to move around on your knees comfortably, and they protect your knees from construction debris and prolonged contact with hard floors. They should be comfortable enough to wear all day.

A headlamp (battery-powered) is invaluable in tight, dark spaces where you should have both hands free.

A safety harness should be attached to solid framing when you are working on roofs with a 6/12 pitch or steeper, over open framing, or on any other high, unstable workplace.

A first-aid kit should be secured to a prominent place at the work site so you can find it quickly when you need it.

Cleanup tools. You'll need a household broom, a push broom, a dustpan, a heavy-duty rubber garbage can, a flat shovel for scooping debris, and a large-capacity (12-gal. to 16-gal.) wet/dry shop vacuum. You'll find Dumpster™ tips at the end of this chapter.

Tarps. Buy at least one 9-ft. by 12-ft. tarp and one 45-in. by 12-ft. runner. Get good-quality, heavy canvas duck. Paint will soak through cheap fabric tarps, and sheet plastic is too slippery to work on.

You may not need all of the following tools, but it's good to know what each can do.

A framing square with stair gauges is a basic layout tool for plumb and level cuts. It also enables you to set the rise and run for stairs as well as to make repetitive layouts such as for rafter ends.

Mason's string has many uses, whether to support a line level or to temporarily tie things together.

An **adjustable square** is a smaller version of a framing square and is somewhat less versatile.

A **stud-finder** enables you to find studs you need to find or want to avoid.

A **small combination square** fits easily into a tool belt and enables quick and accurate 45° and 90° cuts on small pieces. It also doubles as a depth gauge for getting notches to a certain depth, setting door stops to jamb edges, establishing "reveals," and so on.

An **adjustable bevel gauge** copies odd angles and transfers them to workpieces.

A **try square** is a precise tool that's more of a shop or bench tool, handy for making sure that a table-saw blade is perfectly square to the table.

A **chalkline box** contains chalked line that you snap between points to mark straight chalklines on sheet materials or layout lines for framing. The line itself can double as a stringline. And, in a pinch, the box and line can also serve as a plumb bob.

A **folding rule** with sliding insert is great for accurate, inside measurements like inner cabinet or window widths. Because the folding rule is rigid, it will hold the dimension you set. The sliding brass insert doubles as a depth gauge.

Ladder Safety

Don't scrimp on ladders. For greatest safety and durability, buy a type IA, which is a construction-grade ladder rated for 300 lb. Avoid household-grade ladders, which can be unsafe.

Although fiberglass ladders are more expensive than wood or aluminum, most pros prefer fiberglass because it's sturdy and nonconductive, and it's midweight compared to wood and aluminum. Wood stepladders are okay for indoor use, but wood ladders used outside can deteriorate quickly. Aluminum ladders are a reasonable compromise in price and weight but are the most electrically conductive of the three. *Note:* All ladder materials can conduct electricity if they're dirty or wet.

Safe working-lengths of ladders are always less than their nominal lengths. When using an 8-ft. stepladder, for example, stand no higher than 6 ft. on it, and certainly

don't stand on the top step—which usually has a label stating, "This is *not* a step." Likewise, a 32-ft. extension ladder is only 26 ft. to 28 ft. long when extended. Ladder sections overlap about one-quarter, and a ladder leaning against a building should be set away from the wall about one-quarter of the ladder's extended length.

Ladders must be solidly footed to be safe, especially extension ladders. After setting up the ladder so that its sides are as plumb as possible, stand on the bottom rungs to seat the feet. *Adjustable leg levelers,* as shown, are available for leveling ladders on slopes. If you're at all unsure about the ladder's footing, stake its bottom to prevent "creeping."

Finally, as you work, always keep your hips within the ladder's sides.

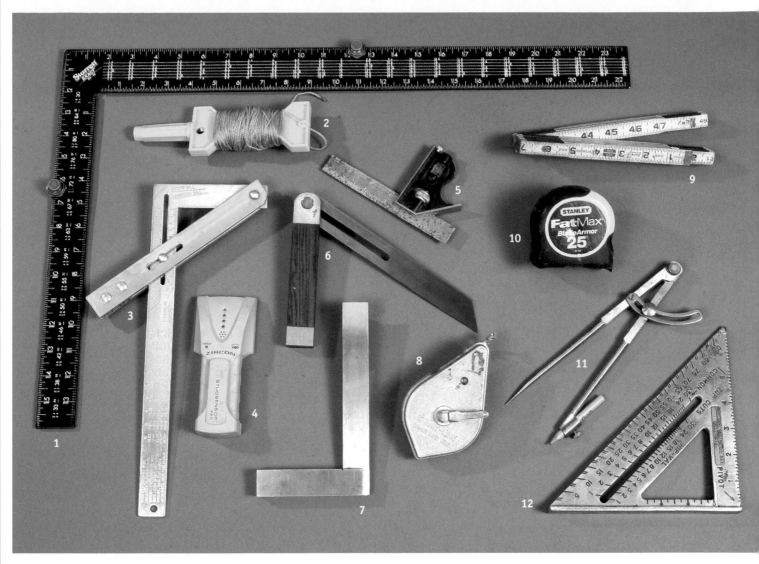

Measuring and layout tools: 1, framing square with stair gauges; 2, mason's string; 3, adjustable square; 4, stud-finder; 5, combination square; 6, adjustable bevel gauge; 7, try square; 8, chalkline box; 9, folding rule with sliding insert; 10, tape measure; 11, compass; 12, Swanson Speed™ Square.

Tape measures are a must. A 16-ft. one will do for most jobs; but the wider tape of a 25-ft. model can span 7 ft. without collapsing, thereby allowing you to take an approximate reading across a span opening.

A **compass** draws circles or doubles as a scribe so you can fit flooring or sheet materials to the curved or irregular profile of a wall, cabinet, or baseboard.

A **Swanson Speed™ Square** enables quick 45° and 90° angle layouts. And with a little practice, you can set rafter pitches. Indestructible, this fits snugly in any tool pouch and is easily one of the most popular tools since the 1970s.

PLUMB AND LEVEL

A **plumb bob** takes patience to use, but it's a compact, accurate tool. The plumbed string is also a useful reference line you can measure out from. The Gammon Reel® shown in the photo on the next page automatically reels in the string so it can't tangle up in a tool pouch.

A **4-ft. spirit level** is a good, all-purpose level, long enough to level accurately across joists, check for level and plumb of door and window casings, and so on.

A **2-ft. spirit level** enables you to level window sills, door head jambs, and other tight spaces where a 4-ft. level won't fit.

A **standard torpedo level** is small and fits into a tool pouch. Though it's not as accurate as a longer level, it's good for a quick reference in

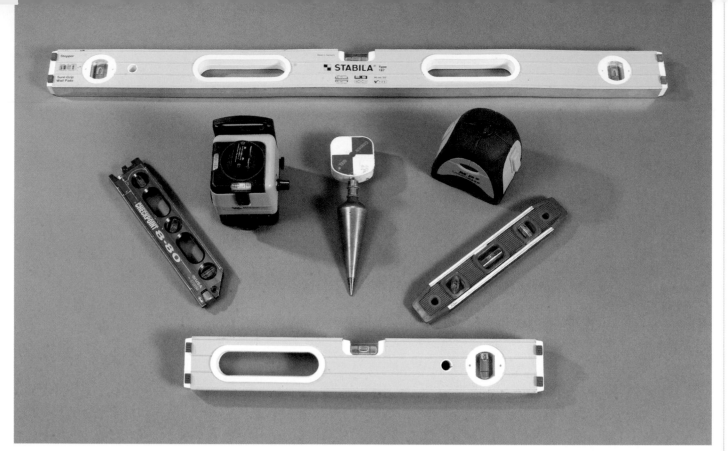

Levels and plumbing devices. Top: 4-ft. spirit level; bottom: 2-ft. spirit level. Center, from left: torpedo level with laser, rotating laser, plumb bob with Gammon Reel, 5-beam self-leveling laser, and standard torpedo level.

tight spaces. Magnetic versions can stick to cast-iron pipe.

A torpedo level with a laser has the same limitations as any torpedo level, but its laser allows plumbers to set the tool on a pipe that's pitched correctly and extend that pitch (indefinitely) to other pipe sections.

POWER SAWS

Circular saws are generally characterized as either *worm-drives* or *sidewinders* and are often called Skilsaws®, the name of a popular brand.

Among professional builders, especially on the West Coast, worm-drive circular saws are favored for cutting framing lumber. They tend to have bigger motors and more torque. They also spin slower, bind less, and run quieter than sidewinders. If you're right-handed, worm-drive saws make it easier to see the line you're cutting.

Sidewinders are generally lighter and more compact, so they're easier to handle and a good choice for the occasional builder. But because the blade is turning at 90° to the motor shaft, it is more likely to bind if your cut wanders off the line. For that reason, a rip fence is a nice accessory.

Beam saws are called "sidewinders on steroids" because they can accommodate 10-in. blades that cut smoothly through 4× lumber in one pass. It's not a must-buy item, but wow, what a tool!

Circular saws. From left: sidewinder, beam saw, and worm-drive.

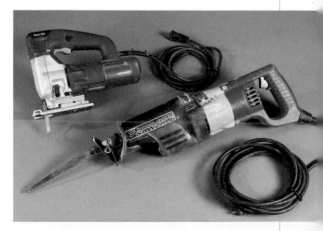

Jigsaw and reciprocating saw.

For circular-saw blades in general, the more teeth, the smoother the cut. If you buy just one, make it carbide tipped; it will stay sharp far longer and give cleaner cuts. There are specialty blades for almost anything you'd want to cut: tile, concrete, metal, and wet or pressure-treated lumber (has a Teflon™ coating). Remodelers' blades cut through wood and the occasional nail without being damaged.

A reciprocating saw, also called a Sawzall® after a popular make, is *the* indispensable demolition saw. A marvel in tight spaces, it can remove old pipes, cut through studs or joists or, with a bimetal blade, cut through nails *and* studs in one pass. (Blades break, so get extras.) A "recip" saw is also useful in new construction to notch studs for pipes, cut plywood nailed over rough openings for windows and doors, and so on.

Jigsaws, sometimes called saber saws, are useful for notches, curving cuts, and odd-shaped holes. Typical uses include cutting out holes for sinks in countertops and holes in cabinet backs so pipes or ducts can pass through. The blades are thin and prone to snap, so buy extras.

HANDSAWS

The following inexpensive handsaws are handy to have:

Coping saws cut curves into any thin stock, although their primary use is coping trim so intersecting pieces fit snugly. They take both metal- and wood-cutting blades.

A hacksaw is most often used to cut metal, especially bolts or nails. Sawblades will last longer if you use the full length of the blade.

A Japanese saw cuts on the pull stroke. Its thin, flexible blade is perfect for cutting flush shims and other thin stock. Most are two-sided, with rip and crosscut teeth.

A handsaw is still worth having in your toolbox, preferably a 10-pt. crosscut saw. Even if you depend primarily on a circular saw, a handsaw is handy for finishing cuts that don't go all the way through a rafter or joist.

A dovetail saw makes clean crosscuts in small molding, doorstops, and casing beads.

A keyhole saw can cut holes in drywall for electrical boxes, without predrilling.

ROUTERS

Full-size routers are probably too expensive for casual remodelers, but trim routers and rotary tools are versatile and reasonably priced. Safety goggles are a must with any router.

Laminate trimmers are also called trim routers. In addition to trimming laminate edges, these lightweight routers are great for mortising door hinges and strike plates.

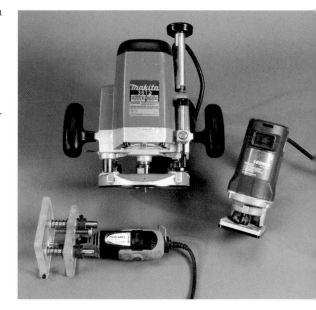

Routers. Clockwise, from top: large plunge router, laminate trimmer, and Dremel® rotary tool with plunge base.

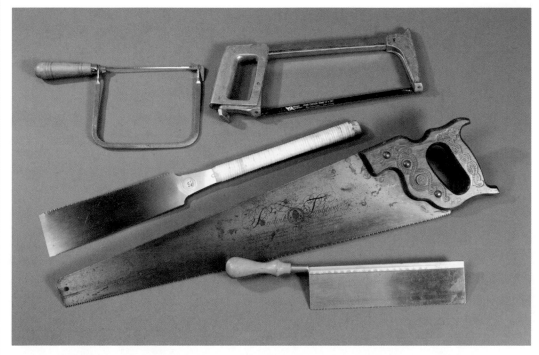

Handsaws. Clockwise, from lower right: dovetail saw, crosscut saw, Japanese saw, coping saw, and hacksaw.

Plunge routers can lower to precise depths in the middle of a workpiece, making them ideal for wood joinery, edge shaping, mortising door hinges, and so on.

Dremel™, variable-speed rotary tools can dislodge tired tile grout and remove stubborn paint from beaded or ornate woodwork. There are hundreds of specialized accessories for this tool.

HAND CUTTING AND SHAPING TOOLS

Power tools can do a lot, but you often need a hand tool to finish the job.

Chisels clean up the corners of a hinge mortise that a router can't reach and quickly notch plates so washers sit flush. Be sure to sheathe cutting edges so they stay sharp and don't cut you when you reach for them.

Mallets can strike chisels without damaging their handles.

Utility knives are indispensable. Quick-blade-change knives dispense fresh blades so you don't need to unscrew the knife's body. Don't use knives with cheap, snap-off blades (often sold at stationery or office-supply stores) to cut construction materials; such blades can break unexpectedly and injure you.

Rat-tail files smooth and enlarge holes and create an oval slot after two holes are drilled close to each other.

Flat files take burrs off newly cut bolts and the like, so you can start a washer.

Four-in-one rasps contain two flat and two curved rasps in one wood-shaping tool.

Block planes shave off tiny amounts of wood from door edges, casings, and other thin stock, allowing tight, final fits of materials.

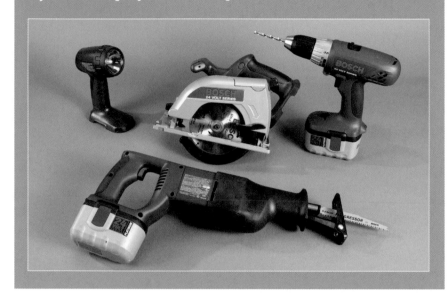

Cordless TOOLS

It's astounding how powerful and hefty cordless tools have become. There are now 24-volt drills, circular saws, and reciprocating saws. But the trade-off remains between workload and battery life: Corded tools are still better if there's a lot of cutting and drilling to do. But when you have only a few joists to cut, holes to drill, or joists to notch, grab your cordless, and go for it.

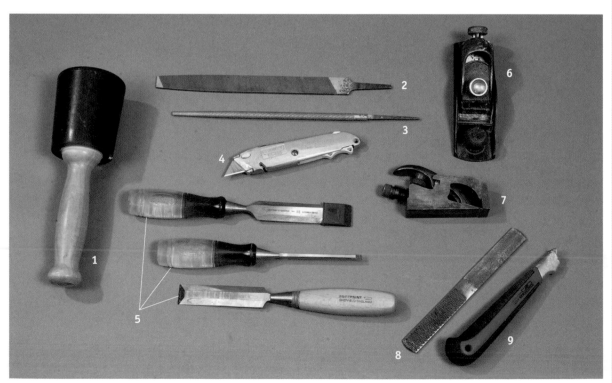

Cutting and shaping tools: 1, mallet; 2, flat file; 3, rat-tail file; 4, utility knife; 5, chisels; 6, block plane; 7, bullnose plane; 8, 4-in-1 rasp; 9, carbide scraper.

Bullnose planes can fine-shave wood edges in tight places. Bullnose blades are the same width as plane shoes. You can remove the bullnose front piece, allowing you to plane right up to the juncture of an adjoining piece.

Bahco® by Snap-On®, carbide scrapers are not intended to shape wood, but their blades are so sharp that you can. Instead use them to remove dried putty or excess Bondo™ or to clean up the spurs of medium-density fiberboard (MDF) that screws sometimes kick up.

DRILLS

A ⅜-in. cordless drill is a must. These days, builders use screws to install almost everything from exterior trim to decks and drywall. You can get more voltage and bigger chucks, but this size has a good weight to power ratio. Get a reversible, variable-speed model with a keyless chuck, adjustable clutch, and an extra battery.

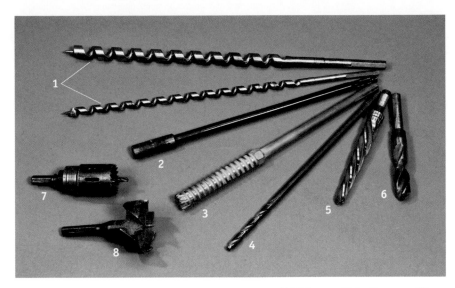

Drill bits. 1, self-feeding auger bits; 2, drill bit extension; 3, rebar-cutting bit; 4, long twist drill bit; 5, ½-in. by ¾-in. reamer; 6, ¾-in. twist drill bit; 7, hole saw; 8, plumber's bit (wide self-feeding bit).

A ⅜-in., corded, pistol-grip drill has the sustained run-time that cordless drills lack, more power, and a side handle to help you control its torque. It drills 1-in. or 1½-in. holes easily, but use a ½-in. right-angle drill if you're roughing in plumbing systems.

A ⅜-in. close-quarter cordless drill is best for tight spaces like cabinet interiors. Its right-angle configuration extends your reach when you are hanging upper cabinets.

DRILL BITS

A standard drill nest contains 1/16-in. to ¼-in. twist drill bits. From there, you're on your own. The following specialized bits are quite useful.

Vix® bits have spring-loaded drives that accurately center holes predrilled for hinges, striker plates, window pulls, etc.

Self-feeding auger bits drill through posts for bolts and through wall plates for hold-downs. A 12-in. by ¼-in. auger doubles as an exploratory bit.

Hole saws drill large-diameter holes in finish materials such as doors and countertops. The pilot bit in the middle emerges on the backside first, so you can retract the bit and center it to finish drilling from the other side. This lets you avoid wood "bust-through," splintering backsides.

A plumber's bit is a wide, self-feeding auger bit good for rough-in framing work.

Reamers are tapered bits that enlarge an existing hole in metal or wood.

Large twist drill bits, also called aircraft bits, are best suited for drilling metal.

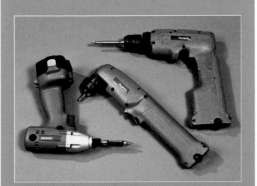

Cordless drills and drivers. From left: Impact driver, close-quarters right-angle drill, standard drill.

Drilling and screwing accessories. 1, Allen wrenches; 2, magnetic bit holders; 3, extension bit holder; 4, flexible bit holder; 5, stubby screwdriver; 6, 4-in-1 screwdriver; 7, ratchet-handle bit driver.

Clamps. Clockwise, from lower left: spring clamp, bar clamp, quick-release bar clamp, C-clamp, and hand screw.

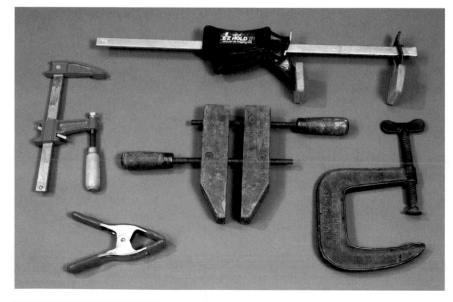

DRILLING AND SCREWING ACCESSORIES

Magnetic bit holders magnetize drill bits so screws don't fall off the bit. Some types also have a collet that keeps the screw centered as you drive them in.

Extension bit holders enable you to drive screws where drill/drivers won't fit.

Flexible bit holders drive screws at angles drill/drivers can't reach.

Drill bit extensions enable you to drill deeper with the bits you've got.

A ratchet-handle bit driver can turn Phillips- or hex-head screws in tight spaces. They're also great for turning the leveling devices on refrigerator legs.

A stubby screwdriver has a reversible bit: one side Phillips-head, the other slotted.

A 4-in-1 screwdriver is the screwdriver to own, if you have only one.

Allen wrenches tighten Allen screws on a lot of tools, including drill bit extensions.

CLAMPS

Quick-release bar clamps are a second set of hands on the job site. Use them to hold work to a bench, temporarily join two boards, align stair balusters, or mock up rafter pairs. Their rubber jaws won't mar surfaces on fine work.

Standard bar clamps slide jaws to approximate position and use a threaded handle to draw materials tight. They're a little slower than quick-release clamps, but they apply more force.

Spring clamps are the quickest to operate for relatively thin materials that don't require an especially tight a grip.

Hand screws apply even pressure to a relatively broad area. Excellent for gluing, they hold work well and won't damage wood. Open and close such clamps with two hands rotating, almost like pedaling a bicycle.

C-clamps apply a very strong force and are especially suitable when the workpiece absolutely mustn't move. Insert scrap wood between the jaws and workpiece to protect it from jaw damage.

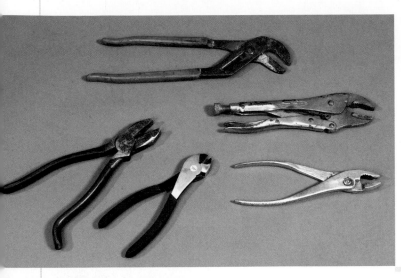

Pliers and cutters. Clockwise, from top: Channelock™ slip-joint pliers, Vise-Grip locking pliers, slip-joint pliers, side cutters, lineman's pliers.

Lineman's pliers are an electrician's mainstay, great for twisting and cutting wire.

Aviation snips, also known as tinsips, cut sheet metal; use them for flashing and duct work.

HAMMERS

Choose a hammer with a grip and weight that feel right for you. Bigger heads and longer handles can deliver greater impacts when nailing and so require fewer swings to drive nails. But they also require greater torquing force from you and so may cause tendonitis.

Twenty-six-ounce framing hammers are as big as anyone needs. Titanium framing hammers are in vogue these days because they transfer less shock to your arm, though more to your wallet.

Twenty-ounce framing hammers are light enough to double as trim hammers. But, truth is, pros prefer trim guns (pneumatic nailers) for finish work because they free-up one hand to steady the work and don't ding the trim, like hammers do.

Sixteen-ounce finish hammers are fine for a small amount of trim.

Hand sledges are handy for knocking shoring or partitions a few inches over and for breaking loose stubborn foundation forms.

Hammer tackers are a quick way to staple building paper, insulation, and sheet plastic (see the photo on p. 68).

WRECKING AND PRYBARS

 Disconnect plumbing pipes and electrical cables in areas about to be demolished—and check with a voltage tester to be sure the power's off. Be methodical and work slowly.

Wrecking bars have differing lengths and end configurations. Most are crowbars with crooked

Hammers. Left: hand sledge. Top to bottom: 26-oz. framing hammer, 20-oz. framing hammer, 16-oz. finish hammer, and small hand sledge.

PLIERS AND CUTTERS

Slip-joint pliers are Old Reliables. Our grandfathers used the same design.

Channelock® slip-joint pliers have long, offset handles and jaws that open wide for the slip-nut under the kitchen sink...or wherever.

Vise-Grip® pliers have an adjustable tension mechanism that lets you lock the tool's jaws on work, such as stripped screws. They can double as a temporary clamp, but don't overtighten.

Side cutters are designed to cut wire or small nail shanks. But they're also great nail pullers if you don't squeeze too hard.

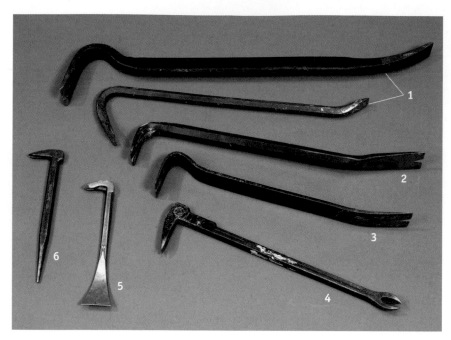

Wrecking and prybars. 1, Crook–neck wrecking bars; 2, L–bar; 3, flat bar; 4, cat's paw; 5, 8–in. prybar/nail puller; 6, cat's paw with punch point.

pipe cutter, large and small adjustable open-end wrenches (commonly called Crescent® wrenches), slip-nut pliers, and a pair of pipe wrenches.

Earth tools include round-point shovel, pickax, hatchet or ax, and wheelbarrow.

Tools to Rent

Most contractors own the tools listed in this section, but occasional users should probably just rent them. The decision depends on how often or how long you may need the tools and how passionate you are about collecting them.

SAFETY, SCAFFOLDING, AND JACKS

Inside or out, scaffolding gives you secure footing and peace of mind. Instead of hanging precariously from a ladder, you can concentrate on the task at hand. That said, anyone who's not comfortable working at heights, shouldn't. As one contractor put it, "If it feels unsafe on a roof, it probably is."

Pipe-frame scaffolding. Have the rental company set up and tear down exterior scaffolding. It takes experience to set scaffolding safely, especially on uneven ground, and units must be attached to the building.

Pipe scaffolding typically consists of two rectangular end frames and diagonal braces secured with wing nuts or self-locking cleats. Once the first stage is assembled, the installer adjusts the self-leveling feet until the platform is level.

To raise successive stages, the installer stacks end frames over coupling sleeves and locks the pieces in place with uplift and cotter pins. Additional lock arms may join the bracing. Platforms should be planked their entire width with 2× lumber or metal planks provided by the rental company. Guardrails are a must on all scaffolding. If your platform is 10 ft. or higher, most safety codes require mid-rails and toe boards as well.

Interior scaffolding has rollers that let you move it around a room (see the photo on p. 351). Before you mount a platform, always lock the roller locks, and dismount before unlocking the locks for any reason. It's unwise to move an unlocked scaffold while someone is atop it.

Ladder jacks. Ladder jacks offer an inexpensive, quickly adjustable setup, which can be safe if both ladders are well footed. Many jack brackets pivot so that scaffolding planks can rest under or over the ladder. Consult the operating instructions supplied with your ladder jacks. In general, avoid platform heights higher than 8 ft.

Pump jacks. Pump jacks work fine when new, but after a few seasons of rain and rust, they often bind, which produces eye-popping free falls

ends for better leverage. The longer the bar, the better the leverage.

L-bars are wrecking bars with a flat L-shaped end instead of a crook. Drive the L into lumber that's nailed together and twist the tool to pry the pieces apart.

Flat bars (also called Wonderbar® or handy bars) are the best tool to ease off delicate trim without damaging it. Pry the trim up gradually along its length.

A cat's paw is the tool of choice if you're pulling a lot of nails out of framing. It bites into wood pretty deeply, so don't use this tool on trim.

A small cat's paw with a punch point is small enough to remove finish nails, and its pointed end doubles as a nail punch.

An 8-in. prybar/nail puller lifts trim gently and pulls finish nails.

MISCELLANEOUS TOOLS

Sawhorses support work at a comfortable height. The metal-leg variety, which nail to lengths of 2×4, are sturdy and easy to collapse and store. Black & Decker's® Workmate® has an integral clamp in its benchtop; it also folds flat for compact storage and transport.

Electrical and plumbing tools are covered in other chapters. But don't be without a *voltage tester* (see the bottom photo on p. 235) to make sure the power's off, slot and Phillips-head screwdrivers with insulated handles, and needle-nose and lineman's pliers. And every toolbox should have a

Rotating laser on a job site. Note the laser lines on nearby studs.

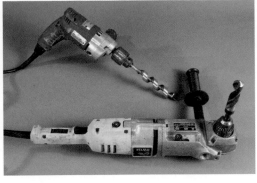

Corded drills. From top: ³⁄₈-in. pistol-grip drill and ¹⁄₂-in. right-angle drill.

Sliding compound-miter saw.

Pneumatic nailers. From left: finish nailer and framing nailer.

or blind rage, when you're 15 ft. in the air and the jacks refuse to go up or down. Consequently, most rental pump jacks have been hammered silly for their failings. Granted, such abuse does not improve any equipment, but where the issue is your safety, be wary of rental pump jacks.

LASER LEVELS

Laser levels, ingenious layout devices, are usually too expensive for nonprofessionals; but once you see one in action, you'll want one. A self-leveling five-beam laser shoots a beam straight up (plumb) and four beams perpendicular to it (and each other). A rotating laser can be mounted to a wall or a tripod, from which it will project a level reference line all around the room, which is invaluable if you're setting cabinets.

SLIDING COMPOUND-MITER SAW

A 10-in. sliding compound-miter saw is the ultimate tool for a wide range of finish work. The extended crosscut length, combined with adjustable angle and bevel settings, allows complicated cuts in larger materials such as 6-in. by 6-in. deck posts, 10-in.-wide siding boards, and large crown molding.

POWER PLANERS

Moderately priced and incredibly useful, a power planer can plane down studs to create a flat plane for drywall, trim a little off an exterior door, and quickly cut a slot so the nailing flange of an electrical box is flush to the edge of a stud (see the photo on p. 167).

RIGHT-ANGLE DRILL

Renting a ¹⁄₂-in. right-angle drill will let you avoid burning out your own drill while roughing in plumbing and electrical runs. The right-angle drill is a godsend in the tight spaces between framing members, and the drill's long handle gives you more leverage to control the torque of this slow-drilling powerful machine.

When drilling through framing, self-feeding, double-spiral bits clear wood well, but use a hole-cutting bit when bigger holes are required. Whatever bit you use, wear goggles and watch for nails. The better right-angle drills will have a clutch that disengages if the bit meets a certain level of resistance.

PNEUMATIC NAILERS

It may take 20,000 to 30,000 nails just to sheath an average house. Add to that the nails needed

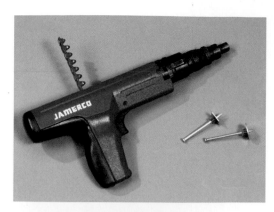

A powder-actuated tool with drive pins and (at top of gun) a strip of cartridges.

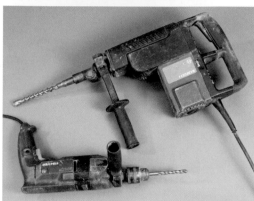

Rotary hammers. From left: ½-in. hammer drill and 1½-in. hammer drill.

for framing, roofing, and shingling, and you can begin to imagine the number of hammer strokes required. Pneumatic nailers, commonly called nail guns, can reduce those strokes to a small fraction.

Control of the workpiece is the other big advantage of these nailers—with a hammer and nail, you need one hand for each. A pneumatic nailer delivers the nails, giving you a free hand to hold a stud or top plate in place. The nail goes in quickly without requiring hammer blows that cause the wood to "drift."

And unlike hammer heads, pneumatic nailers won't slip and ding expensive pieces of trim. Consequently, among professionals, pneumatic finish nailers have all but replaced the hand nailing of door and window casings.

There are framing nailers, finish nailers, and brad nailers (also called pin tackers). These nailers are powered by air hoses running to a compressor and calibrated by a pressure adjustment on the nailer. Staff at rental companies can explain such adjustments as well as safety features and correct operation.

Hard hats, safety glasses, and hearing protection are musts.

POWER-ACTUATED TOOLS

Potentially very dangerous, powder-actuated tools are useful for shooting nails into concrete, as when framing an interior wall on a concrete slab or securing pressure-treated lumber to a foundation wall. But such connections need to be nonstructural. Engineers specify bolts instead for all structural connections to concrete.

A reputable rental company will demonstrate the tool's safe use, describe (and rent) safety equipment, answer your questions, and supply appropriate cartridges and drive pins. Some local codes prohibit renting powder-actuated tools to nonprofessionals.

When using this tool, wear safety glasses, hearing protection, and a hard hat.

ROTARY HAMMERS

A rotary hammer is also known as a hammer drill or RotoHammer®, after a brand name. On

the hammer setting, the tool punches as it turns, somewhat like a jackhammer.

Smaller hammer drills (½ in.) typically offer two settings: rotation only and hammering with rotation. Such drills are adequate to drill small holes in concrete, for anchoring door thresholds to slabs and for predrilling pilot holes for masonry screws.

Larger hammer drills (1½ in.) usually offer only hammering with rotation. If you need to drill dozens of ¾-in. holes for standard ⅝-in. anchor bolts, this is the tool. Get a model with padded handles as well as vibration reduction.

Wear safety glasses, hearing protection, heavy gloves, and hard hat.

CONCRETE BREAKER AND COMPRESSOR

Whenever you need to replace defective concrete, change the configuration of foundations, or get down to soil level to put in new drainage, rent a concrete breaker (see the photo on p. 215) and special high-volume compressor.

SOIL TAMPER

Use a gasoline-powered soil tamper tool before you pour a concrete slab, lay a brick walk, and so on.

DUMPSTERS

Although you can rent Dumpsters by the day or week, carefully plan (and stick to) demolition schedules so you fill and get Dumpsters removed as quickly as possible. Other people's debris has a way of filling your Dumpster when it sits too long, so don't even order one until you're well into tearout and have accumulated a half week's worth of debris.

If you're demolishing masonry, rent a "low boy," which is a small unit (10 cu. yd.) specially built for the great weight of concrete, brick, and the like. For other jobs, rent the largest size available, usually 20 cu. yd. Be advised that you'll also pay for the dumping fee the company must pay to your municipality.

Nailer TRIGGERS

Pneumatic nailers have several types of triggers. The safest is a restrictive trigger, which you must squeeze and release to shoot a nail. A second type, a bounce-fire trigger, shoots a nail each time you depress the gun's nosepiece. Bounce-fire triggers are usually favored for sheathing, which requires a lot of 8d nails (2½ in. long) spaced relatively close to one another. Until you become accustomed to nailers, restrictive triggers are far safer.

Building Materials

This chapter offers an overview of the materials needed to frame and sheath a house. Materials include standard lumber; engineered lumber; sheet materials, such as plywood and particleboard; and fasteners, including nails, screws, and construction adhesives.

There's never been a wider choice of building materials or more readily available information on using them, whether you need to size ceiling joists or find an environmentally safe adhesive that can bond frozen lumber. Just type your requirements into a Web site calculator or ask at your lumber supplier for a recommendation. Many related techniques are covered in Chapter 8.

Standard Lumber

Wood is a superb building material. It is strong, economical, and easily worked. Whether as a tree or as lumber, wood can withstand great loads, yet it's resilient enough to regain its shape when loads are removed. *Standard lumber* is lumber sawn from logs in the traditional manner; whereas *engineered lumber* is often an amalgam of peeled, shredded, or reassembled wood pieces and strong adhesives.

LUMBER GRADES

After lumber has been milled, each piece is visually graded according to established performance standards and then stamped. This grade stamp is important because building inspectors won't approve structures built with unstamped lumber. Otherwise they'd have no way of knowing what loads the wood can support. In brief, grading is based on the presence of warping, knots, holes, decay, or other imperfections that could weaken the lumber and reduce its load-bearing capacity. Generally, dimension lumber grades are based on

Dimension lumber is sawn from logs and then milled to a thickness and width that is slightly less than its nominal end cross sections. For example, the ends of these 2×6s actually measure 1½ in. by 5½ in.

strength, appearance, or both. The more imperfections, the lower the grade.

Grade stamps indicate lumber grade, tree species, moisture content when the lumber was surfaced, sawmill, and regional agency certifying the grading standards. Lumber that is stress rated by machine will have additional information.

Structural framing lumber grades run from Select Structural (the best looking and strongest) through No. 1, No. 2, and No. 3. An architect might specify Select Structural 4×8s, for example, when beams will be exposed in a living room. In most grading systems, No. 1 and No. 2 are equally strong, though No. 1 has fewer cosmetic flaws. Thus if appearance is not a factor, you can order "No. 2 and better" without sacrificing strength. No. 3 is the weakest and least expensive grade in the structural category; you won't save much by using it, because you'll have to order larger dimensions to carry the same loads as No. 1 and No. 2 grades.

Light framing lumber, which is used for plates, sills, and blocking, has lower strength requirements than structural framing members. Light framing members are 4 in. (thick or wide) or less. Grades are Construction (the best), Standard, and Utility. Contractors often order "Standard and better."

Stud lumber is graded Stud or Economy Stud. In general, avoid Economy grade lumber of any kind. Although okay for temporary use, its inferior quality makes it unreliable in any sustained load-bearing situation.

LUMBER SPECIES

Species are denoted by abbreviations such as PP (ponderosa pine), DF (Douglas fir), and HEM (hemlock). Often, manufacturers will group species with similar properties. S-P-F (spruce, pine, fir) is by far the most common Canadian grouping, and HEM-FIR (hemlock-fir) is common throughout the United States. Because lumber is heavy and expensive to ship, lumberyard sources tend to be from nearby mills. Since your lumberyard is likely to carry only a mixed stock of sizes and grades, your choice may be limited to what's on hand.

MOISTURE CONTENT

Each day, a mature living tree can pump a ton of water into the atmosphere, so it's no surprise that logs arrive at the mill with moisture contents of 30 percent to 55 percent. Consequently, a sawmill will rough-cut logs into lumber, air dry or kiln dry it, and then grade the lumber's moisture content before planing (surfacing) it.

Moisture content of 15 percent to 19 percent is optimal because that approximates the moisture content of ambient air in much of North America, except in the dry U.S. Southwest. Most often, lumber will be marked S-DRY or KD (kiln dried), indicating that its moisture content is 19 percent or less. KD-15 or MC-15 indicates a moisture content of 15 percent or less. Of course, even MC-15 lumber may be sopping wet if rained on during storage or transport. Wood that's drier than MC-15 (say, 7 percent to 8 percent MC) may be a problem because it could swell after absorbing moisture on the job site—unless you live in the Southwest.

Select structural quality

Certifying agency

Kiln dried

Mill number

Douglas fir (northern species)

Lumber grade stamps.

PRO TIP

Different species have different density, elasticity, and load-bearing capacity, so their lumber grades are not interchangeable. For example, a No. 1 HEM-FIR 2×10 may not have the same load/span capacity as a No. 1 southern pine 2×10. That's why structural engineers routinely specify both the grade *and* species of lumber (or species group) needed to satisfy requirements in building codes.

▌▌▌▌

Yard TALK

Here's some standard lumberyard lingo:

▸ **BOARDS** are less than 2 in. thick and are used as trim, sheathing, subflooring, battens, doorstops, and such.

▸ **LUMBER** (dimension lumber) is 2 in. to 4 in. thick and is used for house framing: studs, posts, joists, beams, headers, rafters, stair carriages, and so on.

▸ **FACTORY OR SHOP LUMBER** is wood milled into window casings, trim, and other elements.

▸ **TIMBER** is at least 5 in. thick in its smallest dimension.

▸ **STOCK** applies to any building material in its unworked form, as it comes from the lumberyard or mill.

▸ A **STICK** is jargon for a piece of lumber, such as a 2×4: "If that stick is too warped, go get another."

Most construction lumber is called *softwood*, which is the lumber industry's term for wood from conifers, the needle-leaved evergreens such as pine, fir, spruce, and hemlock. For the most part, these softwoods are softer and less dense than most hardwoods, which come from broad-leaved deciduous trees such as maple, oak, and walnut. That said, some softwoods, namely southern yellow pine, are much harder than some hardwoods, such as basswood.

(chromated copper arsenate). But the U.S. Environmental Protection Agency (EPA) determined that CCA leaches arsenic into the soil; as a result, industry leaders agreed to stop using that treatment by the end of 2003. More benign types of pressure-treated lumber, such as .40 ACQ (alkaline copper quat) and CBA (copper boron azole) are available. Both biocides are arsenic free.

Whatever lumber treatment you consider, consult its product data sheets for the relative safety of the chemicals used and whatever care you should take when handling, storing, cutting, and applying it. In fact, it's smart to capture and safely dispose of the sawdust.

ORDERING LUMBER AND CALCULATING BOARD FEET

The price of long thin pieces of wood, such as molding or furring strips, is based on their length, or *lineal feet* (lin. ft.). Sheet materials such as plywood and composite board are sold by the *square foot*, which is length times width; sheet thickness affects price, but it is not computed directly. Roofing and siding materials are often sold in *squares* of 100 sq. ft. Most yard lumber is sold by *board feet*, according to this formula:

$$\frac{\text{width (in.)} \times \text{thickness (in.)} \times \text{length (ft.)}}{12}$$

A grade mark of S-GRN (surfaced green) indicates a moisture content more than 19 percent. Green lumber is hell to work with because it's heavy (a green 8-ft.-long 2×4 can weigh 40 lb.), likely to distort, and certain to shrink—wreaking havoc with finish surfaces and trim. Thus S–GRN is a risky choice for renovations.

LUMBER SIZES

Lumber's final size depends on milling processes. In smaller mills, lumber is often sawn, stickered, and allowed to air dry for 4 months to 6 months. If it's not milled further, it's called *rough-cut lumber*. Depending on the accuracy of the sawyer, the size may vary slightly, but the *nominal size* of, say, a rough-cut 2×4 is usually a full 2 in. by 4 in.

However, most lumber is rough cut and then *surfaced* (run through a planer to achieve uniform thickness) before being kiln dried. At each stage, the lumber size decreases. Thus when you order a 2×4 (nominal size), you receive a piece with a 1½-in. by 3½-in. cross section (*actual size*). Still, you pay for the nominal size.

Another way to size wood, especially hardwood and Select finished woods, is by quarter-inch increments: 2/4, 3/4, 4/4, 5/4 , 6/4, and so on. The nominal actual difference is present here, too: For example, a nominal 5/4 stair tread is actually 1 in. thick.

PRESSURE-TREATED LUMBER

Lumber may also be marked as pressure treated. Such wood, after treatment, may be left exposed to weather, used near the foundation, or otherwise subjected to moisture, insects, or extremes of climate. If the wood will remain in contact with the soil, be sure that it is also rated for Ground Contact.

Since the 1940s, roughly 90 percent of all pressure-treated lumber was treated with CCA

Nominal and Actual Sizes of Softwood

NOMINAL	ACTUAL (in.)
1×2	¾×1½
1×4	¾×3½
1×6	¾×5½
1×8	¾×7¼
1×10	¾×9¼
1×12	¾×11¼
2×4	1½×3½
2×6	1½×5½
2×8	1½×7½
2×10	1½×9½
2×12	1½×11½

In the two examples below, each board contains 1 board foot (bd. ft.):

$$\frac{12 \text{ in.} \times 1 \text{ in.} \times 1 \text{ ft.}}{12} = 1 \text{ bd. ft.}$$

$$\frac{6 \text{ in.} \times 2 \text{ in.} \times 1 \text{ ft.}}{12} = 1 \text{ bd. ft.}$$

In each of the following two examples, the dimensions given yield 2 bd. ft.:

$$\frac{12 \text{ in.} \times 1 \text{ in.} \times 2 \text{ ft.}}{12} = 2 \text{ bd. ft.}$$

$$\frac{2 \text{ in.} \times 4 \text{ in.} \times 3 \text{ ft.}}{12} = 2 \text{ bd. ft.}$$

When calculating the total board feet of several pieces of lumber, multiply the numerator (top part) of the fraction by the total number of pieces needed. Thus here's how to calculate the board feet of 10 pieces of 2-in. by 6-in. by 12-ft. lumber:

$$\frac{2 \text{ in.} \times 6 \text{ in.} \times 12 \text{ ft.} \times 10}{12} = 120 \text{ bd. ft.}$$

Salvage Lumber

Salvage materials have striking advantages and disadvantages—the major plus being low cost; the major minus being prep time. Salvaging molding, flooring, and other materials from your own home is a good way to match existing materials, but be picky in selecting materials from other sources.

Reuse centers are popular these days. One example is Habitat for Humanity's nonprofit stores, which offer tax deductions to donors and savings up to 75 percent off the original price of materials.

However, make sure all materials are structurally sound. Be sure to use a pocketknife to test lumber for rot or insects. Also treat with preservative any salvaged lumber that you'll use as sills or that will be exposed to moisture.

Salvage materials usually aren't worth the effort if they are in small quantities or if, after removing them, you find that they will be too short. Used 2×4s, for example, normally aren't worth the trouble. By the time you yank them free from plates, remove nails, and cut off split ends, the studs may be only 7 ft. long.

Some materials just aren't worth removing. For example, siding and other exterior trim is rarely worth saving, for it's usually old and weather beaten. Barn board, in vogue years ago, is hardly charming when it is half-rotted, warped, and crawling with carpenter ants. If there is any danger of your destroying a piece of salvage by removing it, leave it alone. Parts of many beautiful old places that were restorable have been ruined by people who didn't know what they were doing.

If you have any qualms about the structural strength of a building, stay out of it. Dismantling a building is a special skill, and inexperienced people who undertake the task can get hurt. Perhaps the best advice for would-be users of salvage materials is to buy it from a salvage yard. In this case, somebody has already done the dirty and dangerous work of removal.

Engineered Lumber

Like any natural product, standard lumber is quirky. It has knots, holes, and splits. And it twists, cups, and shrinks. As mature old-growth timber was replaced by smaller, inferior trees, lumber quality became less reliable—much to the dismay of builders.

In response, the lumber industry combined wood fiber and strong glues to create engineered lumber (EL), including I-joists, engineered beams, plywood, and particleboard. EL spans greater distances and carries heavier loads than standard lumber of comparable dimensions. In addition, EL won't shrink and remains straight, stable, strong and—above all—predictable.

Still, EL has two main drawbacks: It's heavy, so dense that it must often be predrilled, and it costs considerably more than sawn lumber. Even so, EL is here to stay.

Seven Steps for On-Site Salvage

If you are determined to do on-site salvage, here are a few suggestions:

▶ Get a tetanus shot and wear a long-sleeved shirt, heavy pants, thick-soled shoes, goggles, dust mask, gloves, and hard hat.

▶ Always cut power to the affected areas. Then use a voltage tester in outlets, fixtures, and switches to make sure there's no current flowing through them.

▶ Don't hurry. Look at the joints involved and remove the pieces slowly, bit by bit.

▶ As you free each piece, remove its nails immediately. Remember, footing on construction sites is chancy at best, and you don't want to land in a bed of nails when descending from a ladder in a hurry.

▶ If the piece is complex, such as a fireplace mantel, photograph it and then label the elements while carefully removing them.

▶ Before cutting salvage wood, scrutinize it closely for nails. Insert a pocket knife or an ice pick into suspect holes and check for hidden nails with a magnet. Then, still being concerned for hidden nails, use a carbide-tipped demolition sawblade and wear safety goggles.

▶ Most salvage is old, dry, and highly vulnerable to rot. Because it is dry, it will absorb moisture and rot before you know it. So get it under cover at once.

TRUSSES

The most common truss is the prefabricated *roof truss*, which is a large triangular wood framework that serves as the roof's support structure. Its short web-like reinforcing members are fastened by steel truss plates. Trusses are lightweight, cheap, quick to install, and strong relative to the distances they span. Thus they eliminate the need for deep-dimensioned traditional roof rafters and complex cutting.

▶ *Advantages:* Trusses can be prefabricated for almost any roof contour, trucked to the job site, and erected in a few days. In addition, you can route ducts, pipes, and wiring through openings in the webbing—a great advantage in renovation work.

▶ *Disadvantages:* Roof trusses leave little living space or storage space in the attic. Adding kneewalls on the sides will gain some height, but your design options will be limited. Roof trusses should be engineered and factory built and never modified, unless an engineer approves the changes; otherwise, unbalanced loads could cause the trusses—and the roof—to fail.

Floor trusses, on the other hand, are often open webs spaced 24 in. on center. Although their spanning capacities are roughly the same as I-joists of comparable depth, it's much easier to run ducts, vents, wiring, and plumbing through open-web trusses.

I-JOISTS

I-joists are commonly called TrusJoists®, after a popular brand (now a subsidiary of Weyerhaeuser®). Typically, I-joists are plywood or OSB (oriented strand board) webs bolstered by stiff lumber flanges top and bottom, which add strength and prevent lateral bending.

Although I-joists look flimsy, they are stronger than solid-lumber joists of comparable dimensions. Whereas solid joists are spaced 16 in. on center, I-joists can be laid out on 19½-in. or 24-in. centers. They are also lightweight, straight, and stable. Floors and ceilings constructed with I-joists stay flat because there's virtually no I-joist shrinkage; hence almost no drywall cracks, nail pops, or floor squeaks.

Installing I-joists is not much different from installing 2× lumber, but blocking between I-joists is critical. (They must be perfectly perpendicular to bear loads.) You can drill larger holes in I-joist webs than you can in solid lumber, but religiously follow manufacturer guidance on hole size and placement. And *never* cut or nail into I-joist flanges.

Alternatives to Solid-Wood Joists

I-JOIST

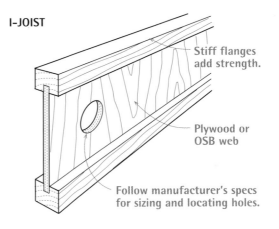

Stiff flanges add strength.

Plywood or OSB web

Follow manufacturer's specs for sizing and locating holes.

OPEN-WEB FLOOR TRUSS

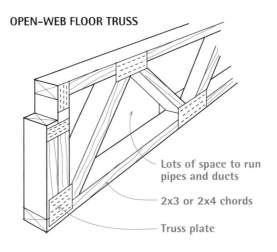

Lots of space to run pipes and ducts

2x3 or 2x4 chords

Truss plate

Manufacturers continue to develop more economical I-joist components. Webs may be plywood, particleboard, or LVL (laminated veneer lumber). Flanges have been fabricated from LVL, OSB or—back the future!—solid lumber (2×3s or 2×4s) finger-jointed and glued together. I-joists with wider flanges are less likely to flop and fall over during installation. Plus they offer more surface to glue and nail subflooring to.

ENGINEERED BEAMS

The most daunting part of using engineered beams may be the wide selection. Fortunately, lumberyard staff can usually explain the merits of each type and help you determine correct size.

Glulams, or glue-laminated timbers, are the granddaddy of engineered beams. They've been used in Europe since the early 1900s. In North America, they're fabricated from relatively short pieces of dimension lumber (often Douglas fir or southern pine), which is overlapped or finger-jointed, glued, and pressure clamped. Glulams come in stock widths 3⅛ in. to 6¾ in., but you can obtain them in almost any size or shape, including curves and arches, as well as pressure treated.

Glulams are expensive, but their stability and strength make them suitable for high loads in clear spans as great as 60 ft. Obviously, you'd need a crane to move such a behemoth.

LVL (Microllam®) is fashioned from thin layers of wood veneer glued together—much like plywood, except the wood grain in all LVL layers runs parallel. It's stronger than sawn lumber or laminated strand lumber of comparable size, though it's roughly twice the cost of sawn lumber.

LVL is usually milled as planks 1¾ in. wide, so it's typically used as rim joists, cantilever joists, or in-floor headers and beams. It's a good choice for medium-span beams up to 16 ft., and because individual beams are easy to handle, a small crew can join LVL planks on site to create a built-up girder. LVL is available in other widths, from 3½ in. to 5½ in. Depths range up to 20 in.

▶ *Disadvantages:* **LVL can't be pressure treated and shouldn't be used on exteriors. If it gets wet, it will cup. For this reason, keep it covered till you're ready to use it.**

PSL (parallel strand lumber, Parallam®) is created from wood fiber strands 2 ft. to 8 ft. long, running parallel, and glued together under tremendous pressure. PSL is the strongest and most expensive of any structural composite lumber.

Standard PSL sizes are 7 in. to 11 in. wide, up to 20 in. deep, and they can be fabricated to virtually any length—66 ft. is not uncommon. Because they're stronger than glulams, PSLs are

This engineered beam is a 4-in. by 14-in. Parallam girder secured with a Simpson™ CCQ column cap.

built without camber (a curve built-in to anticipate deflection under load), so they're easier to align during installation.

PSL beams can be pressure treated and thus can be used outside.

LSL (laminated strand lumber, Timberstrand®) is fabricated from 12-in. wood strands from fast-growing (but weaker) trees, like aspen and poplar, and then glued together in a random manner. Consequently, LSL carries less load than the beams noted previously, and it costs less. Still, it is stronger than sawn lumber, though more expensive.

LSL is available in 1¾-in. to 3½-in. widths and in depths up to 18 in., but it's most often used as short lengths in undemanding locations, such as door or window headers, wall plates, studs, and rim joists.

LSL headers are stable, so they'll probably reduce nail pops and drywall cracks around doors or windows. But for small openings of 10 ft. or less and average loads, sawn-lumber headers are usually more cost-effective.

Framing with Steel

The use of steel framing in residential renovation is increasing, but it's still rare and generally not advised for novice builders unless working with a builder experienced with it.

LIGHT STEEL FRAMING

Light steel framing consists primarily of C-shaped metal studs set into U-shaped top and bottom plates, joined with self-drilling pan-head screws. Fast and relatively cheap to install, light steel framing (20 gauge to 25 gauge) is most often used to create non-load-bearing interior partitions in commercial work.

Its advocates argue that more residential contractors would use it if they were familiar with it. In fact, light steel framing is less expensive than lumber; it can be assembled with common tools, such as aviation snips, screw guns, and locking pliers; and it's far lighter and easier to lug than dimension lumber. To attach drywall, use type-S drywall screws instead of the type W screws specified for wood.

If you want to hide a masonry wall, light steel framing is ideal. Masonry walls are often irregular, but if you use 1⅝-in. metal framing to create a wall within a wall, you'll have a flat surface to drywall that's stable and doesn't eat up much space.

That said, light steel is quirky. You must align prepunched holes for plumbing and wiring before cutting studs and, for that reason, you must measure and cut metal studs from the same end. If you forget that rule, your studs become scrap. Finally, if you want to shim and attach door jambs and casings properly, you need to reinforce steel-framed door openings with wood.

FLITCH PLATES

Flitch plates are steel plates sandwiched between dimension lumber and are through-bolted to increase span and load-carrying capacity. Flitch plates are most often used in renovation where existing beams or joists are undersize. (You insert plates after jacking sagging beams.)

Ideally, a structural engineer should size the flitch plate assembly, including the size and placement of bolts. Steel plates are typically ⅜ in. to ½ in. thick; the carriage bolts, ½ in. to ⅝ in. in diameter. Stagger bolts, top to bottom, 16 in. apart, keeping them back at least 2 in. from beam

edges. Put four bolts at each beam end. To ease installation, drill bolt holes ⅟₁₆ in. wider than the bolt diameters.

Flitch plates run the length of the wood members. The wood sandwich keeps the steel plate on edge and prevents lateral buckling. *Note:* Bolt holes should be predrilled or punched—never cut with an acetylene torch. That is, loads are transferred partly through the friction between the steel and wood faces, thus the raised debris around acetylene torch holes would reduce the desired steel–wood contact.

STEEL I-BEAMS

Although lately eclipsed by engineered-wood beams, steel I-beams, for the same given depth, are stronger. Consequently, steel I-beams may be the best choice if you need to hide a beam in a relatively shallow floor system—say, among 2×6s or 2×8s—or if clearance is an issue.

Wide-flange I-beams are the steel beams most commonly used in residences, where they typically range from 4⅛ in. to 10 in. deep and 4 in. to 10 in. wide. Standard lengths are 20 ft. and 40 ft., although some suppliers stock intermediate sizes. Weight depends on the length of the beam and the thickness of the steel. That is, a 20-ft.,

Heavy STEEL FRAMING

Load-bearing steel framing is heavier (14 gauge to 20 gauge) and costs much more than lumber. Plus it requires specialized tools and techniques. Metal conducts cold, so insulating steel walls can be a challenge. For exterior and load-bearing walls, you're better off with wood framing.

Veneer grade

Certifying agency

Thickness

Span rating
(rafters/studs)

Exposure rating

Mill number

Plywood grade stamps.

Sorting Out Panel Names

Structural panels

▶ **Plywood** is a sandwich of thin veneers sliced from logs, with veneers stacked perpendicularly to one another (cross-grain) in alternating layers and glued. Each layer is a ply. Alternating wood grain direction adds stiffness and strength.

▶ **OSB** (oriented strand board) is made from logs shredded into long strands. The strands are oriented in the same direction, mixed with resins, and pressed into thin sheets. As with plywood, strands in alternating layers run perpendicularly.

Nonstructural panels

▶ **Particleboard** (also known as chipboard) is fabricated from mill wastes, mixed with resins, and hot pressed. Because of its stability and uniform consistency, particleboard is an excellent core material for veneered cabinets, laminated countertops, and bookcases.

▶ **MDF** (medium-density fiberboard) is a mixture of fine, randomly oriented wood fibers and resins, hot pressed for a smooth surface. It is used as interior trim and cabinetry stock.

▶ **Hardboard** (such as Masonite®) is a high-density fiberboard created by steaming wood chips and then hot pressing them into sheets. The hard, smooth surface is well suited for underlayment, interior trim, and paneling. Hardboard used as exterior siding has been plagued by warping, delamination, and other moisture-related problems.

▶ **MDO** (medium density overlay) is typically a laminated veneer lumber core with a resin/paper overlay. It is touted as an exterior trim, but the jury is still out on its long-term durability (see p. 131).

8×4 I-beam that's 0.245 in. thick weighs roughly 300 lb.; whereas, a 20-ft., 8×8H I-beam with a web that's 0.458 in. thick weighs 800 lb. If you order a nonstandard size, expect to pay a premium.

Before selecting steel I-beams, consult with a structural engineer. For installation, use a contractor experienced with these beams. Access to the site greatly affects installation costs, especially if there's a crane involved.

Structural and Nonstructural Panels

Plywood and OSB are the structural panels most often specified to sheathe wood framing and increase its shear strength. For example, a 20-ft. wall sheathed with 7⁄16-in. plywood can withstand more than a ton of lateral force pushing against the top of the wall.

PLYWOOD

Structural plywood is made by laminating softwood plies. Each panel is stamped to indicate veneer grade, species group or span rating, thickness, exposure durability, mill number, and certifying agency.

Veneer grades. Veneer grades range from A to D, with letters appearing in pairs to indicate the front and back veneers of the panel. "A/B Exterior," for example, has a grade A front veneer, a grade B back veneer, and grade C inner plies. When you buy CDX (C/D exterior-grade), it's advisable to place the grade C side toward the weather—or up, if used as subflooring.

Most roof and wall sheathing and subflooring is CDX. If a panel is also stamped PTS, its imperfections have been plugged and touch sanded. Lower veneer grades have more plugs and bigger knots.

Grade D is the lowest grade of interior plywood panels; it should not be exposed to weather.

Species grade or span rating. Plywood's strength may be indicated by two marks. One is a species group number (1–5). Group 1 is the strongest and often contains Douglas fir or southern yellow pine.

The second mark, a span rating, is more common. The two-digit rating looks like a fraction, but it's not. Rather, a rating of 24/16 indicates that a panel can sheathe rafters spaced 24 in. on center and studs spaced 16 in. on center.

Another common stamp is Struc I, which stands for Structural I sheathing, a five-ply CDX that's tested and guaranteed for a given shear value. If an engineer specifies Struc I, it must be used. *Note:* Plywood used for structural sheathing must have a minimum of five plies. Avoid three-ply, ½-in. CDX. Although it is widely available and cheaper than five-ply, it's vastly inferior.

Thickness and length. APA (American Plywood Association) panels rated for Struc I wall sheathing, roof sheathing, and subflooring range from ⅜ in. to ²³⁄₃₂ in. thick. Although 4×8 panels are the most common, 4×9 or 4×10 sheets enable you to run panels vertically from mudsills to the rim joists atop the first floor, thereby reducing the shear-wall blocking you might need behind panel edges and greatly improving the shear strength of the wall. (*Shear walls* are specially engineered walls that brace a building against lateral seismic and wind forces.) Although the square-foot price of 4×9 and 4×10 panels is higher than that of 4×8s, the larger panels enable you to work more quickly.

Exposure durability. How much weather and moisture a wood-based panel can take is largely a function of the glues used. *Exterior-grade* panels can be exposed repeatedly to moisture or used in damp climates because their plies are bonded with waterproof adhesives. *Exposure 1* is suitable if there's limited exposure to moisture—say, if construction gets delayed and the house doesn't get closed in for a while. *Exposure 2* panels are okay for protected applications and moderate construction delays. *Interior-grade* panels will deteriorate if they get wet; use them only in dry, protected applications.

OSB PANELS

OSB and plywood have almost exactly the same strength, stiffness, and span ratings. Both are fabricated in layers, and they weigh roughly the same. Both can sheathe roofs, walls, and floors. Their installation is almost identical, down to the blocking behind subfloor edges and need for H-clips between the unsupported edges of roof sheathing. Exposure ratings and grade stamps

YET MORE Panel STAMPS

▸ **T&G:** tongue and groove

▸ **G2S:** good two sides

▸ **G1S:** good one side

▸ **PRP 000:** performance-rated panel (number follows)

▸ **SEL TF:** select tight face

▸ **SELECT:** uniform surface, acceptable for underlayment

▸ **SHG:** sheathing

Formaldehyde-Free PANELS

Many engineered panels, including particleboard and MDF, are bonded with urea-formaldehyde resins, which outgas (give off formaldehyde gases). This is a problem for people with chemical sensitivities, especially in airtight houses. Also, formaldehyde in high concentrations is probably a carcinogen. Fortunately, there are now formaldehyde-free panels: Medite II, and Medex®, MDF (SierraPine™) are three of the better known. Visit the Internet or your local lumberyard for more choices.

are also very similar. But in some respects, OSB is superior to plywood. It rarely delaminates, it holds screws and nails better, and it has roughly twice the shear values. (That's why I-joists have OSB webs.) So given OSB's lower cost (10 percent to 15 percent cheaper, on average), it's not surprising that OSB grabs an increasing market share every year.

But OSB has one persistent and irreversible shortcoming: Its edges swell when they get wet and appear as raised lines (ghost lines) through roofing. To mitigate this swelling, OSB makers seal the panel edges; but when builders saw panels, the new (unsealed) edges swell when wet. Buildings under construction get rained on, so edge swelling is a real problem. Swollen edges can also raise hell in OSB subflooring or underlayment if it absorbs moisture, as commonly occurs over unfinished basements and uncovered crawl spaces. Thus many tile and resilient-flooring manufacturers insist on plywood underlayment.

Given the huge market for OSB, however, count on solutions before long. At this writing, J.M. Huber AdvanTech®, Louisiana-Pacific Top Notch®, and Weyerhaeuser Structurwood® are all tongue-and-groove-edged OSB panels purported to lie flat, install fast, and have minimal "edge swell." Stay tuned.

NAILING STRUCTURAL PANELS

Your local building code will have the final say on sizing structural panels. To accommodate heavy loads, choose a panel rated for a higher span. A span rating of 32/16 indicates that the panel is strong enough to sheathe rafters spaced 32 in. on center and studs 16 in. on center and, therefore, can support far greater live loads than a 24/16-rated panel, even though a 32/16 panel is only ½ in. thicker.

Nailing schedules for different uses of plywood are the same: Nail every 6 in. around the perimeter, not closer than ⅜ in. to the edge; elsewhere, nail every 12 in. For subflooring, annular ring or spiral nails hold best; use hot-dipped galvanized nails for all exterior purposes. An 8d nail is sufficient for ½-in. to ¾-in. plywood. For structural shear walls, follow the engineer's specifications for nailing. Shear walls often require tighter nailing around the edges of the panel—and, sometimes, thicker nails (10d).

Leave a gap of 1/16 in. between sheets, for expansion; more where humidity is high. (Tongue-and-groove panels may not need gaps.) For greatest strength, run the length of a 4×8 sheet perpendicular to the structural members you are nailing to, and always stagger the butt ends of the sheets. In the intervals between framing, support plywood edges in floors and walls with solid blocking; on roofs, place *blocking clips* (also called ply-clips or H-clips) between the sheets' edges unsupported by solid wood.

Pneumatic nailers (also known as nail guns) are widely used to nail down plywood, and they save a lot of time. But one thing a nailer won't do is "suck up" a piece of plywood to framing. This is worth noting because almost all plywood is warped to some degree. So after you nail down plywood with a pneumatic nailer, go back over the surface and give each nail an additional shot with a 20-oz. framing hammer. The hammer head, being larger than the striker of the nailer, will help drive the plywood down as well.

As important, don't drive a nail too deeply. If the nailer's pressure is set too high, the nail may be driven through the face ply, diminishing the shear value and holding capacity of that nail.

Thus set the nailer's pneumatic pressure a little lower than would be needed to drive the nail flush. Then finish each nail with a hammer blow.

HARDWOOD PLYWOOD

Hardwood plywood is not intended to be structural, but since you may need some during renovation, here's a brief overview. As with softwood plywood, there's a great variety, classified by species, face plies (appearance), core material (MDF, LVL, particleboard), and glues. The range of uses is suggested by the many thicknesses—from 1/16-in. aircraft plywood to 2-in. door stock.

Most hardwood plywood is used indoors, so appearance grading and careful handling are crucial. Be sure to specify the grade of both faces, and check the stock carefully for damage. Because this plywood is extremely expensive, sheets are often used right up to the edges. Thus check to ensure that edges aren't damaged or frayed. Here's a list of hardwood grades:

▶ *Specialty.* **You can special order closely matched flitches (veneer surfaces that can be laid together in sequence) that allow repetitions of face grain for visual effect.**

▶ *Premium (A).* **Grain patterns and colors are matched precisely.**

▶ *Good (No. 1).* **Colors of matched veneers on a face do not vary greatly, but patterns are less closely matched than premium grade.**

▶ *Sound (No. 2).* **Although colors and patterns are not matched, there are no open flaws.**

▶ *Utility (No. 3).* **These may have small flaws, tight knotholes, discoloring, and splits that can be filled, but no rot.**

▶ *Backing (No. 4).* **Defects are allowed as long as they don't weaken the sheet or prevent its use; the backing side may be from a different tree species than that of the exposed face.**

Metal Connectors

If wood is the universal building stock, metal is the universal connector. Nails of many types as well as screws and bolts are discussed in this section. Specialty plates that reinforce structural members are also described. Later in this chapter is a review of construction adhesives, which, some say, are destined to supplant metal connectors.

NAILS

As they're driven in, nail points wedge apart wood fibers. The ensuing pressure of the fibers on the nail shank creates friction, which holds the joint together. Nails also transmit shear loads between the building elements they join. Where nails join major structural elements, such as

Nail types. Top row from left: 60d galvanized spike, 40d common, 20d common, 16d galvanized, 16d common, 12d vinyl-coated sinker, 12d galvanized box, 10d galvanized common, 8d galvanized box, and 4d galvanized siding. Bottom row, from left: concrete nail and six joist-hanger and metal-connector nails (also called Teco™ nails). Longer nails may be required when sheathing covers framing.

Nail Sizes

NAIL LENGTH (in.)	PENNY SIZE (d)
1	2
1½	4
2	6
2½	8
3	10
3¼	12
3½	16
4	20
4½	30
5	40
6	60

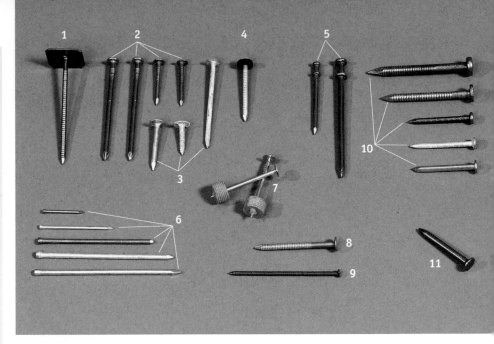

Specialty nails. 1, Simplex nail for roofing underlayment and thin foam insulation; 2, copper flashing nails; 3, galvanized roofing nails; 4, gasketed nail for metal roofing and some skylight flashing; 5, duplex nails; 6, finish nails (the middle one is vinyl coated); 7, furring nails for stucco wire; 8, ring-shank nail; 9, stainless-steel nail color matched to wood siding; 10, joist-hanger nails (Teco® nails); 11, case-hardened masonry nail.

rafters and wall plates, the loads can be tremendous; where nails attach finish elements, such as trim, loads are usually negligible.

There are hundreds of different nails, which vary in length, head size, shank shape, point, composition, and purpose.

Length. Length is reckoned in penny sizes, abbreviated as *d*. The larger the nail, the greater the penny rating. Nails 20d or longer are called *spikes*.

Heads. The shape of a nail's head depends on whether that nail will be exposed or concealed and what type of material it's designed to hold down. Smaller heads—such as those on casing, finish, and some kinds of flooring nails—can easily be sunk below the wood surface. Large heads, like those used to secure roofing paper or asphalt shingles, are needed to resist pull-through.

Shanks. Nail shanks are usually straight, and patterned shanks usually have greater holding strength than smooth ones. For example, spiral flooring nails (with screw shanks) resist popping, as do ring-shank nails. (By the way, it takes more force to drive spiral nails.) Spiral and ring-shank nails are well suited to decks and siding because changes in wood moisture can reduce the friction between wood fibers and straight shanks.

Points. Nails usually have a tapered four-sided point, but there are a few variations. For example, blunt-point nails are less likely to split wood than pointed nails because the blunt points crush the wood fibers in their path rather than wedging

them apart. You can fashion your own blunt points by hammering down a nail point. However, the blunt point reduces the withdrawal friction on the nail shank.

Composition. Most nails are fashioned from medium-grade steel (often called *mild steel*). Nail composition may vary, according to the following situations:

▶ *Material nailed into.* **Masonry nails are case hardened. That's also true of the special nails supplied with joist hangers and other metal connectors. Do not use regular nails to attach metal connectors.**

▶ *Presence of other metals.* **Some metals corrode in contact with others because of galvanic action (see "Galvanic Action," on p. 70). So try to match nail composition to the metals present. The choice of nails includes**

see "Galvanic Action," on p. 70

Pilot HOLES

Whenever you need to avoid bending nails in dense wood like southern pine and when you're worried about splitting a joist because you're nailing too close to the end, simply predrill a pilot hole. There's no absolute rule to sizing pilot holes: 50 percent to 75 percent of the nail shank diameter is usually about right, letting the friction between nail and wood provide adequate grip.

aluminum, stainless steel, brass, copper, monel metal, and galvanized (zinc coated).

▶ *Exposure to weather and corrosion.* Neither stainless-steel nor aluminum nails will stain wood. However, stainless is very expensive, and aluminum is brittle and somewhat tricky to nail. Galvanized nails, which are reasonably priced, will stain only a modest amount where the hammer chips the coating off the head. Therefore, you should seal galvanized nails as soon as possible with primer. Galvanized nails are also specified when framing with redwood or treated lumber, both of which will corrode common nails. If you're installing costly redwood or cedar siding, use stainless steel, especially if you'll be sealing walls with a clear finish.

▶ *Holding power.* Nails that are rosin coated, cement coated, or hot-dipped galvanized hold better than uncoated nails. Vinyl-coated nails both lubricate the nail shaft as you drive it in (friction melts the polymer coating) and acts as adhesive once the nail's in place.

Sizing nails. Common sense dictates the size of most nails. Generally, length should be about three times the thickness of the piece being nailed down. For sheathing ½ in. to ¾ in. thick, use 8d nails (which are 2½ in. long). Use 6d nails if the sheathing is ⅜ in. thick or less. Nail points should not protrude through the second piece.

The workhorse of framing is the 16d common, although 12d or 10d nails are good bets if you need to toenail one member to another. Use 10d or 12d nails to laminate lumber, say, as top plates, double joists, and headers.

When nailing near the edge or the end of a piece, avoid splits by using the right size nail, staggering nails, not nailing too close to the edge, blunting nail heads, or drilling pilot holes. Box nails, which have smaller-diameter shanks than common nails, are less likely to split framing during toenailing.

Pneumatic framing nails. When you've got a lot of nailing to do, say, to sheathe an addition, you may want to rent a pneumatic nailer. As noted earlier, it's best to set nailer pressures so that nail heads stop just shy of a panel's face ply. Then use a framing hammer to drive each nail flush. Most pneumatic framing nails are vinyl coated to make them hold well. And some pneumatic nail heads are colored, so you know immediately which size you're loading.

Pneumatic nails differ slightly from common nails, however, so you may want to check your local building code before you rent a nailer. For example, pneumatic nailers load either coils of nails (coil nailers) or nails aligned in diagonal strips (stick nailers). Both work well, but some stick nailers accept only nails whose heads have been partially clipped. (Clipped-head nails pack more tightly.) Clipped-head nails are rarely a problem when nailing 2× lumber together, but plywood secured by the smaller nail heads is more likely to pull through under stress.

Second, pneumatic nail shanks are often thinner than those of common nails. In fact, some pneumatic 16d nail shanks are roughly the same thickness as 8d common nails used for nailing by hand.

Recommended Nailing Schedule*

APPLICATION	FASTENER
Joist to sill or girder (toenail)	▶ 3-8d
Ledger strip	▶ 3-16d at each joist
1×6 subfloor or less to each joist (face-nail)	▶ 2-8d (or two 1¾-in. staples)
Wider than 1×6 subfloor to each joist (face-nail)	▶ 3-8d
2-in. subfloor to joist or girder (blind- and face-nail)	▶ 2-16d
Sole plate to joist or blocking (face-nail)	▶ 16d at 16 in. o.c.
Top plate to stud (end-nail)	▶ 2-16d
Stud to sole plate (toenail)	▶ 4-8d
Sole plate to joists or blocking	▶ 3-16d at 16 in. o.c.
Doubled studs (face-nail)	▶ 10d at 24 in. o.c.
Doubled top plates (face-nail)	▶ 16d at 16 in. o.c.
Doubled top plates, lap spliced (face-nail)	▶ 8-16d
Continuous header, two pieces	▶ 16d at 16 in. o.c., along each edge
Rim joist to top plate (toenail)	▶ 8d at 6 in. o.c.
Ceiling joists to plate (toenail)	▶ 3-8d
Continuous header to stud (toenail)	▶ 4-8d
Ceiling joists, laps over partitions (face-nail)	▶ 3-16d
Ceiling joists to parallel rafters (face-nail)	▶ 3-16d
Rafter to plate (toenail)	▶ 3-8d
Built-up corner studs	▶ 16d at 24 in. o.c.
Built-up girders and beams	▶ 20d at 32 in. o.c., along each edge

* UBC content reprinted courtesy of International Conference of Building Officials (adapted from 1997 UBC Table 23-II-B-1).

SCREWS

Screws have revolutionized building. Thanks to a flood of specialized screws, builders can now quickly attach, detach, adjust, and reattach almost any building material imaginable. This is especially important in renovation, when you are scribing cabinets or setting door casing to walls that aren't plumb—jobs that require patience and test positionings.

Heads. The increased use of cordless screw guns has made slotted screws almost obsolete. That's because screws with traditional slot-drive heads let the driver blade slip out of the slot when torque is applied, but drive heads with centered patterns completely surround the point of the driver tip, holding it in place. Among the most popular drive heads are Phillips, square-drive, and six-pointed Torx®.

These days, screws are often engineered to specific uses. Trim-head screws have small heads like casing nails so they can be countersunk easily. Drawer-front screws have integral washers so they won't pull though. Deck-head screws are designed to minimize "mushrooming" of material around the screw hole. Some structural screws have washer heads with beveled undersides so the screws will self-center in predrilled hinges or connector plates.

Threads. Screw threads are engineered for the materials they join. Traditionally, screws for joining softwoods are made of relatively soft metal with threads that are steep pitched and relatively wide in relation to the screw shaft. Screw threads for hardwoods and metal tend to be low pitched and finer. (The steeper the thread pitch, the more torque needed to drive the screw.) If you're screwing into dense particleboard or MDF, predrill and then use Confirmat® screws, which have thick shanks and wide, low-pitched threads.

Many screws now feature self-tapping tips, in which a slotted screw tip drills its own pilot hole. Another ingenious design is a W-cut thread in which the threads nearest the tip are serrated like tiny saw points, so they cut through wood fiber as they advance. Such self-tapping features make it easy to drive in screws, without compromising holding power.

There are even screws that cut into concrete. Granted, you need to use a hammer drill to predrill an exact pilot hole, but once the pilot is drilled, you can use a 12-volt or 18-volt cordless screw gun, a standard ½-in. screw gun, or an impact screw gun to drive the screw the rest of the way. The threads grab the concrete and hold fast; the trick is not overtightening and breaking screws.

Coatings. Coatings matter most on screws used outdoors or in high-humidity areas. Although

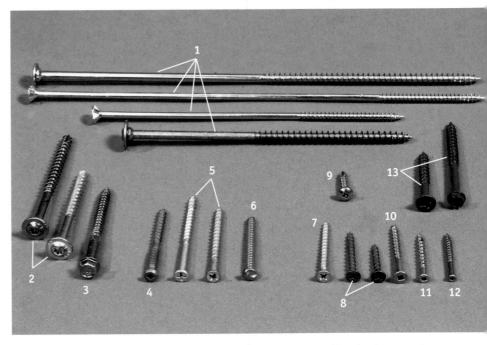

A sampling of screws. 1, Structural screws long enough to join timbers; 2, Torx-head structural screws with integral washers; 3, hex-head structural screw; 4, square-drive deck screw with two different thread pitches; 5, deck screws; 6, one-way screw; 7, galvanized drywall screw; 8, standard drywall screws; 9, square-drive sheet metal screw; 10, stainless-steel square-drive flathead screw; 11, stainless-steel square-drive trim screw; 12, brass Torx-head trim screw; 13, concrete screws.

galvanized screws do resist rusting and are relatively inexpensive, don't expect them to last much more than 8 years to 10 years on a deck—fewer years if used near saltwater. GRK Fasteners® promises "25 years in most applications" for its Climatek® coated screws. Makers of epoxy-, polymer-, and ceramic-clad screws offer varying life spans. The king of exterior screws is stainless steel—expensive, by far the most corrosion resistant, and the only suitable screw to prevent stains after attaching cedar or redwood.

BOLTS

Bolts are used to join major structural members, though with the advent of structural screws, the differences between the two are blurring. In general, machine bolts and carriage bolts have non-tapering, threaded, thick shanks. Some bolts are more than 1 in. in diameter and longer than 2 ft. Allthread (threaded) rod comes in lengths up to 12 ft. and can be used with nuts and washers at each end. Carriage bolts have a brief section of square shank just below the head. Lag screws (also called lag bolts) have a hex head, but the lower half of the shank tapers like a wood screw.

WALL ANCHORS

Wall anchors employ small bolts or screws to attach light to medium loads (towel racks, mirrors, curtain rods) to drywall and plaster walls. None is designed for structural use. With the exception of *drive anchors,* most require a predrilled hole, and all expand in some manner so they won't pull out easily. Molly bolts, drive anchors, and toggle bolts are best for attaching a light load to hollow walls. Wedge anchors, on the other hand, expand in solid masonry walls.

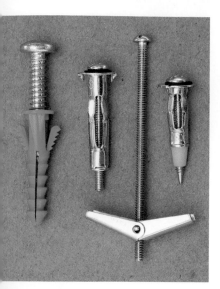

Anchors and bolts for light loads. From left: plastic anchor with screw, molly bolt, toggle bolt, and drive anchor.

WOOD CONSTRUCTION CONNECTORS

Wood construction connectors are commonly called Simpson™ Strong-Ties™ after the company that popularized them. For a complete overview of available connectors from Simpson, go to www.strongtie.com. Professionals swear by these ingenious connectors for three main reasons.

▶ They offer wood-to-wood connections superior to most traditional construction methods. For example, unlike toenailing, metal connectors are unlikely to split lumber ends or loosen under stress. These galvanized steel connectors are strong and durable.

▶ They greatly strengthen joints against earthquakes, high winds, and other racking forces. They can tie rafters to walls, walls to floor platforms, and the substructure to its foundation.

▶ Most can be attached to existing framing, a great boon to renovators, and in many cases steel connectors are the only cost-effective way to bolster the existing structure and tie additions to the original structure.

Joist hangers are indispensable in renovation when you want to add joists but can't end-nail, either because access is limited or because you're using engineered lumber, which is too thin in cross section to end-nail successfully. (Sawn-lumber joists and I-joists require different hangers.) There are joist-hangers for single joists, double joists, 4×10 beams, joists intersecting at a 45° angle, and so on. You also have the choice of face-mount or top-flange hangers. Top flanges are popular because they effortlessly align the tops of I-joists with the top of a header or beam.

Strap ties come in myriad shapes—tees, right angles, twists—but all help keep joints from pulling apart. Install flat strap ties where wall

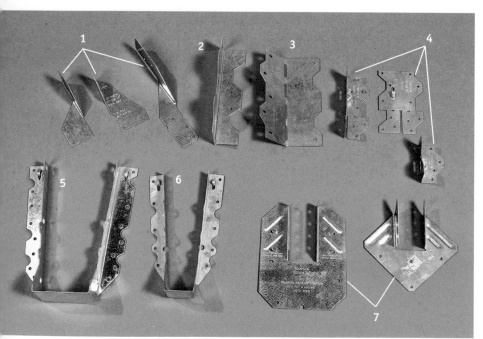

Wood construction connectors. (Contractors generally refer to them by their Simpson catalog numbers.) 1, H2.5, H4, and H8 hurricane ties; 2, L90 reinforcing angle; 3, LS70 skewable angle (bend one time only); 4, A35, A35F, and A34 framing angles; 5, U410 face-mount hanger for 4×10 beam (or double 2×10s); 6, LU28 face-mount hanger for 2×8 joist; 7, H10 and H1 hurricane ties.

Straps, ties and angles. Clockwise, from lower left: T-strap (post-to-beam connector), SST22 light-gauge strap, ST6224 (24-in.) strap, MST24 heavy-gauge strap, twist strap, and heavy-gauge L-straps.

plates are discontinuous or where rafter pairs meet at the ridge. Strap ties also keep floor platforms from separating, much as shear walling does. *Hurricane ties,* or twist straps, have a 90° twist to join rafters to top plates, thereby fighting the tendency of roofs to lift during a strong crosswind. T-straps and L-straps are face-nailed to members joining in a right angle.

Framing angles are used extensively to reinforce wood connections at 90° intersections. For seismic strengthening and on shear walls, framing angles help prevent floor framing from slipping off walls and supports during an earthquake.

Hold-downs are massive steel brackets that anchor framing to foundations and, when used with long threaded rods, join framing on different floors. When retrofitting to a foundation, use epoxy to attach hold-down bolts to concrete, as shown in the bottom left photo on p. 219.

Clips vary by function. *H-clips* are an alternative to solid blocking when installing roof sheathing. They also act as 1⁄16-in. spacers so roof sheathing can expand. *Drywall clips* allow you to eliminate some blocking in corners, but it's best to use these clips sparingly; solid blocking is much stronger. *Deck clips* are nailed to deck joists, and then 2×4 decking is driven onto the sharpened

Simpson Top-Flange Hanger

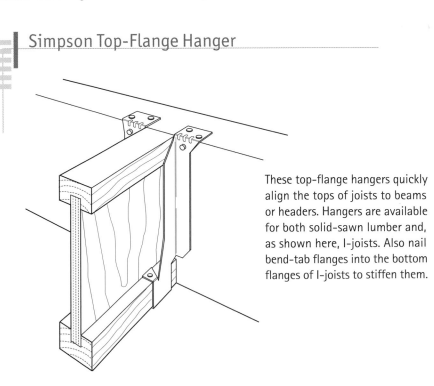

These top-flange hangers quickly align the tops of joists to beams or headers. Hangers are available for both solid-sawn lumber and, as shown here, I-joists. Also nail bend-tab flanges into the bottom flanges of I-joists to stiffen them.

TECO Nails

When attaching metal connectors, wear safety glasses and use only the special nails supplied by manufacturers, commonly called Teco nails after an early manufacturer. These nails are harder and squatter than regular nails and are less likely to shear under pressure.

point of the clip. Thus you can lay down decking without having to face-nail it; the clip also acts as a spacer so that water can clear.

Post bases and caps provide strong connections while eliminating the need to toenail posts, which tends to split them. Post bases are typically set in concrete, with posts then bolted or nailed to the base. Bases also reduce post rot, for their raised *standoffs* elevate the post and so double as a moisture shield. Post caps resemble a pair of U-brackets set at right angles to each other: One U, upside down, straddles the top of the post, while the other, right side up, receives the beam on which the joist will sit.

Miscellaneous metal connectors are often needed. Where you absolutely must notch stud edges to accommodate plumbing, a metal *shoe plate* reinforces the stud and protects the pipe from errant nails. Speaking of protection, this discussion would be incomplete without mentioning *nail plates,* which protect wires and pipes from stray nails when finish walls go up.

Adhesives, Caulks, and Sealants

Common adhesives, caulks, and sealants look the same, but their formulations are complex and carefully formulated for specific materials and expected conditions. They all generally come in 10-oz. cartridges that fit into an applicator (caulk-

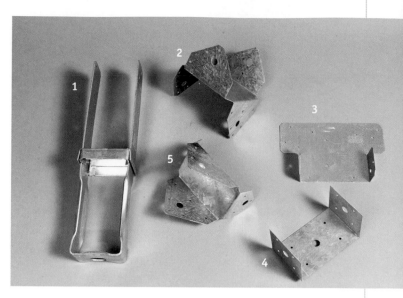

Caps and bases. 1, A CBSQ44 post base anchors a 4×4 to concrete; 2, BC6 post cap and base; 3, AC6 post-to-beam connector, which can be attached after the members are in place; 4, BC460 half-base; 5, BC46 post cap and base.

ing gun). You then simply cut the cartridge nozzle to the desired diameter and squeeze the long pistol-grip trigger to lay down beads of the stuff.

CONSTRUCTION ADHESIVES

Construction adhesives bond to a remarkable variety of materials, including standard lumber, treated lumber, plywood and OSB panels, drywall, wall paneling, rigid insulation, concrete and masonry, tile, metal, and glass.

Construction adhesives are a boon to builders. Instead of nailing sheathing every 6 in. around panel edges and every 10 in. "in the field," builders using adhesives need nail only every 12 in. Being flexible, adhesives fill surface irregularities and double as sealants. Structurally, panels bonded with adhesive are stiffer and capable of bearing greater loads than panels that are only nailed. Floor sheathing and stair treads so bonded are far less likely to flex, pop nails, or squeak. Drywall ceilings bonded with adhesives do a better job of deadening sound and cutting air infiltration.

A number of considerations should determine your choice of adhesives: the materials being joined, strength, durability, flexibility, shrinkage, conditions on the work site (especially temperature and humidity), workability, curing time, ease of cleanup, and odor.

Most solvent-based adhesives create waterproof bonds and clean up with mineral spirits. Most water-based adhesives create water-resistant bonds and clean up with water. Because solvent-based adhesives often have strong odors that are problematic for people with chemical sensi-

Made of 16-gauge steel, nail plates protect plumbing pipes and electrical wires from being punctured by nails.

tivities, there's a growing selection of solvent- and odor-free adhesives—and whole lines of environment-friendly adhesives.

Fortunately, you don't need to be a chemist to find a suitable adhesive. Many manufacturers now offer on-line interactive product selectors on their Web sites, such as the Titebond™ company (www.titebond.com). Choose the adhesive features you want, and the on-line selector will choose the most appropriate product. Once you pick an adhesive, download product specs and study them: particularly application, curing times, cleanup, and safety advice.

A POTPOURRI OF ADHESIVES

Here's a primer on common adhesives you may encounter.

Polyurethanes are often touted as all-purpose waterproof adhesives, capable of bonding wood, stone, metal, ceramics, Corian®, and so on. Strong, versatile, and easy to use, polyurethanes are favorites with builders and woodworkers. Since they require some moisture to set up, it's possible to glue up wet wood with polyurethanes. In fact, you should moisten extremely dry wood joints before application.

Acrylics are good for outdoor use. They're quick drying, strong, and completely waterproof.

Epoxy resins are famous for their strength. Typically mixed from two components, epoxies can bond to materials on which almost nothing else will—that is, when the surface areas to be bonded are small or when dampness is extreme. Epoxy products are especially important in foundation repairs and seismic strengthening (for more information, see Chapter 10).

Resorcinol is a strong, waterproof glue used by boatbuilders, among others. Like epoxy, it is a two-part glue that is very difficult to remove once it has set. Wood parts fastened with resorcinol will probably shear before the glue itself does.

Styrene-butadiene is a good all-purpose exterior and interior glue for joining materials of low porosity, such as tile and masonry.

Contact cement is commonly used to bond veneers and laminates to a base material, often particleboard. Once the sheets come in contact with each other, separation or realignment is all but impossible.

Hot-melt glues are applied with an electric glue gun and are excellent for tacking surfaces quickly. However, strength and water resistance are only so-so, because hot glues are applied only as spots. Still, they're great for building templates out of thin plywood strips (see Chapter 13).

Sticky NAMES

▶ **CAULKING** was the first on the market, so that's the default word for materials that fill gaps and keep out weather.

▶ **SEALANTS** generally refer to high-performance compounds like silicones and polyurethanes.

▶ **ADHESIVES** stick things together; their fancy name is quite a mouthful: elastomer-based extrudable mastics. **ELASTOMER** indicates that the product will stay flexible and rubbery, and **MASTICS** is a general term denoting any pasty or gooey adhesive. That noted, adhesives also seal and sealants adhere, though that's not their main mission.

SEALANTS AND CAULKS

As noted in "Sticky Names," above, sealants and caulks do pretty much the same thing: fill gaps, keep moisture at bay, and reduce air infiltration. Sealants tend to last longer, perform better, and cost more. In this brief section, we'll look at the strengths and weaknesses of three major types of caulk.

Although caulks aren't quite so diverse as construction adhesives, they do have varying formulations and properties. For specifics, go on-line or visit your lumberyard.

Silicones are arguably the most durable and most water resistant of any caulk. They are especially suitable for window glazing and slick bathroom and kitchen surfaces.

▶ *Advantages:* Silicones are incredibly tenacious on nonporous materials like glass, glazed ceramic tiles, and metal. There's little shrinkage, and they can be applied at -40°F. Silicone sealants specified for metal flue pipe function at 500°F. And silicones have the best long-term flexibility, UV resistance, and weatherability. Also, molds won't grow on them.

▶ *Disadvantages:* Silicones are messy to work with; wear rubber gloves to protect your skin. Once silicones have cured, it's almost impossible to remove them. Plus, they are bond breakers—that is, because nothing will stick to an area they've tainted, think twice about trying them on wood, concrete, or other porous surfaces they don't adhere well to. Avoid inhaling acetoxy silicones, and don't use them on metal because they'll corrode it. Pure silicones can't be painted, although siliconized acrylics can.

Polyurethanes are versatile multipurpose caulks but are not as tenacious as silicones.

▶ *Advantages:* Because they attach equally well to wood, masonry, and metal, they're good for caulking joints where dissimilar

PRO TIP

Use the same gun to apply caulking and construction adhesive, but use a different technique. Because caulks and sealants fill gaps, *push* the gun away from you as you apply them, pushing caulk into gaps. But to get an evenly sized bead of construction adhesive, *pull* the gun toward you, in a "lazy S" motion. Where two panels meet over a framing member, apply a tight zigzag of adhesive so both edges will seat well.

materials meet. Polyurethanes won't corrode metal. They're easy to work, though polys get pretty stiff as temperatures approach freezing. Shrinkage is negligible. They're great for skylight flashing and metal roofs. And they can be painted. Also, they're easier to work than silicones, even though solvent based.

▶ *Disadvantages:* Polyurethanes have poor UV resistance, though additives or painting can improve that dramatically. While they are a good all-purpose caulk, they don't have the durability or shelf life of silicones.

Latex acrylics are a good balance of performance, price, and workability.

▶ *Advantages:* Latex acrylics are water based, hence nontoxic, largely odor free, and very easy to apply (you can shape caulk joints with your finger). They clean up with soap and water. They adhere well to a range of materials, have good UV resistance, and can be painted. Durable once cured, they are best used in protected areas in temperate climates. They are paintable.

▶ *Disadvantages:* Expect significant shrinkage (up to 30 percent) and long curing times. Although good as bedding caulk under door or window casing, they're iffy as exterior caulk or shower and tub caulk. Properties vary widely from product to product. Although some manufacturers tout spectacular performance specs, check out on-line contractor chat groups for real-life performance ratings.

Floor Joists*

30-lb. Live Load   10-lb. Dead Load   L/360

Species or Group	Grade	2x6				2x8				2x10				2x12			
		12 in.	16 in.	19.2 in.	24 in.	12 in.	16 in.	19.2 in.	24 in.	12 in.	16 in.	19.2 in.	24 in.	12 in.	16 in.	19.2 in.	24 in.
Douglas fir–larch	Sel. Struc.	12–6	11–4	10–8	9–11	16–6	15–0	14–1	13–1	21–0	19–1	18–0	16–8	25–7	23–3	21–10	20–3
	No. 1 & Btr.	12–3	11–2	10–6	9–9	16–2	14–8	13–10	12–10	20–8	18–9	17–8	16–5	25–1	22–10	21–4	19–1
	No. 1	12–0	10–11	10–4	9–7	15–10	14–5	13–7	12–4	20–3	18–5	16–9	15–0	24–8	21–4	19–6	17–5
	No. 2	11–10	10–9	10–1	9–3	15–7	14–2	13–0	11–8	19–10	17–5	15–11	14–3	23–4	20–3	18–6	16–6
	No. 3	9–11	8–7	7–10	7–0	12–7	10–11	10–0	8–11	15–5	13–4	12–2	10–11	17–10	15–5	14–1	12–7
Douglas fir (South)	Sel. Struc.	11–3	10–3	9–8	8–11	14–11	13–6	12–9	11–10	19–0	17–3	16–3	15–1	23–1	21–0	19–9	18–4
	No. 1	11–0	10–0	9–5	8–9	14–6	13–2	12–5	11–6	18–6	16–10	15–10	14–5	22–6	20–6	18–9	16–9
	No. 2	10–9	9–9	9–2	8–6	14–2	12–10	12–1	11–3	18–0	16–5	15–5	13–10	21–11	19–8	17–11	16–1
	No. 3	9–8	8–5	7–8	6–10	12–4	10–8	9–9	8–8	15–0	13–0	11–10	10–7	17–5	15–1	13–9	12–4
Hem-fir	Sel. Struc.	11–10	10–9	10–1	9–4	15–7	14–2	13–4	12–4	19–10	18–0	17–0	15–9	24–2	21–11	20–8	19–2
	No. 1 & Btr.	11–7	10–6	9–10	9–2	15–3	13–10	13–0	12–1	19–5	17–8	16–7	15–5	23–7	21–6	20–2	18–3
	No. 1	11–7	10–6	9–10	9–2	15–3	13–10	13–0	12–1	19–5	17–8	16–7	14–10	23–7	21–1	19–3	17–2
	No. 2	11–0	10–0	9–5	8–9	14–6	13–2	12–5	11–4	18–6	16–10	15–6	13–10	22–6	19–8	17–11	16–1
	No. 3	9–8	8–5	7–8	6–10	12–4	10–8	9–9	8–8	15–0	13–0	11–10	10–7	17–5	15–1	13–9	12–4
Spruce-pine-fir (South)	Sel. Struc.	11–0	10–0	9–5	8–9	14–6	13–2	12–5	11–6	18–6	16–10	15–10	14–8	22–6	20–6	19–3	17–11
	No. 1	10–9	9–9	9–2	8–6	14–2	12–10	12–1	11–3	18–0	16–5	15–5	14–1	21–11	19–11	18–3	16–3
	No. 2	10–5	9–6	8–11	8–3	13–9	12–6	11–9	10–10	17–6	15–11	14–9	13–3	21–4	18–9	17–2	15–4
	No. 3	9–3	8–0	7–3	6–6	11–8	10–1	9–3	8–3	14–3	12–4	11–3	10–1	16–6	14–4	13–1	11–8
Western woods	Sel. Struc.	10–9	9–9	9–2	8–6	14–2	12–10	12–1	11–3	18–0	16–5	15–5	14–3	21–11	19–11	18–6	16–6
	No. 1	10–5	9–6	8–11	8–0	13–9	12–4	11–4	10–1	17–5	15–1	13–10	12–4	20–3	17–6	16–0	14–4
	No. 2	10–1	9–2	8–8	8–0	13–4	12–1	11–4	10–1	17–0	15–1	13–10	12–4	20–3	17–6	16–0	14–4
	No. 3	8–5	7–3	6–8	5–11	10–8	9–3	8–5	7–6	13–0	11–3	10–3	9–2	15–1	13–1	11–11	10–8

* **Design Criteria:** Strength – 30 lbs. per sq. ft. live load, plus 10 lbs. per sq. ft. dead load. Deflection – Limited in span in inches divided by 360 for live load only.

This table is used courtesy of Western Wood Products Association (www.wwpa.org) and is excerpted from Western Lumber Span Tables of Floor and Ceiling Joists and Roof Rafters. For more information about lumber grades, see pp. 47 and 48.

Roofs

A roof is a building's most important layer of defense against water, wind, and sun. Properly constructed and maintained, a roof deflects rain and snowmelt, and routes them away from other house surfaces. Historically, roof materials have included straw, clay tile, wood, and slate. Although many of these materials are still used, most roofs installed today are asphalt-based composites.

If roofs consisted simply of two sloping planes, covering them would be easy. But today's roofs have protruding vent pipes, chimneys, skylights, dormers, and the like—all potentially water dams and channels that need to be *flashed* to guide water around them. Then as runoff approaches the lower reaches of the roof, it must be directed away from the building by means of overhangs, drip-edges, and—finally—gutters and downspouts.

This chapter assumes that the house foundation and framing are stable. Because structural shifting or settling can cause roofing materials to separate and leak, you should fix structural problems before repairing or replacing a roof.

Roof Safety and Equipment

Among the building trades, roofing is considered the most dangerous—not because its tasks are inherently hazardous—but because they take place high above the ground. The steeper the roof pitch, the greater the risk. If heights make you uneasy or if you're not particularly agile, hire a licensed contractor.

Although these wood shingles seem randomly placed, the installer is taking great pains to offset the shingle joints between courses and to maintain a minimum exposure of 5 in. so the roof would be durable as well as distinctive.

COMMONSENSE SAFETY

► Stay off the roof unless you have a compelling reason to be on it. Besides being hazardous to you, walking on a roof can damage roofing materials.

► If you must work on a roof, have a second person within earshot in case you fall or need occasional help.

► Don't venture up when the roof is wet or near freezing or extremely warm. When wet, most roofing materials are slippery. Cold asphalt shingles are brittle; warm asphalt can stretch and tear. Always wear shoes with soft nonslip soles.

► Position ladder feet securely away from the building about one-quarter of the ladder's extended length. Never lean sideways from a ladder. If you can't reach something while keeping your hips within ladder sides, move the ladder.

► When installing a roof, use scaffolding with a safety rail. The most dangerous part of a roofing job—apart from tearing off shingles and underlayment—is applying the first few courses along eaves.

► When walking on a roof, try to "walk on nails." In other words, try to walk directly over the rafters, where the sheathing is nailed. The roof will be less springy over rafters, and you'll be less likely to break through rotten sheathing.

► Follow the manufacturer's installation instructions, which often provide time- and money-saving tips. Also, if a material fails after correct installation, manufacturers are more likely to honor their warranties.

EQUIPMENT

Unless you are installing roofing systems that need to be "torched" (heat-sealed with a propane torch) you won't need a lot of specialized equipment or tools. Most of the items discussed here are safety related.

Pneumatic nailers have gauge stops on their bases that you can adjust to the correct shingle exposure. For example, when the gauge stop is snug to the butt of a shingle, the next shingle above, placed on the nose of the tool will be correctly positioned to nail.

Footwear should be sneakers or other soft-soled shoes that grip well on a roof. Old-time roofers prefer boots with thick soles that are less likely to be punctured by stray nails, but such boots are inflexible and don't grip as well.

Scaffolding can make applying the first few courses along the eaves far safer. After the lower courses are installed, the scaffolding serves mainly as a staging area for materials and tools.

Roofing jacks enable you to work safely on roofs with a 6-in-12 pitch or steeper. Several different roof pitches are shown in "Gutter Lip and Roof Pitch," on p. 149. Jacks are also indispensable platforms for storing materials. As you work up a roof, install additional pairs of jacks whenever you must stretch to nail the next course. As shown in the photo on p.65, many roofers leave jacks installed till the job is completed.

Full-body harnesses, also known as personal fall-arrest systems (PFAS), may be required by local building authorities if a roof exceeds a certain pitch or if the eaves are more than a specified height above the ground. If harnesses are required, have someone at the rental company demonstrate correct use.

Kneepads, sturdy ones with integral plastic cups, will spare you a lot of pain. In addition, a Malco Shingle Pad®, an insulated foam pad you can sit or kneel on while shingling, protects shingles from abrasion and has a little lip to keep tools from sliding south.

PRO TIP

Many roofers prefer hand nailing the first half dozen shingle courses, rather than pneumatic nailing. That's because the hose of a pneumatic nailer makes footing more treacherous along the eaves, where there's little time to catch yourself before rolling over the edge.

REPUTATION, LICENSE, AND Insurance

Before hiring a roofing contractor, call your local office of the Better Business Bureau to see if complaints have been lodged and check with the state licensing board to determine if the contractor is properly licensed and bonded. Ask to see current certificates of liability insurance coverage and workers' compensation. Otherwise, even if a contractor misrepresents his credentials, you could be liable for injuries the contractor and his crew sustain on your property.

A pneumatic nailer, which you can rent, speeds the job along. Have the rental company recommend nails and explain the nailer's correct use.

Shingling hatchets in the hands of a pro can fasten shingles almost as fast as a pneumatic nailer.

Miscellaneous tools include a utility knife with hooked blades, a straightedge or framing square, a hammer, a chalkline, a tape measure, caulk guns, work gloves, safety glasses, and hearing protection.

Preparing to Install a New Roof

Daily temperatures on a roof or in an unventilated attic can swing from 50°F to 150°F, thereby causing tremendous expansion and contraction of roof materials. Improving ventilation under the roof, as shown in "Roof Venting," on p. 76, can prolong shingle life somewhat, but the key to a long-lasting roof is the quality of the materials.

In the long haul, shingles with a 30-year warranty are a smarter buy than 20-year shingles because they last significantly longer, even though they cost only a little more. And most of a job's cost is the labor.

WHEN IT'S TIME TO TEAR OFF

Short-term, you can save money by installing a new roof over an old one if local codes allow. However, new roofing applied over old (see p. 83) rarely lasts as long as roofing installed on a stripped and properly prepared substrate.

You *must* tear off existing roofing under the conditions at right:

Roof Longevity

MATERIAL	LONGEVITY (years)
Slate and tile*	80
Wood shingles or shakes	30–40
Metal	40–50
Asphalt shingles	20
Three-ply built-up roof	15–20
Four-ply built-up roof	20–25

**Underlayment quality also determines how many leak-free years you can expect. With 15-lb. building paper underneath, a tile roof might start leaking in 15 years; modified bitumin under tile could help create an 80-year roof.*

Warranty ISSUES

If you observe product defects such as premature wear or curling, ask the company that installed the shingles to inspect them and advise you on warranty issues. (Always keep records of installations.) If the company is reputable, it probably has a longstanding relationship with the manufacturer and can exert more pressure to settle disputes than you could. If you don't know or can't find the installation company, hire another licensed roofing contractor to inspect the roof and, if possible, identify the shingle type and manufacturer. If that contractor concurs that the shingles are defective—rather than installed incorrectly—contact an attorney who specializes in building-related claims to explore your options.

The roof already has two roofing layers. Two is the limit for most local codes, because it's virtually impossible to install a third layer that will lie flat. Even if you could, three layers would be a nightmare to flash and nail correctly. Underlying shingle layers are a springy substrate to nail through, and old wood shingles often split and migrate. Besides, if the bottom layer is wood shingles over *skip-sheathing* (1-in. boards with spaces between), only half of the new roofing nails would be likely to hit sheathing. Consequently, additional layers would be poorly attached and therefore wouldn't last.

Sheathing and rafters show extensive water damage. When you can't determine exactly what's been causing leaks, it's time to strip. The previous roofers may have installed flashing incorrectly or not at all. Or reroofers may have left tired old flashing in place. Whatever the cause, if the remedy is stripping back extensive sections of roofing in order to replace faulty flashing, reroofing may be the most cost-effective cure.

Rafters and sheathing are undersize. If rafters are too skimpy, the roof will sag, especially along the ridge. If the sheathing is too thin, the roof will sag between rafters and look wavy. In either case, consult a structural engineer. The remedy may be stripping the roof and nailing ½-in. plywood over old sheathing or bolstering undersize rafters with new lumber; but let a professional make the call.

Shingles are prematurely worn, curling, or missing. If a roof is relatively new and these symptoms are widespread, suspect product

A stripping shovel is a flat-nose shovel whose blade is serrated to peel off shingles and grab nail shanks. The fulcrum on the back increases leverage as you pry up roofing.

defects, inadequate ventilation, faulty installation, or a combination of those factors. A layer of new shingles won't lie flat over curling ones. So if shingles are curling—even if there is only a single layer of roofing—tear them off.

Adjacent roof sections must be replaced. This is a judgment call. When a house has additions that were roofed at different times, their need for replacement rarely coincides with that of the older roof—one section always has a few extra years left. Likewise, south-facing roof sections age 20 percent to 30 percent faster than north-facing ones. If you see signs of leaks, strip the whole roof, install flashing, and reroof.

STRIPPING AN OLD ROOF

Roof stripping is one of the nastiest, dirtiest, most dangerous jobs in renovation. If you can afford it, hire an insured contractor for this. Most roofing contractors know of tear-off crews that will obtain permits, rip off the old roof, and cart away the debris, or you might be able to subcontract the job through a roofer. Professional stripping takes at most a couple of days, and it's money well spent to allow the start of new work.

If you must strip the roof yourself, remove all drain gutters and then minimize the mess by buying a heavy 6-mil plastic tarp to catch shingles and old roofing nails. So you won't be picking shingle shards and nails from the lawn for years to come, lay tarps from the house to the Dumpster as well. To protect plants around the house, place sawhorses or 2×4 frames over them and cover with bed sheets or cloth drop cloths. *Caution:* Don't cover plants with plastic or they'll bake. Finally, lean plywood in front of windows so falling objects don't break them. When the job is done, rent a *magnetic roller* (also called a magnetic nail broom) and roll the lawn to locate roofing nails—before your lawn mower does it for you.

And don't forget the inside of the attic. Spread plastic tarps over attic floors, especially if there's insulation between the joists. During tearoff, an immense amount of debris and fine dust falls into an attic. Unless you catch it in plastic and remove it, you could breathe it or smell asphalt-shingle residue for years.

Other than that, stripping is mostly grunt work. Most strip-

pers use a specially designed tear-off shovel, starting at the top and working down, scooping shingles as they go. Tear-off shovel blades have a serrated edge that slides under nail heads and a fulcrum underneath that pops nails up. Be sure to tear off all old building paper (felt or rosin paper), too.

SHEATHING

Once you've stripped off roofing, survey the sheathing for damage and protruding nails. As you pound down nails, be sure to place your feet directly over rafters. Probe suspect sheathing and replace any that's soft. Cut bad sections back to the nearest rafter centers. For this, wear safety glasses and use a circular saw with a carbide-tipped, nail-cutting blade because the blade will hit a lot of nails. Replacement pieces of sheathing should be the same thickness as the original.

If the old roof was wood-shingled, it probably had skip-sheathing, which is 1×4s spaced 5 in. on center. Skip-sheathing allows air to circulate under the shingles. If the boards are in good shape, you can nail on new wood shingles after stripping old ones. But many contractors prefer to sheathe over the 1×4s with ½-in. exterior-grade plywood (for rafters spaced 16 in. on center) or ⅜-in. plywood (for rafters 24 in. on center). This stiffens the roof and makes it safer to work on, but plywood virtually eliminates air flow under shingles. Consequently, some builders install a synthetic mesh, CedarBreather®, over plywood to increase circulation, before nailing on wood shingles.

A hammer tacker allows you to staple building paper quickly, so it won't slide down the roof as you roll it out. Later, secure the paper with tabbed roofing nails.

Run plywood lengths perpendicular to rafters, centering plywood edges over rafter centers. Nail every 6 in. with 8d galvanized nails. Elsewhere, use H-clips to support panel joints and create ¹⁄₁₆-in. expansion gaps. Sweep the roof well and hammer down nail pop-ups.

UNDERLAYMENT

Once limited to building paper, underlayment now includes self-adhering rubberized sheets that replace metal flashing in some cases. Thus you can base your choice of underlayment on climate, composition, and position on the roof.

Weather-resistant underlayment. Traditionally, underlayment has been 36-in.-wide, 15-lb. or 30-lb. felt paper used as a *weather-resistant layer* with several purposes. It keeps sheathing dry till shingles are installed, serves as a backup layer when water gets under shingles or flashing, and separates sheathing and shingles and so prolongs shingle life. (Without underlayment, shingle asphalt can leech into wood sheathing, or resins in sheathing can degrade the shingle.) Heavy-duty, 30-lb. felt paper is often specified in high-wear, high-water areas such as eaves and valleys. A standard roll of 3-ft.-wide, 15-lb. felt paper covers roughly 400 sq. ft.; the same-size roll of 3-ft.-wide, 30-lb. paper covers only 200 sq. ft. because it's roughly twice as thick.

Because unreinforced lighter grades of building paper (15 lb.) tear easily and wrinkle when wet, some types are now reinforced with fiberglass. Moreover, all asphalt-impregnated building papers dry out and become less water resistant when exposed to sunlight, so the sooner they're covered by shingles, the better. Building paper was never intended to be an exterior membrane.

When installing building paper on a sloped roof, have a helper and work from the bottom up. As you roll the paper out, it will tend to slide down the roof, so be sure to unroll it straight across the roof. The first course of paper should overlap a metal drip-edge nailed along the eaves. Align the paper's lower edge to the lower metal edge and unroll the paper, stapling as you go. Staples are only a temporary attacher, to help you keep the paper from bunching or sliding. Then nail the underlayment, using the tabbed roofing nails (also called Simplex® nails) shown on p. 57. Along roof edges and where the ends of the building paper overlap, space nails every 6 in., insetting them 1 in. from the edge. Elsewhere, drive nails in a zigzag pattern, spacing them 12 in. to 15 in. apart.

For steep-slope roofs (4-in-12 or steeper), overlap horizontal courses of building paper 2 in.

Eaves, Rake, and Underlayment Details

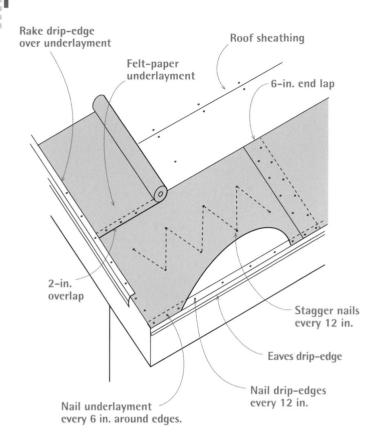

Rake drip-edge over underlayment

Roof sheathing

Felt-paper underlayment

6-in. end lap

2-in. overlap

Stagger nails every 12 in.

Eaves drip-edge

Nail underlayment every 6 in. around edges.

Nail drip-edges every 12 in.

Overlap ends of seams (end laps) at least 6 in. To prevent water backup on low-slope roofs (less than 4-in-12), building codes often specify two plies of 36-in.-wide underlayment, with horizontal seams overlapped at least 19 in. and (vertical) end seams overlapped 12 in. Check your local code to be sure, for it may also specify self-sticking waterproof shingle underlayment along the eaves.

If you're installing wood shakes or slate, use *shake liner:* 18-in.-wide rolls of 30-lb. building paper alternated between roofing courses.

Waterproof shingle underlayment (WSU). WSU is a heavy peel-and-stick bituminous membrane that protects roof areas most likely to leak because of concentrated water flows in valleys, ice dams at eaves, or high winds at eaves and rake edges. Many building codes also specify WSU in lieu of building paper where asphalt shingles are installed on low-slope roofs. In addition to being self-adhering, WSU also self-seals around nails, making it a truly waterproof membrane.

Installing WSU along valleys is vastly easier and superior to lining them with unwieldy roll roofing or aluminum flashing. And with WSU,

PRO TIP

As you prepare to install roofing components, imagine rainwater running down the roof. To prevent water's running underneath underlayment, flashing, or shingles, roofing materials upslope must always overlay those below.

Tack one side of the WSU to the sheathing, fold it in half lengthwise, and then peel off the release sheet for that half. Roll out the untacked half, smoothing it from the valley outward. Pull free the stapled half and repeat.

there's no need to trowel on 3-ft.-wide swaths of roofing cement between 30-lb. building-paper layers to protect eaves from ice-dam damage. Snap a chalkline to position the WSU. Then unroll and cut the membrane to length, align it to the chalkline, peel off its release-sheet backing, and press the material down. Most manufacturers recommend rolling it once it's down.

WSU is more easily installed with two people, but if you're working alone, fold the WSU in half, lengthwise, and temporarily staple one edge of the membrane to a chalked guideline. Peel off the release-backing from the unstapled half of the WSU, and flop the adhesive side of the membrane over onto the sheathing. Finally, yank free the stapled edge, peel off the backing from the second half, and stick it to the sheathing. Because WSU is self-adhering, you needn't nail it; you need to use staples only to keep the sheet from sliding around before sticking it down.

WSU comes in 9-in. to 36-in. widths. Brand names suggest usage, for example, CertainTeed Winterguard™, W.R. Grace Ice & Water Shield™, and GAF Weatherwatch™.

Roof Flashing

Because underlayment directs water away from sheathing, it's technically flashing, too. More often, however, *roof flashing* refers to sheet metal that protects building seams or edges from water penetration or diverts water around pipes, chimneys, dormers, and so on. Metal flashing is widely used because it's durable and relatively easy to cut and shape. Always replace old flashing when installing a new roof.

PRO TIP

Some WSU membranes may be degraded by petroleum-based roofing cements. If you need to caulk near WSU, urethane caulks are probably the best choice; but check your WSU installation specs to be sure.

MATERIALS

Various sheet materials are suitable for flashing. Unformed, they come in sheets 10 ft. long or in rolls of varying lengths, widths, and gauges. Copper is the longest lasting and most expensive. Lead is the most malleable but is also the most vulnerable to tears and punctures. Galvanized steel ranks second in longevity, but it's so rigid that you should buy it preshaped or rent a metal-bending brake to use on site. Lightweight aluminum is commonly shaped on site and is a good trade-off in expense and durability. There's also painted steel flashing, in case you don't like the glare of bare metal.

When installing flashing, use the fewest nails possible and avoid nailing in the center of a flashing channel, where water runs. If possible, always position nails so they can be overlapped by roofing above. Where you must leave nail heads exposed—say, when installing skylight flashing or wall cap-flashing—put urethane caulk under the nail heads before driving them down or use gasketed roofing nails.

DRIP-EDGE FLASHING

You want water to drip free from roof edges, rather than being drawn by capillary action back up under shingles or sheathing. Drip-edge also covers and protects sheathing edges from gutter splashback and ice dams along the eaves and gives *rake edges* a clean, finished look. The

Galvanic ACTION

A number of metals, if paired, will corrode one another in a process called *galvanic action*. To be safe, use nails or clips that are the same metal as the flashing you install. Because water is an electrolyte, any moisture present will increase corrosion. The following metals make up a group known as the electrolytic sequence.

1. ALUMINUM
2. ZINC
3. STEEL
4. IRON
5. NICKEL
6. TIN
7. LEAD
8. COPPER
9. STAINLESS STEEL

When you pair up materials, the metal with the lower number will corrode faster. If you must pair two different metals, you can retard galvanic action by insulating between the metals with a layer of heavy (30-lb.) building paper.

Drip-edge flashing allows water to drip free from roof edges. Here, copper drip-edge is being retrofitted under an existing roof before being fastened with 3d copper flashing nails. An uninstalled piece is shown lying atop the shingles.

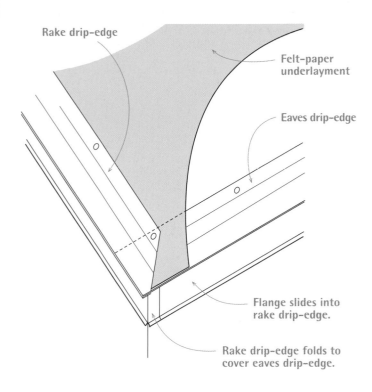

Underlayment runs over the eaves drip-edge, and rake drip-edge runs over the underlayment. Thus, at lower corners the rake drip-edge will overlay the eaves drip-edge.

crimped edge of drip-edge flashing also resists bending and thus supports overhanging shingles.

Drip-edge is sold in varying widths and comes in an L-shape or a lopsided T-shape. Install drip-edge along the eaves first, nailing it directly to sheathing, using 4d big-head roofing nails. Space nails every 18 in. or so. Underlayment along the eaves thus overlaps the drip-edges. Along the rake edges of a roof, install underlayment before applying rake drip-edge. In the corners, where rake edges meet eaves, run the rake drip-edge over the eaves drip-edge. Slitting the vertical leg of the rake drip-edge makes it easier for you to bend it over the leg of the eaves drip-edge.

In general, drip-edge flashing 6 in. wide or wider is better than narrower flashing because it enables you to nail well back from the edge of the flashing—always desirable.

VALLEY FLASHING

There are basically two types of valleys: *open*, where the valley's flashing is exposed, and *closed*, where flashing is covered by shingles. Each has advantages. Open valleys clear water well, are easy to install, and work especially well beneath wood shingles, shakes, and laminated asphalt shingles, which are thicker and harder to bend than standard three-tab shingles. In woven valleys, shingles from both roof planes meet in the valley in alternating overlaps and are slower to install, but offer double-shingle protection and are favored for low-slope roofs. And there are variations, such as the *closed-cut valley* of the two valleys shown in "Closed Valleys," on p. 73.

Prepare all valley types by sweeping away debris, hammering *all* sheathing nails flush, and then lining the valley with underlayment. Traditionally, this lining was 30-lb. building paper.

But, as mentioned earlier, peel-and-stick WSU, though more expensive, is simpler to install and far more durable. Because it's self-sticking, WSU doesn't need to be nailed; moreover, it self-seals around shingle nails, preventing leaks. Though it comes in varying widths, install 36-in.-wide WSU for valleys, centering a single piece down the length of the valley and overlapping the drip-edge flashing at the bottom.

If you instead line the valley with 30-lb. building paper, run a continuous piece of 36-in.-wide paper down the valley or overlap pieces below by at least 6 in. Using tabbed roofing nails, nail down the paper, keeping nails 6 in. away from the center of the valley. The 15-lb. building paper underlayment used elsewhere on the roof will overlap the outer edges of this heavier "valley paper."

Install metal valley flashing that's 18 in. to 24 in. wide on most slopes, so that each side of the valley is 9 in. to 12 in. wide. If the roof pitch is steep or if you live in an area that gets much

An Open Valley

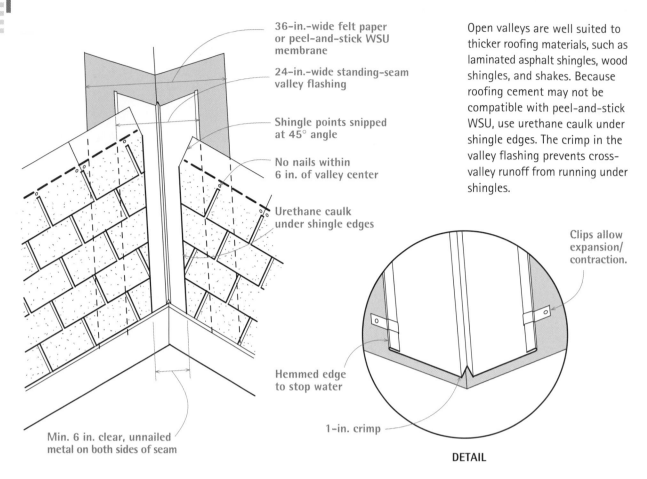

36-in.-wide felt paper or peel-and-stick WSU membrane

24-in.-wide standing-seam valley flashing

Shingle points snipped at 45° angle

No nails within 6 in. of valley center

Urethane caulk under shingle edges

Min. 6 in. clear, unnailed metal on both sides of seam

Open valleys are well suited to thicker roofing materials, such as laminated asphalt shingles, wood shingles, and shakes. Because roofing cement may not be compatible with peel-and-stick WSU, use urethane caulk under shingle edges. The crimp in the valley flashing prevents cross-valley runoff from running under shingles.

Clips allow expansion/contraction.

Hemmed edge to stop water

1-in. crimp

DETAIL

Vent-pipe flashing overlaps shingles below and is overlapped by shingles above. To keep water from entering the snipped metal collar, seal it with urethane caulk.

rain, have a metal shop fabricate valley flashing with an inverted V-crimp down the middle. This crimp helps prevent heavy runoff from one side running across the valley and up under shingles on the other side. Overlap lower sections of flashing 8 in. to 9 in. The heavier the metal, the more durable the valley: 26-gauge is standard for pre-fabricated pieces, but the heavier 24-gauge is better.

Avoid driving nails through metal valley flashing. Rather, place nail shanks snugly against the edge of the flashing and drive nails till their heads touch, but don't dent, the metal. Space nails every 12 in. to 16 in. along both edges or use clips that interlock seams along the edge. Not nailing through the metal allows it to expand and contract freely and leaves no nail holes for water to penetrate. To prevent corrosive galvanic action, use nails or clips of the same metal as the flashing.

VENT-PIPE FLASHING

Vent-pipe flashing (also called jack flashing) is usually an integral unit with a neoprene collar atop a metal base flange. Some pros prefer all-metal units because UV rays won't degrade them

and their taller collars are less likely to leak on low-slope roofs.

Neoprene combos are easier to install. In both cases, shingle up to the base of the vent pipe and slide the unit down the pipe. Nail the top edge of the base, and then overlap it with shingles above. Neoprene collars slide easily over the pipes, but metal collars must be snipped and spread to receive the pipe, before being caulked with urethane to prevent leaks. For either base, don't nail the lower (exposed) edge; instead, apply a bead of urethane caulk beneath the flange, to seal it to the shingles beneath.

CHIMNEY FLASHING

Chimneys must be *counterflashed* (see p. 74). The upper pieces of counterflashing are usually tucked into chimney mortar joints and made to overhang various pieces of *base flashing*, which are nailed to the roof deck. Counterflashing and base pieces overlap but aren't physically joined, so they can move independently yet still repel water. (This independence is necessary because houses and chimneys settle at different rates, causing single-piece flashing to tear and leak.)

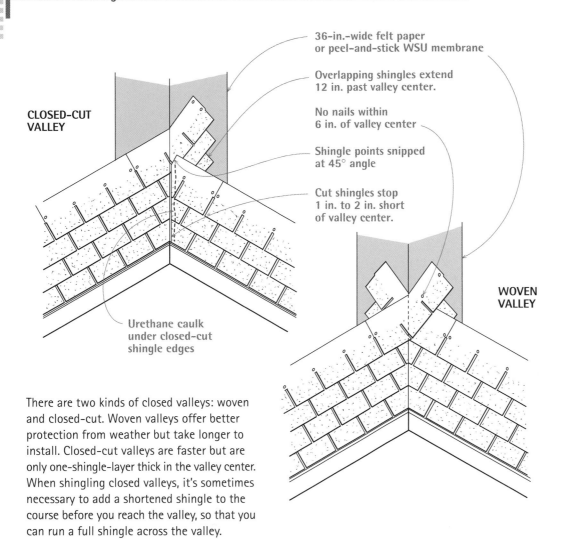

CLOSED-CUT VALLEY

36-in.-wide felt paper or peel-and-stick WSU membrane

Overlapping shingles extend 12 in. past valley center.

No nails within 6 in. of valley center

Shingle points snipped at 45° angle

Cut shingles stop 1 in. to 2 in. short of valley center.

WOVEN VALLEY

Urethane caulk under closed-cut shingle edges

There are two kinds of closed valleys: woven and closed-cut. Woven valleys offer better protection from weather but take longer to install. Closed-cut valleys are faster but are only one-shingle-layer thick in the valley center. When shingling closed valleys, it's sometimes necessary to add a shortened shingle to the course before you reach the valley, so that you can run a full shingle across the valley.

Replace counterflashing and base flashing when reroofing. To avoid damaging the chimney, use the gentlest possible method to remove counterflashing. If mortar is weak and crumbling, you may be able to pull the flashing out by hand; in that case, repoint the mortar before replacing counterflashing. If the mortar is sound and the counterflashing firmly lodged, try using either a cold chisel or a carbide-tipped bit in a pneumatic air chisel to cut out the flashing and as little of the mortar as possible.

You need to remove base flashing because you'll be stripping the roofing and building paper at the same time. Base flashing has several components: a continuous sheet-metal *apron* across the chimney's downslope face, L-shaped *step-flashing* running up both sides, and (when the chimney sits below the roof ridge) a *cricket* (or saddle) running across the upslope face. A cricket is sloped like a tent roof to deflect water around

the chimney. Use a claw hammer, a flat bar, or a cat's paw to pry up old base flashing. Then hammer down any nails you can't pull.

Reattach base flashings first. As shingles butt against the chimney's downslope face, place the apron over them. The apron's bottom flange should overlap shingles at least 4 in.; its upper flange should run at least 12 in. up the face of the chimney. Prefabricated aprons usually have "ears" that wrap around chimney corners and are nailed to the deck sheathing. As shingles progress up both sides of the chimney, they overlap the bottoms of L-shaped pieces of step-flashing.

Keep nails as far back from the flashing crease as possible. Use a single nail to nail down each piece of step-flashing and the shingle covering it. When shingle courses along both sides of the chimney reach the back (upslope) face of the chimney, the lower flanges of the cricket overlap them.

Chimney Flashing

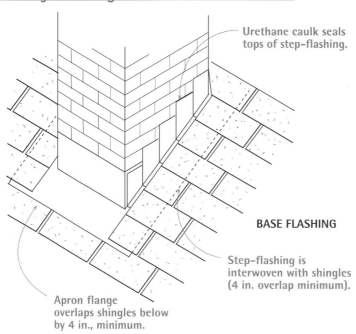

Urethane caulk seals tops of step-flashing.

BASE FLASHING

Step-flashing is interwoven with shingles (4 in. overlap minimum).

Apron flange overlaps shingles below by 4 in., minimum.

COUNTERFLASHING

Cricket flange extends up under shingles by 6 in., minimum

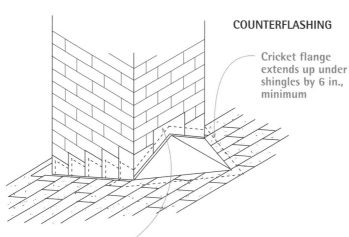

Tops of apron, cricket, and step-flashing are covered by counterflashing.

The apron flashing along the downslope of the chimney wraps around the corners of the chimney and is itself overlapped by step-flashing coming down each side. The cricket on the upslope side is also complex; it wraps corners and overlaps step-flashing below. Have a sheet metal shop solder all seams so they'll be watertight.

If a self-supporting cricket is fabricated from heavy 20-gauge galvanized steel, predrill the nail holes in the cricket's lower flange. Nail it down with ring-shank roofing nails spaced every 6 in., down 2 in. from the top edge. Then cover the top edges of the cricket flange with a strip of peel-and-stick bituminous membrane, and overlap that with shingles. Finally, caulk the top edges of apron, step-, and cricket flashings with urethane caulk to seal them to the chimney.

There are several ways to install counterflashing. Counterflashing should overlap the base flashing by 4 in. Traditionally, a mason used a *tuck-pointing chisel* to remove chimney mortar to a depth of 1½ in. and then inserted a folded lip of counterflashing into the mortar joint. The joint was then packed with strips of lead to hold the flashing in place, followed by fresh mortar applied with a *striking tool* (also known as a slick). This method can work well, but you need to be careful not to damage the surrounding bricks. Caulk with urethane caulk once the mortar has set.

Alternatively, you can use an abrasive wheel in a handheld grinder to cut narrower slots in the mortar joints; then insert counterflashing with its lip folded back so sharply that it resembles the barb of a fishing hook. This barbed lip friction-fits tightly into the slot, so mortar is unnecessary.

The transition step-flashing that turns the corner on a dormer sidewall is complex and inclined to leak, so have it prefabricated by a sheet-metal shop. Seal the top of the step-flashing with 9-in.-wide peel-and-stick membrane, and then overlap that with housewrap before covering it with siding.

Instead, fill the slot with urethane caulk, which adheres well and seals out water.

FLASHING ADJOINING STRUCTURES

Where roof sections abut other roofs or walls, there are various ways to flash but only one underlying principle: Allow water to run downhill freely.

Where a shed roof abuts a wall, you'll need to open up the wall or remove siding nails so you can slide the upper leg of the flashing up at least 4 in., under both underlayment and siding—8 in. in snow country. The lower leg of the flashing goes over the uppermost course of shingles on the shed roof. Secure flashing with gasketed roofing nails 2 in. from its lower edge. Stop the siding at least 1 in. above the shingles of the shed roof.

Where a gable-end addition abuts a vertical sidewall, install step-flashing on both sides of the gable. Fashion L-shaped step-flashing by folding in half 5-in. by 10-in. pieces of sheet metal; alternate pieces of flashing and shingles, as you would chimney step-flashing. Again, you'll need to pull siding nails or cut back the siding to fit the upper legs of the flashing up under wall underlayment and siding. Place nails as far as possible from the flashing folds. Use two nails to attach each piece of step-flashing: one nail (into the sidewall) 1 in. from the top edge of the upper leg and the other nail through the bottom leg and the shingle overlapping it. Apply urethane caulk under any flashing legs or shingle edges that don't lie flat.

SKYLIGHT AND RIDGE FLASHING

Skylight flashing is discussed in Chapter 6, where you'll see an installation from framing to flashing. As a general rule, follow the instructions in the flashing kit provided by the skylight manufacturer.

Traditionally, ridges were flashed with a continuous strip of 12-in.-wide, 30-lb. building paper folded lengthwise, which straddled the ridge and overlapped the top courses of shingles. The build-

Flashing a Shed Roof That Abuts a House Wall

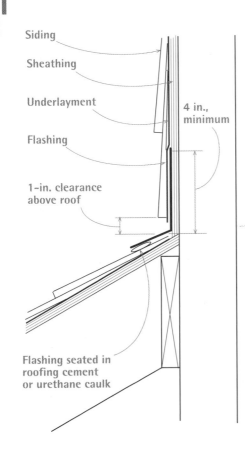

Siding

Sheathing

Underlayment

Flashing

4 in., minimum

1-in. clearance above roof

Flashing seated in roofing cement or urethane caulk

CHIMNEY FLASHING

1. As you roof along a chimney, alternate shingles and L-shaped pieces of step-flashing. Counterflashing will cover the tops of the step-flashing. For extra protection, run a bead of urethane between the step-flashing and the chimney. Press the flashing into the urethane to achieve a positive seal.

2. This grinder is poised to grind out an old chimney mortar joint. Once the abrasive wheel hits mortar, you'll see nothing but grit. So wear goggles.

3. Counterflashing is held in place by a folded-back lip jammed into the mortar joint. For good measure, the mason hammered masonry nails into the mortar, and then used a cold chisel to set them deeper.

4. Finally, run a bead of urethane caulk such as Vulkem® 116 to fill the joint and seal out water. Once the caulk has set a bit, you can tool it with your thumb.

Roof VENTS

Ridge and soffit vents allow hot air under the roof to rise and exit, thus moderating under-roof temperatures, extending the life of roofing materials, reducing ambient moisture in the attic—a big source of mold—and preventing ice dams from forming along the eaves.

Roof Venting

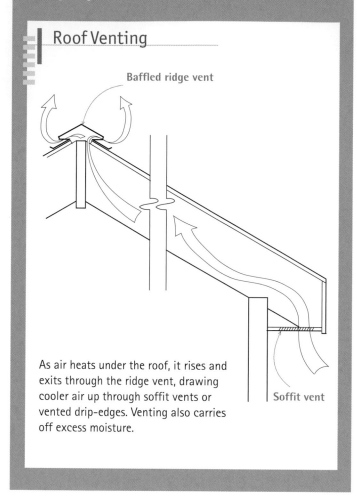

Baffled ridge vent

As air heats under the roof, it rises and exits through the ridge vent, drawing cooler air up through soffit vents or vented drip-edges. Venting also carries off excess moisture.

Soffit vent

ing paper was then covered with a shingle saddle or overlapped ridgeboards. Metal flashing was sometimes used instead of building paper.

These days, ridges aren't sealed by flashing. Instead they are often covered with ridge vents that allow hot air to escape, as shown on p.82.

Asphalt Shingles

On residences, two primary types of asphalt shingles are used. Until recently, most were *three-tab shingles* with two slots dividing the exposed part of the shingle into thirds. But today, *laminated shingles* (also called architectural and dimensional shingles) are gaining in popularity. Consisting of two bonded layers, laminated shingles are thicker, more wind resistant, and somewhat easier to install because they have a random pattern,

with no shingle cutouts to line up. When installed, they look distantly like wood shakes.

MATERIALS: ROUGH NUMBERS

Shingle dimensions vary by maker. Three-tab shingles are typically 12 in. by 36 in. Laminated shingle dimensions are often metric, roughly 13 in. by 40 in. Most shingles are installed with a 5-in. exposure, though shingles with metric dimensions may specify a 5⅝-in. exposure.

Calculating shingles needed for a complex roof is. . .complex. Begin by measuring the roof accurately, making a to-scale sketch on graph paper as you measure. Note valleys, ridges, chimneys, skylights, plumbing vents, and other elements that require flashing, waterproof membranes, or special attention. With that sketch, a building supplier can develop a final materials list for shingles, nails, underlayment, flashing, vents, and so on.

Asphalt shingles come three to five bundles to the *square* (100 sq. ft.), depending on shingle dimensions. Thus you need to calculate the square footage of roof surfaces and divide that number by 100 to get the number of squares needed to shingle the *field*. In addition, you'll need materials to reinforce shingles along eaves and rake edges—either by installing a double layer of shingles along the roof perimeter or by applying a heavy *starter strip* before shingling.

If you're installing laminated shingles, use three-tab shingles as an underlayer along the eaves and rakes. For this purpose, three-tab shingles are far cheaper than laminated shingles and will lie flatter. If you're installing woven valleys, you'll interweave roughly one bundle of shingles per 16 linear (lin.) ft. of valley. Finally, add two extra bundles for waste, ridge and hip caps, and future repairs.

Shingle colors often vary from one production lot to another. So, to avoid having a new roof with a patched-together look, specify that all bundles come from the same lot when you order. Then when your order arrives, check the lot numbers on the bundles and open a few bundles from different lots. If lot numbers don't match and the color variation is noticeable, call the supplier and ask it to rectify the situation. If the color varies only slightly, you might mix lots every other shingle during installation. Finally, have shingles delivered directly to the roof. Many suppliers will place bundles on the roof by means of truck booms or conveyor belts.

Roofing nail quantities vary according to method: hand nailing, power nailing, or some combination of both. Typically, use 4 nails per shingle, or about 2 lb. of nails per square if you're hand nailing. However, high-wind areas require

Have a boom truck deliver roofing supplies directly to the roof. Stack materials along the ridge so the rest of the roof will be clear to work on.

6 nails per shingle or 3 lb. per square. Roofing nails come in 5-lb. and 50-lb. quantities. Boxes of pneumatic nails typically contain 120 nails per coil and 60 coils per box. At 4 nails per shingle, you'll need about 3⅓ coils (400 nails) to attach a square of shingles.

Use corrosion-resistant roofing nails at least 1¼-in. long for new roofs; 1½-in. nails if you're roofing over a previous layer. Ideally, nails should sink three-quarters into sheathing or stop just short of penetrating all the way through for ½-in.- to ⅝-in.-thick sheathing. Hence, if the roof has an exposed roof overhang (you can see the under-side of the sheathing), use ¾-in. ring-shank nails

PNEUMATIC Staples? NO THANKS.

Many local codes don't allow pneumatic staples to attach roofing, and for good reason. Slight variations in compressor-line pressure or setting depth will blow staples right through shingles, and even if staple depth is correct, shingles can easily work loose from the skinny crown holding them down. Roofing nails are vastly superior.

Shingling Terms

These definitions will help you make sense of roofing terms.

▶ **Course:** a horizontal row of shingles.

▶ **Butt edge:** the bottom edge of a shingle.

▶ **Exposure:** typically, the bottom 5 in. of the shingle, left exposed to weather. Shingles with metric dimensions are usually exposed 5⅝ in.

▶ **Cutouts:** slots cut into the exposed part of a three-tab shingle, to add visual interest and allow heat expansion.

▶ **Offset:** the distance that shingle slots or ends are staggered from course to course.

▶ **Self-seal strip:** the adhesive on the shingle face which, when heated by the sun, fuses to shingles above and prevents uplift.

▶ **Fastener line:** on shingles with a 5-in. exposure, a line roughly 5⅝ in. up from the butt edge. Nails along this line will be covered by the shingles above. (If shingles don't have such lines marked, nail just below the self-seal strip.)

▶ **Control lines:** chalklines snapped onto underlayment to help align courses and cutout lines.

Three-Tab Shingles

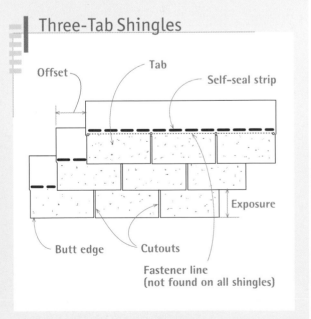

Offset · Tab · Self-seal strip · Exposure · Butt edge · Cutouts · Fastener line (not found on all shingles)

(along the overhang) for a new roof; 1-in. ring-shank nails for roofovers.

When ordering, don't forget tabbed roofing nails for underlayment and metal-compatible nails for attaching flashing or valley clips.

SHINGLE LAYOUT

We'll assume that the roof has been stripped of old shingles, that failed sheathing has been replaced, and that the roof is safe to walk on.

Reconnoiter the roof. Use a tape measure to see whether the roof is square, the ridge is parallel to eaves, the rake edges are parallel, and whether—overall—the width of the roof requires shifting shingle courses left or right. *To determine square,* measure diagonally from both ends of the ridge down to the opposite eaves corner; if the readings are roughly equal, chances are the roof is square. *If the ridge is parallel to eaves* within ½ in., run shingle courses right up to the ridge. But if ridge-to-eaves readings differ by ¾ in. or more, you'll need to compensate by adjusting shingle-exposures as you approach the ridge.

The last two measurements, for parallel rakes and roof width, are of most concern if you're installing three-tab shingles. Because three-tab shingle patterns align vertically, avoid cutting shingle tabs less than 2 in. wide along either rake edge—such short tabs look terrible. It's far better to shift the shingle layout (and thus the vertical control lines) slightly right or left, so the shingle piece is larger. For additional strategies for installing three-tab shingles, see Mike Guertin's fine book, *Roofing with Asphalt Shingles.*

Establishing control lines. After installing drip-edges along the eaves, many pros measure only once, to establish a horizontal *control line* parallel to the eaves, to which they nail the shingle *starter course.* After the starter course is down, they put away their tape measure and use only the exposure gauge of their pneumatic nailer or shingle hatchet to position successive courses.

But, to keep courses evenly spaced and straight, you should mark horizontal lines at regular intervals on the underlayment. If your shingle exposure is 5 in., snap chalklines for every course or every third course—whatever works for you. Snapping lines doesn't take much time and will help ensure professional-looking results.

If you're installing three-tab shingles, it's also wise to snap a pair of parallel, vertical control lines 6 in. apart, to line up the slots of alternating shingle courses, as shown in "Laying Out Three-Tab Shingles," at left. With a 6-in. offset, the slots of every other course line up, creating a strong visual pattern. If slots don't align, the installation will look sloppy. On the other hand, laminated shingles have no slots to align and so don't need vertical control lines.

INSTALLING SHINGLES

After attaching drip-edge flashing to the eaves and rolling out underlayment over the drip-edge, install the starter course along the eaves. You'll cover the starter course with the first course of shingles. Running starter courses along the rakes isn't imperative, but it's smart because starters stiffen the overhanging shingle edges and create a cleaner line.

The starter course. First determine how much the starter course will overhang the drip-edge: ¼ in. to ¾ in. overhang is typical, but some roofers allow as much as 1 in. if eaves or rake boards are badly bowed. The starter course will be 7 in. high. Extend your tape measure past the drip-edge the amount of the overhang, and make crayon marks on the underlayment at 7 in. and at 12 in. Do this at both ends of the roof and snap chalklines through both sets of marks. The 7-in. line indicates the top of the starter course; the 12-in. line indicates the top of the first course of shingles.

PRO TIP

Score shingles on the backside, using a utility knife. If you try to cut through the granules on the front, the blade will go awry and soon dull. When you score along a straightedge and snap along the cut, you'll get a straight, clean edge.

Laying Out Three-Tab Shingles

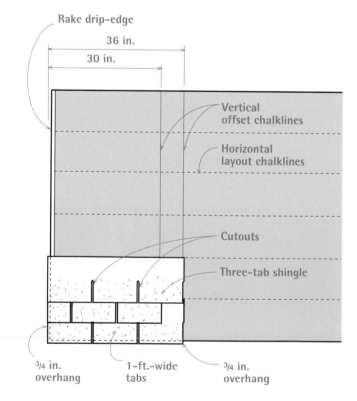

Aligning three-tab shingle cutouts can be as easy as snapping two vertical chalklines 6 in. apart. Because individual shingle tabs are 1 ft. wide, a 6 in. offset will line up shingle cutouts every other course.

Starter courses can be three-tab shingles with the bottom 5 in. cut off or a *starter strip* that comes on rolls in various widths. Starter strips have the advantage of stiffening shingles above and, viewed from below, providing a clean, unbroken line. Still, trimming three-tab shingles is cheaper, so here's a quick look at that method.

First, use three-tab shingles as a starter course, rather than laminated shingles, which cost more and don't lie flat. Traditionally, the starter course was just a full shingle turned upside down so its tabs faced up, but that placed the shingle's self-seal strip too high to do much good. Far better to measure down 7 in. from the top of the shingle, trim off the bottom 5 in., and snap off the shingle tabs.

Secure the starter course by aligning the shingles' top edges to the 7-in. control line and nailing them down, four nails per shingle. If you're installing a starter strip, align its top edge to the 7-in. control line. Next, install starter courses over rake drip-edges, using the same overhang you used for eaves. Rake starter strips overlap eave starter courses when they meet at lower corners. Along both ends of the roof, measure up from the 12-in. control line and snap exposure chalklines for the shingle courses to come. That done, you're ready to install the first course of shingles.

Shingling the field. Install the first course of shingles over the starter course. If you're right-handed, start at the left side of the roof and work right; otherwise, you'll be reaching across yourself continually. Left-handers, of course, should start right and work left.

After installing drip-edge along the eaves, double the first course of shingles or, as shown, install a starter strip. The lower edge of the starter strip overhangs the drip-edge by ¼ in. to ¾ in., or even 1 in. if bowing eaves or rake boards require it.

Instead of doubling shingles along the roof rakes, install a starter strip. It's stiff enough to resist wind uplift. And, seen from below, it presents a much cleaner, straighter line than individual shingles.

Using a Pyramid Pattern Layout

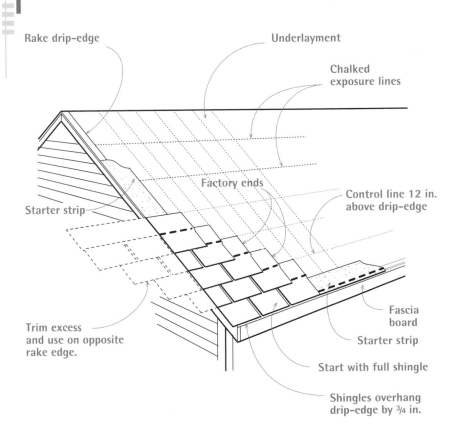

Rake drip-edge

Underlayment

Chalked exposure lines

Factory ends

Control line 12 in. above drip-edge

Starter strip

Fascia board

Starter strip

Trim excess and use on opposite rake edge.

Start with full shingle

Shingles overhang drip-edge by ¾ in.

A pyramid pattern is best for installing laminated shingles that don't have distinct cutouts. As you build the pyramid along the rake edge, trim excess from the rake end so a factory end always leads off each course. Align shingles to horizontal chalklines you snap, not to lines printed on building paper. This method is also shown in the photo sequence on p. 80.

Using Pneumatic Nailers

Because pneumatic nailers can easily blow nails through shingles, some codes specify hand nailing. And it's safer to hand nail the first five or six courses along the eaves, where stepping on a pneumatic hose could roll you right off the roof. Wear goggles when using nailers. Those concerns aside, pneumatic nailers are great tools if used correctly. Here's how:

▶ Don't bounce-fire a nailer till you're skilled with it. (To bounce-fire, you hold the trigger down and press the nailer's nose to the roof to fire the nail.) Shingles must be nailed within a small zone—below the sealer strip but above the cutouts, if any—and it's hard to hit that zone if the nailer is bouncing around. Instead, position the nailer nose where you want it, and then pull the trigger.

▶ Trigger-fire the first nail of every shingle. Do this to keep shingles from slipping, even if you're skilled with pneumatic nailers. Once the first nail is in, you can bounce-fire the remaining ones.

▶ Hold the nailer perpendicular to the roof so nails go in straight, and keep an eye on nail depth as the day wears on. Nail heads should be flush to the shingle; if they're underdriven or overdriven, adjust the nailer pressure.

▶ Nailing schedule: four nails per shingle is standard; six nails for high-wind areas. Trimmed-down shingles must have at least two nails. Place the first and last nails in from the edges at least 1 in. All nails must be covered by the shingle above.

INSTALLING SHINGLES IN A PYRAMID PATTERN

Carefully align the first shingle (which is uncut) to the edges of both eaves and rake starter strips.

Shorten the second shingle in the pyramid by the offset dimension (5 in.). Use the gauge-stop on the bottom of the pneumatic nailer to establish the correct exposure between courses.

At this point, you could run courses all the way across the roof, but most roofers prefer to work up and out, maintaining the diagonal. Although this veteran roofer didn't need to snap horizontal chalklines across the roof to keep courses straight, novices should.

PRO TIP

If you mistakenly shoot a nail through a shingle, cover the nail head with roofing cement and drive a new nail within 1 in. If a nail is crooked, hammer its head flush. Then apply roofing cement and a new nail within 1 in. If a nail is too low to be covered by the shingle above, dab cement on its head and sprinkle loose shingle granules on the cement so the head won't be noticeable.

There are many ways to lay out and install shingles. If you're installing laminated shingles, a *pyramid pattern* is best. With this method, you precut a series of progressively shorter shingles, based on some multiple of the *offset dimension*. Because each successive course is, say, 5 in. or 6 in. shorter, the stepped pattern looks like a pyramid. Typically, pyramids start along a roof edge, with the first shingle in each course flush to the rake starter strip.

Once the pyramid is in place, the job goes fast. Just place a full shingle against each step in the pyramid and keep going. Because the offset is established by those first shingles, you can install full shingles till you reach the other end of the roof. But most roofers prefer to work up and out, maintaining the diagonal. If there are color variations among bundles, they'll be less noticeable if the shingles are dispersed diagonally.

The frequency of a pyramid pattern's repeating itself depends on how random you want shingles to look. Traditionally, patterns repeat every fourth course, that is, every forth course begins with a full shingle. Whatever pattern you choose, trimmed pyramid shingles should be at least 8 in. wide; otherwise they'll look flimsy.

Keeping things lined up. As you work up the roof, align the top of each shingle to a horizontal exposure line. Chalklines wear off quickly, so don't snap them too far in advance; snapping chalklines each time you roll out a new course of building paper is about right. However, to get the measuring done all at once, you can measure up from that original 12-in. line and use a crayon to mark off exposure intervals along the rake edges on both ends of the roof, and then snap chalklines through those marks later.

Alternatively, if you snap chalklines only every second, third, or fourth course, use the gauge on the underside of your pneumatic nailer or on your shingle hatchet to set exposures for intervening courses. If your shingling field is interrupted by dormers or such, always measure down to that original 12-in. line to reestablish exposure lines above the obstruction. Finally, if the ridge is out of parallel with the eaves by more than ¾ in., stop shingling 3 ft. shy of the ridge and start adjusting exposures so that the final shingle course will be virtually parallel with the ridge. For example, if there's a discrepancy of 1½ in., then at 3 ft. below the ridge, you'll need to reduce exposures on the narrow end of the roof by ¼ in. in each of six courses.

Valleys. Both open valleys (in which metal valley flashing is exposed) and closed valleys should be lined, as described in "Underlayment," on p. 69. Closed valleys are more weathertight but slower

Closed-cut valleys are faster to install than woven ones because you don't need to weave shingles from two converging roof planes at the same time.

Roofing Jacks

Roofing jacks provide safe, affordable platforms, even on slopes. Typically, install a pair of jacks for every 8 to 10 courses you go up the roof. To attach the jacks, level the pair by aligning the jacks to horizontal chalklines, and drive two 10d galvanized common nails through each jack into rafters. (Jacks nailed only to sheathing are unsafe because they may pull out under load.) Place jack nails above the fastener line on the shingle because the nails will stay in place after jacks are removed.

If you space each pair of jacks 8 ft. apart horizontally, they can be spanned by 10-ft.-long planks that allow a 1-ft. overhang on each end. However, install the two shingle courses above the jacks before you insert the plank; otherwise the plank will prevent your nailing those courses. To prevent a plank from sliding out of a jack, nail through the hole in the front of the jack arm, into the plank.

Plank-and-jack removal is a two-person job, especially in windy weather. Above all, play it safe, first removing the plank to a secure location. To remove a jack, sharply hammer its bottom upward, thereby driving the slotted jack holes off the 10d nails. Then, while being careful not to disturb the overlapping shingles, slide the jack out. It's a good idea to drive jack nails flush, but not imperative. To drive them flush, slide a flat bar under the overlapping shingle, placing it atop the nail head; then strike the bar's handle with a hammer. This may require several blows.

to install, so they've become less popular. Open valleys are faster to install and better suited to laminated shingles, which are too bulky and stiff to interweave in a closed valley.

Once you've installed valley flashing, snap chalklines along both sides to show where to trim overlying shingles. Locate chalklines at least 3 in. back from the center of the valley; oncoming shingles cover valley flashing at least 6 in. When nailing shingles, keep the nails back at least 6 in. from the valley centerline—in other words, 3 in. back from the shingle trim line—so nails can be covered by shingles above. To seal shingle ends to the metal flashing, run a bead of roofing cement under the leading edge of each shingle, and put dabs of cement *between* shingles. Ideally, you should not nail through the metal at all, but that could leave an inordinately wide area of shingles unnailed. Besides, self-adhering waterproofing membranes beneath the metal flashing will self-seal around the nail shanks.

As a shingle from each course crosses a chalkline, use a utility knife to notch the shingle top and bottom. Then flip the shingle over and, using a straightedge, score the back of the shingle from notch to notch. Or, to speed installation, run shingles into the valley, and then, when the roof section is complete, snap a chalkline along their ends to indicate a cut line. To avoid cutting the metal flashing underneath, put a piece of scrap metal beneath shingle ends as you cut, use a hooked blade in the utility knife, or use snips.

Finally, codes in wet or snowy regions may require that valleys grow wider at the bottom. In that case, move the bottom of each chalkline away from the valley center, at a rate of ⅛ in. per ft.

RIDGE VENTS

To install a ridge vent, cut sheathing back at least 1 in. on either side of the ridgeboard. Run underlayment and shingles to the edge of the sheathing. Then nail the ridge vent over the opening, straddling the shingles on both sides. In most cases, the ridge vent is covered by cap shingles. Because shingles folded in this manner tend to split over time, it's wise to double them.

Chapter 14 offers more information on ventilation. But, in brief, you need a minimum of 1 sq. ft. of ventilation per 300 sq. ft. of roof surface. Install half the vent area as soffit vents on the underside of the eaves, and half as ridge vents. For example, if the roof surfaces total 2,500 sq. ft., vent surfaces should be 2,500÷300, or 8.33 sq. ft. Ridge vents would therefore be half that, or 4.16 sq. ft. Your building supplier can explain the calculations, but 4.16 sq. ft. corresponds roughly to 33 lin. ft. of ridge vents, based on net free vent area (NFVA) charts.

ASPHALT SHINGLE REPAIR

Most roofs are repaired in response to leaks caused by a missing shingle or, more often, worn-out or missing flashing. Or, in some cases, it's necessary to disturb shingles to install a roof vent or a plumbing vent.

When removing a shingle, or a course of shingles, disturb surrounding shingles as little as possible. First break the adhesive seal between courses, by sliding a mason's trowel or a shingle ripper (see the left photo on p. 121) under the shingles and gently slicing through the adhesive strips. It's best to do this when shingles are cool and the adhesive is somewhat brittle and easier to break. If you attempt this when the roof is hot, you're more likely to tear the shingles. However, actually working with the shingles—lifting them to remove nails or slide in new shingles—is best done when the shingle is warm and flexible.

To remove a damaged shingle, raise the shingles above and tear the old one out. If it doesn't tear easily, use a utility knife to cut it out. Remove the nails that held the damaged shingle by inserting a shingle ripper against the nail shafts and prying up. Keep in mind that those nails are actually going through two shingle courses—the one you're trying to remove and the top of the course below. If you extricate the shingle and the nails don't come up with a reasonable amount of trying, just knock them down with your hammer and a flat bar.

Fill old nail holes with roofing cement, and slide the new shingle into place. Gently lift the course above and position nails so they'll be overlapped by that course. Once you've inserted a new shingle, use the flat bar to help drive them down, placing the flat bar atop the nail head and striking the bar with a hammer.

Wood Shingles

There's romance in wood shingles. Despite wood's tendency to mold, grow moss, and catch fire and despite the diversity and durability of laminated asphalt shingles, wood remains popular.

PRO TIP

As shingles run diagonally into an open valley, their leading edges often end in sharp points, under which water can run. To prevent that, use a utility knife with a hooked blade to clip points at a 45° angle.

Ridge vents allow hot air—and excess moisture—to exit the building. Here, a perforated plastic ridge vent gets capped with shingles.

This classic wood shingle roof has an open valley. Shingle caps cover the roof hip.

PREPARING THE ROOF

Be sure to read the earlier sections on sheathing, underlayment, and flashing. And review the methods of asphalt-shingle installation, for they have much in common with wood shingling.

If the old roof was once covered with wood shingles, they were likely nailed to skip-sheathing, which consists of widely spaced 1-in. boards that allow air to circulate under the shingles and dry them. These days, most roofers cover skip-sheathing with plywood because it stiffens the roof and is safer to walk on. But nailing shingles directly to plywood or building paper impedes air circulation and may lead to cupping (shingles' undersides will dry much more slowly than the tops), rotting, and shortened shingle life.

The answer to this dilemma is a layer of ¼-in.-thick synthetic mesh between the building paper and the shingles. CedarBreather is one brand, which comes in 39-in.-wide rolls. Roll the mesh out over 30-lb. building paper, tack or staple it down, and you're ready to shingle. The mesh retains enough loft to allow air to circulate freely around the shingles, so they can dry. To attach shingles over the mesh, you'll need longer nails: 6d shingle nails should do, but check the product's literature to be sure.

Flash a wood shingle roof as you would an asphalt roof, including WSU along the eaves, rakes, and valleys and metal drip-edge along the eaves and rakes.

ESTIMATING MATERIALS

Use only No. 1 (blue-label) shingles on roofs because they're free of sapwood and knots. Lesser grades are fine for siding but may leak on

New Roofing over Old

Although "roofovers," placing new roofing over old, may be allowed by some codes, roofovers tend to be inferior. As noted earlier, you must strip a roof if there are two or more layers or if existing shingles are curling. That said, laminated shingles are usually better than three-tab shingles for roofovers because their random appearance hides minor irregularities in the old roof.

Before beginning, replace or flash over old flashing as follows:

▶ Use aviation snips to cut away flashing around plumbing vents.
▶ Use a cold chisel to remove chimney counterflashing.
▶ Along the eaves, install a new drip-edge over the butt ends of existing shingles.
▶ Along the rakes, install a new J-channel drip-edge, which wraps around the old rake flashing and starter courses.
▶ Leave the old valley flashing in place, and install new over it.

To level out an existing asphalt roof, rip down (reduce the height of) two courses of shingles, as shown in the drawing. Because asphalt shingles are routinely exposed 5 in., rip down the first strip (the starter course) so that it is 5 in. high. Then lay it over the original (old) first course so that the strip is flush against the butts of the original second course above. Next rip down a second strip (second course) 10 in. high and put it flush against the butts of the original third course. You now have a flat surface along the eaves. The third course of new shingles—and all subsequent shingles—need not be cut down, just butted to an original course above and nailed down. Use 1½-in. roofing nails for roofovers.

New Shingles over Old

When installing a new roof over an old one, avoid a wavy-looking job by reducing the height of the first two courses to establish a flat surface.

After installing drip-edge flashing, double the first course of wood shingles along the eaves. Along eaves and rakes, the drip-edge overhangs sheathing or trim boards by ½ in. to ¾ in., and shingles extend at least 1 in. beyond the drip-edge.

Wood Shingle Details

If the old wood shingle roof was attached to skip-sheathing, cover it with plywood for safety and stability. A layer of synthetic mesh allows the underside of the wood shingles to dry out.

Solid plywood sheathing

Old skip-sheathing

Felt paper

Mesh allows shingles to breathe

Two nails per shingle, in ¾ in. from edges

¼-in. gap

Double first course of shingles along eaves.

Fascia board

Offset shingle joints 1½ in., minimum.

Shingles overhang 1 in. at eaves and rake.

a roof. Shingles come 16 in., 18 in., and 24 in. long, with recommended exposures of 5 in., 5½ in., and 7½ in., respectively, on roofs with a 4-in-12 slope or steeper. Ultimately, slope determines exposure and thus the number of bundles per square (100 sq. ft.).

In general, four bundles will cover a square. To calculate the number of squares you'll need, calculate the square footage of the roof and divide by 100. Because shingles are doubled along eaves and rakes, add an extra bundle for each 60 lin. ft. of eaves or rake. For valleys, add an extra bundle for each 25 lin. ft. For ridges and roof hips, buy preassembled ridge caps, sold in bundles that cover 16 lin. ft. One Canadian supplier, WoodRoof™ (www.woodroof.com) offers information about hip and ridge caps, precut "fancy butt" shingles, specialty tools, and more.

You'll need 2 lb. of 4d or 5d galvanized shingle nails per square of shingles. For shingle caps along ridges and hips, use 6d shingle nails to accommodate the greater thickness of materials. Have your supplier deliver the materials in a lift-bed truck, so that you can unload the shingles right onto the roof.

INSTALLING WOOD SHINGLES

Double the first courses of shingles along the eaves, extending them beyond the drip-edge by 1 in.; and double shingles along rakes, overhanging rake trim by 1 in. In addition, install metal drip-edge along eaves and rakes. When nailing the bottom course of doubled shingles along the eaves, nail them about 1 in. up from the butt edges; if possible, sink the nails into the edge of the fascia board. Those two nails will be covered by the top course of doubled shingles. Nail that course with two nails placed 1½ in. above the exposure line.

WOOD Shingle BASICS

No matter how wide the shingle, use only two nails—placed ¾ in. in from the edge, and 1½ in. above the exposure line. To allow for expansion, leave a ¼-in. gap between shingles, unless they are wet, in which case you can place them snug against each other because they'll shrink. Offset joints between successive courses at least 1½ in. Shingle joints that line up must be separated by two courses—in other words, shingle joints can line up every fourth course, but not sooner. Finally, nail heads should touch but not crush shingle surfaces; deeper, they may split the wood.

You could snap chalklines to indicate exposures for successive courses, but chalk can be unsightly and slow to fade. Instead, get a straight board as wide as the shingle exposure (5 in., for example), place its bottom edge flush to the bottom of the last shingle course, and position the next course of shingles by simply placing them atop the board. Move loose shingles around till all their joints are correctly offset to the courses below. Then nail them down.

When you start stretching to install courses above, install roof jacks as described on p. 81. Because wood shingles do not have fixed lengths as asphalt shingles do—just the same bottom line—several workers can work on a course at the same time. As you get within 6 ft. of the top, measure up to the ridge. If the ridge is not parallel to the eaves, there may be a discrepancy of several inches between measurements at one end of the roof and the other. If so, start adjusting exposures so that the final course of shingles will be more or less parallel to the ridge. If there's a discrepancy of 2 in., for example, you should reduce exposures on the narrow end of the roof by ¼ in. per course.

Open valleys. Refer to previous sections in this chapter on underlayment and valley flashing before you start. For most renovations, an open valley is the way to go: The exposed metal flashing of an open valley clears water well and is not likely to clog with debris and to dam up water. In addition, shingles running alongside an open valley require less fitting and cutting than those in closed valleys.

You can shingle out from a valley or into a valley from roof planes on either side. In either case, start by snapping parallel chalklines along both sides of the metal valley flashing, each line should be at least 3 in. from the center fold of the flashing. As each course approaches the valley, don't nail the last four or five shingles immediately; just arrange them so that wide shingles end in the valley. Where shingles cross a chalkline, use a utility knife to notch the shingle at those points.

Keep nails as far as possible from the valley center: 5 in. away is minimum. A bead of urethane caulk under the leading shingles should keep the edges from lifting.

Closed valleys. Run shingles into the valley until they meet oncoming shingles from the other side. At that juncture, rough cut each shingle about ¼ in. wide to establish the correct angle. Then use a block plane to back-bevel its leading edge. By cutting and planing, you create a compound angle so that the shingles fit tightly; this can be done only on the roof, shingle by shingle—a slow job. For best weathering, alternate miters right and left, from course to course. Build up several courses in the valley and shingle out to the rest of the field.

Ridge treatments. Be sure to read the comments on venting a ridge on p. 76. In brief, cut back sheathing at least 1 in. on either side of the ridgeboard. Then run underlayment and shingles to the edge of the sheathing before nailing a ridge vent over the opening.

▶ *Shingle caps.* Use a pneumatic nailer to attach preassembled shingle caps over the vent. Because the mesh underlayment and the ridge vent are compressible, they would move if you tried to hand nail them. Shoot 2-in. to 2½-in. galvanized shingle nails through the shingle caps; nails should penetrate the roof sheathing at least ½ in.

▶ *Ridgeboards.* These butt to each other; for a weather-tight fit, they should be mitered. To establish the miter angle, lap two pieces of scrap at the peak and, using an adjustable bevel, transfer this angle to your table saw.

Ventilating a Wood Shingle Ridge

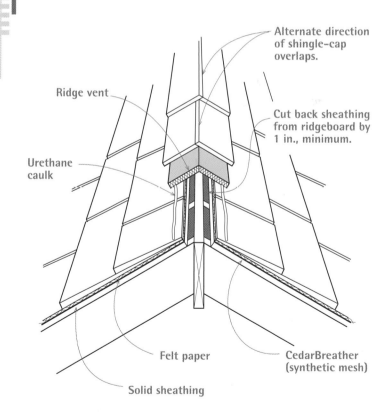

- Alternate direction of shingle-cap overlaps.
- Ridge vent
- Cut back sheathing from ridgeboard by 1 in., minimum.
- Urethane caulk
- Felt paper
- CedarBreather (synthetic mesh)
- Solid sheathing

Use a pneumatic nailer to attach preassembled ridge caps over the ridge vents because hand nailing the caps could split them.

Test-cut several pieces of scrap till the fit is tight; then rip down the ridgeboards on the table saw. Because ridgeboards should be as long as possible, get help nailing them down. If it takes several boards to achieve the length of the ridge, bevel joints 60° and caulk each with urethane caulk.

Using 8d galvanized ring-shank roofing nails, nail the ridgeboards to the rafters; use two nails per rafter. Then go back and draw the beveled joint together by nailing it with 6d galvanized box nails spaced every 12 in. As you work, push down on the ridgeboards to force them together. To avoid splitting boards, predrill them or use a pneumatic nailer to shoot nails through the roofing layers into the rafters.

SHINGLE REPAIRS

To remove wood shingles, use scrap blocks to elevate the butt ends of the course above. Work the blade of a chisel into the butt end of the defective shingle, and with twists of your wrist, split the shingle into slivers. Before fitting in a new shingle, remove the nails that held the old one. Slide a hacksaw blade or, better, a shingle ripper (also known as a slate hook) up under the course above and cut through the nail shanks as far down as possible. If you use a hacksaw blade, wear a heavy glove to protect your hand.

Wood shingles should have a ¼-in. gap on both sides, so size the replacement shingle ½ in. narrower than the width of the opening. Tap in the replacement with a wood block. If the replacement shingle won't slide in all the way, pull it out and whittle down its tapered end, using a utility knife. It's best to have nail heads covered by the course above, but if that's not possible, place a dab of urethane caulk beneath each nail head before hammering it down. Use two 4d galvanized shingle nails per shingle, each set in ¾ in. from the edge.

GOT MOSS?

Moss-covered shingles and shakes are common in moist, shaded areas. Hand scrape or use a wire brush to take the moss off. Keep it off by stapling 10-gauge or 12-gauge copper wire to a course of shingle butts all the way across the roof. Run one wire along the ridge and another halfway down. During rains, a dilute copper solution will wash down the shingles, discouraging moss. A nice alternative to toxic chemical treatments.

A Medley of Roofing Types

Although this section contains a few modest repairs a novice can make, most of the roof types discussed here should be installed by a roofing specialist. You'll also find suggestions for determining the quality of an installation as well as a few inspired tips.

FLAT ROOFS

Actually, no roof should be completely flat, or it won't shed water. But *flat roof* is a convenient term for a class of multimembrane systems. At one time, *builtup roofs* (BURs) once represented half of all flat roof coverings. BURs consisted of alternative layers of heavy building paper and hot tar. Today, modified bitumin (MB) is king, with cap membranes torched-on to fuse them to fiberglass-reinforced interplies or base coats. MB systems are durable and adhere well to dissimilar materials and difficult joints, but an inexpert torch user can damage the membranes and set a house on fire. For that reason, future roofs are likely to employ hot-air welding, cold-press adhesives, and roll membranes with self-sticking edges.

Causes of flat-roof failure. Whatever the materials used, flat roofs are vulnerable because water pools on them, people walk on them, and the sun degrades them unless they're properly maintained. Here are the primary causes of membrane damage:

▶ Water trapped between layers, because of improper installation. This is caused by installing roofing too soon after rain or when the deck was moist with dew. The trapped water expands, resulting in a blister in the membrane. In time, the blister is likely to split.

▶ Inadequate flashing around pipes, skylights, and adjoining walls.

▶ Drying out and cracking from UV rays—usually after the reflective gravel covering has been disturbed.

▶ People walking on the roof, or roof decks placed directly on a flat roof membrane. Roof decks should be supported by "floating posts" bolted through the sheathing to rafters and correctly flashed.

Repairing roof blisters. If there are no leaks below and the blister is intact, stay away from it! Don't step on it, cut it, or nail through it. However, if it has split, press it to see what comes out. If the roof is dry, only air will escape; if the roof is wet, water will emerge. In the latter case, let the inside of the blister dry by holding the side open with wood shims; if you're in a hurry, use a hair dryer. Once the blister has dried inside, patch it.

LAYING A FLAT ROOF

Once the granular membrane is down, its overlapping edges are often lifted and torched again to ensure sound adhesion and a waterproof seam.

In the final phase of a MB roof, an installer torch-welds a granular surface membrane to an interply sheet or directly to a base sheet. The granular surface is somewhat more expensive at installation, but it is cost-effective in the long run because it doesn't need periodic recoating.

Roofers refer to the molten material being forced out by the pressure of the trowel as wet seams—the mark of a successful installation.

The intersection of flat and sloping roof sections is worth extra attention. Run MB membranes at least 10 in. (vertical height) up the sloping section. Then overlap those membranes with the underlayment materials and asphalt shingles.

Professionals repair split blisters with a three-course patch, which requires no nails.

1. Trowel on a ¼-in.-thick layer of an elastomeric mastic, such as Henry 208 Wet Patch®, carefully working it into both sides of the split. Extend the mastic at least 2 in. beyond the split in all directions.

2. Cut a piece of "yellow jacket" (yellow fiberglass roofer's webbing) slightly longer than the split and press it into the mastic; this reinforces the patch.

3. Apply another ¼-in. layer of mastic over the webbing, feathering its edges so it can shed water.

A three-course patch is also effective on failed flashing, where dissimilar materials meet, and for other leak-prone areas.

TILE AND SLATE ROOFS

Tile and slate are relatively brittle, expensive, and easily damaged if you don't know what you're doing. And they're slippery when wet. In most cases, hire a pro to make repairs.

Tile and slate are so durable that they often outlast the underlayment and fasteners. So when repairing or replacing these roofs, prolong the life of the installation by using heavy underlayment (30-lb. building paper or a self-adhering bituminous membrane), copper attachers, and copper flashing. Although these materials are expensive, if the roof lasts upward of 60 years without leaking, it's money well spent.

Roof tiles weigh about three times as much as asphalt shingles. So if you're thinking of installing a new type of tile or tiling a roof for the first time, have a structural engineer evaluate your situation. Your roof framing may need bolstering to support the additional load.

Tile-Roof UNDERLAYMENT

A rubberized asphalt underlayment reinforced with fiberglass, layfastSBS®, is getting a lot of buzz among professionals. Specified for tile roofs, it's installed in two layers (double-papered) with 36.-in.-wide sheets overlapped by 19 in. Tiles often gouge building paper underlayment during installation, but not this stuff, which is also specified for shake, shingle, and metal roofs.

Tiles are available as two-piece, mission-barrel tiles; as one-piece, low-profile concrete tiles; and as flat-shake tiles, which mimic wood shakes. Tiles overlap to direct rain into tile channels. Traditionally, tiles were set without nails on wood battens or skip-sheathing. But today they are commonly nailed to plywood sheathing, especially if the roof pitch is 5-in-12 or steeper. Two-piece mission tiles are nailed in two manners: *Trough tiles* are nailed directly to sheathing. *Cap tiles*, which sit atop trough tiles, are attached to intervening copper wires nailed to the roof.

Slate roofs are most often damaged by tree limbs. You can usually make repairs safely if the damage is along an edge and hence reachable without requiring that you walk on the roof. If you note a number of missing slates and concomitant rust stains on the roof, the nails may be rusting through, creating an extremely dangerous situation. Call a slate specialist at once.

If properly installed over a durable membrane—such as the fiberglass-reinforced underlayment shown below—a tile roof can last 80 years.

To repair incidental damage, buy a slate hook. Work the head of the tool up under the damaged piece until the tool's hooked head catches a nail shank. Then strike the handle of the tool with a hammer to cut through the nail shank. When both shanks are severed, slide out the damaged slate, being careful not to disturb adjacent pieces.

Once the damaged slate's on the ground, transfer its dimensions onto a replacement slate. Then rent a *tile-cutting saw* to cut the new piece, wearing goggles. Or ask a tile dealer to cut the piece for you. Ideally, the new piece should be the same size as the one it's replacing, but old nail shanks may prevent sliding a full-size replacement piece into place. In this case, trim the replacement piece further.

When replacing sections of slate or slate-like materials, alternate courses with strips of 30-lb. building paper. Century-old sheathing can get pretty hard, so if copper nails bend or deform, use stainless-steel roofing nails instead.

That done, align the bottom edge of the replacement slate to others in the course. Predrill two nail holes, each one 1 in. from the edge and about 1 in. below the course above; you'll probably be drilling through two layers of slate, so take it slow. (A cordless drill is ideal for this task.) Size the drill bit just slightly larger than the thickness of the nail shank. Because this pair of nails won't be covered by the slate above, caulk all holes with urethane before inserting nails. Drive the nails down just snug and no more, so you don't split the slate.

METAL ROOFS

Although metal roofs tend to be quite durable, nail maintenance is key to their longevity. Most leaks occur when wind and ice lift the sheeting and pop nails up.

At least once a year and after major storms, study the roof with binoculars, and nail down any pop-ups. For extra security, put a dab of urethane caulk beneath nail heads. (Although roofing cement works too, it would be unsightly.) If popped nails seem loose, upsize the nail or use a screw. To avoid galvanic-action corrosion, use nails or screws that are compatible with the roof metal. By the way, nail or screw metal roofing only at the raised crests, not in troughs where the water runs.

If the roofing is rusted but serviceable, use a wire brush on the surface to remove the rust and paint on an elastomeric roof coating, such as Gacoflex® acrylic latex. An elastomeric coating is necessary because metal expands and contracts. Incidentally, such coatings can also extend the life of metal gutters.

Individual mission-barrel tiles are irregular, so it's smart to snap horizontal chalklines to align tile courses and vertical lines to line up trough tiles, which are nailed directly to the roof deck. Cap tiles, which lie atop trough tiles, are secured to the roof deck with copper wire. To prevent galvanic corrosion, use nails and wires of the same material.

Doors, Windows, and Skylights

6

Doors, windows, and skylights are asked to do a lot. They must be solidly attached yet movable, let light in while keeping rain out, admit guests but deny drafts. Because these units are so complex, it's impossible to shoehorn everything one might say about them into one chapter. You'll find more about flashing in Chapters 5 and 7; more on adding openings to exterior walls, replacing rot, and structural carpentry in Chapter 8; and more on installing interior casing in Chapter 17.

This chapter begins with installing interior doors—among the last things you'd do in a renovation—but a task so similar to hanging *exterior* doors that these two procedures belong side-by-side.

Ordering Doors: An Overview

Door *frames* consist of several pieces: two side pieces, or *side jambs,* and a *head jamb* (or *frame head*) running across the top; exterior doors also have a *sill* spanning the bottom. (The sill may also

have a *threshold*, but more about that later.) Jambs are further distinguished by the hardware they bear: The jamb on which the door is hung is the *hinge jamb;* the jamb that receives the latch is the *latch jamb* (also called *strike jamb* or *lock jamb*).

From door to door, parts names are similar. On a common frame-and-panel door, the thicker vertical elements are called *stiles*; hence, *hinge stile* and *latch* (or *strike*) stile. Horizontal elements are called *rails*. Glass panes in French doors are called *lights,* and the wood strips between lights are called *muntins.* Consider the following factors when ordering doors.

Interior vs. exterior. Exterior doors are generally thicker (1¾ in. vs. 1⅜ in.), more expensive, more weather resistant, and more secure than interior doors. Because they must withstand weather, exterior doors may have water- or UV-resistant finishes and are often insulated and weatherstripped. Don't use doors designed for interiors outside—they won't last.

If water is a house's greatest enemy, cap (head) flashing may be one of its greatest allies, for it diverts water around doors, windows, and skylights, thus preventing leaks at the top of the unit. Building paper and stucco will overlay the top flange of this cap flashing.

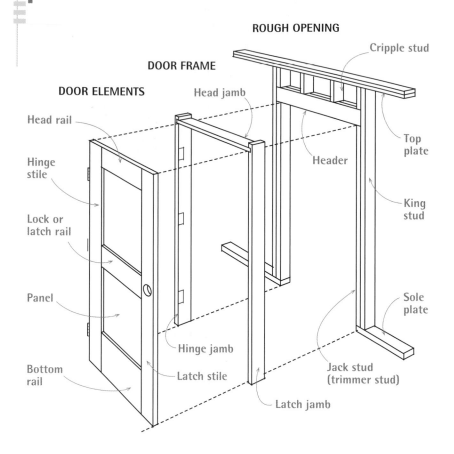

ROUGH OPENING

DOOR FRAME

DOOR ELEMENTS

Cripple stud

Head jamb

Head rail

Hinge stile

Lock or latch rail

Panel

Bottom rail

Hinge jamb

Latch stile

Latch jamb

Top plate

Header

King stud

Sole plate

Jack stud (trimmer stud)

Prehung. Prehung (preframed) doors come fitted to a frame, with hinges mortised into a jamb. Ordering prehung doors can save huge amounts of time. However, if doorways are already framed, specify unframed doors (see "Hanging a Door to an Existing Frame," on p. 110).

Knock-down prehung doors arrive with the frame head cut to the correct width and all other parts milled with correct clearances around the door, but the parts are not assembled. This allows you to trim the jambs down to the right length for your flooring and threshold heights. Suppliers will cut exterior sills to fit if you ask them to, but many contractors prefer to buy sills separately and fit them on site.

Width. Door widths increase in 2-in. increments. When door dimensions are stated as a pair of numbers, width always comes first—for example, 2 ft. 8 in. by 6 ft. 8 in. (this is sometimes abbreviated as 2868).

Standard *interior* doors are 2 ft. 6 in. and 2 ft. 8 in. wide. For doors leading to busy hallways, architects often specify 2 ft. 10 in. or 3 ft. 0 in. If you need access for wheelchairs, order special doors 3 ft. 6 in. wide. Narrow doors (2 ft. 0 in. to 2 ft. 4 in.) are available for half baths and closets; and narrower ones (1 ft. 4 in. to 1 ft. 10 in.), for linen closets and such.

Standard *exterior* doors are 3 ft. 0 in. wide, though side doors are sometimes 2 ft. 8 in. or 2 ft. 10 in. wide. Again, wheelchair-access exterior doors need to be 3 ft. 6 in. or 4 ft. 0 in. wide.

Installation, in a Nutshell

Today, most doors, windows, and skylights are preassembled in factories and delivered preframed, which makes installation much easier. Basically, you screw or nail the unit's squared frame to a rough opening (RO). If the opening is in an exterior wall, weatherproof it first—wrap, flash, and caulk. Rough openings are typically ½ in. to 1 in. wider and taller than the outside dimension of the door or window frame being installed.

However, rough openings are rarely square or perfectly sized, so you need to insert shims (thin, tapered pieces of wood) between the square frame and the out-of-square opening. Shimming takes patience. But if you install shims well, doors, windows, and skylights will operate freely, without binding. Once a preframed window or door is installed in its RO, insulate or spray foam between the frame and the RO to further block moisture and drafts. Then cover those gaps with casing (or trim) inside and out.

In general, avoid precased units, which have casing pre-attached to frames. It's difficult to shim between the frame and the rough opening if casing's in the way.

As you level and plumb windows and doors, use pairs of tapered shims to hold units in the rough openings. Use trim-head screws when tacking frames. They are easier to remove when adjusting shims and less likely to bend than finish nails. And their small heads are easy to sink, fill, or cover with a stop.

This is a pair of prehung single-panel fir interior doors.

Swing. Door swing indicates which side you want the hinges on. Imagine facing the door as it swings open *toward you:* If the door knob will hit your right hand first, it's a *right-handed* door; if your left hand grabs the knob, then it's a *left-handed* door.

Type and style. *Hinged single doors* are by far the most common type, but they need room to operate. If space is tight, consider *sliding doors, pocket doors,* or *bifolds.* For wide openings, note that *hinged double-doors* individually weigh less and take less room to swing open than one massive door.

Try to match existing doors or those on houses of similar architectural periods. In general, frame-and-panel doors tend to go well with older houses; whereas flush doors have a more contemporary look. For that reason, sliding doors on older homes are usually placed on the back side of the house so they don't look inconsistent with the front and side facades.

Height. Standard door height is 6 ft. 8 in., for both interior and exterior doors on newer houses. Older houses (1940s and earlier) sometimes had doors 7 ft. high, so that size is still widely available. Of late, 8-ft.-high French doors are in vogue. Of course, you can special-order a door of virtually any size if you're willing to pay enough. Salvage yards are excellent sources of odd-size doors.

Jambs. Wall thickness will determine the widths of door jambs if you order prehung units. Interior door jambs are commonly 4⅜ in. wide, which can span a 2×4 stud wall (actual width, 3½ in.) with ½-in. drywall on both sides—leaving 1/16 in. to spare. Typically, interior door jambs are built from ¾-in.-thick stock (nominal 1 in.).

For 2×6 walls (actual width, 5½ in.), specify 6⅜-in.-wide jambs, which can accommodate two wall-sandwiching layers of ½-in. drywall or—on an exterior wall—½-in. drywall and ½-in. plywood sheathing. Jambs for prehung exterior doors are usually fashioned from 1½-in.-thick stock, rabbeted with an integral doorstop to receive the door when closed.

Standard-width jambs won't work if your old house has full-dimension lumber and plaster walls or if you're covering walls with ⅝-in. drywall. Your choices then become (1) *jamb extensions* to increase the width of standard jambs; (2) *custom-milled jambs,* including ⅛ in. extra to accommodate wavy walls or twisted lumber; and (3) *split jambs,* interlocking half-jambs that can be adjusted to the widths of walls. (An integral doorstop covers the gap between sections.)

Interior Wall Cross Section

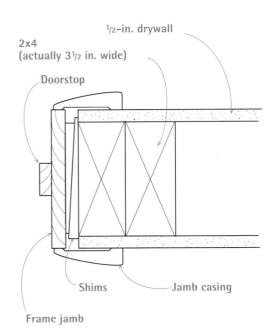

A standard frame jamb, which is 4⁹/₁₆ in. wide, can span a stud wall sandwiched between ½ in. drywall panels

Construction and materials. For exterior doors, wood is the traditional favorite, but it requires a lot of maintenance. Consequently, wood doors come clad in vinyl or aluminum, and good-quality, insulated steel doors are virtually indistinguishable from wood once they're painted. Fire codes require steel doors between living spaces and attached garages or workshops. Exterior doors should have integral weatherstripping.

Given the rise of engineered lumber, it's not surprising that many doors—both interior and exterior—are now made from plywood, hardboard, and so on. They can be stamped to mimic traditional panel doors and insulated to deaden sound and retain heat. They paint up nicely, can be cost-effective, and are generally more stable than solid wood.

Weatherstripping and glazing. Weatherstripping on exterior doors is often rabbeted into jambs, so it's tighter and more energy efficient than anything you could install later. There is also a variety of thresholds and door bottoms available to keep snow or rain out, or to clear water so it doesn't soak and destroy the bottom of the door.

If your exterior door has glass panels, they should be double glazed at the least; triple glazing is more energy efficient but costs more. Double glazing and a storm door may be a better choice. Finally, prefinish exterior doors with a UV- and water-resistant finish; at the very least, prime or seal all six sides.

Hardware. Hardware for prehung doors is pre-installed at the factory; then locksets and door handles are removed to prevent damage during shipping.

As indicated in "Sizing Hinges," below, hollow-core or solid-wood interior doors up to 1⅜ in. thick can be supported by two 3½-in. by 3½-in. (opened size) hinges; whereas 1½-in.-thick exterior doors

usually require three 4-in. by 4-in. hinges. Extra-heavy exterior doors may need even bigger hinges or hinges with ball bearings or grease fittings.

As shown in "Mortise Lockset," on p. 103, and "Cylinder Lockset," on p. 105, *exterior locksets* are most often *cylinder locks,* which require a 2⅛-in. hole drilled into the face of the door, or *mortise locks,* which are housed in a rectangular mortise cut into the latch edge of the door. Mortise locks are more expensive and difficult to install, so they are most often used only on entry doors, with a thumb-lever handle. For added security, supplement exterior door locksets with a *dead bolt* and a *reinforced strike plate.*

Double exterior doors may have *interconnected locksets,* and *flush bolts* or *surface bolts. Interior locksets* are almost always some kind of cylinder lock: *passage locks* or *latch sets* on doors that don't need to be locked and *privacy locks* or *locksets* on doors that do need locking, such as bedroom doors. *Bathroom locks* are specialized locksets with a chrome bathroom-facing knob to match plumbing fixtures.

Installing an Interior Door

There are many ways to hang a door. Thus, the installation sequences that follow occasionally offer alternative methods.

ASSESSING AND PREPPING THE OPENING

Prehung doors usually come preassembled with the door hung on hinges in the jamb and held tight by a screw through the latch jamb into the door. Or the door may be secured with a removable plastic plug through the predrilled hole where the lock will go.

1. Start by measuring the height and width of the opening. Rough openings (ROs) are typically ½ in. to 1 in. wider and taller than the outside dimensions of the door frame, or about 2½ in. taller and wider than an unframed door.

2. Measure the thickness of the wall, from finish surface to finish surface. Standard 2×4 walls covered with drywall are 4½ in. thick, so standard frame stock is 4⁹⁄₁₆ in. wide, providing an extra ¹⁄₁₆ in. to accommodate wall irregularities—⅛ in. extra would be better. So if you're using ⅝-in. drywall, order 4⅞-in. jamb stock.

3. If the finish floor is not yet installed, determine its thickness so that you'll know how much to cut off the bottoms of the door frame's side jambs. Ideally, side jambs will stand directly on the subflooring or flooring. Jambs are nailed to the RO, but they must be solidly footed so they can't drift down later. If a jamb leg is too short to

Sizing Hinges

OPENED HINGE SIZE (in.)	DOOR THICKNESS (in.)	DOOR WIDTH (in.)
3½	1⅜–1⅜	Up to 32
4	1⅜–1⅜	32–37
4½	1⅜–1⅞	Up to 32
5	1⅜–1⅞	32–37
5, extra-heavy	1⅞ and up	37–43
6, extra-heavy	1⅞ and up	43 and up

reach the subfloor, shim it solidly and trim the shim flush; finish flooring will cover the shim.

Allow ¼ in. clearance above the finish floor, so the door can swing freely. For example, if you're installing a 6-ft. 8-in. door and ⁵⁄₁₆-in. oak flooring, make jambs 80 in. + ⁵⁄₁₆ in. + ¼ in., or 80⁹⁄₁₆ in. long. If you'll be laying heavy carpet and a thick pad, allow 1¼ in. + ¼ in. clearance.

4. Use a level to see if the floor in the doorway slopes; if it does, add the amount below level to the jamb on that side. By doing this, you ensure that the frame head will be more or less level when jambs rest on the floor or subfloor. Check studs and walls for plumb.

FITTING THE FRAME TO THE OPENING

If the door is shipped attached to the hinge jamb, pull the hinges and remove the door before fitting the frame to the opening. (*Another opinion:* Leave the door in its frame, especially if the door is a lightweight hollow core. To mark the bottom

of the side jambs for cutting, lean the frame against the RO. With the door in the opening, you can easily see the exact amount of clearance between the door and the subfloor.

1. Using a circular saw, cut the jambs to length; a small cordless circular saw is perfect for the task. Cut from the back side so you get a nice clean line on the front, and cut through stop pieces, if any.

2. If your door frames are knocked down, fasten the jambs to the head with carpenter's glue and three or four 6d finish nails or 2-in. screws per side.

3. Position the frame in the RO. If stray drywall or sole plates sticking into the RO interfere with the frame, cut them off. If screws from hinge plates protrude through the jamb stock— as they frequently do—remove them so you can slide shims easily. Many carpenters remove the middle screw, insert shims behind it and, later, after the jambs have been shimmed, replace that middle screw with an extra-long one.

Ideally, side jambs (jamb legs) should rest directly on the subfloor or floor. Check the head jamb for level. If it is not level, remove the frame...

...and use a square to mark the bottom of the side jamb; cut off the amount that side is high. Reinsert the door frame in the opening and check the head for level again.

Positioning Door Hardware

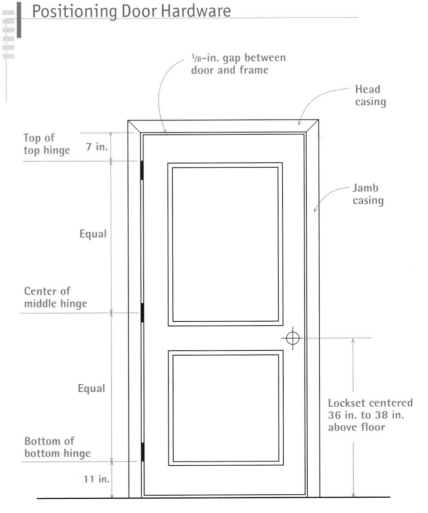

¹⁄₈-in. gap between door and frame

Head casing

Jamb casing

Top of top hinge — 7 in.

Equal

Center of middle hinge

Equal

Lockset centered 36 in. to 38 in. above floor

Bottom of bottom hinge

11 in.

Use a square to see if a jamb edge is flush to the finished wall. If the jamb edge is flush or slightly proud (projecting beyond drywall), casing corner joints will meet. However, if the jamb is shy (shallower than the drywall), mitered joints will gap.

Using a 6-ft. level to check that the jamb is plumb, start shimming frames near the top hinge and work down the jamb, checking for plumb constantly.

If you screw near shims, rather than through them, they can be easily readjusted and won't split. Here, the carpenter replaces a middle hinge screw with a longer one that will grab the framing.

4. Use a Speed Square to determine if the studs on either side of the opening are twisted; if so, you can shim the jambs to make them square. That noted, margin the frame in the opening—that is, center the frame in relation to the wall's thickness. Ideally, a jamb will be slightly wider, so that it is 1/32 in. proud (extending beyond) on each side.

5. With the frame margined in the opening, use 2½-in. finish nails or trim-head screws to tack it in place. Place shims behind the top hinge, and nail or screw just below the shims. By not nailing through the shims, you can still adjust them, and if you center tack nails in the middle of the frame, they'll be covered later by the stop pieces.

SHIMMING THE FRAME

Plumb the hinge jamb first, using a 6-ft. level for accuracy. Or you can hang a plumb bob from a nail in the top of the jamb, as shown in the left photo on p. 102, and measure from the plumb line. When the jamb is plumb, all measurements from the jamb to the line will be equal.

1. If jack studs (trimmer studs) on either side are square to the face of the opening, pair shims so that their tapers alternate, creating a flat surface behind the jamb. However, if jack studs are twisted, you may need to insert an odd number of shims to build up the low edge of the twisted stud. Adjust shims in and out, constantly checking for plumb and square till both the face and the edges of the hinge jamb are plumb. This takes patience. Most installers start shimming behind the top hinge.

Interior doors are commonly shimmed with three pairs of shims along each jamb: behind the two hinges and halfway between them. However, to prevent jambs from twisting should the door fly open suddenly, many carpenters also shim behind the top and bottom corners of each side jamb.

2. After checking that the frame head is level, secure the latch jamb. Margin that jamb, and tack it in place. At this stage, most carpenters rehang the door to the hinge jamb so they can eyeball jamb clearances to the door. Mill specs vary, but there's usually an 1/8-in. gap along the hinge jamb and 1/16 in. to 1/8 in. of clearance along head and latch jambs.

Shim at least three points along the latch jamb; one shim point should be directly behind the strike-plate location. If the latch jamb bows into the opening, add nails or screws to draw it back toward the jack stud. Check for margin,

After tacking the hinge jamb, rehang the door. Adjust the floating jambs till there's uniform clearance around the door. Here double doors complicate the task, as there are two hinge jambs. Adjust the frame to create an even gap on two sides of the first door. Then tack up the hinge jamb for the second door.

When hanging the second door, create an even gap around it by adjusting shims and screws. Your goal is a uniform gap where the doors meet—with both lying in the same plane. The pains you take squaring and plumbing the framing really pay off. Also see "Fine-Tuning French Doors," on p. 102.

square, and plumb as you go. Shim up from the bottom of the jamb as needed to create a uniform clearance along the length of the door and at the upper corner.

3. Shim the frame head, inserting a pair of shims at either corner. *Caution:* If you drive shims too aggressively, you'll cause the top of the door to bind.

4. This is the last chance to check margins and adjust shims, if necessary. Make sure all clearances around the door are uniform. When the door is closed, it should be parallel with the latch jamb. Once you've checked for margin, plumb, level, and clearances all around, secure the frame. Use five pairs of 10d finish nails or trim-head screws: one pair near each hinge, one pair in the middle of the frame, and one pair at each corner. Using a pair of nails or screws at each shimming point will keep the frame from turning.

If you must reduce the width of a door, use a power plane on the hinge stile of the door. Planing down the lock stile is not advisable because locks have specific setbacks from door edges and you'd need to move face bores, too. So, it's far easier to plane hinge stiles.

After planing down the hinge stile, use a small router (laminate trimmer) to mortise the hinge gains deeper. Clamp scrap to the door edge to provide a wider base for the router. You could use a chisel, but a router will get the depth exactly right.

IF THE Door HITS THE LATCH JAMB

If the door hits the latch jamb, the frame head may have been cut a little short. If it's a very slight amount, you may be able to back out latch-jamb shims and hammer the latch jamb outward, using scrap wood to avoid marring it. But if the door still hits, you may need to rip down the hinge stile slightly to reduce the door's width. Because holes for locksets are backset exactly from the edge of the door, don't rip down the lock stile. It's far easier to remove the hinge butts, use a power plane to trim the hinge stile, and then recut the hinge mortises an equal amount.

FINAL TOUCHES

Now you're in the home stretch.

1. Install the lockset in the door, mortise the strike plate into the latch jamb, and shut the door. With the door shut, make light pencil marks on the latch jamb to indicate the door edge when closed. Then place the doorstop back ¹⁄₁₆ in. (about the thickness of a dime) from those marks. The door and its stops should not quite make contact if they're yet to be painted. Evenly space five 4d finish nails to attach the stop to the latch jamb.

2. Set all nails with a nail set (or turn screws slightly below the surface) and fill holes. If you'll be painting, fill the holes with spackling compound; if using a clear finish, fill with wood dough or a stick-type filler.

3. Using a sharp mat knife or a Japanese saw, score the shims along the wall, tight to the frame.

Trimming Doors

When your door swings open, it should not "pattern" your carpet or abrade the finish floor. If it does, trim the bottom rail of the door. To register the height of the carpet on the base of the door, slide a flat builder's pencil across the carpet. The pencil, being flat, won't sink into the carpet as much as a round pencil will. Add ⅛ in. of clearance to that rough line and score the final cutoff line onto the door, using a utility knife drawn along a straightedge. Scoring the door is important, for it prevents vertical grain from splitting and veneer from lifting and splintering. Run the circular saw a whisker below that scored line and you'll get a nice, clean cut.

For best results, use a circular saw with a sharp Mastercut® blade, which has a close configuration of at least four fine teeth and a raker to clear chips. Use a straightedge clamped to the door to guide the blade. Clean the saw sole (base plate) well: de-gum it with turpentine (or paint thinner) and steel wool; then rub it with metal-polishing cloth or paraffin to help it glide across the wood. Smooth the cut, and ease the edge with 220-grit sandpaper, sanding with the grain.

Score as deeply as you can (shingle butts may take several passes); then snap off the waste. Don't try to snap shingles that are too thick, or you may torque the jamb out from the opening. Then install the interior trim (see Chapter 17).

Installing a Basic Exterior Door

Installing a prehung exterior door builds on the information just presented, so if any step is insufficiently explained here, consult the preceding section.

ASSESSING AND PREPPING THE OPENING

Cover finish floors with heavy cardboard or particleboard when installing an exterior door, and cover the work area with tarps to contain the mess.

1. Before ordering the new door unit, measure the height and width of the RO and the thickness of the wall; check the jack studs for plumb, the header for level, and corners for square. You can install a squared door frame into an out-of-square opening. But to allow proper shimming, the RO must be at least 1 in. taller and wider than the frame.

2. Next determine the height of the finish floor. In most cases, prehung doors come with a combination sill–threshold already attached, which sits directly on the plywood subfloor. However, some custom exterior doors come with separate sills set flush to the subfloor, which require installing the sills before the subfloor or notching the subfloor and the framing below the subfloor to accommodate the thickness of the sill.

If you need to build up the bottom of the opening to make the new sill the same height as the finish floor, do so now.

3. The bottom of the RO should be level and weather tight. If there's an overhang to protect the door, just line the bottom of the RO with building paper. If there's no overhang, install a floor pan across the bottom of the RO. The pan can be as simple as a peel-and-stick flexible membrane applied to the subfloor or, if your region gets driving rains, a prefabricated metal pan (usually aluminum).

Whatever the pan material, fold its ends and back edge up so it will confine any water that gets under the sill rather than soaking the framing, subfloor, or finish floor. Overlap the pan corners and caulk them for good measure. (Make sure the caulk is compatible with the flexible membrane.) Solder or caulk the metal pan seams. Finally, the outer lip of a floor pan should overlap the deck or other exterior flashing beneath the sill.

4. The sides of the RO are often weatherproofed by folding building paper or housewrap into the opening, as described in Chapter 7. To direct water away from the framing, the building paper or housewrap should overlap the upturned ends of the floor pan. Caulk that seam, too.

If the subfloor isn't level—common in remodeling jobs—one option is shimming beneath a sill–threshold combo and then filling between shims with a cementitious mix. Cedar shims are okay over a dry concrete subfloor. But if the doorway is damp or unprotected, use plastic shims.

Floor Pan for Exterior Door

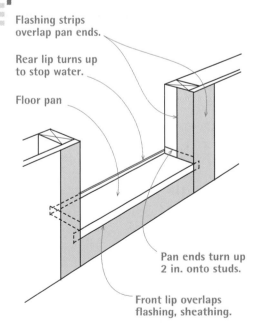

Flashing strips overlap pan ends.

Rear lip turns up to stop water.

Floor pan

Pan ends turn up 2 in. onto studs.

Front lip overlaps flashing, sheathing.

Whether fabricated from sheet metal or bituminous membrane, floor pans can protect doorway openings from getting soaked by standing water.

Replacing an Exterior Door

To replace an exterior door, first remove the interior and exterior casing to expose the door frame and the rough opening. Proceed carefully, minimizing damage to the siding and finish surfaces whenever possible. Exposing the rough opening enables you to measure it exactly and inspect for water damage or rot, which must be repaired before installing a new unit.

To remove casing without breaking it, use a flat bar to raise it slightly; then use a reciprocating saw with a metal-cutting blade to cut through the casing nails. (Wear safety glasses.) Cutting nails is far easier on surrounding surfaces than prying alone. However, some casing can't be removed without destroying it—stucco molding, for example.

In many older houses, the sill will be a 2-in.-thick board notched into the framing so that it sits flush with the subfloor. If it is in decent shape, leave it. If it has rot, cut out the sill and install a floor pan over the framing before installing a replacement sill that's flush to the subfloor. If there's a sloping threshold atop the sill, remove it. It will probably be weathered, and anyway, the new preframed door must sit on a level surface. (New exterior doors typically have a combo sill–threshold preattached to the side jambs.)

To install the new door unit, remove the existing door frame, preferably by cutting through the nails holding it to the rough opening so that you can pull out the frame in one piece. That way, should the new frame not fit, you can easily replace the old frame and rehang the door so you won't be without a door while you correct the problem.

Leveling a Doorsill

There are several ways to level an exterior doorsill. After you've installed a floor pan, place a spirit level across the bottom of the rough opening (RO) and insert pressure-treated wood shims under the tool till it reads level. Tack shims to plywood subflooring to keep them from drifting, and then install the prehung door unit. If the subfloor is concrete, use construction adhesive to spot-tack the shims. Or you can place the door frame into an unlevel opening, use a flat bar to raise the low end of the frame sill, and insert shims under the sill till it's level. To prevent flexing between shims, space shims every 12 in. beneath aluminum/combination or oak sills, or every 6 in. beneath sliding-door sills.

The problem with any of these solutions is that many sills—especially hollow aluminum ones—are so thin that they may flex between shim points. If there's ¼ in. to ½ in. of space under the sill, use a ¼-in. tuck-pointing trowel (see the photo on p. 198) to push dry-pack mortar into the spaces between the shims, compacting the mortar as best you can. Or fill under the shimmed-up sill with nonshrinking mortar, such as an epoxy mortar/grout.

The only way to correct an out-of-level opening without shims is to rebuild it, which is rarely simple. For example, you can remove the subfloor and power-plane down the tops of joists till they are level and then install pressure-treated plywood atop them, but if nearby floors are out of level, you may need to level them next. Jacking is another option.

Before installing a prehung exterior in-swing door, remove the door and test-fit the frame in the opening. The 2×4 cleats nailed to the sheathing act as depth gauges, so jambs will be flush to sheathing.

PRO TIP

If the door edge does not close evenly against the stop—the top or bottom of the door hits first—the frame or rough opening may be slightly *cross-legged* (out of plane). If the top of the door hits first, pry out the top of the hinge jamb or pull back the top of the latch jamb. However, if the walls around the opening are not plumb, gently use a sledgehammer to knock them into plumb.

▌▌▌▌

PRO TIP

Caulk around the rough opening, rather than the door frame or casing; if you instead caulk the frame, you're likely to get sticky fingers lifting it into place. If it's necessary to remove a frame after pressing it into caulking, reapply a continuous bead of caulking around the opening.

▌▌▌▌

EYEBALLING THE FRAME

Once you've prepped the opening, place the door unit in it to see what needs tweaking. This is a dry run, so frame jambs needn't be perfectly plumb or level—just close.

1. Test-fit the door frame in the opening. Center it right to left in the RO; then margin the frame. There should be ¼ in. to ½ in. of clearance around the frame so it can be shimmed to the RO. Jamb edges should ¹⁄₁₆ in. proud of the interior wall surfaces to accommodate framing quirks.

2. Is the door frame square? If the frame is square, there should be an even space between the door and the frame jambs; if not, the frame is skewed. To resquare it, remove the frame from the opening, and— with the door still hung—tilt the frame to one side until acute corners (less than 90°) become square and the door fits evenly.

3. Remove the unit, make necessary final adjustments to the RO, and then caulk the bottom of the opening. If the door unit is precased, apply a bead of caulking to the exterior wall around the RO, inward about ½ in. from the edges of the opening. If the prehung door unit is uncased, don't caulk around the opening yet, just caulk the bottom of the RO.

INSTALLING AN EXTERIOR FRAME

As with interior doors, there is no one right way to install a prehung exterior door. Some carpenters prefer to install door frames with doors hung. Others prefer to remove the door, plumb and attach the hinge jamb, rehang the door, then attach the other jambs. Though the accompany-

ing photos show the second method, both methods are described here.

Method 1: The door stays hung. Pry off the shipping blocks, remove the plastic plugs from the lock bore, and place the unit into the RO. (At this point, assume the doorsill is level.) Center the unit left to right in the opening; press the casing into the caulking; and then, while a helper keeps the unit from tipping, drive a 10d galvanized finish nail (or 3-in. screw) into each side jamb about 6 in. above the sill, or into nailing fins (flanges). Leave the nail heads sticking up so you can pull them if needed.

Hold a 6-ft. level against the inside of the hinge jamb to see if it's plumb. If not, insert a flat bar between the frame and the RO near the top of the frame, and pry the frame out on one side till the jamb is plumb. Then drive a nail into the top of each jamb, about 6 in. below the top of the frame. Finally, eyeball the inside of the door frame to make sure there's a uniform clearance (usually ¹⁄₁₆ in. to ⅛ in.) between the door and the frame. Use nails to draw the frame to the RO or adjust the shims until the clearance is uniform.

Speaking of shimming, precased units can be shimmed only from the inside. Unbacked by shims, frames can twist as the door swings. To shim from the inside, insert a shim, fat end first, till it butts

Shim and secure the hinge jamb first, checking for plumb often. Here, installers place shims slightly above and below the hinges so the hinge screws sticking through the jamb won't snag on the shims. Screwing the jambs to the framing facilitates adjustments.

against the back of the casing; then slide additional shims, thin edge first, till shims are tight. Nail or screw *below* each stack of shims; then close the door and see if it seats evenly against the frame. Once you've corrected that, secure the frame to the rough opening, and finish the exterior.

Method 2: Remove the door. After leveling and prepping the opening, pull the hinges and remove the door from the frame. Screw temporary *cleats* to the outside of the frame—or to the exterior sheathing itself—so that when the frame is placed into the RO, the outer edges of its jambs will be flush to the sheathing.

Center the frame left to right in the opening, and check the jambs for plumb and the sill for level. If it's necessary to shim the doorsill to level, place the first shim *under the jamb* on the low side. Plumb and attach the hinge jamb first, inserting the first set of shims behind the top hinge. Remove the middle hinge screw(s) so you can slide the shims freely as you adjust them. Then drive a 10d galvanized finish nail or a 2½-in. screw just *below* the shims, in the center of the hinge jamb; this holds the shims snugly, but you can still adjust them. Shim behind the bottom hinge, check for plumb, and then shim behind the middle hinge. Adjust the shims as needed to attain plumb; then shim behind the corners of the hinge jamb, top and bottom.

With the hinge jamb securely attached, rehang the door. (Get help; exterior doors are heavy.) Close the door and note how it fits the frame. Without weatherstripping, there should be an even gap, ⅟₁₆ in. to ⅛ in. wide, around the door, and the corners of the frame should be square. If the door hits the edge of the latch jamb, that jamb may be bowing into the RO or the shims behind the hinge jamb may be too high. Adjusting an uncased exterior door frame is very similar to "working" an interior door frame.

Shim the latch jamb and then the head jamb. When all is okay, secure the frame with two

After plumbing and securing the hinge jamb, rehang the door so you can use it as a gauge to align the latch jamb correctly. This method is particularly helpful if the door is slightly twisted or warped, because you can align the latch jamb to the door.

As you adjust latch and head jambs, make sure there's an even gap (typically ⅛ in.) between the door and the jambs all around.

Shim the head jamb after plumbing the latch jamb. If the frame is uncased, you can insert shims from both sides and easily slide them in and out. The white line inside the jambs is kerf–in weatherstripping.

Shimming Exterior Doors

Shim exterior door units at five points down each side jamb. Along the hinge jamb, shim behind each hinge and at top and bottom corners. Space shims along the latch jamb at roughly the same intervals, but don't shim directly behind strike plates or deadbolts. Shim the head jamb midway and at both corners.

Exterior door frames are often installed with a pair or 10d or 16d galvanized nails spaced every 16 in.; using two nails at each interval keeps the frame from twisting. Other builders favor 3-in. stainless-steel trim-head or plated flathead screws, because they grip better and can be removed if needed; countersink flathead screws. In addition, many builders remove the middle hinge screws, shim behind the hinge, and replace the original screws with 3½-in. screws that sink deep into the rough-opening framing.

Here are some fine points to consider:

▶ It doesn't matter whether you screw or nail below shims or through them, as long as the shims are snug and won't move; if you screw through shims, predrill them to reduce splits.

▶ Even if jack studs are plumb, shim between the door frame and the rough opening; a shimmed frame is easier to modify or replace later.

▶ Always shim the head jamb so it won't bow into the opening or jump when you nail casing to it.

To cut shims flush to finish surfaces, score the shims with a utility knife. Then, with a flick of the wrist, snap off the waste. Or use a Japanese saw.

16d galvanized finish nails spaced every 16 in. and in 1 in. from the edge. Then seal the frame to keep out weather, apply casing, and flash it, as described in the next section.

FINISHING THE EXTERIOR

If you installed an uncased unit, now seal the outer jamb edges and install the casing.

1. If the unit's sill has horns that extend beyond the side jambs, cut down each horn so that it is as long as exterior casing is wide plus ¼ in. for a reveal (the amount that the casing is set back from the inner edge of the frame jamb). Casing legs sit on horns, so cut casing bottoms at the same angle as the sill. (Use an adjustable bevel gauge to record the angle.)

2. Before attaching casing, however, run a single bead of siliconized acrylic caulking along the side and head jamb edges. Keep the caulking back at least ¼ in. from the inner edge of the jambs so it's not visible in the ¼-in. reveal.

3. Next, cut two fiberglass-reinforced flashing strips 4 in. to 6 in. longer than the length of the side jambs. Press a strip against the caulked jamb edge, again holding back the strip at least ½ in. from the inner edge of the jambs. Staple the portion of the flashing strip that overlaps the sheathing so the strip doesn't blow off.

4. Attach casing to both sides of the jam. Create a reveal by setting back the inner edges of casing ¼ in. from the jamb edges. Then nail up the head casing. If the corners are mitered, nail through the joint to draw the jambs together, as shown in the left photo below. *Note:* There's no flashing strip under the head casing; it's applied over the cap flashing to direct water away from the sheathing.

5. Once the head casing is up, attach the cap flashing (head flashing), which is often prefabbed from vinyl or metal. It's easy enough to make your own from 26-gauge aluminum or galvanized steel; use aviation snips to cut and fold it and a rubber mallet to shape it. Caulk the head casing/sheathing joint, and then press the cap flashing down onto the casing. Use big-head roofing nails to nail the top flange of the flashing. Then staple strip flashing over the top flange of the flashing, and run housewrap and/or siding over that.

At this point, you're ready to install hardware, insulate between the jambs and the RO (use a mild-expanding spray foam), and attach the interior casing.

Installing French Doors

Installing double doors requires more plumb and level readings, shim adjustments, and—above all—more patience than hanging a single door, but the procedure is much the same. So we'll zip through the steps covered earlier to get to the heart of the matter: figuring out why the doors don't meet perfectly in the middle and what to do about it.

INSTALLATION: A QUICK RECAP

▶ Measure the RO to make sure it's big enough to install the door frame.

▶ Using a 6-ft. spirit level, see if the floor is level and the sides of the RO are plumb. Also check the walls on both sides of the RO for plumb. If the bottom of the opening is more than ⅛ in. out of level, correct the situation. French doors are wide and heavy and need to rest solidly on a level opening. Otherwise, they can rack and bind.

Secure the frame, trim the shims flush, remove the temporary cleats, and apply a bead of caulk to the jamb edges. Keep the caulk back at least ¼ in. from jamb faces.

Apply fiber-reinforced flashing paper to the edge of each side jamb so that it beds in the caulking. However, before applying exterior casing, apply a second bead of caulking over the flashing paper. Double-caulking virtually eliminates air and water infiltration.

As you install casing, drive a finish nail through corner miter joints to keep them from separating. You can also glue the joint, but here, stucco will help keep the joint from moving. Note the ¼-in. reveal between the casing and the edge of the jamb.

Install cap flashing atop the head casing, nailing its upper flange as high as possible. Here, this flashing will be overlapped by flashing paper and stucco. Cap flashing should overhang the casing slightly along the front and at the ends of the casing, so water drips free.

▶ The sides of the RO can be shimmed, but if the wall framing isn't plumb, place a 2×4 block against the base of the wall and strike the block with a sledgehammer. Go easy: Numerous gentle hits will cause less damage than one mighty blow.

▶ Remove the doors from the frame, center the frame in the RO, and tack it up with one 10d finish nail at the top of the frame on each side.

▶ Plumb and shim one side of the frame first. Shim behind the top hinge first, then the bottom, then the middle hinge—rechecking that the jamb is plumb, square, and flush to the wall as you go. Nail (or screw) the frame at each shim point. Shim and *tack* the other side jamb; shim and tack the head jamb, placing shims at thirds of the RO width.

▶ Next, rehang the doors. If everything is perfect, the doors will be in the same plane. There will also be a uniform $\frac{1}{16}$-in. to $\frac{1}{8}$-in. clearance around the doors and an even $\frac{3}{16}$-in. gap where they meet at the center. More likely, you'll need to re-adjust shims. When the fit is perfect, use a utility knife to score the shims before snapping them flush to the finish walls.

Door-Casing Reveal

Finished wall

Side jamb

Gap between door frame and RO

Head jamb

Casing

$\frac{1}{4}$-in. reveal

Doorstop

When installing casing, set it back $\frac{1}{4}$ in. from the jamb edges. This setback, called a reveal, tricks the eye: Even if jambs or casings are not straight, their joints look straight.

FRENCH DOOR

Because French doors are wide and heavy, it's crucial that the subfloor of the opening be level. Insufficiently supported, French-door thresholds can flex, misalign, and admit water.

Barely above grade, this opening needed thorough waterproofing. Self-adhering bituminous water-proofing membrane seals the sheathing/foundation joint (just visible, lower left); this membrane is further covered by galvanized sheet metal. The rough-opening bottom is being wrapped with foil-faced peel-and-stick flashing, which extends up 4 in. onto the studs at each end.

Tilt French doors into place. Tack the cleats to the upper corners of the frame to keep the unit from falling through the opening and to ensure that the jambs will be flush with the sheathing.

Prime and paint all six sides of exterior doors—especially the top and bottom edges—before putting on the hardware and weatherstripping. Protect unfinished wood with at least one coat of primer and two coats of good-quality oil-based paint. Also carefully prime lock holes, leaf gains, and all edges. Finally, caulk panels after priming and before painting so there's no place for water to penetrate.

▐▐▐▐

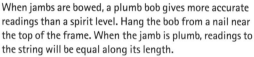

When jambs are bowed, a plumb bob gives more accurate readings than a spirit level. Hang the bob from a nail near the top of the frame. When the jamb is plumb, readings to the string will be equal along its length.

When there's too much of a gap where French doors meet in the middle, use a flat bar to ease the jambs toward the middle so you can slip shims behind them. Tweak and reshim the doors till they seat correctly and close evenly in the center.

Bending a Hinge Knuckle

If the door binds on the latch jamb yet the hinges are tight, a hinge leaf may be bent. Use an adjustable wrench to bend a hinge-leaf knuckle on the door.

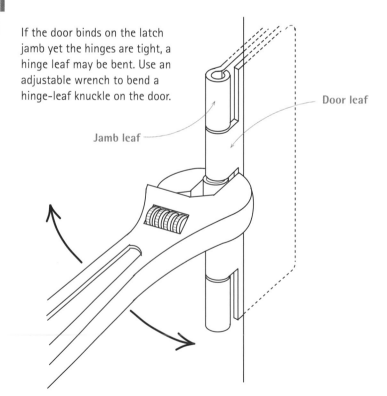

Door leaf

Jamb leaf

FINE-TUNING FRENCH DOORS

Now it's time for fine-tuning the installation or, as the pros call it, *working the frame*. Here are a few things you might see and what to do about each:

▶ *Doors hitting in the center.* Ease off the shims behind the jambs. If the problem is a bowed jamb, use additional nails to pull it back toward the RO or, better yet, use 2½-in. screws.

▶ *Doors too far apart in the center.* Shim out from the RO more. If that doesn't work or if you must shim so much that the center of the jamb bows, the head jamb was probably milled too long and should be cut down. The gap between the double doors should be ³⁄₁₆ in. or whatever the manufacturer suggests.

▶ *Wider gap between doors near the top.* Shim out behind a top hinge on one side.

▶ *Uneven door heights, binding in a corner.* One corner is lower than the other; drive a shim in under the jamb on the low side. Less likely, one jamb is too long. If you use a Japanese saw, you can cut the jamb in place; pull the nails tacking the jamb to the RO and then pry down from the top corner of the cut jamb.

▶ *Doors aren't in plane.* The frame or RO is twisted. Use a level to see which element is out

After the doors are set and the casing is installed, apply foil-faced, peel-and-strip flashing over the top flange of the head casing if the doors aren't protected by an overhang. Note that this flashing overlaps the fiber-reinforced flashing on each side. To facilitate painting, the manufacturer premasked the lights with plastic film.

Mortise Lockset

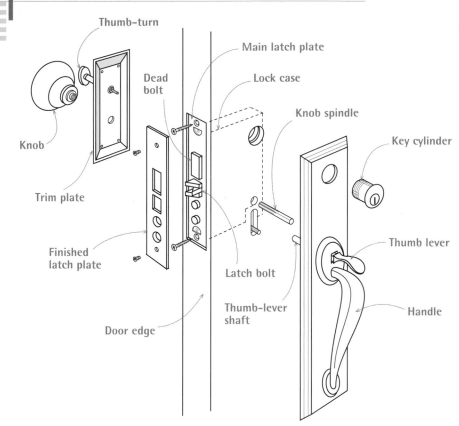

Mortise locksets combine security and convenience, because you can use a single key to operate both a latch bolt and a dead bolt.

of plumb. If it's the frame, pull the nails holding it in place and push the high edges in and the low ones out. If the RO is racked (out of plane), use a sledgehammer as described earlier in this chapter to move the bottoms of the walls until you plumb them. Finally, if the walls and frame jambs are plumb, the door may be warped.

▶ *The door won't stay shut, or one hinge binds while the others work fine.* See if the jamb is twisted. You may need to reset the shims until the jamb is square to the door. Otherwise, the hinge may be irregular. To correct it, use an adjustable wrench or locking pliers to bend the knuckles on one of the hinge leaves. Bend the leaf on the door, though, because you'll probably split the jamb if you try to bend a leaf attached to it.

Installing Hardware

Specifics vary, but most locksets come with paper templates that locate the center of the holes drilled in the face of the door (*face bores*) for handle spindles or cylinders and holes drilled into the edge of the door (*edge bores*) for latch assemblies. A second paper template locates holes drilled in the latch jamb of the door frame. Although the directions given in this section are typical, follow the directions supplied by your lock maker. *Note:* Measure the door thickness before buying locksets or key cylinders; some mechanisms are adjustable; others fit only specific door thicknesses.

PRO TIP

Before drilling, chiseling, or routing a prehung door, insert wedges beneath it so it can't move. Alternatively, you can pull the hinges, remove the door from the frame, and support it in a pair of homemade *door bucks,* also called door-holding jigs.

When you need to hang lots of doors, this router jig saves a ton of time. It has three adjustable metal templates—one for each hinge. With the templates positioned, you can move the jig onto doors or jamb stock to mortise evenly spaced hinge gains (or recesses). Here, a homemade buck is wedged to support the door.

MORTISE LOCKSETS

Mortise locksets house latch bolts and dead bolts in a single casing and can be operated with a single key turn. Mortising a lock case into the edge of the door takes some work, but the unit is very secure. The door stile must be solid wood for this type of lock.

1. Using the template, mark the edge of the door to indicate the outline of the lock case. Then mark a line running exactly in the center of the edge. Along this centered line, use a ⅞-in. spade bit to drill holes to the depth of the lock case. Overlap holes slightly to minimize the need for chiseling.

2. Use a chisel to square up the edges of the lock-case mortise. As you chisel, test-fit the lock case periodically to avoid chiseling away any more than necessary. When the lock case fits all the way into the hole, trace the outline of the main latch plate onto the edge of the door. Use a router to mortise the latch plate. *Note:* If the door edge is beveled, adjust the tilt of the latch plate to match the bevel beforehand.

3. Remove the lock case. Again, using the template, mark knob/spindle and key/cylinder holes on the face of the door stile. Use a hole saw to cut the cylinder hole and a Forstner bit or spade bit to cut the smaller spindle hole, holding drill bits perpendicular to the stile. Drill the holes

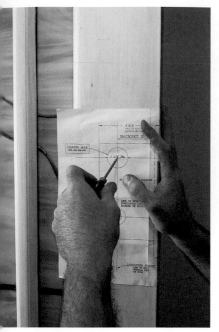

Use the paper template supplied with your lockset to center face bores on the door stile and edge bores on the door edge. The template gives the exact setback and hole sizes. Use an awl to mark the hole centers. Prehung doors often come with lock cases premortised.

Drill the face bores, which were positioned by using a paper template. Use a hole saw for the larger, key/cylinder hole and a Forstner bit for the spindle or thumb-lever hole. The small round level taped to top of drill helps the installer drill perpendicular to the door face.

Properly installed, the holes in the lock case will align with the holes drilled into the door face. If they don't line up, use a rat-tail file to gradually enlarge the face bores.

Once you've mortised the lock case into the edge of the door, use a router and a template to mortise the latch plate into the edge.

Use a chisel to square up the rounded corners of the latch-plate mortise.

until the point of the bit just starts through the other side. To prevent splintering of the stile face, back the drill out and finish drilling from the other side.

4. Reinsert the lock case and screw it to the edge of the door. Then insert the spindles, slide the escutcheons over the spindles, attach the handles or knobs to the spindles, and see if they turn freely. Once they do, screw on all the trim hardware. Typically, door handles or thumb levers are 34 in. to 38 in. high.

Strike plates are closely matched to the locksets they're supplied with. Typically, the larger opening receives the dead bolt. For added strength and security, use 3-in. screws that will reach framing.

Reinforced Strike-Plate Assembly

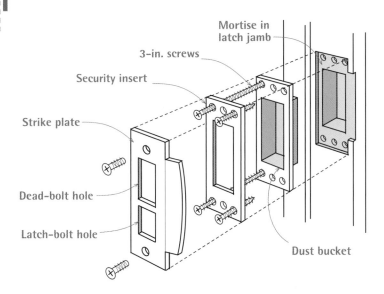

Because 3-in. screws anchor this assembly to framing behind the door frame, this strike plate can't be dislodged by a kick.

5. You will also find a strike-plate template. The plate is often mortised into the latch jamb about 1 in. below the top of the latch plate; use a router to mortise the strike plate into the jamb. To more accurately position the leading edge of the strike plate, rub pencil lead on the latch edge; when the latch is released against the jamb, it will leave a pencil mark. For greater security, buy a unit with a strike-plate reinforcer and 3-in. mounting screws.

CYLINDER LOCKSETS

Cylinder locksets (also called *tubular* or *key-in-knob* locks) are popular because they're cheap and easy to install. Better models have a spring-loaded *dead latch* that prevents the bolt from

DEAD Bolts

Exterior doors should have a dead bolt with a minimum 1-in. throw (extension) and a reinforced strike plate that screws into the framing behind the door frame. Single-cylinder deadbolts have a thumb-turn on the interior that is easy to open in the event of a fire. Unfortunately, such thumb-turns can easily be turned by a burglar breaking a glass side light. Double-cylinder models, which require a key on both sides, are more secure but are frequently banned by fire codes.

Cylinder Lockset

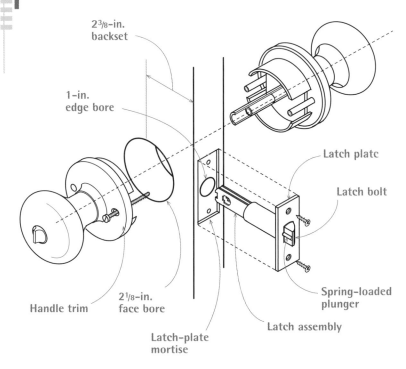

Cylinder locks are relatively inexpensive and easy to install. Many interior doors come with the large face bore predrilled.

being retracted by slipping a plastic credit card between the door edge and the frame. But no cylinder lock is secure, because all can be snapped off with a pry bar or a swift kick. To be safe, install a dead bolt, too.

1. Using the template supplied by the manufacturer, mark the centers of holes to be drilled into the face of the door (face bore) and the edge (edge bore). Use a 2⅛-in. hole saw to drill the face bore. But after the tip of the hole saw bit emerges on the other side, prevent splitting by backing the bit out and finishing the hole by drilling from the other face.

2. Use a ⅞-in. spade bit to drill the edge bore, keeping the bit perpendicular to the edge. (Buy or rent a boring jig if you have a lot of locks to install.) Insert the latch/bolt assembly into the hole and use a utility knife to trace around the latch plate. Rout the inscribed area so that the plate is flush to the edge of the door.

3. Screw down the latch plate and insert the lock mechanism through the latch assembly. Try the handle; it should turn freely. Next, position the strike plate on the jamb. To locate the strike plate exactly, rub a pencil on the end of the latch bolt, shut the door, and release the bolt against the jamb.

4. Using a ⅞-in. spade bit, drill a latch hole ½ in. deep into the jamb. Center the strike plate over the hole and trace around it with a utility knife. Use a router to mortise the strike plate. *Note:* When the door is shut, the latch bolt should descend into the strike plate hole; the small spring-loaded plunger next to the latch bolt should not. Rather, the plunger should be stopped short by a lip on the strike plate.

5. For greater security, install a unit with a strike-plate reinforcer and 3-in. mounting screws. To install the reinforcer, you'll need to drill through the frame jamb into the framing behind; likewise, the extra-long screws will grab the framing.

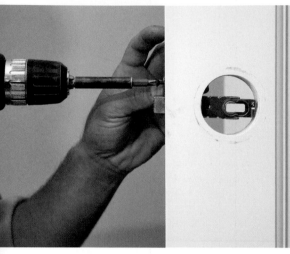

The 2⅛-in. face bore for a cylinder lockset is often predrilled at the mill, using a hole saw. So you may need only to screw the latch plate to the edge of the door...

...then insert the lock body into the spindle hole of the latch assembly, and screw the two handles together. Follow the instructions supplied with your lockset.

Weatherstripping Door Frames

Air infiltration (drafts) can account for 20 percent to 30 percent of the total heat loss of an insulated house. If your budget is tight, caulking gaps and installing weatherstripping should be your first priority, even before insulating. The *single* most crucial piece of weatherstripping is a tight-fitting door threshold.

WEATHERSTRIPPING JAMBS

Today, there are three main types of weatherstripping: *tubular, metal-leaf,* and *kerf-in.* Most are easy to install and require few special tools. Prehung doors usually come with weatherstripping attached, which can be a nuisance when installing the unit and trying to establish a uniform gap between the door and its jamb all around. Thus many installers remove kerf-in weatherstripping before beginning the installation; it's easy enough to slide the strips back into the kerfs when the job is done. Door shoe gaskets (which seal the bottom of a door) are removed for the same reason.

Tubular is the easiest to install on old doors and the least expensive type of permanent weatherstripping. The reinforced part of the strips is usually metal, with slots for attaching screws; slots allow you to adjust the stripping so it fits tight to windows or doors. To install tubular weatherstripping, shut the door and press the strip's flexible seal against the door, then screw the reinforced part to the jamb; if it's metal, use a hacksaw or aviation snips to cut it. Don't buy tubular stripping that nails up or has round holes (not slots), because it can't be adjusted.

Metal-leaf, commonly called a V-bronze or metal-tension strip, is a thin metal strip folded lengthwise and nailed with brads to door jambs. When the door shuts, it compresses the metal, stopping drafts. Metal tension strips are durable

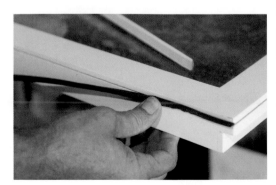

Kerf-in weatherstripping is essentially the same for doors and casement windows. Both compress the flexible stripping as they shut, sealing out drafts and moisture.

Door Weatherstripping

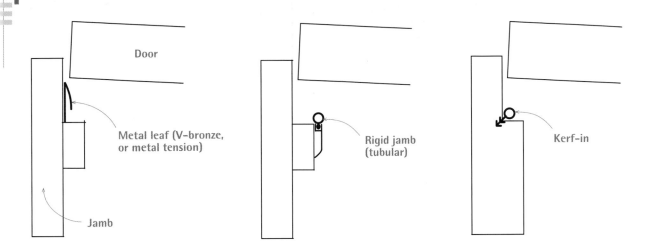

Door

Metal leaf (V-bronze, or metal tension)

Jamb

Rigid jamb (tubular)

Kerf-in

and, because they fit between the door or window and its frame, are hidden when the door is shut. When installing it, place the leaves flush to the doorstop, spacing brads every 3 in. Install the head piece first, then the sides. To keep the leaves from snagging where they meet in the corners, snip them back at a slight angle (5°). In time, the leaves flatten, but they can be raised by running a flathead screwdriver down the center of the fold.

Kerf-in features flexible stripping (silicone, vinyl, foam) that slides into a kerf (slot) between the jamb and the doorstop. Kerf-in is the preferred weatherstripping for new prehung doors because it seals tightly and can be easily replaced if the

stripping gets worn out. To cut kerfs into existing frames, use a *kerfing tool,* which looks like a laminate trimmer on an angled base. Silicone stripping is a good choice for retrofits because it compresses so small that old doors shut easily without doorstop adjustments. At head-jamb corners, cut stripping at 45° angles so it lies flat.

SEALING DOOR BOTTOMS

Weatherstripping beneath exterior doors must be weather tight and durable, this because of the heavy traffic it must bear in normal use. Elements that attach to door bottoms are called *shoes* or *sweeps;* those that attach to the floor,

Weatherstripping Thresholds

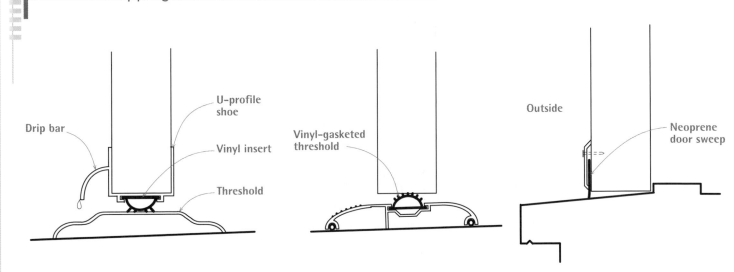

Drip bar

U-profile shoe

Vinyl insert

Threshold

Vinyl-gasketed threshold

Outside

Neoprene door sweep

Door shoes are usually sized for the 1¾-in. thickness of the exterior door. The shoe is cut back about ½ in. from both sides of the door so the shoe's drip cap will clear the thicker part of the jamb as the door closes.

By turning the screws of this adjustable threshold, you can raise and lower the oak strip to get a good seal to the door bottom, thus stopping drafts and water.

thresholds. If the doorway is protected by an overhang, installing a *shoe/threshold combination* will significantly cut drafts under the door. However, if the doorway is exposed or there are signs of water damage around an existing threshold, cover it with the *water-return threshold* shown on p. 111. Also see "Floor Pan for Exterior Door," on p. 97.

Attaching sweeps and shoes is straightforward. The simplest are *flap sweeps* that are nailed or screwed to the bottom of a door while it's shut. On an outswinging door, cut the sweep to length and hold it against the bottom edge of the door so the sweep touches the threshold. Flap sweeps are not terribly durable, but they're cheap and easy to install.

Installing shoes is somewhat more complicated because most types cover the bottom edge of the door and have a vinyl seal. Moreover, you need enough space between the door and the threshold to accommodate the thickness of the shoe and its seal (usually ½ in., but check manufacturer's specs). If not, plane or cut down the door.

If there is enough space under the door, pull its hinge pins, and lift the door out. Then, using a hacksaw, cut the shoe to length (½ in. shorter at each end than the width of the door). Shoes have screw slots that let you adjust their height; attach the shoe with one screw at each end. Rehang the door, lower the shoe till its seal makes solid contact with the existing threshold, tighten the screws at that height, and then open and shut the door. The door should drag slightly as you operate it, and you shouldn't see daylight under the shut door. When you're satisfied with the shoe positioning, insert and tighten the rest of the screws in their slots.

Retrofitting a water-return threshold is a bit more work. A three-piece threshold can be installed over an existing threshold. Consisting of a sill cover, a drain pan, and a threshold with weep holes, the assembly is sloped to send water back outside; hence the name *water return.*

The retrofit requires accurate measurements and careful cutting so all three pieces fit snugly to the existing door frame. To start, measure the widest point of the doorway opening and rough cut the sill cover to that length; then hold one end of the sill cover square to the base of a jamb and scribe the jamb's profile onto the metal sill. Use a small circular saw with a metal-cutting blade to cut the first end before scribing and cutting the other end. The sill cover must slope about ⅛ in. toward the outside so it will shed water. Hold a torpedo level on the sill cover while you temporarily shim its back edge up.

Measure and cut the threshold (not the drain pan) next. Usually, the threshold lines up to the outside edge of the doorstop, so when the door shuts, it fits snug to the threshold, as well. As you did with the sill cover, scribe the profile of the jambs onto both ends and cut them out. With the threshold resting on the sill cover, lightly scribe the outside edge of the threshold onto the sill cover, using an awl or a pocketknife. The outer edge of the drain pan should sit just shy of this scribed line. Remove the threshold and scribe the profiles of the jambs onto the drain pan; use aviation snips to cut the pan—it's very thin.

With all three threshold pieces in place (and sloping toward the outside), measure up ½ in. onto each jamb and make pencil marks. The ½ in. indicates the thickness of the door shoe you'll attach to the bottom of the door. Remove the

(continued on p. 112)

Hinges are manufactured so there will be a ¹⁄₁₆-in. gap along the hinge jamb when the hinge leaves are mortised flush to the jamb and the door. In other words, when the door is shut, hinge leaves do not quite touch.

Quick Door Fixes*

SYMPTOM	CAUSE OR SIGNIFICANCE	WHAT TO DO
Hinged doors, general		
Door binds against top of latch jamb or scrapes floor	Loose hinges allowing door to sag into opening	Rescrew hinge to jamb, replacing inner screws with ones long enough to reach studs, if needed
Hinge-screw holes in jambs are stripped	Larger-diameter screws won't fit holes in hinges	Use longer screws or fill holes with white glue, insert toothpicks, allow to dry, and rescrew
Door binds along latch jamb, but hinges are tight	Hinge may be bent	Use adjustable wrench to bend hinge-leaf knuckles on door
Door binds on latch jamb; hinges are tight; big gap seen along hinge jamb	Hinges not mortised deep enough into door or frame	Remove hinges, chisel hinge gains (recesses) deeper, and reattach hinges
Door binds along hinge jamb	Hinge leaves set too deep	Remove hinges, place cardboard shims under hinges, and reattach
Door binds because door frame is racked (out of square)	Foundation has settled or framing has shrunk	Scribe and trim door to fit skewed opening or replace old frame with squared, prehung door unit
Door shuts but won't latch	Strike plate is misaligned	Raise or lower strike plate
Pocket doors		
Door slides roughly	Built-up dirt or floor wax on floor	Vacuum track thoroughly
Door slides roughly; floor abraded under door	Top track sagging or mechanism needs adjustment	Remove trim to expose top-hung mechanism; adjust to raise door
Door does not slide at all; hard to operate	Door has fallen off track	If bottom track, lift door back onto it; if top track, remove trim and set tracking wheels up onto track
Door drags, balking at certain points; wheels squeal	Wheels not turning freely or are rusty; track bent or broken	Remove trim, swing door out, and oil or replace wheels; use flashlight to examine track inside pocket
Door face abraded; door difficult to operate	Door off track or stud has bowed into pocket	Lift door onto track; if problem persists, remove finish wall on one side—may need to replace stud
Exterior doors		
Drafts around door	Door not fitting tightly to frame	Install weatherstripping or new threshold
Water damage to wood doorsill, finish floors, and subfloor	Water collecting around doorsill area, soaking wood	Replaced damaged materials; install water-return threshold to keep water from getting in
Water stains on interior walls, especially around top of door	Absent or poorly installed cap flashing on exterior	Remove siding above top of door frame and retrofit cap flashing
Heavy condensation on metal sliding door; floor is water damaged	Metal frames conduct cold; moisture condenses on them	Upgrade to vinyl-clad door with better insulating properties
Door frame not square; casing tilts; large diagonal cracks at corners of doors or windows	Possible foundation settlement	Have structural engineer check foundation

* For additional quick-diagnostic charts like this one, see House Check: Finding and Fixing Common House Problems by Michael Litchfield with Roger Robinson (Taunton Press).

PRO TIP

Metal thresholds are thin enough to cut with hacksaws or jigsaws. But a small (3⅜-in.) cordless circular-saw blade is wide enough to track properly and cut square, yet agile enough to notch door-frame profiles. *Play it safe:* Don't hand-hold stock while cutting it. Clamp it down so your hands are free. And by all means, wear eye protection and work gloves when cutting metal.

PRO TIP

If hinges are loose because the screw holes are stripped, fill the holes with epoxy putty. Allow that to harden before predrilling and replacing the screws. Don't bother filling holes with standard wood putty, since it won't hold.

Hanging a Door to an Existing Frame

Hanging a new or recycled door to an existing frame is a common renovation task, but not always feasible. At the very least, the hinge jamb must be straight. If it's badly bowed and you can't draw the bow back with screws, you may need to remove the old frame (and its casing) and replace it with a prehung unit.

Creating a Template

The most reliable way to fit a door to an out-of-square frame is to create a template. (Read "The Beauty of Templates," on p. 317, for some tips.) Use 4-in.-wide, ⅛-in.-thick strips of doorskin plywood; tack-staple the plywood strips to the edges of the doorstops the door will seat against. Where they cross, join the strips with fast-setting hot-melt glue. In addition, run a horizontal strip across the bottom of the door opening from jamb to jamb, and diagonally cross-brace the strips so they will retain the outline of the frame opening after you pull the staples.

As you transfer the outline of this template to the face of the door, subtract ⅛ in. from the top and sides of the template to create an ⅛-in. clearance between the door and the jambs; subtract ¼ in. from the bottom edge of the template for clearance above the finish floor or threshold. If the floor isn't level, you may need more clearance. Place a 4-ft. spirit level across the opening to see how much out of level the floor is.

Trimming the Door

Trim the door rails of the door, then the stiles. To prevent splintering, first score along cut-lines with a utility knife (see the photo on p. 96). Then use a 7¼-in circular saw with a sharp, 40-tooth carbide blade to make the cut. For best results, cut 1/16 in. beyond the cut-line. Then use a belt sander with 80-grit sandpaper to trim the edge exactly to the cut-line. Some carpenters instead trim door edges with a handplane or power plane. If you use a power plane, go slowly to remove the wood gradually, making several shallow passes.

Cutting the Hinge Gains

Cutting hinge gains (recesses) is best done with a router and a template (see the photo on p. 103), but a hammer and chisel are easy enough if you're hanging just one door. If the door frame already has hinge gains, transfer their locations to the door; otherwise, mortise the hinge gains into the door before transferring hinge marks to the frame. To transfer hinge locations, use shims to position the door snug against the hinge jamb—with an ⅛-in. gap. Then use a utility knife to mark the top and bottom of the hinge leaves in both the frame and the door. Typically, the top of the top hinge is 7 in. from the top of the door; the bottom of the bottom hinge, 9 in. to 11 in. from the bottom of the door (see "Positioning Door Hardware," on p. 93). If there's a third hinge, it's equidistant from the other two.

Pull the hinge pins so you can work with one hinge leaf at a time. Set the hinge leaf slightly back from the edge of the door, as shown in "Hinge Setbacks." The setback from the hinge to the doorstop should be slightly greater than that from the hinge to the edge of the door, so there is room for several coats of paint. Use a combination

Hinge Setbacks

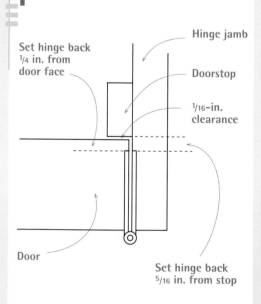

Set hinge back ¼ in. from door face

Hinge jamb

Doorstop

1/16-in. clearance

Door

Set hinge back 5/16 in. from stop

Leave a slight gap between the door and the doorstop, so the door won't bind.

A spring-loaded, self-centering Vix bit is the best way to center pilot holes for hinge screws. Otherwise, screws that drift off-center can cause hinges to twist and misalign with the other hinges.

square to mark setback lines on doors and jambs. Finally, when mortising hinges, it's best to set the router slightly shallow and then use a chisel to pare away the last little bit of wood so the hinge leaf is just flush. Setting hinges too deep can cause the door to bind.

Hanging the Door

Screw down all the hinge leaves using a self-centering Vix-bit®, which centers screws perfectly in the hinge holes. Then lift the door into the frame and mate the door's hinge leaves with those on the frame, starting with the top hinge. Insert the hinge pins loosely, then eyeball the hinges as you open and shut the door. If the clearance between the door and the hinge jamb is excessive, remove the door and set the hinges a little deeper.

Water-Return Threshold

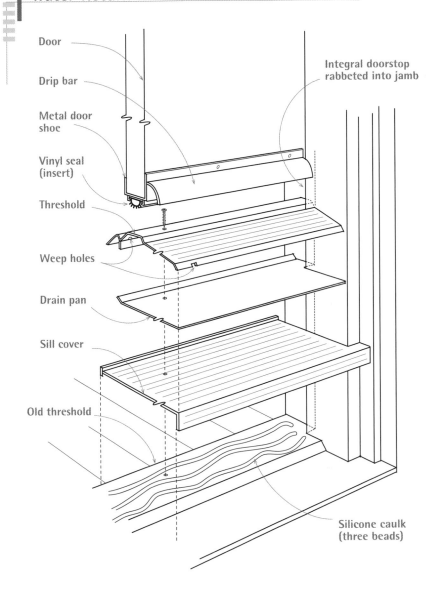

- Door
- Drip bar
- Metal door shoe
- Vinyl seal (insert)
- Threshold
- Weep holes
- Drain pan
- Sill cover
- Old threshold
- Integral doorstop rabbeted into jamb
- Silicone caulk (three beads)

This three-piece threshold fits over an existing threshold and can withstand just about anything short of Noah's Flood. For success, carefully fit and caulk the unit's pieces.

When Hinges Fail

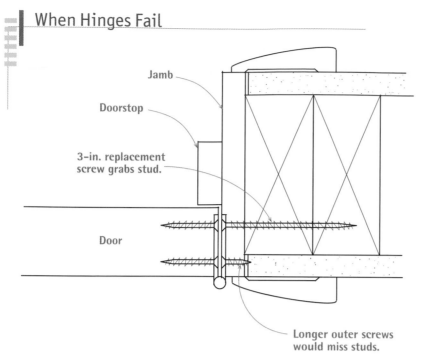

Jamb

Doorstop

3-in. replacement
screw grabs stud.

Door

Longer outer screws
would miss studs.

Replacing a short hinge-screw with one long enough to grab
the framing should be your first "cure" when hinge leaves
pull free from door jambs.

Top-mounted pocket door
mechanisms need oiling and a little
ingenuity to keep them rolling. Here,
an installer retrofitted a new
machine bolt, sawing a slot into its
head so the bolt can be easily turned
to raise or lower the door.

The mortise in this pocket door's
bottom rail will house an adjustable
wheel mechanism. The hole bored in
the face allows access to raise or
lower the wheels and thus the door.

threshold and the drain pan, shut the door and
spread a scriber to the distance from the top of
the sill cover to the mark(s) on the jambs. Then
scribe the bottom of the door to indicate the
amount that you'll need to trim off. Cut down the
door, vacuum the existing threshold well, apply
three beads of silicone caulking across the opening, and press the sill cover into it. Then do the
same with the sill drain pan. Also caulk the jamb-
and-pan joints. Finally, screw down the threshold
and install the shoe on the bottom of the door, as
described in the preceding section.

Installing a Basic Window

Some of the terminology for doors and door
frames is common to windows and window
frames. For example, frames are made of *jambs*,
a head, and *a sill*, with *stops* to guide or seat window sashes. *Window sashes,* like door frames,
have horizontal *rails* and vertical *stiles*.

WINDOW CHOICES

Windows arrive installed in a preassembled
frame, complete with the hardware necessary to
operate them. Unlike door installation, there is
no need to trim window jambs, so the sill is
always preattached. You can order windows *precased* (casing preattached), but such units can be
tricky to shim properly. Uncased units are better
suited to renovation: Local mills will offer a
wider range of casings than window manufacturers, and you'll have more latitude in adjusting
casings to irregular walls or out-of-square frames.

Wood windows are the sentimental favorite.
They're also pleasant to work with and good
looking, but they take a lot of maintenance. On
the other hand, vinyl-clad and aluminum-clad
wood units are virtually maintenance-free,
though they cost more. Of late, all-vinyl units
have become popular, and are an especially
good choice in rainy regions. Metal windows,
on the other hand, seldom look good as retrofits
in older houses; and because they encourage
condensation and heat loss, they're a poor choice
in cold climates.

Clad window units come in a variety of
durable prefinished colors, eliminating costly
exterior painting. Many manufacturers will cus-
tomize a range of factory-built window units to
your specifications. Options include a choice of
fixed, double-hung, single-hung, sliders, bow,
bay, casement, awning, and hopper styles; single-
or double-glazing; many configurations of lights
and muntins; custom glass for sound or UV light
attenuation; safety glass; custom jamb widths;
extended sill horns to accommodate various exterior casing details; and mulled units (windows

ganged together to create larger units). These factory-built wood windows are generally made to tighter tolerances than shopbuilt windows, ensuring good weather tightness and insulation values.

PREPPING THE OPENING

Before ordering windows and again just before installing them, check the ROs for level and plumb. Most window units will need some shimming, but if the sill is level, the rest of the installation will be relatively easy. Typically, an RO is 1 in. taller and wider than the window frame.

WEATHERPROOFING OVERVIEW

Water is persistent, so always wrap exterior wall openings with moisture barriers before installing windows, and use cap flashing on the frame heads to direct water around the opening. The order in which you install weatherproofing materials depends on several variables: Is exterior sheathing exposed or covered by building paper

and siding? And are window units uncased, precased, or surrounded by a continuous nailing flange?

If the sheathing is exposed, run housewrap or building paper at least 4 in. into the RO, and staple it to the framing. However, leave the housewrap *over* the top of RO unstapled because it will overlap the window's cap flashing later.

Alternatively, you can first flash the perimeter of the RO with strips of fiberglass-reinforced flashing or with *self-adhering membrane*. Self-adhering membrane is more expensive, so it's often reserved for flashing sills and head casing, which are more likely to leak. Flash the sill first, folding the strip ends so they extend at least 6 in. up onto the jack studs. Then flash the jack studs, overlapping the upturned ends of sill flashing. (But don't flash the head of the opening yet; that needs to wait till the window is installed.) Then run housewrap or building paper up to the edges of the opening, overlapping the strip flashing just installed.

If the exterior is already covered with building paper and siding, you'll need to fit flashing strips and cap flashing under it. If there's lap siding such as clapboards, or wood shingles, this is relatively easy: Drive a *shingle ripper* up under siding courses to cut the nails holding them, slide flashing strips under the existing building paper and siding, and then caulk and install the unit, as described in the next section. Cut siding nails back at least 4 in. around the opening, although you may want to cut back shingles 12 in., allowing you to offset the shingle joints correctly.

Before installing windows, carefully remove the packaging and shipping blocks.

Sizing Windows

Window catalogs list several dimensions for windows, including a *callout size*, which indicates the size of rough opening (RO) required, and a *unit size*, which denotes the outer dimensions (width and height) of the window frame. Window dimensions are stated as pairs of numbers; the first number is always width.

Thus a window with a callout size of 4030 needs an RO 40 in. wide by 30 in. high. Typically, the unit size of a window (frame) is ½ in. less in height and width than the callout size, but always check manufacturer's specs to be sure. *Note:* Window sashes are usually 1⅜ in. thick unless otherwise noted.

When ordering window units, measure the width of the ROs in three places from top to bottom and the height in three places from side to side. Window manufacturers usually prefer the smallest reading in each direction but, again, follow the manufacturer's ordering instructions to the letter. Also measure the thickness of the walls, from interior finish surfaces to exterior sheathing; you may need jamb extensions as well.

Measure openings and order windows well in advance. If your window units are in odd sizes or otherwise unusual, they may require a special order, which could delay your job.

Cut back stucco to replace and correctly flash windows. Here, the roof leaked because the corner of the window was too close to the roof, where a lazy roofer just stopped the step-flashing. The replacement window won't be as tall, so its sill will be at least 4 in. above the roof.

PRO **TIP**

Windows are usually installed by setting the bottom onto the sill of the opening and tipping the unit up into place. But if you're installing a flanged unit, which has integral cap flashing, slip the cap flange up under the housewrap and siding first; then swing the bottom of the unit onto the sill. Obviously, you'll need to slit the housewrap or pry out the siding nails above the opening to insert the flange.

||||

Replace and renail the siding, as necessary; then caulk and install the window as described in the next section.

If there's stucco, the only way to retrofit flashing successfully is to cut back the stucco and wire lath 6 in. to 8 in. around the opening, using an *electric chipping hammer* (see the top photo on p. 145). After installing the new unit, insert flashing beneath the existing building paper (especially the cap flashing), tie new wire to the old, and patch the stucco.

INSTALLING THE WINDOW UNIT

Before installing window units, remove the packaging, shipping blocks, screens, storm windows, and so on. If the unit is uncased, screw temporary *cleats* to the outside edges of the frame so that when it is placed in the opening, its jamb edges will be flush to the sheathing. Window installation is a two-person job—one inside, one outside.

1. Dry-fit the window first. Set the bottom of unit onto the RO sill and tilt the window up into place. There should be roughly ½ in. of space on both sides of the unit and ½ in. to 1 in. above. Using a spirit level, the person outside quickly checks for level and plumb. If there are no glaring problems, set the unit aside and caulk around the opening.

2. Caulking details will vary. For most precased or flanged units, apply a continuous ⅜-in. bead of siliconized acrylic caulk along the sides and top of the RO, back ½ in. from the edge, and press the casing or flange of the new unit into the caulking for a good seal. If the unit is uncased, caulk only along the bottom of the opening, at this stage.

3. Now install the window. As the outside person supports the unit, the inside person uses a small flat bar inserted between the RO and the frame to center the unit in the opening. That done, the person outside uses a spirit level to check the window's sill and head for level, while the person inside uses the flat bar and adds shims as needed. Once the unit is level and plumb, the outside person uses a tape measure to check the frame's "diagonals" (opposite corners of the frame). If diagonal measurements are equal, the frame is square.

4. When the unit is level and plumb, nail the upper corners of precased units and units with nailing fins. Tack uncased units with a nail or screw centered in each side jamb, down about 4 in. from the top of the frame. Open and close the window to see if it binds. Where the frame binds, use screws to draw it out or shims to push it into the opening. If you are installing a double-hung window, make sure the meeting rails meet evenly.

Dry-fit the window first to make sure it fits and that there's enough space in the opening to level and shim the unit. That done, set the window aside, and caulk around the opening. The temporary diagonal cleats at the upper corners keep the jambs flush to the sheathing.

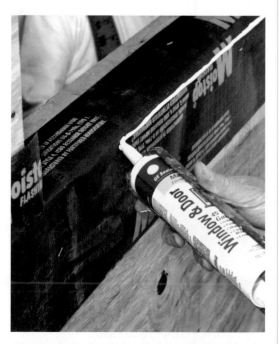

After dry-fitting the window, flash the sill of the RO and run a bead of siliconized acrylic latex caulk near the corner so the window seats in it. Once the window is in place, apply an additional bead of caulk to the underside of the windowsill to cut air infiltration.

Once the unit is shimmed and screwed into final position and the window opens and closes freely, cut the shims flush with the inside face of the framing. Do the same outside.

After applying a bead of caulking along the outside edge of the jambs, seat fiber-reinforced flashing paper in the caulking, as shown. Apply a second bead of caulking over the paper. Then install the casing and head flashing as shown on p. 89.

FINISHING TOUCHES

Use a Japanese saw or a utility knife to cut the shims flush to the interior finish surfaces and exterior sheathing. Set the nails or sink the screws holding the frame to the opening, and then fill the holes. Use a mild-expanding polyurethane spray-foam sealant to stop air infiltration around the unit. This type of foam is less likely to bow window frames than a foam that expands aggressively (see Chapter 14).

Now weather-seal the outside of the opening. If you installed a precased unit, it's already set in caulking, so you're ready to install the cap flashing. If the unit has continuous nailing flanges, seal the sides and sill with strips of self-adhering membrane. But install cap flashing before applying a self-adhering membrane strip across the top of the unit.

If the unit is uncased, like the unit shown in the photos, caulk the side jamb edges with siliconized acrylic caulk (run the beads back ½ in. from jamb edges), press fiberglass-reinforced strip flashing into the caulk, and nail the side casing to the jambs, using 8d galvanized finish nails. Then apply a bead of caulking to the edge of the head jamb and nail up the head casing to the side casings. To keep the joints from pulling apart, send one nail diagonally through each joint, too. Then apply the cap flashing (usually metal or vinyl), nailing through its top leg. Flashing strips, self-adhering membrane strips, or housewrap overlaps that top leg. Finally, apply a bead of surface caulk to the frame/sheathing joints all around.

Shimming Windows

All window frames must be shimmed securely. Pairs of tapered shims allow you to plumb and level window frames in out-of-square openings; supporting frame jambs and preventing deflection even as you drive screws or nails through them.

Ideally, you should shim each side jamb within 4 in. of its top and bottom corners, and every 16 in. in between—a minimum of three shim points along each jamb. If the rough sill is level and uniformly supports the windowsill, don't shim underneath it. Window makers disagree about shimming the head jamb. Some recommend that you shim head jambs at the same intervals as side jambs; others suggest not shimming at all because if the header sags, shims beneath it could deflect the head jamb. To be safe, follow the installation instructions that come with your window.

As explained on p. 94, you can nail through or below shims as long they're snug. At each shimming point, use a pair of 10d galvanized finish nails or 3-in. galvanized or stainless-steel trim-head screws to keep the jambs from twisting. Screws are more expensive but allow you to make adjustments easily. If the shims are green or "yard wet," there's no need to predrill them to avoid splits; otherwise, predrill. You can easily fill and paint dimpled nail heads and countersunk screw heads in the jambs. Or you can remove the inside window stops, nail through the jambs, and replace the stops to hide the nails.

After installing cap flashing, cover its top flange with self-adhering peel-and-stick membrane or, as shown, fiber-reinforced flashing paper. The siding will overlay the flashing.

Window Repairs

Old houses often have ailing windows, unopenable because they're swollen shut or entombed in paint. Try to repair windows during a sunny stretch, but have a roll of sheet plastic on hand to tack over the openings in case a storm catches you by surprise. Above all, be patient, use force very sparingly on balky windows, and wear goggles and gloves.

FREEING SASHES

The window may just be painted shut. Rap around the perimeter of the sashes with a hammer, using a wooden block to prevent marring. Then run a scraper or a putty knife along the sash edges.

If the lower sash still won't move, remove the *inside stop,* which is usually screwed on, if you can find the screws under all that paint. If you can't pry up the stop, use a chisel to cut it out; stops are easy to replace. But try not to damage the jamb. Once the inside stop is out, pull out the lower sash and disconnect the sash cord if it hasn't already rotted away. Use a narrow scraper to remove paint or debris from the sash channel. With a putty knife, clean up the sash channels, and then lightly sand them. Try the sash to see if it now slides more smoothly. If so, wax the chan-

PRO TIP

Retrofitting cap flashing takes dexterity. Cut back the siding nails 2 in. to 4 in. above the opening, and pry up the siding so you can slide the top flange of the Z-bar cap flashing under the building paper and siding, while simultaneously holding up the window unit. You can nail the top flange of the Z-bar through the siding, but that's not imperative. Wedged into place, the cap flashing won't go anywhere.

Double-Hung Window Elements

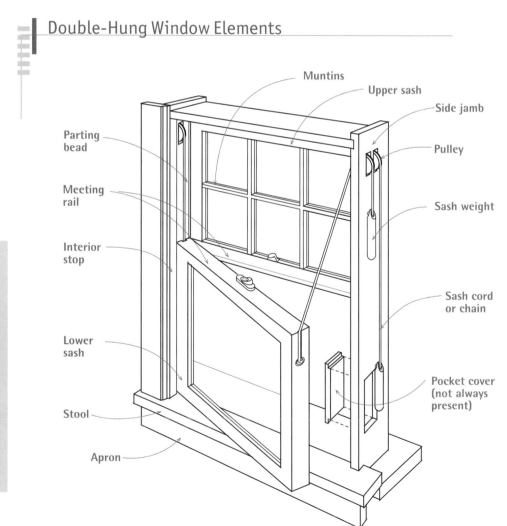

Muntins

Upper sash

Side jamb

Parting bead

Pulley

Meeting rail

Sash weight

Interior stop

Sash cord or chain

Lower sash

Pocket cover (not always present)

Stool

Apron

nels (a piece of candle works fine) and the sides of the sash, replace the sash, and reattach the inside stop.

If a sash weight has come loose from its cord or chain, reattach it while the sash is out. Access to these weights varies, but there is often a removable panel toward the bottom of each jamb. If there is no such panel, pry the jamb trim off.

REPLACING GLASS

Wear goggles and gloves when replacing damaged glass and dried-out putty (glazing compound). Although a *glazier's chisel* will easily remove most putty, use paint stripper or an *electric putty softener* to dislodge the tough stuff. (But do not use chemical stripper *and* heat at the same time.) Because direct heat can crack glass, cover nearby panes with a piece of hardboard wrapped in protective foil. After removing the old putty, glazier's points, and damaged glass, sand the frame lightly, using 180-grit sandpaper.

Prepping the frame. Before applying new glazing compound to weathered sashes, brush the exposed wood with a sealant or a half-and-half mixture of alcohol (or turpentine) and linseed oil. This will prevent the dry wood from sucking the oil out of the fresh putty. Let the sash dry for an hour or two. Then spread a thin bed of putty along the lip that receives the glass. This bed of putty will prevent rattling and seal air leaks. The replacement pane should be ⅛ in. smaller than the width and length of the frame.

Cutting the glass. After scribing the glass with a glass cutter, gently rap the ball end of the cutter along the underside of the cut—up and down its length—until a clear line develops. Then, with the cut directly over a table edge, quickly snap the waste portion free. If the waste piece is too small to grip, use glass pliers. *Note:* Old glass is imperfect and often hard to cut because it's irregular and often doesn't break cleanly.

As you place the glass in the frame, press around the edges so that the putty will seat evenly beneath the pane. With a putty knife held almost flat against the glass, push in new glazier's points until they are half-buried. (Never hammer the points in; you may break the glass.) Sink a point every 6 in., or at least one for each side of the glass. Be particularly careful when pushing points into *muntins* (the wooden strips between panes); if you push a point in too far, you could crack the adjacent pane. Glass in metal-frame windows is usually held in place by metal spring clips, which can be reused.

Once the replacement pane is held fast by glazier's points, apply putty generously. Scoop out a palmful of putty and knead it in one hand until it is soft and pliable. Use your thumb to press the putty into the frame, applying moderate pressure. You'll recover any excess when you trim, so use a lot of putty now to ensure getting a good seal.

To trim off the excess, hold the knife blade at an angle of about 45° to the glass, with a corner of the blade touching the glass and the middle of the blade resting on the frame. Pull the knife evenly toward you, plowing a steady furrow through the putty. Go back and touch up the corners after removing most of the excess. You

Using a straightedge to guide your cut, pull the glass cutter, with an even pressure, toward you. One pass of the cutter should do it. Then use the ball end of the cutter to rap lightly along the line.

Wearing gloves and safety glasses, place the scribed line over a table edge and snap the glass sharply; it will break along the line.

shouldn't be able to see putty from the inside of the window once it has been trimmed.

If the putty doesn't stick, either you're holding the knife handle too high or there is dust on the frame or the glass. If the problem is just the drag of the knife blade across the putty, a bit of saliva on the blade will lubricate it. When the putty has cured for a week, overpaint it slightly onto the glass to seal the putty from weather.

Installing a Skylight

By letting in light, skylights can transform a room, making a bathroom seem larger, a kitchen warm and cheery, or a bedroom a place to watch the stars. And because of marked improvements in flashing and quality control, skylights can now

Double-sided, self-adhering foam tape has largely replaced putty in production glazing. Tape, unlike putty, is uniformly thick, quick to install, and won't degrade the seals of insulated glass.

However, once the glass is placed in glazing tape, it's difficult to reseat. So seat the panes carefully if you use tape.

be installed without fear of leaks from outside or excessive heat loss from within.

Where you put the skylight is partly aesthetic and partly structural. If it's a kitchen unit, catch the morning sun by facing it east. If placed in a hallway, even a small unit provides enough light to let you do without electric light during the day. In a bathroom, privacy is the main issue. Avoid skylights in south-facing roofs unless you're designing for passive solar gain; such skylights can roast you in the summer. Similarly, skylights in west-facing roofs may create too much heat in the South and Southwest United States. Avoid skylights that straddle a ridge because they are difficult to flash and likely to leak.

SELECTING A SKYLIGHT

Consider a number of things when buying a skylight, not least of which is the manufacturer. Although sizes have become pretty much standard, quality varies greatly—so ask local contractors or lumber suppliers which brands they prefer. Here are a few aspects to investigate:

▶ Do you want *ventilating* (openable) or *fixed* (closed) skylights? Skylights that open can vent excess heat. And *turn-tilt* models pivot so they're easy to clean.

▶ Is it energy efficient? Most units come with doubled thermal-pane glass, but units should also have a thermal break to minimize loss by conduction. A metal frame that's continuous (inside to out) will wick off a lot of indoor heat. A better bet is sealed wood.

▶ Does it have step-flashing along its sides (desirable for shingle roofing) or strip flashing, which must be caulked to keep water out? If the unit is wide (more than 32 in.), does the maker supply a cricket to deflect water around the skylight head?

▶ Does the unit have tempered glass? That's an important consideration if a tree limb overhangs your roof. Your building code may require such glass.

▶ If the unit will be installed beyond reach, how easy is it to open and close? Remote-controlled units with motors can be programmed to open at a given temperature, and shut when an electronic sensor detects rain, but such units are more expensive and more temperamental than manually operated ones.

▶ Can you get units with screens, blinds, shades or polarizing tints? *Low-E coatings* selectively admit light while reflecting heat. *Note:* There are different coating types for cold and hot climates, so ask your supplier which is appropriate for your area.

Skylights dramatically change rooms. Because drywall joints and nail holes will be illuminated, too, apply joint compound generously and sand carefully. Heat buildup in the lightwell can cause compound to shrink, so you may need to apply an extra coat.

Replacement Windows

If existing sashes have deteriorated and you'd like to avoid the major headache of ripping out existing frames, casing, finish surfaces, and siding, then replacement windows can be a cost-effective solution. These units come encased in frames, which you insert into existing wood frames, after removing the old sashes and pulling the parting beads so that old jambs are reasonably flat. Just cut the sash cords and leave old sash weights in the wall.

Start by measuring the existing window frames carefully, because replacement units fit snugly inside them. Old frames are frequently out of square, even if their jambs are parallel. Thus, in addition to measuring height and width, note which way a frame leans, so you can order the biggest rectangle that will fit into that opening. To install most replacement units, apply a ⅜-in. bead of siliconized acrylic caulk along the inside faces of the interior or exterior window stops and across the sill in line with those stops. Set the new window in bottom first, tilt it up into place, and then press its vinyl frame into the caulking so there's a good seal. There's little shimming; many models have adjustable screw jacks that hold side jambs tight to the opening. Use a mild expanding polyurethane foam to seal the gaps around the unit.

Admittedly, these units are something of a compromise. If existing frames and casings are parallel but not plumb, replacement windows are commonly installed slightly off-plumb. Replacement sashes tend to be narrower than old-fashioned wood ones, so there's also an aesthetic compromise. That noted, vinyl- or Fiberglas®-clad replacement units are typically one-half the cost of custom-milled wood sashes, require little maintenance, and cut drafts and energy costs dramatically. Their color range is limited—white—but you can paint Fiberglas. Aluminum-clad units come in dozens of colors but are the most expensive option, and salty coastal air will eventually corrode the metal.

SIZING SKYLIGHTS

Folks often order skylights larger than they need to be. Keep in mind that even the smallest unit brightens a room greatly. Moreover, much of the light gain comes from reflections off the sides of the *lightwell* (or lightshaft), which is why wells are usually painted white. You can increase the amount of light markedly by flaring out the sides of the well. If you need more light than one narrow skylight will yield, consider "ganging" several, side by side, in adjacent rafter bays. Smaller skylights are easier to frame out, and the fewer rafters you disturb, the better.

Most skylights are sized incrementally to fit between rafters spaced 16 in. or 24 in. on center. Thus skylights routinely come in 24-in., 32-in., and 48-in. widths. Skylights 32 in. wide are the most popular size because you need to cut only one rafter to accommodate the unit. Velux®, for example, has several models whose inside curb dimensions are 30½ in. wide—the same distance between rafters spaced 16-in. on center, if one rafter in between is removed. Aligning the inner faces of skylight curbs and rafters also makes installing drywall much easier. Attached to the roof sheathing with L-shaped mounting brackets, the sides of Velux units sit right over rafters.

FRAMING A SKYLIGHT OPENING

This section provides general guidance related to the framing procedures shown in the photos. Usually, it doesn't matter whether you cut ceiling joists or rafters first, as long as they're adequately supported. Some pros prefer to frame out the lightwell completely before opening the roof; whereas others place the skylight first and measure down from that.

Insulation. Remove the ceiling insulation. Then disconnect and cap any wires and pipes that will need to be rerouted around the opening. (Use a voltage tester to be sure the power's off.) Where possible, work from a stepladder rather than sitting on ceiling joists; that way, you'll be less likely to crack the finish ceiling. The job will go faster if one worker on a ladder measures carefully and calls out measurements for headers, trimmers, lightwell studs, and the like to a second worker on the floor, who does the cutting.

Before cutting ceiling joists, support them with a *strongback*, which is a piece of dimension

Skylight Positioning

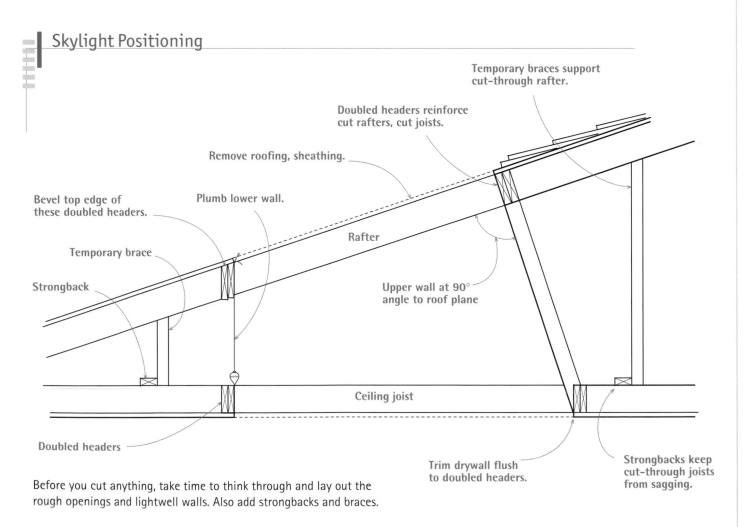

Temporary braces support cut-through rafter.

Doubled headers reinforce cut rafters, cut joists.

Remove roofing, sheathing.

Bevel top edge of these doubled headers.

Plumb lower wall.

Temporary brace

Rafter

Strongback

Upper wall at 90° angle to roof plane

Ceiling joist

Doubled headers

Trim drywall flush to doubled headers.

Strongbacks keep cut-through joists from sagging.

Before you cut anything, take time to think through and lay out the rough openings and lightwell walls. Also add strongbacks and braces.

lumber nailed to the tops of ceiling joists to keep them from sagging, as shown in "Skylight Positioning," at left. The strongback should run perpendicular to the joist grid, be placed within 1 ft. of the cut joist ends, and rest on uncut joists beyond the opening to distribute the load. To tie the strongback to the joists, you can use steel *hurricane ties* (see the photo on p. 61).

Joists. Cut out the ceiling joists after attaching the strongbacks. Use a framing square to make sure the cuts are square. Cut the ceiling joists so their ends will be set back 3 in. from the final opening in the ceiling. This setback ensures that the doubled headers (3 in. wide) at both ends will be flush with the edges of the finish ceiling. Use three 16d common nails to nail the first board of each doubled header to the joist ends; nail the second header of each pair to the face of the first. Once the headers are in place, nail into their ends, through the trimmer joists. Use steel double-joist hangers for greater strength. Then double the trimmer joists along each side, making sure the nails don't protrude into the opening.

Roof opening. Cutting out the roof opening is relatively easy if the roof pitch is low (5/12 or less). But if it's steep, use *roof jacks* to create a safe working platform. Once on the roof, snap chalklines through the four 16d nails you drove through earlier, as described in "Skylight above a Flat Ceiling," at right. Then use a hooked blade in a utility knife to score the asphalt shingles, along the chalklines. Scoring allows you to remove the

Skylight above a Flat Ceiling

Positioning a skylight above a flat ceiling is an inexact science. Situating the skylight between rafters is easy enough, but because lightwells flare out, sizing and positioning the ceiling opening can be tricky if you've never done it before. Here are a few tips to demystify and simplify the process.

▶ Use a pencil or painter's tape to roughly outline the lightwell opening on the ceiling. Push nails up through the corners of the opening so you can spot them from above.

▶ Go into the attic or crawl space above to find the four corner nails and determine if there are wires, pipes, and ducts that would be a problem to relocate. Avoid positioning skylights where roof planes converge, by all means. It's far easier to reposition the skylight.

▶ If the space over the ceiling is inaccessible, *turn off the electricity* and use a cordless recip saw (or a hammer) to punch a hole big enough for your head, so you can take a better look before enlarging the hole.

▶ If you can position skylight openings to avoid cutting rafters or ceiling joists, do so. If you must cut more than one rafter, have an engineer review your plans. Otherwise, double up headers and trimmers around the rough opening(s) to redistribute the loads, and use steel connectors to ensure solid connections.

▶ Flare the top and bottom of the lightwell but, if possible, leave the sides vertical. To simplify layout further, make the upper (end) wall of the lightwell perpendicular to the rafters and the lower (end) wall, plumb, as shown in "Skylight Positioning," at left. It's possible to flare all four surfaces, but compound-angle cuts on all studs are a monster to do correctly.

▶ When you have a better sense of the lightwell's location, enlarge the hole in the ceiling but don't cut it to its final size yet. To mark the corners of the opening in the roof, drive 16d nails up through the sheathing. *Note:* Thus far you've cut into finish surfaces only, not into framing.

After snapping chalklines to outline the rough opening, use a utility knife with a hooked blade to cut the shingles. Then use a shingle ripper (left) or a flat bar (right) to pry up the shingle nails and remove the shingles within the cutout area. Kneepads are a must for most roof work.

Unless you are highly skilled with a reciprocating saw, like this pro, use a circular saw to cut through the roof sheathing. To avoiding gumming up a blade, remove the building paper before cutting. Be sure to wear eye protection.

Standing outside the cutout area, pry up the sheathing and pass it through the hole to your helper inside. By the way, many old–timers don't like sneakers because nails can pierce the thin soles; on the other hand, sneakers can improve your footing. Your call.

After removing the sheathing, the installer used a hooked blade to cut back the shingles more precisely so the Velux skylight's mounting brackets could sit on the flat plane of the roof sheathing, rather than on an uneven shingle surface.

Here, all four lightwell walls will flare out toward the bottom (none plumb). Using his level as a straightedge, the installer marks the rafter cuts; the level runs from the edge of the roof opening to the doubled headers in the ceiling opening. After cutting the rafters, he'll attach a doubled header behind the cut-line.

PRO TIP

Cut the length of the lightwell a little long. It's difficult to know exactly where the grooved lower edge of the skylight curb will meet the finish surface on the plumbed lower wall, so you're better off cutting the opening long and shimming it up as needed, using thin pieces of plywood. Ultimately, ½-in. drywall edges should fit perfectly into curb grooves.

shingles within the RO without disturbing those around the perimeter.

Once you've removed the shingles within the RO, use a circular saw with demolition blade set to the depth of the roof sheathing. If you're skilled, you can use a reciprocating saw with a bimetal blade to cut through the sheathing, as the pro is doing in the photo on p. 121, but don't cut through a rafter while you're standing on it! Whatever tool you use, wear eye protection because you're likely to hit nails. After you've cut around the perimeter of the RO, use a claw hammer or a flat bar to pry out the sheathing.

Next slide a shingle ripper under the shingles around the RO, gently breaking the self-sealing shingle spots and pulling out any nails within 1 ft. of the opening. This nail-free perimeter will enable you to properly flash the skylight curb with building paper or self-adhering bituminous flashing. Finally, if you're installing a skylight with L-shape mounting brackets, cut back the shingles an additional 1½ in. to 2 in. around the RO so the brackets can sit on a uniformly flat surface and be screwed easily into sheathing.

Framing. Frame the roof opening and the lightwell. Before cutting through the rafters, install temporary braces to the ceiling joists below; those rafter braces stay in place till the rafters are headered off. If the upper wall of the lightwell will be perpendicular to the rafters, use a framing square to mark a square cut back 3 in. from the edge of the opening (a doubled header is 3 in. wide).

The lower end of the lightwell is a bit trickier to frame because it intersects the roof plane at an obtuse angle (greater than 90°). Hold a 4-ft. level plumb against the lower edge of the roof RO, and then mark that angle onto the face of the trimmer rafters on each side of the opening. Bevel-cut the top edges of the doubled headers at that same angle. Once you've headered off the top and bottom of the RO, double up the trimmer rafters along the sides of the opening, using as long a board as possible. (Space is tight in an attic.)

Finally, install studs running from the RO in the roof to the RO in the ceiling below. If you install the four corner studs first, you can run taut strings between them to align the intervening studs. If the lightwell sidewalls are plumb, rather than flared out, you will have saved yourself a lot of work.

INSTALLING AND FLASHING SKYLIGHTS

Follow the manufacturer's instructions when installing and flashing your skylight, so the warranty will be honored should the unit leak. Installations shown are fairly typical.

Screw the mounting brackets to the sides of the skylight curb; most brackets are adjustable. Then, with one worker on the roof and one in the attic, pass the skylight out through the opening. As the worker outside raises or lowers the brackets till the top and bottom of the unit are level, the worker inside centers the unit in the opening.

Different skylight, same installer. Here, he frames out the lightwell before cutting a hole in the ceiling because it was raining. First he headered off the ceiling joists, then the rafters around the roof opening, before angle cutting the studs between the two openings. (He cut the four corner studs first.)

The same lightwell after the roof has been opened: Note the doubled headers around all sides of the opening. Because all walls flare, this is a complicated piece of framing.

Skylight Framing

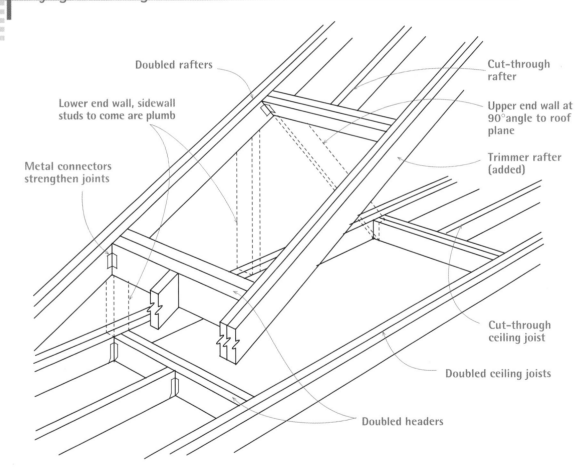

- Doubled rafters
- Lower end wall, sidewall studs to come are plumb
- Metal connectors strengthen joints
- Cut-through rafter
- Upper end wall at 90° angle to roof plane
- Trimmer rafter (added)
- Cut-through ceiling joist
- Doubled ceiling joists
- Doubled headers

In addition to doubling headers at the ends of rough openings, double up rafters and joists running along the sides of openings. Framing out a lightwell will be somewhat easier if side walls and the lower end wall of the lightwell are plumb.

Velux units have integral curbs and proprietary flashing kits. This one is "directional"—that is, with a top and bottom. Having slipped head flashing under shingles above, the installers will slip the unit's head underneath. Small L-shaped brackets along the curb will mount to the sheathing.

That done, the outside installer screws the bottom legs of the brackets to the sheathing.

Wrapping the curb with building paper or self-adhering membrane underlayment gives you an extra layer of protection before installing the unit's apron, side flashing, and head flashing. Apply four 12-in.-wide strips of underlayment, one on each side, folding each so that it runs up onto the curb about 2 in. Apply the bottom piece first, which overlaps the shingles below; then place the side pieces and, finally, the top piece. If possible, slide the top piece of self-adhering membrane up under the building paper so you adhere it directly to the sheathing. Slit the folded strips where they overlap the curb corners so the strips lie flat, and apply a dab of roofing cement to adhere the slit pieces.

Install the apron flashing first, which runs along the lower edge of the skylight and overlaps the shingles below it. Holding the apron snug against the curb, attach it to the curb—not the roof—using a single screw (or nail) on each side. Although it's usually not necessarily to caulk under the apron's lower flange, follow the manufacturer's advice for your unit. Ideally, the apron will line up with a course of shingles, but in renovation that's not always possible.

Install step-flashing along the sides, weaving the L-shaped flashing between the shingle courses. Ideally, shingle courses should stop ¼ in. shy of the curb so that water can run freely along the sides. The vertical leg of each piece of step-flashing should extend up high enough so it will be protected from rain by *curb caps;* the horizontal leg should extend under the shingles at least 4 in. As with all flashing, avoid nailing in the channel where water will run. Rather, nail overlapping pieces of step-flashing to the curb only and high enough so the nails will also be protected by curb caps. If necessary, trim the last (uppermost) pieces of step-flashing so they don't extend beyond the curb.

Install the head flashing by slipping its upper flange under the next full course of shingles above and pressing the head flashing snug to the curb. Attach the head flashing to the curb with one screw or nail at each corner. Then install a strip of building paper—or a second strip of self-adhering membrane—over the head flashing's flange before shingling over it. *Note:* Stop the flashing strip and shingles 2½ in. to 4 in. above the skylight curb, so there is a clear expanse of metal to clear leaves and accelerate runoff.

Installing cladding (curb caps) is the last step. These pieces cover and seal the tops of apron and side (step-) flashing and, on some models, the top of the head flashing as well. Follow your skylight's installation guide religiously. In some fixed models, the head flashing is the last piece to go on, covering the upper ends of the side cladding pieces. Details vary, but caps snap or screw on. *Note:* Better-quality units have self-sticking foam gaskets that are applied to the top of the curb before the caps are installed, which reduces air and dust infiltration.

Once the unit's mounting brackets are screwed to the sheathing, wrap the curb with building paper or self-adhering membrane as described in the text. (Note: Because rain began falling during this photo session, the curb wasn't wrapped until later.) Here, the apron's bottom flange overlays the shingles below.

Working from the bottom up, apply L-shaped step flashing along the side. Each overlaps the one below and is nailed with a single nail to the side of the curb. The last pieces of step-flashing slide up under the head flashing. When all the step-flashing is placed, counterflashing strips fit down over them, sealing the unit.

Slip the flange of the head flashing under adjacent shingles, and then press the head flashing snug to the curb, attaching it with one screw or nail at each corner.

Skylight Cladding

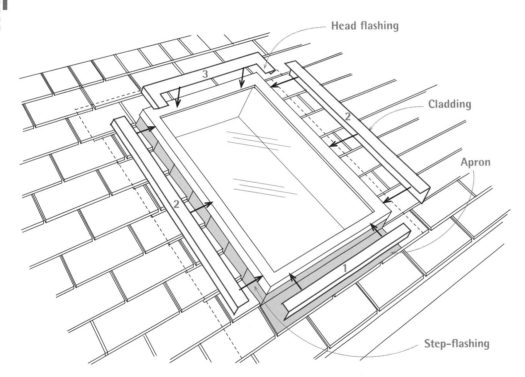

Cladding covers and seals the top legs of apron and step-flashing and—on some operable models—it covers the head flashing as well. Read installation instructions closely. Numbers on the cladding indicate the installation sequence.

Finish off with a couple more tasks. To reflect light, lightwells should be covered with drywall and painted a light color. Insulate around the lightwells to reduce heat loss and condensation. Because condensation is common around sky-lights, cover the lightwell with water-resistant (WR) drywall, often called *greenboard* for its color. Stiffen the well's outside corners with metal *cornerbeads*.

7 Exteriors

The exterior wall of a house is a multi-layered membrane, weatherproofing the house much the way a roof does. In addition to protecting underlying elements from damage by sun and wind, the exterior intercepts and directs water away from the underlying sheathing and framing. The visible exterior layer consists of siding and trim. Beneath the siding, ideally, is either building paper or plastic housewrap, which is relatively water repellent. In addition, flashings seal transitions from one material to another or redirect water around potential dams, such as window and door headers, vent fans, and outdoor outlets. Finally, various sealants fill gaps, adhere materials, or cut air infiltration. Of course, windows and doors are exterior elements, too. But as "openings" in the exterior, they are the principal subjects of Chapter 6.

Although drain gutters may be considered part of the roof, they are discussed at the end of this chapter because gutters "attach to" and protect the exterior. Gutters also direct water away from foundations, thus reducing moisture there and mold in basements and crawl spaces while preventing excess water from undermining foundations.

As with other building systems, maintenance is crucial. Each autumn after the leaves have fallen and each spring, clean gutters and downspouts; if needed, do this more often to keep them flowing freely. Every year, survey and recaulk building seams as needed. Paint or stain wood siding periodically. Trim trees and shrubs so they don't retain moisture next to the siding or restrict air circulation. Slope the soil away from the foundation to help direct water away. Adjust lawn sprinklers so they don't spray siding.

It still takes a skilled eye to install siding. For this job, pneumatic nailers, as shown, have largely replaced hammers and drill drivers.

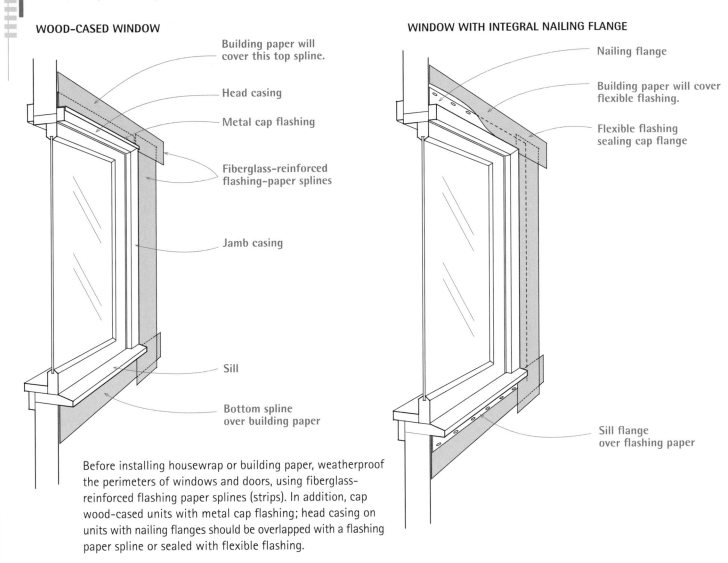

WOOD-CASED WINDOW

Building paper will cover this top spline.

Head casing

Metal cap flashing

Fiberglass-reinforced flashing-paper splines

Jamb casing

Sill

Bottom spline over building paper

WINDOW WITH INTEGRAL NAILING FLANGE

Nailing flange

Building paper will cover flexible flashing.

Flexible flashing sealing cap flange

Sill flange over flashing paper

Before installing housewrap or building paper, weatherproof the perimeters of windows and doors, using fiberglass-reinforced flashing paper splines (strips). In addition, cap wood-cased units with metal cap flashing; head casing on units with nailing flanges should be overlapped with a flashing paper spline or sealed with flexible flashing.

Weather Barriers

No matter how well siding is installed, sooner or later water will work its way behind. Typically this happens when storms drive rain into building seams or gaps around doors or windows. But water can also be drawn inward and even upward by capillary action before trickling down behind siding. For these reasons, builders protect exterior sheathing with building paper (15-lb. building paper is most common) or plastic housewraps such as Tyvek® or R-Wrap® to repel water.

Both building paper and plastic housewrap do a good job of reducing air infiltration. That is, both are permeable enough to allow excessive moisture behind the siding to escape, and both are sufficiently water repellent to protect sheathing from wind-driven rain. Bottom line: It doesn't matter whether you use building paper or housewrap, as long as it's correctly installed and conforms to local building codes, which may require

that they are compatible with finish materials. For example, beneath stucco, many building codes require a double layer of Grade D kraft paper or a fortified paper such as Fortifiber's Super Jumbo Tex® 60 Minute.

Typically, this weatherproofing membrane is installed after windows and doors have been installed and their perimeters weatherproofed with fiberglass-reinforced flashing paper. As shown in "Wood-cased window," above, building paper overlays *cap flashing* and fits under the *sill flashing*. Cap flashing, also called *head flashing*, is especially important because it redirects water that might otherwise dam behind a door or window head casing, leading to stains and mold on interior surfaces, swollen sashes, peeling paint, and rot.

Replacing all siding, flashing, and building paper is the surest way correct such water-related damage, but if that's not in your budget, retrofitting flashing around individual windows and doors may do the trick. In that case, cut back the siding far enough around the perimeter of the door or window to install 6-in.-wide flashing paper, as described next.

INSTALLING BUILDING PAPER

Installation techniques for housewrap and building paper are much the same; in this chapter, both materials are often referred to generically as *building paper.*

Before starting, survey the sheathing and knock down protruding nail heads and wood slivers that could puncture the paper and admit water.

Installation is two-person job, especially if you're working with 9-ft.-wide rolls of Tyvek. As one person unrolls the material, the other aligns and staples it. Start at the bottom of the wall, overhanging the bottom edge of the sheathing by about 1 in. Position the building paper, tack an upper corner in place, roll out about 8 ft., and raise or lower the roll till the edge of the building paper is roughly parallel to the bottom edge of the sheathing. When it's in position, staple the paper every 16 in. along the edges and every 24 in. in the field; use ¼-in. or 5⁄16-in. staples. Thereafter, roll out 3 ft. to 4 ft. at a time, stapling as you go. Trim the 1 in. overhang later.

As you roll out the building paper, make sure it lies flat to the sheathing. Otherwise, puckers can elevate the siding or trim applied over them, compromising weather tightness. Typically, the person holding the roll maintains a slight tension on the building paper to prevent puckers. Also, take care to avoid tearing the membrane while handling and stapling it—more of a problem with paper than with plastic housewrap, which stretches.

Overlapping and taping seams. Overlap vertical end seams by 4 in. to 6 in.; overlap horizontal seams 6 in. to 8 in. As you work up the wall, applying courses of building paper, upper courses should always overlay those below so any water that gets behind the siding is directed out and down, away from the sheathing. Building paper should also overlay any flashing, especially cap flashing over doors and windows.

Seal building-paper seams, tears, and punctures with seam tape; smooth down the tape to make sure it adheres well. If you're installing plastic housewrap, use a seam tape recommended by the manufacturer. If you tear building paper, just staple a patch of the same material over it and apply caulking over the top edge. Last, install siding as soon as possible after installing the building paper because wind can lift and stretch it, especially plastic housewraps.

To weatherproof windowsills, fold flashing paper strips into the rough opening, staple the paper down, and apply caulking. When the window is installed, its sill will compress the caulk, creating a positive seal. Tuck building paper or housewrap up under sill flashing.

Corners and rough openings. Take special pains with corners. Although a 4-in. overlap is often adequate for corners, you'll be safer to overlap outside corners by 1 ft. In addition, many builders reinforce corners with a self-adhering flexible flashing to keep water out should corner boards or siding gap. To prevent the material's bunching in inside corners—a common problem with building paper—use a straight furring strip to press the paper into the corner before stapling it. That done, tape the corner seams immediately—before wind has a chance to lift the paper.

Builders installing plastic housewrap usually roll it right over rough openings (ROs) for windows and doors, cutting an *X* in the middle of the opening and folding the housewrap into the sides of the framing. Well, that method can't hurt. But it's doubtful that it truly waterproofs the opening. If you're installing metal windows, maybe a layer of housewrap will isolate the moisture that condenses on cold metal. But if flashing paper is correctly installed about the perimeter of the window or door, water shouldn't enter the RO in the first place.

INSTALLING FLASHING PAPER

Flashing paper is available in several forms, the most convenient being fiberglass-reinforced rolls either 6 in. or 9 in. wide. (These strips are sometimes called felt splines.) There's also a plethora

After installing a wood–cased window, carefully caulk its jamb edges and overlap those edges about halfway with flashing paper strips.

Before installing jamb casing, run another bead of caulk atop the flashing paper.

of peel-and-stick flexible flashings; but because they're expensive, they tend to be used mainly as cap flashing for the tops of doors and windows. Foil-faced flexible flashings like Polyken® Foil-astic, for example, adhere aggressively and seal head joints so water can't back up behind them.

Uncased windows are commonly used in renovation when it's desirable to install casing that matches an existing style. Since precased units offer a limited range of casing styles, many builders install uncased windows and buy appropriate casing from a local mill.

Flash the rough sill before installing an uncased window. Tuck the paper into the kerf at the bottom of the sill (if there is a kerf) or fold the paper into the RO, caulk its edge, and set the sill onto it. This provides an unbreachable seal, and apron casing or siding will cover the edge of the paper later.

To seal side jambs, consider the double-caulking method shown above. Caulk each jamb edge, embed a flashing-paper spline in the caulk, and then run another bead of caulk atop the spline before installing the jamb casing. This caulk-and-spline sandwich stops infiltration effectively. Finally, caulk the edge of the head jamb before installing the head casing, but do not insert a spline between the head jamb and the casing—that could direct water behind the head casing.

After the window is cased, add the (metal) cap flashing over the head casing. Before installing flashing paper over metal flashing, careful

builders first caulk the upper flange of the flashing. This will prevent water that gets under the siding from wicking back up under the paper when it hits the window head. This is especially important with stucco siding, which is water permeable and often collects water between the stucco and the building paper. Chapter 6 offers more specifics about cap flashing.

Should jamb flashing go over or under the building paper covering the sheathing? It doesn't really matter because the strip flashing is extra protection. But under the windowsill, leave the lower edge of the flashing spline unstapled so it can overlay the building paper or housewrap below.

Windows and doors with integral nailing flanges require slightly different detailing. If the flanges are metal, apply fiberglass-reinforced flashing paper along the bottom and sides of the RO first. Then apply a bead of exterior caulk around the perimeter of the paper—close to the edges of the opening—and set the unit over the flashing paper. Position and shim the unit; then nail or screw through the flanges, into the sheathing. Install cap flashing (some units have an integral cap flashing) over the head of the unit, caulk its upper flange; then install flexible flashing over that cap flange. Building paper above will overlay the flexible flashing. *Note:* Most flanged windows don't have casing per se. Unlike wood-cased windows, flanged units have jambs that protrude above the surface of the sheathing, so siding (or casing) is butted to the sides of these protruding jambs.

Exterior Trim

In appearance, exterior trim is sometimes ornate and complex, but its basic function is to cover critical building seams.

GENERAL PREPARATION

Exterior trim can be applied in many different ways, depending on the design of the house and the type of siding. For wood shingles or clapboards, use trim boards that are thicker than the siding, and apply trim to the sheathing before putting up the siding. For flat shiplap and board-and-batten sidings, apply trim boards over the siding. In general, try to use the same materials and installation methods that were used on the house originally.

Solid-wood exterior trim should be a rot-resistant species such as redwood, cedar, or hard pine and sufficiently dry to avoid shrinkage, cupping, and checking. For those reasons, avoid sugar pine, knotty pine, hemlock, fir, and the like. If you'll be painting the trim, you may find it cost effective to use finger-jointed trim stock fabricated from shorter lengths of high-grade wood. Such stock is widely available and can be durable if you keep it sealed with paint. For best results, specify vertical-grain heartwood grade because it

Prime all faces and edges of exterior trim and siding, including the back faces. Back priming is especially important because moisture trapped between back faces and sheathing can lead to paint or sealer failure, cupping or—in extreme cases—structural rot. After cutting trim or siding, be sure to prime the cut edges as well.

resists decay, holds paint well, and is the most stable dimensionally. *Caution:* If this trim is allowed to absorb moisture, its finger joints may separate.

BACK-PRIMING AND PAINTING

Apply primer to all faces and edges of exterior wood (and engineered wood) siding and trim, including the back faces. Back-priming is critically important because wood will cup (edges warping up) when the sun dries out the exposed front face, while the back unexposed face retains moisture. The greater the moisture differential between front and back faces, the more likely the cupping.

While cutting trim or siding, keep a can of primer and a cheap brush nearby to seal the ends after every cut; unprimed end grain can absorb a lot of moisture. (It's especially easy to forget to prime cut edges when you're using preprimed trim.) Ideally, apply at least two top coats of acrylic latex paint after priming to seal trim and siding. If you want stained or clear-finished trim or siding, use cedar or heart redwood.

ATTACHING TRIM

As a rule, for best attachment, secure exterior trim to framing. In those rare instances where you have only sheathing to nail to, angle the nail so that it will be less likely to pull out.

Choosing attachers. Pick a nail meant for exteriors. If you'll be using a transparent finish, making nail heads visible, stainless-steel nails are the premier choice; though expensive, they won't

PRO TIP

Apply caulk around rough openings, rather than to the back of window or door casings. If you caulk the back of the casing instead, you're more likely to get sticky fingers while handling the unit. *Caution:* Positioning and shimming windows and doors may break caulk seals, so you should recaulk the perimeter once you've secured the unit.

Eaves Trim

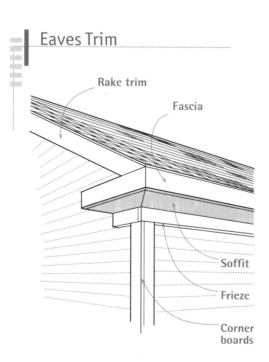

Rake trim

Fascia

Soffit

Frieze

Corner boards

Fascia, soffit, and frieze boards are collectively called the eaves trim.

rust. Aluminum nails won't stain but are somewhat more brittle and more likely to bend. Galvanized nails are the most popular because they're economical, stain minimally, and grip well. Many nail types (including stainless) also come in colors matched to different wood types—cedar, redwood, and so on. Ring-shank nails hold best.

For stained exteriors, some contractors prefer galvanized finish or casing nails because their heads are smaller and less visible. Box nails are a good compromise. Their larger heads hold better than finish nails, yet their shanks are smaller than those of common nails, making box nails less likely to split wood. There are also "splitless" siding nails that come with preblunted points to minimize splits. (The blunt point smashes through wood fibers, rather than wedging them apart.)

Where trim is exposed—say, at cap trim atop a half wall—and you want maximum grip, use stainless-steel trim-head screws instead of nails.

Pneumatic nailers. Most pros use pneumatic nailers to attach exterior trim. Using a finish nailer with galvanized nails allows you to tack up trim exactly where you want it. Anyone who has spent time trying to simultaneously hold and nail a 16-ft. corner board in place while balancing on a ladder will appreciate this tool. Nailers also drive nails quickly and accurately, reducing splits and eliminating errant hammer blows that mar trim. After setting the trim with finish nails, you can always can go back and hand nail with headed nails to secure the trim further. Or you can use headed siding nails in the nailer.

Nailing schedules. To face-nail nominal 1-in. trim (actual thickness, ¾ in.), use 8d box nails spaced every 16 in. Nail both edges of the trim board to prevent cupping, placing nails no closer than ½ in. to the edge. If the trim goes over siding, say, at corners, use 8d to 10d box nails. To draw board edges to each other, use 6d nails spaced every 12 in., and drive them in a slight angle. If you'll be painting the trim, also caulk this joint or glue it using an exterior urethane glue, such as Gorilla Glue®.

Engineered Trim: A Primer

Just as engineered lumber revolutionized structural materials, there's now an engineered trim rated for exteriors. Many such trim products are perfectly straight, flat, and factory primed on all six sides. If you're accustomed to working with wood, engineered trim requires getting used to, and the jury is still out on its long-term stability and durability, especially that of the hardboards. Here's an overview of types:

▶ **Laminated veneer lumber** (LVL) is made from thin wood veneers glued so the grain runs in the same direction, faced on one side with a medium-density overlay (MDO) of resin-impregnated paper. LVL trim is available in 1-in. and 1¼-in. (5/4) thicknesses; in standard widths from 4 in. to 12 in., in 2-in. increments; and in standard lengths of 16 ft. and 20 ft. It's easy to cut, drill, nail, and handle, and its MDO face paints wonderfully. However, LVL is expensive. Clear Lam® is one well-known brand.

▶ **Hardboard, fiberboard, or wood-fiber composite** is fashioned from wood chips steamed, pressed, and glued. There are many brands in this category, including TrimCraft®, MiraTEC®, PrimeTrim®, ChoiceTrim®, and ProTrim®, and product features vary greatly. Composites tend to be available in 1-in. and 1¼-in. thicknesses, in standard widths of 4 in. to 12 in., and in 16-ft. standard lengths. Some are primed on all sides, some not; some have MDO-like paper facing, some not—so check with your distributor.

Hardboard sidings have had widespread problems with moisture retention, swelling, and degradation, so hardboard-trim makers have worked hard to improve their products. That noted, however, take pains to prime all sides and the cut edges. Drive corrosion-resistant nails just flush to the trim surface; nails driven deeper may need caulk to keep out moisture. Last, gap butt joints ⅛ in. to allow expansion; then caulk and paint the trim ASAP.

▶ **Fiber-cement trim** is wood fiber mixed with Portland cement and sand, and it's virtually indestructible. Few people would mistake it for wood, but it's rot, insect, and fire resistant; strong; lightweight; and very stable. HardiTrim® is available in thicknesses from ⅞₆ in. to 1 in.; in widths of 4 in., 6 in., 8 in., and 12 in.; and in lengths of 10 ft. and 12 ft. Nail it with galvanized nails; cut it with a carbide-tipped blade, always wearing goggles and a dust mask.

Preassemble corner boards, soffit-and-fascia boards, and other exterior trim on the ground whenever possible. The joined pieces will be tight and square, even if the framing and sheathing behind them isn't.

▶ **TIP 1.** Join trim boards on the ground, especially in these situations: The joints are complex, the heights are daunting, the house framing is out of square, and/or the boards are long and unwieldy. To do this most easily, place the trim stock on sawhorses to shape, assemble, and prime it. The resulting joined pieces will be a little heavier to raise than single pieces, but the assembly will be straight and crisp, even if the framing isn't. Use an exterior glue such as Gorilla Glue and 6d galvanized box nails to draw the boards tight.

▶ **TIP 2.** If your trim run is longer than individual boards, join the boards with bevel joints, which won't show wood shrinkage as obviously as butt joints. When using beveled joints on vertical boards—say, corner boards—make the top bevel slant down, away from the building, so water can't collect. Last, stagger trim joints by at least 32 in. so they'll be less obvious.

About nail heads. Taking the time to line up nail heads makes the job look neater. For example, when nailing up jamb casing, use a combination square to align nail pairs. If you're putting up a long piece of trim that runs perpendicular to studs, snap chalklines onto the building paper beforehand so that you'll know stud positions for nailing. If the trim will be painted, take the time to set the nail heads slightly below the surface, using a flathead punch. Then use exterior wood filler to fill the holes. If you don't set the heads slightly, they may later protrude as the wood shrinks, compromising the paint membrane and admitting water. On larger jobs, carpenters are usually expected to set nail heads. Painters fill and paint them.

EAVES TRIM

Because eaves trim is often complex and can impact framing, roofing, ventilation, and the house's aesthetic integrity, draw a cross-section of it as early as possible.

There is no single correct way to construct the eaves, but the boxed eaves on the facing page are a good place to start. First, a fascia board that overhangs a soffit by ⅜ in. to ½ in. enables you to hide rafter irregularities—rafters are rarely perfectly straight or cut equally long. Second, that overhang accommodates a rabbeted fascia–soffit joint, which protects the outer soffit edge, even if the wood shrinks slightly. Third, if you rabbet out the back edge of a frieze board or build it out using blocks, the frieze will conceal the top edge of the siding. A built-out frieze also creates an inconspicuous space to install an eave vent.

Ventilation channels at eaves allow air to flow up under the roof and exit at ridge or gable-end vents. This airflow is beneficial because it lowers

attic temperatures and helps remove excess moisture from the house, thus mitigating mold, ice dams, and a host of other problems. To keep insects out, soffits need screening. In a wide soffit, there's plenty of room for screened vents in the middle. In a narrower soffit, you may need to leave a ¾-inch space at the front of the soffit or at its back, hidden behind a built-out frieze board.

If the house has exposed rafter tails rather than soffits, cut down the blocking between rafters so air can flow over the top. Again, staple fine mesh screen or corrugated vent strips behind ventilation passages to keep insects out.

WATER TABLE

The water table is horizontal trim running around the base of a building below the siding, and not all houses have it. Depending mostly on regional preferences, the water table takes several forms. In the West, it typically looks like windowsill ears (the parts that stick out) and is often used to separate different types of siding materials, such as shiplap siding from wood shingles above. This strip-like water table usually runs continuously around the building and is mitered at the corners. It often has a rabbeted heel, which fits over the top of the wood siding below, and a

Water-table trim often finishes off the bottom of a wall and provides a level base for the first course of siding. To forestall rot, cap the water table with metal or vinyl flashing before installing the siding.

beveled top, which is overlain with shingles or clapboards.

In the East, water tables are also called splashboards; they usually are 1-in. boards 8 in. to 12 in. wide and may be capped to shed water. Splashboards are most common in wet regions, where roof runoff often splashes back along the base of a house. (Some primal carpenter may have reasoned it would be easier to replace a single rotted board than to disturb several courses of siding or that a thicker board would simply last longer.)

Whatever shape of water table you prefer, flash its top with a metal drip-edge that extends at least ½ in. beyond the face of the board. The section where corner boards sit atop the water board is especially rot prone. Prime and paint the boards thoroughly.

CORNER BOARDS

Corner boards are usually 1-in. boards butted together. Siding is then butted against them, making an attractive and weathertight corner.

Not all buildings have horizontal trim below the bottom of the siding. For example, the first (bottom) course of shingles is often doubled and

overhangs the sheathing slightly. In that case, run corner boards 2 in. to 3 in. below the bottom edge of the sheathing; then, after you nail up the first course of shingles, trim the corner board ends level to the shingles' butts. If the house has a water table or splashboard, measure from its top edge up to the underside of the soffit to determine the length of the corner boards.

If you're installing shingles, whose overlapping courses have a higher profile than clapboards, use 5/4 corner boards, which are full 1 in. thick. To give the illusion that corner boards are the same width at each side, rip down the overlapped board by the thickness of the stock. And for a crisp, straight corner, preassemble corner boards before installing them, as explained earlier.

Occasionally, corner boards are nailed over siding. This can be a problem because nails driven through the trim are likely to split the thinner siding. Besides, corner boards can't seal well if nailed over an irregular surface. This method was commonly used on Victorian homes with flat, shiplap siding. Careful nailing and liberal doses of caulk will help ensure a weathertight seal. To minimize splits, predrill the board nails.

PRO TIP

Trim on older buildings is rarely level or parallel. Thus new trim may look better if it's installed slightly out of level, so that it aligns visually with what's already there. For example, when stretching a chalkline to indicate the bottom of the water table, start level; then raise or lower the line till it looks right in relation to nearby windowsills and the like. Once the chalkline looks more or less parallel to existing trim, snap it on the building paper, and extend it to corner boards.

Boxed Eave: Detail 1

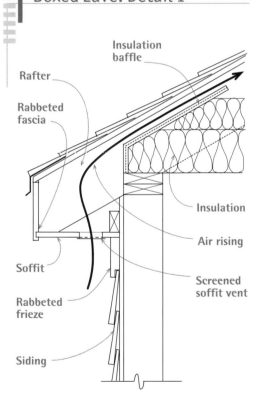

A strip of continuous screen in the soffit allows air to circulate into the attic. The rabbeted frieze conceals and protects the top of the siding.

Boxed Eave: Detail 2

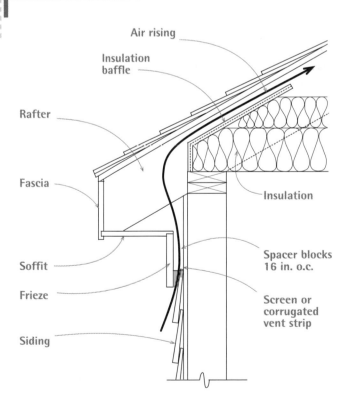

You can create ventilation channels behind the frieze by spacing it out ³/4 in., using blocks spaced every 16 in. on center. This also conceals the top of the siding.

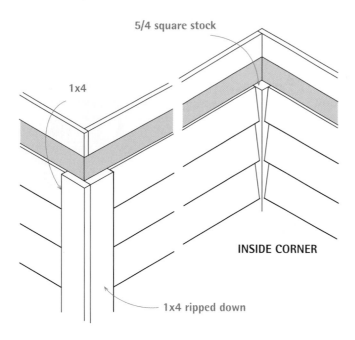

5/4 square stock

1x4

INSIDE CORNER

1x4 ripped down

OUTSIDE CORNER

Butt siding to the corner boards to avoid complex miter cuts. In outside corners, rip down the overlapped board by the thickness of the stock, and both boards will look equally wide.

EPOXY REPAIR

After wire brushing away loose material, inject liquid consolidant into the wood till it becomes saturated. After allowing the consolidant to set, apply the paste–like filler to build up the damaged area.

Use a taping knife to compress and smooth the filler. The galvanized metal tacked to the sill keeps the filler in place until it dries and doubles as a screed strip to which you can level the filler (see the text for more details).

The corner boards described thus far cover outside corners. Inside corners aren't as exposed to weather, so wide boards aren't necessary. Instead, nail 1-in. by 1-in. strips (or 1¼-in. by 1¼-in. strips) to the inside corners, and butt the siding to that. That's much faster than cutting compound miters in the clapboards or interweaving shingles.

REPAIRING EXTERIOR TRIM

Although it may be tempting to rip out exterior trim that's badly weathered or rotten, repair is often a better option if replacement trim would be expensive or difficult to remove. Before deciding either way, survey the extent of the rot and address its cause. Otherwise you're treating only the symptom.

Replacing rotted sections is a good option when the bottom of an otherwise sound trim board has rotted away. Flat and square trim is easier to replace and match than molded trim. Rotted bottoms of corner boards and splashboards are usually easy to cut free and replace, whereas punky doorsills or windowsills are probably best repaired in place, using epoxy, as described in the next section.

Replacing the bottom of a rotted board is straightforward. Draw a line across the face of the board, 6 in. above the bad section. After setting your circular-saw blade to the thickness of the board, use a Speed Square to guide the saw shoe, making a 90° cut. Wear goggles and use an old blade because it may hit nails. The replacement piece should be the same thickness, width, and—preferably—species as the original trim. To join the new section to the old, use a router with a slot-cutting bit to cut a biscuit slot in both board ends. Dry-fit everything, prime all surfaces with epoxy primer, and allow the primer to dry well. Then epoxy the pieces together. Hold the boards in place with a piece of scrap screwed to both. Give the epoxy a day to cure (or whatever the manufacturer suggests), and you're ready to sand and paint.

In-place epoxy repairs are appropriate when the rotted area is relatively small (epoxy is expensive!) and the trim would be difficult or costly to replace. Rotted windowsills or sashes are tough to remove because both are captured by surrounding elements. Epoxy applications vary considerably, so visit the manufacturers' Web sites (try Abatron®, ConServ®, and Advanced Repair Technology®, for example) for specifics or get recommendations at your local home center.

Use a chisel or awl to dislodge loose, crumbling wood. Suck up debris with a shop vacuum. Allow the wood to dry thoroughly before proceeding. Although it's desirable to cut back to solid wood, soft punky wood can often be reinforced by impregnating it with a liquid consolidant. Typically, you'd drill a series of small-diameter holes into the wood and then inject consolidant into them till the wood is clearly saturated. In time, the impregnated wood will become as hard as a rock.

But, for the best bond between the consolidant and the two-part epoxy filler that follows, apply the putty-like filler while the consolidant is still tacky. Avoid getting epoxy on your skin, and by all means wear a respirator mask with replaceable filters when applying or sanding it. After the filler dries and you've sanded it to its final shape, prime and paint it. Though otherwise tough, some epoxies are degraded by UV rays, and whatever original wood remains still needs protection from the elements.

Siding

This section addresses installation of the three most common traditional sidings: wood shingles, clapboards, and stucco. Vinyl and aluminum sidings are cost-effective alternatives to traditional sidings; they're also durable and virtually maintenance-free if correctly installed. But they're normally a whole-house job most efficiently handled by specializing contractors and so aren't further addressed here. Aesthetics are another consideration. Although popular in new construction and renovation, faux-grained vinyl looks phony to traditionalists. If that's your reaction, too, consider untextured sidings, which, when painted, more closely resemble painted wood.

The information that follows assumes that building paper or plastic housewrap covers the wall sheathing and that windows, doors, and exterior trim are already installed.

LAYING OUT WOOD SHINGLES AND CLAPBOARDS

For clapboards and shingles, the two most important parts of the layout are establishing level for the bottom course and varying the exposure of subsequent courses so that they align with door or window trim, if possible. If a leveled water table has already been installed, skip the next section.

Establishing level. If there's no water table on the house (see p. 132), the bottom of the first course of siding typically overhangs the sheathing by ¾ in. to 1 in. Because the bottom edge of sheathing is seldom level, use a laser level or a water level to establish a level base line. Simple tripod-mounted laser levels are relatively inexpensive and offer quick layout over long distances without needing a helper. When set up correctly, they're also quite accurate, usually within ⅛ in. in 100 ft.

Lay out the front of the building first. Pencil in an appropriate siding overhang on one corner board. Then, using the level, transfer that mark to all the other corner boards. When you're done, use a combination square to draw light lines through your pencil marks, across the faces of the corner boards. These lines indicate cut-off lines for the corner boards and the bottom of the first course of siding. To align that first course of siding, stretch a chalkline through the marks and snap it onto the building paper. Or, if you've used housewrap, which won't chalk well, drive a nail into a pencil line at each corner and stretch a taut line between them. Place clapboards or shingle butts slightly above, but not touching, the line so it won't be distorted.

Varying subsequent courses. By aligning siding courses to window and door trim, you can minimize funky-looking notch cuts at door and window

PRO TIP

Epoxy filler can be applied with a putty knife. But this filler is easier to shape to match existing contours by hand—hands protected by latex gloves, that is. Restorationist Tom O'Brien suggests donning three or four pairs of disposable latex gloves at the start of the job and peeling them off as they become gunked up.

Wood siding is pleasant to work with and requires few specialized tools. Though power nailing has largely replaced hand nailing, there's still plenty of hand crafting and fitting to do, such as the shingle shaving shown here.

Aligning Siding Courses

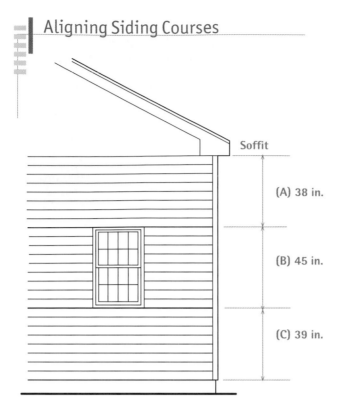

Soffit

(A) 38 in.

(B) 45 in.

(C) 39 in.

For best visual effect, align siding courses with the top and bottom of windows and doors. This may require three separate calculations for exposures, as represented by A, B, and C and explained in the text. Whether installing clapboards or shingles, it's customary to mark course lines lightly on corner boards and then snap chalklines between them.

corners. (But when installing wide-board siding, notch cuts are sometimes unavoidable.) Achieve these alignments by increasing or decreasing the exposure of individual courses. Of course, there are physical restrictions. For example, clapboards must overlap at least 1 in. But as long as exposure adjustments are no more than ¼ in. between courses, they'll look evenly spaced.

The following steps refer to the illustration above:

1. Measure the full height of the wall, from the cutoff at the base of a corner board to the underside of the soffit. Let's say the height is 10 ft. 2 in. (for calculation purposes, 122 in.). Because shingle exposures are customarily 5 in., that wall will have roughly 24 courses.

2. The wall has three windows and a door. Fortunately, their head casings happen to align 84 in. above the base line. This creates three separate areas for which shingle exposures need to be adjusted, as shown in the drawing: (A) from the top of head casings to the soffit, 38 in.; (B) from the top of the window head casing to the bottom of sills, 45 in.; and (C) from the bottom of windowsills to the base line, 39 in. Total: 122 in.

3. Calculating exposure adjustments is easy. Round off each measurement to the nearest increment of 5 in. Then increase or decrease the shingle exposure accordingly. Thus area A yields a 4¾-in. exposure (38÷8 = 4¾); area B is exactly 5 in. (45÷9); and area C is roughly 4⅞ in.

The easiest way to keep track of such measurements and adjustments is by penciling them onto a *story pole,* a long straight board (a 1×2 is fine) whose length equals the distance between the top of the water table (if any) to the underside of the soffit or frieze. First mark the tops and bottoms of window and door casings onto the story pole, then the adjusted course heights between.

As you work around the house, align the bottom of the story pole to each corner board and transfer marks from the pole to each board. If the house has windows set at varying heights, story-pole marks will better align with casing on some walls than on others; give precedence to the house's most prominent facade. Where courses just won't line up with casing joints, notch the siding around them.

INSTALLING WOOD SHINGLES

Before you start shingling, make sure that windows and doors are correctly flashed, that sheathing is covered with building paper—most pro shinglers prefer 15-lb. felt paper—and that exterior trim is installed.

Materials. For best results, use No. 1 grade cedar shingles. For a standard 5-in. shingle exposure, figure four bundles per *square* (100 sq. ft.). Always inspect the visible shingles on a bundle to make sure they're uniformly thick (⅜ in.) at butt ends, of varying widths (on average, 6 in. to

CUTTING SHINGLES CROSS-GRAIN

Cross-grain cutting is a snap with shingles. Score them with a utility knife...

12 in.), knot free, and reasonably straight grained. Installing shingles requires a lot of trimming, so you don't want to be fighting knots and wavy grain. Shingle butts should also be cut cleanly and squarely across, not angled or ragged. Send back bundles that look inferior or contain mostly narrow shingles.

To save a little money, however, you might want to use No. 2 shingles for the bottom layer of doubled starter courses. In this case, order one bundle per 50 lineal (lin.) ft. of wall. Typically, the starter course of shingles along the bottom is doubled, with vertical joints between the two shingle layers offset by at least 1½ in.

Also, pick up a bundle to see how dry it is. Relatively wet shingles are fine, as long as they're good quality, but they'll shrink. In fact, most shingles shrink. Though how-to books are fond of telling you to leave a ¼-in. gap between shingles during installation, many shinglers don't bother; unless the shingles are bone-dry, installers assume that all shingles will shrink some.

Use two 1¼-in. galvanized nails or staples per shingle, whatever its width. Because nails must be covered by the course above, place shingle nails in ¾ in. from either edge and 1 in. above the eventual butt line of the course above. Where nails will be visible—say, on interwoven corners or the top course below a window—use siliconized bronze ring-shank nails or stainless-steel nails. Again, 1¼-in. nails are fine, unless you're also nailing through a gypsum layer to reach the sheathing on a fire-rated wall.

Installation. If you've got a water table (see p. 132), set your first course of shingles atop it, even if it's not level. That way you eliminate unsightly gaps along the trim, and it's easy

enough to level the next course of shingles. If there are corner boards, snap chalklines between them to mark shingle courses, and off you go. However, if there are no corner boards, weave shingles at the building corners, alternating shingle edges every other course. This requires more skill and patience than just butting shingles to the boards but produces corners that are both handsome and weather-tight. Weave the corners first; then nail up the shingles in between. Because the starter course overhangs the bottom of the sheathing ½ in. to 1 in., measure down that amount at each corner, using a laser level to establish level. After establishing the correct exposure, as described above, shingle up each corner. As you work up the wall, snap a chalkline from corner to corner to line up shingle butts.

As you did on the first course, offset the vertical shingle joints at least 1½ in. between courses. If you have a partner, you'll find it easier if each of you works from a corner toward the middle. Only the last shingle will need to be fitted.

When you weave the corners first, leveling the shingle courses in between is largely a matter of snapping chalklines between shingle butts at either end of the wall. If you snap the chalkline slightly high, as shown, the shingle butts will cover the chalk.

Wood Shingle Details

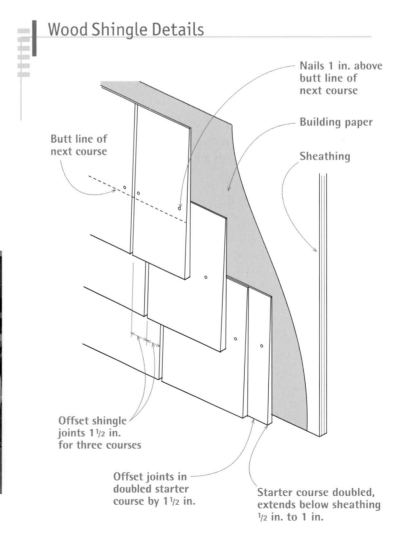

Butt line of next course

Nails 1 in. above butt line of next course

Building paper

Sheathing

Offset shingle joints 1½ in. for three courses

Offset joints in doubled starter course by 1½ in.

Starter course doubled, extends below sheathing ½ in. to 1 in.

... and snap them sharply over your knee. Use a cordless jigsaw for complex cuts around windowsills and exterior light fixtures.

Fit shingles closely to window and door casings. The top of the shingle course under a windowsill should butt squarely to the sill. Because this course needs to be shortened and will be susceptible to splits, caulk the back sides. It's also wise to caulk the shortened top course of shingles under the eaves. Ideally, the tops of those shingles will also be protected by a rabbeted-out or built-up frieze.

If you need to angle cut shingle butts for use along gable-end walls and dormers or need to angle cut shingle tops to fit under rake trim, use an adjustable bevel to capture the roof angle and transfer it to shingles. Such angle cuts are best

The Art of Weaving Corners

To weave shingles tightly on corners, nail them up, and shave them in place. As you place each shingle, use a torpedo level to level its butt, overlapping the adjacent wall by about 1 in., and nail the shingle down. Despite using only two nails per shingle in other places, it's okay to use three or four here because you don't want the shingles turning while you're shaving them down. As before, use stainless-steel, brass, or bronze nails wherever the nails will be exposed; ring-shanked nails hold best.

Use a utility knife to rough trim the excess. Then continue with a block plane till the shingle edge is almost flush to the shingle it overlaps on the adjacent wall. To prevent splits and to draw overlapping shingles tight, drill a pilot hole in ¼ in. from the edge and up 2 in. from the butt of the shingle. A push drill (also called a Yankee drill) is perfect for the task. Alternate the edge that overlaps, from course to course.

Because there's not room to use a block plane on the bottom and top course of corners, use a cordless jigsaw to precut shingle edges or butts. And because the top course of shingles will be quite short (about 4 in. long) and susceptible to splits, caulk the back sides with a durable urethane caulk, in addition to nailing.

Alternate shingles overlap at the corners. Nail each shingle up. Then use a utility knife to trim all but ¼ in. of excess, before finishing up with a block plane. Stop planing when the edge is barely proud of (above) the oncoming shingle. On the top course, where a block plane won't fit, use a jigsaw to precut the shingle to the correct angle.

PRO TIP

Some pros align shingles by tacking up a straight 1×2 for each course and resting shingle butts on it. This allows nailing to go a bit faster, but you must still snap a chalkline or measure up from the bottom course periodically to level the 1×2. Most pros prefer to snap a chalkline and then barely cover that line with the shingle butts so the chalk doesn't show.

Draw the shingle corners together with a single nail driven through the overlapping shingle. To prevent splits, predrill with a push drill.

Because the nails joining corners or finishing the top course of shingles will be exposed, use either stainless-steel, brass, or bronze nails at those junctures.

made all at once, on the ground, using a table saw. To notch shingles around windowsill ears and the like, use a cordless jigsaw. Finally, leave a ½-in. gap beneath dormer-wall shingles and adjacent roofing; otherwise, shingles resting directly on roofing can wick moisture and rot.

INSTALLING CLAPBOARDS

The following discussion assumes that you've read this chapter's earlier sections on layout and that you've installed door and window flashing, building paper, and exterior trim. It also assumes that the building has corner boards that you can butt the clapboards to. Otherwise, the clapboard corners will require compound-miter joints, which is a considerable amount of work.

Materials. Clapboards are a beveled siding milled from redwood, red cedar, or spruce; for best results, use Grade A or better. Preprimed finger-jointed clapboards are a cost-effective alternative, joining shorter lengths of high-quality wood. Clapboards come in varying widths and thickness, but all are nominally 1-in.-thick boards that have been planed down. Thus a 1×6 is actually ⅜ in. thick (at the butt) by 5¼ in. wide; a 1×8 is actually ½ in. by 7½ in., and so on. Traditional clapboards come in varying lengths, whereas finger-jointed products are manufactured in 16-ft. lengths; all are sold by the lineal foot.

To estimate the amount you need, calculate the square footage of your walls, less window and door openings. Then consult the table below, which assumes ½ in. of overlap for 1×4 clapboards and 1-in. to 1⅛-in. overlap for all other sizes. It also factors in 5 percent waste. Order preprimed (or prestained) clapboards. Prepriming seals out moisture, saves tons of time otherwise lost to priming and waiting for primer to dry, and keeps the job moving. You will need a small amount of primer on hand to touch up newly cut ends.

Clapboard Needed to cover 100 Sq. Ft.

CLAPBOARD SIZE	LINEAL FEET
1x4	440
1x6	280
1x8	200
1x10	160

REPLACING Shingles

If you split a shingle while installing it (or if you need to remove shingles to install an exhaust vent for a fan), break out the shards, hammer down the nail heads, and replace the shingle. To remove a few damaged shingles on an otherwise intact wall, use a shingle ripper (also called a slate hook), shown in the photo on p. 121. Slide its hooked head up under surrounding the shingles till you can feel it hook around a nail shank. Then hammer down on the tool's handle till the hook cuts through the shank. To avoid damaging the replacement shingles as you drive them into place, hold a scrap block under the shingle butt to cushion the hammer blows.

Nails. Buy 5d stainless-steel, ring-shank siding nails, whether you're painting the clapboard or not. True, stainless-steel nails cost four or five times as much as galvanized nails, but that premium buys you peace of mind. Galvanized nails are fine 99 percent of the time. But if their coating breaks off, the nail will rust. Moreover, the tannins in cedar and redwood can chemically react with galvanization, which causes staining. Same with galvanized staples. For every 1,000 lin. ft. of siding, buy 5 lb. of 5d nails.

Installation. Worth repeating: Standard clapboard exposure is 4 in. for 1×6 clapboards (actual width, 5¼ in.), but you may want to vary that exposure by ¼ in. or less between courses to help align the clapboards with the window and door casings.

The first course of clapboards typically sits atop a water table. First flash the top of the water table with metal drip-edge to forestall rot. To establish the correct pitch for that first course, rip a 1¼-in.-wide beveled starter strip from the top of a clapboard. (Save the 4-in.-wide bottom waste rip for the top of a wall.) Tack the strip atop the water table, and you're ready to nail up the first course. The water table may not be level, but that's okay; better to avoid a noticeable gap between a level first course and an off-level water table. In that case, take pains to level the second and all successive courses.

Start at one corner board and work all the way across the wall, nailing clapboards to each stud center they cross. All butt joints should be square cut and centered over a stud so that the ends of both boards can be securely nailed.

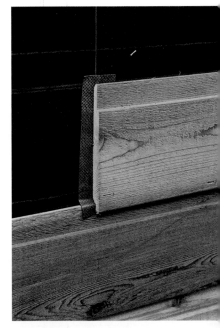

Clapboards and other horizontal lapped sidings are less likely to cup if nailed to stud centers—here, indicated by the vertical red chalkline. Install strips of building paper or waterproofing membrane behind such joints to keep water out.

Clapboard Details

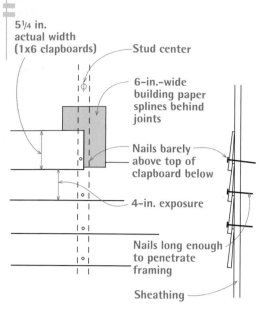

5¼ in. actual width (1x6 clapboards)

Stud center

6-in.-wide building paper splines behind joints

Nails barely above top of clapboard below

4-in. exposure

Nails long enough to penetrate framing

Sheathing

Position clapboard joints over stud centers. For the most weathertight joints, bevel-cut ends. Note: For clarity in this drawing, building paper between clapboards and sheathing isn't shown.

Homemade Clapboard Gauge

Scribe this line.

To fit clapboards closely to jamb casing, make a gauge from 1-in. stock. Slip the gauge over the clapboard, slide it next to the casing, and mark the casing edge onto the clapboard.

Remember to stagger joints by at least 32 in. To further weatherproof the joints, back them with strips of building paper; the paper overlaps the top of the clapboard beneath by ½ in.

For clean, square cuts, rent or buy a 10-in. radial-arm saw with a 40-tooth or 60-tooth carbide-tipped blade. And be prepared to recut joints. When fitting the second board of a butt joint, leave it a little long till you're satisfied with the joint. If it isn't perfectly square on the first try, you'll have excess to trim.

When butting clapboards to corner boards and jamb casings, use the homemade gauge shown below at left. Using the gauge to hold the clapboard tight to the trim, scribe the cutoff line with a utility knife. Never fit clapboards so tightly to the casing that you need to force them into place: Too tight trim can cause window sashes to bind. Where top courses abut the underside of eave or rake trim, rabbet or build out the trim to receive the top edges of the clapboards, as illustrated on p. 133. Caulk all building joints well with latex acrylic or urethane caulk before nailing up the top course of clapboards.

The Science of Nailing Clapboards

Even though clapboard nailing isn't rocket science, four carpenters will give you five opinions on how to do it. Here's what you need to know:

▶ Place clapboard nails roughly 1¼ in. from the bottom so they don't enter the tip of the clapboard underneath, especially if you're installing 1×8 clapboards or wider. Wide clapboards are particularly likely to split if they are inadvertently nailed at top and bottom.

▶ Nail clapboards to stud centers. For guidance, snap vertical chalklines on the building paper over the stud centers; offset the clapboard butt joints by at least 32 in. Lined-up nails look better, especially if you're using a clear finish.

▶ Carpenters set nails; painters fill and paint them. Setting nails makes painters cranky, and if there are 1,000 to set, painters will miss some.

Rain-Screen Walls

In humid regions where housewrap and back-primed siding are not enough to prevent rotted siding, some builders have retrofitted rain-screen walls to remedy paint failure and soaked sheathing. Basically, rain-screen walls employ furring strips to space clapboards out from the building-paper membrane, allowing air to circulate freely behind the siding and dry it out. The reasoning is sound, and field reports are encouraging.

As sensible as this solution is, it's not for every renovation. Rain screens require careful detailing and a skillful crew. For example, if furring strips raise the siding roughly ⅜ in., existing trim needs to be oversize already (5/4 stock) or built up to compensate for the increased thickness of siding layers. Another option: Home Slicker®, or CedarBreather, a thin layer of nylon mesh, raises siding off the building paper and doesn't need furring strips.

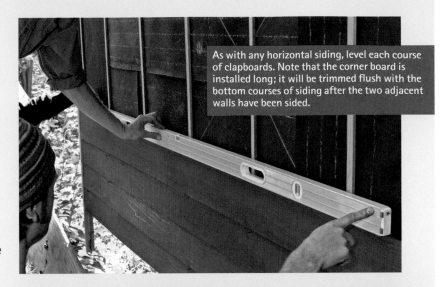

As with any horizontal siding, level each course of clapboards. Note that the corner board is installed long; it will be trimmed flush with the bottom courses of siding after the two adjacent walls have been sided.

Note the rain-screen corner-stop. These clapboards were too thin (⁷⁄₁₆ in., butt end) to miter, and the builder didn't want corner boards. So a clever carpenter fashioned this corner-stop with his table saw. The stop legs are the same thickness as the furring strips affixed to the wall studs. To avoid splits, the corner-stop was predrilled and attached with stainless-steel screws.

Rain-screen walls allow air to circulate behind the siding, thereby allowing its back face to dry thoroughly. Here, thin wood furring strips raise the siding above the building paper; each strip is centered over a stud.

A layer of nylon mesh over the building paper allows better air circulation under wood shingles and siding. (Note that the mesh and building paper overlay the cap flashing below.)

STUCCO REPAIRS

PRO TIP

Don't use plastic housewrap as a membrane beneath stucco. Otherwise, stucco in contact with housewrap will bond to the housewrap, filling its pores and allowing water to pass through it via capillary action. Stucco also contains surfactants (surface-active substances) that reduce the water-shedding qualities of housewrap.

Stuccoing a whole house requires skills that take years to learn, but stucco repairs are well within the ken of a diligent novice. If you spend a few hours watching a stucco job in your neighborhood, you'll pick up useful pointers.

A basic description. Stucco is a cementitious mix applied in several layers to a wire-lath base over wood-frame construction or to a masonry surface such as brick, block, or structural tile. Like plaster, stucco is usually applied in three coats: (1) a base (or scratch) coat approximately ½ in. thick, scored horizontally to help the next coat adhere; (2) a brown coat about ¾ in. thick; and (3) a finish coat (called a dash coat by old-timers) ⅛ in. to ¼ in. thick. For repair work and masonry-substrate work, two-coat stucco is common.

The mix. The mix always contains Portland cement and sand, but it varies according to the amount of lime, pigment, bonders, and other agents, which are described in the following text. See "Stucco Mixes," below, for standard mixes.

The consistency of a mix is easy to recognize but hard to describe. When you cut it with a shovel or a trowel, it should be stiff enough to retain the cut mark yet loose enough so it slumps into a loose patty when dropped from a height of 1 ft. It should never be runny.

Building paper. Stucco is not waterproof. In fact, unpainted stucco will absorb moisture and wick it to the building paper or sheathing underneath. Always assume that moisture will be present under stucco, and apply your building paper accordingly.

Basically, you want to cover the underlying sheathing with two layers of building paper before attaching the metal lath. Two layers of Grade D building paper will satisfy most codes, but you're better off with two layers of a fiberglass-reinforced paper such as Super Jumbo Tex 60 Minute. Although 60-minute paper costs more, it's far more durable. Typically, the stucco sticks to the first layer of paper, exposing it to repeated soakings till it largely disintegrates; the second layer is really the only water-resistant one, so you want it to be as durable as possible.

Take care not to tear the existing paper around the edges of the patch. Tuck the new paper under the old at the top of the patch, overlapping old paper at the sides and bottom of the patch. If the old paper is not intact or the shape of the patch precludes an easy fit, use pieces of reinforced flashing paper as "shingles," slipping them up and under the existing stucco and paper and over the new. Caulk new paper to old at the edges to help keep water out.

Lath. Metal lath reinforces stucco so it's less likely to crack and also mechanically ties the stucco to the building. *Lath* is a general term; it encompasses wire mesh or stucco netting (which looks like chicken wire) and expanded metal lath (heavy, wavy-textured sheets). When nailing up wire mesh, use galvanized furring nails with a furring "button" that goes under the mesh. When you drive these nails in, you thus pinch the wire mesh between the nail head and the button, creating a space behind the mesh, into which the scratch coat oozes, hardens, and keys. *Note:* Don't use aluminum nails, because cement corrodes them. Use about 20 nails or staples per square yard of lath, spacing nails at least every 6 in. Overlap mesh at least 2 in. on vertical joints, and extend it around corners at least 6 in.

Expanded metal lath is a thicker, stronger lath used in situations requiring greater strength—for example, to cover soffits, where you're fighting gravity while applying stucco. That is, expanded metal lath won't sag. It typically comes in 2-ft. by 8-ft. sheets, is somewhat more work to install, and costs more. Expanded metal lath is stapled or nailed up; no need for furring nails because it's self-furring.

The perfect stucco mix is stiff enough to retain a trowel mark yet loose enough to slump into a loose patty when dropped from a height of 1 ft. This mason is using his trowel (left) to load stucco mix onto his hawk, which he'll carry to the wall. With a trowel, he'll apply the mix in sweeping motions.

Stucco Mixes

PORTLAND CEMENT	MASONRY CEMENT	LIME	SAND
1 part	—	¼ to 1 part	3¼ to 4 parts
1 part	1 part	—	3¼ to 4 parts

Applying the brown (second) coat takes a lot of skill. The mason starts with a very irregular scratch coat and builds it up till the surface is flat and within ⅛ in. of its final thickness.

After applying the rough, brown coat with a hand trowel, the mason steel-trowels the surface to make the thickness uniform and the surface relatively flat. After the mortar sets, he'll rough up the surface slightly with a wood- or rubber-faced float.

Base coat. Here's how to apply the base (scratch) coat:

1. Cover the sheathing with building paper and attach the lath.

2. Establish screed strips, which are guides for the stucco's final surface thickness. Screeds can be existing window edges, corner boards, or strips manufactured for this purpose.

3. Mix and trowel on a thick first coat, pressing it to the lath.

4. When the mud has set somewhat, screed it (meaning get it to a relatively uniform thickness) using screed strips as thickness guides.

5. Even out the surface further with a wood- or rubber-surfaced float.

6. Press your fingertips lightly against the surface; when it is dry enough that your fingers no longer sink in, steel trowel the surface. Steel troweling compacts the material, setting it well in the lath and driving out air pockets.

7. Scratch the surface horizontally.

Brown coat. Installing the brown (second) coat requires the most skill, care, and time because this stage flattens the surface and builds up the stucco to within ⅛ in. of its final thickness.

To apply the brown coat, trowel on the stucco, screed it to a relatively uniform thickness, float the surface further, and steel-trowel to improve the uniformity. Then roughen the surface slightly with a wood or rubber float. As the stucco sets up, you will be able to work it more vigorously to achieve an even, sanded texture that will allow the finish texture coat to grab and bond. Do not leave the brown coat with a smooth, hard-troweled surface. Otherwise, the finish coat won't stick well.

Finish coat. The finish coat is about ⅛ in. thick, and textured to match the rest of the building.

Stucco Details

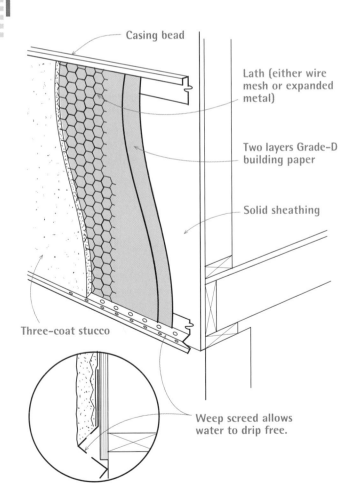

Casing bead

Lath (either wire mesh or expanded metal)

Two layers Grade-D building paper

Solid sheathing

Three-coat stucco

Weep screed allows water to drip free.

When attempting to match an existing texture, you may need to experiment. If at first you don't achieve a good match, scrape off the mud and try again until you find a technique that works. Textures are discussed at the end of this stuccoing section.

Stucco trim. If doors or windows in stucco walls are cased with wood trim, flash their head casings with self-adhering flexible flashing. Metal windows in stucco usually have no casing to dam up water and so need no head flashing; metal windows usually have an integral nailing flange that serves as flashing after being caulked. If you need to cut back stucco siding to repair rot or install a new window, install flexible flashing over the head casing, and install fiberglass-reinforced paper along the sides and under the sill.

Helpful materials. The following materials are particularly useful for repair work and are available from any masonry supplier.

▶ *Weep screed* is a metal strip nailed to the base of exterior walls, providing a straight edge to which you can screed stucco. Because it is perforated, it allows moisture to "weep" or migrate free from the masonry surface, thus allowing it to dry thoroughly after a rain.

Weep screeds are an easy way to make the bottom edge of stucco look crisp and clean. And because the weight of the stucco flattens the screed down against the top of a foundation, the screed provides a positive seal against termites and other pests. (Stucco's tendency to retain moisture makes rot and insect infestation particular problems.) Weep screed is also a good solution for the frequently rotted intersection of stucco walls and porch floors.

Weep screed isn't difficult to retrofit, but you'll need to cut away the base of walls 6 in. to 9 in. high in order to flash the upper edge of

the screed strip properly. Cut the screed with aviation snips, and fasten it with large-head 8d galvanized nails.

▶ *Wire corners* are preformed corners (also called corner aid) that can be fastened loosely over the wire lath with 6d galvanized nails. Set the corner to the finished edge, taking care to keep the line straight and either plumb or level.

▶ *Latex bonders* resemble white wood glue. They are either painted into areas to be patched or mixed into batches of stucco and troweled onto walls. To ensure that the mixture is distributed uniformly, stir the bonder into water before mixing the liquid with the dry ingredients. Reduce the amount of water accordingly, as recommended by the manufacturer.

To ensure that a patch will adhere well, brush bonder full strength all around the edges of the hole or crack you'll fill with new stucco. Merely applying patch stucco without bonder creates a "cold joint," which is likely to fracture. In most cases, you must apply new stucco before the bonder dries; otherwise, the joint won't be as strong, although products such as Thorobond® and Weldcrete® will reemulsify when moistened by the next stucco coat.

▶ *Prepackaged stucco mix* is helpful because it eliminates worry about correct proportions among sand, cement, and plasticizing agents. However, you will need to add bonder to the mix.

▶ *Color-coat pigment* (also known as LaHabra™ color or permanent color top coat), is a pigmented finish coat, available in a limited range of colors. Its principal advantage is its ease of mixing and its depth of color, which is as deep as the finish layer. But precolored top coats usually aren't of much use to renovators because their colors aren't likely to match older colors on a house. Yet, if a house is already painted white, white pigmented stucco will require fewer coats of paint to blend in.

▶ *Masonry paint and primer*, which is alkali resistant, can be used on any new masonry surface. You should still wait at least 2 weeks or 3 weeks for the stucco to "cool off" before painting it. (Follow the manufacturer's recommended wait times.) Use two coats of primer and two coats of finish paint.

The repair. Before repairing damaged areas, first diagnose why the stucco failed. Then determine the extent of the damage by pressing your palms firmly on both sides of the hole or crack. Springy areas should be removed. Continue pressing till you feel stucco that's solidly

Diagnosing STUCCO PROBLEMS

Here are some common symptoms of stucco problems and their probable causes.

▶ **DIAGONAL CRACKS** from the corners of door or window trim indicate a shifting foundation; call a structural engineer.

▶ **CRUMBLING STUCCO** along the base of a wall suggests standing water and probable deterioration of the sheathing. Cut back the damaged area and install a weep screed so water can exit.

▶ **LARGE PATCHES FALLING OFF** suggest faulty flashing, rotted sheathing, or lath that's insufficiently attached. *Note:* If you see a shiny surface beneath a section of stucco that fell off, the installer likely waited too long to apply that coat, mistakenly letting the bonder dry. In this case, roughen the surface with a chisel before applying new bonder and a stucco patch.

Used correctly, an electric chipping hammer enables you to fracture stucco without destroying the underlying wire mesh and waterproofing membrane.

attached. When removing damaged areas, be deliberate and avoid disturbing surrounding intact stucco. Avoid damaging existing lath so you can attach new lath to it. Also avoid ripping the old building paper if possible. *Safety note:* Whether removing old stucco or mixing new, wear eye protection, heavy leather gloves, and at least a paper dust mask.

You can use a hammer and a cold chisel to remove a small section of damaged stucco. But for larger jobs, rent an electric chipping hammer with a chisel bit. *Important:* The bit should just fracture the stucco, not cut through it. Ideally, the underlying wire mesh and building paper will remain undamaged.

Let's say you're removing stucco to expose a rotted mudsill. Using a chipping hammer, fracture the stucco surface in two roughly parallel lines. On the first pass, delineate the top of the stucco to be removed. Then make a second pass, 6 in. lower. Basically, you'll eventually demolish all the stucco below the top cut-line and restucco it after you replace the mudsill. But if you carefully remove the top 6 in. of the damaged stucco, you'll preserve the wire mesh in that section, giving you something to tie the new mesh and stucco to.

Cut through the wire mesh exposed by the second pass, insert a pry bar under the stucco, and pry up to detach the stucco from the sheathing. Because the first pass of the chipping hammer separates damaged stucco from intact stucco, prying up this 6-in. corridor of stucco will not disturb the solid areas above it.

Now the strenuous work begins. Using a mason's hammer or a beat-up framing hammer, carefully pulverize the corridor of pried-up stucco.

Stucco is hard stuff, so whacking it in place with a hammer is more likely to drive it into the wood sheathing than to pulverize it. However, if you pry up the stucco slightly, you can slide a hand sledge under it to serve as an anvil. Then, between a hammer and a hard place, the stucco will shatter nicely. After you've removed all old chunks of stucco, you'll have a 6-in.-wide section of unencumbered wire mesh and, ideally, a layer of largely intact building paper under that. Once you've replaced the rotted framing (and sheathing), insert new paper, tie new mesh to the old—just twist the wire ends together—and nail both to the sheathing. Now you're ready to apply the new scratch coat.

If only the finish coat is cracked, wire brush and wet the brown coat, apply fresh bonding liquid, and trowel in a new finish coat. But if the cracks are deeper, the techniques for repair are much the same as those for patches, except that you need to undercut the cracks. That is, use a cold chisel to widen the bottom of each crack. This helps *key in* (hold) the new stucco. Chip away no more than you must for a good mechanical attachment. Then brush the prepared crack well with bonding liquid.

Texturing and finishing. To disguise new stucco patches, it's often necessary to match the texture of the surrounding wall. Before texturing the finish coat, steel-trowel it smooth and let it set about a half hour—although the waiting time depends on temperature and humidity. Cooler and more humid conditions delay drying. Stucco allowed to cure slowly is far stronger than fast-cured stucco. So, after applying the finish coat, use a hose set on a fine spray to keep the stucco

To remove stubborn chunks of old stucco from the wire mesh, pry up the mesh enough to slide the head of a hand sledge underneath so it can serve as an anvil. Hammered stucco will then pulverize. Wear eye protection and a paper respirator mask.

After completing the repairs, texture the wall to blend the patch to the surrounding stucco. Here, plastering cement, LaHabra color, and water were mixed repeatedly, poured into a hopper, then sprayed onto the wall to create a stippled effect.

damp for 3 days. Here are descriptions of the three common textures:

▶ *Stippled.* For this effect you'll need rubber gloves, an open-cell sponge float like those used to spread grout in tiling, a 5-gal. bucket, and lots of clean water.

After dampening the sponge float, press it into the partially set finish coat and quickly lift the float straight back from the wall. As you lift the float, it will lift a bit of the stucco material and so create a stippled texture looking somewhere between pebbly and pointy. Repeat this process over the entire surface of the patch, feathering it onto surrounding (old) areas as well, to blend the patch in.

Rinse the float often. Otherwise, its cells will pack with stucco, and the float won't raise the desired little points when you lift it. Equally important, the sponge should be damp and not wet. If you want a grosser texture than the float provides, use a large open-cell natural sponge. If you notice that the new finish is more pointy than the old surrounding stucco, that's probably because the old finish has been softened by many layers of paint. To improve the match, knock the new texture down a little by lightly skimming it with a steel trowel.

▶ *Swirled.* Screed (level) the patch's finish coat to the surrounding areas, and feather it in. After you've made the patch fairly flat, comb it gently with a wet, stiff-bristled brush. For best results, use a light touch and rinse often; otherwise you'll drag globs of stucco out of the hole. By varying the pressure on the brush, you can change the texture.

▶ *Spanish stucco or skip troweled.* Visually, this texture looks rather like flocks of amoebas or clouds. To achieve this look, screed off the patch so it's just 1⁄16 in. below the level of surrounding areas. Then, using a steel trowel, scoop small amounts of stucco off a mortarboard and, with a flick of the wrist, throw flecks at the wall. Skim the flecks with a swimming pool trowel because its rounded edges are less likely to gouge the stucco as you flatten the flecks slightly.

Ideally, this will give you an irregular pattern of miniature mesas, matching that of the original surface. Another approach is to use a wet, sandy mix and load it onto your steel trowel unevenly. (Beforehand, coat the hole well with bonder so the new material adheres well.) Again, using a swimming pool towel, you'll see the material "skipping" over the sand particles, leaving flattened patches of texture and gaps. To get the right texture, you'll need to experiment with trowel pressure, mix stiffness, and wrist movement.

Rain Gutters

Gutters direct water away from the house, preventing water from collecting next to the foundation and thereby possibly undermining it. The two most common gutter profiles are half-round and K-style, in which the gutter has a squared-off back and an ogee front. For appearance's sake, try to match the profile of new gutters to old.

To clear water adequately, gutters must be sized properly and cleared of leaves and debris twice a year—in spring and in fall. Your lumberyard probably has elaborate gutter-sizing charts based on regional rainfall, roof square footage, and pitch. But you might remedy chronically overflowing downspouts simply by upsizing the gutters from a standard 5-in. width to a 6-in. model and installing larger downspouts. To keep

Begin any gutter installation by checking the slope of roof edges and trim and then measuring the areas to receive gutters. Typically, gutters extend beyond the roof section 1⁄2 in. on each end. As you reconnoiter, consider where downspouts will be least obtrusive.

Most metal gutter stock is relatively lightweight, so it can be cut, drilled, and attached easily with a modest assortment of tools. When using a hacksaw on gutters, cut from the back and bottom sides forward, so you'll be cutting the shaped (thicker) edges last. Aluminum and copper are soft and easy to work; galvanized steel is more challenging.

Use a hole saw in a cordless drill to create openings for downspout outlets. In a pinch, you can also start holes by hammering an old chisel into the metal, then use aviation snips to complete the cutout.

roof runoff from running behind gutters and rotting fascia, extend the roof drip-edge flashing so it overhangs the gutter.

If gutters are spaced too far from the roof edge or slope away from the drip-edge, you can place an L-shaped piece of metal flashing over the back of the gutter and tuck its upper edge up under the drip-edge. (Notch that flashing so it fits around the roof hangers.) Some K-style gutters also come with an integral flange that runs under the roofing and serves the same function as a drip-edge.

MATERIALS

Metal gutters can be fabricated on site by a gutter specialist with a mobile machine. Or you can assemble them from 10-ft. or 20-ft. prefab lengths, using pop rivets and exterior caulking. Plastic gutter sections need cementing. Gutter runs that are longer than 40 ft. need an expansion joint to keep them from buckling. Here are the materials most commonly used.

Aluminum. By far the most popular, aluminum resists corrosion, is easily worked, is reasonably priced, and is durable—though it will dent. It comes prepainted in a range of colors. Standard thickness is 0.028 in., but spending a little more for 0.032 in. is prudent, especially if heavy snows and ice dams are common in your area.

Galvanized steel. Stronger and harder to dent than aluminum, galvanized steel rusts if you don't keep it painted. There are prepainted varieties, generally in the same colors as painted metal roofs. The minimum thickness is 26 gauge.

For gutters, a pop riveter is indispensable for joining because, unlike screws, pop rivets don't intrude into the gutter or downspouts and so won't snag leaves and cause clogs. Predrill pop-rivet holes.

Copper. Handsome when new, copper acquires a beautiful green patina as it weathers. It's malleable, durable, and about five times as expensive as aluminum. This gutter is usually formed from 16-oz. sheet copper. Copper resists salt air but may be corroded by cedar-shingle runoff.

Plastic. Plastic comes in 8-ft. and 10-ft. lengths, with matched fittings. You can join sections either with liquid cement or with neoprene gaskets. It's virtually maintenance free and durable, if the plastic contains a UV inhibitor. Its expansion joints can accommodate a wide range of movement.

Gutter Hangers

Gutter sections need to be supported by hangers at least every 32 in.; closer if there's a heavy snow or ice load. The many variations can be grouped into two general types: roof mounted, which employ a strap nailed to roof sheathing, and fascia mounted, which screw or nail directly to fascia boards or rafter tails. Whatever type hanger you use, gutters are less likely to pull free if you nail or screw the attachers to framing behind the fascia or roof sheathing. Here are profiles of four common hanger types:

▶ **Spike-and-ferrule hangers** nail directly into rafter ends or through fascia boards. Although this is a simple system, its detractors point out that 7-in. spikes leave large holes, encourage rot, and—in the end—don't hold well.

▶ **Roof-mounted strap nailers** support gutters well and are an alternative to end-nailing rafters—in fact, they're the only option when there's no fascia. If you're reroofing, nail them to the roof sheathing and apply shingles over them. Or, if the rafter tails are exposed, nail the straps atop the rafters, and install flashing over the straps to forestall rot.

▶ **Hidden hangers** are favored for hanging K-style aluminum gutters. They can be inserted into the gutters on the ground and, thanks to integral screws, attached to the fascia one-handed. But because they clip inside the gutter channels—rather than supporting them underneath—these

hangers are best used with heavier, 0.032-in. gutter stock, which is stiffer and less likely to flex or sag than the lighter stock.

▶ **Bracket hangers** are usually lag screwed to fascia boards. They range from plain 4-in. brackets that snap over the back gutter lips to cast bronze brackets ornamented with mythical sea creatures. Brackets simplify installation because you can mount them beforehand—snap a chalkline to align them—and then set gutters into them.

Hidden Gutter Hanger

Hidden hangers are commonly used with K-type gutters. They can be prepositioned in the gutter and quickly screwed or nailed to the fascia. Because hangers are not visible, gutter lines are clean.

Prefab Gutter Pieces

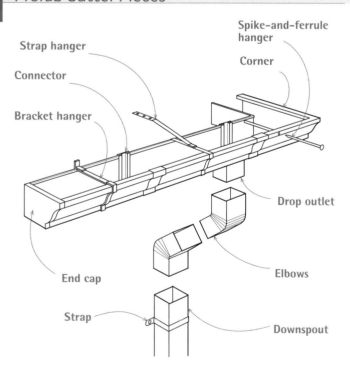

Strap hanger

Connector

Bracket hanger

Spike-and-ferrule hanger

Corner

Drop outlet

End cap

Elbows

Strap

Downspout

Prefabricated gutter pieces facilitate assembly. Use the hanger type most appropriate to your eaves detailing.

SLOPING AND PLACING GUTTERS

Ideally, gutters should slope down toward downspouts 1 in. per 16 ft., but this is not always possible. For starters, this may not look good: Next to a level fascia board, the steeper the slope of the gutter, the more it looks out of whack. As long as there is a slight pitch—say, ½ in. in 20 ft.—with no low spots en route to the downspout, a gutter will drain. If a house settles so that its roof edge or trim slopes away from downspouts, either install new gutters with downspouts properly located or raise or lower the gutters so they slope toward existing downspouts.

Place the front lip of the gutters below the roof plane, low enough so the sliding snow won't tear them off yet high enough so the rain runoff won't overshoot them. The distance below the projected roof plane varies with pitch: For a gently sloped 5/12 pitch, place the front lip of the gutter ¾ in. below the projected roof plane; for a steeper 7/12 pitch, ½ in. below the plane; for a 12/12 pitch, ¼ in. The front lip of a gutter should always be about 1 in. lower than the back. That way, if the gutter overflows, water will spill over the front lip rather than soaking the fascia and siding behind.

INSTALLING GUTTERS

Reconnoiter the roof. Measure the length of the roof the gutter will service, and check the fascia (if any) and roof edge for level. Try to place the downspouts in an inconspicuous place, away from foot traffic. In positioning downspouts, the biggest challenge is usually on the uphill side of the house, where downspouts often require

underground drains to carry water beyond the outside house corners.

Next determine where you want seams, which should also be placed inconspicuously. Because gutter stock comes in 10-ft. or 20-ft. lengths, it might look better to join a 15-ft. length and a 10-ft. length to achieve a gutter 25-ft. long, rather than tacking a 5-ft. length onto the end of a 20-ft. length, if that joint would be near the front door.

Although gutter sections are light enough for one person to carry, the job is safer and more

Gutter Lip and Roof Pitch

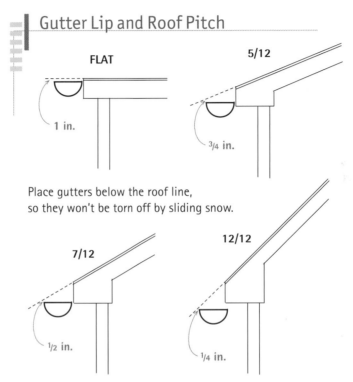

Place gutters below the roof line, so they won't be torn off by sliding snow.

PRO TIP

Though it's desirable to secure the gutter hangers to the framing, you might not be able to see the rafter-center marks if you're holding the gutter section over the fascia. Instead, beforehand, use a builder's crayon to mark the framing centers along the edge of the roofing.

▮▮▮▮

Don't try this at home on a windy day. Pros know how to raise and attach long sections safely, but the rest of us will do well to have a helper or two.

After securing gutters, use screws to attach the downpouts to the outlets. Screws allow you to disconnect this joint later. Have the downspout brackets handy so you can immediately secure the downspouts to the siding.

Unless you're an experienced sheet-metal worker, buy pre-formed corners (such as this one) as well as preformed miter strips, and so on. After pop-riveting such connections, caulk them liberally, including the rivet holes.

Consequently, use rivets to join the gutter sections, downspout outlets, and miter strips. And use the shortest screws feasible to join the downspouts to the gutter outlets. To avoid galvanic corrosion, use screws that are the same material as the gutter; otherwise, use stainless-steel screws. Because elbows slow water and tend to clog, use as few as possible. Place the vertical sections above the elbows so falling water can pick up speed to flush debris out of elbows. Apply gutter caulk freely to seal the joints, rivet holes, and the like. And where you see holes left by earlier gutter hangers, fill them with exterior wood filler or color-matched acrylic latex caulk.

GUTTER REPAIRS

If gutters are rusty but otherwise intact, use a wire brush to remove rust. Then rinse well and allow the gutters to dry. Paint gutters with an elastomeric roof coating such as Gacoflex acrylic latex, which can handle the expansion and contraction of metal gutters.

You may be able to get a few more years from metal gutters beginning to rust through by patching them with a compatible-metal patch. First, vigorously wire-brush the rusted area till you uncover solid metal, wipe the area clean with a rag damped with paint thinner, and prime with metal primer. After the primer dries, spread epoxy around the hole, and press the patch into it. Or simply wire brush the rusted area clean and apply a foil-faced, self-adhering bituminous membrane; such waterproofing membranes are often used to flash skylights, plumbing pipes, and other roofing elements. They're easily shaped to the contour of a gutter.

Wooden gutters should be inspected every year for deterioration and repainted every 2 years or 3 years. They must be thoroughly dry before painting; otherwise, paint will seal in moisture and promote rot. So it's best to paint gutters after a dry spell, after allowing the morning dew to evaporate.

Begin work by sanding the wood well and wiping away grit with a rag dampened with paint thinner. Next, apply a water-repellant preservative, prime, and apply two finish coats of paint. If you find rot, your problem is compounded if the gutter also doubles as exterior trim and abuts sheathing or framing. Short of replacing such integral gutters, you may be able to prolong their life by lining them with peel-and-stick waterproofing membrane.

predictable with two workers, especially if it's windy. Snap a chalkline along the fascia to indicate the level of the hanger brackets and install a bracket at either end of the roof. Otherwise, snap a chalkline to indicate the back lip of the gutter. If your gutter hangers fit into the gutters, position them before you carry gutter sections aloft; also, preassemble the end caps, downspout takeoffs, and so on.

Once you've secured either end of the gutter and checked its position, add hangers every 32 in. (every other rafter); in snow country, install a hanger every 16 in. The hangers you choose will determine exactly how you secure gutters. Most modular gutter systems can be cut to length with a hacksaw and joined with poprivets or self-tapping sheet-metal screws. *A disadvantage of screws:* Their points protrude, snagging leaves and causing blockages. *An advantage:* Screws can be removed to disconnect the sections.

Structural Carpentry

This chapter is mostly about wood, the king of building materials. Built amid virgin forests, the first wood houses were fashioned from massive ax-hewn timbers that took half a neighborhood to raise. Because iron was scarce, those great post-and-beam frames were joined without nails. Instead, they were fitted tightly and then fastened with whittled wooden pegs. The technology was crude, but the houses survived, in large part because of the mass and strength of wood.

Early in the nineteenth century came plentiful iron nails and circular-sawn lumber of uniform, if smaller, dimensions. Although such lighter components needed to be spaced closer than rough-hewn timbers, their reduced weight made it possible for three or four people to raise a wall. Balloon framing was the earliest of milled lumber houses, with long studs running from one story to the next, and is rarely used today. Since the beginning of the twentieth century, platform framing (also called western framing) has been the most widely used method. Here, each story is capped with a floor platform. Because the studs of a platform-framed house run only one story, they are shorter and easier to handle.

Understanding Structure

A house must withstand a variety of loads (forces): the *dead load* of the building materials; the *live loads* of the people in the house and their possessions; and the *shear loads* from earthquakes, soil movement, wind, and the like, which exert racking (twisting) forces on a building. There are

If there's room, assembling a wall on a flat surface and walking it upright is the way to go. This crew nailed restraining blocks to the outside of this second-story platform beforehand, so the sole plate couldn't slide off the deck.

other, finer distinctions, including *point loads*, where concentrated weights dictate that the structure be beefed up, and *spread loads*, in which a roof's weight, say, pushes outward with enough force to spread walls unless counteracted.

Loads are transferred downward by *framing members*, primarily by exterior walls sitting atop a perimeter foundation and by interior *bearing walls*, often supported by a secondary foundation consisting of a girder, posts, and pads. Generally, a *girder* runs the length of the house, and supports floor joists running perpendicular to it. *Nonbearing walls*, as their name denotes, are not intended to bear anything but their own weight. *Headers* (or lintels) are bearing beams that carry loads across openings in walls. A *partition* is any interior dividing wall, bearing or not.

Before you decide to demolish old walls or frame up new ones, determine what is a bearing wall and what's not. This will influence how you frame up, for example, the size of headers, whether you need shoring, whether you need additional support below the walls being removed, and whether you should disturb the structure at all. Get as much information as you can before you commit to a plan because there are always surprises once you start. If you plan to remove walls, be sure to hire a structural engineer to review your plans.

Exploring Your Options

To assess the framing hidden behind finish surfaces, go where it's exposed: the basement and the attic. Joists often run in the same direction from floor to floor.

Generally, a **girder** (also called a carrying timber or beam) runs the length of the house, with joists perpendicular to it. Some houses will have framed **cripple walls** (short walls from the top of a foundation to the bottom of the first-floor joists) instead of a girder. Main bearing walls often run directly above the girder, but any wall that runs parallel to and within 5 ft. of a girder or cripple wall is probably bearing weight and should be treated accordingly.

Bearing walls down the middle of the house are also likely to be supporting pairs of joists for the floors above. That is, most joists are not continuous from exterior wall to exterior wall—they end over bearing walls and are nailed to companion joists coming from the opposite direction. This allows the builder to use smaller lumber—2×6s rather than 2×8s, for example—to run a shorter span. If you cut into such a bearing wall without adding a header, the joists above will sag.

Large openings in obvious bearing walls are often spanned by a large beam or a header that supports the joists above. These beams, in turn, are supported at each end by posts within the wall that carry the load on down to the foundation. These **point loads** must be supported at all times. Similarly, large openings in floors (stairwells, for example) should be framed by doubled headers and trimmers that can bear concentrated loads.

Finally, it may be wise to leave a wall where it is if pipes, electrical cables, and heating ducts run through it. Look for them as they emerge in unfinished basements or attics. Electrical wiring is easy enough to remove and reroute—but disconnect the power first! However, finding a new home for a 3-in. or 4-in. soil stack or a 4-in. by 12-in. heating duct may be more trouble than it's worth.

Framing Walls

The framing of walls is arguably the most common carpentry task in renovation, and it employs many of the layout and assembly techniques you'd use elsewhere to construct walls, floors, and roofs. For a deeper look at carpentry, consult Rob Thallon's *Graphic Guide to Frame Construction* or Mike Guertin and Rick Arnold's *Precision Framing*, both published by The Taunton Press.

Basically, wood-frame walls are an array of vertical studs nailed to horizontal top plates and sole (bottom) plates. Depending on whether walls are bearing or nonbearing, plates may be doubled. Although 2×4 walls are more common and less expensive, 2×6 walls allow you to install thicker insulation and route pipes more easily. To simplify matters, the examples in this section assume 2×4 framing.

HANDLING LUMBER

Here are a few lumber-handling tips that'll save energy and make the job go quicker.

Minimize moves. Lumber is heavy. Tell your lumberyard to load the delivery truck so that the lumber you'll use first—say, floor joists—will be on the top of the load. Clear a level place close to the work site where the truck can unload. Many suppliers have boom trucks that can unload lumber stacks directly onto a work deck.

Sort your lumber. Lumber today is often bowed, so eyeball each piece for straightness—and sort it into like piles. Save the straight stock for kitchen and bathroom walls—especially those that will get cabinets or be tiled—and for corners, top wall plates, and jack studs along rough openings (ROs). Pieces with slight bows (¼ in. in 8 ft.) can be used as studs and joists, but draw an arrow on the face of the lumber to indicate which way the lumber bows so you remember to place slightly bowed joists crown (bow) up, so they'll be less likely to sag when loaded. Set aside stock that bows more than ¼ in. in 8 ft., which you'll cut shorter and use as headers, cripple studs, and blocking. Return corkscrew (twisted) studs to the lumberyard for credit.

Be methodical. Snap chalklines onto floors to mark wall plates. Cut top and bottom plates. Then mark stud locations and ROs onto the plates. Make a cutting list: By cutting same-length lumber all at once you'll save a ton of time. If possible, cut lumber or plywood right atop the stack that the lumberyard truck delivered.

NAILING IT

On larger renovations these days, pneumatic nailers do most of the work, but it's worth knowing how to use a hammer correctly. Then you'll create fewer bent nails, splits, and *dings* (dented wood when the hammer misses the nail), and perhaps avoid a smashed thumb, tendonitis, and joint pain.

The perfect swing. If you're driving large nails such as 16d commons, start the nail with a tap. Then, with a relaxed but firm grip on the end of the hammer handle, raise the hammer head high and swing smoothly from your shoulder. If you're assembling stud-wall elements, spread them out on a deck, put one foot on the lumber to keep it in place, bend forward slightly, and let the falling hammer head's weight do some of the work. Just before striking the nail, snap your wrist slightly to accelerate the swing.

However, if you're driving smaller nails (6d or 8d), you won't need as much force to sink them. So choke up on the handle and swing from the elbow. Choking up is particularly appropriate if you're driving finish nails because you'll need less force and be less likely to miss the nail and mar the casing. It's also necessary to choke up when there's not enough room to swing a hammer freely or where you must drive a nail one-handed in a spot that you need to stretch to reach.

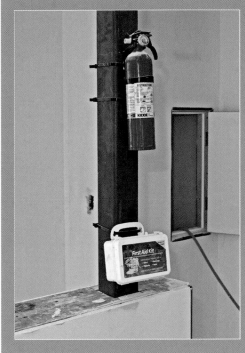

Work SAFELY

Put first-aid kits and fire extinguishers in a central location where you can find them quickly. Likewise, gather hard hats, safety glasses, hearing protection, and respirator masks at the end of each workday so they'll be on hand at the start of the next.

PRO TIP

Precut studs save labor and time; they're available in several lengths. Buy 92¼-in. studs if finished ceiling heights are 8 ft. (92¼ in. + 3 in. for two wall plates = 95¼ in.), 88-in. studs if the ceilings are 7 ft. 6 in., and 104-in. studs if the ceilings are to be 9 ft.

Loads and Structure

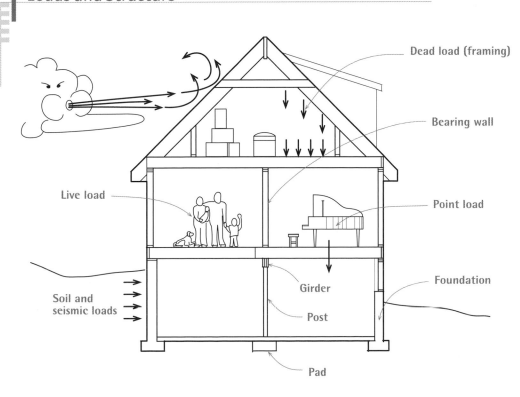

Dead load (framing)

Bearing wall

Live load

Point load

Soil and seismic loads

Girder

Foundation

Post

Pad

NAILING Plywood SHEATHING

To nail plywood panels ½ in. thick or less, most codes specify 6d common nails spaced every 6 in. along the panel edges and every 12 in. in the field. Panels thicker than ½ in. require 8d common nails spaced in the same pattern. (Structural shear walls are typically nailed with 10d nails 4 in. to 6 in. on center along the edges and 12 in. on center in the field, but an engineer should do an exact calculation.)

Don't overdrive nails. Ideally, nail heads should depress but not crush the face ply of the plywood. Panel strength isn't affected if nail heads are overdriven by $\frac{1}{16}$ in. or less, but if more than 20 percent of the nail heads are $\frac{1}{8}$ in. or deeper, the American Plywood Association recommends adding one extra nail for each two overdriven ones. Pneumatic-nailer pressure that's too high is the most common cause of overdriven nails. It's far better to set the nailer pressure so the heads are flush, and then use a single hammer blow to sink each nail just a little deeper.

The right nail. The nailing schedule given in "Recommended Nailing Schedule," on the facing page, suggests the size and number of nails you need for various framing tasks, but local building codes will have the final say. When joining two pieces of framing lumber, nails should be long enough to penetrate the second piece of wood, without sticking out its other side. Properly sized nails are also less likely to split board ends. As the table indicates, use two 16d nails to end-nail a stud through a plate, and four 8d nails, which are shorter and skinnier than 16d nails, to toenail stud ends to sole plates. Speaking of splits, you can reduce them by first hammering nail points to blunt them.

Removing nails. Everybody inadvertently bends nails now and then, especially when nailing at an odd angle or in a tight space or nailing into a hard wood like southern pine. To remove a bent nail, slip a block under a claw hammer head to increase the leverage as you pull out the nail; if the nail head is buried too deep to grasp with a claw hammer, use a cat's paw, which has pointed claws, to dig it out.

LAYING OUT WALLS

Wall layout varies, depending on whether you're erecting walls in open space (say, framing an addition) or within existing space (adding a parti-

NAILING TIPS

To nail where it's hard to reach, start the nail by holding it against the side of the hammer and smacking it into the wood. Once the nail is started, you can finish hammering with one hand.

A blunted nail point is less likely to split wood because it will crush the wood fiber in its path rather than wedging it apart, as a sharp nail point does.

A wood block under your hammer head makes nail-pulling easier.

tion). In both cases, use house plans to position walls. Snap chalklines onto subfloors (or floors) to indicate wall sole plates. If you're building a wall within a room, next measure from existing framing to determine the height and length of the new wall, as described in "Reinforcing and Repairing the Structure," on p. 165. Finally, mark the locations of ROs, *wall backers* (blocking you nail drywall corners to), and studs into plates.

The easiest way to frame a wall is to construct it on a flat surface and tilt it up into place. Once the wall is lifted, just align its sole plate to a chalkline on the floor sheathing. This construction method is also stronger, because you can end-nail the studs to the plates rather than toe-nailing them. Sometimes, there's not enough room to tilt up walls, a situation which is addressed later in this chapter.

Assembling a wall on the ground is no guarantee that lumber edges will line up. Here, a builder uses his hammer to raise the top plate flush to the header, before nailing. Wear safety glasses when using a pneumatic nailer.

Stud-Wall Elements

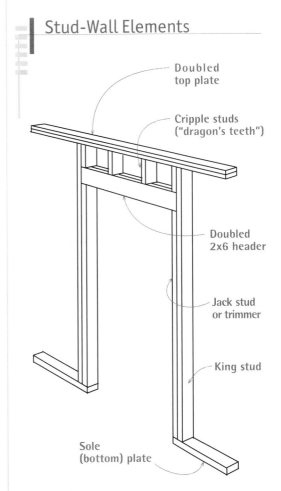

- Doubled top plate
- Cripple studs ("dragon's teeth")
- Doubled 2x6 header
- Jack stud or trimmer
- King stud
- Sole (bottom) plate

If you use doubled 2x6s for your header in a rough opening in standard 8-ft. wall framing, you need cripple studs to support the doubled top plate. If you use a 4x12 instead, it will support the top plates. Although code may allow a single top plate for nonbearing walls, a single plate offers little to nail drywall to, if the ceiling is finished before the wall.

Recommended Nailing Schedule*

APPLICATION	SCHEDULE
Joist to sill or girder (toenail)	3-8d
Ledger strip	3-16d at each joist
1×6 subfloor or less to each joist (face-nail)	2-8d (or 2-1¾ staples)
Wider than 1×6 subfloor to each joist (face-nail)	3-8d
2-in. subfloor to joist or girder (blind-nail and face-nail)	2-16d
Sole plate to joist or blocking (face-nail)	16d at 16 in. o.c.
Top plate to stud (end-nail)	2-16d
Stud to sole plate (toenail)	4-8d
Sole plate to joists or blocking	3-16d at 16 in. o.c.
Doubled studs (face-nail)	10d at 24 in. o.c.
Doubled top plates (face-nail)	16d at 16 in. o.c.
Doubled top plates, lap-spliced (face-nail)	8-16d
Continuous header, two pieces	16d at 16 in. o.c. along each edge
Rim joist to top plate (toenail)	8d at 6 in. o.c.
Ceiling joists to plate (toenail)	3-8d
Continuous header to stud (toenail)	4-8d
Ceiling joists, laps over partitions (face-nail)	3-16d
Ceiling joists to parallel rafters (face-nail)	3-16d
Rafter to plate (toenail)	3-8d
Built-up corner studs	16d at 24 in. o.c.
Built-up girders and beams	20d at 32 in. o.c. along each edge

From the Uniform Building Code/1997. Whittier, California. International Conference of Building Officials. Reproduced with permission of the International Code Council. All rights reserved.

A Speed Square is used to mark stud locations on a pressure-treated mudsill (sole plate) and a top plate. An X usually indicates regular studs 16 in. on center; a J, jack studs; a K, king studs; and a C, cripple studs. The sole plate has been predrilled so it will fit over the anchor bolts when the wall is assembled and lifted into place.

STUD-AND-PLATE LAYOUT

Mark stud edges on plates so that stud centers will be spaced 16 in. on center (O.C.).

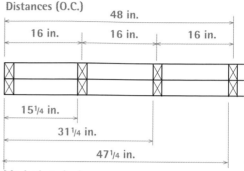

Distances (O.C.)

48 in.

16 in. | 16 in. | 16 in.

15¼ in.

31¼ in.

47¼ in.

Marked stud edges

CORNER-STUD LAYOUTS

Corners require at least three studs to provide adequate backing for finish materials. In the first example, the middle stud need not be continuous, so you can use pieces.

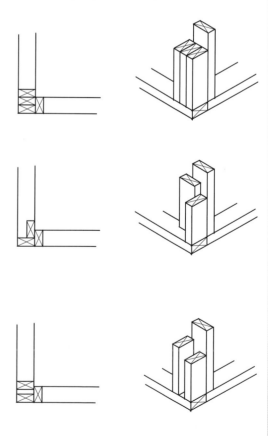

Mark rough openings. Place the sole plate, face up, next to a chalkline; then place a top plate next to it, so that edges butt together and the ends align. Use a square to mark the top plate and the sole plate at the same time. (If the top plate is doubled, there's no need to mark the upper top plate.) Using a tape measure, mark the ROs for doors and windows. Rough openings are so named because they are about 1 in. wider and 1 in. higher than preframed doors or windows (so units can be shimmed snug) and 2½ in. wider and higher than unframed units.

As you mark the width of the RO on the plates, keep in mind that there will be a *king stud* (full length) and a shortened *jack stud* (also called a trimmer stud) to support the header on each side of the opening. After marking the ROs, mark the *corner backers* (also called wall backers)—extra blocking for drywall where partitions intersect with the wall you're framing. "Corner-Stud Layouts" shows several backer configurations.

Mark studs on the plates. After marking the first stud, which is flush to the end of the plates, mark the subsequent studs ¾ in. back from the red 16-in.-interval highlights on your measuring tape. (In other words, mark stud edges at 15¼ in., 31¼ in., 47¼ in., and so on.) By marking stud edges ¾ in. back, you ensure that stud centers will coincide with the edges of drywall or sheathing panels, which are usually some multiple of 16 in., for example, 48 in. by 96 in.

Mark studs every 16 in. on center on plates—through the ROs as well—so that drywall or sheathing panels running above or below openings can be nailed to cripple studs at regular intervals. At window openings, you'll mark cripple studs on both the top and the bottom plates. But on door openings, you'll mark cripple studs on the top plates only. *Note:* For door openings, where 16-in. on-center studs occur within 2 in. of a king stud, omitting the 16-in. on-center stud will not weaken the structure.

HEADERS

Every opening in a wall must have a header over it. Headers must be able to carry a cumulative load and transfer it downward without warping, flexing, or pulling away from the sides of the opening. Thus headers must be sized according to the loads they carry and the distances they span. Your local building code will have the final say in sizing them.

That noted, many builders in North America use this rule of thumb when sizing headers for single-story buildings with 2×4 walls and a 30-lb. live load on the roof: The nominal depth a 4× header in inches equals the span in feet of the opening. For example, if a builder uses No. 1 grade Douglas fir on edge, its spans look like this:

Douglas Fir Header Spans

HEADER SIZE (in.)	SPAN (ft.)
4×4	4
4×6	6
4×8	8
4×10	10
4×12	12

Oversizing headers. Span tables establish minimum requirements. In the field, however, experienced builders routinely oversize headers—using 4×12s to span all openings, interior and exterior. This is a considerable overkill, say, for a 4-ft.-wide window. But it has important advantages:

▶ Same-size headers ensure that the tops of most exterior openings will be at the same height, which is aesthetically pleasant.

▶ The additional cost of using an oversize beam is more than offset by the peace of mind it brings. That is, there won't be any cracks in finish surfaces caused by undersize beams.

▶ The reasons for using a 4×10 or 4×12 for a partition are equally compelling. Should a nonbearing partition become point-loaded because of structural shifts, its header should bear the additional load easily.

▶ Even in nonbearing walls, the header is the weakest point, structurally. Each time you shut a door, you compress the air in the room causing the wall to flex. The more solid wood you've got to nail to, the stronger the connection. (Code requires at least five 16d nails through-nailed into each end of a header.)

▶ But the most compelling reason is time. Cutting an oversize header from solid stock is far quicker than cutting and laminating two pieces of 2× lumber to a ½-in.-thick plywood core. (The ½-in. core makes the whole package exactly 3½ in. thick, the width of a nominal 2×4.) You also save time because you don't need to cut *dragon's teeth,* the term pros use for cripple studs between a header and the top plate.

STANDARD Framing

For standard 8-ft. wall framing, cut studs 92¼-in. long. One bottom plate and two top plates will be roughly 4½ in. thick, creating a wall height of 96¾ in. This height accommodates one drywall panel (½ in. to ⅝ in. thick) on the ceiling and two 4-ft.-wide drywall panels run horizontally on the wall. If you install a 4×12 header directly under the top plates of a standard wall, the rough opening height will be 82½ in. This is just right for a 6 ft. 8 in. door, and door head heights will match that of the windows.

ASSEMBLING THE WALL

After marking the top and bottom plates, and cutting full-length studs, start assembling the wall. Place the plates on edge, roughly a wall height apart. Then insert the studs on edge between them. Again, use straight studs at wall ends and cabinet locations; elsewhere, place slightly bowed studs crown (bow) up so that stud ends will rest on the deck when it's time to nail them to the wall plates.

Nailing studs. Position studs to the squared marks along the plates. Then end-nail studs through the sole plate, using two 16d common nails at each end. Space nails ½ in. to 1 in. from the edge of the plate. If you stand on the stud as you nail it, it will stay put. As you nail, be sure that stud and plate edges are flush, or the resultant wall plane won't be flat. When you've nailed all studs to the sole plate, nail the top plate. *Important:* If the sole plate will sit on concrete, it should be pressure-treated lumber or a naturally rot-resistant wood such as redwood. Moreover, all nails set into redwood or pressure-treated

When nailing the top plate to studs, lift the studs as needed so their edges align with the top plate's. Flush studs and plates allow drywall finishing to go smoothly. This exterior wall will have a doubled top plate; the second plate is nailed on once the wall is up, tying this wall to another.

After using five 16d nails to end-nail the header through the king stud, face-nail the trimmer stud to the king.

Because a 3×4 mudsill is too thick to end-nail through, toenail studs instead. Here, pneumatic nailers really shine: They nail so quickly that studs won't drift off stud marks, as they frequently do when you're hand-nailing them.

Half-Cutting the Sole Plate

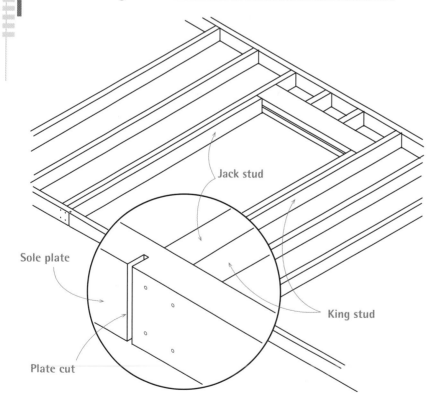

Jack stud

Sole plate

King stud

Plate cut

A stud wall a with continuous sole plate is less likely to flop around as you raise it, but it's difficult to cut through a plate once it's resting on a subfloor. The solution? Cut halfway through the sole plate before you nail it to studs, and finish the cuts after the wall is up.

plates must be galvanized so they won't be corroded by chemicals in the wood.

Framing the rough opening. After cutting the header, end-nail the king studs (through the plates), on both sides of the RO. If you're installing a full-height header such as a 4×12, insert the header between the king studs and nail down through the top plate into the header, to draw it tight to the plate. Then nail through the king studs into the ends of the header, using at least five nails per end. Next, to determine the length of the jack studs, measure from the underside of the header to the top of the sole plate. Cut the jack studs slightly long; tap them into place; and face-nail them to the king studs, making sure their edges are flush.

If the header requires cripple studs between it and the top plate, install king studs, then jack studs, then the header. Holding the header tight to the top of the jack studs, nail through the king studs into header ends. If the header is laminated from pieces of 2× lumber, each piece should get two or three nails per end. Then cut and toenail the cripple studs that run between the top of the header and the top plate. If you're framing a rough opening for a door, you're done.

However, if you're framing a rough opening for a window, your final steps will be leveling and toenailing the sills (also called saddles) to jack studs and then nailing cripple studs between the sills and the sole plate. Again, space cripples according to the 16-in. on-center markings along the plates.

Leaving the sole uncut. You're now ready to tilt up the assembled wall. Note, however, that sole plates haven't yet been cut and removed within door ROs, and for good reason: It's far easier to raise a wall if its sole plate is continuous. Thus cut only halfway through the sole plate while it's flat on the deck, as shown in "Half-Cutting the Sole Plate." Finish the cut once the wall is up and nailed down.

After leveling and toenailing the lower plate of a windowsill, end-nail cripple studs under the sill. After all cripple studs are in, face-nail the upper plate of the sill. Doubled sill plates are common in the western United States; elsewhere, they're usually reserved for wider windows only.

PLUMBING AND SECURING THE WALL

Once the wall is up, nail the bottom of the brace so the wall will stay upright as you fine-tune its position. Use a sledgehammer to tap the sole plate till it aligns with your chalkline on the floor. As you adjust, continuously check for plumb, using a 6-ft. level. If you unnail the brace to plumb the wall, have workers support the wall until you've renailed it.

Once the bottom plate lines up with the chalk-line, drive two or three 20d nails through the plate, into the joists or blocking below, so the wall can't drift. Methods for securing the top of the wall vary. If you're framing an addition and have wide-open space, typically two walls inter-secting at right angles are raised, plumbed, and braced, and then tied together by overlapping top plates.

But if you're raising a partition in an existing room, you'll usually nail the top plate to ceiling joists. Invariably, space is tight indoors, and you'll often need to gently sledgehammer the par-tition into place, alternating blows between top and sole plates till the wall is plumb. Alterna-tively, you can gain room to maneuver by first nailing the upper 2×4 of a doubled top plate to the exposed ceiling joists—use two 16d nails per joist—before raising the wall. Tilt up the wall, slide it beneath the upper top plate, plumb the wall, and then face-nail the top plates together using two 16d nails per stud bay. Finally, finish

Raising walls

Two workers can raise an unsheathed stud wall 8 ft. to 10 ft. long. But if it's much longer than that or if it's sheathed, assemble a larger crew or use wall-lifting jacks to raise it.

Raising walls safely takes prep work: Clear the deck of tools, scrap lumber, and other items you might trip over. Nail the top of a diagonal brace 1 ft. below the top plate, using a single 16d nail so that the brace can pivot as you raise the wall; and prenail a 2× block into floor framing so you can quickly nail the bottom of the diagonal brace once the wall is plumb. If you are raising an exterior wall, first nail 2× stops to the outside of the platform so the bottom plate can't slide off the deck during the operation.

If you are raising a partition within an existing structure, expose the ceiling joists or end-wall studs you'll nail the partition to. If joists run parallel to the new partition, add blocking between the joists beforehand, as shown in "Partition Parallel with Joists" and "Blocking for Sole Plates" on p. 166.

Here are three tips for raising walls:

▶ As shown in the photo below, several workers straddling the top plate should drive hammer claws into the top plate, lift in unison, and slide 2× blocks beneath the top plate so they can get a good grip before actually lifting.

▶ Lift with your legs, not with your back.

▶ If your crew is small, set two sawhorses nearby, perpendicular to the wall; the horses will support the wall once the crew has raised it waist-high, allowing them to reposition themselves so they can push the wall up the rest of the way.

After constructing a wall on the ground and walking it up, the crew must now lift it up 3 ft. and align the mudsill holes to the bolts in the foundation wall. Have a lot of workers on hand, and lift with your knees, not your back.

Several workers hold the wall plumb while one worker adds diagonal braces on both ends. After plumbing and bracing both ends and tightening sill bolts, they'll run a string between ends to ensure the wall is straight. The top plate needs to be straight so the rafters will line up.

nailing the sole plates, driving two 16d nails into the joists or blocking below. In the corners, use 10d or 12d nails to toenail the corner studs to blocking or existing studs; use 16d nails if you can face-nail them. Adding blocking to existing framing is discussed on p. 165.

ALTERNATIVE FRAMING METHODS

In renovation, it's not always possible to assemble a wall on the deck and tilt it up. There may not be enough room, shoring may be in the way, or sloping floors may frustrate attempts to cut studs accurately in advance. In those cases, it may be easier to build the wall in place, piece by piece.

Building a partition in place. Start by positioning the plates and tack nailing them to joists (or blocking) above or below. Although it's most common to snap a chalkline on the floor and plumb up to the top plate, it doesn't really matter which plate you attach first, unless there's a compelling structural or design reason. If you're erecting a bearing wall, for example, center its sole plate over the appropriate girders or bearing walls below. But if you're trying to align a non-bearing partition with a rafter above, set the top

plate first and plumb down to establish the sole plate. If possible, face-nail the plates with two 16d nails at each joist crossing.

Mark the stud intervals onto the plates, and then—especially if floors or ceilings slope—measure the stud lengths individually. Cut the studs slightly long (1/16 in) so that they fit snugly. Toenail each end of the studs with three 10d nails or four 8d nails, angling them roughly 60° from horizontal. Use a spirit level to level the headers. Use three 16d nails to end-nail a header through the king studs on either side. Then face-nail trimmer studs to the kings, staggering 10d or 12d nails every 16 in.

Framing beneath slopes. Framing beneath stair stringers and rafters isn't difficult if you measure carefully and use an adjustable bevel. Mark off 16-in. intervals along a 2×4 sole plate, nail it to the floor, and then plumb up to the underside of the rafter or stringer to mark the top plate. Cut the top plate to length, and nail it to the underside of the sloping rafter or stair stringer before using a plumbed board to mark off stud intervals along the top plate.

To establish the angle at which you'll cut the top of the studs, plumb a piece of 2× stock in

Sizing Gable-End Studs

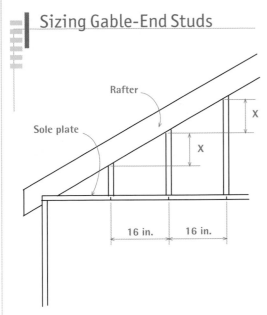

After marking off 16-in. stud centers onto the sole plate, plumb up and transfer the stud marks to the rafter or top plate. Once you've cut two consecutive studs, you'll know the difference in length between adjacent studs, indicated by "X."

front of the top plate and use an adjustable bevel to duplicate the acute angle at which they intersect. (Set your circular saw to the angle of that bevel.) Holding a straight board against 16-in. on-center marks on the sole plate, plumb and mark the tops of two adjacent studs. The difference in their lengths—represented by the X in "Sizing Gable-End Studs," above—will be constant for all successive pairs. Toenail the studs with four 8d nails on each end.

Establishing kneewalls. Kneewalls are short partitions, about knee high, which isolate the largely unusable space where the rafters approach the top plates of the exterior walls. Kneewalls usually run parallel to the roof ridge and consist of a single top plate and sole plate, with studs spaced 16 in. on center. Position the sole plate and plumb up to the underside of the rafters to mark the top plate. Using an adjustable bevel, copy the angle at which the rafters intersect, using a plumbed spirit level or board.

Nail the top plate with two 16d nails per rafter and the sole plate with two 16d nails per joist. Cut across the faces of the studs in the angle established by the bevel gauge. (*Note:* This is not a bevel cut, but a square cut at an angle.) To attach the studs to the plates, toenail each end with 8d nails.

Demolition

Before demolishing an old wall or framing up a new one, determine whether it's a bearing wall. If so, erect shoring if needed, and have a plan for rerouting electrical cables, pipes, or heating ducts in existing walls. ⊘ Above all, shut off the electrical power before cutting into finish surfaces—and use a voltage tester to be sure the power's off.

GETTING READY FOR DEMOLITION

Living in a house that's being torn apart and renovated isn't fun, and it can be murder on marriages. But you can minimize the stress caused by disruption, noise, confusion, and dirt. If you don't need to be around the house during the demolition, don't be; that's a good time to take a vacation. If you just bought the house and can afford the expense of keeping your old place until the demo is done, do so. But if you're there for the duration, create a clean room—usually a bedroom—in which you do no work at all.

Isolate the zone by covering the doorway with sheet plastic held up by duct tape or by installing temporary plastic walls with zippered doorways such as the Zipwall System®. Situate your Shangri-La upstairs if you can, because dust settles downward. If you are beneath a room being renovated, particularly one in bad repair, tape plastic to the ceiling. In the clean zone, store clothes, stereo equipment, art—anything that

Kneewalls

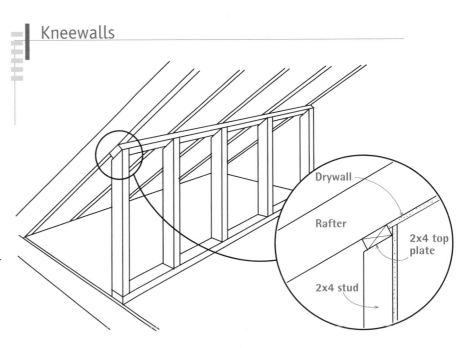

When nailing a kneewall top plate to the underside of a rafter, align the leading edge of the top plate with the inner edge of studs. Drywall will cover the small triangular voids where the plate meets the rafter.

could get ruined by the omnipresent dirt of tearout. At the end of the day, go there and relax.

LAST-MINUTE PRELIMINARIES

Take care of these items before you start:

▶ Notify gas, water, and electric companies if you haven't done so already. Utility representatives can tell you what temporary hookups are safe and who must do them.

▶ If you've newly purchased the building and if inspection reports indicated signs of insect infestation, have a pest-control professional treat the condition before you move in.

▶ Make sure your general contractor is properly covered by insurance. Or, if you're acting as your own GC, check with your insurance company to make sure you and any helpers are covered.

▶ If you don't have a cell phone, have a telephone installed so you can call for help in an emergency. Have a first-aid kit and fire extinguisher handy. Ensure that everyone on site has had a tetanus shot.

USEFUL TEAR-OUT TOOLS AND EQUIPMENT

Many of the tools mentioned here are shown and discussed at greater length in Chapter 3.

Safety. Be sure you have a voltage tester, hard hat, goggles or safety glasses, a respirator mask with changeable filters, sturdy work gloves, a droplight, and shoes with thick soles.

Dismantling. Your kit should include wrecking bars of various sizes (see the photo on p. 44), a flat utility bar, cat's paw, hand sledge, full-size sledgehammer, and heavy scrapers. If you're tearing out masonry, rent an impact hammer with carbide-tipped bits.

Work aids. Rent scaffolding if you're doing a lot of tearout over your head. Have a good supply of rolls of sheet plastic, duct tape, and heavy tarps; heavy cardboard, Masonite or ⅛-in. doorskin plywood can be used to protect finish floors. Gather heavy rubber trash cans (they work better than metal ones), wheelbarrows, push brooms, dustpans, square-nose shovels for scooping debris, stepladders, and planks. Rent a Dumpster for big jobs.

Cutting. Wear goggles when cutting out materials, for you're likely to hit nails. Most blade makers sell demo blades, which are often carbide tipped and frequently thicker than standard blades. Reciprocating saws with demolition blades are the workhorses of renovation. Such blades typically have pointed ends that enable plunge-

Demolition is incredibly dusty and disruptive, so seal off one room where you can store your stuff.

cutting (gradually lowering a blade into a surface) and bimetal construction that can cut through nails without shattering.

ELECTRICAL SAFETY

⊘ Before you cut into finish surfaces, *always shut off electrical, water, and gas service* to that area. After disconnecting electrical power and *using a voltage tester* to make sure the power's off, start slowly and proceed carefully. If any procedures described in the following sections are unclear, please read Chapter 11 and especially "Using a Voltage Tester," on p. 235, before continuing.

Circuits. Identify circuit breakers or fuses controlling electricity to the construction areas. This will require one person at the panel to flip breaker switches or unscrew fuses while another person watches a light fixture or a voltage tester inserted in a receptacle to see if the light goes out. If you use cell phones to communicate, you won't need to scream instructions between floors.

Receptacles and switches. ⊘ Plug-in voltage testers allow you to quickly see if a receptacle is energized. Always test a tester first on an outlet you know is hot, to be sure the tester is working correctly. To double-check a receptacle or to check a switch, however, you'll need to remove the cover plate. To do so safely, follow the procedures described in Chapter 11.

Junction boxes. 🚫 As you break open drywall or plaster or pull up flooring, you may find junction boxes. To get at the wires, remove the junction box cover. The wires inside will either be spliced together with wire nuts or be tape wrapped. Using pliers with insulated handles, carefully pull wire groups out of the box and remove wire nuts or tape to expose wire ends. (If you are at all uneasy about handling wires, turn off all the electricity in the house and remove the wire nuts before proceeding.) Touch your voltage tester to the black and white wires simultaneously, then to each wire group and the metal box.

There are also pen-like voltage detectors that can detect electrical current through a wire's insulation. You simply place the tester sensor near the wire.

Hidden wires. 🚫 If you unexpectedly discover cables hidden in a wall you are demolishing, stop and turn off all power in the house. Then snip the cable in two with a pair of insulated wire cutters, but *never* do this when the power is on. After testing both ends of the snipped cable with a voltage

tester to make sure that there is no live current, separate the black and white wires, and wrap the individual wires with electrical tape or cap them with wire nuts. While the power is off, also pull any staples holding the cable to the studs so that you can remove the studs later without damaging the cable.

With the cable thus severed and protected, you may proceed with the demolition. If the cable is to be discarded, disconnect it from the entrance panel. If the cable is to be reconnected, reroute it after the structural work is complete—and house all new connections in a junction box. Again, consult Chapter 11 for further details.

CONTAINING THE MESS

Managing mess is crucial to a successful renovation. Torn-out plaster and drywall are nasty stuff to handle and worse to breathe. The dust gets everywhere, and the volume of debris is prodigious. If you're sloppy as you renovate, you'll pay later: Finish floors are particularly vulnerable to grit that isn't swept up and to nails that go astray. Lath with nails sticking out creates a hazardous workplace. Heed these tips and your life will be a lot easier:

▶ **Cover floors with heavy plastic, thick floor-covering cardboard (it comes in rolls), or hardboard panels duct-taped together.**

▶ **Isolate the demolition area by duct-taping clear plastic over door and window openings to contain the dust. Clear plastic lets in light.**

▶ **Clean up as you tear out.**

▶ **When demolishing outside, drape heavy tarps to protect your plants and to avoid a lot of raking later on. After discarding large pieces of debris, two people can lift the tarp and shake the remnants directly into the trash.**

Organize your debris. Maximize Dumpster loads by first putting in dense materials such as plaster, concrete, and soil. Place lighter, bulkier items on top. If your community has a recycling center, set aside recyclable materials such as unpainted wood, brick, glass, or metal. That may be cheaper than sending them to a landfill.

TEAROUT

Before you construct anything in renovation, it's usually necessary to tear out part of what's there and beef up what remains. No sooner have you torn out plaster than you're nailing up blocking for partitions to come. This natural flow from demolition to construction is a little frustrating for how-to writers who like to pigeonhole everything, but it's a fact of life if you're renovating. Frequently, you're doing both at the same time.

A roof-stripping shovel's serrated edges punch through and pry off drywall plaster lath easily. Wear goggles for this job, and disconnect the electricity before you begin.

Conserve when you can. If most of a plaster surface is sound, avoid damaging adjacent areas when removing loose plaster, exposing framing, or adding openings. For example, if you're adding a medicine cabinet, set your circular-saw blade to the depth of the old plaster and lath, and cut back those materials to the nearest stud centers on both sides so the plaster edges can be renailed before you patch the opening.

On the other hand, if at least half of a room is to be affected by demo or if the existing plaster walls are cracked and damaged, it is often better to gut the room. When wires, pipes, framing, and rotted areas are exposed, new framing and drywall go in faster and finish better. It's tough and time-consuming to patch extensively.

REMOVING DOORS AND TRIM

Doors, hardware, and trim (casing) make a house distinctive. Remove and store them till you are done with tearout and rough framing. Remove doors and hardware worth saving and clearly mark them "Salvage" so they don't get tossed. Most of the time, it's easy to pop hinge pins and lift doors out of the frame. But if that's not possible and hinge leaves are encrusted with paint, use an old screwdriver or a chisel good for little else to chip away paint from the screw heads. Or apply paint stripper.

To gently remove trim, first run a stiff putty knife between the frame and the trim to break the paint seal. Don't use anything with a sharp blade, because a sharp blade will slice into the trim. Then gently tap a flat 8-in. prybar behind the trim, as shown in the photo below, preferably near the nails holding it down. Pry up along the entire length of the trim, raising it little by little. Be patient. As you remove trim pieces, use a permanent marker to number the back of each so you can reinstall trim assemblies correctly.

Old trim is likely to be dry and brittle, so be patient when removing it. Use a flat bar to pry it out from the framing it's nailed to, gradually raising its entire length.

REMOVING PLASTER AND DRYWALL

Whether you're cutting a large hole for a skylight or gutting the whole ceiling, try to minimize the mess. Using a reciprocating saw with a demo blade to cut out 2-ft. by 2-ft. sections of drywall or plaster, you'll create a lot less dust and have a compact load to carry to the trash. But that's not always possible.

If the old plaster falls off the lath as you try to cut out sections, go ahead and break it out. Pull the lath and plaster down together, using a pick or crowbar, or use a hand sledge or a 2×4 to pound it down from the attic space above (place planks across the attic joists) or from the back side of the wall, if it's exposed. After separating and bundling the lath, shovel the plaster into buckets.

Dress for the job: hard hat, goggles, dust mask, heavy gloves, long-sleeved shirt. Wear thick-soled work boots when gutting plaster: Lath nails are ubiquitous and razor sharp, and they'll puncture tennis shoes in a flash.

Ceilings. 🚫 If ceiling joists are exposed in the attic, first take out the insulation from the area to be removed. If it's loose insulation, use a dustpan to shovel it into a garbage bag.

If you work on the ceiling from below, use movable scaffolding for ceilings 10 ft. or higher. Otherwise stand on 2-in.-thick planks straddling sawhorses or stepladders. If the plaster is solidly adhered to the lath, use a reciprocating saw to "outline" sections. Then rock them from side to side till the nails holding them to joists work free. Hand the removed section to a helper on the floor. Then proceed to the next plaster section.

If plaster is sound but sagging in a few spots, you may be able to reattach it with washered screws or cover it with ¼-in. drywall, as described in "Attaching Top Plates," on p. 166.

Walls. 🚫 Walls are easier to gut than ceilings because debris won't rain on you. Start at the top of each wall and work down, periodically carting out debris before it restricts your movements. Again, use a reciprocating saw to cut out 2-ft.-sq. sections if possible; otherwise break them out. Tile walls, you'll need to break out. If you'll be putting up new drywall or plaster, this is the time to pull old nails. Likewise, remove any old wires and pipes.

A skillful integration of old and new framing: After stripping interior surfaces and removing a wall to enlarge the room, carpenters installed a new 4×4 window king post and a third top plate to raise the old wall's framing. Note: Old and new window headers line up.

Before removing bearing walls, first shore up the joists or other loads they support. But if you're removing a nonbearing partition, you can do so after stripping plaster or drywall. Cut through the middle of each stud, using a reciprocating saw; its thin blade is less likely to bind than a circular saw's. With studs cut, pull them away from their plates. To remove plates, pry them up with a wrecking bar (goggles and a hard hat are musts). Use a metal-cutting blade in a reciprocating saw to cut through any remaining nail shanks.

REMOVING WOOD FLOORING

If they're solidly attached, old wood floors are generally left in place, to be refinished later or floored over. However, it's sometimes necessary to pull up a few boards so you can install joists or blocking, run wires, or patch-repair floor sections elsewhere. Partitions installed over finish flooring make it difficult to pry out floorboards.

If you'll be reinstalling the floorboards, try to pry them up in an inconspicuous spot, such as along the base of an existing wall. Remove the baseboard trim and try to insert a flat bar under the leading edge of a floorboard. You may need to destroy the first row of boards to get them out if they're face-nailed or, at the very least, break off the tongue on tongue-and-groove flooring. Successive courses will likely be toenailed through the tongue.

If you're gutting wall surfaces, the space between studs is a good place to fit the curved head of a wrecking bar, to pry up a first row of floorboards.

Reinforcing and Repairing the Structure

This section focuses on upgrading nonbearing structural elements: adding blocking, leveling ceilings, straightening stud walls, bolstering joists, and treating rotten or insect-damaged wood.

ADDING BLOCKING

In renovation, it's common to add *blocking* (short pieces of wood) to bolster existing joists or studs, to give new framing something to nail to, and to provide backing for the drywall or plaster lath to come.

Attaching top plates. To attach the top plate of a new partition, first cut back finish surfaces to expose ceiling joists. Snap two parallel chalklines to indicate the width of the top plate. If joists run perpendicular to the partition, cut out a 4-in.-wide slot to receive the top plate. Remove plaster or drywall sections, relocate insulation (if any), and pull nails sticking out of the joists. Use a utility knife to clean up ragged edges before nailing up the top plate, using two 16d nails at each point the plate crosses a joist.

If joists run parallel to the partition, cut back finish surfaces to joist centers on either side of the proposed plate so you can add blocking. Snap chalklines to indicate joist centers, and cut along those lines. (Set a plaster-cutting circular-saw blade to the thickness of the ceiling drywall or plaster. Wear eye protection.) Install blocking that's the same depth as the joists, spaced 24 in. on center. Cut blocking square for a tight fit, and make sure that its lower edges are flush to the

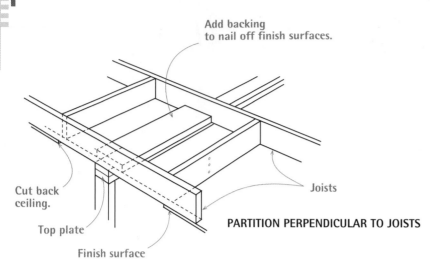

Add backing
to nail off finish surfaces.

Cut back
ceiling.

Top plate

Finish surface

Joists

PARTITION PERPENDICULAR TO JOISTS

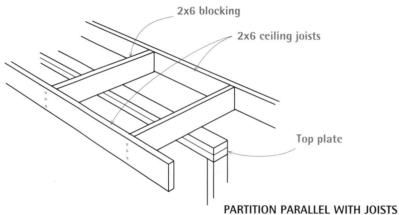

2x6 blocking

2x6 ceiling joists

Top plate

PARTITION PARALLEL WITH JOISTS

Where a partition runs perpendicular to joists, nail its top plate at each joist crossing. Remember to add backing for drywall or plaster lath, to which you can screw finish materials when you patch the ceiling. Where a partition runs parallel to joists, add 2× blocking to nail top plates to.

underside of the joists. If there's access, end-nail each block with three 12d nails, through adjacent joists. If you toenail them, use four 8d nails on each end. A pneumatic palm nailer is ideal for driving nails in such tight spaces.

Finally, add backing for the ceiling patch to come and reattach plaster or drywall edges along joist centers, as needed. Metal drywall clips (see the photo on p. 360) are a good alternative to blocking. Nail them to the top edge of the top plate.

Blocking for walls. 🚫 To effectively nail off a new wall where it abuts an existing one, first cut into the existing wall to expose the framing. Start with a small exploratory hole to determine exactly where the studs are. Then cut back finish surfaces to the nearest stud center on either side.

Even if your new wall runs directly to a stud in place, add blocking for metal drywall clips to reattach drywall patches.

If, as is more likely the case, there are no studs in the spot where you need a nail off, add them, as shown in the drawing "Where Walls Meet," at right. These nailers will be stronger if you preassemble them and then sledge them into place. Face-nail them together with 16d nails staggered every 16 in. Full-length nailers should be toenailed with three 10d or four 8d common nails top and bottom. Or prenail metal L-angles to tie nailers to plates.

Blocking for sole plates. Nail partition sole plates to the framing below, not merely to flooring or subflooring. If the partition runs perpendicular to the joists, use two 16d nails at each point the sole plate crosses a joist. (See p. 169.)

However, if the wall is parallel to the joist grid, try to locate it over an existing joist. If that's not possible, add blocking between the joists so there's something solid to nail the sole plate to. If the partition is nonbearing, use blocking the same depth as the joists, spaced on edge every 24 in. on center. Cut the blocking square so that it fits snug, flush to the underside of the subflooring. Use two or three 16d common nails to end-nail blocking through the joists. Blunt the nail points to prevent splits.

Note: Bearing walls should be supported by two full-length joists, on edge, running directly under the sole plate. Add blocking to adjacent joists to keep the new joists from rotating, and attach both ends with a double-joist hanger. Because doubled joists are, in effect, a girder, they may also need post support beneath; see "Beam Span Comparison," on p. 213, which offers sizes and spans. But because local codes have the final say, consult a structural engineer in your area.

LEVELING CEILINGS

The older the house, the more likely its ceiling joists are sagging. If you're gutting the old finish ceiling, the easiest way to create a flat, level plane for the drywall that will follow is to fasten lightweight steel studs to the old joists at a uniform height below the lowest joist (see p. 168).

With the aid of a helper, stretch a taut, level stringline perpendicular to existing joists at each end of the room and position each string lower than the bottom of the lowest joist so the studs won't deflect it as you work. Here's how:

1. Use a self-leveling laser level to establish a level line around the room that is ¼ in. below the lowest point of your ceiling joists.

Where Walls Meet

Existing studs

New studs

New partition

Existing studs

Finish surface

Where a new partition abuts an existing wall, cut back finish surfaces to the centers of the nearest stud on either side, and add studs to nail the partition to.

2. At this height, drive nails into the corners of the room. Stretch a taut string perpendicular to the ceiling joists at both ends of the room.

3. Line up the bottom edges of the steel studs $\frac{1}{16}$ in. above these taut strings, as you and your helper screw studs to the faces of the ceiling joists. (The $\frac{1}{16}$-in. gap is necessary to avoid moving the string and misaligning studs.)

4. Unless the ceiling is badly out of level (more than $1\frac{1}{2}$ in.), use 4-in.-wide steel studs. Lift the studs over the leveled strings, and lower each stud till its bottom edge is $\frac{1}{16}$ in. above the strings.

5. Once the stud is correctly positioned, use 1-in. screws to attach it to the joist; stagger screws every 16 in. along the length of the stud. Place the screws back at least $\frac{1}{2}$ in. from the lower edge of the joist. Use aviation snips to cut light (20-gauge to 25-gauge) steel framing.

Note: If the ceiling joists are undersize, rotted, or very springy, fix those conditions first. Screwing light steel to the joists won't strengthen them appreciably.

STRAIGHTENING STUDS

Before installing drywall on recently gutted or newly erected stud walls, scrutinize them to make sure they're flat. Stud variations of $\frac{1}{8}$ in. (from flat) are generally acceptable, unless they're in bathroom or kitchen walls—where studs should be within $\frac{1}{16}$ in. of flat. There, plumbed cabinets will make high and low spots glaringly obvious. Granted, you can scribe cabinet backs to fit wavy walls, but it's easier to straighten studs while they're still exposed.

Eyeball walls for obvious discrepancies. Then stretch taut strings across the stud edges at several heights. If the studs aren't flush to the top or sole plates, hammer them flush and screw on steel reinforcing-angles (see the photo on p. 61) to attach studs to the new position; more toenailing might split them. Next stretch a taut string, chest high, across the wall plane to find really high (protruding) and low (receding) spots. Mark them with a pencil. Finally, use a 6-ft. or 8-ft. level or straightedge to assess individual studs for bowing. Scribble symbols directly on stud edges, indicating high spots to be planed down, where studs bow toward you, and low spots to be built up, where studs bow away from you. Use special cardboard furring strips to build up the low spots.

Plane down high spots. Before power planing the high spots, use a magnet to scan the old studs for nails. Nails will destroy planer blades, so if the nails are too rusty or deep to pull, use a metal-cutting blade in a reciprocating saw to shave down the stud edges—a tedious process. If studs are nail free, plane down the high spots in several passes, starting at the middle of the high spot and gradually tapering out. Because knots are hard, they'll take more passes. Use your straightedge to check your progress, and use taut strings to check the whole wall again after building up or planing down the studs. *Caution:* Wear eye protection when using a power planer.

When studs bow into the room, use a power planer to plane down the high spots. Make the first pass over the high point of the bow; then make several successively longer passes to feather out the surface.

Common sense and "feel" are a big part of the straightening process: If all the studs in the wall have a slight bow inward or outward, the wall won't be flat, but drywall covering it may look flat. In that case, leave the studs as they are.

BOLSTERING JOISTS

Widespread sagging or excessive springiness in a floor is probably caused by joists that are too small for the span or by post, pad, and foundation failure, as covered in Chapter 10. Isolated joist failure is usually caused by insect or water damage; an earlier renovator cutting into the joist; or point loading, in which a heavy piece of furniture or a tub causes joists to sag. If there's infestation or rot, correct that condition first.

Sistered joists. The most common way to reinforce a weakened joist is to nail a new one to it—a "sister" of the same dimension and length. The new sister needn't be the exact length of the original but should be long enough to be supported on both ends by the perimeter foundation or a girder. For this reason, short sections "scabbed on" don't work and are usually prohibited by local building codes.

To insert the new joist, remove blocking or bridging between the affected joists, and bend over or snip off flooring nails protruding from the underside of the floor. Then eyeball the new sister joist and note its crown: If its arc is excessive, power plane it down so that you don't bow up the floor as you drive the joist into place. Beveling the leading top edge of the joist will also make sledging into place easier. Once the new joist is in position, use bar clamps to draw it tight to the old joist; then face-nail them, staggering 16d nails every 12 in. If there's no room to swing a hammer, use a pneumatic palm nailer to the drive nails most of the way.

Angled-end joist. Where joists will rest on a foundation mudsill at one end and hang from a girder at the other (rather than sitting atop it), angle-cut the end destined to rest on the mudsill so it will fit between the mudsill and subfloor. Cut the other end square to butt to the girder. Place the angle-cut end of the joist on edge over the mudsill; then lift the squared end and slide it toward the girder till it butts against it. Thus angle cut joists must be a few inches shorter than the original joist you're sistering to.

Leveling a Ceiling with Steel Studs

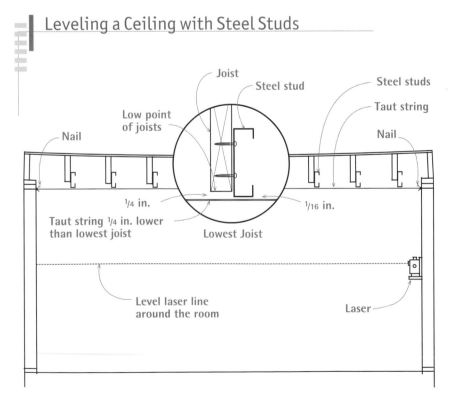

Steel studs let you establish a level plane of nailers for eventual drywall. As detailed in the text, measure up from a level laser line, drive a nail at each room corner, and stretch a string perpendicular to the joists at each end of the room.

Here, new joists are sistered to both sides of existing joists, with a 3-ft. overlap. The red chalkline down the center of the joists indicates the center of a new girder to come.

You may need a plumbed adjustable column or a screw jack to raise the joist till it's flush to the underside of the subflooring. Once it is flush, use a double-joist hanger to join the new joist (and its sister) to the girder. Face-nail the two joists, staggering 16d nails every 12 in. Remove jacks and replace blocking between joists. Should one flange of the double-joist hanger overlap a hanger already there, predrill the metal so that you can nail through both hangers with case-hardened hanger nails. To learn more about jacking safely, see Chapter 10.

Flitch plates. Steel flitch plates are sometimes used to reinforce undersize beams or joists. Because they are typically ⅜-in. to ½-in. thick and must be predrilled, they're not well suited to casual installation by nonspecialists. There's more on flitch plates on p. 53.

TREATING INSECT INFESTATIONS

If you see signs of an infestation, hire a pest-control professional to assess and remedy it. Pesticides are often toxic, and anyone unfamiliar with insect habits may not destroy all their nesting sites or may apply pesticides inappropriately

Nailing Off Sole Plates

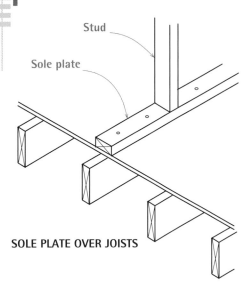

SOLE PLATE OVER JOISTS

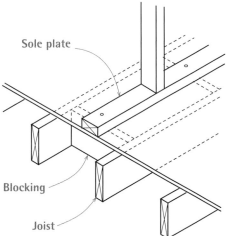

SOLE PLATE OVER BLOCKING

When a partition runs parallel to the joists, try to position it over a joist so you'll have something to nail the sole plate to. If you can't reposition the wall, add blocking between the joists.

Finishing Basement Walls

Basement walls are usually masonry, rarely plumb, and often damp. If you want finished basement walls, here's a skeletal outline of the principal steps (see Chapter 14 for insulation tips).

1. Eliminate external sources of water such as clogged gutters, inadequate drainage, and improper grading. Repair foundation cracks that could admit water.

2. Trowel or roll a cementitious coating onto foundation walls to damp-proof them. Using construction adhesive, install rigid foam insulation panels to isolate cool foundation walls and prevent condensation. Cover the panels with a plastic waterproofing membrane.

3. Erect wood-frame or light-steel stud walls within—but not touching—the foundation walls. Use pressure-treated sole plates on wood walls. Or, if space is tight, consider installing 1⅝-in.-wide steel studs. (Covered with drywall, they're sturdy and stable.)

4. Powder-actuated tools quickly attach sole plates to concrete floors, but such tools are dangerous because most powder loads are the equivalent of a .22 cartridge. Plus you're shooting steel fasteners into concrete. Get instruction in using these tools safely, read the accompanying safety manuals, and wear appropriate safety equipment—including eye and hearing protection.

As furring for basement walls, light–steel studs have advantages: They won't rot, and 1⅝-in.-wide studs don't waste much space. Here, a powder–actuated tool attaches a metal sole plate to a concrete floor. Because of risks in misusing such tools, follow the manufacturer's operating instructions exactly.

Sistering Joists

SISTER JOIST SITS ATOP SILL AND HANGS OFF GIRDER

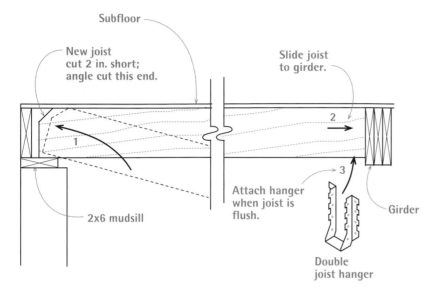

To sister a new joist when one end will rest on a mudsill and the other will hang from a girder, angle cut the mudsill end and slide it into place. Then raise the other end till it's flush with the girder before attaching with a hanger.

SISTER JOIST SITS ATOP SILL AND GIRDER

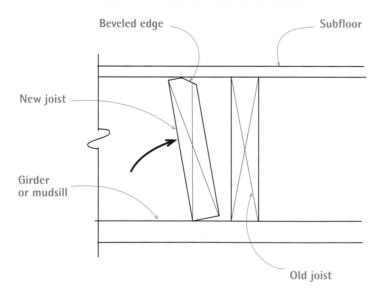

To "sister" a new joist to one that sits atop a mudsill on one end and a girder on the other, bevel the leading top edge so it will "sledgehammer" into place.

or unnecessarily. Moreover, local codes may require a professional.

It's often difficult to tell whether an infestation is active or not. For example, if a subterranean termite infestation is inactive, a prophylactic treatment may suffice. But if the infestation is active, the remedy may require eliminating the conditions that lead to the infestation (such as excessive moisture and earth–wood contact) and an aggressive chemical treatment. Treatment usually consists of applying a chemical barrier on the ground that repels the termites or a "treated zone" whose chemical doesn't repel them initially but later kills or severely disrupts them.

Termites, the most famous of insect pests, include drywood, subterranean, and Formosan types. Because subterranean termites need access to the moisture of the soil, they build distinctive dirt tubes up along the surface of foundations. When they eat into the wood, they usually proceed with the grain. Termites swarm in spring or fall. Discourage the return of subterranean termites by lowering soil levels around foundations, footings, and the like.

Drywood termites hollow out chambers separated by thin tunnels and often travel cross-grain; they eject fecal pellets through kick-out holes, forming a pyramid-shaped pile under the holes. Fumigation is effective for drywood termites, but it's ineffective for treating subterranean termites because their colonies are located in the ground and fumigation gas does not penetrate the soil.

Formosan termites, whose colonies may exceed 1 million individuals, are wreaking havoc along the Gulf Coast of the United States; they live in the ground or in buildings and build huge, hard nests.

Carpenter ants are red or black, ¼ in. to ½ in. long. Sometimes confused with termites, these ants have narrow waists and, when winged, wings of different sizes. While they do tunnel in wet or rotting wood, they do not eat it as food and are therefore less destructive than termites. To locate their nests, look for borings rather like coarse sawdust. Professionals will often drill into nests and spray them with an insecticide safe enough for inside use; dusting with boric acid is another common treatment.

Powder-post beetle holes look like tiny BB-gun holes; their borings resemble coarse flour. Because these insects favor the sapwood, evidence of borings may be only superficial until you prod with a pocketknife. Still, holes are not a sure sign of an active infestation. One approach is to remove the damaged wood, sweep up borings, paint the area, and monitor it for a year. If holes reappear, it's an active

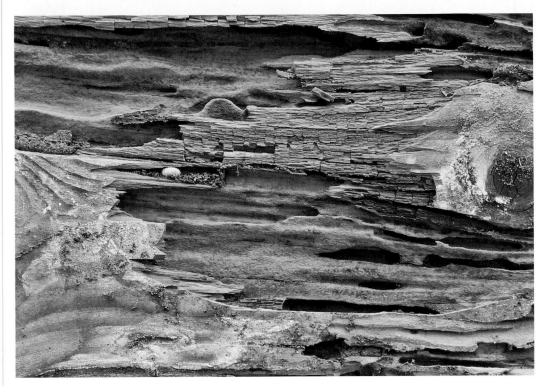

This wall sheathing shows evidence of fungi and insect damage. After failed window flashing allowed water behind a stucco exterior, wood-destroying fungi grew quickly. Then subterranean termites tunneled, consuming the moist, fungus-damaged wood. Cross-grain checking just above center is a typical sign of fungus damage. A beetle larva showed up too.

infestation: A professional will need to fumigate the wood or apply a pesticide.

DEALING WITH ROT

If wood is spongy, contains wispy fibers that look like cotton, or disintegrates without reference to the grain, it is infested by a rot fungus. The white strands are spores.

If the rot is limited to a few spots, suspect leakage and look for other clues above. Water may be entering from inadequate roof flashing, blocked gutters, or—quite common in older houses—windows or doors that lack flashing altogether, in which case there will probably be fungus damage to walls and ceilings inside. Also, look for structural damage beneath tubs, sinks, and water heaters; if you find any, make sure the damage hasn't progressed into subflooring and floor framing.

Rotted wood, unsightly as it is, poses no threat to healthy wood nearby, as long as you control the moisture that encouraged the rot fungus. Cut out deteriorated sections, but don't bother to remove discolored wood that is solid; leave it in place, especially if flooring is nailed to it. You can reinforce existing joists by sistering on new ones, but before doing so, allow the old joists to dry thoroughly.

Water, Insects, Rot, and Mold

Whether structural damage is caused by insects or rot fungi, excess water is usually the heart of the problem. Thus, before treating the specific agent causing the deterioration, reduce excess water by maintaining gutters, improving drainage, grading the soil away from the building, eliminating wood–soil contact, improving ventilation, and so on.

The fungi that rot wood reproduce by airborne spores, so they're virtually everywhere. But they can't establish colonies on wood with a moisture content (MC) less than 28 percent; and they go dormant if the MC drops below 20 percent or the air temperature drops below 40°F. Household molds, also caused by fungi, thrive in a similar moisture and temperature range. So if moisture-meter readings in your basement or crawl space are too high, reducing excess moisture may solve both wood rot and mold problems.

How you reduce moisture, however, is something experts can't agree on (see Chapter 14 for more on mitigating moisture and mold). Many building codes recommend covering dirt floors in crawl spaces or basements with sheet plastic and installing screened vents to circulate air and disperse moisture: 1 sq. ft. of vent per 100 sq. ft. of floor space is the standard formula. Whereas another group of builders argues that it makes more sense—especially in the humid South—to close vents, insulate crawl space or basement walls, seal air leaks, and install a dehumidifier. That, they argue, will stop mold from colonizing and migrating to living spaces. Best bet: See which approach builders in your region favor.

Stair Repairs

Stairs are complicated to build, and problems can be tricky to diagnose. For example, it may be possible to repair squeaky stairs with glue and a few screws. But if squeaking is widespread, stairs tilt to one side, and there's a gap along a stairwell wall, the diagonal supports beneath the staircase may be failing. In that case, you'll probably need to expose those supports to find out.

SQUEAKY STEPS

If the underside of your staircase is covered and you have only a few squeaks, try fixing them without tearing out finish materials. Many people mistakenly attempt to fix squeaks by nailing down offending treads with finish nails, but nails alone won't work. The nails may split the nosing, and they'll almost certainly pull loose. It's far better to predrill and countersink Torx screws through the tread into a riser or center carriage beneath.

If stairs can be painted or carpeted over, caulk the squeaky joint with subflooring adhesive. This doesn't bind the pieces together as well as screws do, but the adhesive cushions them, in effect. Keep people off the stairs until the compound has cured. If that doesn't eliminate squeaking, expose the underside of the staircase to examine its underpinnings.

What you do next depends on the construction of the stairs. If there are blocks glued along the riser–tread joint, it's likely the glue has failed. First, eliminate tread movement by nailing through the back side of risers into treads: predrill, and use two or three 6d finish nails per tread. Then reglue errant blocks with white glue or, better yet, with construction adhesive.

REPLACING BALUSTERS

Broken balusters can usually be doweled, glued, and filled. But if you're disappointed with the repair, see if your lumberyard can order a replacement in the same pattern. Stair parts have been mass-produced for a century or more, so there are catalogs full of stock balusters. Custom mills can create new balusters to match old ones, but the process is labor intensive and costly. Thus, if you have many damaged or missing balusters and can't find stock replacements, consider replacing all with another pattern.

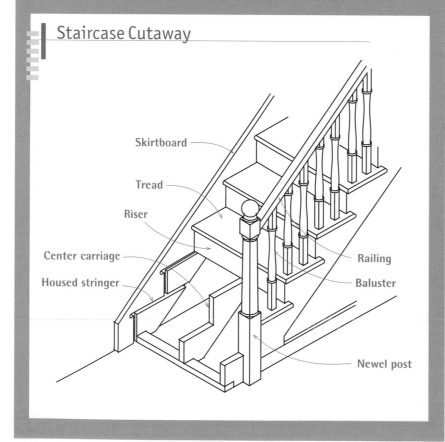

Stair LINGO

As shown below, stringers and carriages support steps. Stringers serve as the diagonal support frames on each side. And carriages carry by means of a sawtooth pattern cut into them. Stringers and carriages are often fastened together. Another option is a housed stringer, in which a stringer has routed grooves that receive and support tread and riser ends.

Staircase Cutaway

- Skirtboard
- Tread
- Riser
- Center carriage
- Housed stringer
- Railing
- Baluster
- Newel post

The rough cap atop this baluster section of a custom-built staircase will be covered by a three-piece railing assembly. The short fillet strips between the baluster tops can be removed, should balusters need replacing later.

If balusters are intact but shaky, remove and reglue them; simply nailing them won't do much good. To get at balusters, pry free the return molding at the end of the tread by inserting a putty knife or small chisel into the nosing seam. Once you start prying, you'll see small finish nails holding the nosing in place; remove these nails. Then gently tap out the bottom of the baluster, which is usually joined to the tread by a dovetail joint or a dowel. The top of the baluster is held in place by fillet strips that fit tightly between baluster tops and are toenailed with tiny finish nails to the *plow* (routed channel) in the underside of the railing. Pry out the *fillets* first, shown in the photo on the facing page.

To fit the baluster back in place tightly, lightly coat both ends with white glue and replace the tenoned or doweled end first. Replace fillets to evenly space the tops of the balusters. Replace the return molding and wipe off the excess glue. To prevent marring during this operation, cushion blows with a rubber mallet or scrap wood.

TIGHTENING NEWEL POSTS

If many of the balusters are loose, check the railing and the newel post: They may not be firmly attached. Or if the upper end of the railing dead ends into a wall on the floor above, the railing may be anchored with a bracket beneath. Make sure this bracket is tight.

If the newel post is shaky, try shimming underneath its base or screwing the post down

Anatomy of a Hollow Newel Post

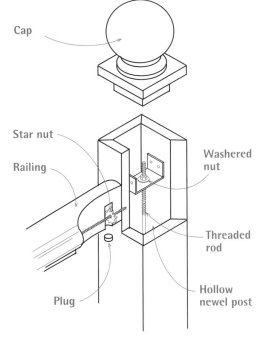

Cap

Star nut

Railing

Washered nut

Threaded rod

Plug

Hollow newel post

Unlike modern newel posts, older ones are often hollow and attach to railings in various ways. One common way is a star nut centered in the end of a railing, which is accessed by removing a plug on the underside. The bottom of the post may be screwed to a stringer or held fast by an adjustable rod-and-plate assembly running down the middle of the post.

This three-piece railing assembly mockup has two skirt (side) pieces that cover the tops of the balusters and a cap. This unusual assembly will create a massive, magisterial look.

The doweled end of this square-cut baluster fits precisely into a hole predrilled into a stair tread.

To cut a tread out, first remove the balusters from the step's open end, saving that end as a template for the new tread. Drill into the middle of the tread and, driving a chisel with the wood grain, split out the old tread. Clean up any old glue or wood fragments. After fabricating the new tread and testing its fit, apply glue to its edges and to the tops of the carriages on which it will sit. To each carriage, screw down the tread with two or three trim-head screws, predrilled to prevent splitting. Reinsert and glue balusters and nosing.

SAGGING STAIRS

If the staircase has several of the ailments described in preceding sections, it may also have major troubles underneath. Investigate further. If the stairs tilt to one side, the carriage on the low side is having difficulty: That is, nails or screws holding it to the wall may be pulling out, the wood may be rotting or splitting, or the carriage may be pulling free from the stringer. Sagging on the open side of a stairway is common, for there's no wall to bolt its carriage to. If there are large cracks or gaps at the top and bottom of the stairs, you're seeing symptoms of a falling carriage.

To learn more, remove the finish surfaces from the underside of the staircase. But before cutting into anything, rent a Dumpster for the rubble and confine the mess by sealing off the stairwell with sheet plastic. When you cut, set your circular saw just to the depth of the finish materials so that you don't cut into carriages. Wear goggles and use a Carborundum™ blade to cut out the surface in 2-ft. squares.

You can probably save any decorative plaster molding along the staircase by cutting parallel to it—about 1 in. from its edge, thus isolating the section of lath nailed to the underside of the outer carriage. Leaving a 1-in. strip will also make it easier to disguise the seam when you reattach the ornamental border after repairing the stairs.

With the underside of the stairs exposed, you can see exactly what the problem is. If the carriages have pulled loose from adjacent walls, you'll see a definite gap. Replace wood that is rotted or badly cracked, especially wood cracked across the grain. If the wood sags or is otherwise distorted, bolster it with additional lumber; it may also need to be reattached. All of these repairs are big ones. To do them right, you'll need complete access to the substructure, from one end of the carriages to the other.

Starting at the top, remove all nosing, balusters, treads, and risers. You could theoretically bolster undersize carriages without removing all the treads, risers, and balusters, but it's better to

With skirt pieces glued and clamped to both sides of the rough cap, the finish railing cap is test-fitted.

with predrilled 3-in. Torx screws. If this easy repair doesn't suffice, see if the internal hardware needs tightening. Quite often newel posts are hollow, with a long, threaded rod inside, as shown in "Anatomy of a Hollow Newel Post," on p. 173. You may be able to tighten the upper end of this rod, concealed by the post cap, by turning a nut against a restraining plate. Because you may have difficulty finding the cap joint under many years of polish and grime, loosen the cap by rapping the side of it with a rubber mallet. The bottom end of the threaded rod often emerges on the underside of the subflooring—if it's exposed, have a look.

On occasion, newel posts also connect to another plate-and-rod assembly on the inside of the nearest stair carriage. About the only way to get at that assembly (if it exists at all) is to pull up the first tread. Where the railing meets the newel, the railing is held tight by wood joinery or by a double-ended hanger bolt accessible through a plug on the underside of the railing.

REPLACING STAIR TREADS

Treads crack because they aren't supported correctly or they weren't made from good stock. To replace them, you'll need to pry or cut them out. Prying is preferable but rarely possible, especially if the treads are rabbeted to risers or housed in stringers.

remove them. Otherwise, misaligned or distorted carriages will be held askew by all the pieces nailed to them. So remove the treads and risers, and jack up the distorted carriages to realign them. (You may want to stretch taut strings as an alignment aid.)

Number all parts as you remove them, grouping pieces according to the step number.

REALIGNING AND REINFORCING CARRIAGES

If the outside stair carriage has bowed outward, use a 2×4 jammed against a near wall to push the carriage back into place. You can instead use an adjustable screw column horizontally to push the carriage back, but nail the column's top plates so it can't fall.

Where a carriage has separated from its stringer, clamp the pieces together; then add two ¼-in. lag bolts, staggering the pairs of bolts every 18 in. along the length of the boards. If a carriage has pulled free from a stud wall, reattach it with washered lag bolts. Where a carriage is attached to a masonry wall, drill through the carriage into the masonry, using a carbide-tipped masonry bit. Slip a lead sleeve into the hole and expand the sleeve by tightening a washered ⅜-in. lag bolt into it. To forestall rot, slip a piece of 30-lb. building paper behind the carriage before bolting it down.

Occasionally, stringers or carriages come loose at the top and bottom. In a well-built staircase, the upper ends of carriages are nailed to the inside of the header above; the lower ends of those carriages sit on, and are nailed to, the doubled joists of the rough opening below.

However, sometimes the lower ends of center carriages are mistakenly nailed to the inside of a RO header; in time the nails pull free and the carriages slip down. Jack up the fallen carriages, using a plumbed, adjustable column securely footed on the floor or atop a 4×8 beam on edge. To create a flat jacking surface for the top of the column, screw a triangular piece (with the same slope as the stairs) to the underside of the carriage. Should old nails resist your effort, cut through them with a metal-cutting blade in a reciprocating saw. Goggles, please.

Jack up the center carriage and join its lower end to the header with steel connectors or ¼-in. right-angle mending plates. Secure the plates to the header with ⅜-in. lag bolts and through the bottom of the carriage with ¼-in.-diameter carriage bolts. It's not usually necessary to use mending plates on the upper end of the carriage because the lower end is bearing most of the weight.

Bolstering a Center Carriage

⅝-in. plywood
tread supports screwed
on alternate sides

2x6 or 2x8
center carriage

¼-in.
steel angle plate

⅜-in.
carriage bolts

3-in. x ⅜-in.
lag screws

If the center carriage isn't notched, it may not support treads well. In this case, screw plywood tread supports to alternate sides. Also, if the center carriage was only nailed to the face of a header originally, it may have slipped down. If so, jack it up and reattach with a ¼-in. steel angle plate.

Inadequate support for the middle of a staircase can lead to split treads or major failures. Where a center carriage is not sawtoothed to receive treads, add plywood supports beneath each step. Cut support blocks from scrap plywood ½ in. thick. Then glue and screw them to alternate sides of the carriage—one per tread. If the stair sags in the middle and has no center carriage, add one.

You can replace finish surfaces after the carriages are bolstered and reattached and the stairs and balusters are reinstalled. Be sure that the nailing plane on the underside of the carriages is flat, shimming as needed. To reattach plaster lath or drywall, use type W drywall screws (hammering drywall nails can crack surrounding materials).

Shoring

Shoring temporarily supports loads carried by bearing walls while you modify them—say, to add a window or a door opening. Typically, shoring is installed after removing finish surfaces and rerouting pipes and wires but before cutting into a bearing wall. If you're not sure if the wall is bearing or whether it can be safely modified, have a structural engineer inspect the house and review your remodeling plans. This is hard-hat work.

For first- and second-floor walls, two types of shoring are common: *screw jacks* used with top and bottom plates, and temporary stud walls built from 2×4s. In either case, position shoring back 2 ft. to 3 ft. from the wall you're working on so you'll have room to move tools and materials.

▶ **If you're using screw jacks,** doubled 2×6 top plates will distribute loads better. Here's how to laminate the top plates in place: Use two or three

Screw jacks and a doubled 2×6 top plate pick up loads so a window opening can be safely enlarged. The floor shown is concrete. If yours is wood, use a 2×6 plate under the jacks, as well.

In the foreground is a 2×4 shoring with a horizontal brace.

16d common nails to nail the upper 2×6 directly to the ceiling joists; then face-nail the second 2×6 to it. Ideally, the top plates should extend one joist beyond the new opening on both sides. Don't over-nail, you're just holding up the plates till you get jacks underneath. Plumb down to mark the location of the single 2×6 sole plate. Place jacks every 4 ft., and plumb them. Tack-nail the top of each jack so it can't fall over. Then raise one jack in tiny increments before moving to the next. Raise ceiling joists no more than ⅛ in.—just enough to take pressure off the bearing wall.

▶ **Building a temporarily stud wall** is simi-lar: Tack-nail the top plates; then plumb down to mark the bottom plate. (To keep the bottom plate in place, tack-nail it to the joists underneath.) Cut studs ¼ in. longer than the distance between the plates because, here, the studs do the lifting. Toenail the studs to the top plate on 16-in. or 24-in. centers. Then use a sledge to rap the bottom of each stud till the stud is plumb. Recheck each stud for plumb as you progress, and monitor them periodically.

Once shoring supports the loads above, remove the studs from the bearing wall as needed to enlarge openings, add headers, and the like. If the bearing wall transfers loads from upper stories down into girders or foundation walls, study the lengthy sec-tion on jacking and shoring in Chapter 10.

Structural Remodeling

Once shoring is in place, you should be safe in removing bearing walls. Check with a structural engineer if you have any doubts. Again, wear safety gear (hard hat, eye protection, work boots with thick soles, and so on) and test the electrical outlets to be sure the power is off. If you need to do any jacking, read Chapter 10.

FRAMING A DOOR OR WINDOW OPENING

After cutting back interior surfaces to expose the framing in the exterior wall, outline the RO by snapping chalklines across the edges of studs. If you can incorporate existing studs into the new opening—an old stud might become the king stud of the new opening, as shown in the photo on p. 165—you can save time and materials.

To remove old studs within the new opening, use a sledge to rap the bearing wall's top plate upward, thus creating a small gap above the studs (and old header, if any). That should create enough space to slip in a metal-cutting reciprocating-saw blade and cut through nails holding studs to the top plate. Though sheathing or siding may be nailed to the studs, they should still pull out easily.

Start framing the new opening by toenailing the king stud on both sides, using three 10d nails or four 8d nails top and bottom. Laminate the header package or cut it from 4× stock. (The procedures described here employ terms illustrated in "Stud-Wall Elements," on p. 155.) Precut the jack studs, and face-nail one to a king stud; lean the second near the other side of the opening. Place one end of the header atop the jack stud in place. Then slide the second jack under the free end of the header. Raise the header by tapping the second jack into place. Or, as an alternative, you can use a screw jack to hold the header flush to the underside of the top plate. Check for level; then measure and cut both jack studs to length.

If there are cripple studs over the header, nail up one jack stud, use a level to establish the height of the jack stud on the second side, and nail it up. Install the header; then cut the cripple studs to length and install them. If you're framing a window opening, there will also be cripple studs under the sill. So level and install the sill next, using four 8d nails on both sides for toenailing the sill ends to the jack studs. End-nail through the sill into the top of the cripple studs; toenail the bottoms of the cripple studs to the sole plate.

To mark the rough opening outside, cut through the sheathing and the siding, using a reciprocating saw. Or, if you want to strip most of the siding in the affected area first, drill a hole

PRO **TIP**

Today, rough openings are usually 82½ in. high, which accommodates a standard 6 ft. 8 in. preframed door. But if your house is nonstandard, instead try to line up new or enlarged openings in exterior walls to the tops of existing doors and windows. The underside of a new header will usually be 2 in. to 2½ in. above the window or door frame, but check your unit's installation instructions.

IS IT A Bearing WALL?

As noted in "Exploring Your Options," on p. 152, bearing walls and girders usually run parallel to the roof ridge and perpendicular to the joists and rafters they support. And in most two-story houses, joists usually run in the same direction from floor to floor.

Things get tricky, however, when rooms have been added piecemeal and when previous remodelers used nonstandard framing methods. For that, you'll need to explore. Use an electronic stud-finder or note which way the heating ducts run (usually between joists) to figure out joist direction. If all else fails, go into a closet, pantry, or other inconspicuous location and cut a small hole in the ceiling so you can see which way the joists run.

Finally, nonbearing walls sometimes become bearing walls when homeowners place heavy furniture, book shelves, appliances, or tubs above them. If floors deflect—slope downward—noticeably toward the base of such walls, they're probably bearing.

through each corner of the RO. Outside, snap chalklines through the four holes. Remove siding within that opening—plus the width of the new exterior casing around all four sides. Nail the sheathing to the edges of the new frame. Finally, run a reciprocating saw along the chalklines to cut sheathing flush to the edges of the RO. Now you're ready to flash the opening and install the door or window. Chapter 6 will guide you from there.

REPLACING A BEARING WALL

Bearing-wall replacements should be designed by a structural engineer and executed by a contractor adept at erecting shoring and handling heavy loads in tight spaces. In the two methods presented in the following text, beam-and-post systems replace bearing stud walls. In the first method, the bearing beam is exposed because it supports joists from below. In the second method, the beam is hidden in the ceiling, and joist hangers attach joists to the beam.

Once you've cut electrical power to the affected area, installed shoring on both sides of the existing bearing wall, and inserted blocking under support post locations, you're ready to remove the bearing wall and replace it with a new beam. However, if you're installing a hidden beam, your job will be easier if you leave the old wall in place a bit longer to steady the joist ends as you cut through them.

Installing an exposed beam is the easier of the two methods. Because ceiling joists sit atop an exposed beam, it's not necessary to cut the joists—as it is when installing a hidden beam. After removing the bearing wall, snap chalklines on the ceiling to indicate the width of the new beam—say, 4½ in. wide for a beam laminated from three 2×10s or 2×12s. Cut out the finish surfaces within this 4½-in.-wide slot so the joists can sit directly on the beam. Chances are, the slot won't need to be much wider than the width of the top plate of the wall just removed.

Because the beam extends into end walls, notch the beam ends so they will fit under the end-wall top plates, which may also support joists. Notching ensures that the top of the beam, the top plates, and the bottom of the ceiling joists will be the same height. If end walls have doubled top plates, the notch will be 3 in. to 4 in. deep. Before notching the beam, eyeball it for crown and place it crown up. Before raising the beam, be sure to have blocking under each post to ensure a continuous load path down to the foundation.

A laminated 2×12 beam can weigh 250 lb., so have enough helpers to raise it safely. Once the top of the beam is in place, flush to the underside of the joists above, temporarily support it with plumbed screw jacks or 2×4s cut ¾ in. long and wedged beneath the beam—have workers tack-nail and monitor the 2×4s so they can't kick out! (Put 2× plates beneath the jacks or the wedged 2×4s to avoid damaging finish flooring.)

Measure from the underside of the new exposed beam to the floor or subfloor. Then cut 4×4 posts ¹⁄₁₆ in. longer than the height of the opening, and use a sledgehammer to tap them into place. (Ideally, cut posts the exact length; but a little long is preferable to a little short.) Plumb the posts, and install metal connectors such as Simpson Strong-Tie A-23 anchors to secure the post ends to the top and sole plates. Add studs to both sides of each post, as shown in "Supporting an Exposed Beam," to "capture" it and keep it from moving; nail these studs to the plates and to the 4×4s as well.

Installing a hidden beam takes more work than installing an exposed beam but yields a smooth ceiling. To summarize, after erecting stud-wall shoring on both sides of the bearing wall to be replaced, cut all the ceiling joists to create a slot for the hidden beam, assemble the beam on the ground, and then lift it into place. Here, joists will hang from the sides of the beam rather than

Supporting an Exposed Beam

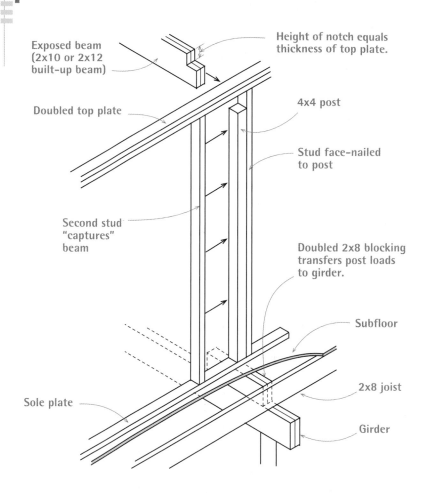

Exposed beam (2x10 or 2x12 built-up beam)

Doubled top plate

Second stud "captures" beam

Sole plate

Height of notch equals thickness of top plate.

4x4 post

Stud face-nailed to post

Doubled 2x8 blocking transfers post loads to girder.

Subfloor

2x8 joist

Girder

After notching and then raising an exposed beam with jacks, cut 4x4 posts to support it at both ends. There must also be blocking under each post, to transfer post loads to the girder and other foundation elements.

Checking THE LOAD PATH

Because loads will be concentrated on support posts beneath each end of the new beam, those posts must be supported continuously all the way down to girders and to concrete pads, footings, or foundation walls. To make sure there is adequate support below proposed post locations, strip the bearing wall to its studs and insert shoring along both sides before removing corner studs at both ends of the bearing wall. Leave the rest of the wall alone for now.

Using a long auger bit (18 in. by ⅜ in.), drill down through a sole plate at each end, where a post will stand. (In fact, the posts may be hidden in end walls at either end of the bearing wall.) If the bit hits a girder, posts should have adequate support. But if the bit hits air or only a single joist, add solid blocking. That blocking may be a 6x6 atop a girder or a new post and concrete footing—but let a structural engineer decide. Fit the blocking tight to the underside of the subflooring beneath the posts so there can be no deflection when loads are transferred to them.

Hidden Beam

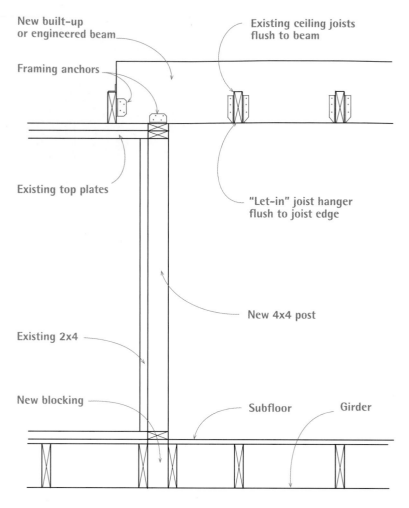

New built-up or engineered beam

Framing anchors

Existing ceiling joists flush to beam

Existing top plates

"Let-in" joist hanger flush to joist edge

New 4x4 post

Existing 2x4

New blocking

Subfloor   Girder

A hidden beam allows you to remove a bearing wall and still have a smooth expanse of ceiling. A continuous load path—from the beam, through the posts, to the foundation—is crucial to a successful installation.

sitting atop it, so the hidden beam will rest on top of end-wall top plates.

Thus install 4×4 posts between the top and the sole plates—and blocking under the posts—before raising the beam. Snap chalklines on the ceiling to indicate the width of the beam plus 4 in. extra on each side so you can slide joist hangers in later. Cut out drywall or plaster within that slot to open up the ceiling and expose joists. After installing shoring, as explained in earlier sections, go up into the attic.

1. Make the attic workspace safe and comfortable. Place 2-in.-thick planks or ⅝-in. plywood walkways on both sides of the area where you'll insert the beam. Tack-nail the walkways so they can't drift. Clamp work lights to the underside of rafters and add ventilation. For necessary ventilation, you may first need to install gable end louvers and buy a fan—especially if it's summer. If roofing nails protrude from the underside of roof sheathing, wear a hard hat.

If there's enough room in the attic, assemble the beam in place and lower it down into the slot you'll create by cutting back joist ends. However, if you must assemble the beam on the floor below—or if you're raising an engineered beam—use a nylon web sling and a chain fall (see the photo on p. 53) bolted through the rafters to raise the beam up through the cutout in the ceiling. Angle-brace rafters to keep them from deflecting under the load, and don't attach a chain fall to rafters that are cracked or already sagging.

2. Snap a chalkline to mark the beam location onto the top edges of joists. Snap a first line to mark the centerline of the beam. Then measure out half the beam width plus ⅛ in. on both sides, and snap chalklines to indicate cut-lines on the joists. Using a square, extend these lines down the face of each joist. Use vivid chalk so the marks will be visible.

Because thin reciprocating-saw blades wander, use a circular saw to ensure square cuts across joists. It's hard to see the cut-line of a saw you're lowering between two joists, so clamp a framing square to each joist to act as a guide for the saw shoe. Some renovators prefer a small chainsaw for this operation, but hitting a single hidden nail in a joist can snap a chainsaw blade and send it flying at you. Whatever you use to cut the joists, wear hearing and eye protection and, ideally, have a similarly protected helper nearby shining a light into the cut area.

3. Get help to raise the beam one end at a time. If your cuts are accurate, you should be able to raise the beam between the severed joists and onto the top plate of one end wall and then the other. But, invariably, the beam gets hung up on something. Here, a chain fall is invaluable because it allows you to raise and lower one end of the beam numerous times without killing your back or exhausting your crew.

When the first end of the beam is up, nail cleats to both sides of the beam so it can't slip back through the opening as you raise the other end. Raise and position the other end of the beam atop the other end wall and directly over

PRO TIP

Before attaching joist hangers, make a single pass of a power plane across the underside of each joist end, where it abuts the new beam. The planed area, roughly the width and thickness of a joist hanger "stirrup," ensures that the joist hangers will be flush to the bottom of the joists and the beam and that the patched ceiling will be evenly flat.

IIII

As a chain fall and a nylon sling support one end of the beam, master builder John Michael Davis and his helper lower the other end into the tight space between newly cut joist ends. Both ends of the beam will sit on a doubled-top-plate-and-post assembly that transfers loads down to foundation components.

the 4×4 support post. Then use a metal connector such as a Simpson BC4 or an A-34 anchor (see the top photo on p. 60) to secure the beam to the top plates.

4. Fine-tune the height of individual joists till their lower edges are flush to the bottom of the beam. This operation is easiest with one worker downstairs using a 2×4 to raise or lower the joist ends as a worker in the attic directs. As each joist is correctly positioned, attach it to the beam using joist hangers and the case-hardened nails supplied with the hangers. Before attaching joist hangers, however, use a power planer to cut a shallow slot into the underside of each joist, to let in the hangers so they're flush to the under-side of the joists. If there's not much room to swing a hammer between joists, use a pneumatic palm nailer to drive the nails most of the way. Finally, along the edges of the beam slot, center and end-nail 2×4 backing between the joists for the finish-surface patches to come.

For more details on this complex operation, see John Michael Davis's article "Removing a Bearing Wall," in *Fine Homebuilding*, No. 152.

Heavy Metal

Steel connectors are an important part of renovation carpentry, often joining new and old framing members.

Straps such as Simpson Strong-Tie LSTA strap ties are frequently used where wall plates are cut, at wall intersections, and as ridge ties. Pros often use them to splice new rafter tails to existing rafters, to replace sections that rotted at the wall plate. After cutting rafter tails at the correct angle, toenail them to the top plate and use 12-in. or 18-in. strap ties to tie new tails to the old rafters. After the sheathing is nailed on, such reinforced rafter tails will stay in line indefinitely.

The 4×14 Parallam beam sitting atop a 2×4 top plate at right is much like the hidden beam dis-cussed in "Installing a Hidden Beam" in the text. In the old days, beams of this size would have been merely toenailed to top plates. So the Simpson BC4 post cap now specified by engineers is quite an

improvement. It's simple to install and strong enough to resist uplift and lateral movement. Note, too, the 4×4 post directly under the beam—it's part of the load path that goes all the way down to the foundation.

9 Masonry

Modern masonry employs a range of materials, including stone, brick, tile, concrete, and other minerals that become strong and durable when used in combination. The craft of masonry is ancient. The oldest surviving buildings are stone, but stone is heavy and difficult to work with. Brick, on the other hand, is less durable than stone but lighter and easier to lay up. And clay, the basic component of brick, is found almost everywhere.

Technologically, the switch from stone to brick was a great leap in several respects. First, masons began with a plastic medium (mud and straw) that they shaped into hard and durable building units of uniform size. Second, brick-making is one of the earliest examples of mass production. Third, basic bricklaying tools, such as trowels, were so perfectly designed that they've changed little in 4,000 or 5,000 years.

Terms, Tools, and Tips

Unless otherwise specified, mixes and methods in this chapter are appropriate for brickwork as well as concrete-block work. But most of this chapter is about brick and poured concrete because concrete-block work is uncommon in renovation.

TERMS

Here's a handful of mason's lingo that's frequently confused:

Portland cement. The basic component of all modern masonry mixtures. When water is added to cement, it reacts chemically with it, giving off heat and causing the mix to harden, thus bonding together materials in contact with the mix. By varying the proportions of the basic ingredients of a concrete mix, the renovator can alter the concrete's setting time, strength, resistance to

Masonry needn't always be straight lines. Here, clinker bricks, fieldstones, and tile playfully conceal a drab concrete retaining wall. (For more on this technique, see "Dressing Up a Concrete Wall," on p. 199.)

certain chemicals, and so on. Portland cement is available in 94-lb. bags.

Masonry cement. Also called mortar cement, a mix of portland cement and lime, although exact proportions vary. The lime plasticizes the mix and makes it workable for a longer period. Once dry, the mix is also durable.

Aggregate. Material added to a concrete mix. Fine aggregate is sand. Coarse aggregate is gravel. Concrete aggregate is typically ¾-in. gravel, unless specifications call for pea gravel (⅜-in. stone).

Mortar. Used to lay brick, concrete block, stone, and similar materials. As indicated in "Mortar Types," on p. 187, mortar is a mixture of masonry cement and sand or of portland cement, lime, and sand. It's usually available in 60-lb. bags.

Grout. A mix of portland cement and sand or of masonry cement and sand. Mixed with enough water so it flows easily, grout is used to fill cracks and similar defects. In tiling, grout is the cementitious mixture used to seal joints.

Concrete. A mixture of water, portland cement, sand, and gravel. Supported by forms until it hardens, concrete is afterward a durable, monolithic mass.

Reinforcement. The steel mesh or rods embedded in masonry materials (or masonry joints) to increase resistance to tensile, shear, and other loads. In concrete, the term usually refers to steel rebar (reinforcement bar), which strengthens foundations against excessive lateral pressures exerted by soil or water.

Admixtures. Mixtures added to vary the character of masonry. They can add color, increase plasticity, resist chemical action, extend curing time, and allow work in adverse situations. Admixtures are particularly important when ordering concrete, because mixes may contain water reducers, curing retardants, accelerators, air entrainers, and a host of other materials that affect strength, curing times, and workability.

BASIC MASONRY TOOLS

Most of the tools listed in this section are hand tools. Chapter 3 describes impact drills, rotary hammers, and other useful power tools. *Important:* Wear goggles and a respirator mask when striking, grinding, or cutting masonry. Errant chunks of masonry can blind you, and masonry dust is not stuff you want to breathe.

Trowels are indispensable masonry tools. If you have no other tool, a trowel can cut brick, scoop and throw mortar, tap masonry units into place,

A bricklayer's tool kit (clockwise, from upper left): 4-ft. brass-bound level, tool bag, 6-ft. folding rule, statistical booklet, 11-in. steel trowel, 5½-in. pointing trowel, brick hammer, two convex jointers, 4-in. brick set, box of line clips, yellow stringline.

and shape mortar joints. A good-quality trowel has a blade welded to the shank. Cheap trowels are merely spot welded. Bricklayer's trowels tend to have blades that are 10 in. to 11 in. long. Pointing trowels, which look the same, have blades roughly 5 in. long; they're used to shape masonry joints. Margin trowels are square-bladed utility trowels used for various tasks.

Jointers (striking irons) compress and shape mortar joints, some of which are shown in "Mortar Joints," on p. 189. The most common are bullhorn jointers, shown in the photo on p. 190, and convex jointers, shown in the photo above. The half-round, concave mortar joint they create sheds water well.

Tuck-pointing trowels are narrow-bladed trowels (usually the width of a mortar joint, ⅜ in.) used to repoint joints after old mortar has been cut back. Because it packs and shapes mortar, this tool is both trowel and jointer and has more aliases than an FBI fugitive: tuck-pointing trowel, jointing tool, repointing trowel, striking slick, slicker jointer, slicker, and slick.

Tuck-pointing chisels partially remove old mortar so joints can be repointed (compacted and shaped) to improve weatherability. Angle grinders and pneumatic chisels also remove mortar.

THE Point OF IT ALL

When you see the term *pointing* in masonry texts, someone is doing something to mortar joints—usually shaping or compressing them so they weather better. Repointing or tuck-pointing refers to adding (and shaping) new mortar after old, weak mortar has been partially removed from a joint, usually with a tuck-pointing chisel or a tuck-pointer's grinder

Mason's hammers score and cut brick with the sharp end and strike hand chisels with the other. The blunt end is also used to tap brick down into mortar.

Brick sets have a cutting edge beveled on one side, so you can cut bricks precisely or dislodge deteriorated brick without damaging surrounding ones.

Brick cutters are rentable levered tools that precisely cut or "shave" brick, as you often must do when fitting firebricks to fill gaps in a firebox.

Line blocks (or pins) secure a long, taut line to align masonry courses. They're less important in renovation masonry, where you're often filling in between existing courses or laying short runs, such as the sides of a chimney.

Mason's levels are indispensable for leveling courses and assessing plumb. Generally 4 ft. to 6 ft. long, better quality levels have an all-metal casing and replaceable vials. During work, be sure to wipe wet concrete or mortar off a level before it hardens and affects the readings.

Brick tongs enable you to carry up to 10 bricks comfortably, as if they were in a suitcase.

Concrete tools include floats (used to level concrete), finishing trowels (for smoothing surfaces), and edgers (short tools that contour edges). You'll also need a strike-off board (usually a straight 2×4) for leveling freshly poured pads. Action photos of these tools appear in Chapter 10.

Miscellaneous tools include goggles, knee pads, rubber gloves, rubber boots (concrete work), a flat bar, and a homemade mortarboard (a platform that holds mortar near the work) made from scrap plywood. You'll also need sheet plastic to cover sand or cement, a concrete mixer or a mortar pan, a wheelbarrow, square-nose shovels, buckets, a garden hose, stiff-bristle brushes, and so on.

PREP TIPS

The following tips will help your job go smoothly.

Code. Check local building codes and get necessary permits.

Water. Protect materials from rain as soon as possible. Because water causes cement to set, sacks of portland or mortar cement left on the ground—or on a seemingly dry concrete floor—will harden and become useless. If outdoors, ele-

Brick tongs let you carry bricks as if they were a suitcase.

vate sacks on a pallet or scrap lumber and cover the pile with sheet plastic, weighting down the edges with rocks.

Although bricks should be wetted before being laid, don't leave them uncovered in a downpour. They will absorb too much water, which can dilute the concrete and weaken the bond. (Concrete blocks, on the other hand, should be laid dry. Don't wet them beforehand.)

Sand and gravel are little affected by water, but if they absorb a lot of water, you'll need to reduce the amount of water you must add to a mortar or concrete mix. Damp sand won't ball up when you squeeze a fistful; it contains about 1 qt. of water per cubic foot. Wet sand will ball up and will contain about 2 qt. of water per cubic foot. Dripping wet sand oozes water when you squeeze it and will contain about 3 qt. of water per cubic foot. Of greater concern is the purity of these aggregates: Unload them onto an old sheet of plywood or a heavy (6-mil) plastic tarp to keep them from being contaminated with soil or other organic matter.

Weight. Masonry materials are heavy. To save labor, have materials delivered close to the work site. Likewise, have a mortarboard within 3 ft. of your work area and about waist high so you don't need to bend over to scoop mortar. For this reason, scaffolding is a sensible investment if you will be working higher than shoulder height. If you're not strong or in good shape, divide materials into loads you can handle without straining, and use ramps and wheelbarrows when possible. As you lift, get close to the object and lift with your knees, not your back.

Game plan. Before mixing mortar, complete preparatory work, such as chiseling out old joints, removing old brick, and brushing dust off receiving surfaces.

Curing. Give masonry time to cure. Because freezing compromises strength, plan your work so the mortar joints or new concrete will set before temperatures drop that low. Admixtures can extend the temperature range in which you can work, but exterior masonry work is easiest when the 24-hour temperature range is 40°F to 80°F. On hot summer days, start early—preferably on a shady side of the house—and follow the shade around as the day progresses. Cover fresh work with burlap sacks, dampened periodically, or with sheet plastic. The longer masonry stays moist, the stronger it cures.

Protecting surfaces. Spread tarps to catch mortar droppings. And if you're working on a chimney, tack plywood over the windows to protect glass from falling bricks, tools, and such.

Cleanup. At the end of the day, clean tools well. Wet them down and use a wire brush as needed to remove hardened materials. Before lunch breaks or at the end of the day, run a few shovelfuls of gravel and a few buckets of water in the concrete mixer to loosen caked materials. Then dump it out, ensuring that the barrel wall and mixer blades are clean.

Working with Brick

Common brick-related repairs include repointing mortar joints, repairing chimney tops, rebuilding chimneys and fireboxes, and cleaning bricks. You may also have to repair or add flashing where the chimney meets the roof, as shown in Chapter 5. Less common repairs include filling openings after the removal of doors or windows. If you want to create an opening to a brick wall, leave that to a structural engineer and a licensed and insured mason.

To conserve resources and get the best-looking results, respect existing masonry. Match existing bricks and mortar as closely as possible, including the thickness of mortar joints. When repointing brick, choose a mortar of appropriate strength.

TYPES AND TERMS

Of the many types of brick available, renovation calls mainly for *building brick,* also called common brick. Building brick is classified according to its weathering grade: SW (severe weathering), MW (moderate weathering), and NW (nonweathering). SW grade should be used where brickwork will be below grade—that is, in contact with the soil and hence subject to freezing in cold climates. Use SW on all floors, whether indoor or outdoor. MW grade is used indoors or on exteriors above grade. NW is used only indoors, though not as flooring.

Standard-size brick is nominally 8 in. by 4 in. by 2⅔ in.; but it is actually 7⅝ in. by 3⅝ in. by 2¼ in., to accommodate mortar joints ⅜ in. thick. Thus three courses of brick (and mortar) will be 8 in. high.

Brick is also named according to its positioning, whether it is laid on its face, end, or side. *Stretcher* and *header* are the most common placements, with *rowlock* patterns often being used to finish courses beneath windowsills or to cap the tops of walls where coping isn't used.

In masonry work, the word *bond* has several different meanings. Mortar bond denotes the adhesion of brick (or block) to mortar. Structural bond refers to the joining or interlocking of individual units to form a structural whole. If there are two *wythes* (pronounced *w-EYE-ths*) of brick

(a double wall), the wythes may be bonded structurally by steel ties, or by header bricks mortared into both wythes, or by grout poured into the cavity between the two wythes. Finally, pattern bond indicates brick placement, as shown in "Bond Patterns," on p. 186.

If you're laying up a typical brick pattern—say, running bond—you will need about 6¾ bricks per square foot of wall; figure 7 bricks per square

Bricklaying Terms

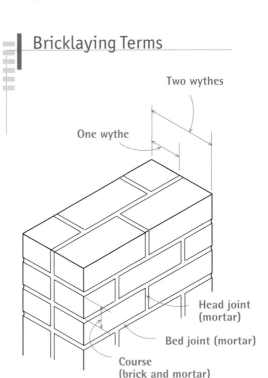

Two wythes

One wythe

Head joint (mortar)

Bed joint (mortar)

Course (brick and mortar)

Brick Names Based on Positioning

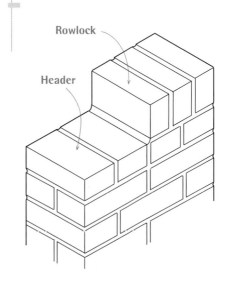
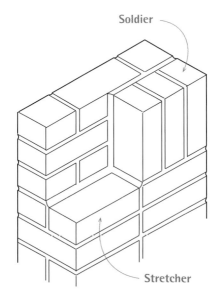

Rowlock

Header

Soldier

Stretcher

foot in order to have enough extra for waste. As you handle bricks, inspect each for soundness. All should be free of crumbling and structurally significant cracks. When struck with a trowel, bricks should ring sharp and true.

BASIC BRICKWORKING TECHNIQUES

You should wet bricks before using them so they won't absorb moisture from the mortar mix. Hose down the brick pile once a day (more often in hot, dry weather), but don't overdo it. If the bricks become too wet, they will slide around on the mortar bed.

Cutting bricks. Wear goggles when cutting bricks. If you're cutting across brick faces, rent a brick cutter, a levered tool that cuts easily. Otherwise, cut bricks by hand.

An experienced mason can score and cut bricks with only a trowel, but you'll probably find that a brick set works better. Placing the

brick on a bed of sand makes the brick less likely to jump when you strike the brick set. After marking the cut-line on the face of the brick, hold the brick set perpendicular to the brick and strike it with a 4-lb. hand sledge. Because the edge of the brick set is beveled on one side, keep the bevel on the waste side of the line. You can also use a mason's hammer as shown in the top photo at right, controlling the cut by using the hammer point to score entirely around the brick. Then rap the scored line sharply to break the brick.

Bond Patterns

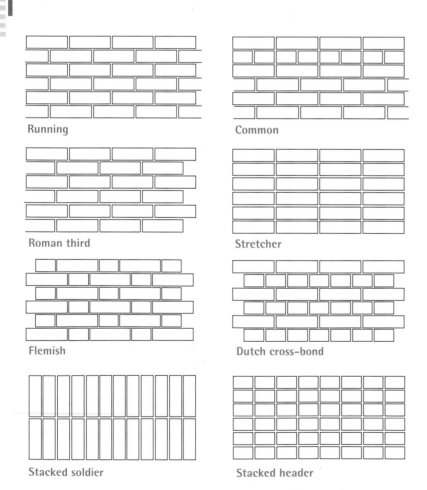

Running

Common

Roman third

Stretcher

Flemish

Dutch cross-bond

Stacked soldier

Stacked header

Running, common, Roman third, Flemish, and Dutch cross-bond are stronger because their head joints are staggered.

Mortar Types

Mortar is usually classified according to its strength and weatherability: The table at right describes the correct proportions of ingredients for each.

▶ **Type M** has the highest compressive strength, at least 2,500 pounds per square inch (psi). This durable mix is recommended for load-bearing walls, masonry below grade, and masonry that is not reinforced with steel.

▶ **Type S** has a relatively high compressive strength (1,800 psi) and the best tensile strength of any mortar listed here; so it best resists wind and soil movement .

▶ **Type N** offers medium compressive strength (800 psi) and is suitable for all above-grade uses, including those subject to heavy weathering, such as chimney mortar.

▶ **Type O** has a low compressive strength (325 psi) and is limited to non-load-bearing, interior uses. However, it is sometimes specified for repointing chimneys with soft, old brick that would be destroyed by stronger mortar (see "The mortar mix," on p. 190, for more information).

▶ **Type K** is an extremely low strength (100 psi) mortar and is not recommended.

Of the mortar types listed here, type N is the most versatile. A simplified version of its proportions is 1 part portland cement, 1 part lime, and 6 parts sand (or 1 part masonry cement and 3 parts sand). Before portland cement became widely used in the nineteenth century, mortar was usually a mixture of lime and sand (animal hair was often added to reduce cracking). If brickwork 100 years old or older needs repointing, use type O so it won't destroy the brick (roughly, 1 part portland cement, 2 parts lime, and 4 parts fine sand).

Dry mixing. When mixing mortar, mix the ingredients dry first to ensure a uniform mixture. That done, create a pocket in the middle, and add water gradually. As you add water, be fastidious about turning out the material in the corner of the mixing pan, so that there will be no dry spots. Mortar should be moist, yet stiff. A batch that's too wet will produce a weak bond. Once the mix is nearly right, its texture will change radically if you add even a small amount of water.

TWO WAYS TO CUT BRICK

Using a mason's hammer, score all the way around the brick, then strike the scored lines sharply. Such cuts will be more accurate if you place the bricks on a bed of sand.

Using a brick-cutting tool, slice small amounts of a brick to ensure a close fit. This tool is safer and quieter than using a diamond blade in a power saw.

Mortar Types (ASTM C 270-68)*,†

TYPE	PORTLAND CEMENT	MASONRY CEMENT	HYDRATED LIME or LIME PUTTY	AGGREGATE‡
M	1	1	—	Not less than 2¼ and not more than three times the sum of the combined volumes of lime and cement used
	1	—	¼	
S	½	1	—	
	1	—	>¼–2	
N	—	1	—	
	1	—	>½–1¼	
O	—	1	—	
	1	—	>1¼–2½	
K	1	—	>2½–4	

* Adapted from the publications of the American Society for Testing and Materials, as are the compression figures given in the text.

† Parts by volume.

‡ Measured in a damp, loose condition.

Mortar will remain usable for about 2 hours, so mix only about two buckets at a time. If the batch seems to be drying out, "temper" it by sprinkling a little water on the batch and turning it over a few times with a trowel. As you seat each course of bricks in mortar, use the trowel to gently scrape excess mortar from joints and throw it back into the pan or onto the mortarboard. Periodically turn that mortar back into the batch so it doesn't dry out. Don't reuse mortar that drops on the ground.

Trowel techniques. Hold a trowel with your thumb on top of the handle—not on the shank or the blade. This position keeps your thumb out of the mortar, while giving you control. Wrap your other fingers around the handle in a relaxed manner.

There are two basic ways to load a trowel with mortar. The first is to make two passes: Imagine that your mortar pan is the face of a clock. With the right-hand edge of the trowel raised slightly, take a pass through the mortar from 6:30 to 12:00. Make the second pass with the left-hand side of the blade tipped up slightly, traveling from 5:30 to 12:00. According to master mason and author Dick Kreh, a trowelful of mortar should

Throwing Mortar

As you turn the trowel to unload the mortar, pull it toward you quickly, thus stringing the mortar in a line.

resemble "a long church steeple, not a wide wedge of pie."

The second method is to hold the trowel blade at an angle of about 80° to the mortarboard. Separate a portion of mortar from the main pile and, with the underside of the trowel blade, compress the portion slightly, making a long, tapered shape. To lift the mortar from the board, put the trowel (blade face up) next to the mortar, with the blade edge farthest away slightly off the board. With a quick twist of the wrist, scoop up the mortar. This motion is a bit tricky: If the mortar is too wet, it will slide off.

To unload the mortar, twist your wrist 90° as you pull the trowel toward you. This motion spreads, or strings, the mortar in a straight line. It is a quick motion, at once dumping and stringing out the mortar, and it takes practice to master. If you are laying brick, practice throwing mortar along the face of a 2×4, which is about the same width as a wythe of brick. Each brick course gets a bed of mortar as wide as the wythe.

After you've strung out the mortar, furrow it lightly with the point of the trowel to spread the mortar evenly. Trim off the excess mortar that hangs outside the wythe, and begin laying brick.

Laying brick. If the first course is at floor level (rather than midway up a wall), snap a chalkline to establish a baseline. Otherwise, align new bricks to existing courses.

Throw and furrow a bed of mortar long enough to seat two or three bricks. If you're filling in an opening, "butter" the end of the first brick, to create a head joint, as shown in the bottom left photo at right. Press the brick into posi-

tion and trim away excess mortar that squeezes out. Both bed and head joints are ½ in. to ⅝ in. thick until the brick is pressed into place, with a goal of compressing the joint to about ⅜ in. thick.

Use both hands as you work: One hand maneuvers the bricks, while the other works the trowel, scooping and applying mortar and tapping bricks in place with the trowel handle. If you use a stringline to align bricks, get your thumb out of the way of the string just as you put the brick into the mortar bed. As you place a brick next to one already in place, let your hand rest on both bricks; this gives you a quick indication of level.

When you have laid about six bricks in a course, check for level. Leaving the level atop the course, use the edge of the trowel blade to tap high bricks down—tap the bricks, not the level. Tap as near the center of the bricks as the level will allow. If a brick is too low because you have scrimped on mortar, it's best to remove it and reapply the mortar.

Next plumb the bricks, holding the level lightly against the bricks' edges. Using the handle of the trowel, tap bricks till their edges are plumb. (Hold the level lightly against the brick, but avoid pushing the level against the face of the brick.) Finally, use the trowel handle to tap bricks forward or back so that they align with a mason's line or a level held lightly across the face of the structure

The last brick in a course is called the *closure brick*. Butter both ends of that brick liberally and slide it in place. The bed of mortar should also be generous. As you tap the brick into place with the trowel handle, scrape excess mortar off, ensuring a tight fit. If you scrimp on the mortar, you may need to pull the brick out and remortar it, perhaps disturbing bricks nearby.

Striking joints. Striking the mortar joints, also called tooling the joints, compresses and shapes the mortar. Typically, a mason will strike joints every two or three courses, before the mortar dries too much. To test the mortar's readiness for striking, press your finger into it. If the indentation stays, it's ready to strike. If the mortar's not reading for striking, wet mortar will cling to your finger and won't stay indented.

Use a jointer to strike joints. First strike the head joints and then the bed joints. The shape of the joint determines how well it sheds water. As suggested in "Mortar Joints," joints that shed water best include concave (the most common), V-shaped, and weathered joints. Flush joints are only fair at shedding water. Struck, raked, and extruded joints shed poorly because they have shelves on which water collects.

Mortar Joints

Flush

Raked and tooled   "V"

Extruded   Struck

Concave   Weathered

Experienced masons lay up bricks from the corners in, moving string guides up as they complete each course.

Before the mortar is compressed, it is ¹/₂ in. to ⁵/₈ in. thick, as shown. Press the brick into the mortar to create a good bond, compressing the mortar to ³/₈ in. thick.

After using a bricklayer's trowel to throw and furrow a mortar bed, butter one end of the brick to create a head joint.

After using the end of the trowel handle to tap the brick down, trim off the excess mortar.

REPOINTING MORTAR JOINTS

Even materials as durable as brick and mortar break down in time, most commonly near the top of a wall or chimney, where masonry is most exposed to the elements. Often, the structure wasn't capped or flashed properly. If the bricks are loose, remove them till you reach bricks that are solidly attached. If joints are weathered but bricks remain firmly attached, repoint (or tuck-point) the joints by partially cutting back the mortar, adding new mortar, and shaping the joints. If the brick is painted, see "Stripping Painted Brick," on p. 191. Finally, if vertical or diagonal cracks run through several courses, there may be underlying structural problems, which must be corrected before repointing. In this case, consult a structural engineer.

Raking old mortar. For best results, rake out (scrape out) mortar joints in an inconspicuous area as a test, starting with the least destructive tool. If the mortar is soft enough, an old screwdriver may be all you need. But if the mortar is as hard as the brick, you'll need to be patient. Cut

Tools FOR RAKING MORTAR

Before you can repoint joints, you must rake (cut back) old mortar, preferably without damaging surrounding brick. You've got several options:

▶ TUCK-POINTING (PLUGGING) CHISELS are usually thinner than mortar joints. Used with a 2-lb. hand sledge, they're slow but exact.

▶ ANGLE GRINDERS with an abrasive wheel cut quickly into old mortar, but they can easily damage soft brick and leave a ragged line.

▶ PNEUMATIC AIR CHISELS represent a good balance of speed and control, but you'll need to special-order mortar-removal bits. Trow & Holden (Barre, VT) offers a set that includes ¹/₈-in. and ¹/₄-in. cape chisels, a ¹/₄-in. swept cape chisel, and a 4-tooth ripper. Wear safety glasses and a respirator mask when cutting mortar.

After the mortar joints have set enough to retain a thumbprint, strike (tool) them to compress the mortar and improve weatherability. Strike the head joints, as shown, before striking the bed joints. (This tool is a convex jointer.)

joints 1 in. deep, and try to cut a square trough (not a V-groove) in the old mortar.

Once you've raked the joints to the correct depth, brush them out well, using a whisk broom or a wallpaperer's brush, which you can also use to wet down the joints before adding fresh mortar. Remove debris with an air hose or a heavy-duty vacuum. Of course, wear safety glasses and a respirator mask for this work.

The mortar mix. Try to match the old mortar mix when repointing an older brick building. Before portland cement was widely used, mortar joints were usually a resilient mix of hydrated lime and sand, which compressed slightly as the bricks expanded during summer and expanded slightly as the bricks contracted during cool weather. Soft, lime-rich mortars also show *autogenous healing*, an ability to self-repair hairline cracks caused by seasonal temperature shifts. Mortar joints with portland cement, on the other hand, are relatively hard and inflexible: As old bricks heat up, they have no room to expand, so they crack and *spall* (flake).

Although mortar analysis is the best way to match old mixes—historic preservation agencies can suggest mortar analysts—type O mortar (described earlier in this chapter) should be a close match for most old mortars. For this, mix 1 part portland cement, 2 parts hydrated lime, and 8 parts fine sand. The mix should be fairly stiff as mortar mixes go, keeping its shape when squeezed into a ball. If the mix becomes too stiff to work, periodically sprinkle on and stir in small amounts of water.

If you're repointing only a section of a structure, however, and don't want it to stick out like a sore thumb, experiment with combinations of mortar dye, cement, sand, and lime, carefully labeling the proportions of each batch and allowing it dry for a month before committing to a recipe. Masonry supply houses stock such materials; they also carry new bricks manufactured to look old, should you need to replace bricks as well.

Repointing technique. Using a spray bottle or a brush, dampen the newly cleaned-out joints before applying fresh mortar. There are two ways to fill joints with new mortar. If you're repointing a relatively small area, use a bricklayer's trowel as a palette for the mortar and a tuck-pointing trowel to push the mortar into the joint. (See the photo on p. 198.) Press the mortar firmly, so that it will stick.

If you're repointing a large area, use a grout bag to squeeze the mortar into the joint. A grout bag looks like the pastry bag used to dispense fancy icing onto cakes. You force the mortar out by twisting the canvas bag. But you'll need strong

Use a tuck-pointing (or plugging) chisel to cut back eroded mortar before repointing joints. The tool's narrow blade fits easily into joints and so is unlikely to damage brick faces.

WORKING MORTAR INTO JOINTS

Option 1: Let your bricklayer's trowel serve as a palette as you scoop mortar from it with your smaller pointing trowel and press mortar into joints. Two trowels are useful when repointing old joints.

Option 2: Or you can use a grout bag if you've got a lot of joints to fill. But this is hard work: The bag is heavy, and you need to twist hard to force the mortar out a small opening—a bit like wringing water from a stone.

Here a bullhorn jointer compresses mortar joints.

hands and forearms to twist the filled 5-lb. to 10-lb. bag. And you may need to thin the mix slightly so it will flow easily through the bag. After using a grout bag, you'll still need to tuck-point the mortar joints.

When the mortar has dried enough to retain the imprint of your thumb, tool the joints. In most cases, use a jointer that creates mortar joints the same shape as the old ones. Point the head joints first, then the bed joints. As you work, use a trowel to clean the mortar from the brick faces, but don't disturb the mortar joints. Then wait 2 hours or 3 hours before using a stiff plastic-bristle brush to remove the mortar still stuck to the brick faces.

CLEANING AND SEALING EXTERIORS

Use the gentlest, least damaging cleaning agents, chemicals, steam cleaner, or water pressure that works. Determine this by testing on an inconspicuous area. If the gentlest method doesn't work, move to the next stronger. If mortar joints are eroded, a pressure washer may make them leak. After cleaning, allow the brickwork to dry for two days or three days; then caulk gaps around doors and windows and replace worn flashing. *Safety note:* Whatever cleaning method you choose, wear a face shield, rubber gloves, protective clothing, and a respirator mask before you begin.

Cleaning brick surfaces. Get bids on hiring an authorized cleaning service. Because cleaning solvents can be hazardous and must be disposed of according to EPA and local environmental standards, hiring professionals will spare you those headaches. Moreover, the service will be responsible for achieving the desired results, however long it takes. If you've got a tight budget or an adventurous spirit, consider the DIY options described next; they're listed more or less in order of gentleness. Wear safety glasses and rubber gloves for all procedures, and read operating manuals carefully before using pressure washers, steam cleaners, and the like.

Use a garden hose to soak the surface, and then scrub with a nylon scrub brush. The warmer the water and the longer the soak, the more dirt you'll remove.

If the hose wash isn't sufficient, try a pressure washer on a low setting. Increase the pressure slightly—say, to 300 psi to 400 psi—and you'll remove yet more. *Note:* If you see sand in the runoff water, lower the machine's pressure settings immediately. Otherwise, you may be stripping the mortar joints. Likewise, monitor the inside of the building, especially around windows, for leaks; it's easier to lower the pressure than to replace drywall.

Steam cleaning is especially effective if surfaces are mossy, or have ivy "trails" or built-up grime. Although somewhat slower than pressure washing, steam doesn't generate the volume of runoff and won't penetrate as deeply into brick surfaces or cracks.

If you're in an urban area where soot and auto exhaust have soiled the building, try a nonionic detergent with a medium pressure (1,000 psi) next. Nonionic detergents such as GAF's Igepal®, Union Carbide's Tergitol®, and Rohm & Haas' Triton® won't leave visible residues, as household detergents and TSP (trisodium phosphate) will. Again, scrub with a synthetic-bristle brush, and rinse well.

If these methods don't produce the results you want, proprietary chemical cleaners are the next step. They usually involve a three-step process—wetting surfaces, applying the cleaner and scrubbing it in, and then rinsing—repeated as many times as needed. If you apply the cleaner, follow manufacturer's instructions to the letter. Instructions will be quite specific about safety garb, dilution rates, dwell times (how long the chemical remains on), washer settings, temperature ranges (most don't work well below 50°F.), and so on. Before committing to a cleaning system, visit the manufacturer's Web site and call its tech-support number.

Sealing exteriors. Are water-repellent or waterproof coatings necessary on exterior masonry walls above grade? Mostly, no. There may be a few 200-year-old buildings in every city whose porous brick would benefit from being coated, but most masonry exteriors won't admit water if rain is directed away from the structure by gutters, downspouts, and other standard drainage details and if the masonry is properly flashed, caulked, and detailed.

First of all, so-called exterior sealants, loosely divided into water-repellent and waterproofing coatings, don't fully seal masonry surfaces, nor would you want them to. A perfect seal could trap water inside the walls. Moreover, masonry walls with water trapped inside and walls that are wicking moisture from the ground will, in time, exude soluble salts in the masonry as powdery white substances called *efflorescence*.

Water-repellent coatings, which are usually clear, penetrate masonry pores and so keep rain from penetrating to a large degree, while allowing water vapor from living areas to escape through the wall. Most water-repellent compounds are water-based, formulated from silanes, siloxanes, and silane/siloxane blends. Both premixed and concentrated coatings are available—typically applied in several coats. Some water-repellent coatings double as graffiti barriers, though they tend to be shiny.

Waterproof coatings come closer to being true sealers because they're usually pigmented or opaque and form a thin elastomeric (flexible) film. Chemically, they run the gamut from water based to bituminous. Bituminous varieties are widely applied below grade on building foundations and, to a lesser extent, to interior basement walls where mild leaks have occurred.

Chimneys

Masonry chimneys are freestanding units that carry exhaust gases out of the house. To prevent superheated gases from escaping, chimneys should be tile lined and free from cracks or gaps, or they should have insulated stainless-steel flues. Annual inspections and maintenance are crucial to chimney health: If you discover mortar or flue tiles that are cracked or missing, the chimney is unsafe. Chimney flashing and roof safety are further discussed in Chapter 5.

A professional chimney sweep needs a variety of brushes. The reel at the right contains a 50-ft. flexible rod that can push and pull brushes.

These days, new and retrofit chimneys are often nonmasonry. There are several reasons for this transition: building code and insurance requirements; a shrinking pool of qualified masons; the inherent inflexibility and tendency of masonry to crack and compromise safety when structurally stressed; and, perhaps most important, a host of safe, cost-effective, and easily installed insulated metal chimneys now available. That noted, the review here is limited to masonry chimneys.

CLEANING A CHIMNEY

Chimneys and their flues should be inspected at least once a year and cleaned as needed—ideally, before the heating season. Better chimney-cleaning services will get up on the roof, inspect the chimney top, and in some cases lower a videocamera into the flue linings. That video is very helpful if the chimney needs relining because homeowners can see the damage for themselves and make an informed decision.

Because chimney cleaning takes serious elbow grease, working atop the roof is often the most effective way to brush clean a chimney. But working on a roof is inherently dangerous to you and your roof shingles, which can be easily abraded, torn, and dislodged, leading to leaks. Moreover, because many people put off cleaning a chimney till it's almost heating season, they frequently go aloft when the weather is inclement or the roofs are slick after a rain. For all these reasons, you're probably better off hiring an insured professional, certified for cleaning and inspecting.

However, if you are determined to clean the flues yourself, first turn off the furnace and other appliances (such as water heaters) that vent to the flues and disconnect their vent pipes. Using duct tape, tape plastic over the thimbles that open into living spaces, to prevent dislodged soot from entering. If you have a fireplace, open its damper to allow dislodged soot to fall into the fire pit. Then firmly tape sheet plastic around the fireplace opening. But before you start, suit up. Dislodged creosote and soot are highly carcinogenic, so wear a respirator mask with replaceable cartridges, tight-fitting goggles, gloves, and disposable coveralls.

To clean a chimney thoroughly, you'll need special brushes, which scrub flue surfaces without damaging them. Today, many professional sweeps favor polypropylene brushes to clean sooty flues and stiff steel-wire brushes for flues with heavy use and creosote buildup. These brushes come in various sizes to match the most common flue cross sections. You can screw them onto a series of 3-ft. to 4-ft. rod sections or to a continuous flexible rod (on a reel) up to 50 ft. long.

About Chimney Fires

Chimney fires occur when imperfectly burned materials in wood smoke condense and stick to the inside of a chimney. The chief culprit in chimney fires is creosote, a sticky brown or black substance that may harden to resemble fragile glass. Incomplete combustion also produces tar, ammonia, methane, carbon monoxide, toluene, phenol, benzene, and eventually, turpentine, acetone, and methyl alcohol.

If the chimney isn't cleaned for a while, creosote accumulates until it's heated enough to combust in a flash fire, often in excess of 2,000°F. For homeowners, a chimney fire is a terrifying experience, for it may literally roar for extended periods inside the entire flue, flames shooting skyward from the chimney top as though from an inverted rocket. If there are cracks in mortar or flue tiles—or no flue tiles at all—those superheated gases can "breach the chimney" and set fire to wood framing. At that point, the whole house can go up in smoke.

Fortunately, you can prevent chimney fires, simply by inspecting and cleaning the chimney regularly. In general, don't burn green (unseasoned) or wet wood. Give a fire enough air to burn completely. Each time you start a fire, open the dampers and air controls until the fire is burning well. Don't burn Christmas trees (whose unburned resins collect as sticky masses inside flues), wrapping paper, or glossy-coated papers because their emissions can corrode stovepipes

This flue tile and mortar cap were cracked by a chimney fire in a flue overdue for cleaning.

and attack mortar joints. Above all, never use chimneys whose tiles or mortar joints are cracked or chimneys that have no flue lining.

If you're considering buying a house, have its chimney professionally inspected if you see signs of a chimney fire such as creosote flakes on the roof or the ground, scorched or cracked flue liners or chimney crowns, warped dampers or charred studs or joists near a chimney. Many local codes require inspections before homeowners fire up new woodburners.

After you've brushed the flues well, allow the dust and debris to settle before removing the plastic covering the fireplace and other openings. Shovel up the soot and debris at the bottom of each flue and from the fireplace; then vacuum all areas thoroughly. Don't forget the soot that may be resting in thimbles or on the fireplace smoke shelf.

REPLACING A CHIMNEY CROWN

A masonry crown is a beveled flue collar at the top of the chimney, sloping gently to direct water away from flue tiles. When crowns weather and crack, water can drain between flue tiles and brick, seep into mortar joints, and freeze, thereby cracking flue tiles, bricks, and mortar joints. In warmer seasons, this water can leak into living spaces, stain walls, and linger as acrid combustion smells. Replacing the crown is easy enough if the chimney is not too tall—and the roof not too high or too steeply sloped. Otherwise, you'll need rooftop scaffolding—which a pro should install—before tearing down the chimney to sound masonry and rebuilding from there.

Note: In warmer regions, uncovered flues and crowns are common. However, for winters in cold climates, flues should be capped to prevent the entry of rain and sleet that can damage flues during freeze–thaw cycles.

In most cases, a few hammer blows will dislodge old mortar crowns. Put the debris into a bucket. Then sweep the top of the chimney clean. If some mortar joints need repointing, attend to that. If many mortar joints are soft and badly eroded, tear down the chimney to the roofline, clean the bricks, install new flashing, and rebuild it. If bricks are cracked or broken, replace them with new SW grade bricks. It's okay to reuse old bricks if they're solid, but if you must replace more than a handful, rebuild the chimney with new bricks. They'll look more uniform and last longer.

Installing a new crown. Spread sheet plastic around the base of the chimney to catch falling mortar. There are essentially two types of crowns. If your region gets a lot of precipitation, pour an in-place concrete crown, which overhangs the chimney 1 in. to 1½ in. and acts as a drip cap, keeping rain and sleet off bricks near the top. Otherwise, use a trowel to build a sloping mortar crown that runs flush to the chimney faces. A flush crown isn't as durable as an overhanging crown but is much quicker to build.

To construct an overhanging crown, as shown on p. 194, measure the outside dimension of the chimney top and build a frame from 2×2s that slides snugly over the chimney top. Shim from below to wedge the frame in place so its upper face is flush to the top of the chimney. This 2×2 frame (actual dimension, 1½ in. × 1½ in.) creates a 1½-in. overhang. Next, cut strips of plywood 3½ in. wide and as long as the sides of the frame; using a cordless screwdriver, screw these strips to the frame so that they stick up 2 in. above the top of the frame. The resultant plywood frame keeps the concrete in place and creates a 2-in.-thick edge.

Wet the bricks with a brush or a spray bottle, and you're ready for the concrete. Use a cement-rich, fairly stiff concrete mix: 1 part portland cement, 2 parts sand, and 2 parts ⅜-in. gravel is about right. To prevent cracks, mix in a handful (¼ cup) of fiberglass fibers, which concrete suppliers carry. As you place the concrete into the plywood frame, use a trowel to force it into the corners and to drive out air pockets.

Important: Whether you build a mortar crown or pour a concrete one, wrap the flue liners with polyethylene bond-breaker tape or closed-cell foam strips. This prevents the mortar and concrete from bonding to the tile liners and thereby provides an expansion joint. Without this gap, heat-expanded flue tiles can crack a new crown in a single heating season.

If you're building up a mortar crown, use a premixed mortar mix. For a slightly more flexible, crack-resistant crown, substitute a liquid latex fortifier for part of the water.

Both types of crowns should be sloped away from the flue liners and troweled to a smooth finish; and both will cure slower and stronger if you cover them with a damp burlap sack or plastic to protect them from rain and sun. Caulk the gap between the flue liners and the crown with a good urethane sealant.

Chimney caps should match the style of the house: chimneys on colonials and capes are often covered with slabs of bluestone bedded into corner tiers of mortared brick. Whereas, for newer homes or those with stainless-steel liners a stainless-steel or copper cap may be more appropriate. If there are multiple flue liners, you may need multiple caps or an overall custom cap.

RELINING A CHIMNEY

While inspecting a chimney, you may find that it has no flue-tile lining or that existing tiles are cracked or broken and too inaccessible to replace. Because superheated gases can escape

Overhanging Chimney Crown

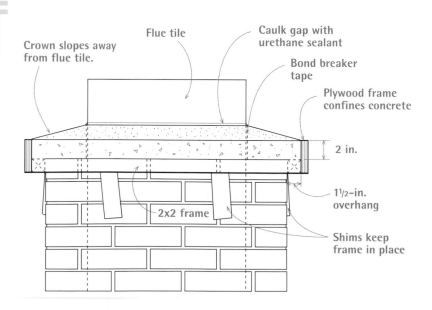

Crown slopes away from flue tile.

Flue tile

Caulk gap with urethane sealant

Bond breaker tape

Plywood frame confines concrete

2 in.

1½-in. overhang

2x2 frame

Shims keep frame in place

A simple 2x2 and plywood frame creates a 1½-in. overhang and a 2-in.-thick edge for this site-built concrete crown. To make frame disassembly easy, use drywall screws to fasten it.

As two unseen helpers on the other side of this double-sided fireplace steady the Franklin stove, the mason tips it upright. She placed heavy sheet metal over the hearth and slid the stove on its back into the fireplace.

through gaps, such a chimney is unsafe to use. In this case, your options are:

▶ **Seal up the chimney** so it can't be used and add a new, properly lined chimney elsewhere. Or tear that chimney out and replace it.

▶ **Install a poured masonry liner.** In this procedure, a heavy-gauge tubular rubber balloon is inflated inside the chimney, and the void is then filled with a cementitious slurry. After the mixture hardens, the tube is deflated and removed. Poured masonry creates a smooth, easily cleaned lining and can stiffen an old chimney whose strength is suspect. Poured masonry systems are usually proprietary, however, and must be installed by someone trained in that system. Finally, this method is expensive.

▶ **Which brings us to stainless-steel pipe,** a sensible choice if you want a solution that's readily available, quickly installed, effective, and about one-third the price of a poured masonry liner. Interchangeable rigid and flexible pipe systems enable installations even in chimneys that aren't straight.

Installing a stainless-steel liner. Steel flue liners and woodstoves are often installed in tandem, correcting flue problems and smoky fireplaces at the same time.

Start by surveying the chimney's condition, including its dimensions. After steel flue pipe is installed, there should be at minimum 1 in. clearance around it. Thus a 6-in. pipe needs a flue at least 7 in. by 7 in. Note jogs in the chimney that might require elbows or flexible sections. Also note obstructions, such as damper bars, that must be removed before you insert the pipe.

If you're installing a woodstove, too, measure the firebox carefully to be sure the stove will fit and that there's room for the clearances required by local code and mentioned in the stove manufacturer's instructions. You'll also need room to insert the stove, with or without legs attached, and raise it up into its final position. Stoves are heavy—300 lb., on average—so give yourself room to work. Fireboxes often need to be modified to make room for a fireplace insert or stove. Install the stove or fireplace insert before installing the flue liner.

Assemble the flue pipe on the ground, joining pipe sections with four stainless-steel sheet-metal screws per joint, so the sections stay together as you lower them down the chimney. Although pop rivets could theoretically join such pipe, they'd likely fail under the stress and the corrosive chemicals present in wood smoke.

Next insulate the flue pipe, as necessary, with heat-resistant mineral batts and metal joint tape.

INSTALLING AN INSULATED FLUE PIPE

To keep internal temperatures constant and prevent condensation, insulate stainless-steel flue liners with heat-resistant mineral wool batts and metal tape. Note: The flexible flue section that attaches to the woodstove outlet does not need to be insulated.

Don't try this on a windy day. The entire length of flue liner is preassembled and screwed together on the ground, carried aloft, and then lowered into the chimney...

...while the flexible lower section (above) and an adjustable elbow will enable you thread the pipe through a slightly offset chimney and still connect to the woodstove outlet.

To increase directional draw and prevent rain blow-in, the big monsoon cap (right) is clamped to the top of the metal flue liner. A steel top plate sealed to the top of the terra-cotta tile centers the steel flue liner in the opening and stabilizes it.

Heat ratings vary. Temperatures inside flue pipes intermittently reach 2,000°F. Thus flue pipes are insulated to keep temperatures constant inside and prevent condensation, which also prevents accretion of creosote and creosote's corrosive effects. Generally, the first pipe section coming off the woodstove is not insulated because temperatures are so high that there's little danger of condensation. Toward the top of the pipe, stop the insulation just before the pipe clears the chimney—you don't want to expose the insulation to the elements.

Carry the flue-pipe assembly onto the roof and lower it down the chimney. This is a two-person job, especially if it's windy. Once the lower end of the flue pipe nears the woodstove, one team member can go below to fit the lower end over the woodstove's outlet.

Although installation details vary, a metal top plate centers the pipe within the chimney and is caulked to the chimney top with a high-temperature silicone sealant. The juncture between the pipe and the top plate is then covered with a storm collar, which typically employs a band clamp to draw it tight. That's caulked, as well. Finally, cap the top of the flue pipe. The monsoon cap shown on p. 195 maintains a fairly uniform updraft even when winds shift suddenly.

REBUILDING A FIREBOX

If you can see broken firebricks or missing mortar inside your fireplace, it's time to rebuild the firebox. You'll need to decide which bricks to leave and which to replace. But you'll almost certainly need to replace the back wall, which suffers the highest temperatures as well as the most physical abuse—from logs thrown against it.

This job requires a respirator mask, eye protection, and—at least during demolition—a hard hat. A head sock is also a good idea because you'll be sitting in the dusty firebox during most of the repairs. Finally, you'll need a droplight that can withstand abuse.

Measure. Measure the firebox before you start tearing out old bricks. Note its height, width, depth, and angle at which sidewalls meet the back of the firebox. And if the back wall also tilts forward, take several readings with a spirit level

NINE Fixes FOR SMOKING FIREPLACES

▶ Open a window. New houses are often so tightly insulated that there's not enough fresh air entering to replace the smoke going up the chimney. So smoke exits only sluggishly if at all. Alternatively, you can install an air-intake vent near the hearth.

▶ Use dry wood. Burning wet or green wood creates a steamy, smoky fire whose low heat output doesn't create enough of an updraft and promotes creosote buildup.

▶ Clean chimneys at least once a year, so their flue diameters aren't choked down with creosote. Cleaning also removes obstructions, such as nests.

▶ Have a properly sized flue. Flues that are too large won't send volatiles upward at a fast enough rate and often allow smoke to drift into living spaces. Although flue pipes are sized to match woodstove flue outlets (6 in. or 8 in.), sizing fireplace flues is trickier. In general, a fireplace flue's cross section should be one-eighth to one-tenth the area of a fireplace opening.

▶ Reduce air turbulence inside the smoke chamber, above the metal damper by giving the corbeled bricks on the front face a smooth parge coat. To do this, brush, vacuum, and wet the corbeled bricks before applying a smoothening heat-resistant mortar such as Ahrens® Chamber-Tech 2000. (You'll need to remove the damper for access.)

▶ Replace the chimney rain cap. Clogged or poorly designed metal or masonry caps can create air turbulence and prevent a good updraft.

▶ Increase the height of the chimney. A chimney should be a minimum of 3 ft. above the part of the roof it passes through and a minimum of 2 ft. above any other part of the roof within 10 ft.

▶ Rebuild the firebox with Rumford proportions. Count Rumford was a contemporary of Ben Franklin and almost as clever; however, he bet on the British and left the colonies in a hurry. But not before he invented a tall, shallow firebox that doesn't smoke and radiates considerably more heat into the living space than low, deep fireboxes. Search the Internet for companies that sell prefab Rumford-style fireplace components—or build your own.

▶ Install a Franklin woodstove. Charming as they are, fireplaces are an inefficient way to heat a house. Install an efficient, glass-doored stove and you can watch the flames without getting burned by wasted energy costs.

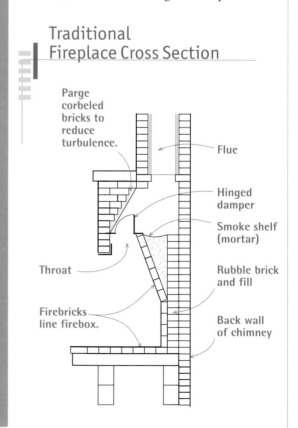

Traditional Fireplace Cross Section

Parge corbeled bricks to reduce turbulence.

Flue

Hinged damper

Smoke shelf (mortar)

Throat

Rubble brick and fill

Firebricks line firebox.

Back wall of chimney

to determine how much off-plumb it is. Finally, note the height and dimensions of the chimney throat, the narrowed opening at the top of the firebox, usually covered by a metal damper. Knowing the location and dimensions of the throat is particularly helpful—it tells you the final height of the back wall of the firebox.

Tear out. Starting with the back wall of the firebox, use a flat bar to gently dislodge loose firebricks—most will fall out—and place them in an empty joint-compound bucket for removal. Rebuild with only new firebricks. Remove the damper, and if it's warped, replace it. As you remove firebricks from the back wall, you may find an intermediate wall of rubble brick between the firebox and the outer wall of the chimney. And, as likely, the rubble bricks will also be loose, their mortar turned to sand. You can save, clean, and reuse these bricks when you rebuild the rubble wall.

Next remove loose or damaged firebricks from the sidewalls and floor of the firebox. But, again, if the bricks are intact, it's a judgment call. If repointing the joints is all that's needed, leave the bricks in place. Firebricks on the floor, which have been protected by insulating layers of ash, often need only repointing. Once you've removed loose bricks, sweep and vacuum the area well. (Rent a shop vacuum.) Using a spray bottle, spritz all surfaces with clean water till they're damp.

Bricks and mortar. Firebricks (refractory bricks) are made of fire clay and can withstand temperatures up to 2,000°F. They're bigger and softer than conventional facing bricks and less likely to expand and contract and hence are less likely to crack from heat. Yet, because they are soft, they can be damaged by logs thrown against

This is a partially dismantled fireplace firebox. To the left, the firebrick sidewall is solid enough to be left in place, though its mortar joints need repointing. The back-wall firebricks have already been removed, revealing the back of the chimney. (An intervening wall of rubble bricks was also removed.)

them. Firebrick walls need tight joints of $\frac{1}{16}$ in. to $\frac{1}{8}$ in. thick and thus require exact fits. To achieve this, rent a lever-operated brick cutter.

For firebricks, two kinds of mortar are used. Until recently, most masons just threw a few handfuls of fire clay into a conventional portland cement–based mortar, such as Quikrete® Mason Mix. (Fire clay helps resist burnout and smoothes easier.) However, adding too much fire clay makes a mix so sticky it's difficult to scrape off your trowel. The second mortar, refractory mortar, comes premixed in cans or pails and is roughly the consistency of joint compound. With names such as Heat Stop® and Alsey Air-Set Refractory

This mason is building a rubble-brick wall between the firebox she's building and the back wall of the chimney. Firebrick mortar joints are thin, typically, only $\frac{1}{16}$ in. to $\frac{1}{8}$ in. thick, because the firebricks do virtually all of the insulating.

Traditionally, the back walls of fireboxes start tilting forward at the third or fourth course to promote heat reflection and circulation into the room. To create this tilt, apply the mortar bed more thickly at the back, canting the course of bricks forward. Periodically, scrape off excess mortar.

Gently use a mason's hammer to seat firebricks in the mortar. At this point, the back wall's forward tilt is very similar to that of the sidewall, at left. Angle-cut firebrick to fill any voids between the sidewalls and the back wall. (A rented brick cutter is ideal for this.)

Fireplace Mortar, these mortars can withstand high temperatures without degrading. Heat tolerance aside, the biggest difference between the two mortar types is drying time: Refractory mortars set very quickly—in 15 seconds or 20 seconds—so there's little time to re-adjust bricks once in place. If you're new to bricklaying, a conventional mix will be more forgiving.

Openings in Brick Walls

If you want to add a door or window to a brick wall, hire a structural engineer to see if that's feasible. If so, hire an experienced mason to create the opening; this is not a job for a novice. If the house was built in the 1960s or later, the wall will likely be of brick veneer, which can be relatively fragile because the metal ties attaching a brick veneer to wood- or metal-stud walls tend to rust out, especially in humid or coastal areas. In extreme cases, steel studs will rust, and wood studs will rot. Thus, when opening veneer walls, masons often get more of a challenge than they bargained for.

Brick homes built before the 1960s are usually two wythes thick (with a cavity in between), are very heavy, and have very likely settled. Undisturbed, such walls may be sound; but openings cut into them must be shored up during construction, adequately supported with steel lintels, and meticulously detailed and flashed. Moreover, openings that are too wide or too close to corners may not be feasible, so a structural engineer needs to make the call.

To close off an opening in a brick wall, remove the window or door and its casings, and then pry out and remove the frame. Prepare the opening by toothing it out—that is, by removing half bricks along the sides of the opening and filling in courses with whole bricks to disguise the old opening. The closer you can match the color of the existing bricks and mortar, the better you'll hide the new section. As you lay up bricks, set two 6-in. corrugated metal ties in the mortar every fourth or fifth course, and nail the ties to the wood-frame wall behind. Leave the steel lintel above the opening in place.

Build up. The rest is basic bricklaying technique. String a bed of mortar as wide as the edge of a firebrick across the back of the firebox and press the bricks firmly into it, working from one side to the other. Bricks should be damp but not wet. Butter the ends of each brick to create head joints, and when you've laid the first course, check for level. Use the handle of your trowel or mason's hammer to tap down bricks that are high. Typically, you'll need to cut brick pieces on each side of the back wall, to "tooth into" the staggered brick joints on the sidewalls, but that step can wait till the back wall is complete. As you lay up each course of firebrick, lay up the rubble brick courses, which needn't be perfect, nor do you need to point their joints.

Unless yours is a tall, shallow Rumford fireplace, firebricks in the back wall should start tilting forward by the third or fourth course. To do that, apply the mortar bed thicker at the back. Build up the firebox and rubble-brick walls till you reach the throat opening. Then fill in any space between the firebox and rubble-brick walls with mortar, creating a smoke shelf. The smoke shelf can be flat or slightly cupped.

Once the back wall is up, fit piece bricks where the back wall meets sidewalls. Clean and repoint the mortar joints as needed. With a margin trowel serving as your mortar palette, use a tuck-pointing trowel to "cut" a small sliver of mortar and pack it into the brick joints. Allow the mortar to dry a month before building a fire. Make the first few fires small.

After cutting back deteriorated mortar joints, pack them with fresh mortar. Fill a margin trowel with refractory mortar, as shown. Then use a thin tuck-pointing trowel to scrape mortar from it into the joint. Refractory cement is so sticky that it will cling to the margin trowel's blade even if held vertically.

Dressing Up a Concrete Wall

If you're bored with the drab band of foundation concrete around the bottom of your house, dress it up with a glued-on brick or stone facade. A number of adhesive materials will work well.

In the project shown here, the mason used SGM Marble Set™, intended for marble or heavy tiles, but epoxies would work too. Whatever adhesive you choose, check the manufacturer's instructions for its suitability for exterior use in your area, especially if you have freezing winters. Use exterior-grade bricks, too.

How traditional or freeform you make the facade depends on your building's style and your sense of fun. The clinker brick, tile, and stone facade shown completed on p. 182 nicely complemented the eclectic style of the Craftsman house. It would probably also look good on the foundation of a rambling brown shingle, a Gothic revival house, or a more whimsical sort of Victorian.

Not relying on mortar joints to support the courses gives you a certain freedom in design, but it's still important that you pack joints with mortar and compress them with a striking tool so they shed water—especially if winter temperatures in your region drop below freezing.

Today's masonry adhesives are so strong that they can adhere heavy materials—such as brick, stone, and tile—directly to concrete. Freed from needing to support much of anything, mortar joints can be as expressive as you like.

Butter the backs of masonry elements with adhesive, in this case, a mortar designed to adhere marble and heavy tile to concrete.

Use short sticks to space bricks, stones, and tiles. This prevents what little slippage may occur before the adhesive sets and creates a joint wide enough to pack mortar into. Compress and shape the mortar to make it adhere and keep the weather out.

10 Foundations and Concrete

Foundation issues can be complex. So before starting extensive remedial work, such as replacing failed foundation sections or adding a second story to your house, have a structural engineer evaluate your foundation. In addition, bring in a soils engineer if the site slopes steeply or if the foundation shows any of the following distress signs: bowing, widespread cracking, uneven settlement, or chronic wetness. Engineers can also assess potential concerns such as slide zones, soil load-bearing capacity, and seasonal shifting.

An Overview

A foundation is a mediator between the loads of the house and the soil on which the foundation rests. A well-designed foundation keeps a house's

wood underpinning above the soil so it doesn't rot or get eaten by insects. And it should be sturdy enough to keep walls plumb and floors level despite wind, water, soil movement, and earthquakes.

FOUNDATION TYPES

Foundations should be appropriate to the site. For example, on sandy well-drained soil, unmortared stone foundations can last for centuries. But an unstable clay hillside may dictate an engineered foundation on piers extending down to bedrock.

The tee, or spread, foundation is perhaps the most commonly used type, so named because its cross section looks like an inverted *T*. It's remark-

These concrete forms are half complete, showing oiled inside form boards, a new mudsill nailed up, and the bottom outer form board in place. Rebar, as shown, will be wire-tied to anchor bolts after they've been inserted into predrilled holes in the mudsill.

ably adaptable. On a flat site in temperate regions, a shallow tee foundation is usually enough to support a house, while creating a crawl space that allows joist access and ventilation.

Where the ground freezes, foundation footings need to be dug below the frost line, stipulated by local codes. Below the frost line, footings aren't susceptible to the potentially tremendous lifting and sinking forces of freeze–thaw cycles in moist soil. (Thus most houses in cold climates often have full basements.)

When tee foundations fail, they often do so because they're unreinforced or have too small or too shallow a footprint. Unreinforced tee foundations that have failed are best removed and replaced. But reinforced tees that are sound can be *underpinned* by excavating and pouring larger footings underneath a section at a time.

Slab on grade is a giant pad of reinforced concrete, poured simultaneously with a slightly thicker perimeter footing that increases its load-bearing capabilities. Beneath the slab, there's typically a layer of crushed gravel and sheet plastic over that to prevent moisture from wicking up from the soil. Slabs are generally installed on flat lots where the ground doesn't freeze because, being above frost line, shallow slabs are vulnerable to frost heaves. Although shallow, the large footprint of a slab sometimes makes it the only feasible foundation on soils with weak load-bearing capacity. Because slabs sit on grade, their drainage systems must be meticulously detailed.

Drilled concrete piers in tandem with grade beams are *the* premier foundation for most situations that don't require basements. These foundations get their name because pier holes are typically drilled to bearing strata. This foundation type is unsurpassed for lateral stability, whether as replacement foundation for old work or for new construction. Also, concrete piers have a greater cross section than driven steel piers and hence greater skin friction against the soil, so they're much less likely to migrate. The stability of concrete piers can be further enhanced by concrete-grade beams resting on or slightly below grade, which allow soil movement around the piers, without moving the piers.

The primary disadvantages of drilled concrete piers are cost and access. In new construction, a backhoe equipped with an auger on the power takeoff requires 10 ft. or 12 ft. of vertical clearance. Alternatively, there are remote-access portable rigs that can drill in tight quarters, even inside existing houses, but they are labor intensive to set up and move, increasing the cost.

Foundation Types

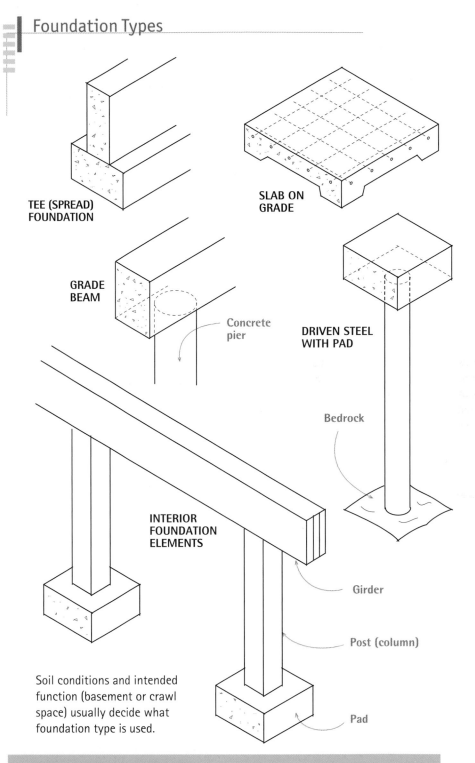

TEE (SPREAD) FOUNDATION

SLAB ON GRADE

GRADE BEAM

Concrete pier

DRIVEN STEEL WITH PAD

Bedrock

INTERIOR FOUNDATION ELEMENTS

Girder

Post (column)

Pad

Soil conditions and intended function (basement or crawl space) usually decide what foundation type is used.

Pouring VERSUS PLACING CONCRETE

Every trade has its jargon. Concrete snobs, for example, insist on using the phrase *placing concrete,* though concrete coming out of a 4-in. hose looks more like a pour, albeit a sluggish one. Perhaps "placers" want to emphasize that concrete is so weighty that you should place it as close to its final location as possible. Point taken. But to denote the general movement of concrete from truck to forms, pour us a tall one.

This pier and grade-beam foundation was built on a sloping site with expansive clay soil, so the engineer specified parallel-grade beams and a more massive grade-beam perimeter. (The piers go down 15 ft.) Integral concrete post piers atop grade beams support 4×6 joists spaced 3 ft. on center.

Before the pour, the rebar spine of this foundation wall is still visible. The green bolt holders will position anchor bolts in the middle of the mudsill.

Driven steel pilings are used to anchor foundations on steep or unstable soils. Driven to bedrock and capped, steel pilings can support heavy vertical loads. And, as retrofits, they can stabilize a wide range of problem foundations. There are various types of steel pilings, including *helical piers,* which look like giant auger bits and are screwed in with hydraulic motors, and *push piers,* which are hollow and can be pushed in, strengthened with reinforcing bar, and filled with concrete or epoxy.

IMPORTANT ELEMENTS

In many parts of North America, building codes don't require steel reinforcement in concrete foundations, but steel is a cost-effective means of avoiding cracks caused by lateral pressure on foundation walls.

Steel reinforcement and fasteners. *Steel reinforcing bar* (rebar) basically carries and distributes loads within the foundation, transferring the loads from high-pressure areas to lower-pressure areas. It thereby lessens the likelihood of *point failure,* either from point loading above or from lateral soil and water pressures. *Anchor bolts* or threaded rods, tied to rebar, attach the overlying structure to the foundation. *Steel dowels* are usually short pieces of rebar that pin foundation walls to footings, new sections to existing foundations, and so on.

There are also a number of metal connectors—such as Simpson Strong-Ties—that tie joists to girders, keep support posts from drifting, and hold down mudsills, sole plates, and such. Several are shown in Chapter 4.

Quality. Concrete quality is critically important, both in its composition and in its placement. Water, sand, and aggregate must be clean and well mixed with the cement. Concrete with compressive strength of 2,500 psi to 3,500 psi (pounds per square inch) is common in residential foundations, yet there are many ways to achieve that strength, including chemical admixtures. Discuss your needs with a concrete supplier who's familiar with soil conditions in your area, and read "Ordering Concrete," on p. 222.

Drainage. The drainage system is not technically a part of the foundation, but the flow of water alongside and under a foundation is important to its success. In some soils, it's essential to mediate water flow. At the very least, water seeping through foundations can cause damp basements and encourage mold. Worse, excessive water can rot framing, undermine footings, and cause unreinforced foundations to crack, bulge inward, or fail altogether. Often moisture problems can be mitigated simply by keeping gutters and downspouts clear, grading the soil away from the foundation, and improving drainage around basement window wells. Beyond that, the "cures" are increasingly expensive, such as excavating along the outside of the foundation to add gravel and perimeter drainpipe and to apply waterproofing treatments.

INDOOR SYMPTOMS OF FOUNDATION FAILINGS

Most foundations that fail were poorly designed, poorly constructed, or subjected to changes—especially hydrostatic pressure or soil movement—that exceeded their load-bearing capacities. Exact causes are often elusive.

Localized springiness or low spots in flooring are probably caused by an undersize pad or by a deteriorated or absent post beneath a girder. If you find wet rot or insect damage at the base of the post, correct that situation first.

Widespread springiness in floors and joists sagging in mid-span are caused by joists too small

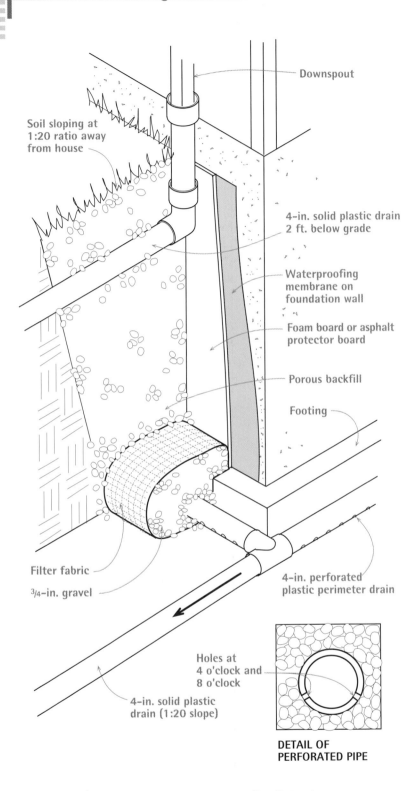

Soil sloping at 1:20 ratio away from house

Downspout

4-in. solid plastic drain 2 ft. below grade

Waterproofing membrane on foundation wall

Foam board or asphalt protector board

Porous backfill

Footing

Filter fabric

³/₄-in. gravel

4-in. perforated plastic perimeter drain

4-in. solid plastic drain (1:20 slope)

Holes at 4 o'clock and 8 o'clock

DETAIL OF PERFORATED PIPE

If you're willing to excavate, you can retrofit a first-rate drainage system such as this.

for a span or by a failed or absent girder. If an existing girder seems sound, adding posts or new pads may fix the problem. Otherwise, add a girder to reduce the distance joists span.

Flooring that crowns above a girder, sloping downward toward the outside walls; doors and windows that are difficult to open; and cracking at the corners of openings are often caused by a failure of all or part of the perimeter foundation.

Foundation cracks often signal foundation failure. Cracks may range from short surface cracks to through-the-wall cracks that should be examined by a structural engineer. Here are some common symptoms and remedies:

▶ Narrow vertical or diagonal surface cracks with aligned sides are likely caused by foundation settlement or soil movement but are probably not serious. If water runs from cracks after a storm, fill cracks with an epoxy cement, and then apply a sealant.

▶ Wide cracks in foundations less than 2 ft. tall indicate little or no steel reinforcement, a common failing of older homes in temperate climates.

▶ Large, ½-in. or wider, vertical cracks through the foundation that are wider at the top usually mean that one end of the foundation is sinking—typically at a corner with poor drainage or a missing downspout.

▶ Large vertical cracks through the foundation that are wider at the bottom are usually caused by footings that are too small for the load. You may need to replace or

reinforce failed sections.

▶ Horizontal cracks though a concrete foundation midway up the wall, with the wall bowing in, are most often caused by lateral pressure from water-soaked soil. This condition is common to uphill walls on sloping lots.

▶ Concrete-block walls with horizontal cracks that bulge inward are particularly at risk because block walls are rarely reinforced with steel. If walls bulge more than 1 in. from vertical and there's a chronic water problem, foundation failure may be imminent.

▶ In cold climates, horizontal cracks through the foundation, just below ground level, are usually caused by adfreezing, in which damp soil freezes to the top of the foundation and lifts it. If these cracks are accompanied by buckled basement floors, the foundation's footings may not be below the frost line for your region.

Gaps between the chimney and the house are usually caused by an undersize chimney pad. If the mortar joints are eroded, too, tear the chimney down and replace it.

Jacking and Shoring

Jacking refers to raising or lowering a building so you can repair or replace defective framing or failed foundations or to level a house that has settled excessively. *Shoring* refers to a temporary system of posts, beams, and other structural elements that support building loads. *Temporary* is the crucial word: Shoring supports the building between jackings. Once repairs are complete, you need to lower the house and remove the shoring as soon as possible. If repairs are extensive—say, replacing foundation sections—have a structural engineer design the new sections; specify jack size; and specify the posts, beams, and bracing needed to safely jack and shore the building.

Jacking a house is nerve-wracking. It requires a deep understanding of house framing and how structures transfer loads. It also requires superb organizational skills and a lot of specialized equipment. For that reason, foundation contractors routinely subcontract house-raising to house movers who have crews who know what they're doing and have on hand thousands of cribbing blocks, scores of hydraulic jacks, and cranes to lift steel I-beams for bigger jobs. Structural engineers will usually know qualified house movers. (By the way, these specialists are still called *house movers* even when the house stays on the site.)

PRO TIP

If you're not sure that a foundation crack is active (moving), epoxy a small piece of glass to both sides of the crack. If the glass breaks, the crack is active. A glass microscope slide is perfect for this test. Or substitute a scrap of window glass.

This dramatic crack through the corner of this building was caused by a downspout that stayed clogged for decades, water that undermined the footings, and a sinking corner.

If your foundation upgrade will require big steel I-beams, hire house movers. They'll have the cranes, beam rollers, cribbing, and expertise to handle I-beams safely.

MATERIALS AND TOOLS

Basically, timbers used for jacking and shoring stages are the same size. For example, once you have jacked the building high enough with 4×4 *jacking posts*, you can plumb and insert 4×4 *shoring posts* next to the jacking posts. Then, with shoring posts solidly in place, you can slowly lower the jacks of the jacking posts and remove each jacking component.

Posts and beams. To support a single-story house, 4×4 posts with 4×8 or 4×10 beams should be adequate. Because harder woods compress less when loaded, shoring should be Douglas fir, oak, or a wood with similar compressive strength. You'll also need *footing blocks* under each post: typically, two 2-ft.-long 4×12s placed side by side, with a 2-ft.-long 4×6 placed perpendicular atop the 4×12s. Footing blocks of that size are wide enough to accommodate a jacking post and a shoring post side by side while you make the transition from jacking to shoring.

For two-story houses or heavy single-story houses, most professionals specify W6×18 or W8×18 steel I-beams to support the loads. (A heavy single-story house might have a stucco exterior, a plastered interior, and a tile roof.) Because steel beams can span greater distances than wood, they require fewer posts underneath, which frees space under the house and improves access for workers. However, if you use steel

Patching Foundation Cracks

Determine the cause of the crack and fix that first; otherwise the crack may recur. Shallow foundation cracks less than ⅛ in. wide are usually caused by normal shrinkage and needn't be patched, unless their appearance disturbs you or they leak water. However, you should repair any cracks that go all the way through the foundation: Probe with a thin wire to see if they do.

Of the many crack-repair materials, there are three main types: cement-based, epoxy, and polyurethane foams. When working with any of these materials, wear disposable rubber gloves, eye protection, and a respirator mask with changeable filters.

Cement-based materials such as hydraulic cement are mixed with water and troweled into cracks. To ensure a good connection, first use a masonry chisel and hand sledge to enlarge the crack; angle the chisel to undercut the crack, making it wider at the back, like a rabbet joint in woodworking. Then wire-brush the crack to remove debris. Next, dampen the surfaces, fill the crack with hydraulic cement, and feather out the edges so the repaired area is flat. Work fast because most hydraulic cement sets in 10 minutes to 15 minutes and expands so quickly that it can stop the flowing water of an active leak.

Epoxies range from troweled-on pastes to *injection systems* that pump epoxy deep into cracks. Application details vary, but many injection systems feature *surface ports,* which are plastic nozzles inserted into the crack along its length. You should space ports 8 in. apart before temporarily capping them. Then seal the wall surface with epoxy gel or hydraulic cement, which acts as a dam for the epoxy liquid you'll inject deep into the wall through the ports. Working from the bottom, uncap each surface port, insert the nozzle of the applicator, and inject epoxy till it's visible in the port above. Cap the port just filled, and then move up the wall, port by port.

Epoxy is famously strong. The manufacturer of Simpson Crack-Pac™ claims that its injected epoxy achieves 11,000 psi compressive strength when cured for 7 days. (Foundation concrete averages 3,000 psi to 4,500 psi.) Consequently, injected epoxy, which bonds to both sides of the crack, is a true structural repair, not just a crack filler. There are a couple of disadvantages: cost and curing time. Epoxy takes hours to harden, so it can ooze out the back of the crack, if there's a void between the soil and the foundation wall—as there often is. If

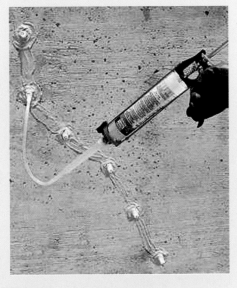

your main concern is water leaks and not structural repairs, polyurethane foam is probably a better choice.

Polyurethane foam is applied in many ways, including the surface-port injection just described for epoxies. Polyurethane sets up in minutes, so it's unlikely to sag or run out the back of the crack. It's largely unaffected by water, so you can inject it into a damp crack. Unlike epoxy or cement-based fillers, polyurethane is elastomeric (meaning it stays flexible), so it's great for filling foundation cracks that expand and contract seasonally. One disadvantage is that it has little compressive strength and hence does not create a structural repair.

beams, stick with wood posts: Fir 6×6s are less likely to migrate than steel columns.

Cribbing. Cribbing refers to a framework of usually squared timber (often 6×6s) stacked perpendicular in alternate layers to create a stable platform for jacking or shoring house loads. In earthquake country, foundation contractors "shear wall" cribbing higher than 8 ft.—that is, they temporarily nail ½-in. plywood to the cribbing, using duplex nails. The precaution is worth the trouble: in 1989 a California house resting on 13-ft.-high shear-walled cribbing remained standing through a 7.1 quake.

Braces and connectors. To keep posts plumb and prevent structural elements from shifting, builders use a variety of braces and connectors such as these:

▶ Diagonal 2×4 braces 3 ft. or 4 ft. long are usually nailed up with double-headed nails for easy removal.

▶ Plywood gussets are acceptable if space is limited.

▶ Metal connectors such as Simpson hurricane ties, post caps, and post-to-beam connectors are widely used because they are strong and quick to install.

Jacks. House-raising screw jacks and hydraulic jacks are by far the most common types. For safety, all jacks must be placed on a stable jacking platform and plumbed.

Screw jacks vary from 12 in. to 20 in. (closed height), and extend another 9 in. to 15 in. Never raise the threaded shaft more than three-quarters

its total length because it would be unstable beyond that. Screw jacks are extremely stable: Of all types, they are the least likely to fail or lower unexpectedly under load. But they require a lot of muscle and at least 2 ft. of space around the jack for operation.

Hydraulic jacks are the workhorses of foundation repair and are rated according to the loads they can bear, such as 12 tons. In general, hydraulic jacks are easier to operate than screw jacks, and they fit into tighter spaces. They are lowered by turning a release valve and so can't be lowered incrementally. Because hydraulics release all at once, many house movers use hydraulics to raise a house and screw jacks to lower it gradually.

Because the head of a hydraulic jack is relatively small, you need to place a 4-in. by 4-in. by ¼-in. steel plate between it and the wood it supports so the head doesn't sink in during jacking. *Safety note:* Before lowering the jack, have a helper remove the steel plate as pressure is released. Otherwise, the plate could fall and injure the jack operator. Alternatively, have the plate predrilled so you can screw or nail it to the underside of the beam.

Unsafe! Although post jacks such as this are widely used as temporary shoring, they are not strong enough for house loads. Here footing blocks are also undersize, and the post is badly out of plumb.

Jacks. Left: a hydraulic jack, the workhorse of house raising. Right: a screw jack. Textured heads on both reduce chances of post slippage.

Unsuitable for raising a house. *Post jacks* employ a screw mechanism but are of flimsier construction than the compact screw jack described in the previous section. They tend to be fashioned from lightweight steel, with slender screws that could easily distort when loaded beyond their capacity. So use post jacks only for low-load, very temporary situations.

JACKING SAFELY

For safe jacking, you need to proceed slowly and observe the following precautions.

Preparatory steps

▶ Survey the building, noting structural failings and their probable causes as well as which walls are load bearing. Also determine whether joists or beams are deflecting because of heavy furniture, such as a piano; which pipes, ducts, or wires might complicate your repairs; where the gas pipe shutoff is; and so on.

▶ Have a plan that anticipates everything. If excavation is necessary, who's going to do it? And where will you put the displaced dirt? (Disturbed dirt has roughly twice the volume of compacted soil.) Will you need to rent equipment, such as jacks, compressor, and jackhammer? Where will you store materials? How will rain affect the materials and the work itself? Can a concrete-mixer truck reach your forms or will you need a separate concrete pumper, an auxiliary pump on wheels that pumps (pushes) the concrete from the mixer truck to the pour?

▶ Assemble safety equipment. This is mostly hard-hat work. You'll also need safety glasses that don't fog up, sturdy knee pads, and heavy gloves. For some power equipment, you'll need hearing protectors. Update your tetanus shot. Set up adequate lighting that keeps cords out of your way—and, on a post near a suitable light, mount a first-aid kit. Even though a cell phone is handy if trouble strikes, never work alone. Workers should stay within shouting distance.

▶ Have all necessary shoring materials on hand before you start jacking. Remember, jacks are for lifting, not supporting. Within reason, level the ground where you'll place footing blocks or shoring plates. As soon as a section of the house is raised to the proper level, be sure to set, plumb, and brace the shoring. Hydraulic jacks left to support the structure too long may slowly "leak" and settle or—worse—kick out if bumped or jostled.

Jacking basics

▶ Support jacks adequately. The footing blocks or cribbing beneath the jacks must be thick enough to support concentrated weights without deflection and wide enough to distribute those loads. It's difficult to generalize how big such a support must be; a 4×12 footing block 3 ft. long or two layers of 4×4 cribbing should adequately support a jack beneath the girder of a single-story house. In this case, the soil must also be stable, dry, and level. If the soil isn't level, dig a level pit for the cribbing, as shown on p. 208. (Avoid precast concrete piers as jacking blocks because their footprints are too small and the concrete could shatter when loaded.)

▶ Don't place jacking or shoring platforms too close to the edge of an excavation. Otherwise, the soil could cave in when the timber is loaded. The rule of thumb is to move back 1 ft. for each 1 ft. you dig down. Also, don't put jacks or shoring where they could be undermined later. For example, if you need a needle beam to support joists parallel to the foundation, excavate on either side of what will be your new foundation, and place jacking platforms in those holes. In that manner, you can remove foundation sections without undercutting the jacking platforms.

Jacking Components

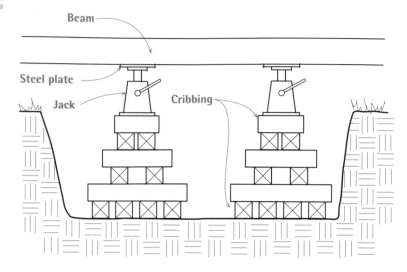

Jacks must be supported on a level, stable platform. Here, cribbing beneath the jacks and steel plates atop them disperse loads to larger surface areas. Without the steel plates to spread the load, jack heads can sink into wood beams.

DON'T DO THIS!

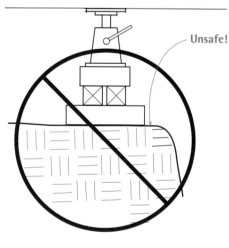

When the jack is loaded, bearing blocks placed unsafely close to the edge of an excavation can cause it to collapse.

FOOTING PIT

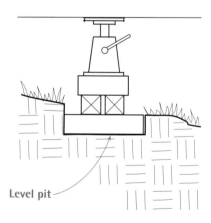

Where you must jack on a slight incline, dig down into the soil to create a level pit. The pit will also surround the bearing blocks, giving them no place to go when loaded.

▶ Level support beams, and plumb all posts. The logic of this should be evident: When loads are transmitted straight down, there is less danger that jacks or posts will kick out, injuring someone and leaving shoring unsupported. Accordingly, cut the ends of the posts perfectly square, plumb the posts when you set them, and check them for plumb periodically as the job progresses.

Where the ground slopes, dig a level footing pit into the soil, as shown in the bottom drawings at left, so footings or cribbing can't migrate under pressure. (Typically, the foundation contractor digs the pits and prepares the site before the house mover arrives to install the cribbing.) Surrounded by the walls of the pit, the bearing blocks have no place to go.

▶ Keep checking for level and plumb as you jack. If supports sink into the soil, posts tilt, or the jack starts "walking" under pressure, lower the jack, reset those elements and begin anew. First thing each day, check jack supports and shoring for plumb and level.

Diagonal bracing, plywood gussets, and metal connectors will each help posts stay plumb. When cross bracing temporary posts and beams, use screw guns or pneumatic nailers to attach braces. Hand nailing braces could knock posts out of plumb or cause beams to rotate or jack heads to migrate.

▶ Raise jacks in small increments—say, ¼ in. per day—to minimize damage to finish surfaces inside the house. When you're jacking a structure to be repaired, as when replacing a mudsill, jack just enough to lift the weight off the sill to be removed. If many jacks are involved, raise them simultaneously if possible, so excessive stress (and damage) doesn't accrue above any one jack.

Steps in jacking and installing shoring.
Setting jacking equipment varies according to the type of jack; the structural elements to be raised; and site conditions, such as ceiling height, access, and soil stability. That noted, the following observations hold true in most cases.

1. Position the jacks and jacking beams as close as possible to the joists, girders, or stud walls you're jacking. If you're adding posts under a sagging girder, support may be directly under the girder; but more often, it will need to be offset slightly—say, within 1 ft. to 2 ft. of joist ends—to give you working room. In other words, close enough to joist ends so they won't deflect, yet far back enough to let you work. Again, don't put jacks or shoring where they could be undermined by unstable soil later.

Needle Beams

When replacing a mudsill or sections of a foundation whose joists run perpendicular to that foundation wall (see p. 210), place a 4×8 or 4×10 carrying beam on edge under the house, within 2 ft. of the foundation. A jack every 6 ft. under the beam should suffice.

When joists run parallel to the foundation wall being replaced, you'll need to run *needle beams* through exterior walls, and support each beam with one post underneath the house and a second post outside, roughly 2 ft. beyond the foundation wall. For this, you'll need to remove sections of siding so you can insert a beam every 6 ft. to 8 ft. If the siding is stucco, you'll need to punch large holes through it. To keep the rim (outer) joist from deflecting under the load, nail a second rim joist to it, doubling it before jacking. Also, add solid blocking from those doubled rim joists to the first adjacent joist. Use metal connectors to affix the blocking and 10d nails to face-nail the rim joists.

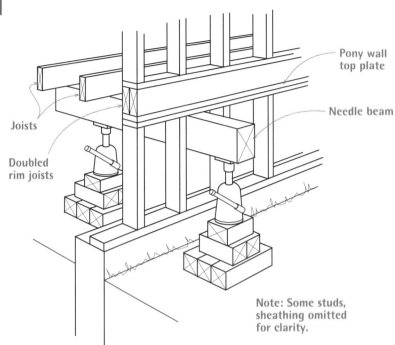

Pony wall top plate

Needle beam

Joists

Doubled rim joists

Note: Some studs, sheathing omitted for clarity.

Where joists run parallel to the foundation wall, remove a section of siding and run a temporary needle beam through the wall as shown. To prevent its deflection under pressure, double the rim (outer) joist and run solid blocking to the next joist inward.

This big needle beam needed to fit under the top plate of the pony wall (short wall) on the right. As a result, the top of the beam needed to be built up with a 4×4, which now supports the floor joists.

Joists Perpendicular to a Foundation Wall

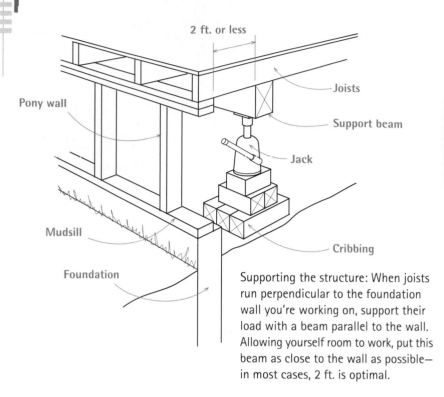

Supporting the structure: When joists run perpendicular to the foundation wall you're working on, support their load with a beam parallel to the wall. Allowing yourself room to work, put this beam as close to the wall as possible—in most cases, 2 ft. is optimal.

To determine the height of the shoring posts, jack the beam to the desired height, level the footing block, and measure between the two. Nail the post cap on before inserting the post. Because this needle beam is simply holding a wall in place—not raising it—it was jacked just snug to a wall plate.

2. Level and set the footing blocks or cribbing on compacted soil. Each jack base should be about 2 ft. by 2 ft. Or, if you're using a single timber block, use a 4×12 at least 3 ft. long or, if the soil is crumbly, at least 4 ft. long. If you spend a little extra time leveling the footings, the posts will be more likely to stay plumb. To support a single-story house, set posts every 5 ft. or so beneath an adequately sized beam—typically, a 4×8 or 4×10 set on edge.

3. Positioning a jacking beam requires prep work. Ideally, the crew should raise the beam into place and then immediately plumb and set the jacks. But they may need to catch their breath or gather equipment before setting the jacking posts. In that event, cut two 2×4s approximately ½ in. longer than the distance from the underside of the beam to the top of the cribbing plates and use a sledgehammer to wedge a 2×4 under each end of the beam. *Caution:* This setup is inherently unstable, so workers should monitor both 2×4s continually to make sure they don't kick out.

4. As soon as the beam is in place, cut posts 10 in. shorter than the distance from the underside of the beam to the top of the footing blocks. This 10 in. is roughly the (closed) height of a hydraulic jack plus a little room to move. With a helper, place jacks and posts under both ends of

the beam, plumb the posts, and start jacking. Center each jack on its footing blocks so there's plenty of room for the shoring post(s) that will follow shortly. (If you use hydraulic jacks, you can position the shoring posts 3 in. to 4 in. from the jacking posts.) As you jack, try to raise both ends of the beam evenly, using a 4-ft. or 6-ft. spirit level to check for level.

The amount you raise the beam beyond that depends on whether you're leveling floors, taking weight off joist ends before replacing a foundation, or just supporting the structure where it is. When the beam is at the desired height, measure down to the tops of footing blocks to determine the height(s) of the shoring posts. (If you jack up an additional ⅛ in., you'll find it easier to slide shoring posts in.)

5. After you're done jacking, install the shoring posts, which are more stable than jacks on posts. To keep the shoring posts in place, nail steel caps to their tops before installing them. Once you've placed the posts under the footing beams, attach the post caps to the beams, and add cross bracing or plywood gussets to keep the beam from rotating. Once you've plumbed the shoring posts and braced the beams, lower the jacks slowly till they no longer bear weight, and then remove them.

With shoring supporting all necessary bearing members, you're ready to begin repairs.

Note: Some foundation contractors install two shoring posts—one on either side of the jacking post—for greater stability. Once the jack is removed, nail two 3-ft. long 2×4 diagonal braces between the two shoring posts; for this, use a pneumatic nailer. Hammer blows could dislodge the posts.

6. When your repairs are finished, begin to remove the shoring by reinserting the jacking apparatuses and then simultaneously raising all the jacks slowly and evenly to take weight off the shoring. Leave the cross bracing in place till those loads are removed. Then, keeping the jacking posts plumb, carefully remove the post-and-beam bracing and carefully lower and remove those elements. Gradually lower the building onto its new pads, posts, and foundation, and then remove the jacks.

Minor Repairs and Upgrades

The category *minor repairs* includes anything short of replacing a failed foundation, which is covered in the next section. Repairing surface cracks is explained on p. 205.

REPLACING POSTS AND PADS

If floors slope down to a single point, there's a good chance that a post or pad has failed. If a floor slopes down to an imaginary line running down the middle of the house, there's probably a girder sagging because of multiple post or pad failures. Fortunately, the cures for both conditions are relatively straightforward.

Post repairs. The most common cause of wooden post failure is moisture wicking up through a concrete pad, rotting the bottom of the post. To replace a damaged post, use the techniques just described in "Jacking and Shoring." Place footing blocks as close as possible to the existing pad, and jack just enough to take the load off the post—plus ⅛ in. Remove the rotted post, measure from the underside of the girder to the pad (remembering to subtract the ⅛ in.!), and cut a new post—preferably from pressure-treated lumber.

To keep this new post from rotting, cut a sheet-metal plate to put under the bottom of the post; use aviation snips to cut the 22-gauge sheet aluminum. The metal will prevent moisture from seeping up through the concrete. Place the plate

PRO TIP

It's generally safer to place jacks atop posts rather than under them. As jacking pressures increase, there's increasing danger that posts sitting on jacks will kick out. However, if the load is light, either way is okay. For example, in the photo on the facing page, the jack is merely holding a needle beam in place while workers measure and set a shoring post.

Cutting into a Concrete Floor

To enlarge an existing load-bearing pad or create one where none was, you may need to cut through a concrete floor. Depending on the condition and thickness of that floor, the job will range from nasty to horrible. Cutting concrete is noisy, dirty, and dangerous; and the tools are heavy and unpredictable. Wear safety glasses, gloves, hearing protectors, and a respirator mask. Adequate ventilation and lighting are a must.

If the floor was poured before the 1950s, you'll likely find that it is only 3 in. or 4 in. thick and is without steel reinforcing. The floor may also be badly cracked. In this case, you can probably break through it with a pickax, but to minimize floor patching later, rent an electric concrete-cutting saw with a diamond blade to score around the opening. Then finish the cut (the saw-blade rarely cuts all the way through) with a hand sledge and a chisel.

Be advised, however, that a concrete-cutting saw cuts dry and thus throws up an extraordinary amount of dust. Therefore, you may need to seal off the basement with plastic barriers and then spend an hour vacuuming afterward. Alternatively, you can rent a gasoline-powered wet-cut saw, which keeps down the dust but fills the basement with exhaust fumes. And, if the concrete floor is a modern slab, 5 in. thick and reinforced

with rebar, you can spend a day accomplishing very little. Well . . . you get the picture.

Fortunately, for a few hundred bucks you can hire a concrete-cutting subcontractor to cut out a pad opening in about an hour. (Don't forget to allow for the thickness of the form boards when sizing the opening.) The subcontractor can also bore holes needed for drainpipes and such.

A gasoline-powered wet-cut saw has a diamond blade and attaches to a water supply (via the yellow fitting), which reduces dust when cutting concrete.

under the post (a dab of silicone caulking will hold it in place while you plumb and position the post); then lower the jack so the new post bears the load. Or replace the wooden post with a preprimed metal column. However, if basement floors are wet periodically—suggested by sediment lines along the base of walls—build up or replace the existing pad with a taller one to elevate the base of the post. Add a sump pump, too, as explained on p. 224.

Replacing pads. Replace concrete pads that are tilting or sinking because they are undersize for the loads they bear. Likewise, you'll need to pour a new pad, if there was no pad originally and an overloaded post punched through the concrete floor. Pads for load-bearing columns should always be separated from floors by isolation joints.

Load-bearing pads should be 24 in. by 24 in. by 12 in. deep, reinforced with a single layer of No. 4 (½-in.) rebar arranged in a tic-tac-toe grid. Pads supporting a greater load (such as a two-story house) should be 30 in. by 30 in. by 18 in. deep, with two layers of no. 4 rebar; in each layer, run three pieces of rebar perpendicular to three other pieces. In either configuration, keep the rebar back 3 in. from the edges of the pad.

Line the forms with sheet plastic so that the water in the concrete won't drain into the soil and weaken the pad. (Plastic also prevents soil moisture from later migrating through the pad and rotting the post.) If you carefully level the tops of the form boards and screed off the concrete to them, the top of the pad will be level as well. Allow the concrete to cure before putting weight on it: 3 days minimum; 7 days recommended.

ADDING A GIRDER

Adding a girder beneath of a run of joists shortens the distance they span, stiffens a springy floor, and reduces some loading on perimeter foundations. If your floors are springy and joists exceed the following rule-of-thumb lengths, consider adding a girder.

JOIST SIZE	TYPICAL SPAN (ft.)
2×6	8
2×8	10
2×10	12
2×12	14

PRO TIP

Before adding a girder to correct springy floors, go under the house and see if there's solid blocking or cross bridging between joists. If not, add it, and that may be all you'll have to do to stiffen the floors. If floors sag *between* joists, the subflooring may be too thin.

An engineer can size the girder for you. "Beam Span Comparison," on the facing page, shows maximum spans for built-up girders in two-story houses.

Ideally, the new girder should run beneath the midpoint of the joist span, but if existing ducts or drainpipes obstruct that route, avoid them by shifting the girder location a foot or two. Once you locate the girder, snap a chalkline to mark its center, and plumb down from that to mark positions for pads and posts. Place posts at each end of the girder and approximately every 6 ft. along its length. If you create a girder by laminating several 2×s, keep at least one member of the "beam sandwich" continuous over each post.

Size and reinforce pads as described in the preceding section. After the pad's concrete has cured 1 week, bring in the girder or laminate it on site from 2-in. stock. Prescribed widths for built-up girders are usually three 2× boards (4½ in. thick when nailed together). For built-up girders and beams, the Uniform Building Code recommends the following nailing schedule: 20d nails at 32 in. on center at the top and bottom and two 20d nails staggered at the ends and at each splice.

Whether solid or laminated, if the girder has a crown, install it crown up. Installing a new girder is essentially the same as positioning a temporary shoring beam, except that the girder will stay in place. Have helpers to raise the girder and support it till permanent support posts are in place. Properly sized, the pad will have more than enough room for jacks and posts, so place jacking posts as close as possible to the permanent post's location. Raise the girder approximately ⅛ in. higher than its final position, to facilitate insertion of the new posts.

STEEL BEAMS

If there's limited headroom or clearance under the house, steel beams provide more strength per equivalent depth than wood beams. For steel beams, hire an engineer to size them and a specialist to install them: Steel I-beams are expensive and heavy, and they can be problematic to attach to wood framing, without special equipment to drill holes, spot-weld connectors, and so on. For commonly available sizes and some sense of the weights involved, see "Steel I-Beams," on p. 53.

Replacing a Shallow Foundation

If you decide to replace a shallow foundation, begin by checking local building codes for foundation specs appropriate for your area. Before beginning foundation work, be sure to review this chapter's earlier sections on shoring and jacking. Then survey the underside of the house and the area around the foundation for pipes, ducts, and other potential obstructions. If you can reposition jacks or move shoring slightly to avoid crushing or disconnecting drains, water pipes, and the like, do so.

Remember, jacking timbers and shoring are *temporary* supports. Complete the job and lower the house onto foundation elements as soon as possible. Work within your means, skills, and schedule: If you can't afford a house mover to raise the house and replace the whole foundation, do it one wall at a time.

REPLACING MUDSILLS

Mudsills are almost always replaced when foundations are. With the framing exposed, it's easy to install new pressure-treated or redwood mudsills that resist rot and insects. At the same time, replace rotted or insect-infested pony-wall studs . (If just a few studs are rotted, cut away the rot and nail a pressure-treated sister stud to each. If the bottom 1 in. or 2 in. of many studs has rotted, you might also install a thicker mudsill to make up for the amount you cut off stud bottoms.) If the siding is in good shape, remove just enough to expose the mudsills and rotten studs; the siding holds the pony-wall studs in place and keeps them from "chattering" while you cut them. (Pony walls shown on p. 209.) You'll also need to punch through the siding to install temporary needle beams, discussed earlier in this chapter.

Girder (Beam) Supports

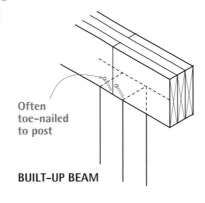

BUILT-UP BEAM

Often toe-nailed to post

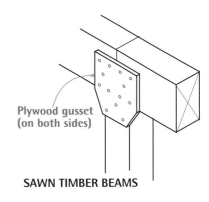

SAWN TIMBER BEAMS

Plywood gusset (on both sides)

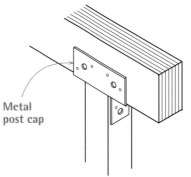

LVL BEAM (engineered lumber)

Metal post cap

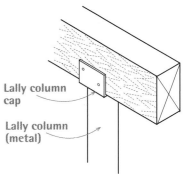

PSL BEAM (engineered lumber)

Lally column cap

Lally column (metal)

When it's necessary to construct a girder from several pieces of lumber, support each girder joint by placing a post or column beneath it. Many building codes also require metal connectors or plywood gussets at such joints to join posts to beams.

Beam Span Comparison

Typical joist

Beam

Header or other support

Header

Joist span y

Joist span x

Beam supports ½ of each joist span, or x/2 + y/2. See table at right.

Header supports ½ of single joist span

Use this drawing and table for estimating beam sizes and comparing beam types for uniform floor loads of a 40-psf (pounds per square foot) live load and a 15-psf dead load. Have a structural engineer calculate your actual loads.

Beam Span Comparison

| BEAM TYPE | JOIST SPAN (x/2+y/2) | | | |
| | 8 FT. | 10 FT. | 12 FT. | 14 FT. |
	BEAM SPAN (ft.)			
(2) 2x8 built-up beam	6.8	6.1	5.3	4.7
4x8 timber	7.7	6.9	6.0	5.3
3⅛ in. x 7½ in. glue-laminated beam	9.7	9.0	8.3	7.7
3½ in. x 7½ in. PSL beam	9.7	9.0	8.5	8.0
(2) 1¾ o=in. x 7½ in. LVL (unusual depth)	10.0	9.3	8.8	8.3
4x8 steel beam (W8 x 13 A36)	17.4	16.2	15.2	14.1

Once you've jacked up and shored the house framing, lay out the height of the new sill by snapping chalklines across the pony-wall studs. Use a laser level to indicate where the chalk marks should go or, if the old foundation is level, measure up from it. Although the line should be as level as possible, small variations will be accommodated when the concrete is poured up to the bottom of the mudsill.

With the siding removed, use a square to extend the cutoff marks across the face of the studs; a square cut optimizes load bearing from the stud onto the mudsill. Use a reciprocating saw to make the cuts. If the first stud chatters as you attempt to cut through it, tack furring strips to all the studs, just above the cut-line to bolster successive studs. Then remove the old mudsill and rotted stud sections. Chances are the old mudsill will not be bolted to the foundation.

The replacement sill should be foundation-grade heart redwood, pressure-treated Douglas fir, or yellow pine to resist insects and moisture and should be end-nailed upward into the solid remnants of each stud, using two 16d *galvanized* common nails. Use a pneumatic nailer to nail up the new mudsill; it does the job quickly. However, predrill anchor bolt holes into the new

This old mudsill rotted out because the foundation was too close to the ground. After using a laser level to transfer the height of the new foundation, this builder snapped a chalkline across the pony-wall studs to indicate the height of the new sill.

mudsills before nailing them to stud ends. Anchor bolts will secure house framing to the foundation after you pour it.

REMOVING OLD FOUNDATIONS

To tear out an old foundation, you've got several options. All require safety glasses, hearing protection, heavy gloves, a mask, patience, and a strong back. Before acquiring heavy and expensive equipment, try to break out a section of the old foundation using a 9-lb. sledgehammer and a 6-ft. pointed steel bar. Old concrete without rebar is often cracked and soft. Once you've removed a small section, the rest may come out easily.

If the concrete is too thick and hard, rent a towable air compressor and jackhammer. A 90-lb. jackhammer will break almost anything, but it's a beast to maneuver; a 60-lb. hammer is light enough to lift onto a foundation wall and almost always strong enough to break a wall apart. A 60-lb. electric jackhammer is less powerful than a compressor-driven one, but it may have enough muscle to get the job done.

Or you can rent a gas-powered saw with a 10-in. concrete-cutting blade that cuts 4 in. to 5 in. deep, letting you cut the concrete into manageable chunks. A third option is rotohammering a line of $\frac{5}{8}$-in. holes across the foundation and then splitting along that line with a large mason's chisel and a hand sledge.

Should you encounter rebar, you'll either need an acetylene torch to cut through it or a metal abrasive wheel in a circular saw or grinder. Rebar cutting is monstrously hard work. With the old foundation removed, you can excavate new footings from outside the house and install forms for the concrete.

PRO TIP

If a new foundation section isn't terribly long or deep, use an *electric demolition hammer with a shovel bit* to excavate the trench. This tool is particularly helpful when there's no room to swing a pick. Shovel bits cut a nice, clean edge and dig themselves in, even in heavy clay. Then you simply shovel out the loosened soil.

Leveling a House

In theory, you can level a house using individual hydraulic jacks. And if the house has only one or two low spots, you may succeed. However, the framing of a house will usually have sagged and settled, increasing the likelihood that jacking one area will raise an adjacent area too high. Heavily loaded points in multistory houses may resist being raised at all and when they finally do move, it's often sudden, loud, and frightening.

Leveling a house is far more likely to succeed if done by a house mover with a *unified hydraulic jacking system,* in which jacks are interconnected, via hoses, to a central console that monitors the load on each jack. Thus, instead of 12 workers trying to turn 12 jacks at exactly the same time, a single operator at the console can ensure that the jacks rise at the same—or variable—rates, to the desired height.

That desired height is determined beforehand by the foundation contractor, house mover, structural engineer, and—on occasion—the architect. Most often, the house mover works from a *master reference point* outside, against which house corners are read to determine whether they need raising or lowering. (For example, corner 1 might be listed as +¾ in.; corner 3, as -½ in.; and so on.) Once the corners are leveled, the framing in the middle of the house is fine-tuned.

Even when professionals level a structure, there's invariably damage to the finish surfaces inside, such as cracked plaster or popped drywall seams, door latches that no longer meet strike plates, trim that's askew, and windows and doors that bind during opening or shutting. Consider all this before you jack. Raising only the most out-of-level areas may be more cost-effective than leveling floors perfectly. Moreover, gently sloping floors may add character to an older house.

Once the needle beams are in place to pick up the loads that were previously carried by the pony wall, you can cut the pony-wall studs and remove the sill.

CONCRETE FORMWORK

Correctly positioning 1½-in.-thick form boards can be tricky, and there are myriad ways to do so. Here's a relatively foolproof method, in which you first erect the inner (house side) form walls, by nailing them to 2×4 *form-hangers* nailed to joists. This method also enables easy access for tying rebar, reattaching sills, and the like.

Inner form walls. If floor joists run perpendicular to the foundation wall, start by nailing 2×4 form-hangers into the joists at both ends of the foundation wall section being replaced. The 2×4s should extend down into the foundation trench, stopping 1 in. or 2 in. above the tops of footing forms, if any. Position each 2×4 so its edge is exactly 9½ in. from the outside face of the foundation (8-in.-thick concrete plus 1½-in.-thick form board). First nail the bottom form board to the 2×4s; then add 2×4 form-hangers between the first two. Spacing 2×4 form-hangers every 32 in., use two 16d nails to nail them to each joist. Then stack additional form boards atop the first until the top board is slightly above the bottom of the mudsill. As shown in "Concrete Forms for a Shallow Foundation," on p. 217, run diagonal 2×4 braces from joists to the 2×4 form-hangers to stiffen the inner form wall, thereby keeping it plumb and in place (see also the photos on p. 200 and on p. 216, left).

If the joists instead run parallel to the foundation, first add blocking between the rim joist and the first joist back, across the top of the pony wall. Nail the 2×4 form supports to the blocking, much as just described for perpendicular joists. Once the inside forms are complete, you can cut, bend, and assemble the rebar; attach the mudsill to the pony-wall studs; and insert anchor bolts before building the outside form walls. Even if local building codes don't require steel-reinforced foundations, adding steel is money well spent (see "Adding Steel," on p. 217).

Outer form walls. If your foundation is shallow and the sides of its trenches are cleanly cut, you may not need form boards for footings. But if your footings will have form boards, install them before building the foundation's outer form walls.

If there are no footing form boards, drive 4-ft.-long perforated steel stakes down into the footing area to secure the bottom form boards for the outer form walls. Plumb and space these stakes out 1½ in. from the outside face of the foundation, to allow for the thickness of the form boards. Use two stakes per form board to get started. Use 8d duplex nails to attach form boards to the steel stakes. Install this first outer form board a little higher than the inner form board initially; then hammer the stakes down to achieve level. *Note*: You may need several tries to drive stakes that are plumb and accurately positioned because, during driving, stake points are often deflected by rocks. Use a magnetic level to plumb the stakes.

Once the steel stakes are correctly positioned and the bottom form boards are nailed to them, add 2×4 form-hangers so you can hang additional form boards above. But first, nail spacers to the pony-wall studs, to compensate for the thickness of the 1½-in.-thick form boards. If the pony-wall studs are sheathed,

A 60-lb. jackhammer is powerful enough to bust concrete yet light enough to lift onto the foundation. Jackhammering is bone-rattling work, so have workers take turns at it.

POSITIONING Foundation FACES

Traditionally, the outside face of a foundation wall is flush to the edge of the house framing, allowing sheathing to overhang the foundation 1 in. or so, covering the joint between foundation and framing. However, contractors who install a lot of stucco argue that a foundation face flush to the outer face of the sheathing better protects the sheathing edge and creates a stucco edge that's less bulky—that is, one that sticks out less beyond the foundation wall.

Whichever detail you prefer, drop a plumb bob to establish the foundation's outside face. If the foundation wall is 8 in. thick, measure back 8 in. from the plumb line to mark the foundation's inside face.

nail 1½-in.-thick spacer boards to the studs, so the back face of the form boards lines up with the exterior sheathing. If the studs aren't presently sheathed, nail up 2-in.-thick spacers to accommodate the thickness of the form boards and the sheathing to come. If the outer face of the foundation wall aligns to the face of the sheathing, you can easily cover that often-troublesome joint with siding.

As you install each form board atop the preceding one, set the form ties that tie together inner and outer form boards. Form ties are designed to space the form boards exactly the right distance apart; they are available in 6-in., 8-in., 10-in., and 12-in. lengths. Use wire to tie the form ties to each vertical rebar, typically spaced 32 in. on center. At the ends of each form tie, insert metal wedges into the slots to keep

forms from spreading when filled with concrete. The top form board should overlap the mudsill slightly.

The outer form boards are braced by the plumbed 2×4 form-hangers, which are in turn supported by diagonal braces running back down to perforated steel stakes or to 2×4 stakes driven into the ground. Under the house, diagonal braces run from the inner form-hangers to the joists.

Note: After the pour, you'll be able to remove form boards and steel stakes if you first sprayed them with form-release oil. But be careful not to spill the oil onto the rebar, anchor bolts, or old foundation, because the oil will weaken the bond with new concrete.

Use prelooped wire ties to splice lengths of rebar, overlapping rebar sections at least 12 in. Note the cleanly cut sides of this trench, which will serve as forms for the poured foundation footings. An electric demolition hammer with a shovel bit was used to cut this dense soil.

Ready for concrete—the form walls are up and braced. Metal wedges inserted into the ends of the form ties will keep the form boards from spreading. The next step is to pour the footings before pouring the foundation walls.

ADDING STEEL

Structural steel used in renovated foundations includes *rebar*; *anchor bolts,* to attach framing to concrete; *pins* (or dowels), which tie old foundations to new ones; and a plethora of *metal connectors,* including the popular Simpson Strong-Ties), which strengthen joints against earthquakes, high winds, and other racking forces.

Rebar. Rebar in foundations is not specified by all building codes, but it's cost-effective insurance against cracking caused by lateral pressures of soil and water against foundations. Rebar can also eliminate concrete shrinkage cracks. Common sizes in residential construction are No. 3 (⅜ in. in diameter), No. 4 (½ in.), and No. 5 (⅝ in.). One common configuration is No. 4 rebar spaced every 32 in. or 48 in. on center.

In footings and foundation walls below grade, place rebar back 3 in. from forms and at least 3 in. above the soil. On the inner side of the foundation walls, rebar can be within 1½ in. of the forms. You should run rebar the length of a foundation, tying the lengths together after overlapping them at least 12 in. Use *prelooped wire ties* to join them. (Wire ties don't lend strength; they simply hold the bars in place before and during the pour.) Use wire ties to attach rebar to the anchor bolts, pins, form ties, and the like. Use a *cutter-bender* to cut and bend bars on small jobs. When rebar is delivered, store it above the ground—dirty rebar doesn't bond as well.

Concrete Forms for a Shallow Foundation

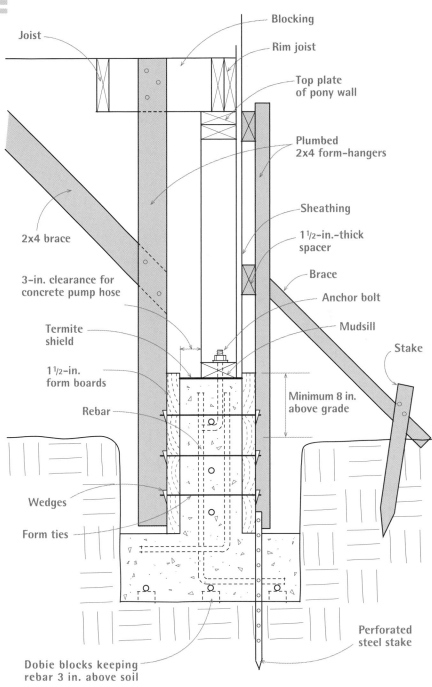

In this example, foundation walls are flush to the sheathing, and the trench walls serve as forms for the footings. Details will vary slightly, depending on the direction of joist, (as described in the text) and on other framing particulars.

To use this rebar cutter–bender, you feed rebar parallel with the base arm for bending, as shown, and perpendicular to the base arm when cutting.

Masonry anchors. 1, anchor bolt holder (monkey paw); 2, anchor bolt holder; 3, Simpson SSTB anchor bolt, used with seismic hold-downs; 4, J-bolt anchor; 5, square plate washers; 6, concrete screws (high-strength threaded anchors); 7, lag screw within expansion shield; 8, pin-drive expansion anchor; 9, wedge expansion anchor; 10, expansion shields for machine screws.

PRO TIP

If you're retrofitting anchor bolts to existing mudsills, begin with a wood-cutting bit to drill through the sill. Then switch to a rotary hammer bit to drill into the concrete foundation. Because the tip of the wood bit invariably hits concrete as it clears wood, you'll ruin the bit before long. But rotary hammer bits are too slow and ineffective at cutting wood.

Anchor bolts. Place ½-in. or ⅝-in. anchor bolts no more than 6 ft. apart in one-story house foundations and no more than 4 ft. apart in two-story foundations. In earthquake zones, 4-ft. spacing is acceptable, but conscientious contractors space the bolts every 3 ft. There should also be an anchor bolt no farther than 1 ft. from each end of the sills. For maximum grip, use square washers. When pouring a new foundation, use J-type anchor bolts; the plastic bolt holders shown in the photo on p. 202 will position the anchor bolts in the middle of the foundation wall.

When retrofitting bolts to existing foundations, use ⅝-in. *all-thread rod* cut to length. Rod lengths will vary according to code specs and sill thickness. For example, a 10-in. rod will accommodate a washer, nut, and 1-in.-thick mudsill and will embed 7 in. in the concrete. You can also buy precut lengths of threaded rod, called *retrofit* bolts, which come with washers and nuts. Drill through the mudsill into the concrete, clean out the holes well, inject epoxy, and then insert the rods and bolts. The procedure is essentially the same for epoxying rebar pins to tie new concrete to old.

Because bolts, all-thread rods, and other tie-ins are only as strong as the material around them, you should center bolt holes in the top of the old foundation and drill them 6 in. to 8 in. deep, or whatever depth local codes require. Use an impact drill if you're drilling concrete. Drill

holes ⅛ in. larger than the diameter of the bolt so there's room for epoxy. For example, for ⅝-in. all-thread rod, drill ¾-in. holes; for ½-in. rod, drill ⅝-in. holes. Even if you oversize such holes, the bond probably won't be weaker, but you may waste a lot of expensive epoxy.

Note: To anchor mudsills in retrofits, threaded rod and epoxy have largely replaced expansion bolts. These chemical bonds are almost always stronger than mechanical ones, and epoxy's compressive strength is roughly four times greater than that of concrete.

Pins. Concrete *cold joints* are inherently weak. Cold joints occur when new concrete is butted against old or when separate pours create seams. To keep cold joints from separating, you need to join them with rebar pins. When drilling lateral holes to receive rebar pins that tie old walls to new (or secure a foundation cap), angle the drill bit slightly downward, so the adhesive you'll inject into the hole won't run out and so pins will be less likely to pull out.

Local codes and structural engineers will have the final say on sizing and spacing rebar pins. But, in general, drill ⅝-in. holes for ½-in. rebar to be epoxied; drill holes at least every 18 in. and embed rebar at least 7 in. into the top of foundations, and at least 4 in. into the side of 8-in.-thick walls. Extend rebar epoxied into the old foundation at least 18 in. into new formwork, and overlap rebar splices at least 12 in.

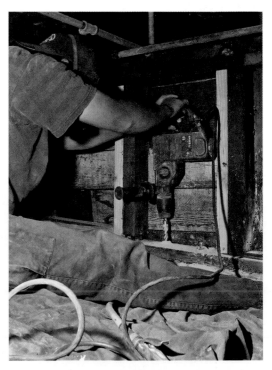

Retrofitting anchor bolts requires drilling in tight spaces. Bolts should be centered in the sill and embedded at least 7 in. into the concrete.

ATTACHING THE MUDSILL

Builders may attach new mudsills at different stages of form assembly. But here are the essentials. Before nailing up the mudsill (to the bottom of the pony-wall studs) predrill for anchor bolts, as described earlier, making sure that no bolt occurs under a stud. If local codes require metal termite shields, tack them to the underside of the mudsill after first predrilling it with anchor-bolt holes. Then, using a pneumatic nailer, end-nail the sill to the studs, using two 16d nails per stud. If there isn't enough room to end-nail upward into the sill, jack the mudsill tight to the studs and toenail down from the studs into the mudsill.

Once the mudsill is nailed to the studs, insert anchor bolts into the predrilled holes, screw on washers and nuts, and tie the free ends of the bolts to the rebar. At this point, the nuts should be just snug; you can tighten them down after the concrete has cured. If you end-nailed the mudsill, make sure the studs are tight to the top plates above: Jack up any studs that have separated. You may also need to brace the pony wall if it's loose, which is often the case if you have to demolish siding to remove it. Pony walls should be plumb and aligned with the forms.

POURING CONCRETE

After installing the outside form boards, you are almost ready to pour. If you are using a 2-in. hose (interior diameter) to pump the concrete to the site, make sure there is at least a 3-in. clearance between the edge of the form board and the outside edge of the new mudsill, to accommodate the width of the pump nozzle. If necessary, notch the forms so the nozzle can fit. The top of the form should be slightly higher than the bottom of the mudsill.

Fill the footing to the bottom of the wall forms before filling the forms. Some concrete may slop over from the walls onto the footing and bottom form boards, but slopover isn't a problem if you remove the concrete from the form bottoms before it sets up. That will allow easy removal of the forms once the concrete has cured.

When the concrete begins to set, but is not completely hard, pull out the perforated steel stakes holding the bottom form boards in place. To do this, remove the duplex nails and then use either a pipe wrench to grip the stakes or a commercial *stake puller*. If you leave the stakes in till the next day, you'll likely be able to pull them only if you remembered to oil them first.

GETTING A GOOD Epoxy BOND

When you're done drilling into the foundation, you need to clean each hole well because dust clinging to the hole's sides will greatly reduce the epoxy's bond strength. For this, use compressed air to blow dust from each hole and then a hole-cleaning brush in a repeating blow–brush–blow–brush–blow cycle. Before blowing, put on a respirator mask and eye protection. Then fit a tube into the hole and attach a blow nozzle. Continue the cycle until the hole's clean.

To avoid air pockets in the epoxy, fill each hole from its bottom, using a long-nozzle injector. The epoxy should flow in easily. As you insert the threaded rod or piece of rebar, twist it one full turn clockwise to distribute the adhesive evenly.

If no epoxy oozes out of the top of the hole when you've fully inserted your threaded rod, you didn't use enough epoxy or the epoxy leaked out. Leave the failed bolt in place, and drill and insert a new one next to it. Or remove the bolt and refill the hole completely with new epoxy.

This Simpson HD8A hold-down ties framing to the foundation and transfers tension loads between floors.

Rebar epoxied into the old foundation is spliced to steel in a perimeter wall of the new foundation. Part of this new wall's footing underpins (flows under) the old concrete. The chalkline immediately above the rebar marks the top of the foundation (see arrow).

This 2-in. (interior diameter) concrete-pump hose is easier to handle than a 3-in. hose. But its smaller diameter requires smaller, ³⁄₈-in. aggregate in the mix. Although a 2-in. hose is much lighter than a 3-in., tons of concrete pass through it—so you'll need helpers to support the hose and move it to the pouring points.

PRO TIP

If you have a septic tank, show the driver of the concrete-mixer truck where the tank and fields lie, so he or she doesn't drive over and crush them. After the pour, make sure the driver doesn't rinse and empty the truck's residue on your yard. You may want to plant a lawn there someday.

Capping a Foundation

Capping an old foundation with new concrete is relatively rare but is done when the existing foundation is in good condition and needs to be raised because the house's framing is too close to the ground, allowing surface water to rot sills and siding.

To raise wood members sufficiently, the new cap must be 8 in. above grade. At the very least, that means shoring up the structure, removing the existing mudsill, shortening the pony-wall studs, drilling the old foundation, epoxying in rebar pins to tie the new concrete to the old, and pouring new concrete atop or around some part of the existing foundation. That's a lot of work. So if the existing foundation is crumbling or lacks steel reinforcement, you should replace it altogether.

On the other hand, if the house lacks pony walls and the joists rest directly on the foundation, you have basically two options: (1) grade the soil away from the house to gain the necessary height, which may not be possible if the foundation is shallow, or (2) jack up the house at least 8 in., which means hiring a house mover. Here again, replacing the foundation is usually more cost effective.

Otherwise, cut the tops of the stakes off and leave the rest embedded in the new concrete.

Hammer the outside of the form boards and then use a *concrete vibrator*, to drive out the air pockets. For this, insert the hose-like vibrator into the forms. As the concrete approaches the tops of forms, signal the pump to shut off so that the concrete doesn't spill over the sides. When the forms are full and vibrated, use a trowel to flatten the top of the wall and sponge off any globs on the stakes and forms. Allow the concrete to cure 3 days at a minimum and 7 days for the optimum, before removing the forms and shoring, replacing the siding, and tightening down the washered anchor bolts. For further protection against moisture, apply below-grade waterproofing to the outside wall and footing before backfilling.

Concrete Work

Concrete is a mixture of portland cement, water, and aggregate (sand and gravel). When water is added to cement, a chemical reaction, called *hydration*, takes place, and the mixture hardens around the aggregate, binding it fast. Water makes concrete workable, and cement makes it strong. The lower the water to cement ratio (w/c), the stronger the concrete.

POURING A CONCRETE SLAB

Pouring (or placing) a concrete slab is pretty much the same procedure, whether for patios, driveways, basements, or garage floors. Most slabs consist of 4 in. of concrete poured over 4 in. of crushed rock, with a plastic moisture barrier between. In addition, garage floors are often reinforced with steel mesh or rebar to support greater loads and forestall cracking.

PREP STEPS

As with any concrete work, get plenty of help. Concrete weighs about 2 tons per cubic yard, so if your slab requires 10 cu. yd., you'll need to move and smooth 40,000 lb. of concrete before it sets into a monolithic mass. Time is of the essence, so make sure all the prep work is done before the truck arrives: Tamp the crushed stone, spread the plastic barrier (minimum of 6 mil), and elevate the steel reinforcement (if any) on

dobie blocks or *high chairs* so it will ride in the middle of the poured slab. Finally, snap level chalklines on the basement walls or concrete forms to indicate the final height of the slab— you'll *screed* to that level.

To pour concrete with a minimum of wasted energy, use a 2-in. (interior diameter) concrete-pump hose. A hose of that diameter is much lighter to move around than a 3-in. hose. Another advantage: It disgorges less concrete at a time, allowing you to control the thickness of the pour better. And a 2-in. hose gives easier access to distant or confined locations. *Important:* As you place concrete around the perimeter of the slab, be careful not to cover up the chalklines you snapped to mark the slab height. And as you

Cubic Yards of Concrete in Slabs of Various Thicknesses*,†

AREA (sq. ft.)	1.0 in.	1.5 in.	2.0 in.	2.5 in	3.0 in.	3.5in.	4.0 in.	4.5 in.	5.0 in.	5.5 in.	6.0 in.
10	0.03	0.05	0.06	0.08	0.09	0.11	0.13	0.14	0.15	0.17	0.19
20	0.06	0.09	0.12	0.16	0.19	0.22	0.25	0.28	0.31	0.34	0.37
30	0.09	0.14	0.19	0.23	0.28	0.33	0.37	0.42	0.46	0.51	0.56
40	0.12	0.19	0.25	0.31	0.37	0.43	0.50	0.56	0.62	0.68	0.74
50	0.15	0.23	0.31	0.39	0.46	0.54	0.62	0.70	0.77	0.85	0.93
60	0.19	0.28	0.37	0.46	0.56	0.65	0.74	0.83	0.93	1.02	1.11
70	0.22	0.32	0.43	0.54	0.65	0.76	0.87	0.97	1.08	1.19	1.30
80	0.25	0.37	0.49	0.62	0.74	0.87	1.00	1.11	1.24	1.36	1.48
90	0.28	0.42	0.56	0.70	0.84	0.97	1.11	1.25	1.39	1.53	1.67
100	0.31	0.46	0.62	0.78	0.93	1.08	1.24	1.39	1.55	1.70	1.85
200	0.62	0.93	1.23	1.54	1.85	2.16	2.47	2.78	3.09	3.40	3.70
300	0.93	1.39	1.85	2.32	2.78	3.24	3.70	4.17	4.63	5.10	5.56
400	1.23	1.83	2.47	3.10	3.70	4.32	4.94	5.56	6.17	6.79	7.41
500	1.54	2.32	3.09	3.86	4.63	5.40	6.17	7.00	7.72	8.49	9.26
600	1.85	2.78	3.70	4.63	5.56	6.48	7.41	8.33	9.26	10.19	11.11
700	2.16	3.24	4.32	5.40	6.48	7.56	8.64	9.72	10.80	11.88	12.96
800	2.47	3.70	4.94	6.20	7.41	8.64	9.88	11.11	12.35	13.58	14.82
900	2.78	4.17	5.56	6.95	8.33	9.72	11.11	12.50	13.89	15.28	16.67
1,000	3.09	4.63	6.17	7.72	9.26	10.80	12.35	13.89	15.43	16.98	18.52

* *This table can be used to estimate the cubic content of slabs larger than those shown. To find the cubic content of a slab measuring 1,000 sq. ft. and 8 in. thick, add the figures given for thicknesses of 6 in. and 2 in. for 1,000 sq. ft.*

† *Courtesy of Bon Tool Company, © 2003, from Statistical Booklet: Contractors, Tradesmen, Apprentices (see also www.bontool.com).*

Ordering Concrete: Be Specific

Concrete has so many different uses (such as floors, foundations, and countertops) and so many admixtures (water reducers, retardants, accelerants, air entrainers, and so on) that the best way to get the mix you need is to specify its use and desired characteristics. That is, when ordering the mix, tell the supplier the quantity you need (in cubic yards), how the concrete will be used (driveway, foundation, patio slab), the loads it will bear, how far it must be pumped, how it will be finished, and other such details.

If you're pouring a slab that will have a smooth finish, you might specify "a 2,500 psi mix, but a true five-sack mix," which will be "creamy" enough to finish with a steel trowel. If you specify a 2,500 psi mix but don't describe the finish, the supplier might use four sacks of cement and a water reducer to attain that strength. However, with less cement in it, the mix would be sandier and more difficult to finish.

Where the concrete will be placed can also affect the mix. For example, concrete for a second-story patio far from the street may require a smaller, 2-in. (inner diameter) hose to pump it, so the supplier may specify smaller aggregate (⅜-in. vs. ¾-in.) to facilitate flow. Aggregate size, in turn, affects load-bearing capacity, so a mix with ⅜-in. gravel is often bumped up, say, to 3,000 psi. If the patio slab will also be steel troweled, the mix thus becomes "a 3,000 psi, ⅜-in. aggregate, true six-sack mix." Well, you get the point: Be specific.

Estimating the amount of concrete in cubic yards is straightforward: The calculation is width × length × depth (in feet) of the area you want to cover. You then divide that result by 27 (as there are 27 cu. ft. in 1 cu. yd.). If you're pouring a slab, "Cubic Yards of Concrete in Slabs of Various Thicknesses," on p. 221, calculates cubic yards based on the slab thickness (in inches).

Most concrete-mixer trucks can hold 9 cu. yd. to 11 cu. yd. So if your pour requires more than one truck, ask the supplier to time deliveries 90 minutes apart so you have enough time to deal with each delivery. Finally, don't shave the estimate too close; far better to have too much concrete than too little.

place concrete in the slab footings, drive out the air pockets by using a concrete vibrator.

Establishing screed levels. If the slab is only 10 ft. or 12 ft. wide, you can level the concrete by pulling a *screed rail* across the top of form boards. Otherwise, create *wet screeds* (leveled columns of wet concrete) around the perimeter of the slab and one in the middle of the slab to guide the screed rails. The wet screeds around the perimeter are the same height as the chalklines; pump concrete near those lines and level it with a trowel. This technique is very much like that used to level tile mortar beds, as explained in Chapter 16.

The wet screed(s) in the middle should be more or less parallel to the long dimension of the slab. There are several ways to establish its height, but the quickest way is to drive 18-in. lengths of rebar into the ground every 6 ft. or so, and then use a laser level or taut strings out from perimeter chalklines to establish the height of the rebar. In other words, the top of the rebar becomes the top of the middle wet screed. When you've troweled that wet screed level, hammer the rebar below the surface, and fill the holes later.

SCREEDING AND FLOATING

Screeding is usually a three-person operation: two to move the screed rail back and forth, striking off the excess concrete, and a third person behind them, constantly in motion, using a stiff rake or a square-nose shovel to scrape down high spots or to add concrete to low ones. You can use a magnesium screed rail or a straight 2×4 to strike off, but the key to success is the raker's maintaining a good level of concrete behind the screeders, so the screed rail can just skim the crest of the concrete, without getting hung up or bowed by trying to move too much material.

Screeding levels the concrete but leaves a fairly rough surface, which is then smoothed out with a magnesium *bull float*, a long-handled float that also brings up the concrete's *cream* (a watery cement paste) and pushes down any gravel that's near the surface. This creates a smooth, stone-free surface that can be troweled and compacted later.

A bull float should float lightly on the surface. As you push it across the concrete, lower the handle, thereby raising the far edge of the float. Then, as you pull the float back toward you, raise the handle, raising the near edge. In this manner, the leading edge of the bull float will glide and not dig into the wet concrete.

Because of the loads it will bear, this garage floor slab is reinforced with rebar 12 in. on center. The stepped forms running along the sides of the slab will create foundation walls roughly 1 ft. above grade.

Fill slab footings first; then vibrate them to drive out any air pockets. Because placing a concrete slab usually entails standing in it, wear rubber boots.

Ready for concrete, this site has 4 in. of gravel over compacted soil, 6-mil plastic atop that, and rebar elevated by concrete dobie blocks so the steel will lie in the middle of the slab.

FINISHING THE SLAB

After the bull float raises water to the surface, you must wait for the water to evaporate before finishing the concrete. The wait depends on the weather. On a hot, sunny day, you may need to wait less than an hour. On a cool and overcast day, you might need to wait for hours. Once the water's evaporated, you have roughly 1 hour to trowel and compact the surface. When you think the surface is firm enough, put a test knee board atop the concrete and stand on it. If the board sinks ¾ in. or more, wait a bit. If the board leaves only a slight indent that you can easily hand float further and then trowel smooth, get to work.

As the photos show, knee boards distribute your weight and provide a mobile station from which to work. You'll need two knee boards in order to move across the surface, moving one board at a time. Then, kneeling on both boards, begin sweeping with a magnesium hand float or with a wood float, if you prefer a rougher finish. Sweep back and forth in 3-ft. arcs, raising the far edge of the float slightly as you sweep away and raising the near edge on the return sweep. The "mag" float levels the concrete.

After you've worked the whole slab, it's time for the steel trowel, which smooths and compacts the concrete, creating a hard, durable finish.

As the concrete dries, it becomes harder to work, so it's acceptable to sprinkle *very small amounts* of water on the surface to keep it workable. Troweling is hard work, especially on the back. When the concrete's no longer responding to the steel trowel, edge the corners and then cover the concrete with damp burlap before calling it a day. If the weather's hot and dry, hose down the burlap periodically—every hour, at

Screeding is a job for three people: Two to level the concrete by moving the screed rail from side to side, and a third with a shovel or rake to fill low spots and pull away excess.

Bull-floating the concrete pushes down gravel near the surface and brings the concrete's cream to the surface.

Finishing the slab. Start with magnesium or wood floats, and finish with a steel trowel for a smooth, hard finish. Knee boards distribute your weight as you work.

An edger compresses and rounds the slab's edge, making it stronger and less likely to chip off than a square corner.

least—and keep the slab under cover for 4 or 5 days. At the end of that time, you can remove the forms. Concrete takes a month to cure fully.

Damp Basement Solutions

To find the best cure for a damp basement, first determine whether the problem is caused by water outside migrating through foundation walls or by interior water vapor inside condensing on the walls. To determine which problem you have, duct tape a 2-ft.-long piece of aluminum foil to the foundation, sealing the foil on all four sides. Remove the tape after 2 days. The wet side of the foil will provide your answer. Chapter 14 has more about mitigating moisture and mold.

CORRECTING CONDENSATION

If the problem is condensation, start by insulating cold-water pipes, air-conditioning ducts, and other cool surfaces on which water vapor might condense. Wrap pipes with preformed foam pipe insulation. Wrap ducts and larger objects with sheets of vinyl-faced fiberglass insulation, which is well suited to the task because vinyl is a vapor barrier. Use duct tape or insulation tape to seal seams.

Next install a dehumidifier to remove excess humidity. For best results, install a model that can run continuously during periods of peak humidity; place it in the dampest part of the basement at least 12 in. away from walls or obstructions. To prevent mold from growing in the unit's collection reservoir, drain it daily and scrub it periodically.

Survey the basement for other sources of humidity. An unvented clothes dryer pumps gallons of water into living spaces; vent it outdoors. Excessive moisture from undervented kitchens and bathrooms on other floors can also migrate to the basement; add exhaust fans to vent them properly. Finally, weatherstrip exterior doors and keep them closed in hot, humid weather.

DAMPNESS DUE TO EXTERIOR WATER

Position and maintain gutters and downspouts so they direct water away from the house. And, if possible near affected walls, slope soil away from the house.

Besides those two factors, water that migrates through foundation walls or floors is more elusive and expensive to correct. Basically, you have three remedial options: (1) remove water once it gets in; (2) fill interior cracks, seal interior surfaces, and install a vapor barrier; and (3) excavate foundation walls, apply waterproofing and improve drainage.

Option one: Remove water. *Sump pumps* are the best means of removing water once it gets

Insulated water pipes conserve energy and reduce condensation in humid basements.

into a basement. If you don't have a sump pump, you'll probably need to break through the basement floor at a low point where water collects, and dig a *sump pit* 18 in. to 24 in. across. Line the pit with a permeable liner that allows water to seep in while keeping soil out, and put 4 in. of gravel in the bottom.

There are two types of sump pumps. *Pedestal* sump pumps stand upright in the pit. They are water cooled and have ball floats that turn the pump on and off. *Submersible* sump pumps, on the other hand, have sealed, oil-cooled motors, so they tend to be quieter, more durable, and more expensive. And because they are submerged, they allow you to cover the pit so nothing falls in. A ⅓-hp pump of either type should suffice.

The type of *discharge pipe* depends on whether the pump is a permanent fixture or a sometime thing. Permanent pumps should have 1½-in. rigid PVC discharge pipes with a check valve near the bottom to prevent expelled water from siphoning back down into the pit. If the water problem is seasonal, many people simply attach a 50-ft. garden hose and run it out a basement window. In either case, discharge the water at least 20 ft. from the house, preferably downhill and not directly into a neighbor's property.

Option two: Interior solutions. If basement walls are damp, try filling cracks as suggested on p. 205 and applying damp-proofing coatings. (However, this approach won't work if the walls are periodically *wet*.) After scrubbing the basement walls, *parge* (trowel on) a cementitious coating such as Thoroseal® Foundation Coating or Sto Watertight Coat® or a polymer-modified system such as Bonsal's Surewall®. These coatings can withstand higher hydrostatic pressures than elastomeric paints or gels. Epoxy-based coatings also adhere well but are so expensive that they're usually reserved for problem areas such as wall to floor joints.

To further control moisture diffusion through the walls, install a vapor barrier. After parging the walls with a damp-proofing material, use construction adhesive to attach heavy (6-mil at a minimum) sheet polyethylene to the foundation walls. Then place sheets of rigid foam insulation over the plastic sheeting. Caulk and tape the foam seams to seal them. If the seams are airtight, the insulation layer becomes a second vapor barrier and makes condensation less likely because it isolates cool basement walls from warm air.

Option three: Exterior solutions. To waterproof exterior foundation walls, first excavate them. At that time, you should also upgrade the perimeter drains, as shown in "Foundation Drainage," on p. 203. Then, after backfilling the excavation, slope the soil away from the house. That is, no waterproofing material will succeed if water stands against the foundation. Before applying waterproofing membranes, scrub the foundation walls clean and rinse them well.

▶ **Liquid membranes** are usually sprayed on, to a uniform thickness specified by the manufacturer, usually 40 mil. That takes training, so hire a manufacturer-certified installer. Liquid membranes are either solvent based or water based. Modified asphalt is one popular solvent-based membrane that contains rubber-like additives to make it more flexible and durable. Asphalt emulsions are water based and widely used because, unlike modified asphalt, they don't smell strong, aren't flammable, and won't degrade rigid foam insulation panels placed along foundation walls. Synthetic-rubber and polymer-based membranes are also water based; they're popular because their inherent elasticity allows them to stay flexible and span small cracks. *Note:* Water-based membranes dry more slowly than solvent-based ones and can wash off if rained on before they are cured and backfilled.

▶ **Peel-and-stick membranes** are typically sheet or roll materials of rubberized asphalt fused to polyethylene. They adhere best on pre-primed walls. To install these membranes, peel off the release sheet and press the sticky side of the material to foundations. Roll the seams to make them adhere better. Peel-and-stick costs more and takes longer to install than sprayed-on membranes, but they're thicker (60 mil, on average) and more durable. Though not widely used on residences, these materials seem justified on sites with chronic water problems. They're often called Bituthene®, after a popular W. R. Grace Construction product.

▶ **Air-gap membranes** aren't true membranes because they don't conform to the surface of the foundation. Rather, they are rigid plastic (polyethylene) sheets held out from the foundation by an array of tiny dimples, which creates an air–drainage gap. Water that gets behind the sheets condenses on the dimples and drips free, down to foundation drains. (For this system to work, you must coat the foundation walls first.) Air-gap sheets are attached with molding strips, clips, and nails; caulk the sheet seams.

▶ Until technology transformed waterproofing compounds, cementitious coatings rivaled unmodified asphalt as the most common stuff smeared onto foundations. These days, acrylic additives make cement-based coatings a bit more flexible, but they will still crack if the foundation flexes. Bentonite, a volcanic clay sheathed in cardboard panels, swells 10 times to 15 times its original volume when wet, keeping water away from foundation walls. Use construction adhesive or nails to attach the panels. These panels are costly and not widely available, and they can be ruined if rained on before the foundation is backfilled.

PRO TIP

Waterproofing membranes are relatively fragile, especially those that are sprayed on. So after they're applied, they're often covered with rigid insulation, drain board, protection board, and the like. These rigid panels protect the membranes during backfilling, and insulate the foundation walls to reduce heat loss.

Pedestal Sump Pump

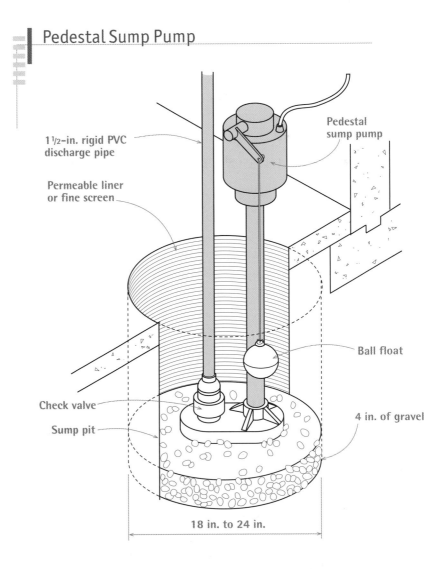

1½-in. rigid PVC discharge pipe

Permeable liner or fine screen

Pedestal sump pump

Ball float

Check valve

Sump pit

4 in. of gravel

18 in. to 24 in.

Electrical Wiring

Electrical work is among the most predictable, pleasant aspects of construction—no heavy lumber to be wrestled, no large sheets that would fit if only your fingers weren't in the way, no quick-drying compounds driving you into a frenzy. Wiring a house is methodical work that requires attention to detail and some dexterity. And you know quickly if you've done the work correctly: bulbs glow and radios play.

Electricity should be respected, and it must be taken seriously. But it is a natural phenomenon, subject to the laws of physics. If you heed the safety precautions in this chapter—especially those about shutting off power and testing with a voltage tester, to make sure the power is off—you'll do fine. If you're new to wiring, take the time to read the whole chapter because important information is not necessarily repeated.

It's imperative that you check with local building code authorities even before buying tools and materials. Although most building authorities do not forbid an owner's doing his or her own electrical work, most require inspections when the system is roughed in—that is, before wires are connected to switches, receptacles, and so on. Besides, building inspectors are usually knowledgeable: They can tell you if local codes conform to the *National Electrical Code®* (NEC) or, if not, how they vary.

If this chapter whets your appetite for more, get copies of Rex Cauldwell's *Wiring a House* (The Taunton Press) and Redwood Kardon, Doug Hansen, and Mike Casey's *Code Check® Electrical* (The Taunton Press).

Understanding Electricity

Electricity is tricky to describe. A physicist might call it "the movement of electrons," but most people find it easier to visualize electricity as something like water flowing through a hose. Using that analogy, here are two useful concepts: (1) Electrical current flows in a circle, making a *circuit,* and (2) it flows most easily along paths of least resistance, but it will follow any path that's available . . . *including you!*

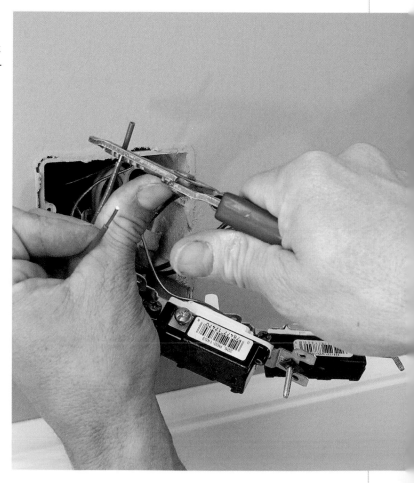

Use a wire stripper to strip ½ in. of insulation off the wire ends before attaching them to the screw terminals on switches. Begin by scoring the insulation with a twist of the wrist. Then use your thumb as a fulcrum to pop the insulation off.

CIRCUITS, FAULT CIRCUITS, AND GROUND FAULTS

Electricity moves in a circle from power source back to power source, whether it travels across the country in great transmission lines or flows through the cables in your walls. In a house, each distinct electrical loop is called a *circuit*.

Most of the time, household electricity flows through copper wires (low resistance) insulated with thermoplastic or rubber (very high resistance). But electrical current is opportunistic. Should a wire's insulation break and a fault circuit of lesser resistance become available, current will flow through it. The current flowing through that fault circuit is called a *ground fault*. The lower the fault circuit's resistance, the greater that current flow will be.

If equipment and appliances are correctly *grounded* (bonded together), this abnormally high *current flow* (amperage) will trip a breaker or blow a fuse, cutting power to the fault circuit—or "clearing the fault," as electricians say.

ELECTRICITY IN THE HOUSE

A modern electrical system consists of three large cables, or conductors, which may enter the house overhead or underground. When fed underground, service conductors are installed in buried conduit or run as USE (underground service entrance) cable. Overhead service running from a utility pole typically consists of a triplex assembly—two insulated hot conductors wrapped around a bare messenger cable that also serves to carry the neutral load—which runs to a weather head atop a length of rigid

WIRES, CABLES, AND Conductors

The terms *wires*, *cables*, and *conductors* are often used interchangeably, but they are not exactly the same. A conductor is anything that carries or conducts electricity. A wire is an individual conductor, and cable is usually an assembly of two or more wires, protected by a plastic or metal cable *sheathing* (also called a *jacket*). Often, cable derives its name from the size of the wires within. For example, *12-gauge cable* contains 12AWG (American Wire Gauge) wire. More specifically, *12/2 with ground* denotes cable with two 12AWG wires plus a ground wire.

Circuits and Ground Faults

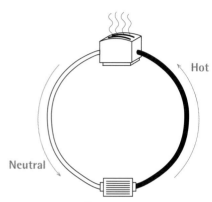

Hot

Neutral

Power source

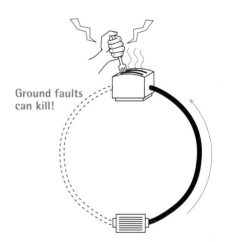

Ground faults can kill!

Power source

Electricity tends to move in a circle (circuit) to and from a power source, flowing through insulated wire. Current flowing through an unintended conductor, such as a person, is called a ground fault. Because only a little current flowing through your heart can kill you, ground faults can be fatal.

conduit. (Overhead service cables are called a *service drop*.) Whether it arrives overhead or underground, three-wire service delivers 240 volts. An old service with only two incoming wires—one hot and one grounded neutral conductor—delivers only 120 volts, which is inadequate for modern household demand and so should be upgraded.

Service conductors attach to a *meter base*. From the meter base runs another length of rigid conduit, or *service entrance* (SE) *cable*, to the *service panel*. Straddling the two sets of terminals on its base, the meter measures the wattage of electricity as it is consumed. (Increasingly common are meter–main combos, which house a meter base and a main service panel in a single box.)

Main service panel. At the main service panel, the two hot cables from the meter base attach to lug terminals atop the main breaker, and the incoming neutral cable attaches to the main lug of the neutral/ground bus, as shown in "Main Service Panel, Unwired," below. In main service panels, neutral/ground buses must be bonded, usually by a main bonding jumper. *Important:* In subpanels and all other locations downstream from the main service panel, ground and neutral buses must be electrically isolated from each other.

In a service fuse box, the hot cables attach to the main power lugs, and the neutral cable to the main neutral lug. Whether the panel has breakers or fuses, metal buses issue from the bottom of the main breaker/main fuse. Running down the middle of the panel, buses distribute power to the various branch circuits. Similarly, neutral/ground buses are long aluminum strips with many screws that ground and neutral wires attach to.

A Service Entrance

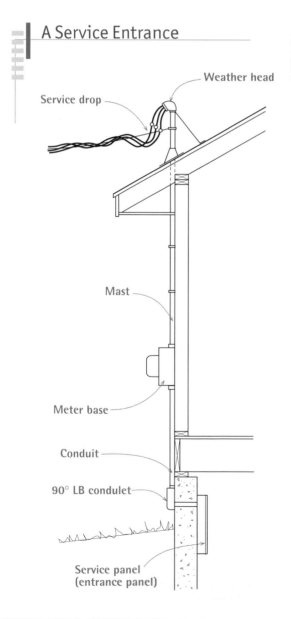

- Service drop
- Weather head
- Mast
- Meter base
- Conduit
- 90° LB condulet
- Service panel (entrance panel)

Main Service Panel, Unwired

- Hot cables from meter attach to lug terminals.
- Main breaker
- Neutral/ground cable attaches here.
- Tie bar
- Main bonding jumper
- Neutral/ground buses
- Hot buses
- Knockouts for circuit cables on all sides of panel

The main panel houses incoming cables from the meter, as well as the breakers and wires that distribute electricity to individual circuits. At the service, neutral conductors (white wires), equipment-grounding conductors (bare copper or green insulated wires), the metal service panel, and the grounding electrode system (grounding rods) must be bonded together.

THE Main BREAKER

All electricity entering a house goes through the main breaker, which is usually located at the top of a main panel. In an emergency, throw the main breaker switch to cut all power to the house. The main breaker is also the primary overcurrent protection for the electrical system and is rated accordingly. (The rating is stamped on the breaker handle.) Thus if the main breaker for a 200-amp panel senses incoming current that exceeds its overload rating, the breaker will automatically trip and shut off all power.

A 200-amp service panel. At the top center, note the two large black hot cables attached to the main breaker. The smaller red and black circuit wires are also hot, the white wires are neutral, and the bare copper wires are grounds. A licensed electrician should make all connections in the panel.

Each fuse or breaker is rated at a specific number of amperes (amp), such as 15 or 20. When a circuit becomes overloaded, its current flow becomes excessively high, causing its breaker to trip or its fuse strip to melt, thereby cutting voltage to the hot wires. All current produces heat, but as current doubles, the heat generated quadruples. If there were no breakers or fuses, current would continue flowing till wires overheated and a fire started. Thus the amperage ratings of breakers and fuses are matched to the size (cross-sectional area) of the circuit wires.

Branch circuits. Branch circuits are conductors that run from the last *overcurrent device* (fuse or breaker) to their outlets. Inside each cable or conduit are several wires color-coded for safety. In most 120-volt circuits, there is one hot wire (coded black), one neutral wire (coded white), and one bare copper (or green) ground wire. Think of hot and neutral wires as parallel wires that must never be joined.

Ground wires (discussed later in this chapter) must also be kept separate from hot and neutral wires as you run branch circuits. (Ground and neutral bus bars are connected in the main panel, but that's another issue.) In 240-volt circuits, such as those "dedicated" to a heavy user like a stove, there are typically two hot wires: one coded black, and the other, red.

Outlets. Each branch circuit serves one or more outlets. At outlets, individual wires connect to various devices such as switches, receptacles, and fixtures. To ensure a safe hookup, the devices' connecting screws or terminals are color coded or otherwise clearly designated: Hot wires attach to gold- or brass-colored screws, neutral wires to silver screws, and ground wires to green screws (when present).

Switches cut or vary the flow of power by interrupting hot lines only. Neutral wires are always continuous, as are ground wires, even though their sections may be connected by wire nuts. *Wire nuts* are insulated caps that twist onto the bare ends of *wire splices* (clusters), thereby joining them mechanically and covering them so those bare ends can't come in contact with other wires, devices, fixture terminals, or the outlet box itself.

THE GROUNDING SYSTEM

A house's grounding system is complex, and understanding it is made more difficult by the imprecise language used to describe it—as noted in "Making Sense of Grounding," on p. 230. If you want a more comprehensive overview of grounding, get a copy of the book *Code Check® Electrical*, mentioned earlier. Here are some of the basics.

Underlying principles. *Fuses* were among the earliest overcurrent devices, and they greatly reduced the incidence of electrical fires by disconnecting current when its flow became too great. But something more was needed to protect people, who were being electrocuted when they came in contact with fault currents unintentionally energizing the metal casing of a tool or an electrical appliance, for example.

Consequently, the industry added equipment-grounding conductors (which we'll call *ground wires*) that bond all electrical devices and potentially current-carrying metal surfaces. This bonding creates a path with such low impedance (resistance) that fault currents zip along it as they return to the power source—quickly tripping breakers or fuses, and clearing the fault. Contrary to popular misconceptions, the human body has a relatively high impedance (compared to copper wire), so if electricity is offered a path of less resistance (a copper ground wire), it will take it.

To sum up: To reduce shock hazards, individual ground wires connect to every part of the electrical system that could become a potential conductor—metal boxes, receptacles, fixtures—and, through three-pronged plugs, the metallic covers and frames of tools and appliances. At the main service panel, these ground wires attach to a neutral/ground bus bar, which is itself bonded to the metal panel via a main bonding jumper. To quote one master electrician, "This bonding jumper is possibly the most important single connection in the whole system."

Grounding electrode system. Also attached to the neutral/ground bus in the service panel is a large, bare copper ground wire —the *grounding electrode conductor* (GEC)—that clamps to a *grounding electrode* (also called a ground rod), which is driven into the earth or is attached to steel rebar in the footing of a foundation. The electrode's primary function is to divert lightning and other outside high voltages before they can damage the building's electrical system.

Note: Although the grounding electrode system (GES) is connected to the equipment-grounding system at the service panel, the GES has virtually nothing to do with reducing shock hazards.

The NEC sizes grounding electrode conductors based on the sizes and types of conductors in the service. Typically, residential GECs are size 6 American Wire Gauge (6AWG) copper. Ground rods are typically ⅝-in. to ¾-in. copper-clad steel rods 8 ft. to 10 ft. long; the longer the rod, the more likely it will reach moist soil, whose resistance is less than that of dry soil. Be sure to install multiple-rod systems in lightning-prone areas.

GROUND-FAULT CIRCUIT INTERRUPTERS

Despite the presence of grounding systems, people were still being killed by electrical shock, particularly when moisture was present. To remedy this problem, the industry developed ground-fault circuit interrupters (GFCIs), which are highly sensitive devices that can detect minuscule current leaks and shut off power almost instantaneously. A ground fault is any failure of the electrical system that leaks current from a hot wire.

Normally, the current in hot and neutral wires is identical. But when there is as small a variance as 0.005 amp (5 milliamperes) between hot and neutral wires, a GFCI can shut off all power within ¹⁄₄₀ of a second. Consequently, the NEC now requires GFCI protection on all bathroom receptacles, kitchen receptacles within 4 ft. of a sink, all receptacles serving kitchen counters, all outdoor receptacles, accessible basement or garage receptacles, and receptacles near pools, hot tubs, and the like.

A GFCI breaker will cut all power to a circuit, whereas a GFCI receptacle will cut power to receptacles downstream if wires are fed through the GFCI receptacle as shown in "Wiring a GFCI Receptacle," on p. 250.

ARC-FAULT CIRCUIT INTERRUPTERS

When electrical connections are loose or corroded or if nails puncture wires, electricity can arc (jump) between points. Arcing may be responsible for many of the 40,000 electrical fires each year. The NEC now requires arc-fault circuit interrupter (AFCI) protection for all 15-amp and 20-amp bedroom circuits. Just as GFCIs cut power to prevent shocks, AFCIs detect minute fluctuations in current associated with arcing

Making Sense of Grounding

Grounding confuses a lot of people, including electricians. Part of the problem is that the word *ground* has been used imprecisely for more than a century to describe electrical activity or components. The term *ground wire*, for example, may refer to one of three different things:

▶ The large, bare-copper wire that clamps to a ground rod driven into the earth or to rebar in a concrete footing. Because the rod or the rebar is technically a grounding electrode, this "ground wire" is better called a *grounding electrode conductor*.

▶ Short conductors that connect one piece of electrical equipment to another to eliminate the possibility of a voltage difference between the two. These wires should be called *bonding conductors*.

▶ The bare copper or green insulated wires in most multiwire circuits, which ultimately connect electrical equipment, such as receptacles and fixtures, to the service panel. These connections create an effective fault path back to the breakers or fuses in the service panel, for example, in case the equipment becomes energized by a hot wire touching a metal cover. In this book, the term *ground wire* refers to this conductor. If reformers in the code world have their way, these wires will soon be called *equipment-grounding conductors*.

Electrical safety devices. From top: arc–fault circuit interrupter (AFCI) breaker, ground–fault circuit interrupter (GFCI) breaker, and GFCI receptacle.

and de-energize the circuits before a fire can start. Installing AFCI breakers is essentially the same as that for GFCI circuit breakers.

Planning and Estimating

The scope of a renovation is always a trade-off between what you'd like and what you can afford. Oversizing the system slightly to accommodate future needs is usually money well spent. Assess the existing system, see what local codes require, calculate future needs, and then map out an upgrade.

ASSESSING THE PRESENT SYSTEM

To assess the situation, start with two questions: Is the electrical system safe? and Is it adequately sized?

Is it safe? Hire a licensed electrician or a qualified home inspector to assess the electrical system and advise you about what needs doing. But before the electrician shows up, do a little *hands-off* looking for yourself and try to answer the following questions:

▶ Is the entrance panel grounded? There should be a large grounding wire running from the panel and clamped to a cold-water pipe and/or a grounding rod.

▶ Is there equipment grounding? Grounding the panel is not enough. For the entire electrical system to be grounded, there must be continuous ground wires running to every device in the house. If there is only two-wire service to the house and you see only two-hole receptacles in use, the system is outdated and has no equipment grounding.

▶ Do bathrooms, kitchens, garages, and outdoor outlets have GFCI receptacles, as required by the NEC?

Major Grounding Elements

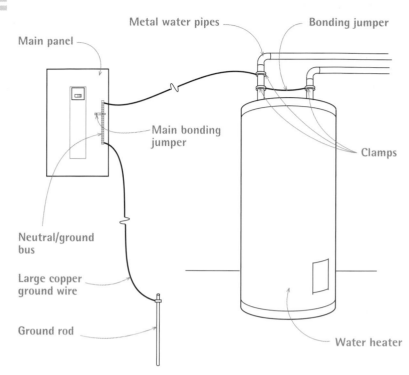

The equipment-grounding system acts as an expressway for stray current. By bonding conductors or potential conductors, the system provides a low-resistance path for fault currents. The abnormally high amperage (current flow) that results trips a breaker or blows a fuse, disconnecting power to the circuit.

▶ Is the equipment in good shape? Rusty entrance panels, receptacles encrusted with paint, and wires with cracked or frayed insulation are as unsafe as they are unsightly.

▶ Is the service panel installed in a wet or damp area? This situation is extremely unsafe. In fact, many electricians refuse to examine service panels if there's standing water nearby.

▶ Is present usage safe? Installing fuses too big for a circuit to prevent blown fuses is a fool's bargain, as are overloaded receptacles, extension cords under carpets, and the like.

Is it adequate? If you've lived in the house for a while, you'll have a fair idea of whether the system is big enough.

▶ Are there enough outlets, or do receptacles teem with multiplug and extension cords? If so, plan to add more receptacles where needed.

▶ Do you blow fuses often, especially when starting up small appliances or power tools? Does your TV screen shrink momentarily when the refrigerator motor or the water

Calculating Total Electrical Load

General-use circuits:

▶ _____ sq. ft. × 3 volt-amp/sq. ft.   _____ *

Small-appliance circuits:

▶ _____ 20-amp circuits × 1,500 volt-amp   _____ *

Laundry circuit

▶ (1,500 volt-amp each)   _____ *

Major appliances/dedicated circuits

▶ Water heater   _____

▶ Cooktop/oven or range   _____

▶ Garbage disposal   _____

▶ Dishwasher   _____

▶ Microwave   _____

▶ Other   _____

Subtotal for all major appliances   _____ *

Note: volt-amp (volt-amperes) = volts × amperes. Asterisks (*) indicate subtotals for distinct groups.

Add the asterisked subtotals of each circuit group. Then multiply any volt-amperes *greater than* 10,000 by 0.40 (because not all outlets are drawing energy at the same time).

▶ Total volt-amperes: 10,000 volt-amp × 0.40   = _____ (A)

▶ Add subtotal A to 10,000 volt-amp   + 10,000   (B)

▶ Subtotal C   = _____ (C)

▶ To subtotal C add the volt-amperage of the heating system *or* the air-conditioner, whichever is greater: + _____ (D)

Total volt-amperes   = _____

To convert this total volt-amperes to amperes, divide by volts:

▶ _____ volt-amp÷240 volts   = _____ amp

Using This Table

To determine the total capacity you need, add up the volt-amperes of (1) general-use circuits, (2) small-appliance circuits, (3) laundry circuit, and (4) major-appliance/dedicated circuits.

Calculate the volt-amperes of general-use circuits first, by determining the square footage of the house; measure outside dimensions and include the areas of all finished living space. Then multiply the area in square feet by 3 volt-amp to obtain general-use volt-amperes. Assign small-appliance and laundry circuits 1,500 volt-amp each. All major appliance name-plates list amperage ratings.

pump kicks in? These symptoms may indicate a system that's close to its present limits.

▶ How many cables run from the utility pole to the house? If there are only two large cables, the electrical service is probably inadequate. As explained in "Electricity in the House," on p. 227, a two-wire service delivers only 120-volt service; whereas a three-wire service delivers 120-volt and 240-volt service.

▶ What is the panel rating on the nameplate? If there's a two-wire service, the panel is probably rated for 30 amps. These days, a 100-amp entrance panel is considered minimal; a 200-amp panel can accommodate future uses.

GENERAL CODE REQUIREMENTS

Licensed electricians use NEC (*National Electrical Code*) formulas to size a house's electrical load. Here's an overview of NEC requirements.

General purpose.

▶ Keep lighting and appliance circuits separate. Calculate lighting loads at 3 watts per square foot, or roughly one 15-amp circuit for every 500 sq. ft. of floor space. When laying out the lighting circuits, do not put all the lights on a floor on one circuit. Otherwise, should a breaker trip, that entire floor would be without power.

▶ General-use circuits are intended primarily for lighting, but small users such as TVs, record players, and vacuums are allowed, as long they don't exceed the capacity of the circuit. Though 14AWG wire is sufficient for lighting and switch runs, electricians often run 12AWG wire on general-use circuits to accommodate future uses.

▶ There must be a receptacle within 6 ft. of each doorway, and no space along a wall in a habitable room should be more than 6 ft. from a receptacle. Any wall at least 2 ft. wide must have a receptacle; and a receptacle is required in hallway walls 10 ft. or longer.

▶ The NEC does not specify a maximum number of outlets on a residential lighting or appliance circuit, though local jurisdictions may. Figure roughly 9 outlets per 15-amp circuit and 10 outlets per 20-amp circuit.

▶ There must be at least one wall switch that controls lighting in habitable rooms, the garage, and storage areas (including attic and basement). And there should be a switch near each outdoor entrance. Three-way switches are required at each end of corridors and at the top and bottom of stairs with six steps or more.

▶ All new 15-amp and 20-amp circuits in bedrooms must have AFCI breaker protection.

Kitchens and bathrooms.

▶ The NEC requires GFCI protection in the following locations: all bathroom receptacles; all receptacles serving kitchen counters; all outdoor receptacles; accessible basement or garage receptacles; and receptacles near pools, hot tubs, and the like. (Check the current NEC for a complete listing.)

▶ Bathroom receptacle outlets must be supplied from a 20-amp, GFCI-protected circuit with no other outlets. However, the NEC allows the circuit to supply required receptacles in more than one bathroom.

▶ There must be at least two 20-amp small-appliance circuits in the kitchen. No point along a kitchen countertop should be more than 2 ft. from an outlet. Every counter at least 12 in. wide must have a receptacle.

▶ All critical-use stationary appliances must have their own dedicated (separate) circuits: water pump, freezer, refrigerator, oven, cooktop, microwave, furnace and/or whole-house air-conditioning unit, garbage disposal, window air-conditioners, and water heater.

▶ If a cable does not attach directly to an appliance, its receptacle must be within 6 ft. of the appliance.

CAN YOU ADD OUTLETS TO A CIRCUIT?

If there's room in the service panel for additional breakers or fuses, adding circuits is largely a matter of running cable and making good mechanical connections along the way. Have a licensed electrician connect new cable runs to the panel.

🚫 To add outlets to a circuit, you must disconnect the power from an existing outlet and fish new cable from it, as described on p. 261. But first determine the load-bearing capacity of the circuit you want to extend.

Begin by identifying the circuit breaker (or fuse) controlling the circuit: 🚫 Turn off the electricity to that circuit and test to be sure it's off. Note the rating of the breaker. If it's a general-purpose circuit, the breaker will probably be 15 amps or 20 amps. A circuit controlled by a 15-amp breaker has a capacity of 1,800 watts (15 amps × 120 volts); a 20-amp breaker, 2,400 watts. The total wattage of all energy users on the newly extended circuit must not exceed these capacities; otherwise, you risk overheating wires. To avoid overloading, load is calculated at 80 percent of capacity. For example, 80 percent

of 1,800 watts is 1,440 watts for a 15-amp circuit; 80 percent of 2,400 watts equals 1,920 watts for a 20-amp circuit. As a rule of thumb, 10 outlets is the maximum for a general-purpose or lighting circuit.

Note: If someone has unwisely oversized a breaker, you can't use breaker size to calculate the circuit's capacity. If you suspect oversizing, hire an electrician to remove the panel cover and determine the size of the circuit wires used. In general, lighting circuits with 14AWG wire should be protected by a 15-amp breaker. Small-appliance circuits with 12AWG wire should be protected by a 20-amp breaker. Most large 240-volt appliances require 10AWG wire, protected by a 30-amp breaker. Always check appliance nameplates for amperage ratings.

Safe Circuit Capacities*

AMPERES × VOLTS†		TOTAL CAPACITY (watts)	SAFE CAPACITY† (watts)
15 × 120	▶	1,800	1,440
20 × 120	▶	2,400	1,920
25 × 120	▶	3,000	2,400
30 × 120	▶	3,600	2,990

* Safe capacity = 80 percent of total capacity.
† Amperes multiplied by volts equals watts.

Volts, Amps, and Watts

At a power plant or a substation, electricity is multiplied (charged) and given pressure (*voltage*); in that form, electricity is potential energy, just like a charged battery. When electricity is put to work at an outlet, electrons flow through the wires, and power is delivered as heat or light. *Amperes* (amp) is the measure of this current flow. The amount of energy consumed at a given point—say, at a toaster or a light bulb—is measured in *watts*. Volts, amperes, and watts are thus interrelated:

▶ **Voltage:** the potential to do work (electrical pressure).
▶ **Amperes:** the rate of electrical flow.
▶ **Watts:** the rate at which energy is consumed.

Or, expressed as mathematical formulas:

$$\text{watts} = \text{voltage} \times \text{amperes}$$
$$\text{amperes} = \text{watts} \div \text{voltage}$$

To reiterate briefly, electricity, impelled by voltage, flows from the power source. Along the way, at outlets, it encounters resistance and does work. It then returns to the power source, its voltage reduced or spent.

Common Electrical Symbols

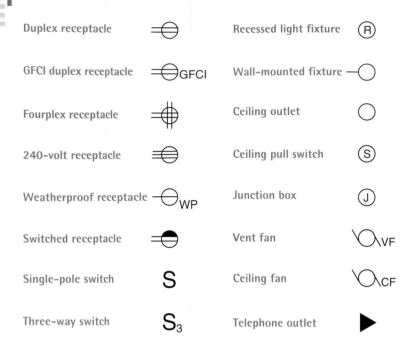

Duplex receptacle	⊖	Recessed light fixture	®
GFCI duplex receptacle	⊖GFCI	Wall-mounted fixture	—○
Fourplex receptacle	⊕	Ceiling outlet	○
240-volt receptacle	⊜	Ceiling pull switch	Ⓢ
Weatherproof receptacle	⊖WP	Junction box	Ⓙ
Switched receptacle	⊜	Vent fan	○VF
Single-pole switch	S	Ceiling fan	○CF
Three-way switch	S₃	Telephone outlet	▶

Symbols for Mapping House Circuits

Numbers indicate separate circuits, or you can use colored markers to differentiate circuits. Dashed lines link switches and the fixture (or receptacles) they control. (Note: "S3" indicates three-way switches, not a circuit number.)

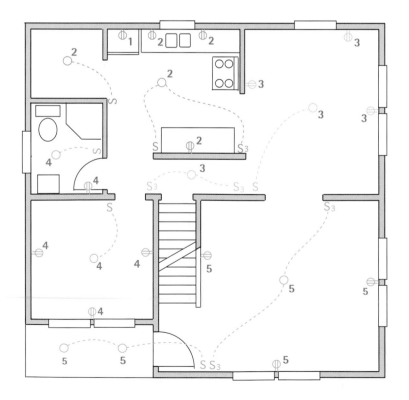

MAPPING THE SYSTEM

Mapping the entire system, including old and new circuits, lets you quickly match outlets, switches, and fixtures to circuits; this is especially helpful later if a circuit breaker trips (or a fuse blows). At the entrance panel, assign a number to each circuit. Then, as a helper flips breakers or removes fuses, map the outlets controlled by each circuit. To save shouting between floors, use cell phones.

Tools and Materials

All tools and materials should bear the Underwriters' Laboratory (UL) stamp, which indicates that a component meets the safety standards of the electrical industry.

TOOLS

You don't need a lot of expensive tools to wire a house successfully. All tools should have insulated handles. Avoid touching the uninsulated parts of tools when they're near potentially hot (energized) wiring.

▶ Wear safety glasses for all tasks that throw up debris, such as cutting through finish materials, drilling, and notching studs. Wearing rubber gloves and using insulated tools can also save your life. But the greatest safety aid is the voltage tester shown on the facing page.

▶ In addition to electrical testers, you should have a continuity tester, which tests wire runs and connectors for short circuits or other wiring flaws—before a circuit is connected to power.

▶ A multipurpose tool is used to strip individual wires of insulation, cut wire, crimp connections, and quickly loop wire around device screws.

▶ Lineman's pliers are the workhorse of an electrician's toolbox. They can cut wire, hold wires fast as you splice them, and twist out box knockouts.

▶ Needle-nose (long-nose) pliers can grasp and pull wire in tight spaces. These pliers can loop wire to fit around receptacle and switch screws. But don't use the tool for heavy twisting because that can misalign its jaws.

▶ Diagonal-cutting and end-cutting pliers can cut wires close in tight spaces; end cutters (sometimes called nippers) also pull out staples easily.

▶ Screwdrivers should always have insulated handles. Get several sizes of slot-head and Phillips-head screwdrivers, plus an offset screwdriver and a nut driver.

Using a Voltage Tester

Two-prong voltage testers are inexpensive, reliable, and available almost everywhere. Whatever tester you use, first test the tester on a circuit that you know is energized. If the tester doesn't indicate voltage on that circuit, the tool may be broken.

Testing Receptacles

When testing receptacles, grasp the insulated part of the tester and insert its probes into the receptacle slots. *Never touch the bare wire tips of tester probes*. If the tester lights up, there's voltage present. Have a helper at the service panel flip circuit breakers (or remove fuses) till you find the one that controls the outlet and the tester light goes out. Use cell phones to communicate, which sure beats screaming between floors.

If the receptacle is faulty or a wire is loose, however, the previous test may not detect voltage present in the outlet box. To be certain, unscrew the receptacle cover plate and the two screws holding the receptacle to the outlet box. Pull the receptacle out from the wall, being careful not to touch the wires, receptacle screw terminals, or metal outlet boxes. Touch the tester probes to screws on opposite sides of the receptacle (gold on one side, silver on the other). Then touch the tester probes to the bared wire ends on the opposite sides (black wires will connect to gold screws, white wires to silver ones). As a final test, touch the tester to the black wire ends and to the metal box.

Testing Fixtures

Remove a fixture by unscrewing the long machine screws holding it to the outlet box. Carefully pull the fixture out from the box. Test the screw terminals on the underside of the fixture as just described for receptacles. If a switch controls the fixture, test it as described in the next section. Unscrew the wire nuts, if any (support the fixture so it can't fall), and then touch the tester probes to the exposed wires.

Testing Switches

To identify the circuit that serves a particular switch, turn on the fixture it controls and have a helper at the service panel flip breakers until the light goes out. If that test is inconclusive or you aren't sure the switch is operable, remove the cover plate and the two screws holding the switch to the box. Test the wires leading to the switch: Be careful not to touch the screws on the side of the switch or the wires leading to them. Switches interrupt hot wires, so apply the tester probes to each screw on the switch as well as to any group of wires spliced together.

MAKING SURE THE POWER IS OFF

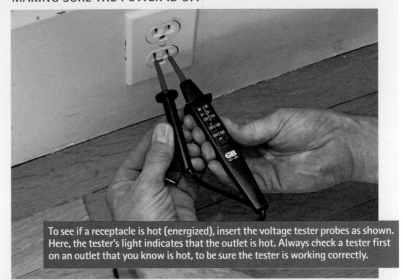

To see if a receptacle is hot (energized), insert the voltage tester probes as shown. Here, the tester's light indicates that the outlet is hot. Always check a tester first on an outlet that you know is hot, to be sure the tester is working correctly.

To double-check a receptacle, remove the cover plate and the screws holding the device to the outlet box. Be careful not to touch the receptacle's sides or metal boxes; use insulated pliers to pull the receptacles out. Hold the tester probes to the screws on opposite sides.

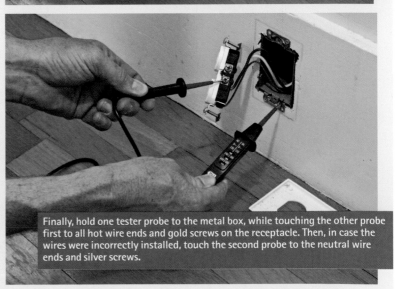

Finally, hold one tester probe to the metal box, while touching the other probe first to all hot wire ends and gold screws on the receptacle. Then, in case the wires were incorrectly installed, touch the second probe to the neutral wire ends and silver screws.

Choosing an Electrical Tester

Testing to see if an outlet is energized is so critical to professional electricians that there are scores of specialized testers to choose from, some of which cost hundreds of dollars. Fortunately, amateur electricians can get a reliable tester for less than $30. Here are five types:

▶ **Neon voltage testers** are inexpensive and versatile. Insert the probes (prongs) into the receptacle slots or touch them to the screw terminals or to a metal outlet box to see if the unit is hot (energized). Buy quality: Better neon testers have insulated handles, whereas cheapies have bare metal probes so short that you risk shocking yourself when using them.

▶ **Plug-in circuit analyzers** can be used only with three-hole receptacles, but they quickly tell you if a circuit is correctly grounded and, if not, what the problem is. Different light combinations on the tester indicate various wiring problems, such as no ground, hot and neutral reversed, and so on. Quite handy for quick home inspections.

▶ **Shirt-pocket voltage detectors** give a reading without directly touching a conductor. Touch the tool's tip to an outlet, a fixture screw, or an electrical cord, and the tip glows red if there's voltage present. Because they depend on battery power, voltage detectors are somewhat less reliable than other options, but all in all, it's an ingenious tool.

▶ **Solenoid voltage testers** (often called "Wiggy's") test polarity, AC, and DC voltage from 100 volts to 600 volts. Most models vibrate and light a bulb when current is present. Solenoid testers don't use batteries, so readings can't be compromised by low battery power. However, because of their low impedance, solenoid testers will trip GFCIs.

▶ **Multimeters,** as the name suggests, offer precise readings in multiple scales, which you select beforehand, although some models are autoranging (they select the correct scale). Extremely sensitive, they can detect minuscule amounts of current. Better models test AC and DC voltage, resistance, capacitance, and frequency.

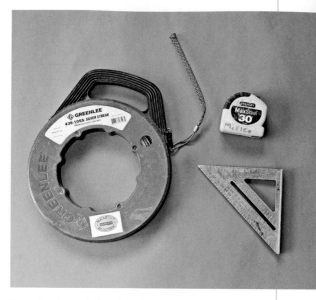

Three for the road. From left: fish tape, tape measure, and Speed Square.

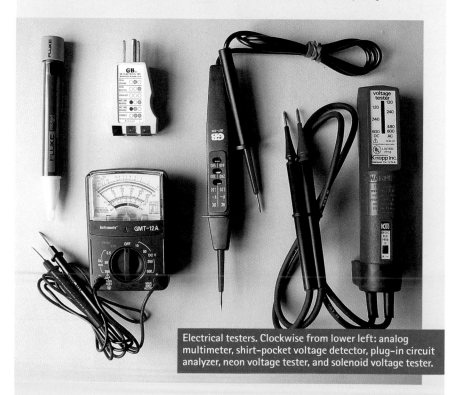

Electrical testers. Clockwise from lower left: analog multimeter, shirt-pocket voltage detector, plug-in circuit analyzer, neon voltage tester, and solenoid voltage tester.

▶ A cable ripper strips the plastic sheathing from Romex® cable without harming the insulation on the individual wires inside. Many pros use a utility knife to strip sheathing, but that takes practice and a light touch to avoid nicking the insulation of individual wires. To strip armored cable, use a Roto-Split® cable stripper, as shown on p. 255; it's vastly superior to the old method of using a hacksaw and diagonal cutters.

▶ Fish tape is used to run cable behind finish surfaces and pull wire in conduit.

▶ A wire wheel, a rotating cable dispenser that nails to a ceiling joist or a stud, is indispensable if you're wiring a whole house (see the photo on p. 245).

Drills. A ½-in. right-angle drill allows you to fit the drill head between studs or joists and drill perpendicular to the face of the lumber (see the bottom photo on p. 244). Pulling cable is much easier when holes are perpendicular to framing and at the same height. Buy a drill with a clutch: Unless there's a clutch to disengage the motor if a drill bit suddenly jams or lodges against a nail shank, the tool body will torque powerfully and could injure you.

Here are some thoughts on drill bits: Spade bits cut quickly, but tend to snap in hard wood. Self-feeding auger bits drill doggedly through hard old wood but won't last long if they hit nails. A ⅞-in. Greenlee Nail Eater™ bit is your best bet if old lumber is nail infested.

Cordless tools. Cordless drills and saws enable you to keep working when the power's off or

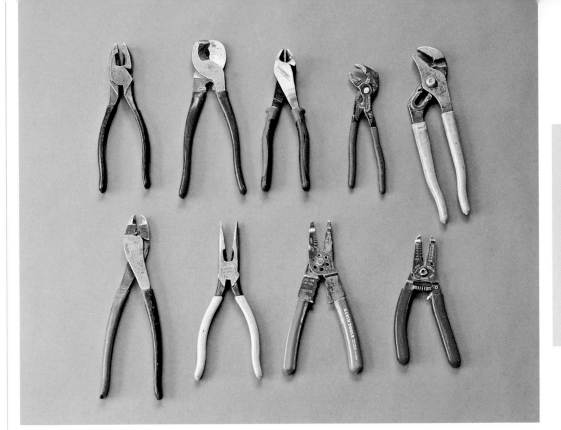

Electrician's cutters and pliers. Top row, from left: lineman's pliers, cable cutters, diagonal cutters, and two slip-joint pliers (also called Channellock® pliers). Bottom row, from left: crimper, needle-nose pliers, and two wire strippers (multipurpose tools).

PRO TIP

In some very old houses, you may find that the neutral wires were attached to a switch—rather than the hot wires, as required by codes today. Thus, when working on old switches or fixtures, test all wires for current. Even if you've flipped a fixture switch off, there could still be a hot conductor in the fixture outlet box.

Miscellaneous tools. From left: two slot-head screwdrivers, tapper (to cut threads in metal box holes), offset screwdriver, nut driver, utility knife, small pry bar/nail puller, plaster chisel, drywall saw, and hacksaw.

PRO TIP

Cordless drills and screwdrivers reduce the tedium of screwing wires to terminals, attaching devices to boxes, putting on cover plates, and connecting myriad other items. But always tighten cable clamps by hand to avoid overtightening them and damaging the incoming wires.

when an outlet is too distant. Cordless tools now have all the power you could want. Besides, they don't need an extension cord and won't electrocute you if you inadvertently drill or cut into a live wire. Cordless reciprocating saws can cut anything from plaster lath to studs; but use a cordless jigsaw if you want to preserve the plaster around a cut-in box opening.

Miscellaneous tools. Other necessary tools include a hammer, tape measure, Speed Square, hacksaw, plaster chisel, drywall saw, nut driver, small pry bar, and spirit level.

Electrical cable. From top: type NM (Romex), type UF (underground), armor clad (AC), and metal clad (MC). Note: The silver wire in the AC cable is a bonding wire, not a ground. In the MC cable, the green wire is ground, the white is neutral, and the red and black are hot.

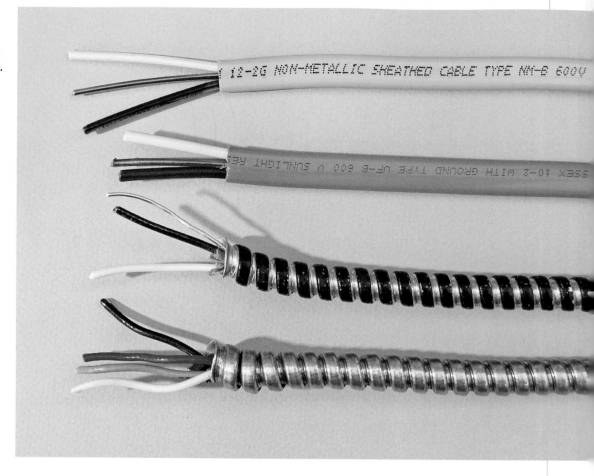

12-2G NON-METALLIC SHEATHED CABLE TYPE NM-B 600V

Reading a Cable

Cables provide a lot of information in the abbreviations stamped into their sheathing; for example, *NM* indicates nonmetallic sheathing, and *UF* (underground feeder) can be buried. The size and number of individual conductors inside a cable are also noted: *12/2 w/grd or 12-2 W/G*, for example, indicates two insulated 12AWG wires plus a ground wire. Cable stamped *14/3 W/G* has three 14AWG wires plus a ground wire. (The higher the number, the smaller the wire diameter.) The maximum voltage, as in *600V*, may also be indicated.

Individual wires within cable have codes, too. *T* (thermoplastic) wire is intended for dry, indoor use, and *W* means "wet"; thus *TW* wire can be used in dry and wet locations. *H* stands for heat-resistant. *N*, for nylon jacketed, indicates a tough wire than can be drawn through conduit without being damaged.

Finally, make sure the cable is marked *NM-B*. Cable without the final "*-B*" has an old-style insulation that is not as heat resistant as *NM-B* cable.

CABLE, CONDUIT, AND WIRING

Most house wiring is flexible cable, but you may find any—or all—of the wiring types described here. Inside cables or conduits are individual wires, or conductors, that vary in thickness according to the amperage of the current.

▶ Nonmetallic sheathed cable (NM or Romex) is by far the most common flexible cable. Covered with a flexible thermoplastic sheathing, Romex is easy to route, cut, and attach.

▶ Metal-clad cable (MC) is often specified where wiring is exposed. *Note:* Some codes still allow armored cable (AC), but that's increasingly rare.

▶ Conduit may be specified to protect exposed wiring; it is commonly thin-wall steel (EMT), aluminum, or PVC plastic. Metal conduit serves as its own ground. Apart from service entrances, conduit is seldom used in home wiring. When connected with weather-tight fittings and boxes, conduit can be installed outdoors.

▶ Knob-and-tube wiring (see the top photo on p. 15) is no longer installed, but there's still plenty of it in older houses. If its sheathing is intact and not cracked, it may still be serviceable. You may even be able to extend it, but have an electrician do the work. Knob-and-tube is eccentric, requiring experience and a skilled hand.

CIRCUIT WIRING

Copper is the preferred conductor for residential circuit wiring. Aluminum cable is frequently used at service entrances, but it is not recommended in branch circuits.

Individual wires within a cable or conduit are color coded. White or light gray wires are neutral conductors. Black or red wires denote hot, or load-carrying, conductors. Green or bare (uninsulated) wires are ground wires, which must be connected continuously throughout an electrical system.

Because most of the wiring in a residence is 120-volt service, most cables will have three wires: two insulated wires (one black and one white) plus a ground wire, usually uninsulated. Other colors are employed when a hookup calls for more than two wires; for example, 240-volt circuits and three- or four-way switches.

BOXES

There is a huge selection of boxes, varying by size, shape, mounting device, and composition. But of all the variables to consider when choosing boxes, size (capacity) usually trumps the others. Install slightly oversize boxes, if possible: They're faster to wire and, all in all, safer because jamming wires into small boxes stresses connections.

Aluminum WIRING

Aluminum wiring was widely used in house circuits in the 1960s and 1970s, but it was a poor choice. Over time, such wiring expands and contracts excessively, which leads to loose connections, arcing, overheating and—in many cases—house fires. If your house has aluminum circuit wiring, the most common symptoms will be receptacle or switch cover plates that are warm to the touch, flickering lights, and an odd smell around electrical outlets. Once arcing begins, wire insulation deteriorates quickly. An electrician who checks the wiring may recommend adding COPALUM® connectors, CO/ALR-rated outlets and switches, or replacing the whole system.

Note: Aluminum *service cable*, thick stranded cable that connects to service panels, is still widely used because it attaches solidly to main lugs, without problems.

Capacity. The most common shape is a single-gang box. A single-gang box 3½-in. deep has roughly 22½ cu. in. capacity: enough space for a single device (receptacle or switch), three 12/2 W/G cables, and two wire nuts. Double-gang boxes hold two devices; triple-gang boxes hold three devices. *Remember:* Everything that takes up space in a box must be accounted for—devices, cable wires, wire nuts, and cable clamps—so follow closely NEC recommendations for the maximum number of conductors per box.

You can get the capacity you need in a number of ways. Some pros install shallow four-squares (4 in. by 4 in. by 1½ in. deep) throughout a system because such boxes are versatile and roomy. If a location requires a single device, pros just add a mud ring cover, as shown in the photo on p. 240. Because of their shallow depth, these boxes can also be installed back to back within a standard 2x4 wall. Thus you can keep even back-

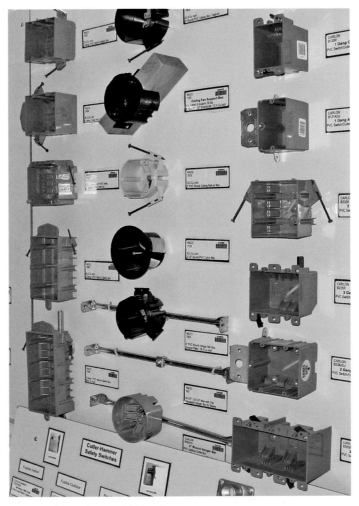

There are hundreds of options for outlet boxes. The sample of blue plastic boxes at right shows (from top) one-gang cut-in, one-gang adjustable, two-gang nail-on, two-gang cut-in, two-gang adjustable, and three-gang boxes. The multicolored boxes in the middle are ceiling boxes.

to-back switch boxes at the same height, from room to room. Shallow pancake boxes (4 in. in diameter by ½ in. deep) are commonly used to flush mount light fixtures.

Mounting devices. The type of mounting bracket, bar, or tab you use depends on whether you're mounting to finish surfaces or structural members. When you're attaching a box to an exposed stud or joist, you're engaged in *new construction* or *new work,* even if the house is old. New-work boxes are usually side-nailed or face-nailed through a bracket; nail-on boxes have integral nail holders. The mounting bracket for Veco® nonmetallic boxes is particularly ingenious (see the photos on p. 244). Once attached to framing, the box depth can be screw adjusted till it's flush to the finish surface.

Adjustable bar hangers enable you to mount boxes between joists and studs; typically, hangers adjust from 14 in. to 22 in. Boxes mount to hangers via threaded posts or, more simply, by being screwed to the hangers. Bar hangers vary, too, with heavier strap types favored in walls, where boxes can get bumped more easily. Lighter hangers, as shown on p. 239, are typically used in ceilings, say, to support recessed lighting cans.

Cut-in boxes. The renovator's mainstay is *cut-in boxes* because they mount directly to finish surfaces. These boxes are indispensable when you want to add a device but don't want to destroy a large section of a ceiling or wall to attach to the framing. Several types are shown in the top photo at right. Most cut-in boxes have plaster ears that keep them from falling into the wall cavity; what vary are the tabs or mechanisms that hold them snug to the back side of the wall: screw-adjustable ears, metal-spring ears, swivel ears, or

Metal VERSUS PLASTIC BOXES

Metal boxes are sturdy and are available in more sizes than plastic boxes. Some metal boxes can be interlocked for larger capacity. Also, metal boxes are usually favored for mounting ceiling fixtures because steel is stronger than plastic. If code requires steel conduit, armored cable (BX), or MC cable, you must use steel boxes. All metal boxes must be grounded.

For most other installations, plastic is king. (Plastic boxes may be PVC, fiberglass, or thermoset.) Electricians use far more plastic boxes because they are less expensive. And, because they are nonconductive, they don't need to be grounded and are quicker to install. However, even if a box doesn't need to be grounded, *all electrical devices within must be grounded* by a continuous ground. Another reason to buy plastic: Box volumes are stamped on the outside.

Box Fill Worksheet*

ITEM	SIZE (cu. in.)	NUMBER	TOTAL
#14 conductors exiting box	2.00		
#12 conductors exiting box	2.25		
#10 conductors exiting box	2.50		
#8 conductors exiting box	3.0		
#6 conductors exiting box	5.0		
Largest grounding device; count only one		1	
Devices; two times connected conductor size			
Internal clamps; one based on largest wire present		1	
Fixture fittings; one of each type based on largest wire			
Total			

* Table based on NEC 370-16(b) and adapted with permission from Redwood Kardon, Douglas Hansen, and Mike Casey, Code Check Electrical® (The Taunton Press).

A four-square box with a mud ring has plenty of room for incoming cables, connectors, and a receptacle. Yet four-square boxes are shallow enough to install back-to-back in a 2×4 wall.

Cut-in boxes and useful accessories. Clockwise from lower left: Grip-Tite™ cut-in box with screw ears, deep plastic cut-in box with swivel ears, standard cut-in box, cut-in box with metal wings, pancake box, goof ring, and bendable metal tabs.

bendable metal tabs (Grip-loks™). *Important:* All cut-in boxes, whether plastic or metal, must contain cable clamps inside that fasten cables securely. That is, it's impossible to staple cable to studs and joists when they are covered by finish surfaces, so you need clamps to keep the cables from getting tugged or chafed by metal box's edge.

Clamps. Every wiring system—whether nonmetallic (Romex), MC, or conduit—has clamps (connectors) specific to that system. Clamps solidly connect the cable or conduit to the box so there can be no strain on electrical connections within the box and, as important, Romex clamps protect cable sheathing from burrs created when a metal box's knockouts are removed.

The exception to this rule is single-gang plastic boxes. If framing is exposed (new construction) and cable can be stapled within 8 in. of the box, code doesn't require cable clamps in a single-gang plastic box. However, two-gang plastic boxes must have cable clamps—typically, a plastic tension clip that keeps cables from being pulled out. And, as noted in the preceding section, all cut-in boxes must contain cable clamps.

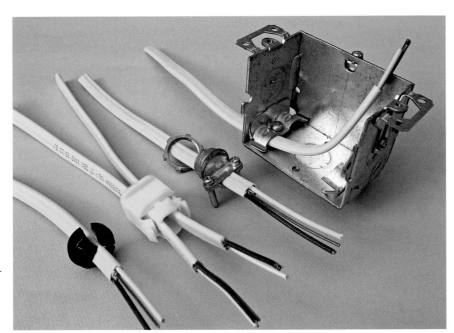

Romex cable connectors. From left: plastic push-in connector, two-cable hit-lock connector, ⅜-in. NM clamp with locknut, and metal box with internal clamps.

GETTING BOX Edges FLUSH

Use an Add-a-Depth ring ("goof ring") to make box edges flush when an outlet box is more than ¼ in. below the surface—a common situation when remodelers drywall over an existing wall that's in bad shape. To prevent the metal goof ring from short-circuiting screw terminals, first wrap electrical tape twice around the body of the receptacle or switch.

Although all UL-rated fixtures, switches, and receptacles will satisfy electrical codes, better-quality devices will last longer. Heavy-duty receptacles, for example, have nylon faces rather than plastic and metal support yokes that reinforce the back of the receptacle.

Receptacles. Most household receptacles are rated for 15-amp circuits and wired with 14AWG or 12AWG wire. The NEC specifies 20-amp protection for kitchen appliance, garage, and workshop circuits.

The NEC specifies GFCI protection for many locations, including bathroom, outdoor, and kitchen counter receptacles, so there are also 15-amp and 20-amp GFCI receptacles. In addition, you can obtain various kinds of specialty 15-amp receptacles, including childproof models that require an adult's grip to uncover them, weatherproof receptacles that combine cover and receptacle in an integral unit, recessed receptacles in which clock wires can be hidden, covered floor receptacles, and many more. In addition, there are receptacles specifically matched to the plugs of 30-, 40-, or 50-amp appliances. Your electrical supplier can tell you what's available.

Fixtures. Lighting fixtures vary greatly, from elaborate multibulb configurations to simple pull-chain porcelain fixtures. Most attach to a ceiling outlet box with two machine screws. Branch-circuit wires attach directly to two screws on the fixture (white wire to silver screw, black to gold screw) or, more commonly, to two color-coded lead wires from the fixture. Metal fixture boxes must be grounded.

Switches. Switches come in a variety of configurations. They include single pole, which control lights from a single location; three-way, which control lights from two locations; four-way, which control lights from three locations; rheostats (dimmer switches), which dim and brighten lights gradually; touch-pad dimmers, which respond to finger pressure rather than a mechanical switch; pilot-light combos, whose small bulbs shine when an attic or basement light is still on; switch–receptacle combos; programmable switches; and space-saver switches.

Before installing any of the more exotic switches, make sure switch amperage matches that of the load (electrical demand of an appliance or piece of equipment) you're feeding. And never run appliances or tools on a rheostat-controlled outlet. Rheostats vary voltage, and without full voltage, appliance or tool motors can burn out.

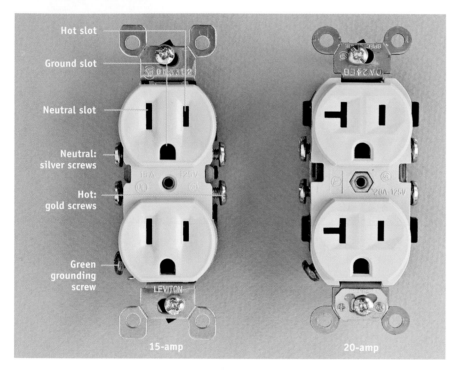

Hot slot
Ground slot
Neutral slot
Neutral: silver screws
Hot: gold screws
Green grounding screw
15-amp
20-amp

The 20-amp receptacle (at right) has a horizontal slot so it can receive a special 20-amp plug in addition to standard 15-amp plugs. Unlike 20-amp receptacles, 15-amp receptacles cannot receive 20-amp plugs. Thus 20-amp receptacles cannot be used on 15-amp circuits.

Polarized FIXTURES AND RECEPTACLES

Fixtures and receptacles are polarized, so they fit together only one way. On a correctly wired light fixture, the neutral wire of the lamp cord connects to the silver screw shell (where the bulb screws in); whereas the hot wire connects to a brass tab inside the bottom of the screw shell. Should you inadvertently touch the side of the screw shell, there's no harm done. Whereas, if you reverse the order in which wires are attached—known as reversing the polarity—the outside of the screw shell becomes hot (energized) and could shock someone changing a bulb.

Receptacles and plugs are also polarized. A receptacle's gold screw terminal connects to hot wires and, internally, to the hot (narrow) prong of a polarized plug. The receptacle's silver screw terminal connects to neutral wires and, internally, to the neutral (wide) prong of a polarized plug. Finally, the green ground screw connects to the ground wire and the U-shaped grounding prong of the plug.

Rough-In Wiring

As noted earlier, electricians distinguish between *new work* and *old work* (remodel) jobs, regardless of the age of the building or the extent of the upgrade. New work means that framing is exposed, so you can attach boxes to studs or ceiling joists and easily drill holes for cable; whereas remodel wiring usually entails mounting cut-in boxes to finish surfaces and fishing cable through walls or floors to add outlets to existing circuits.

Certainly, the two approaches have a lot in common. But to avoid repetition, the following sections discuss their common elements in the context of new work and then examine the specifics of remodel wiring. Assume that nonmetallic cable (Romex) is being installed. Brief sections on installing MC cable and conduit will follow.

OVERVIEW

Electricians further divide installations into rough-in and finish phases. After the rough-in, there's always an inspection by an authority having jurisdiction (AHJ). The following sequences are greatly oversimplified.

Rough-in phase.

1. Locate and mount boxes.

2 Drill holes, and run cable.

3. Feed cables into boxes, staple cables to studs, and clamp cables to boxes.

4. Remove the sheathing of cables inside boxes, group like wires and cut them to equal length, join ground wires, and fold all wires into the boxes.

Finish phase. The finish, or trim, phase takes place after a rough inspection has been signed off by the AHJ and the finish surfaces have been installed and painted.

1. Strip insulated wire ends, and then splice them together—black to black, white to white. Leave switch hot wires unspliced.

2. Attach wires to receptacles, fixtures, and switches.

3. Push wired devices into the boxes, and screw the devices to the boxes.

4. Screw on the cover plates.

LOCATING AND MOUNTING BOXES

After mapping the wiring plan, you can install the boxes. But if you're wiring someone else's house, first do a walk-through with the owners so they can approve the locations. Use a builder's crayon or a heavy marker to indicate boxes or temporarily tack-nail (or screw-fasten) the boxes in place.

Box heights. There are few set rules about locating boxes. Set the bottom of outlet boxes 12 in. above the subfloor, or use a hammer to approximate box height, as shown in the top left photo on p. 244. In housing for disabled occupants, outlet box bottoms should be a minimum of 15 in. above the subfloor. For outlets over kitchen and bath counters, set the box bottoms 42 in. from the subfloor, so they'll end up 8 in. above the counters and 4 in. above a standard 4-in.-high backsplash.

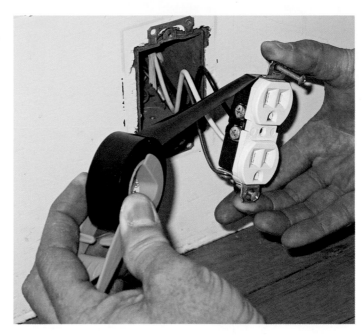

When installing receptacles in a metal box, wrap electrical tape around the sides of the receptacle to cover and insulate the screw terminals.

Test BEFORE YOU TOUCH

Before handling electrical wires or devices—or before cutting into finish surfaces around them—disconnect the power to that area and test with a voltage tester to make sure that the power is off.

Before doing any work in the vicinity of an existing circuit, disconnect the circuit. Flip off the governing breaker or remove the fuse. (*Don't merely loosen fuses. Remove them.*) And leave a note on your service panel announcing work in progress, so that others in the house won't inadvertently turn the electricity back on.

Locate wall switches on the lock side of a door (the side opposite the hinges). If you set the bottoms of the switch boxes 44 in. or 48 in. above the subfloor, the box bottoms will align with the seam of a 48-in.-wide drywall panel installed horizontally—which means you'll need to cut out only one panel. However, if a carpenter has added blocking at that height to nail the panel edges, raise the boxes till they clear the blocking.

Mounting boxes. Mount boxes so they'll be flush with finish surfaces. Most boxes have tabs or gauge marks stamped on the side to indicate different surface thicknesses. If that's not the case, hold a scrap of the finish material—for example, ⅝-in. drywall—next to the front edge of the box as a depth gauge. Unless you're installing nail-in boxes, use screws to mount the boxes so you can make adjustments if you need to. The depth of the Veco box shown on p. 244 can be adjusted after the drywall is up.

To attach ceiling boxes, you have these three choices: (1) screw the box directly to a joist; (2) end-nail a piece of blocking between the

Use a hammer to set the box heights. This is much quicker than measuring, yet almost as accurate. Boxes will be roughly 12 in. above subfloors; set them 15 in. above the floor for disabled persons, if required.

Adjustable boxes can be raised or lowered till they're flush with the finish walls. Here, the adjustment screw is visible below the electrician's thumb. Note the bare wood under the mounting bracket: One pass of a power plane sets the brackets flush to the stud edges.

Drill holes at least 1 ft. above the boxes, so you can feed them with a gentle bend of the cable. Sharp bends can damage wires.

joists, and screw the box to that; or (3) install an adjustable metal hanger bar between the joists, to which the box is mounted. Ceiling boxes must be secured to the structure, not merely to the finish ceiling, so that the fixture will be adequately supported.

DRILLING HOLES

With the boxes in place, drill holes to run cable from the service panel to the outlet boxes. As noted earlier, a ½-in. right-angle drill with a ⅞-in. Nail Eater wood-boring bit is the tool of choice.

For individual circuits, in which a cable serves only one appliance, reduce the amount of hole drilling by drilling up through the top plate(s) above the appliance and running cable through the attic till you're above the service panel. Then drill holes down through the wall plates so you can drop the cable to the panel.

For circuits with many wall outlets, drill through studs 12 in. above the outlet boxes, so the cable can bend gradually toward the boxes. (Avoid sharp bends, which can damage wire insulation.) All holes should be centered in the studs, so that the cable is at least 1¼ in. away from the stud edges; that way drywall screws can't puncture it. If a cable is closer than 1¼ in., nail steel *nail-protection plates* to the studs. Be careful to drill holes at the same height. It's much easier to pull cable through lined-up holes. A right-angle drill will also ensure that the holes are perpendicular to studs.

Sometimes it's easier to run cable around an obstruction. For example, it's possible to run cable through the corner studs if the holes are at the same height and there's no 2× blocking at the point where you drill. But if you're running 12/2 cable or heavier, the cable will be too stiff to pull through the holes at right angles. In this case, drill through the wall plates and go over or under the corner. Likewise, drilling through doubled studs on either side of a door or window opening is a lot of work. So go around.

Finally, drill holes for cable "home runs"— lengths of cable that run from the panel board to the outlet box on each circuit that is closest to the panel.

PULLING CABLE

Pulling Romex cable is easier if you reel it off a wire wheel, a rotating cable dispenser that nails to framing and holds 250-ft. coils. Start by placing the wire wheel near each home-run box and pulling off enough cable to extend roughly 1 ft. beyond each box and 4 ft. beyond the knockout where each cable enters the panel. When in doubt, run cable long. For example, wires inside a service panel may need to run 3 ft. to 4 ft. to reach a neutral or ground bus on the opposite side of the panel.

To run cable for individual circuits, again place the wire wheel near each home-run box, but this time pull cable "downstream"—away from the service panel. Many electricians pull cable through holes to the far end of the circuit and then walk back, pulling out additional cable loops that reach at least 8 in. beyond each box. After running cable to all outlet boxes, cut each loop and feed the cable ends into the box openings or knockouts, so the cables stick out about 8 in. Although most duplex receptacle boxes will contain two cables, double- or triple-gang boxes may have four or more.

Staple cable within 12 in. of most boxes, and every 4½ ft. thereafter. However, if you're using single-gang plastic boxes without internal cable clamps, staple cable within 8 in. of the boxes. Don't overdrive the staples; cable should be just snug. When cable runs parallel to joists, staple it to the sides of the joists. When cable runs perpendicular to joists, drill holes through the joists or staple the cable to the underside of each joist. Alternatively, you can nail a 1×4 board to the underside of the joists and then staple cable to it.

A wire wheel feeds cable freely, without kinking.

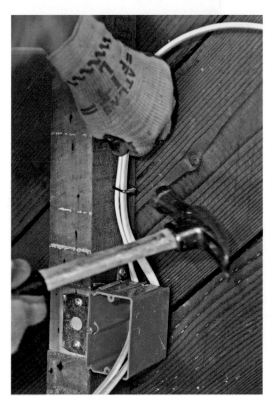

Staple cable within 8 in. of single-gang plastic boxes and within 12 in. for all others. Cables should lie flat beneath the staple; never staple cable on-edge.

PRO TIP

The NEC requires at least 6 in. of "free" wire in a box, and at least 3 in. of it can extend beyond the front of the box. But seasoned electricians usually leave more wire sticking out. For inspectors, short stubby wires are the mark of an amateur.

▐▐▐▐

Identifying Cable Runs

To avoid confusion when it's time to wire devices, identify incoming cables. Use felt-tip markers to write on the cable sheathing or write on masking tape wrapped on grouped wires.

Cables running from the panel board to an outlet should be marked "SOURCE," "FROM SOURCE," or "UPSTREAM." If you're wiring GFCI receptacles, these incoming cable wires attach to GFCI terminals marked "LINE." Cables running on to the next outlet (away from the power source) are denoted "NEXT OUTLET" or "DOWNSTREAM"; they attach to GFCI terminals marked "LOAD."

Double- or triple-gang boxes will have a lot of cables entering, so make the cable descriptions specific: "SWITCH LEG TO CEILING FIXTURE," "THREE-WAY SWITCH #2," and so on.

Use a screwdriver or lineman's pliers to remove the metal box knockouts. Cables entering through such openings must be protected by cable connectors.

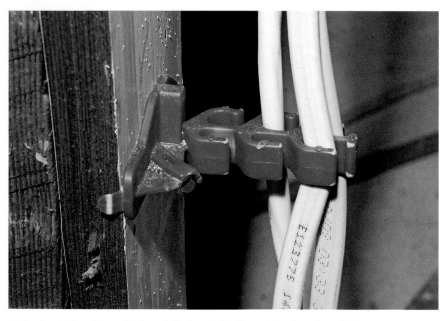

Cable standoffs position cable loosely in the middle of a stud, far from drywall screws or nails. Tightly bundling cables for distances of more than 2 ft. can cause them to overheat.

PRO TIP

Cables should not be stacked tightly under single staples—it's called bundling—for a distance of more than 2 ft. Bundling may cause wires to overheat, thus reducing the amperage they can carry safely. Instead, use a cable standoff, as shown in the photo above, to hold cables loosely apart in the middle of the stud so they can't get pierced by drywall screws.

CABLE CONNECTORS (CLAMPS)

All outlet boxes must have clamps that grip cables, except single-gang plastic boxes whose cables must be stapled within 8 in. of the box. (Several Romex connectors are shown in the photo on p. 243.) Clamps secure cable so its connections can't be yanked—thus preventing strain on connections inside the box. Plastic boxes have tension clamps that allow cable to be pulled in, but not out. When you're fishing wire and installing cut-in boxes, cable clamps are crucially important because it's impossible to staple cable hidden by walls.

Cable clamps in metal boxes also keep wires from being nicked by burrs created when metal box knockouts are removed. (Use a screwdriver to start knockouts and lineman's pliers to twist

them free.) To further protect wire insulation, leave a small amount of cable sheathing—roughly ½ in.—sticking out from under clamps. That is, clamps should tighten down on a remnant of sheathing, not on individual, unsheathed wires. Finally, don't overtighten clamps, which could damage the wire insulation. And if you remove a knockout mistakenly, use a knockout plug to cover the hole; a knockout plug is a thin cap with barbed sides or spring clips that expand after they clear the edge of the knockout hole. Use one cable per clamp unless the manufacturer allows more.

STRIPPING SHEATHING

Many electricians use a utility knife to slit and remove plastic sheathing, lightly running the blade tip down the middle of the cable, over the bare ground wire inside. To remove sheathing with less risk of nicking wire insulation, use a cable ripper to slit the sheathing or a cable stripper to remove a sleeve of sheathing. Use a utility knife or side-cut pliers to cut free any slit sheathing or kraft paper still in the box. Tighten the cable clamps; then group like conductors—hot wires to one side, neutrals to the other, grounds in the middle—and cut all wires to the same length, roughly 8 in.

Use a cable ripper or utility knife to remove cable sheathing and kraft paper. Because cable clamps tighten on sheathing—rather than individual wires—roughly ½ in. of the cable sheathing should stick out under the clamps.

Splicing ground wires. To ensure a continuous ground throughout the system, splice together copper ground wires, using wire nuts or crimps. Ground wires are usually bare copper; if they're green insulated wires, first strip approximately ¾ in. of insulation off their ends.

To use wire nuts, first cut the ground wires to the same length, and butt their ends together, along with a 6-in. pigtail that you'll later connect to the green ground screw of a receptacle. (The grounding pigtail can be bare copper or insulated wire whose ends have been stripped.) Use lineman's pliers to twist the stripped wire ends clockwise. Trim the ends of the grouped ground wires even; then twist on a wire nut, turning it in a clockwise direction. The threads inside the wire nuts cut into and bind the bare wires. Give a gentle tug to be sure the splice is complete.

To crimp ground wires, gather the wires but don't twist them. Feed them through a copper sleeve, use a crimping tool to crimp the sleeve tight before snipping all the wires—except one—even with the sleeve. This one long ground wire emerging from the crimped group will connect to the green ground screw of a receptacle. You can use wire nuts to splice (join) ground wires; but crimping them is faster.

Crimping ground wires is quicker than splicing them with wire nuts. After crimping the sleeve, leave one ground wire long. Then attach it to the green ground screw of a receptacle.

If the box is metal, it too must be grounded. Many electricians simply loop the bare-wire grounding pigtail and screw the loop to a green screw in the metal box. The bare-wire pigtail then continues on, to connect to the grounding screw on the receptacle. Or you can add a second pigtail to the ground-wire splice, so that the first screws to the metal box and the second to the receptacle, but that eats up space in the box and slows down the work.

At this point, most local codes require a rough-in inspection. In addition to outlet boxes, inspectors will examine any connections in junction boxes, typically 4-sq.-in. boxes. All electrical connections must be housed in covered boxes, but you must leave junction box covers off till the rough-in inspection is done.

Splicing neutral and hot wires in outlet boxes is essentially the same as splicing ground wires. Once again, a pigtail runs from both the hot and the neutral wire groups and attaches to the appropriate screw terminal on the receptacle. Because neutral and hot wires are always insulated, use wire strippers to strip the insulation off the wire ends.

Feed the wire into an appropriately sized hole in the tool's jaws, squeeze the handles, and rock the tool so it cuts the insulation but doesn't score the conductor. If you are using wire

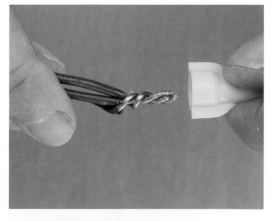

Most electricians use twist-on connectors (also known as wire nuts) to splice like wire groups. Strip the last ¾ in. of insulation from the wire ends. Twist the wires and wire nuts clockwise to fasten.

nuts to splice wire groups, strip roughly ¾ in. of insulation from the wire ends; then twist each wire group together, using lineman's pliers. If you are attaching a pigtail to the receptacle or fixture screws, strip ½ in. of insulation. Back-wired switches and receptacles have stripping gauges on the back that show how much to strip.

At switches, do not splice hot wires; splice only neutral and ground wire groups. Switches turn fixtures off and on by interrupting the current flowing through hot wires. Therefore, you must attach hot wires to switch terminals, not to each other.

Installing Receptacles, Fixtures, and Switches

🚫 Before working around any electrical device, disconnect the power to it and test with a voltage tester to make sure the power is off.

WIRING RECEPTACLES

Before beginning this section, read the previous sections on grouping and splicing wire. The following discussion assumes that each wire group (hot, neutral, ground) in the box is spliced together and has a pigtail that attaches to a receptacle terminal. Connecting wires and devices in this manner ensures that there will be continuous current to outlets downstream, even if a receptacle upstream malfunctions or is temporarily removed.

Method one: Using pigtails. First attach the grounding pigtail to the green grounding screw on the receptacle. If the grounding pigtail is insulated, strip ½ in. of insulation from its end; then use needle-nose pliers or a hole in the wire strip-

per handle to loop the end of the pigtail clockwise, as shown in the bottom left photo on p. 251. Fit the looped wire onto the grounding screw, and then tighten it. (Screws tighten clockwise.) Next strip ½ in. of insulation from the neutral pigtail, loop it clockwise, and attach it to a silver screw on the receptacle. Finally, strip ½ in. of insulation, then loop and attach the hot pigtail to a gold screw on the opposite side of the receptacle.

When all wires are connected, tighten down any unused screws and gently push the wired receptacle into the outlet box, so the wires fold like an accordion. Make sure that the receptacle

Ready for a rough-in inspection: Wires are grouped, spliced with wire nuts, and folded into the box.

A New KIND OF NUT

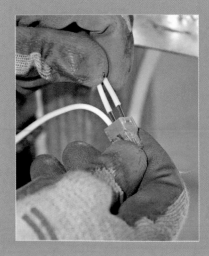

Splicing with twist-on wire nuts can be problematic. It's impossible to tell if the wires have come loose as you twist on the nuts; and stranded wire tends to slide down solid wire when you join solid wires to twisted-strand fixture leads. Wago Wall-Nuts™ simplify the task: Strip the wire ends the specified amount, and then push them into nut ports that hold the wires fast. The clear plastic housing allows you to see if the wires are connected, and the ports grasp both stranded and solid wire well.

Wiring a Receptacle in Midcircuit

Note: In the wiring schematics on pp. 248–255, thin, solid lines denote ground wires, white wires denote neutral conductors, and black, red, or slashed wires denote hot conductors–unless otherwise indicated on an illustration.

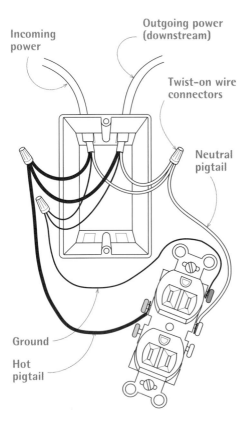

By splicing like wire groups and running pigtails (short wires) to the receptacle, this conventional method ensures continuous current downstream.

face is flat to the wall plane, not tilted, and the receptacle is centered in the box. Push the receptacle into the box by hand: If you use the screws to pull the receptacle into the box, you may strip a screw hole in a plastic box. Later, after the walls have been painted, screw a cover plate to the receptacle.

Method two: Feeding through receptacles. Rather than splicing like wire groups and running pigtails to the receptacles, you can instead attach hot and neutral wires directly to the receptacles. This wiring method—"feeding through receptacles"—is widespread because, on the whole, it is quicker, requires fewer conductors, and results in boxes that are less crowded than those wired with spliced wires and pigtails. It is also acceptable to the NEC.

But feeding wires through receptacles has detractors, who argue that in a circuit so wired, if a receptacle upstream fails or a wire comes loose, receptacles downstream will lose power.

Moreover, there is a voltage drop of about 1 percent per receptacle wired in this manner because receptacles offer more resistance to current flow than wire. If you have 6 or 10 receptacles daisy-chained in this manner, those overheated connections can heat up your electricity bill.

However, in older homes with ungrounded outlets, there's an upside to feeding through receptacles. If you install a GFCI receptacle on the circuit, the GFCI will protect all receptacles downstream. That is, if there's a ground-fault at a receptacle downstream, the GFCI will cut power to it and therefore make the entire circuit safer.

End of circuit. A receptacle at the end of a circuit has only one cable entering the box and none going beyond it. In this case, it's acceptable to attach wires directly to the receptacle terminals, without using pigtails. Attach the ground wire to the green ground screw, the neutral wire to a silver screw, the hot wire to a gold screw.

Feeding Wires through Receptacles

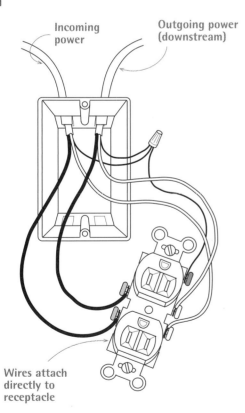

Incoming power

Outgoing power (downstream)

Wires attach directly to receptacle

Attaching hot and neutral wires directly to receptacle terminals is quicker and results in a less crowded box. However, with this wiring method, if the receptacle fails, power can be disrupted to downstream outlets. Note: Ground wires are always spliced to ensure continuity.

Wiring a Receptacle at End of a Circuit

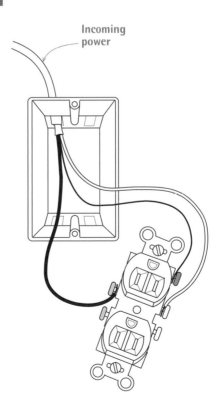

Incoming power

Where there are no receptacles downstream, attach wires directly to the device.

Wiring a Fourplex Receptacle in a Metal Box

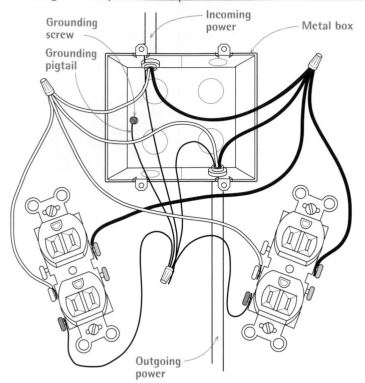

A two-gang box with fourplex (double duplex) receptacles will be crowded. Especially if the box is metal, use insulated ground pigtails, wrap electrical tape around receptacle bodies to prevent screw terminals from shorting out, and always ground the box (see the bottom photo on p. 243).

Wiring a GFCI Receptacle

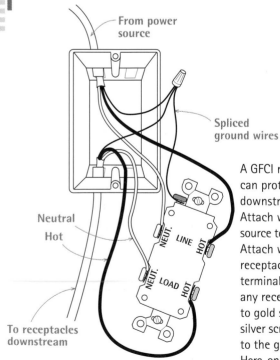

A GFCI receptacle in midcircuit can protect receptacles downstream, if correctly wired. Attach wires from the power source to terminals marked "LINE." Attach wires continuing to receptacles downstream to terminals marked "LOAD." As with any receptacle, attach hot wires to gold screws, neutral wires to silver screws, and grounding wires to the green ground screw. Note: Here, only ground wires are spliced; hot and neutral wires attach directly to screw terminals.

Ganging. By ganging devices you can make the most of limited wall or counter space. Most often, a switch and a receptacle are housed in a single four-square box (4 in. by 4 in.) or in two smaller metal boxes ganged together. Two receptacles will also fit. When in doubt, consult the table "Box Fill Worksheet," on p. 240, to make sure that the box in question is big enough. When ganging two devices, use two pigtails per wire group so you ensure continuity downstream.

INSTALLING A GFCI RECEPTACLE

Important: Read earlier sections about installing standard receptacles before installing a GFCI receptacle. As already mentioned, the NEC requires GFCI protection in the following locations: all bathroom receptacles; all kitchen counter receptacles; kitchen receptacles within 4 ft. of a sink; all outdoor receptacles; accessible basement or garage receptacles; and receptacles near pools, hot tubs, and the like.

Shut off power to the outlet and test with a voltage tester to be sure it's off. Carefully read the instructions that come with your GFCI. Devices vary, and your warranty—and your safety —depends on your installing the device correctly. GFCI receptacles are amperage rated (15 amp and 20 amp) and should match the cable wire size and be correctly sized for the circuit load.

GFCIs are wired in essentially the same manner as standard receptacles—hot wires to gold screws, neutral wires to silver screws, ground wire to grounding screw—except here you'll need to know which incoming cables are line wires (from the power source) and which are load wires (running on to the next outlet). So disconnect the old receptacle *while the power is off* and separate wires from each other. Temporarily turn the power back on and—being careful not to touch the bare wire ends—use a voltage tester to determine which pair of wires are "line." That done, *turn the power off again* and use white tape and a felt-tipped pen to denote "LINE" and "LOAD" wires.

Attach the wires running from the power source to the screw terminals or wire leaders marked "LINE," attach wires continuing to the next outlet to the terminals or leaders marked "LOAD," and attach ground wires to the terminal or leader marked "GROUND" and (if it's a metal box) to the pigtail that grounds the box. If there are no outlets downstream, use wire nuts to cap the two load leaders.

When connections are completed, gently press the device into the outlet box, screw the receptacle to the outlet box, install the cover plate, and turn the power back on. Then test the GFCI by pressing its "on" or "test" button, per the manufacturer's instructions. If the device won't stay on or devices downstream don't work, you have either a short circuit or a defective GFCI. Most makers recommend testing the devices once a month. All GFCI receptacles used outdoors must be housed in gasketed, weatherproof boxes with covers.

CONNECTING TO FIXTURES

Electrical connections to light or fan fixtures are simple: ground wire pigtail to green screw (if any), hot pigtail to black lead wire or gold screw, and neutral pigtail to white lead wire or silver screw. If fixture lead lines are stranded, cut them a little longer than solid-copper pigtails so that both will seat correctly when they're spliced with wire nuts. Push-in Wago Wall-Nuts are a good alternative (see "A New Kind of Nut," on p. 248). Physical connections, such as mounting fixtures

to outlet boxes and attaching outlet boxes to framing, are covered on pp. 260–261.

Wiring fixtures quickly gets complicated when three- or four-way switches control fixtures, as you'll see shortly. If the fixture is a combo—say, a light and fan—each function is usually controlled by a separate switch. Running three-wire cable (for example, 14/3 with ground) to the fixture enables you to run a separate hot wire to both the fan and the light.

INSTALLING SWITCHES

First, turn off the power. Switches interrupt the flow of current through hot wires only. Neutral wires and ground wires are always continuous, never interrupted. Whether a switch controls a receptacle, fixture, or appliance, hot wires only are attached to switching terminals.

Single-pole switch. A single-pole switch is simple to install. Splice the ground and neutral wire groups as described for receptacles, in the preceding sections. Attach the grounding pigtail to a green grounding screw on the switch, if any. Splice the neutral wires together with a wire nut; they need no pigtail because they don't attach to switches. Finally, strip ½ in. of insulation from the ends of the hot wires and attach them to the switch terminals—either by screws or back wiring. It's customary to install a single-pole switch with the manufacturer's name at the top, so that the switch toggle will be up when a light is on and down when off.

WIRING A RECEPTACLE

After finish walls are installed and painted, attach the wires to the devices. Start by stripping the wire ends.

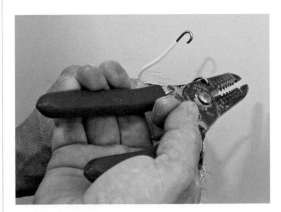

Some wire strippers have a small hole near the handle. Insert a stripped wire, flip your wrist 180 degrees and—voilà!—a perfect loop and faster than needle-nose pliers.

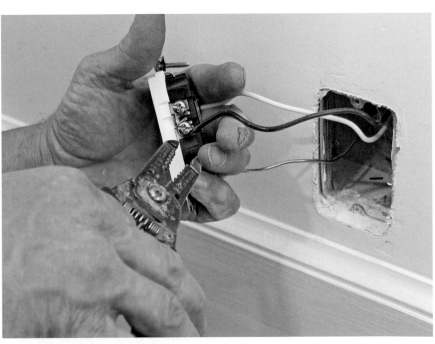

Use the stripper to close wire loops around the screw shanks. It's acceptable to attach wires directly to receptacles at the end of a circuit.

Bending a cardinal rule. When an outlet box is closer to the power source than to the switch box, a single cable may run to the switch, as shown in "Switch at End of Cable," on the facing page. Splice the ground and neutral wires from the source; then attach a neutral pigtail to a fixture lead wire. However, the hot wire from the source should not attach to a fixture lead—instead, the

WIRING A SWITCH

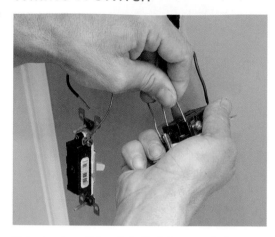

To back-wire switches, first attach the ground wire to the green screw. Then strip the insulated wire ends, using the stripping gauge on the back of the switch. Insert the wires into the terminal holes.

Wiring a Victorian Light Fixture

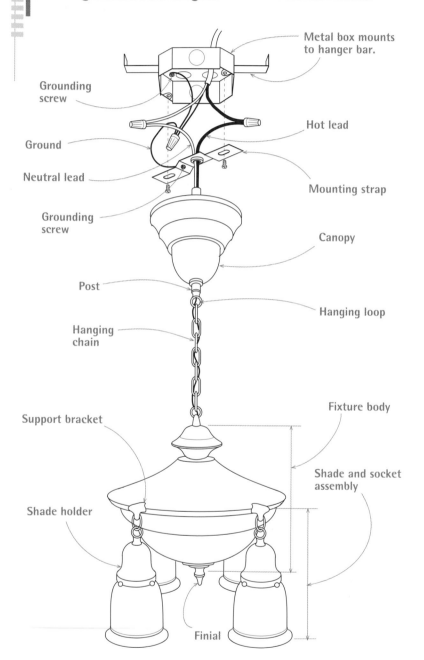

Grounding screw

Ground

Neutral lead

Grounding screw

Post

Hanging chain

Support bracket

Shade holder

Metal box mounts to hanger bar.

Hot lead

Mounting strap

Canopy

Hanging loop

Fixture body

Shade and socket assembly

Finial

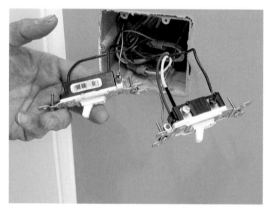

Two types of switches. Left: a single-pole switch; right: a three-way switch. The three-way switch shown has two traveler wires—one red and one white painted black to indicate a hot wire.

Connecting the incoming wires to fixture leads is standard: hot to hot, neutral to neutral, and splice ground wires. All metal parts should be grounded; if you're attaching to a metal box, the grounding pigtail to the mounting strap is optional. Note: Fixture bodies and mounting devices vary considerably.

After wiring the switch, push it into the box to prepack its wires and seat it in the position you want. Caution: Don't be tempted to use box screws to pull the devices in or you'll end up with crooked devices and stripped screw threads.

incoming hot wire is spliced to a cable wire running to the switch.

Here, for convenience, we break the rule of using the white wire only as a neutral wire and instead use black tape on each end of the white wire, to show that it is used as a hot wire. At the switch, attach the black wire and the white wire (taped black) to the switch terminals. This allows you to use inexpensive two-wire cable as a switch loop. Thus painting or taping the white wire black is a breach of the rule in letter only, because both wires are technically hot. We have not mixed actual hot and neutral wires.

More complex switches. Switch wiring gets complex when three- and four-way switches require three- or four-wire cable (plus grounds). If you get confused, redraw each configuration, identifying hot wires with an *H*, neutral wires with an *N*, and so on. At each splice remind yourself: *Neutral wires and ground wires are continuous; switches interrupt hot wires.*

If switches or light fixtures have green grounding screws, run a pigtail to them from the

Use at least a 12–volt cordless drill to cut screw threads into plastic boxes; smaller drills or cordless screwdrivers may not have the torque it takes. (Metal boxes have prethreaded screw holes.)

Light Fixture at End of Cable

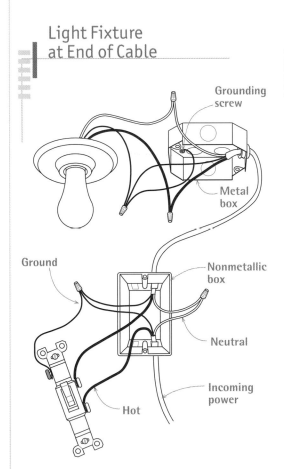

Switch-wiring at its simplest: Incoming and outgoing hot wires attach to the terminals of a single-pole switch. Neutrals and ground are continuous.

Switch at End of Cable

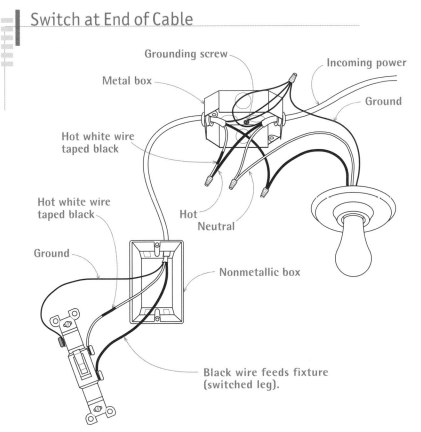

Attach the incoming neutral to a fixture lead; run the hot to a switch at the end of the cable. Use the white wire of a two-wire cable as one of the hot wires attaching to the switch—but tape both ends of the white wire black to show that it's hot.

Two Switches, Two Fixtures

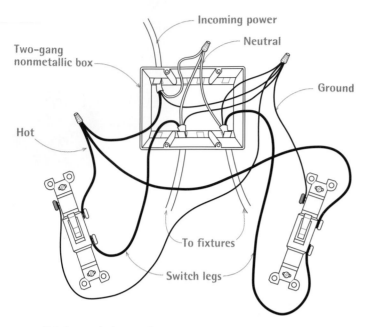

Two-gang nonmetallic box

Incoming power

Neutral

Ground

Hot

To fixtures

Switch legs

This is a typical setup for switches by exterior doors. For example, one single-pole switch controls an exterior light fixture, while the second switch controls an interior fixture.

Three-Way Switch

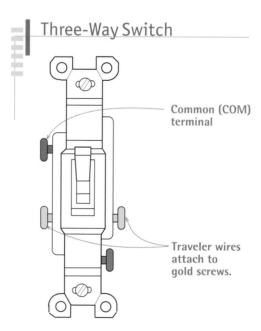

Common (COM) terminal

Traveler wires attach to gold screws.

Three-way switches control power from two locations. Each switch has two gold screws and a black screw (common terminal). The hot wire from the source attaches to the common terminal of the first switch. Traveler wires between the switches attach to the gold screws. Finally, a wire runs from the common terminal of the second switch to the hot lead of the fixture.

ground-wire splice (many older fixtures may not have grounding screws). However, if you're using metal boxes, they must always be grounded: In this case, loop a pigtail from the ground-wire splice to a green screw attached to the metal box.

Conduit and Flexible Metal Cable

The NEC requires that conductors be protected by conduit or flexible metal cable where conductors are exposed, where conductors run through metal studs (and could get nicked), where high moisture could corrode conductors, and so on. Flexible metal cable has factory-installed conductors (wires). But you need to pull conductors through conduit.

FLEXIBLE METAL CABLE

Flexible metal cable is commonly used in remodeling, and it satisfies most code requirements. In addition to its use in branch circuits, MC is

Making Sense of Flexible Metal Cable

There are two main types of flexible metal cable, *armor clad* and *metal clad*. Outside, they look about the same. (For a comparison, see the photo on p. 238.) The main difference is that MC cable contains an insulated ground wire so it can ground equipment and tools with a three-prong plug. MC cable assemblies should be used in exposed dry locations, such as garages and basements. PVC-jacketed MC cable can be used outdoors, but it is so expensive that it is rarely used in residences. *Note: Exposed* doesn't mean "exposed to the elements." Here it means visible and accessible— not hidden behind finish walls.

AC cable, on the other hand, contains no ground wire; rather, its metal sheathing serves as an equipment ground. AC should be used only in dry, indoor locations. The thin, uninsulated copper aluminum wire inside AC is not a conductor; it's a *bonding wire*, which enhances the grounding ability of the armor itself. That is, AC's grounding path is its metal sheathing.

The NEC allows both MC and AC to be used in branch circuits, but for the reasons just cited, many local codes allow only MC in new construction. In the text, *MC* is the default term for any flexible metal cable.

sometimes used as a *whip*, a short section of exposed cable that connects permanent appliances or lighting fixtures to a circuit.

There are at least two ways to cut MC cable. The first method requires looping and squeezing the cable till its coils pucker and then snipping through the pucker with metal shears or diagonal-nose cutters, being careful not to nick the insulated wires inside. The second method is often required by local codes and is far easier: The rotary cable cutter shown in the photo below uses a hand-cranked cutting wheel to cut through metal sheathing. Once the tool cuts through a coil, slide the severed sheathing off the insulated wires inside.

Rough cut lengths of cable about 2 ft. longer than the distance from box to box, to allow for generous loops at turns. After you have removed the metal sheathing, rip free the Mylar® wrap between its outer sheathing and the insulated conductors inside (AC cable has kraft paper surrounding its wires). To prevent the severed sheathing from slicing the insulation of individual wires, insert a plastic or fiber *anti-short bushing* between the wires and the sheathing, as shown below right. *Note:* Anti-short bushings are not required when using UL-listed MC cable clamps, but they are required by code (and manufacturers) for AC cable.

Roto-Split cutters cut through armored cable sheathing quickly and cleanly, without damaging the insulation of individual wires inside.

Three-Way-Switch Wiring

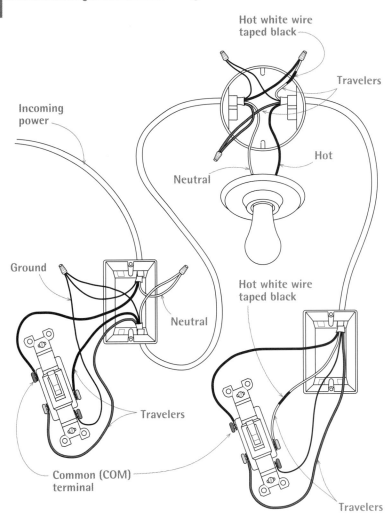

Here's a representative three-way setup (there are many possible configurations). Whenever you use a white wire as a switch leg, tape it black to indicate that it's hot. Here, all boxes are nonmetallic.

Insert anti–short bushings between wires and sheathing, to protect the wire insulation from the sharp edge of the metal sheathing.

Once you've inserted the bushing, attach an appropriate cable connector to the end of the sheathing; most connectors employ a locknut that holds the threaded connector to a metal box. (Pull the BX bonding wire outside the sheathing and wrap it once around the connector screw; the bonding wire doesn't go into the box.) After the cable connector is secured to the metal box, snip incoming wires so they are roughly 8 in. long. Splice and attach them to devices, as you would wires in nonmetallic cable

Because metal cable is flexible, support it every 6 ft. along its run and within 1 ft. of box connections. Staples should be snug but should not crimp the sheathing. The most common method of attaching cable is stapling it to the undersides or sides of joists where the cable runs parallel. When the cable runs perpendicular to framing, drill ⅝-in. holes through the center of the studs or joists and feed the cable through.

Note: Flexible metal cable can be punctured by drywall screws, so keep the cable back at least 1¼ in. from stud or joist edges. Otherwise, use steel nail-protection plates to safeguard the cable.

CONDUIT

There are several types of conduit, including thin-walled electrical metal tubing (EMT), rigid metal conduit (RMC), flexible metal conduit (FMC), and rigid nonmetallic conduit (RNC), which is made of PVC plastic. With metal conduit, the conduit pipe is the equipment ground. Fittings are specific to each type of conduit and may vary further if the conduit is to be used underground or in high-moisture areas. Most types approved for exterior use will have weather-proof compression fittings. All conduit boxes must also be gasketed to keep moisture out.

Because conduit comes without wires inside, you must pull wire through it. Although wire can usually be pushed easily through straight lengths of conduit 10 ft. or less, use fish tape to pull wires around bends or through longer lengths.

First, use a conduit whose diameter is large enough for the number of wires you need to pull: ½-in. interior diameter (I.D.) conduit will suffice for most runs of 12AWG wire; use ¾-in. I.D. conduit for the heavier wires, such as 8AWG or 6AWG wire, needed for stoves and such. Check your local code requirements. Using *pulling compound* (also called pulling lube) will make the task easier, as will having one person to feed wire and one to pull. THHN wire, whose coating is especially slick, is often specified when pulling is necessary. To keep wires from pulling off the fish tape, bend them tightly over the end of the tape, and wrap well with electrical tape.

A conduit bender creates the gentle bends necessary to pull wire through conduits without damaging it.

Pull wire only after you've attached conduit to boxes. If conduit bends more than the equivalent of four 90° bends between two boxes, you'll need a pull box in the middle of the run, through which wires can be pulled. Too many bends creates too much friction to overcome and can stress the wire too much. Such boxes give you access to the middle of the run. To shape bends, use a conduit bender, which slides over the conduit. Bend the conduit, pushing down heavily on the shoe and bend till you achieve the desired curve: For ½-in. EMT conduit, a radius of about 5½ in. is usual for a 90° bend. The bender will have arrows that indicate turning radiuses. Use a hacksaw to cut metal conduit; then use a deburring tool to smooth the cut ends and remove any metal spurs that could nick the conductor insulation.

Support EMT conduit at least every 10 ft. and within 3 ft. of termination. Connections within boxes are essentially the same as those for Romex cable, the principal difference being that the conduit itself, because it is metal, provides the grounding. To ground individual outlets, run a grounding pigtail from the grounding screw on the device to the metal box.

Adding Outlets to Existing Circuits

Adding an outlet may be relatively simple if you can access an existing outlet and run a length of cable to a new outlet in the same wall cavity. But even the simplest setup needs a bit of planning—and some exploration—beforehand.

IMPORTANT PREP STEPS

Here are some tasks to do before working in an existing circuit:

▶ Check local electrical codes, which may not allow extensions of ungrounded circuits. The NEC forbids tying into specialized kitchen, bathroom, or dedicated-appliance circuits. The circuit you tie into must be a 15-amp or 20-amp general-use or lighting circuit.

▶ Using a circuit map like that shown on p. 234 will help you calculate how much power the new circuit will draw. Add up the wattage of all lights and appliances you'll use on the circuit—plus that of tools if it's an outdoor outlet. If the total exceeds 1,440 watts for a 15-amp circuit, you're better off installing a new circuit to serve the new outlets.

▶ 🚫 Turn off the power and test all affected outlets—including switches—with a voltage tester to make sure the power is off (see "Using a Voltage Tester," on p. 235). If you flip a circuit breaker to cut power, tape the service-panel door shut and put up a sign warning others of work in progress.

▶ Using cordless tools with plastic housings also reduces the risk of shock. Wear protection if you use power tools.

▶ After testing verifies that the power is off, unscrew the receptacle and gently pull it from the wall so you can check the capacity of the box. If the box is already crowded—which you can tell just by looking—there may not be room for an additional cable. Consult the table "Box Fill Worksheet, " on p. 240, to be sure. It is possible to replace the existing box with a larger one, but that will complicate the task.

POSITIONING NEW OUTLETS

After deciding where you'd like a new outlet, find an existing outlet close to it. Think spatially: The closest outlet may be on the other side of a wall or on a floor above or below. Any existing outlet

is a likely candidate as long as it is live all the time—and not controlled by a switch upstream.

That decided, next figure out how to run cable with a minimum of drilling, wire fishing, and destroying of finished surfaces. If the nearest existing outlet is on another floor, look for a wall that contains plumbing that runs from floor to floor (a "pipe chase"). Also, there's often room to run cable in the voids around stairwells. Closets that line up vertically are also good places to hide cable, patched walls, and discrete holes.

Drilling through wall plates. If there's an unfinished attic or basement, you may be able to locate a wall in which to run cable by noting where existing cables or pipes emerge, where sole plates have been nailed through a subfloor, or where attic joists rest on wall top plates. When dropping cable down from above, first drill two pilot holes in the top plate—one hole to shine a flashlight into, the other to look into—to see if

PRO TIP

Don't add outlets to circuits that have ungrounded cable; wires with frayed, discolored, or melted insulation; blackened metal boxes or other signs of arcing; or aluminum wire (a soft, dull silver) rather than copper.

▐▐▐▐

A 4-ft. flexible drill bit is one way to drill through wall plates to reach a power source below. Because its diameter is less than ¼ in., the bit shaft tends to wander. Wear heavy gloves so you can guide the bit without hurting your hands. Drill slowly.

INSTALLING A CUT-IN BOX

Ideally, a cut-in box should be positioned so that you need to remove only one complete lath strip and so the box's plaster ears can be screwed into lath strips that are continuous.

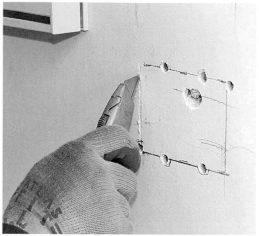

1. After test-drilling to locate the edges of a lath strip, level and outline the box, and drill several holes for a jigsaw blade—the more holes, the better. Before sawing, score the outline to minimize plaster cracking.

there are obstructions such as fire-stops in the stud bay. Professionals sometimes have a helper stand near an outlet they're drilling toward, who lightly places his or her hand on the wall to tell if a bit is on target. (You can feel the vibration of the bit.) Obviously, this takes skill and slow, careful drilling to avoid goring the helper.

Another approach: Drill exploratory holes by facing the outlet and angle drilling a ³⁄₁₆-in. hole at the base (or top) of the wall. Once the ³⁄₁₆-in. bit hits open space, insert a length of coat hanger or wire to find the hole more easily, above or below. If exploratory holes are in the right place, use a ⅞-in. bit to enlarge the holes.

If there's no accessible attic or basement, you may need to cut small holes at the top or base of finish walls so you can angle-drill through wall plates and fish cable. For this you may need to pull back carpeting or remove baseboard molding temporarily.

Behind baseboards. Running cable behind baseboards may be the best way to minimize damage to plaster or drywall. 🚫 First, turn off power to the area, and check to be sure it's off; then remove the baseboard trim. If you use a nail set to drive finish nails through the trim, you'll be less likely to break it. Once the baseboards are off,

use a cordless circular saw to cut along the bottom of the finish wall, 3 in. to 4 in. up from the floor. Set the sawblade to the depth of the finish surface so you don't cut into studs or through electrical cables hidden in the walls. (Wear safety glasses.) Use a flat bar to pry up the finish wall slot.

Next, create a pathway for running the cable by drilling holes through studs; by notching stud edges ½ in.; or by cutting a slot in the back of the baseboard, if it's thick enough. Whatever approach you choose, install ¹⁄₁₆-in. steel nail-protection plates afterward to keep screws or nails from puncturing the cable.

INSTALLING CUT-IN BOXES

Cut-in boxes have special mounting devices that enable you to mount them directly to finish surfaces. But first you've got to cut a hole for them. Hold the new box at the same height as other outlet boxes in the room, lightly pencil trace around the box, and then drill a small exploratory hole to locate studs or wood lath behind. Insert an offset screwdriver or a bent coat hanger in the hole and twirl it. If the tool hits a stud, move the box till it's clear. If you hit wood lath, keep drilling small holes within the opening till you find the edges of the lath. If you position the box

2. Use a cordless jigsaw to cut through the plaster and lath. To avoid pulverizing the plaster, hold the saw shoe slightly above the surface.

3. Before inserting the box in the wall, fish new cable through the box. Tighten down the cable clamps; then screw the plaster ears to the lath. Predrill screw holes to prevent splitting the lath.

correctly, you should need to remove only one section of lath. Cut-in box ears (also called plaster ears) mount to the lath top and bottom, so you may need to adjust the box height to make that happen.

Once you settle on a final location, level the box, trace its outline firmly onto the wall, and use a utility knife to score along the outline to minimize plaster fractures. (If the surface is drywall, don't bother scoring; just go ahead and cut out the opening.) Plaster is delicate stuff, but a cordless jigsaw can cut plaster without pulverizing it if you hold the saw shoe slightly above the surface. (Drill several ¼-in. holes around the outline so you can insert the sawblade.) Finally, when cutting through the lath strip you'll remove, alternate partial cuts from one side of the opening to the other; if you cut completely through one side of the lath first, that end will vibrate wildly and crack the plaster. After you've cut out around the box ears, predrill the lath so the mounting screws don't split it. (If there's metal lath, use a fine-toothed metal-cutting blade, and proceed slowly.)

Before inserting cut-in boxes, remove knock-outs, insert cable clamps, strip sheathing off the ends of incoming cable, feed cable into the cable clamps, and tighten the clamps down. Box mounts vary. Boxes with plaster ears that screw

to wood lath are the most common. Spring-clip types have metal wings that expand once inserted in an opening. Grip-Tite boxes have side-mounted ears that stick out as you turn screws. *Mounting tabs* (also called elephant ears) slip into the space between the box and the edge of the hole; pull them tight against the wall, and bend the tabs into the box, using pliers. Flatten tabs so they cannot touch any terminal screw of the outlet. For good measure, wrap electrical tape around the devices, as shown in the photo on p. 243.

FISHING CABLE

🚫 Once you've cut an opening for a cut-in box—but before inserting the box—fish the cable that will run from the existing outlet to the new one.

Fishing wires is easiest with a helper. As one person feeds metal fish tape down into an outlet cutout, the second person, with another fish tape, tries to catch the first. (Fish tape ends are often bent over to create a hook.) That accomplished, the first tape is pulled through, to have electrical cable attached to it. Bend and then twist the cable wires tightly over the fish tape, as shown in the drawing on p. 261, and wrap them well with electrical tape. Taper the electrical tape to a point

PRO TIP

Don't use cut-in boxes to house receptacles in high-use areas like bathrooms and kitchens. Plugs repeatedly inserted and removed will cause cut-in boxes—and possibly, electrical connections—to work loose. In such locations, you'll need to expose the framing and mount new-work boxes to it.

If you need to run cable between new and old outlets directly over each other, use a lightweight chain or fishing line with a weight rather than fish tape. The weight line or chain will be easy to snag because it will hang freely.

so it will feed more easily into holes. If one person feeds the cable into the opening as the other pulls, the cable should move smoothly.

To pull cable into an existing box, turn the power off, and then unscrew and gently pull the device out from the box and disconnect the wires attached to it. If the box is plastic, use a screwdriver to create a cable slot. If the box is metal, use a screwdriver to remove a knockout and to loosen the cable clamp nearest the knockout. If a metal box has no internal cable clamp, drill and tap a threaded hole so you can add a clamp. Feed the fish tape through the knockout opening; then pull in new cable and clamp it down.

Run a generous length of cable between the two boxes, so at least 1 ft. of cable protrudes from each box. Strip cable sheathing, tighten cable clamps, group like wires, and attach devices as described earlier. Chapter 15 covers patching finish surfaces.

MOUNTING CEILING FIXTURES

How you mount ceiling fixtures depends mostly on the weight of the fixture and whether framing is accessible. New "remodel" fixtures such as that shown below are light enough to mount to drywall or plaster ceilings, but heavier fixtures must be mounted to an adjustable hanger bar attached to ceiling joists or to a metal outlet box secured to the framing. *Note:* To prevent heat buildup and fire, fixtures in insulated ceilings must be rated

IC (insulation compatible) or insulation must be blocked back at least 3 in. from non-IC-rated fixtures.

Recessed lighting fixtures can usually be installed from below. Let's assume that there is cable in the ceiling cavity—either from an old fixture that was removed or from new cable recently fished to that location—and that the cable is not energized.

If there was no old fixture in the location, use a cordless drill to drill a ⅛-in. exploratory hole. Then insert a bent coat hanger into the hole and twirl it to locate nearby joists. Trace the template for the fixture can (housing) onto the ceiling.

Retrofitting a "Remodel" Lighting Fixture

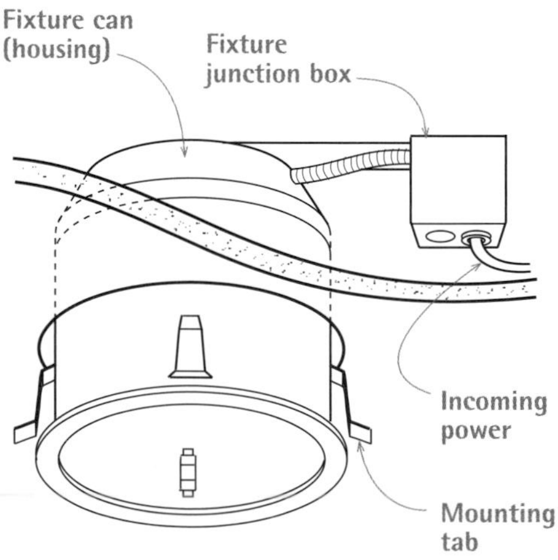

This recessed lighting fixture is a special "remodel" unit, which is light enough to mount to finish surfaces. Attach the fixture leads to the incoming cable wires in the junction box, and then insert the fixture into the opening.

Adding Outdoor Receptacles

To add an outdoor receptacle, find the nearest wall cavity that contains a general-use or lighting circuit, turn off the power, disconnect the receptacle, and fish wire to the new outdoor outlet. However, do not tap into kitchen or bathroom circuits or circuits dedicated to a single appliance. To position the outdoor box, use a utility knife to cut back drywall 2 in. on one side of the existing box; then push aside the insulation in the wall and drill a ⅛-in. hole through the sheathing and the siding. Note anything in the wall that would obstruct a new box. If you can't find a good spot, caulk the hole with urethane, and try another location.

Trace the back of the new outlet box onto a flat section of siding. Then use a reciprocating saw to cut out the siding and—depending on the type of weather-tight box you install—sheathing within that outline. All outdoor receptacles must be GFCIs, housed in "waterproof while in-use" covers. Feed cable into a clamp at the back of the box (12 in. of cable should stick out of the new box), tighten the cable clamp, mount the weatherproof box, and caulk around its perimeter with silicone or urethane caulk.

Wire an outdoor GFCI receptacle as you would an interior one. After screwing the wired receptacle to the new box, attach the gasket and the waterproof cover, splice the new cable to the existing one, and reconnect the indoor receptacle. Turn the power back on, and then test both receptacles to be sure they're correctly wired.

Then use a drywall circle cutter to cut it out. (If you must use a utility knife, the fixture's trim collar will cover up a less-than-perfect hole.)

Open the fixture's junction box. Then strip and splice incoming cable wires to the wires inside the junction box, using the twist-on wire nuts provided. Connections are standard: black wires to black, white wires to white, ground wire to green screw. Close the junction box and feed it through the hole in the ceiling first. Then insert the fixture can into the opening and rotate it till its spring mounting clips engage the ceiling. Insert the fixture's inner baffle, whose mounting springs fit into slots inside the can. Install a light-bulb and the unit's trim collar. Then turn the power on to test.

Mounting heavier fixtures is easier if there's an unfinished attic above. In this case, simply drill an exploratory hole through the ceiling to approximate the desired fixture location. Then go up in the attic and decide whether it's easier to nail a ceiling box to the nearest joist or to run a bar-hanger box between the joists and mount a ceiling box to it. Bar-hanger boxes allow you to position fixtures exactly where you want them, because you can slide the box along the bar. That decided, from the attic, cut out an opening for the ceiling box, which is almost always round. Use a drywall circle cutter for drywall, a cordless jigsaw for plaster.

There are dozens of types of ceiling boxes, from flat 4-in. pancake boxes that screw to the edges of joists to deeper nail-in boxes with brackets that nail to the sides of joists to bar-hanger boxes. Attach the box, fish cable to the location, feed the cable through a knockout in the box, staple the cable to the side of a joist within 12 in. of the box, tighten the cable clamps; then strip the sheathing from the cable, and splice individual wires as described earlier. If the ceiling box is metal, it must be grounded with a ground wire screwed to the box. That done, you're ready to attach the individual cable wires to the lead wires from the fixture and mount the fixture to the ceiling box.

If the cavity above isn't accessible, cut out a larger area of ceiling to expose the ceiling joists, so you can fish cable and mount the box. If the ceiling fixture's location isn't critical, use nail-in boxes with brackets, which have the smallest footprint to patch. If you use a hanger bar, cut a channel in the ceiling from joist center to joist center so you'll have something to attach the patch ends to. If the ceiling is plaster, drill ⅛ in. holes to find the width of one piece of lath, usually 1½ in. wide. You'll reduce patching if you can remove just one lath strip. See Chapter 15 for more about patching plaster and drywall.

PRO TIP

Test new outlets before patching walls or ceilings. If the outlet's not correctly wired, you can repair it without having to rip out a newly installed new patch to get access.

This is a low-voltage recessed lighting fixture, as seen from above. Adjustable hanger bars mount the fixture to the ceiling joists. Because this first-floor ceiling will not be insulated, it's acceptable to use a non-IC-rated fixture.

Fishing Cable to a Ceiling Fixture

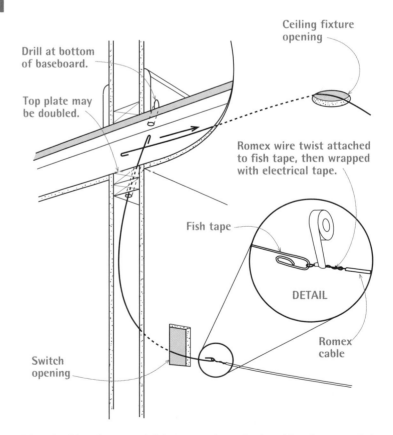

Drill at bottom of baseboard.

Top plate may be doubled.

Ceiling fixture opening

Romex wire twist attached to fish tape, then wrapped with electrical tape.

Fish tape

DETAIL

Romex cable

Switch opening

After catching the second fish tape, twist a single cable wire around that tape so it won't separate; then wrap electrical tape around the splice so it will pull smoothly through holes.

12 Plumbing

Builders have benefited greatly from the standardization of building materials, and nowhere is this more true than in plumbing. Whereas a plumber once had to fashion waste systems from cast iron, oakum, and melted lead, today one needs little more than plastic pipe and solvent-based cement. Such improved technology enables more people to understand, repair, and install plumbing. Would-be plumbers should do two things:

▶ Learn the vocabulary. Some people feel intimidated by the plethora of plumbing terms, especially fitting names. But there's actually a logic to all those names, once you learn what a part does and why it is shaped as it is. Besides, you'll get better service from plumbing-supply clerks if you can speak their language.

▶ Consult local plumbing codes before beginning a project. Codes protect your health and that of your neighbors. They spell out when you need permits, what materials you may use, and at what stages the work must be inspected. There is no national code, so most local building departments often follow the Uniform Plumbing Code (UPC) or the International Residential Code (IRC). Get a copy of local plumbing codes from your building department.

Recommended further reading: Merle Henkenius's *Plumbing* (Creative Homeowner) and two books by Peter Hemp, *Installing and Repairing Plumbing Fixtures* and *Plumbing a House* (both The Taunton Press).

Mother Nature knows a thing or two about plumbing. The larger midrib of this leaf is a naturally occurring trunk line, with smaller veins branching off to supply the leaf.

NEED A Permit?

Local plumbing codes vary greatly. In general, you don't need a permit if you replace a fixture, such as a sink, toilet, or washing machine, without changing existing pipes. However, if you want to add new fixtures or move existing ones, you'll need a permit because you'll need to change pipes.

Replacing a water heater also requires a permit —even if you connect to existing pipes. Here, the issue is safety: Inspectors want to make sure that gas- and oil-fired water heaters are properly vented and that electric heaters are correctly wired. They'll also check that temperature- and pressure-relief (TPR) valves, which keep water heaters from exploding, are correctly rated and installed.

An Overview
of Plumbing Systems

A plumbing system is a loop of sorts, created by supply (or delivery) pipes that carry potable water to the house and its fixtures and by *drainage, waste, and venting* (DWV) pipes that carry waste water, effluvia, and sewage gases away from the *fixtures*—sinks, toilets, lavatories, washing machines, and so on.

These two systems within a system are quite different from each other. DWV pipes are larger and must slope downward so wastes can fall freely (by gravity) and sewage gases can rise through vents. Consequently, large DWV pipes can be difficult to route through framing. By contrast, smaller water-supply pipes are easy to run through studs and joists, and they deliver water under pressure, so there's no need to slope them.

THE WATER SUPPLY

The pipe that delivers water to a house (from a city water main or an individual well) is called the *service pipe*. So it won't freeze, a service pipe must run below the frost line and enter a building through its foundation. Typically, a 1-in. service pipe is controlled by a *main shutoff valve* shortly after it enters a building; but municipal hookups may enter a water meter first. Plumbing codes may also require a *pressure-reducing valve* if water pressure is more than 80 psi (pounds per square inch).

On the other side of the shutoff valve, the service pipe continues as the *main supply pipe,* commonly ¾ in. in diameter. At some point, the main supply pipe enters a tee fitting, at which point it splits, with one leg continuing on as a *cold-water trunk line* and the other feeding into the water heater, where it emerges as the *hot-water trunk line.* From the ¾-in. hot and cold trunks run various ½-in. *branch lines* that serve fixture groups. Finally, individual *risers* (supply tubes) run from branch lines to fixtures. Risers are ⅜ in. or ½ in. in diameter and connect to fixtures with threaded fittings. By decreasing in diameter as they get farther from the trunk lines, supply pipes help maintain constant water pressure.

Before the 1950s, supply pipes were usually galvanized steel, joined by threaded fixtures, but steel pipes corrode and corrosion constricts flow. Consequently, rigid copper piping, which corrodes more slowly, soon replaced galvanized. Joined by *soldering* (sweat fitting), copper was also easier to install and has been the dominant supply piping since the 1950s. Rigid plastic pipe, especially CPVC (chlorinated polyvinyl chloride), has gained market share because it is corrosion

The Water-Supply System

Originating at a service pipe from the street (or from a well), the main supply pipe splits at a T-fitting, with one leg feeding cold-water trunk lines and the other entering the water heater to emerge as the hot-water trunk line.

resistant, less expensive than copper, and easily assembled with solvent cement. But it may be PEX (cross-linked polyethylene) flexible piping that will finally dethrone King Copper (PEX is discussed later in this chapter).

DRAINAGE, WASTE, AND VENTING

The DWV system carries wastes and sewage gases away from the house.

▶ **Every fixture has a drain trap designed to remain filled with water after the fixture empties. This residual water keeps sewage gases from rising into living spaces. (Toilets have integral traps.) As trap arms leave individual fixtures, they empty into branch drains or directly into a soil stack, which, at its base, turns and becomes the main drain. The main drain then discharges into a city sewer main or a septic tank.**

▶ Drainpipes may also be differentiated according to the wastes they carry: soil pipes and soil stacks carry fecal matter and urine, whereas waste pipes carry waste water but not soil. Stacks are vertical pipes, although they may jog slightly to avoid obstacles.

▶ Venting is the *V* in DWV. Without venting, wastes would either not fall at all or, in falling, would suck the water out of fixture traps, allowing sewage gases to enter living spaces. Vents admit an amount of air equal to that displaced by the falling water. Thus every fixture must be vented. In most cases, the trap arm exits into a tee fitting whose bottom leg is a branch drain and whose upper leg is a branch vent. Branch vents continue upward, often joining other fixture vents, until they join a vent stack, which exits through the roof.

Because vents must admit enough air to offset that displaced by falling water, vents are approximately the same size as their companion drains. Branch vents and drains are usually 1½-in. or 2-in. pipes, and main stacks and drains are 3 in. Minimums are indicated in "Minimum Drain, Trap, and Vent Sizes," on p. 281. *Important:* Drainpipes must slope downward at least ¼ in. per foot so that wastes will be carried out; vent pipes usually slope *upward* a minimun of ⅛ in. per foot.

DWV pipes may be of any number of materials. Thus an older house may have drain and vent pipes with sections of cast iron, galvanized steel, copper, or plastic. Because some of these materials are also used for supply, let size be your guide: If an existing pipe's diameter is 1¼ in. to 4 in., it's a drain or vent pipe. DWV pipes installed these days are mostly plastic: white PVC (polyvinyl chloride) or black ABS (acrylonitrile butadiene styrene). Fortunately, there is a host of ingenious fittings that enable you to tightly connect these various materials, should you need to. *Note:* If sound suppression is an issue, you should insulate plastic pipes or install cast iron.

The DWV System (Drainage, Waste, Venting)

Stack vent

Branch vent

2 in.

Vent stack

1½ in. 1½ in.

2 in.

2 in.

Branch drain

2 in. 2 in.

Soil stack

1½ in.

3 in. minimum

To sewer or septic tank

Main drain or building drain

Drainpipes must slope downward at least ¼ in. per foot so wastes can fall freely. Vent pipes must slope upward at least ⅛ in. per foot so sewage gases can rise and exit the building.

A Drain Trap

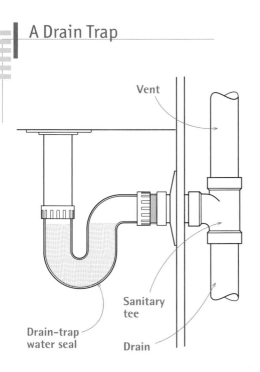

Vent

Sanitary tee

Drain-trap water seal

Drain

Water traps seal sewage gases from living spaces, but they need vents to operate properly. Without incoming air from the vent, falling wastes could suck the water out of traps.

Planning

If you'll be adding or moving fixtures, you'll need to install pipes, and that will require permits and planning. Start by assessing the condition of existing pipes (see Chapter 1), which you can connect to if they are in good shape. Create a scale drawing of proposed changes, assemble a materials list, and then ask a plumbing-supply store clerk or a plumber to review both. If you're well organized, clerks at supply stores will usually be glad to help. However, if you need help understanding your existing system, hire a plumber to assess your system. He or she can also explain how to apply for a permit and which inspections will be required.

IS THERE ENOUGH ROOM?

If you're adding a bathroom, first consider the overall size of the room. If there's not enough space, you may need to move walls. Layouts with pipes located in one wall are usually the least disruptive and most economical because pipes can be lined up in one plane. On the other hand, layouts with pipes in three walls are rarely sensible or feasible unless there's unfinished space above or below in which to run pipes.

FIXTURE ROUGH-IN DIMENSIONS

Once you have a general idea if there's enough room, focus on the code requirements for each fixture, which dictate where fixtures and pipes

Minimum Bathroom Dimensions

PIPES IN ONE WALL

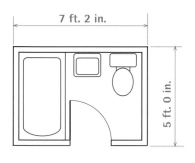

7 ft. 2 in. — 5 ft. 0 in.

PIPES IN TWO WALLS

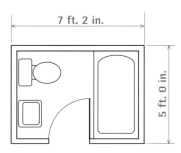

7 ft. 2 in. — 5 ft. 0 in.

PIPES IN THREE WALLS

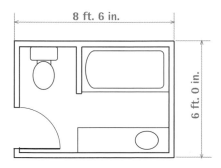

8 ft. 6 in. — 6 ft. 0 in.

FIVE FIXTURES

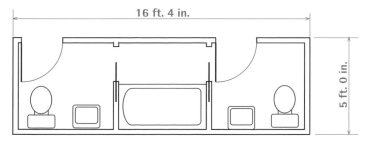

16 ft. 4 in. — 5 ft. 0 in.

must go. It would be aggravating and expensive if code inspectors insisted that you move fixtures after finish floors and walls had been put in place. So install fixtures and pipes to conform with code minimums. The drawings on these two pages show typical drainpipe and supply pipe centers for each fixture and, in most cases, minimum clearances required from walls, cabinets, and the like.

On toilets, the horn—the integral porcelain bell protruding from the bottom—centers in the floor flange. The flange, and the closet bend to which it attaches, should be centered 12 in. from the finish wall for most toilets or 12½ in. from an exposed stud wall. Codes require at least 15 in. clearance from the center of the toilet to walls or cabinets on both sides: In order words, install toilets in a space at least 30-in. wide. There must also be at least 24 in. clear space in front of the toilet.

Toilets with 10-in. and 14-in. rough-in dimensions are available to resolve thorny layout issues (such as an immovable beam underneath) or to replace nonstandard toilets. For example, if you replace a wall-hung toilet with a standard

(close-coupled) unit, there would be an ugly 2-in. gap between the toilet and the finish wall. By installing a *14-in. rough toilet,* whose base is longer, you can use the existing floor flange and eliminate the gap behind the toilet.

Install water-supply risers on the wall behind the toilet, 6 in. above the floor and 6 in. to the left of the drainpipe. If there's a functional riser sticking out of the floor, use it. But floor risers are seldom installed today because they make mopping the floor difficult. Clearances around bidets are the same as those for toilets.

Lavatories and pedestal sinks should be a comfortable height for users. Typically, lavatory rims are set 32 in. to 34. in. above the finish floor; but if a family is tall, raise the lav. (But if you do, remember to raise drain and supply pipe holes an equal amount.) Codes require at least 18 in. clearance in front of a sink; 24 in. is better.

Lavatory drains are typically 18 in. above the floor and centered under the lavatory, although adjustable P-traps afford some flexibility in positioning drains. Center supply pipes under the lav, 24 in. above the floor, with holes spaced 4 in. on center. Pedestal sink drains are housed in the pedestal, so tolerances are tight; follow the manufacturer's installation instructions when positioning pipes.

Bathtubs and showers vary greatly, so follow the manufacturer's guides when positioning the pipes. Most standard tubs are 30 in. to 32 in. wide and 5 ft. to 6 ft. long. Codes require a minimum of 18 in. clearance along a tub's open side(s); 24 in. is better.

Freestanding tubs have exposed drain and overflow assemblies, so their 1½-in. drains can be easily positioned to avoid joists and other design constraints. Standard tubs require a hole approximately 12 in. by 12 in. cut into the subfloor under the tub drain end, to accommodate the drain and overflow assembly. If an existing joist is in the path of the tub drain, you may need to cut through the joist and add doubled headers, as explained further on p. 287.

Positioning supply pipes and valve stems is easier because they're smaller and typically centered on an end wall—although, again, follow the manufacturer's rough-in dimensions for code-required pressure-balancing valves and the like. Place the shower arm 72 in. to 78 in. above the floor so taller users won't need to stoop when taking a shower. Place the tub spout 22 in. high. Tub faucet handles (and mixing valves) are customarily 6 in. above the spout.

Toilet Rough-In Dimensions

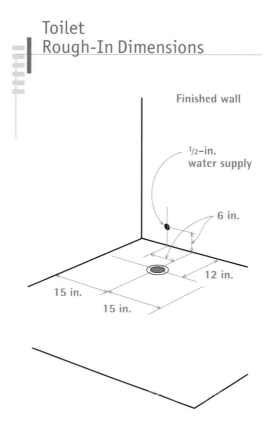

Finished wall

½-in. water supply

6 in.

12 in.

15 in.

15 in.

Center the toilet drain 12 in. from the finished wall behind the unit. Allow at least 15 in. of clearance on both sides of the toilet, measured from the center of the drain.

Lavatory
Rough-In Dimensions

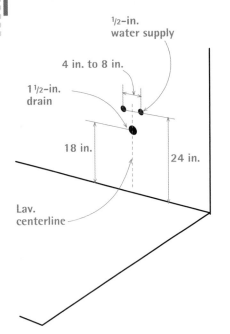

½-in. water supply

4 in. to 8 in.

1½-in. drain

18 in.

24 in.

Lav. centerline

Kitchen Sink
Rough-In Dimensions

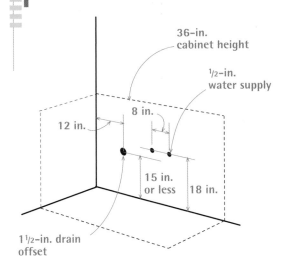

36-in. cabinet height

½-in. water supply

8 in.

12 in.

15 in. or less

18 in.

1½-in. drain offset

Double sinks are most often installed in kitchens, so the drain is often offset under one sink, as shown in the drawing on p. 295. Braided stainless-steel supply lines are very flexible, so you can rough-in water supply stub-outs at any convenient height; 18 in. is common.

Kitchen sinks frequently have double basins, so you can center or offset drainpipes. In standard 36-in.-wide base cabinet, the drain is often offset so that it is 12 in. from one cabinet sidewall, leaving room to hook up a garbage disposer. To make cabinet installation easier, have the drain exit into the wall rather than the floor. A drain that exits 15 in. above the finish floor will accommodate the height of a garbage disposal (11 in.) and the average depth (9 in.) of a kitchen sink. Sink faucet holes are typically spaced 8 in. on center, so align supply pipes with their centerline, roughly 2 in. above the drain height. Supply-pipe height is not critical because risers easily accommodate varying heights.

SKETCHING LAYOUTS

Make a separate sketch of each floor's plumbing; include the basement and attic, too. The easiest way to do this to create an accurate outline of the house's footprint, using graph paper and a scale of ¼ in. per 1 ft. Then use tracing-paper overlays for each floor's plumbing layout. Indicate existing fixtures, drains, supply pipes, water-using appliances, and the water heater. Where pipes are exposed, note the size and dimension of drains and stacks and where the supply pipes exit into

Tub/Shower
Rough-In Dimensions

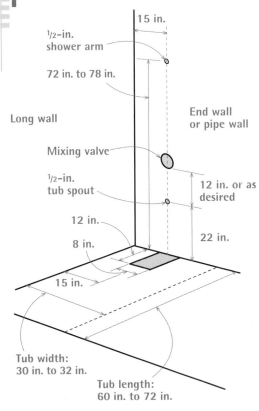

15 in.

½-in. shower arm

72 in. to 78 in.

Long wall

Mixing valve

½-in. tub spout

12 in.

8 in.

15 in.

End wall or pipe wall

12 in. or as desired

22 in.

Tub width: 30 in. to 32 in.

Tub length: 60 in. to 72 in.

The tub drain and stubs in the end wall should be centered 15 in. from the long wall. Mixing valves are typically set 12 in. above the tub spout, whereas individual valve stems are set 6 in. above the spout, 8 in. o.c., or follow the manufacturer's recommended rough-in specs.

Framing Considerations

After positioning fixture drains, see if there's a joist in the drain path. If there is, and you can't reposition the fixture, cut through the joist and install doubled headers to redistribute the load. If possible, avoid running larger drainpipes perpendicular to joists and studs because drilling and cutting weaken the framing. But if drill you must, "Notching and Drilling Limits," on p. 288, shows acceptable hole sizes and locations; "Maximum Sizes for Holes and Notches," on p. 287 will also be helpful.

The trickiest pipe to route is a 3-in. drain, whose outer diameter is 3½ in. If that pipe runs 12 ft. horizontally, sloping ¼ in. per foot, it will drop 3 in. during its run. If it runs between enclosed joists, the pipe will need at least 6½ in. height—plus the height of any fittings. If floor joists are nominally 2×8s (actually, 1½ in. by 7½ in.), things could get pretty tight. When planning pipe runs, consider pipe dimension, slope, space for fittings, and the actual size of the lumber in your calculations.

Plumber's Isometric Sketch of Three-Fixture Bathroom

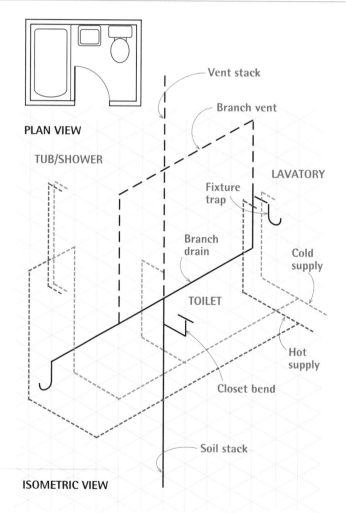

PLAN VIEW

TUB/SHOWER

LAVATORY

Vent stack

Branch vent

Fixture trap

Branch drain

Cold supply

TOILET

Hot supply

Closet bend

Soil stack

ISOMETRIC VIEW

Try to obtain sheets of plumber's isometric paper so you can show bathroom rough-ins in three dimensions. Art or engineering supply stores may carry the paper, but the Internet is probably a better bet.

the floor above. Especially note the location of 3-in. main drains and vents: If you can cluster fixtures around larger DWV pipes within a room—or from floor to floor—you'll shorten the distance that fixture drains must travel and thus reduce the amount of framing you may have to cut or drill when running the new pipes.

If you're moving or adding fixtures, make separate floor sketches for them, too. By laying tracing-paper sketches of old and new plumbing atop each other, you can quickly see if fixtures cluster and, if you're adding fixtures to an existing system, the closest part of a drain or supply pipe to connect to and extend from. Plumbers use isometric paper to draw pipe runs, as shown in "Plumber's Isometric Sketch of a Three-Fixture Bathroom," at left, but any to-scale sketch will give you an approximate idea how long pipe runs will be. Sketches also tell you where you'll need fittings because the pipes change direction, connect to branches, or decrease in size.

Tools

With a modest tool collection, you'll be ready for most plumbing tasks.

Pipe wrenches tighten and loosen threaded metal joints, such as ¾-in. nipples (short pipe lengths) screwed into a water heater, galvanized pipe unions, and so on. A pair of 10-in. or 12-in. pipe wrenches should handle most tasks. Get two: Most of the time, you'll need one wrench to hold the pipe and the other to turn the fitting.

Adjustable wrenches (also called Crescent wrenches) have smooth jaws that grip but won't mar chrome nuts and faucet trim. Get several: A 4-in. adjustable wrench is right for the closet bolts that anchor toilet bowls, a 12-in. wrench gives extra leverage for stubborn nuts, and an 8-in. wrench is appropriate for almost everything else.

Strap wrenches aren't a must-have tool but are useful when you need to grip polished pipe without scarring it.

Slide-nut (sliding-jaw) *pliers* are good utility tools for holding nuts, loosening pipe stubs, and holding a pipe section while it's being soldered.

The jaws of *locking pliers* (or Vise-Grip pliers) adjust and clamp down on fittings, for example, so you can have both hands free to hold a torch and apply solder.

Basin wrenches are about the only tools that can reach water-supply nuts on the underside of sinks and lavs, where supply pipes attach to threaded faucet stems.

Tub-strainer wrenches tighten tub strainer and tailpiece assemblies.

No-hub torque wrenches tighten stainless-steel band clamps on *no-hub couplings*. Many plumbers use a cordless drill/driver to do most of the tightening, but code requires that final tightening be done by hand.

Pipe cutters (also called wheeled tubing cutters) are the best tools for a clean, square cut on copper pipe. Tighten the cutter so that its cutting wheel barely scores the pipe; then rotate the tool around the pipe, gradually tightening until the cut is complete. Many types have a foldaway deburring tool. Use a *close-quarters cutter* (thumb cutter) where there's no room for a full-size one. If you're installing CPVC plastic supply pipe, use *tubing shears* for clean, quick cuts. A *hacksaw* works, but not as well.

A *reaming tool* (if your cutter doesn't have one attached) is used to clean metal burrs after cutting copper. Use a *round wire brush* to polish the inside of copper fittings after reaming and *plumber's sand cloth* to polish the pipe ends. If you're cutting plastic pipe, use a *rounded file* to remove burrs—the steel jaws of an adjustable wrench also work well for deburring plastic pipe.

Wide-roll pipe cutters open wide to receive the larger diameters of plastic DWV pipe. *Plastic-pipe saws* have fine teeth that cut ABS and PVC pipe cleanly—and squarely, if used with a miter box. If you need to cut into cast iron, rent a *snap cutter*, also known as a cast-iron cutter. It's the only tool that cuts cast iron easily. Some models have ratchet heads for working in confined places.

A *cordless drill* and *cordless reciprocating saws* are must-haves if you're working around metal pipes that could become energized by electricity and when working in tight, often damp crawl spaces. Old lumber can be hard stuff to drill or cut, so 14.4-volt cordless tools are minimal. Cord-less drills are perfect for attaching plumber's strap, drilling holes in laminate countertops, and so on.

If you need to drill 2-in. (or bigger) holes, use a *corded drill*. Heavy-duty drilling takes sustained power and more torque than most cordless drills have. A ½-in. right-angle drill supplies the muscle you need in close quarters.

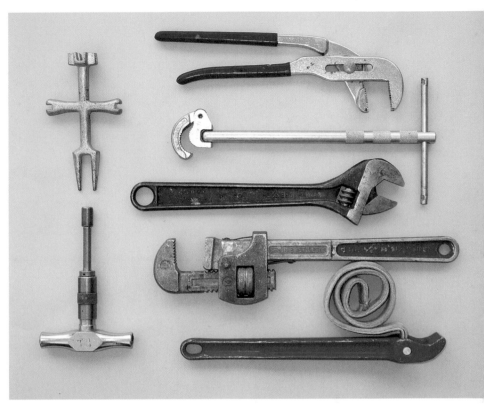

Jaws VII: wrenches and pliers. Clockwise, from upper left: tub-strainer wrench, slide-nut or sliding-jaw pliers, basin wrench, adjustable wrench, pipe wrench, strap wrench (won't mar polished pipe), and no-hub torque wrench.

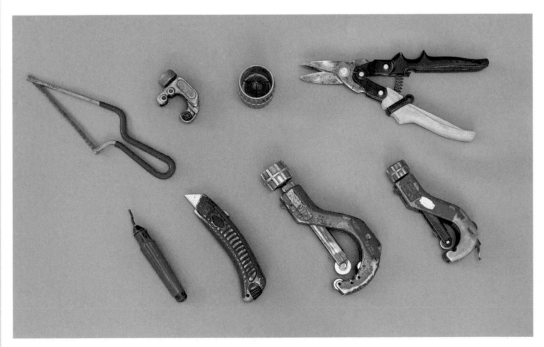

Cutting and reaming tools. Top row, from left: miniature hacksaw, close-quarters cutter, combo chamfer and reamer (cleans burrs from pipe ends after cutting), and aviation snips. Bottom row: reamer, utility knife, large-wheeled tubing cutter (cuts up to 2-in. plastic pipe), and wheeled tubing cutter. The cutting wheels can be changed for different pipe materials.

Miscellaneous tools. Clockwise, from left: torpedo level, hammer, 14.4-volt cordless drill, flint and steel striker (lights torch), MAPP gas soldering torch, tape measure, and plumber's sand cloth (used before fluxing pipe).

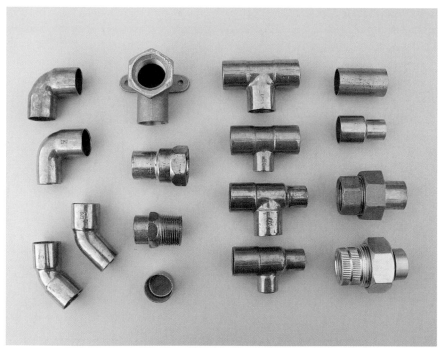

Water-supply fittings. First column, from top: ¾-in. 90, ¾-in. street 90, ¾-in. street 45, and ¾-in. 45. Second column, from top: ¾-in. C × F (copper-by-female) drop-ear 90, ¾-in. C × F adapter, ¾-in. C × M (copper- by-male) adapter, and ¾-in. cap. Third column, from top: ¾-in. tee, ¾-in. by ½-in. tee, ¾-in. by ½-in. by ¾-in. tee, and ¾-in. by ½-in. by ½-tee. Fourth column, from top: ¾-in. coupling, ¾-in by ½-in. reducing coupling, ¾-in. C × F union, and ¾-in. dielectric union.

MAPP (methylacetylene propadiene) *gas torches* have generally replaced propane units (once popular with do-it-yourselfers) and even larger professional rigs with tanks, hoses, and fancy nozzles. MAPP gas torches are perfect for soldering the ½-in. or ¾-in. fittings encountered most often in house plumbing.

Nonasbestos flame shields protect wood framing when soldering joints. It is also important to have a *fire extinguisher* nearby.

Your plumbing kit should also include a handful of other tools. *Aviation snips* are used for cutting perforated strap and trimming gaskets, and a *torpedo level* helps with leveling *stub-outs* (pipe stubs protruding into a room), sinks, and toilet bowls. You'll also want a *hacksaw, screwdriver with interchangeable magnetic bits, utility knife,* and *hammer.*

Working with Copper Water-Supply Pipe

This section focuses on installing rigid copper water pipe: It's strong, easily worked, approved by virtually all codes, and represents nearly 90 percent of residential installations. That noted, you should also consider reading about PEX flexible tubing on p. 279.

Fittings

If you divide fittings into a few categories, their many names start to make sense. Because they do similar things, supply-pipe and DWV fittings often share names.

Fittings join pipes. The simplest fitting is a *coupling,* which joins two straight lengths of pipe. A *reducing coupling* joins different size pipes. A *repair coupling* has no internal stop midway, so it can slide all the way onto a pipe, then slide back over a new piece of pipe inserted to repair a damaged section. A *union* is a coupling you can disconnect.

Fittings change direction. The most common directional fitting is a *90° elbow,* also known simply as a *90* or an *ell.* For a more gradual turn, use a *45° elbow,* also called a *45* or a *⅛ bend.* A *street ell* is a 90° elbow with one hubless end, which can fit directly into another fitting's hub. Ditto, a *street 45.*

Tees join three pipes. *Tees* (also spelled T's) allow you to run branch pipes to individual fixtures or fixture groups. *Reducing tees* accept different size pipes. If you want to sound like a pro, "read a tee" by noting its run (length) dimension first (in inches), then its branch leg. If both ends of the run are the same size, mention that number only once, as in ¾ by ½. But if two legs of a tee reduce, cite all three of the tee's dimensions, for example: a ¾ by ½ by ½.

Adapters join different types of pipe. A *sweat/male adapter* has a soldered end and a

Plumbing Safety

▶ Get a work permit and a copy of current plumbing codes from your local building department. Follow the codes closely; they're there to protect you.

▶ Get a tetanus shot before you start, and dress for dirty work.

▶ Wear protective eyewear when using power tools, chiseling, soldering, and striking with hammers—in short, for most plumbing tasks. Wear heavy gloves when handling drainpipe and disposable plastic gloves when working with solvent-based cements or soldering. Wear a respirator mask (not a mere dust mask) when soldering or working around existing soil pipes; P100 filters are the standard protection.

▶ Use only cordless power tools when cutting into supply pipe. If a power tool shorts out in that situation, it could be fatal. 🚫 Before cutting into finish surfaces, shut off the electrical power to nearby outlets, and test with a voltage tester, as shown on p.235, to be sure power is really off.

▶ Ensure good ventilation when joining pipes because heated solder and solvent-based cements give off noxious fumes. Make sure you have adequate lighting.

▶ When soldering joints in place, place a nonasbestos flame shield behind the fittings to avoid igniting the wood framing. Have a plant spritzer, filled with water, on hand to dampen the wood if you must solder fittings close to framing; make sure there's a fire extinguisher on site. Molten flux or solder can burn you, so be careful.

▶ When connecting to existing DWV pipes, plan the task carefully. Flush pipes with clean water beforehand and have parts ready so that you can close things up as soon as possible. To avoid weakening nearby joints, be sure to support pipes before cutting them.

▶ Be fastidious about washing well after handling contaminated waste pipes and chemicals.

▶ If you smell gas in a home, stop working: Running equipment or doing soldering could spark an explosion. If you can quickly locate the gas shutoff valve outside, shut it off. In any event, clear everyone from the house at once and call the local gas utility.

When soldering copper, prevent fires by placing a nonasbestos flame shield between the fittings and wood framing.

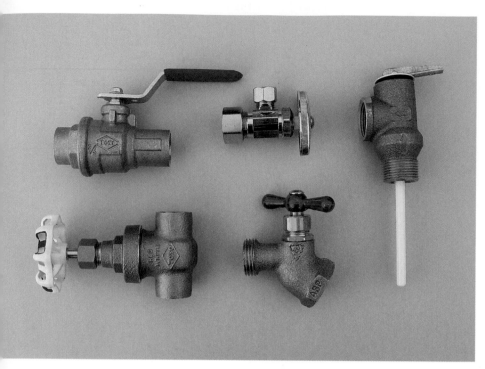

Water–supply valves. Clockwise, from upper left: Lever–handle ball valve, ⅝-in. by ⅜-in. angle stop, TPR valve, female hose bib, and gate valve.

Socket Depths of ABS/PVC Fittings*

SOCKET DIAMETER (in.)	SOCKET DEPTH (in.)
1½	¾
2	⅞
3	1½

Fitting sockets vary, always measure depth to be sure.

threaded end. A *sweat/female adapter* has a threaded receiving end. Adaptors are also called *transition fittings* because they allow a transition in joining, as just described, or a transition in pipe materials. A *dielectric union* can join galvanized and copper, without the electrolytic corrosion that usually occurs when you join dissimilar metals.

Valves are specialized fittings with moving parts. *Gate valves* are the most common type of *shutoff valve,* although *lever-handled ball valves* are gaining popularity because they are easier to operate. *Hose bibs* have a threaded outlet that you can screw a garden hose to. *Angle stops* are shutoff valves that control water flow to lavatories, sinks, bidets, and toilets. TPR (temperature- and pressure-relief) valves are spring-loaded safety valves that keep water heaters from exploding should the water get too hot or the tank pressure too great.

WORKING WITH COPPER SUPPLY PIPE

Type M rigid copper is the most commonly used copper supply pipe in houses, although type L, which is thicker, may also be specified. Type K, the thickest of the three, is usually specified for commercial and industrial jobs.

To cut rigid copper, place a tubing cutter on the pipe, so that its cutting wheel is perpendicular to the pipe. Score the pipe lightly at first, till the cutting wheel tracks in a groove. Gradually tighten the cutting jaw as you rotate the tool, until you cut through. If you tighten the tool too aggressively, you will flatten the pipe or score erratically, thus creating a weak joint.

When the cut is complete, clean the end of the pipe with the deburring attachment on the cutter so that you get a good, solid joint. Leftover burrs also increase turbulence and thus decrease flow through the pipe. Use *plumber's sand cloth* or

Measuring and Fitting Pipe

When measuring water-supply or DWV pipe runs, keep in mind that most pipe slides into fitting sockets. The depth of the socket is its *seating distance* (seating depth), which you must add to the face-to-face measurements between pipe fittings. When running pipe between copper fittings with a seating depth of ½ in., for example, add 1 in. to the overall measurement. Rigid ¾-in. copper fittings have a ¾-in. seating depth.

As important, after you dry-fit pipes so fittings point in the correct direction, use a grease pencil or a builder's crayon to create alignment marks on the pipes and fittings. That way you'll be sure the fittings are pointing in the right direction when you make the final connections. Alignment marks are particularly important when cementing plastic pipe because you must turn plastic pipes one-quarter turn after inserting them into fittings; the marks tell you when to stop turning.

Pipe Fitting

Socket depth

Alignment marks

When measuring pipe, allow for socket depths. Also when dry-fitting pipe assemblies, draw alignment marks on pipes and fittings to help you point the fittings in the right direction when assembled. This is particularly helpful when giving plastic fittings one-quarter turn after glue is applied.

emery paper to polish both ends of the pipe, and a round wire brush to clean the insides of fittings.

To solder copper pipe, first use a flux brush to apply self-tinning flux (soldering paste) to the outside of the pipe and the inside of the fitting. Then slide the fitting over the pipe. If the fitting is a directional fitting, such as a tee or an elbow, make sure that the fitting points in the correct direction.

Heat the fitting (*not* the pipe), moving the soldering torch so that all sides of the fitting receive heat directly. The flux will bubble. From time to time, remove the torch, and touch solder to the fitting seam. When the fitting is hot enough, the solder will liquefy when touched to it. After a few trials, you'll know when a fitting is hot enough. When the fitting is hot, some fluxes change color, from milky brown to dull silver.

Two passes with the solder, completely around the joint, will make a tight seal; more than two passes is a waste. The solder is sucked into the joint, so don't worry if you don't see a thick fillet of solder around the joint. Let solder cool before putting pressure on a joint. After a soldered joint

CUTTING AND SOLDERING COPPER

1. Hold the tubing cutter square to the pipe and score it lightly at first. Once the cutting wheel tracks in a groove, gradually tighten the cutting jaw as you revolve the tool.

2. Ream the inside of the pipe to remove burrs left by cutting.

3. Use a strip of plumber's sand cloth to polish the pipe ends slightly beyond the fittings' seating depths. Put on clean disposable gloves after polishing, because skin oils can impair a solder bond.

4. Use an acid brush to apply flux liberally to the outside of the pipe ends; put a thin, even coat on the inside of pipe fittings, all the way to the bottom of the fitting sockets.

5. Heat the fitting—not the pipe—and apply solder to the lowest fitting hub first. Periodically remove the torch and touch the solder tip to the fitting joint. When the fitting is hot enough, the solder will liquefy and disappear into the joint. (Note: The flame shield behind the fitting was set aside temporarily to get a clearer photo.)

has cooled for a minute, you can immerse it in water to cool it completely; but be careful when handling hot metal.

Soldering in tight spaces can't always be avoided. If a fitting has several incoming pipes—at a tee, for example—try to solder all pipes at the same time. That is, reheating a fitting to add pipes will weaken earlier soldered joints. Clean and flux the pipes, insert them in the fitting, and keep the torch moving so you heat both ends of the fitting equally. If you must reheat a fitting to add a pipe later, wrap the already soldered joint in wet rags to keep its solder from melting. When soldering close to wood, wet the wood first with a plant spritzer filled with water and then use a flame shield to avoid scorching or igniting it.

When space is tight, presolder sections in a vise. Then, when placing the section in its final position, you'll have only a joint or two to solder. If one of the materials being joined might be damaged by heat, solder the copper parts first, allowing them to cool, before making mechanical connections to the heat-sensitive material. For example, if you need to connect copper supply to a pump outtake with plastic or adapters, solder the male (protruding) or female (receiving) adapter to the copper pipe before screwing it in (or on) the pump outtake.

Finally, before soldering pipe to a ball valve or a gate valve, close the valve completely. Otherwise, solder can run inside and keep the valve from closing fully. However, when soldering a shower's pressure-balancing valve or a tempering valve, follow the manufacturer's instructions. Finally, it's helpful to have unions near most valves so that sections can be disconnected without needing to undo soldered joints.

FLEXIBLE COPPER TUBING

Because flexible copper tubing can be bent and run through tight spaces, it's used primarily for short runs to dishwashers (½ in.), ice makers (¼ in. or ⁵⁄₁₆ in.), and so on. Chromed copper tubing is commonly used when supply risers will be exposed because it looks good. Flexible tubing is softer than rigid copper pipe, so take pains when you cut it not to collapse the tubing walls by turning a pipe cutter too aggressively. And use a special, sleeve-like *tubing bender* to shape it so you don't crimp it, as shown in the photo at right.

Flexible copper tubing is most often connected either with *compression fittings* or *flared fittings*. A compression fitting features a *ferrule* of

Copper Pipe: Disconnecting, Reconnecting, and Repairing

To disconnect a soldered fitting, apply heat till the solder melts. Then gently tap the fitting off the pipe. When the metal is cool, clean the pipe end, reflux, reheat, and solder on a new fitting. Unless the fitting is an expensive one, such as a gate valve, don't reuse fittings that have already been soldered.

When disconnecting a fitting on an existing supply line, drain the pipe first; otherwise, the solder won't melt. Draining and reconnecting will be much easier if the pipe section can be isolated with a shutoff valve, but sometimes old valves don't shut perfectly. In that event, ball up a piece of white bread and stick it in the pipe to block the trickle while you solder. Once the water runs again, the bread will dissolve and flush out.

Finally, here's a fix for split pipes that doesn't require soldering at all: Cut out the damaged section of pipe and slide a *compression repair coupling* over the cut pipe ends. (The coupling's inner diameter is the same as the ½-in. rigid copper's outer diameter.) Use a pair of adjustable wrenches to tighten the compression fittings on both ends of the coupling, and you're done.

Repairing pipes split by freezing water is no big deal with a compression repair coupling. Each end of the coupling compresses a brass ferrule to create a watertight seal without soldering.

A Compression Fitting

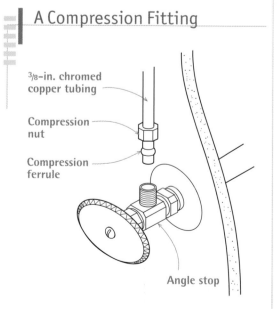

³⁄₈-in. chromed copper tubing

Compression nut

Compression ferrule

Angle stop

Use a tubing bender to shape chrome supply risers; the wire coils of the bender support the soft tubing and keep it from buckling as you gradually shape it.

soft metal that is compressed between a set of matched nuts. A flared fitting requires that you flare the tubing ends with a special tool. When using either type of connector, remember to slide nuts onto the tubing before attaching a ferrule or flaring an end. Both types of connection are easy to disconnect, and so are used where repairs may be expected, such as the supply line to a toilet. Don't reuse ferrules, however; replace them if you need to disconnect fittings.

In most situations, braided *stainless-steel supply lines* are a better choice than flexible copper tubing: Braided lines are strong, look good, and can be connected and disconnected as often as needed.

GALVANIZED STEEL PIPE

Galvanized pipe corrodes and constricts, reducing flow and water pressure, so it is no longer installed as water-supply pipe. If your existing system is galvanized and the water flow is weak, replace it as soon as possible. If you're not quite ready to rip out and replace all of your galvanized pipe, you can replace or extend sections with rigid copper. However, you must use a *dielectric union* (see the photo on p. 272) to join copper sections to steel. Otherwise, electrolysis will take place between the two metals, and corrosion will accelerate.

Today, galvanized pipe is largely limited to gas-supply service. Because of safety considerations and the difficulty of threading pipe without a power threader, *have a licensed plumber install gas-supply service pipes.* A plumber will install *gas shutoff valves* to gas-supply *stubs;* short lengths of flexible *gas-supply pipe* run from there to a fixture.

Most plumbing codes allow CPVC for hot- and cold-water applications, but check with local authorities to be sure. CPVC is a good choice for hard-water areas, because—unlike copper—CPVC won't be corroded by chemicals in the water. *Note:* CPVC is a different material from PVC, which is widely used as drain and waste pipe; PVC may not be used as supply pipe, however, because it releases carcinogens.

That noted, working with CPVC supply pipe is much like cutting and joining plastic DWV pipes, explained at some length later in this chapter. The main difference is that waste pipes are larger. Briefly, here's how to join CPVC: Cut the pipe ends square using a plastic-pipe saw or plastic-pipe cutting shears. Clean the pipe ends as well as the inside of the fitting. Next, apply solvent-based cement to each. Insert the pipe into the fitting, turning either the pipe or the fitting a quarter turn in *one direction only* to spread the cement. Finally, allow the glued joints to set adequately before putting pressure on the line.

Before installing CPVC, make sure that you have the adapters needed to join the new plastic pipes to existing metal pipes and fixtures.

Working with DWV Materials

As mentioned earlier, *DWV* stands for drainage, waste, and venting. ABS and PVC plastic pipe are by far the most common DWV materials, although cast-iron is still specified where sound suppression is important. Plastic pipe is strong, the most corrosion resistant of any DWV pipe; is easy to cut and assemble, using special solvent-based cements; is light enough for one person to handle; is reasonably priced; and is extremely slick inside, which ensures a good flow of wastes. It's by far the favorite DWV material of amateur plumbers—and many pros. But there are few disadvantages. Many codes prohibit using plastic pipe on exteriors because of durability and UV degradation issues, and if you don't spread the cement evenly or allow it to cure before stressing the joints, plastic can leak.

Cast iron is relatively corrosion resistant, though it will rust in time (decades); and its mass deadens the sound of running water. Though it's heavy to work with, it is still specified by many professionals for high-end jobs, where codes allow pipes on building exteriors, and where codes require cast-iron in multistory buildings. Ever since *no-hub couplings* replaced lead and oakum, cast iron has been easier to connect, but it still takes skill and strength to cut cleanly and support adequately. Consequently, it's rarely installed by amateur plumbers. Professionally

ELBOWS

Ell or 90

Vent ell

Street ell

Long-sweep ell

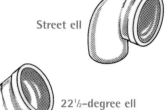

22½-degree ell

45° ell or 45

Closet bend
or 4x3

TEES OR TEE FITTINGS

Sanitary tee

Vent tee

Double tee or cross fitting

Reducing tee

POTPOURRI OF PARTS

P-trap (required for
all fixtures except a toilet)

Trap adapter has a
slip-nut coupling
with a plastic washer

WYE FITTINGS

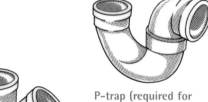

Wye fitting

Double wye

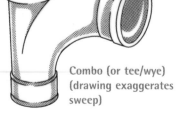

Combo (or tee/wye)
(drawing exaggerates
sweep)

Cleanout adapter

Cleanout plug

Closet flange, which
glues to a closet bend

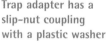

Coupling

The fittings shown are ABS plastic, but their shapes are essentially the same as those of copper and cast-iron DWV fittings of the same name. Drain fittings—such as the long-sweep ell, the combo and the sanitary tee—turn gradually so wastes can flow freely, without clogging. Whereas vent fittings have tighter turning radii because they carry only air. Finally, street fittings have one hubless end that fits directly into the hub of another fitting, which is useful when space is tight.

installed cast-iron systems cost, on average, 30 percent to 50 percent more than plastic pipe installations.

Copper DWV pipe is installed mostly on jobs with bottomless budgets. Copper is lightweight, durable, and undeniably handsome. Because its walls are relatively thin, copper DWV pipe is sometimes specified where there are tight turns. However, copper costs two to three times as much as a plastic DWV installation, and it's less corrosion resistant. Compared to cast iron, copper's thin walls don't suppress sound nearly as well.

PLASTIC DWV PIPE

Cut ABS or PVC pipe with a *plastic-pipe saw* and a miter box, or with a *wide-roll pipe cutter*. If you use a cutter, gradually tighten its cutting wheel after each revolution. Whatever tool you use to cut the pipe, use a utility knife, a rounded file, or a deburring tool to clean off burrs before sanding the cut lightly with emery paper. Use a clean cloth to wipe off any grit.

Dry-fit the pipes and fittings before cementing them together. Dry-fitting allows you to determine the exact direction you want the fitting to point, as well as the depth of the pipe's seat in the fitting. Pipe cement sets so quickly that there's no time to fine-tune fitting locations. Use a grease pencil or a builder's crayon to draw alignment marks on the pipe and the fitting; a yellow or white grease pencil works well on black ABS pipe.

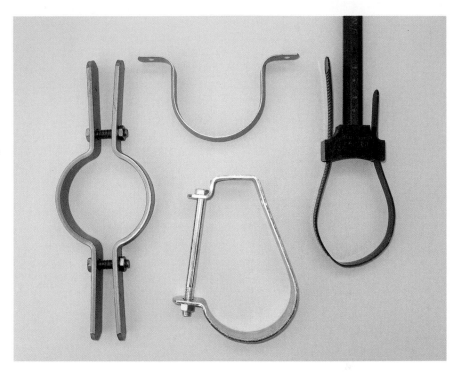

DWV pipe supports. Clockwise from left: riser clamp (stack clamp), steel rigid pipe strap (U-clamp), ABS pipe strap hanger, and J-clamp (often used with all-thread rod).

Here, two horizontal ABS lavatory drains meet at a figure-5 fitting, also called a double-combo. An ABS vent rises out the fitting's top hub, while the drain hub connects to a cast-iron stack via a no-hub coupling. A riser clamp supports the bottom of the cast-iron pipe, and steel nail plates protect the ABS.

PRO TIP

Have a friend help you set plastic DWV pipe. Although plastic is light, it is cumbersome. Once you've applied pipe cement, you have about 30 seconds to position the fittings before it sets. With two people working, one can hold a fitting while the other pushes the pipe and twists it one-quarter turn.

(See "Pipe Fitting," on p. 273). Then take apart the dry-fit pieces and apply the cement.

Apply plastic-pipe primer to the outside of the pipe and to the inside of the fitting. Then, using the cement applicator, apply a generous amount of solvent-based cement to the outside of the pipe and the inside of the fitting hub. Immediately insert the pipe into the fitting so that it seats completely. Then turn the fitting (or the pipe) a quarter turn in *one direction only*—stop when the alignment marks meet. When you are finished, the joint should have an even bead of cement all around. Allow the joint to set completely before putting pressure on it.

One-coat, no-primer plastic-pipe cements are new to the market: They seem promising but as yet are unproven for the long haul. Research them carefully before you commit.

CAST IRON

To the inexperienced eye, all cast iron looks the same, but it's not. If you lightly rap most cast iron with a rubberized tool handle, you'll hear a muffled thud; old "light iron," however, will reverberate somewhat, with a higher, tinny tone. If you suspect that you have light iron, which was widely installed in the northeastern United States till the 1940s, hire a plumber to assess and possibly cut it for you. If you try to cut light iron with a conventional snap cutter, the pipe may crush and collapse.

To cut into cast iron to extend a DWV system or replace a corroded fitting, rent a snap cutter. Many cast-iron joints are hubbed, in which a straight pipe end fits into the flared hub. But increasingly, sections of straight pipe are joined

After dry-fitting DWV pipes and putting alignment marks on the pipes and fittings, disconnect them and apply solvent-based cement to the outside of pipes and the inside of fittings. Wear plastic gloves to protect your skin.

Insert cemented plastic pipes all the way into the fitting and give a quarter turn to spread the cement evenly. The yellow crayon lines are the alignment marks.

A cast-iron snap cutter has beveled cutting wheels along the length of its chain.

PEX: The Rising Star of Supply Pipes

Cross-linked polyethylene (PEX) is a flexible tubing system that's been used in Europe for radiant heating and household plumbing since the 1960s, but it wasn't widely used in potable-water systems in North America till the late 1990s. Within 5 years, though, it had captured 7 percent of the market, even though it was unfamiliar to most plumbers and cost roughly the same as copper. Now approved by all major plumbing codes, PEX could overtake rigid copper pipe in popularity. And as PEX tubing, tools and techniques become more widespread, more and more weekend plumbers will be installing it. There's a lot to like.

PEX Advantages

▶ It installs quickly. Because lengths of flexible tubing easily turn corners and snake through walls, PEX systems require far fewer connections and fittings than do other materials. PEX tubing runs to fixtures from hot- and cold-water manifolds with multiple takeoffs. Most of the fitting is simple, consisting of crimping steel or copper rings onto tubing ends. Fewer fittings also mean fewer leaks and quicker installations.

▶ It's safe: No open flame, no flux, no solder, no pipe cements—in short, nothing toxic to leach into the water supplies. So there's no funny taste. Because it's chemically inert, PEX won't corrode, as metal pipe will, when installed in "aggressive water conditions."

▶ It can take the heat. PEX can withstand water temperature up to 180°F at 100 psi, which is 40°F hotter than recommended water heater settings. And hot water will arrive faster at the tap because, unlike metal pipe, there's minimal heat loss through conduction. Thus it's also less likely to sweat during hot weather.

▶ It's quiet. The tubing expands slightly, minimizing air hammer—the banging that takes place in rigid piping when taps are turned off suddenly and running water stops abruptly. That ability to expand also means less pronounced pressure drops (fewer scalding or freezing showers) and PEX tubing is less likely to rupture if water freezes in it.

▶ It's easier to repair. Because tubing connects to an accessible manifold with a bank of lever valves, you can shut off water to one side of a fixture as simply as flipping an electrical breaker.

PEX Disadvantages

PEX is as costly as copper; you need proprietary connectors and crimping tools for each brand of tubing; and it will break down when exposed to UV light (within 30 days to 90 days), so get it installed and covered quickly. Although PEX can withstand high water temperatures, it will melt when exposed to open flame. Thus it must not be directly connected to gas- or oil-fired water heaters and must be kept away from flue pipes, recessed lights, and other sources of excessive heat.

In PEX water-supply installations, central manifolds distribute hot and cold water to individual fixtures or fixture groups. Flexible tubing requires far fewer fittings than do rigid materials.

PEX tubing does require specialized fittings, such as plastic support elbows at tight bends and proprietary clamps where tubing attaches to metal stubouts.

via no-hub couplings with inner neoprene sleeves, as shown in "Splicing a Branch Drain to a Stack," on p. 285. The new pipe–fitting assembly should be 1 in. shorter than the cutout section.

Before cutting into cast iron, however, support the pipe on both sides of the intended cut to prevent movement, which could weaken joints. Use *stack clamps* (riser clamps), if you're cutting into a vertical section of pipe. Use *strap hangers* (see the top photo on p. 277) if cutting into a horizontal section. Mark cut-lines on the cast iron with a grease pencil. Then wrap the snap-cutter's chain about the pipe, gradually tightening till the chain is snug and the tool's cutting wheels align over the cut-lines. Crank the cutter's handle to continue tightening the chain till the pipe snaps

cleanly. Make the second cut, and remove the old pipe section. *Caution:* Wear goggles during this operation.

Once the cuts are complete, slide the neoprene sleeve of a no-hub coupling over each remaining pipe end. You may need to roll each sleeve back on itself, as you would roll up the cuffs of a long-sleeved shirt. Insert the transition fitting or replacement pipe section, unroll the neoprene sleeves onto the fitting or pipe, and then tighten the steel band clamps. You can also tie into a cast-iron drain without cutting into it, by building out from an existing cleanout, as shown in "Extending a Cast-Iron Main Drain," on p. 286.

Venting Options

Until you expose the framing and actually run the pipe, it's difficult to know *exactly* how things will fit together—especially vents. Because correct venting is crucial, the section discusses several venting options to consider. But first, here are a few terms to keep straight: A stack is a vertical pipe. If the stack carries wastes, it's a *soil stack.* If the stack admits air and never carries water, it's a *vent stack.*

Most of the venting options described next are examples of *dry venting,* in which a vent stack never serves as a drain for another fixture. But there are hybrids; for example, if a vent stack occasionally drains fixtures above it, it is a *wet vent.* Wet vents must *never* carry soil wastes, and many local codes prohibit all wet venting. But when it's legal and the vent is one pipe-size larger than normal to ensure a good flow, wet venting can be safe and cost effective because it requires fewer fittings and less pipe.

NO-HUB Couplings

No-hub couplings (also known as banded couplings, band-seal couplings, and hubless connectors) consist of an inner neoprene sleeve, which fits over the pipe ends or fittings, and an outer corrugated metal shield, which is drawn tight by a stainless-steel band clamp. No-hub couplings are widely used to join cast-iron pipe and no-hub fittings in new construction, but they are also invaluable to renovators.

For example, if you want to add a plastic shower drain to a cast-iron stack, no-hub couplings can accept either a cast-iron or a plastic no-hub fitting and seal it tightly to the pipe ends once you've cut into the stack. (Support both sides of the section to be cut out so it can't shift during cutting and weaken other joints.)

When joining DWV pipes of different materials, use specialized transition couplings whose neoprene sleeves are sized for incoming pipes with different outside diameters, such as the coupling used to join 2-in. copper and 2-in. cast iron, shown in the photo at left.

No-hub couplings. At the upper left, a transition coupling joins DWV pipes with different exterior diameters, a 2-in. copper vent pipe and a 2-in. cast-iron takeoff on a 2 by 3 wye fitting. The other couplings join 3-in. no-hub cast-iron fittings.

BACK VENTING

Back venting (also known as continuous venting), is the dry-venting method shown below, and it's acceptable to even the strictest codes. All the fixtures in the drawing have a branch vent. In a typical installation, the trap arm of, say, a lavatory empties into the middle leg of a sanitary tee. The branch drain descends from the lower leg; the branch vent from the upper. When a branch vent takes off from a relatively horizontal section of drainpipe, the angle at which it departs is crucial. It may go straight up, or it may leave at a 45° angle, to work around an obstruction. But it must never exit from the side of a drainpipe: If it did, it could become clogged with waste.

Back Venting (Continuous Venting)

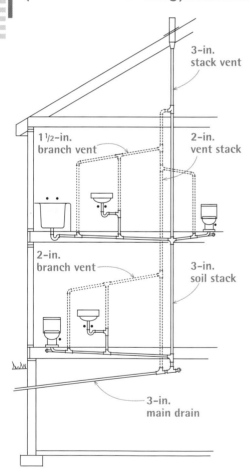

In this illustration of back venting, all fixtures have a dry branch vent—that is, no vent ever carries water. The fixtures on the first floor require a 2-in. branch vent because the toilet's 3-in. drain needs more incoming air to equalize its large waste flow.

Maximum Distance: Trap Arm to Vent*

TRAP ARM DIAMETER (in.)	MAXIMUM DISTANCE TO VENT
1¼	2 ft. 6 in.
1½	3 ft. 6 in.
2	5 ft.
3	6 ft.
4	10 ft.

* Also maximum distance of stack-vented fixture trap arm to stack, based on calculations found in the UPC, T10-1.

Branch vents must rise to a height of at least 42 in. above the floor before beginning their horizontal run to the vent stack. This measurement adds a safety margin of 6 in. above the height of the highest fixture (such as a sink set at 36 in.), so there is no danger of waste flowing into the vent. Since branch vents run to a vent stack, they should maintain an upward pitch of at least ¼ in. per foot; although the UPC allows a vent to be level if it is 6 in. above the flood rim of a fixture.

STACK VENTING

Clustering plumbing fixtures around a central stack is probably the oldest method of venting. In the early days of indoor plumbing, plumbers noticed that fixtures near the stack retained the water in their traps; whereas those (unvented) that were at a distance did not. You can vent three bathroom fixtures (lavatory, tub, and toilet) off a 3-in. stack vent, without additional branch vents—if you detail it correctly, as shown in "Stack Venting," above right.

Note: When stack venting, never place a toilet above the other fixtures on the stack: Its greater discharge could break the water seals in the traps of small-dimension pipes. If you must add fixtures below those already stack vented, add (or extend) vent stacks and branch vents. The maximum allowable distance from stack-vented fixtures to the soil stack depends on the size of the pipe serving a particular fixture; see "Maximum Distance: Trap Arm to Vent," above.

Stack Venting

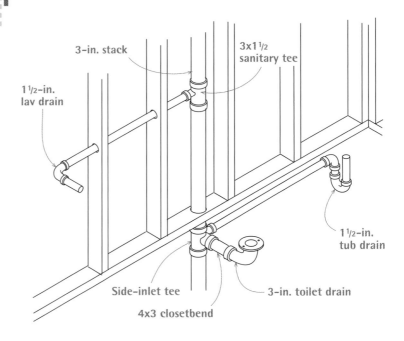

If close enough to a stack vent of adequate size, fixtures can use it for venting (table "Maximum Distance: Trap Arm to Vent") Note: Side inlet serving tub enters above toilet inlet; this fixture group must be the highest on the stack.

Minimum Drain, Trap, and Vent Sizes

FIXTURE/APPLIANCE	DRAIN/TRAP SIZE	VENT SIZE
Toilet	3 in. or 4 in.	2 in.
Bathtub/shower	2-in. drain; 1½-in trap	1½ in.
Shower stall	2 in.	1½ in.
Lavatory	1½-in drain; 1¼-in trap	1¼ in.
Paired lavatories	2-in. drain; 1½-in. trap	1½ in.
Bidet	1¼ in.	1¼ in.
Kitchen sink (with or without disposer)	1½ in.	1½ in.
Dishwasher	1½ in.	1½ in.
Laundry tub	2 in.	1½ in.
Clothes washer standpipe	2 in.	1½ in.
Laundry tub	1½ in.	1½ in.

VENTING TOILETS

Because they have the biggest drain and vent pipes of any fixture, toilets can be the trickiest to route vents for. When space beneath a toilet is not a problem, use a setup such as the one shown below, in "Venting a Toilet," in which a 2-in. vent pipe rises vertically from a 3 by 2 combo, while the 3-in. drain continues on to the house main. The 3-in.-diameter toilet drain, allows the vent to be as far as 6 ft. from the fixture, as indicated in the table on p. 281.

When space is tight, say, on a second-floor bathroom with a finish ceilings below, the drain and vent pipes must descend less abruptly (see "Constricted Spaces," below. Here, the critical detail is the angle at which the vent leaves the 3 by 2 combo: That vent takeoff must be 45° above a horizontal cross section of the toilet drain. If it is less than that, the outlet might clog with waste and no longer function as a vent. As important, the "horizontal" section of the vent that runs between the takeoff and the stack must maintain a minimum upward pitch of ¼ in. per foot.

When you've got two toilets back to back, you can save some space by picking up both with a single *figure-5* fitting (double combo), like the small one in the bottom photo on p. 277. From the top of the fitting, send up a 2-in. or 3-in. vent; from the two side sockets use two 3-in. soil pipes serving the toilets; and use a *long-sweep ell* (or a combo) on the bottom, to send wastes on to the main drain. This fitting is about the only way to situate back-to-back water closets and is quite handy when adding a half bath that shares a wall with an existing bathroom.

OTHER VENTING OPTIONS

Common vents are appropriate where fixtures are side by side or back to back. This type of vent usually requires a figure-5 fitting.

Loop vents are commonly installed beneath an island counter in the middle of a room. The sink

Venting a Toilet

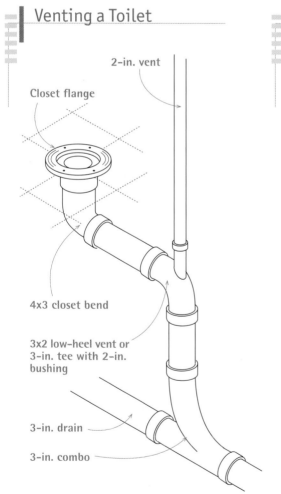

- 2-in. vent
- Closet flange
- 4x3 closet bend
- 3x2 low-heel vent or 3-in. tee with 2-in. bushing
- 3-in. drain
- 3-in. combo

When there's plenty of space under a toilet—say, an unfinished basement—the branch drain can descend steeply.

Constricted Spaces

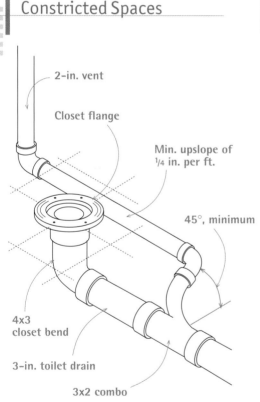

- 2-in. vent
- Closet flange
- Min. upslope of ¼ in. per ft.
- 45°, minimum
- 4x3 closet bend
- 3-in. toilet drain
- 3x2 combo

When a branch drain must travel through a floor platform before reaching a stack, the drain must slope gradually. Here, the angle the vent takes off from the toilet drain is critical—it must not be less than 45°, as depicted in the cross-section drawing at right.

drain is concealed easily enough in the floor platform, but the branch vent, lacking a nearby wall through which it can exit, requires some ingenuity. This problem is solved by the loop shown in "Venting an Island Sink," below.

In addition to the fittings shown in the drawing, note these factors as well: the loop must rise as high under the counter as possible and at least 6 in. above the juncture of the trap arm and the sanitary tee, to preclude any siphoning of wastewater from the sink. The vent portions may be 1½-in. pipe, but the drain sections must be 2 in. in diameter, and drain sections must slope downward at least ¼ in. per foot.

Mechanical vents, also known as air-admittance valves, or pop vents, allow you to use a fixture before the vent runs are complete (say, before you run a vent stack up through the roof). Here's how they work: As water drains from a sink, it creates a partial vacuum within the pipes, depressing a spring inside the vent and sucking air in. When the water is almost gone and the vacuum is equalized, the spring extends and pushes its diaphragm up, sealing off outside air once again.

Mechanical vents are *temporary* vents only. The UPC allows them only if local jurisdictions permit them—and few do. Because valve mechanisms can wear out and allow septic gases into living spaces, mechanical vents must never be used as permanent vents or in enclosed spaces where they cannot draw air easily.

VENT TERMINATION

To reduce chances that vent gases will enter the home, stack tops must be at least 6 in. above the upslope side of the roof and at least 3 ft. above any part of a skylight or window that can be opened. A vent stack must at least 12 in. horizontal distance from a parapet wall, dormer sidewalls, and the like. Finally, stacks must be correctly flashed to prevent roof leaks.

Vent-Takeoff Cross Section

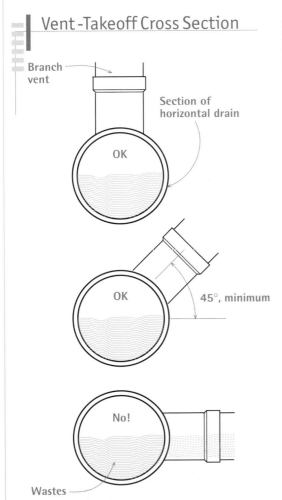

Vents must take off from horizontal drains at a 45° angle minimum. If the take off angle is less than 45°, wastes can block the vent.

Venting an Island Sink

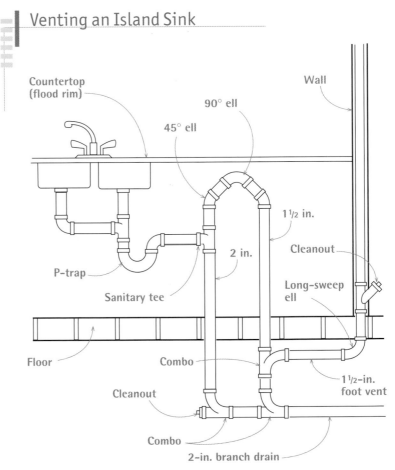

A looped vent is one code-approved way to vent an island sink. The loop should extend as high as possible under the countertop. Loop preassembly makes construction easier. The foot vent must connect to the loop via a combo fitting and slope upward to the stack at a minimum of ⅛ in. per ft.

Roughing-In DWV Pipes

In new construction, pros typically start the DWV system by connecting to the sewer lead pipe, supporting the main drain assembly every 4 ft. and at each point a fitting is added.

Renovation plumbing is a different matter altogether, unless an existing main is so corroded or undersize that you need to tear it out and replace it. Rather, renovation plumbing usually entails tying into an existing stack or drain in the most cost- and time-effective manner. There are three plausible scenarios: (1) cutting into a stack to add a branch drain, (2) building out from the end of the main drain where it meets the base of the soil stack, and (3) cutting into the main drain in mid-run and adding fittings for incoming branch drains.

This discussion assumes that the existing pipes are cast iron and that new DWV pipes or fittings are ABS or PVC plastic, unless otherwise noted. If you're adding several fixtures, position the new branch drain so that individual drains can attach to it economically—that is, using the least amount of pipe and fittings. As noted before, drainpipes must have a minimum downward slope of ¼ in. per foot.

Run clear water through the drains before cutting into them. Flush the toilets several times and run water in the fixtures for several minutes. Then shut off the supply-pipe water and post signs around the house so people don't use the fixtures while work is in progress.

SPLICING A BRANCH DRAIN INTO A STACK

If you're adding a toilet, have a plumber calculate the increased flow, size the pipes, recommend fittings, and—perhaps—do the work. Adding a lav, sink, or tub, on the other hand, is considerably easier and less risky—mostly a matter of splicing a 1½-in. branch drain to a 2-in. or 3-in. stack. The keys to success are clamping the stack before cutting it, inserting a tee fitting into the stack, and joining the branch drain to that fitting.

Let's look at splicing to a cast-iron stack first. Start by holding a no-hub fitting (say, a 2 by 1½ sanitary tee) next to the stack and using a grease pencil to transfer the fitting's length to the stack—plus ½ in. working room on each end. (This will leave a ¼-in. gap at each end, which will be filled by a lip inside the neoprene sleeve.) Install a stack clamp above and below the pro-

PRO TIP

When ordering supplies, order 20 percent more pipe than you think you'll need and at least a half-dozen extra of the more common fittings such as tees, combos, ells, and couplings. You'll also need straps and clamps to support pipe runs and consumables, such as solder or plastic-pipe cement and plumber's sand cloth. Most supply stores accept returns, but check their policy before ordering.

Vent Termination

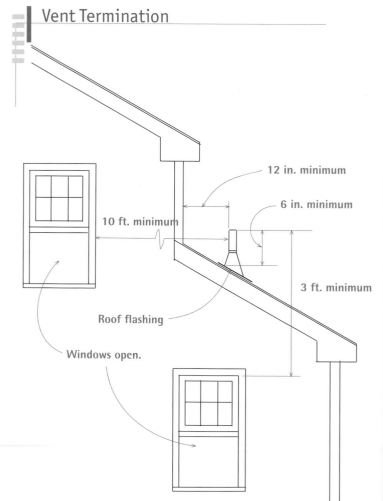

12 in. minimum

6 in. minimum

10 ft. minimum

3 ft. minimum

Roof flashing

Windows open.

So vent gases won't enter the home, plumbing vents must terminate at least 3 ft. above an openable window, or a minimum of 10 ft. horizontal distance from an openable window at the same level.

GOING WITH THE Flow

To optimize flow and minimize clogged pipes, follow these guidelines:

▶ **DRAINAGE FITTINGS.** Use a long-sweep ell (90° elbow) or a combo when making a 90° bend on horizontal runs of waste and soil pipe, and where vertical pipes empty into horizontal ones. Use a standard ell when going from horizontal to vertical. Where trap arms join vent stacks, use sanitary tees. (Long-sweep fittings are not required on turns in vent pipe; regular tees and ells may be used there.)

▶ **CLEANOUTS.** Cleanouts are *required* where a building main joins a lead pipe from a city sewer line or septic tank, at the base of soil stacks, and at each horizontal change of direction of 45° or more. Also, install cleanouts whenever heavy flow increases the possibility of clogging, such as in back-to-back toilets. There must be enough room around the cleanout to operate a power auger or similar equipment.

When splicing a branch to an existing drain, adequately support both sides of the takeoff fitting. Here, J-clamps are on both sides of a combo fitting. Transition couplings join copper to cast iron; you could use similar couplings to splice ABS or PVC drain pipes to cast iron.

Pipe-Support Spacing

PIPE MATERIAL	HORIZONTAL SUPPORTS	VERTICAL SUPPORTS
Water supply		
Copper	6 ft.	10 ft.
CPVC	3 ft.	10 ft. and mid-story guide
PEX	32 in.	Base and mid-story guide
DWV		
ABS or PVC	4 ft. and at branch connections	10 ft. and mid-story guides if pipe ≤ 2 in.
Cast iron	5 ft.	Base and each story; 15 ft.

Splicing a Branch Drain to a Stack

A CAST-IRON STACK

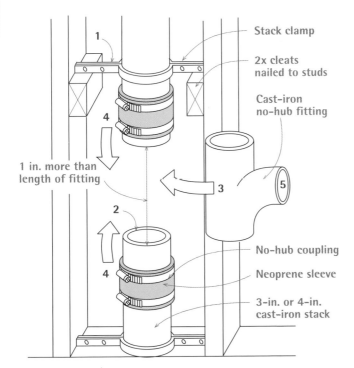

AN ABS-PLASTIC STACK

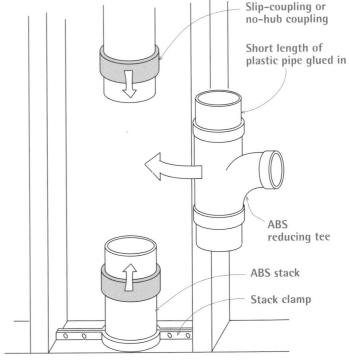

1. Using stack clamps, support the stack above and below the cuts. Mark and cut the stack. 2. Slide no-hub couplings onto cut stack ends (you may need to roll the neoprene sleeves on first). Insert a no-hub fitting. 3. Slide couplings over fitting ends. 4. Tighten. 5. Connect the branch drain to the no-hub fitting.

Glue two short lengths of ABS pipe to a tee. Mark an equivalent length plus ½ in. on both ends onto the ABS stack to indicate cutlines. (Each ABS slip-coupling has an inner lip that nearly fills the ½-in. space). Support and cut the stack. Finally, join the pipes by slipping the couplings in place.

posed cuts. Then use a snap cutter to make the two cuts. Drill through studs as needed to run the branch drain. Next, slide no-hub couplings onto both cut pipe ends; in most cases, it's easiest to loosen the couplings, remove the neoprene sleeves, and roll a sleeve halfway onto each pipe end. (Lips inside the sleeves make them impossible to slide on.)

Extending a Cast-Iron Main Drain

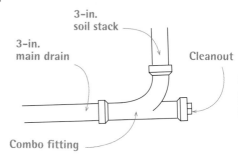

If you build out from a cleanout, you must install a new one at the end of the extension.

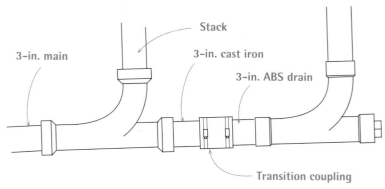

EXTENDING WITH 3-IN. ABS
If the present cleanout is a cast-iron inset caulked with oakum, remove the oakum and the inset and replace it with a short section of 3-in. cast-iron pipe. From there, use a transition (no-hub) coupling to continue with 3-in. ABS plastic.

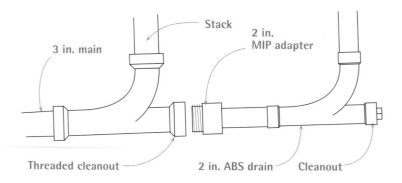

EXTENDING WITH 2-IN. ABS
If there's presently a threaded cleanout opening and you are adding a tub, lav, or sink—but not a toilet—use a plastic MIP (male × iron pipe) adapter.

Insert the no-hub fitting, unroll the sleeves onto fitting ends, slide the banded clamps over the sleeves, orient the fitting takeoff, and tighten the clamps with a no-hub torque wrench. Finally, use a *transition coupling*, which is a special no-hub coupling that accepts pipes of different outer diameters, to tie the new 1½-in. plastic branch drain to the cast-iron no-hub coupling.

Tying into an ABS or PVC stack is essentially the same, except that you'll use a wheeled cutter to cut the stack. And, instead of using a no-hub coupling, glue short (8-in.) lengths of pipe into the tee fitting and then use plastic slip couplings to join the 8-in. stubs to the old pipe. (The slip couplings also glue on, with an appropriate solvent-based cement.) Use a reducing tee, such as a 2 by 1½. Be sure to support the stack above and below before cutting into it.

BUILDING OUT FROM THE MAIN DRAIN

Extending the DWV system out from the end of a cast-iron main drain—where it joins the soil stack—can be the least disruptive way if there's a cleanout at the end of the drain that you can remove. Before cutting the drain, support both sides of the section to be cut, using pipe clamps or strap hangers.

The exact configuration of the end run will depend on the size of the main drain, the fitting currently at the base of the stack, the fixtures you're adding, and the size of the drain needed to serve them. If you are not adding a toilet, the drain extension can be 2-in. pipe, which can be attached with a reducing bushing such as the male-threaded adapters shown in "Extending with 2-in. ABS," at left. If you're adding a toilet, however, the extension must be 3-in. pipe, often inserted with a *ribbed bushing* to ensure a tight fit. If it's not possible to insert the 3-in. pipe into an old cleanout leg, you may need to cut out the existing combo and install a no-hub combo to build out from.

Note: If you build out from an existing cleanout at the end of the main drain, you'll need to add a new cleanout at the end of the extension.

TYING INTO THE MAIN DRAIN IN MID-RUN

Before tying into the main drain in mid-run, flush the drain and support both sides of the section you'll cut into. Then install strap hangers to support both sides of the 3-in. or 4-in. drain. Tying into a cast-iron or plastic drain is essentially the same procedure as splicing into a stack, but it requires different fittings. So here's how to tie into a cast-iron main drain. With one hand, hold the no-hub combo fitting you'll add next to the drain section and, with the other hand, mark cut-lines onto the drain using a grease pencil. The cut marks should be 1 in. longer than the length of the fitting to accommodate the thickness of the stop *lip* inside each no-hub coupling's neoprene sleeve. (If the main drain is cast iron, use a snap cutter to cut it; if it's plastic, use a wheeled cutter.)

After cutting out the drain section, use no-hub couplings to attach the new no-hub combo fitting. Slide a neoprene sleeve onto each end of the cut drain, insert the no-hub combo, and then slide

a sleeve onto each end of the combo. Align the combo takeoff so it is the correct angle to receive the fixture drain you're adding. Finally, tighten the stainless-steel clamps onto the couplings.

CONNECTING BRANCH DRAINS AND VENTS

After modifying the framing, assemble branch drains and vents. Here we'll assume that the new DWV fittings are plastic.

The toilet drain. After framing the tub drain opening, install the 4 by 3 closet bend, centered 12 in. from the finished wall behind the toilet. Install a piece of 2×4 blocking under the closet bend, and end-nailed through the joists on both ends. Use plastic plumber's tape to secure the bend to the 2×4. What really anchors the closet bend, however, is the *closet flange,* which is cemented to the closet bend and screwed to the subfloor.

The flange screws to the subfloor yet will sit atop the finish floor when it's installed. If the finish floor is not in yet, place scrap under the flange so it will be at the correct height. If, on the other hand, the flange is *below* the finish floor, you can build up the flange by stacking plastic *flange extenders* till the assembly is level with the floor. Caulk each extender with silicone as you stack it and use long closet bolts to resecure the toilet bowl. (Check with local codes first, because not all allow extenders.)

PRO TIP

If the neoprene sleeve inside a no-hub coupling won't slide on easily, it may have a small stop lip inside—sort of a depth gauge to stop the incoming pipe in the middle of the sleeve. Soap the inside of the sleeve to reduce friction. You could use a utility knife to trim off the lip, but that would be more time-consuming and you're likely to puncture the sleeve.

Framing for Toilets and Tubs

You may need to cut through joists to accommodate the standard 4 by 3 closet bend beneath a toilet or the drain assembly under a standard tub. In that event, reinforce both ends of severed joists with doubled headers attached with double-joist hangers. This beefed-up framing provides a solid base for the toilet as well. If joists are exposed, you can also add joists or blocking to optimize support.

Toilets

A minimum 6-in. by 6-in. opening provides enough room to install a no-hub closet bend made of cast iron (4½ in. outer diameter) or plastic (3½ in. outer diameter). The center of the toilet drain should be 12 in. from a finish wall or 12½ in. from rough framing. If joists are exposed, add blocking between the joists to stiffen the floor and better support the toilet bowl, even if you don't need to cut joists to position the bend.

Bathtubs

A 12-in. by 12-in. opening in the subfloor will give you enough room to install the tub's waste and overflow assembly. Ideally, there should be blocking or a header close to the tub's drain, that you can pipe-strap it to. To support the fittings that attach to the shower arm and spout stub-outs, add cross-braces between the studs in the end wall. To support tub lips on three sides, attach ledgers to the studs, using galvanized screws or nails. Finally, if there's access under the tub, add double joists beneath the tub foot.

Maximum Sizes for Holes and Notches

FRAMING ELEMENT	HOLE DIAMETER (in.)	NOTCH DEPTH (in.)
Bearing studs		
2×4	1⅜	⅞
2×6	2³⁄₁₆	1⅜
Nonbearing studs		
2×4	2	1⅜
2×6	3¼	2³⁄₁₆
Solid lumber joists		
2×6	1¾	⅞
2×8	2½	1¼
2×10	3⅛	1⅝
2×12	3¾	1⅞

Drilling and Notching Studs and Joists

It's often necessary to notch or drill framing to run supply and waste pipes. If you comply with code guidelines, given in "Maximum Sizes for Holes and Notches," on p. 287, you'll avoid weakening the structure. Although that table is based on the following rules of thumb, remember that local building codes have the final say.

Joists

You may drill holes along the entire span of a joist, provided the holes are at least 2 in. from the joist's edge and don't exceed one-third of the joist's depth. Notches are *not* allowed in the middle third of a joist span. Otherwise, notches are allowed if they don't exceed one-sixth of the joist's depth.

Studs

Drilled holes must be at least 5/8 in. from the stud's edge. Ideally, holes should be centered in the stud. If it's necessary to drill two holes in close proximity, align the holes vertically, rather than drilling them side by side. Individual hole diameters must not exceed 40 percent of the width of a bearing-wall stud, if those studs are doubled and holes don't pass through more than two adjacent doubled studs; hole diameters must not exceed 60 percent of the width of non-bearing-wall studs. Notch width may not exceed 25 percent of the width of a bearing-wall stud or 40 percent of the width of a nonbearing-wall stud.

Edge protection

Any pipe or electrical cable less than 1¼ in. from a stud edge must be protected by steel nail plates or shoes at least 1/16 in. thick, to prevent puncture by drywall nails or screws.

Pipe Slope

DWV pipes slope, so before drilling or notching framing, snap sloping chalklines across the stud edges; then angle your drill bits slightly to match that slope. Drill holes ¼ in. larger than the outside dimension of the pipe, so the pipe feeds through easily. Nonetheless, if DWV pipe runs are lengthy, you may need to cut pipe into 30-in. sections (slightly shorter than the distance between two 16-in. on-center studs) and join pipe sections with couplings. That is, it may be impossible to feed a single uncut DWV pipe through holes cut in a stud wall.

Notching and Drilling Limits

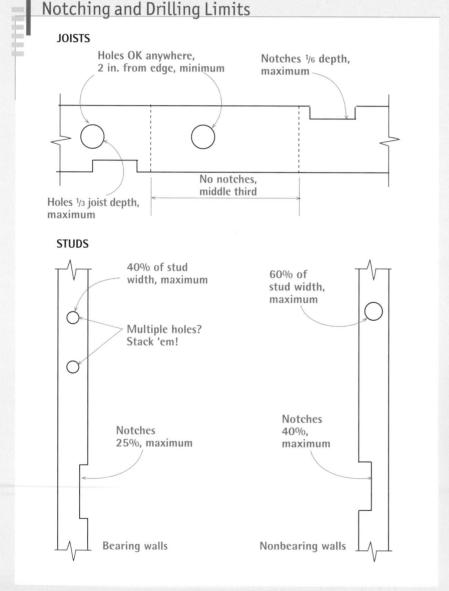

JOISTS

Holes OK anywhere, 2 in. from edge, minimum

Notches 1/6 depth, maximum

Holes 1/3 joist depth, maximum

No notches, middle third

STUDS

40% of stud width, maximum

Multiple holes? Stack 'em!

Notches 25%, maximum

Bearing walls

60% of stud width, maximum

Notches 40%, maximum

Nonbearing walls

When hole diameters exceed maximums allowed by code, reinforce framing with a steel stud shoe.

The toilet flange (orange ring) will sit atop the finish floor. So if the finish floor is not yet installed, place scrap under the flange, elevating it to the correct height. This assembly is essentially the same as that shown in "Constricted Spaces," on p. 282.

Support vent stacks in mid-story by using plumber's strap to tie stacks to blocking between studs.

Once you've secured the closet bend, add pipe sections to the bottom of the bend, back to the takeoff fitting on the main drain that you installed earlier. Maintain a minimum of ¼ in. per foot slope, and support drains at least every 4 ft. Dry-fit all pieces, and use a grease pencil to make alignment marks on pipes and fittings.

Other fixture drains. Next run the 1¼-in., 1½-in., and 2-in. fixture drains up from the main drain takeoff. Drains must slope at least ¼ in. per foot, and all pipe must be rigidly supported every 4 ft. and at each horizontal branch connection. Support pipes with rigid plastic pipe hangers or with plastic-pipe strap, securing pipes to wood blocks beneath them. Support stacks at the base, and in mid-story by strapping or clamping the pipe to a 2× block running between studs.

Run the tub branch drain to the subfloor opening where the tub trap arm will descend. Pipe stub-outs for lavs and sinks should stick out into living spaces 6 in. or so; you can cut them off or attach trap adapters later. All branch drains end in a *sanitary tee*. The horizontal leg of the tee receives the trap arm from the fixture, and the upper leg of the tee is the beginning of the branch vent.

Vent runs. Next assemble vent runs, starting with the largest vent—often the 2-in. or 3-in. pipe rising from the combo fitting below the closet bend. Individual branch vents then run to that vent stack, usually joining it in an *inverted tee fitting*, typically 4 ft. to 5 ft. above the floor. Support all stacks in mid-story with clamps or straps. Horizontal runs of 1½-in. branch vents must be at least 42 in. above the floor, or 6 in. above the flood rim of the highest fixture, and those runs typically slope upward at least ¼ in. per foot. Continue to build up the vent stack, with as few jogs as possible, until it eventually passes through a flashing unit set in the roof. For code requirements at the roof, see "Vent Termination," on p. 284.

TESTING THE DWV SYSTEM

Once you've roughed out the DWV system, but before hooking up fixtures, test for leaks. Filling DWV pipes with water is a common test, which requires that you seal all fixture stub-outs and use a garden hose to fill the largest stack. (All DWV pipes are interconnected, so you need fill only one stack to fill all.) Should you see leaks, drain the system, fix the leaks, and refill. Once

PRO TIP

Use only noncorroding (brass or stainless-steel) screws and bolts to secure the closet flange or the toilet bowl; other materials will corrode. To help you align the bolt holes on the bowl with bolts in the closet flange, buy extra-long, 3-in. by ⁵⁄₁₆-in. closet bolts. They'll be long enough to line up easily, even when the wax ring is in the way, and you can trim excess length without difficulty.

you see no leaks, allow the water to stand at least overnight or until the inspector signs off on your system.

There are several types of pipe seals. The most common and least expensive is a *glue-on cap* that fits inside a DWV pipe stub. Allow pipe cement to dry a day before filling pipes with water. When the test is completed, drain the system by opening a cleanout at the lowest point, and cut off the small sections of drainpipe in which caps are

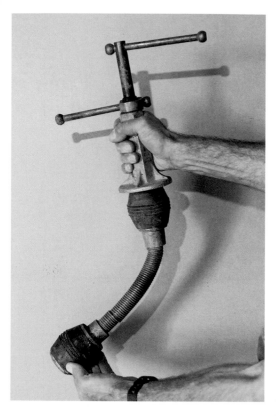

When filling the DWV system for testing, use a double dynamiter to block the combo fitting at the base of the main drain.

Testing plugs. Clockwise, from bottom: 1½-in. test plug, 3-in. test plug, 4-in. test plug, and "jim cap." The first three plugs insert into pipes and expand via a wing nut; the jim cap slips over the outside of a pipe and tightens with a band clamp.

glued. Where a stack is several stories high, this is the only type of cap guaranteed not to be dislodged by a weighty column of water.

Reusable rubber caps or plugs eliminate the need for gluing. A *jim cap* fits over the end of a pipe and tightens with a ring clamp. *Test plugs* fit into pipe ends and are expanded by a wing-nut assembly. A third type, known as a *double-dynamiter* out West, can be rented. It is a spring-loaded device that fits into the combo at the foot of the building drain. As shown in the top photo at left, this tool has two rubber balls that can be expanded or contracted by turn screws on the shaft. Insert the balls so that the forward one lodges in drainpipe, and then expand that ball; the second ball should block the open leg of the combo. To release the water, contract the balls of the double-dynamiter in the order in which you expanded them. Loosened, the forward ball will allow the test water to run down the drain; releasing the second ball allows you to remove the tool. Label the respective turn screws so you don't confuse them: If you release the second ball first, you may get a faceful of waste water.

If there are finish ceilings in place below new pipes and you don't want to risk wetting them with a failed connection, use an *air-pressure test* in which all openings (including stacks) are sealed. Typically, an inflatable bladder attached to a gauge is inserted into a cleanout at the base of the soil stack, and air is pumped into the DWV system. If the gauge shows no pressure loss over a given period, the inspector signs off.

Roughing-In Supply Pipes

Water-supply pipes are easier to run than DWVs because they're smaller and don't need to slope. Metal supply pipes should be bonded to the house's electrical grounding system (see p. 231).

Run supply pipes to fixtures once hot and cold trunk lines are connected. Run ¾-in. trunk lines, using ½-in. pipe for branch lines serving two fixtures or fewer. Individual supply risers for toilets and lavatories are often ⅜ in. You save some money by using smaller-diameter pipes, but the main reason to reduce pipe diameter is to ensure adequate water pressure when several fixtures are used simultaneously. Reducing tees, such as the ¾ by ½ shown in the bottom photo on p. 270, provide a ½-in. branch takeoff from a ¾-in. trunk line.

Support horizontal runs of copper supply pipe at least every 6 ft., but if pipes run perpendicular to joists, plumbers usually secure the pipe every second or third joist. Support vertical runs of copper at every floor or every 10 ft., whichever is

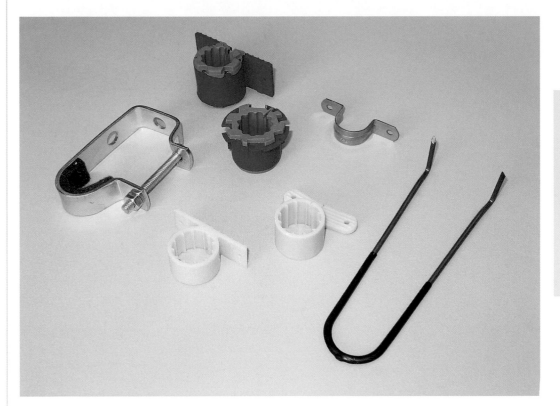

Water-supply pipe supports. Clockwise from upper left: two Acousto-Plumb® clamps (which reduce pipe noise by cushioning vibrations), a copper pipe strap, a ¾-in. by 6-in. plastic-coated wire hook, two plastic suspension clamps, and a felt-lined J-clamp.

SAFETY ALERT

Dielectric unions have insulators inside that will not conduct electricity. If your electrical system is grounded to the water main and you install a dielectric union to join copper pipe to a galvanized steel service pipe, for example, install a bonding jumper to ensure continuous grounding.

less. Support horizontal runs of CPVC supply pipe every 3 ft.; vertical runs should be suported every 10 ft., with clamps or plumber's strap attached to blocking. Support PEX tubing every 32 in. on horizontal runs and every 10 ft. on vertical runs (with mid-story guides).

Keep hot and cold pipes at least 6 in. apart. *They should never touch.* To conserve energy, reduce utility bills, and get hot water sooner at fixtures, install closed-cell foam insulation sleeves on hot-water pipes, as shown in the photo on p. 224. As noted earlier, water-supply stub-outs should protrude at least 6 in. into living space. To hold stub-outs in place, solder them to *perforated copper straps* nailed or screwed to studs.

Code requires shutoff valves for every fixture riser. Supply pipes to outdoor spigots or unheated rooms should have shutoff valves and unions within the main basement so pipes can be drained. Install *water-hammer arrestors* on branch lines to appliances such as washers or dishwashers, whose solenoid valves stop water flow so abruptly that pipes vibrate and bang against the framing.

To test the supply system before installing drywall, solder caps onto fixture stub-outs and turn on the water. (If you're installing CPVC supply,

cement caps onto stub-outs.) If there are no leaks, install steel nail-protection plates over any pipes that lie within 1¼ in. of a stud edge, or use *steel stud shoes* over notched studs. Then install finish surfaces.

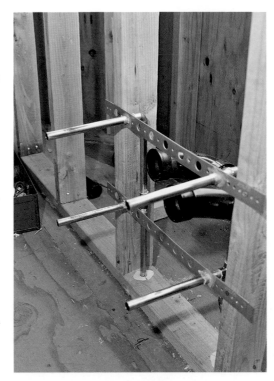

After running DWV branch drains to fixtures, install supply-pipe assemblies and solder stub-outs to perforated strap.

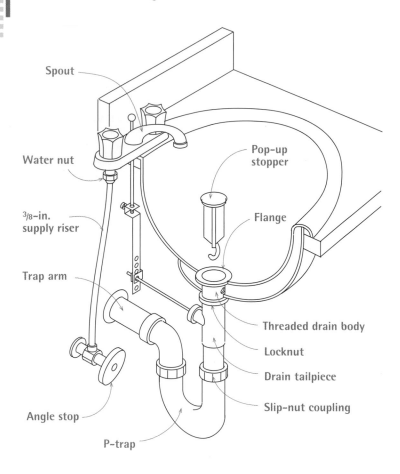

- Spout
- Water nut
- 3/8-in. supply riser
- Trap arm
- Angle stop
- P-trap
- Pop-up stopper
- Flange
- Threaded drain body
- Locknut
- Drain tailpiece
- Slip-nut coupling

Installing Fixtures

Before you can install a new fixture, there's often an old one to remove. If it's necessary to shut off water to several fixtures during installation, capping disconnected pipes will allow you to turn the water back on.

DISCONNECTING FIXTURES

Before disconnecting supply pipes, shut off the valves that control them. As mentioned, code requires a shutoff valve on each fixture riser, but older systems may have only a main valve that shuts off water to the whole house. After shutting off the controlling valve, open the faucets to drain the water.

Lavatory or sink supply pipes may have unions that can be disconnected using two pipe wrenches. Otherwise, *water-supply nuts* (water nuts) will connect the tops of supply risers to threaded faucet stems on the underside of the basin. To loosen water nuts, use a basin wrench, which has a shaft 10 in. to 17 in. long and spring-loaded jaws set at a right angle to the shaft. If the lav is

old and you intend to reinstall it, save the water nuts because the threaded faucet stems may be nonstandard.

To disconnect a fixture's drainpipe, use two pipe wrenches to loosen the slip-nut coupling of the P-trap. If older galvanized couplings have seized up, heat them with a MAPP gas torch and tap them lightly with a hammer to free the joint. Then try again with wrenches. Be sure to wear a respirator mask to avoid inhaling smoke from gaskets and such.

Once you've disconnected the drain and supply pipes, lift the lav/sink off its wall hanger, pedestal, or cabinet base and set it aside. An old cast-iron lav can be quite heavy, so lift it with the aid of helper. Place a plastic bag over the drain pipe stub and secure it with a rubber band to keep sewer gases at bay. Disconnect fittings carefully if you want to reuse them.

To remove a toilet, shut off the water by shutting the chrome *fixture stop* near the base of the unit. Flush the toilet and remove the remaining water with a cup or an inexpensive plastic hand pump. Disconnect the tank from the toilet bowl by loosening the bolts that hold the sections together. If the tank is wall hung, use a wide-jawed *spud wrench* to loosen the slip nut between the tank and the bowl. The toilet bowl is fastened to the floor by two bolts that rise from the floor flange; unscrew the nuts capping the bolts on both sides of the bowl. Rock the toilet bowl slightly to break the wax seal on the bottom. Then lift up the bowl and *immediately* block the drainpipe by stuffing it with a plastic bag containing wadded-up newspapers.

Tub drain assemblies may be hidden in an end wall or they may exit into a hole cut into the subfloor under the drain. The drain and overflow assembly is usually held together with slip couplings, so use a pipe wrench to loosen them. If the drain is solid piece, cut through it. Supply pipes may be joined with unions or they may be soldered; it's easiest just to cut through supply risers. With those pipes disconnected, you can move the tub.

If it's a standard tub (rather than a free-standing tub), you may need to cut into the finish surfaces at least 1 in. above the tub to expose the tub lip, which is often nailed to studs. If you're discarding the tub and don't care about chipping its enamel, use a cat's paw to pull the nails. If the tub is too heavy or tightly fit to slide out of its alcove, you may need to cut the studs of the end wall so you can slide the tub out.

INSTALLING LAVATORIES AND SINKS

Lavatory basins and sinks are supported by pedestals, cabinet counters, legs, wall-mounted brackets, or a combination of these. Cabinet-mounted lavs and sinks are particularly popular because they provide storage space.

Preassemble the hardware. Before mounting a sink or lav, attach its hardware, including faucets, spout, and the drain *tailpiece*. Such connections are easier to make when the fixture is inverted. Insert the threaded faucet stems through pre-drilled holes in the sink or lav body, and tighten the washered nuts on the underside. Many manufacturers supply a rubber gasket; but when that's lacking, spread a generous layer of plumber's

putty between the metal and the porcelain. Don't overtighten. Once the faucets are secure, you can connect the risers loosely to the threaded faucet stems, allowing you to reposition them if needed when attaching their lower ends to the angle stops.

Set the unit. Sink (or lav) installations vary, depending on whether the unit is surface mounted, under mounted, flush mounted, wall mounted, or set atop a pedestal. Once you've attached the hardware, apply a bead of silicone caulk to the sink lip, turn the unit over, and press it flat to the surface (or underside) of the counter. Some sinks need nothing more to secure them, although many have mounting clips similar to

It's much easier to attach hardware to the underside of a sink before mounting it. Here, the plumber uses flexible stainless lines to connect hot and cold faucet valves to the spout inlet. The threaded bottom of each faucet tee—one is visible, at right—receives a ⅜-in. water-supply riser and a water nut that holds it tight.

Apply plumber's putty or silicone under the flange of the drain tailpiece, insert it into the drain hole, and then use sliding-jaw pliers to tighten the locknut on the underside of the basin.

Setting a Pedestal Sink

Installing a pedestal sink takes planning, a lot of adjusting, and two people. For starters, determine well in advance the height of the 2× blocking needed to anchor the sink, so you can cut that board into stud walls well before the drywall goes up.

Preattach the sink's hardware before mounting it on the pedestal. Next, level the pedestal base, shimming it as needed. *Ribbed plastic shims* (also called ribbed stability wedges) work well for this task because their ribs keep them from slipping, even if it's necessary to stack wedges on a badly out-of-level floor. Once the base is level, set the sink atop it and check it for level in two directions—front to back and side to side—using two torpedo levels, as shown in the left photo on p. 295. Chances are, you'll need to reset the sink several times to get it level and stable because sinks and pedestals are often not perfectly mated.

Once you're pleased with the sink's placement, put a pencil in the back of the sink and mark the locations of the lag-screw holes onto the wall. Remove the sink, predrill the holes, start the lag screws, replace the sink, and check for level again. When the sink is level and the lag screws line up to the pilot holes, lift the sink slightly so a helper can slide out the pedestal, attach the drainpipes, slide back the pedestal and reset the sink, and finish tightening the washered lag screws. But don't overtighten or you'll crack the porcelain. Attach the supply risers top and bottom, test for leaks, and you're done.

shown in the left photo on p. 295.

Sink-Mounting Details

For rimless and self-rimming sinks, first set the mounting device or sink edge in plumber's putty, which will compress.

RIMLESS SINK

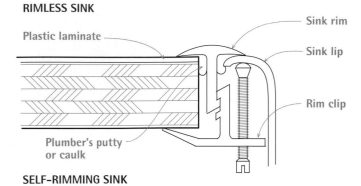

Plastic laminate

Plumber's putty or caulk

Sink rim

Sink lip

Rim clip

SELF-RIMMING SINK

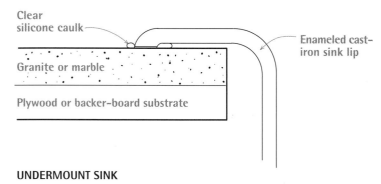

Clear silicone caulk

Granite or marble

Plywood or backer-board substrate

Enameled cast-iron sink lip

UNDERMOUNT SINK

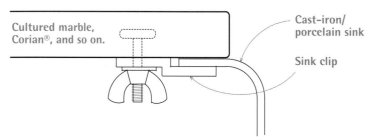

Cultured marble, Corian®, and so on.

Cast-iron/porcelain sink

Sink clip

those shown above. Wall-mounted models slip down into a bracket, which must be lag screwed to blocking attached to studs—preferably *let into* the stud edges. Level the sink front to back and side to side.

Connect the drain. With the sink or lav in place, connect the drainpipe. To the drain stub sticking out of the walls, glue a threaded male *trap adapter*, which will receive a slip coupling. Slide the trap arm into the coupling, but don't tighten it yet. The other end of the trap arm turns down 90° and, being threaded, couples to an adjustable P-trap, which you can swivel so that it aligns to the tailpiece coming down from the lav. The other end of the P-trap has another slip coupling, into which the sink tailpiece fits. When trap

pieces are correctly aligned, tighten the slip couplings.

Kitchen sinks are much the same, except that the upper part of a sink tailpiece is threaded to tighten to the bottom of a strainer body. To drain double sinks, use the hookups shown in "End-Outlet Continuous Waste," on the facing page. Back-to-back lavs or sinks can also share a common drain, by using a figure-5 fitting (see the bottom photo on p. 277).

Connect supply pipes. To each supply pipe stub-out, attach a shutoff valve, typically an *angle stop* with a compression fitting. Slide the angle stop's ½-in. socket over the stub-out, and tighten the fitting so that the ferrule inside compresses and forms a positive seal. Alternatively, you can sweat ½-in. male threaded adapters onto the stub-outs, wrap Teflon tape on the threads, and screw on a shutoff valve with a ½-in. threaded female opening.

Riser attachments depend on whether you install rigid chromed tubing, which inserts into a compression fitting on the angle stop, or a flexible braided supply line, which has nuts on both ends. Rigid tubing must be shaped with a tubing bender and cut to exact length, whereas braided supply can be easily twisted or looped so it fits.

INSTALLING A TOILET

When you're ready to install the toilet, remove the plastic bag you inserted earlier in the closet bend to block sewage gases. Place closet bolts in the closet flange if you haven't already done so.

Set the bowl first. Then attach the tank to the bowl. If you're re-installing an old toilet, as shown in the bottom left photo on p. 296, leave the parts connected, and set the toilet as one piece. But if it's a new toilet, setting the base first is easier on your back. Place the wax ring in the closet flange, so that the ring's plastic funnel centers in the flange. Some manufacturers recommend placing the wax ring on the toilet horn and then inverting the toilet bowl, but the wax ring may not adhere and the funnel may not align.

Have help aligning closet bolts to holes as you set the toilet bowl. Don't rock the bowl when setting it, which could excessively compress the wax ring on one side, creating a gap. Instead, press the bowl down evenly; then use a small adjustable wrench to tighten the nuts gradually, alternating sides, till the bowl is secure. Place a torpedo level atop the bowl edge to see if the unit is level side to side and front to back. If the bowl needs shimming, use plastic shims, which can be chiseled or cut flush to the toilet foot so they're not visible. Don't trim the closet bolts till you've attached the tank and tested the unit for leaks.

It usually takes several tries and some fine-tuning to level the pedestal, level the sink in two directions, and then lag screw the sink to a 2× blocking let into the studs.

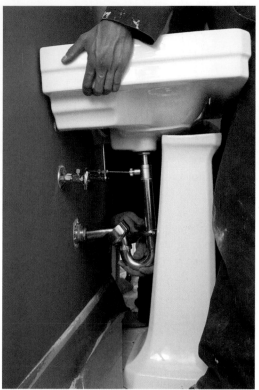

Because the slot in the bank of the pedestal is narrow and the wall is close, there won't be enough room to tighten slip-nut couplings on the drain. Instead, after starting the lag screws, lift and support the front of the sink while a helper slides the pedestal forward. After connecting the drain fittings, slide the pedestal back, and lower the sink.

Check the sink for level one last time, tighten the lag screws to secure the sink, and connect the supply risers top and bottom.

Mount the tank. Standard two-piece toilets have tanks that bolt directly to bowls. In addition to bolt holes, tanks have two fittings on the bottom: a *threaded ballcock stem,* which is screwed to the supply riser, and a larger flush valve, which is tightened to a spud nut. Typically, a rubber spud-nut washer covers the spud nut and cushions the tank–bowl juncture to prevent leaks; there may also be a separate, preinstalled sponge-rubber gasket to cushion the tank and bowl. Tighten the spud nut and position the spud-nut washer, insert the washered tank-mounting bolts into the bottom of the tank, and set the tank atop the bowl so that bolts line up with the holes in the bowl. Carefully follow the manufacturer's instructions about caulking mating surfaces because some caulking compounds may deteriorate the gaskets.

To prevent the tank-bolt threads from turning and cutting into the rubber washers or gaskets, hold the bolts steady with a long screwdriver as you tighten the nuts on the underside of the bowl shelf, using an adjustable wrench. Moving from

FLAWED Toilets

Save fixture invoices and shipping boxes till you've inspected fixtures for flaws. You'll need both to return defective units. Apart from chipped enamel or cracks, the most common toilet flaws are a foot that is not flat, a deformed horn, or bowl and tank surfaces that don't mate correctly.

End-Outlet Continuous Waste

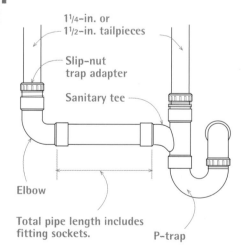

1¼-in. or 1½-in. tailpieces

Slip-nut trap adapter

Sanitary tee

Elbow

Total pipe length includes fitting sockets.

P-trap

A common assembly for double sinks or lavatories.

PRO TIP

Don't overtighten closet bolt nuts or you'll crack the porcelain on the foot. Once the nuts seem snug, gently try to rock the bowl. If it doesn't rock, the nuts are tight enough, though you should return after the toilet's been used for a few weeks and snug the nuts one last time.

INSTALLING A TOILET

Dry-set and shim-level the toilet bowl before centering the wax ring over the closet flange. Once the bowl is placed on the ring, it can't be lifted without your needing to replace the ring.

In most cases, set the toilet base before attaching the tank. Here, an already assembled toilet is being reset onto a new wax ring after a new tile floor was installed. After feeding closet bolts through the bowl, apply even pressure to seat the bowl on the wax ring.

one side to the other, tighten the nuts snugly. Use only brass or stainless-steel bolts and nuts. Connect the water supply, fill the tank, flush the toilet several times, and check for leaks. If there's leaking between the tank and the bowl, tighten the nuts. If there's leaking only near the foot of bowl, the wax ring may have failed: In this case, pull the toilet and replace the ring. If there are no leaks, trim the closet bolts and caulk around the perimeter of the foot.

Toilet supply connections are essentially the same as sink or lavatory risers. The standard toilet supply riser is ⅜-in. chrome tubing that attaches (at the top) to a threaded ballcock stem on the underside of the tank, and a ⅜ by ⅜ angle stop at the bottom. A better option is a ⅜-in. flexible braided stainless-steel supply line: It won't crimp, attaches to the same fittings, and can be easily disconnected.

Bidets. A bidet is easier to install than a toilet. Although a bidet requires hot- and cold-water connections, its wastes are all liquid, so a 1¼-in. drain will suffice. Mount the bidet base securely, but it doesn't need to be seated in a wax ring. In fact, the drain takeoff is similar to that of a tub, which is described next.

INSTALLING A BATHTUB

After framing the three-walled alcove around the tub, attaching 2×4 ledgers to support the tub lip, and cutting an opening in the subfloor for the drain assembly, dry-fit the tub and check for level in two directions. If the tub rocks after its lip is supported by the ledgers, remove the tub, apply 30-lb. building paper over the subfloor, and pour 1 in. to 2 in. of mortar. Place the tub in the mortar before it sets, so the mortar will conform to the shape of the tub. If the tub is made of cast-iron be sure to have at least three workers on hand to move it.

Drain and overflow assembly.
Before the final installation of the tub, preassemble the tub's drain and overflow assembly and test-fit it to the tub openings. Slip-nut couplings make adjusting pipe lengths easy. Once the tub back is in the alcove, install the assembly in the tub: Put a layer of plumber's putty between any metal-to-enamel joint that isn't gasketed. While a helper holds the assembly to the end and underside of the tub, hand screw the threaded strainer into the *tub shoe (waste ell)*. Then use a *strainer wrench*

to tighten it solidly. The overflow plate inside the tub screws to a mounting flange in the overflow ell. There are many types of drain cap (stopper) mechanisms; follow the manufacturer's instructions.

The last drain connection to be made is a P-trap, which slides onto the tub tailpiece descending from the tee. Adjust the trap so that it aligns with the branch drain roughed in earlier. *Note:* If the drain assembly will be inaccessible, code requires a glued-together drain joint. The only exception allowed is the slip-nut coupling that joins the tub tailpiece to the P-trap.

Water supply. Next, attach the tub's supply pipes. Level and mount a *pressure-balancing valve* to the cross brace let into the end-wall studs. (The valve, also called an antiscald valve, is typically set at a maximum of 120°F to prevent scalding.) Follow the manufacturer's instructions for attaching the pipe to the valve. Although gate and ball valves are usually closed when sweating copper pipe to them, balancing valves may need to be open or disassembled before sweating pipe to the valve bodies.

Like most shower/tub valves, a balancing valve has four pipe connections: one each for hot- and cold-supply pipes, one for the pipe that runs to the shower arm, and one that services the spout. To mount shower arms and spouts, screw brass, threaded female drop-eared ells to the cross braces. Because chrome shower arms and spouts can get marred while finish surfaces are being installed, screw in 6-in. capped galvanized nipples. The faucet stem(s) and the balancing valve are protected with a plastic cover till the finish work is done. Turn the water on and test for leaks. Once you're sure there are none, you are ready to close in the walls around the tub.

Once water-supply and DWV pipes are roughed in and 2×4 ledgers are nailed to the studs to support the tub lip, slide the tub into its alcove.

A shower wall at rough-in. A pressure-balancing antiscald valve (which mixes hot and cold water) is shown below. The smaller valve above is a volume control. Note the nail plates to protect the pipes and the stainless-steel screws, which will resist corrosion.

Finishing touches. To avoid marring the surface of a chrome shower arm, insert a sliding-jaw pliers handle into the pipe and turn it into final position. When the bathroom is painted and all brightware is installed, remove the protective plastic from the shower walls.

Replacing a Water Heater

Most municipalities require a permit to replace a water heater, primarily because they want to ensure that the heater's TPR valve is correctly installed. Even though most local codes allow homeowners to replace water heaters, unless you have a lot of plumbing experience, hire a licensed plumber for this job. Plumbers know which brands and hookups require the fewest service calls and can assess the condition of vent pipes and replace them if needed. Besides, thanks to wholesale discounts, plumbers can probably install a new unit for only slightly more than it would cost you if you bought the heater and fittings at retail prices.

Factory-Installed Tank-to-Bowl Connection

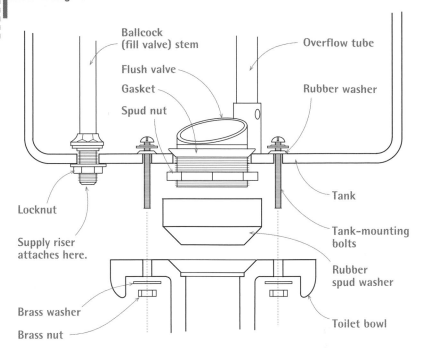

To avoid corrosion, use stainless-steel or brass bolts and nuts.

Tub Drain-and-Overflow Assembly

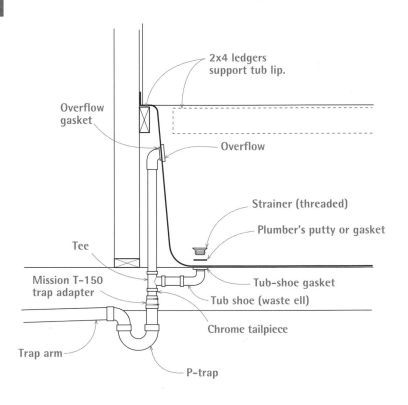

If the tub drain is not accessible, plumbing codes require that joints be glued together, to prevent leaks. To join the tub tailpiece to the trap assembly, use a Mission T-150 trap (1½-in. tubular to 1½-in. pipe).

A plumber should also be willing to peer through the vent thimble with a flashlight and mirror to check the chimney's interior. All manner of debris can accumulate in the bottom of a chimney—from soot to nests—and that debris can block a chimney, hamper flue draft, and possibly force carbon monoxide into living areas. The National Fire Protection Association suggests annual chimney and flue inspections, and whenever a new type of burning appliance is vented into the flue, but inspection is really not a plumber's job. The Chimney Safety Institute of America offers a state-by-state listing of chimney services with certified staff (check out their Web site at www.csia.org).

Above all, installers should follow the water-heater manufacturer's installation instructions closely to ensure a safe installation and to safeguard the unit's warranty should the water heater fail to function properly.

Draining the old water heater. The specifics of disconnecting power or fuel to the old unit will vary, depending on whether the water heater is gas fired, fuel-oil fired, or electric. Once the installer has disconnected the fuel or power source, the water should be shut off and the tank drained. Typically, a hose will be attached to the drain valve at the bottom of the tank. Using a pair of pipe wrenches, unions (if any) on the hot- and cold-water pipes will be taken apart; if there are no unions, pipes will be cut 6 in. to 12 in. above the top of the heater—or a couple inches above the cold-water shutoff valve—by means of hacksaw or a wheeled cutter. *Caution:* Reciprocating saws aren't used because the vibration may weaken nearby pipe joints and cause leaks.

Make way for the new. If the unit is gas or oil fired, the installer will disconnect the draft hood and vent pipe and either wire them up out of the way or set them to one side. As noted earlier, the plumber should inspect the vent pipes. If the hood or pipes are rusty or corroded, they should be replaced. When the old tank is empty, it can be walked out of the way. Be mindful of sharp edges on the newly cut pipes and the area around the old tank. *Note:* If codes require strapping the unit, steel straps should be bolted to the wall behind before putting the new unit in place. Finally, if the pad beneath the old tank is in poor condition or badly tilted, consider installing a new prefab concrete pad. Then the new water heater can be walked into position.

Making connections. What the installer does next depends on the size and condition of the pipes, what fittings are present and, of course, what type of water heater it is. There's no single right way to assemble pipes, but the photos at left show a typical installation in progress for a gas-fired unit. There are ¾-in. brass nipples screwed in the tank inlet holes, flexible stainless-steel lines, sweat-to-threaded male adaptors, valves, and (at the top) ¾-in. rigid-copper trunk lines exiting to the upper floors. Flexible stainless-steel or flexible copper supply lines are highly recommended for top-of-tank connections: Female nuts

Turn off the gas first—the stopcock will be perpendicular to the gas line—before removing an old gas-fired water heater. Use an adjustable wrench to disconnect the gas coupling.

Once the gas line is disconnected, attach a hose to the drain at the bottom of the water heater and drain the tank.

on both ends make them easy to disconnect for future repairs.

Installing a TPR valve. Many new water heaters have preinstalled TPR valves. If there is none, the plumber will install a TPR valve into the threaded outlet atop the unit or in a side outlet a few inches down from the top of the tank, lightly coat the TPR valves threads with pipe compound, and then use a pipe wrench to install the valve. Next, the plumber will install a discharge pipe into the TPR valve's threaded outlet; the pipe may be galvanized or rigid copper—but not plastic!—and must slope downward. The discharge pipe should be terminated about 6 in. above the floor, at a safe location, where it won't scald anyone if it discharges.

Note: Threaded pipe fittings should be coated with pipe compound or wrapped with Teflon™ tape to ensure a positive seal.

Final steps. The plumber will check the water heater for level, shim the base as needed, and tighten the earthquake straps, if any. When all fittings are connected, turn on the cold water to fill the tank. Open the hot-water faucets to expel air. When the tank is full, water will gush from the faucets. At that point, shut the faucets, and reconnect the fuel or power source as specified in the manufacturer's instructions. *Note:* If the installer disconnected the bonding jumper wires from the hot- and cold-supply pipes, those wires should be reclamped now to ensure proper grounding for the house's electrical system.

PRO TIP

When replacing a water heater, put unions and lever-handle ball valves on both the hot- and the cold-water pipes. Code requires a shutoff valve only on the cold-water pipe, but having them on both can make periodic drainage and repairs easier.

A new gas-fired water heater, in mid-installation. The red lever-handled shutoff valve on the cold-water pipe is code required; the tempering valve on the hot-water pipe prevents scalding. After installing the TPR safety valve, plumbers will reattach the vent pipe.

Gas-Fired Water Heater

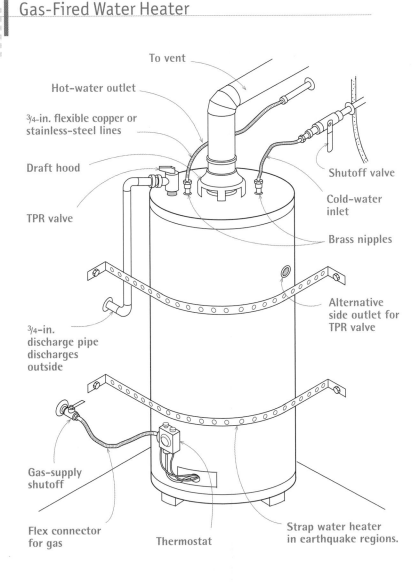

To vent

Hot-water outlet

¾-in. flexible copper or stainless-steel lines

Draft hood

TPR valve

Shutoff valve

Cold-water inlet

Brass nipples

Alternative side outlet for TPR valve

¾-in. discharge pipe discharges outside

Gas-supply shutoff

Flex connector for gas

Thermostat

Strap water heater in earthquake regions.

13 Kitchens and Baths

No other rooms are renovated as often as kitchens and bathrooms, in part, because we've changed the way we live. In the old days, homeowners regarded kitchens and bathrooms as drab utility rooms, best situated at the back of the house, away from guests. Times change. These days, if you throw a party, everybody hangs out in the kitchen. Bathrooms aren't exactly Spartan anymore, either. Today's kitchens and baths contain so many cabinets, counters, fixtures, and appliances that it takes careful planning to make them all fit—and still have room for people to move around. This chapter will help with that.

Built in an Edwardian-Era spirit, this Piedmont, California, kitchen has 11-ft. ceilings; a massive marble and brass stove hood; a porcelain, steel, and cast-iron stove; and 2-ft.-sq. colored cast-concrete floor tiles you can clomp around on in big shoes.

Kitchen Planning

The best kitchens can accommodate your personal tastes and lifestyles as well as your physical characteristics, such as your height.

WHAT GOES ON IN YOUR KITCHEN?

Start planning by imagining a day in the life of your kitchen, being as specific as possible about the activities—and the actors. Do you want a sunny spot to have coffee, read the paper, and wake up? Will the kitchen table double as a desk for homework? Or will the kitchen be a command center in which you field calls and arrange after-school carpools while tossing the salad?

These upper cabinets stand atop a 2-in.-thick stone countertop so they feel like an integral part of the structure, rather than something just screwed to the walls. Yet for all its solidity, the kitchen is light filled and airy. The window above the cabinets helps lower the room's sight lines, as does the pull-down light fixture.

Keep a notebook in your present kitchen and jot down observations about what goes on—as well a wish list for what you'd like changed. Many entries will be cooking specific: Is there enough storage and enough counter space to prep several dishes? Does the cook like company? When you entertain, how large is the crowd? Is there a convenient place for cookbooks? Such considerations will be useful in evaluating your kitchen and establishing priorities for the new one.

CABINET HEIGHTS AND CLEARANCES

Over the years, architects, appliance designers, and builders have adopted a set of physical dimensions that, in theory, make kitchens safer and easier to use. As shown in "Figuring Dimensions" below, these dimensions work for most people but, in the end, may not suit everybody. As a rule of thumb, a counter is the right height if you can place your palms flat on it, with

Figuring Dimensions

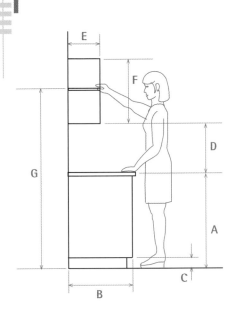

Standard Cabinet Dimensions

REFERENCE*	SPACE	DIMENSION (in.)
A	Height above the finish floor Kitchen countertops Bath vanity countertops	 36 32–34
B	Base cabinet depth	24
C	Height and depth of kick space	4
D	Wall cabinet distance above Standard countertop Sink and cooktop	 18 30
E	Depth of wall cabinet	12–15
F	Typical wall cabinet height (8-ft. ceilings)	30
G	Highest usable shelf	80

* Letter refers to "Figuring Dimensions" at left.

The arched valance over the farmhouse sink picks up curves in other rooms, including the double doors to the dining room, at right. In between, is a quiet alcove with enough room for cookbooks, a chair, and a computer.

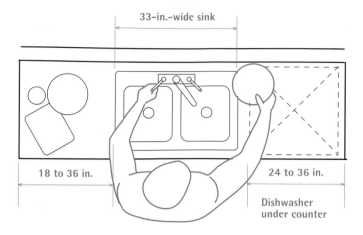

33-in.-wide sink

18 to 36 in.

24 to 36 in.

Dishwasher under counter

Each work area—food prep, cooking, and cleanup—should have adequate counter space so a cook can work efficiently, with enough clearance to move safely. Counters with dishwashers underneath must be at least 24-in. wide; otherwise, 18 in. is the minimum.

Minimum Kitchen Work-Space Clearances

SPACE	DIMENSION (in.)
In front of base cabinet	36
Between base cabinet and facing wall	40
Between facing appliances	48
Work space plus foot traffic	60

a slight bend to your elbow. If the standard counter height of 36 in. above the finish floor isn't right for you, lowering or raising it an inch or two may do the trick. However, if you're thinking of selling the house fairly soon, your ideal counter or shelf height may not appeal to the average buyer.

Equally important are the clearances needed to move easily in a kitchen—clearances that homeowners frequently overlook when laying out new kitchens. Be sure to allow enough room to open cabinet doors fully and still walk around them. Traffic lanes through work areas are vital because cooks frequently handle hot, sharp, or heavy objects: thus keep a 60-in. minimal clearance if the work area doubles as a corridor. Ideally, though, family traffic should bypass the cooking space. So if a kitchen has two or more doors, you may be able to reroute that unwanted traffic by eliminating one of those doorways, while gaining counter and cabinet space in the process.

COUNTER AND CABINET SPACE

Meal preparation consists of food prep, cooking, and cleanup, ideally with counter space for each job. Prepping the food—washing, cutting, and mixing—takes the most time, so give as much space as possible to counters near the sink and the cooktop.

Sink counters should be 24 in. wide on each side of the sink, though 36 in. is better, allowing plenty of room for food prep and the air-drying of pots and pans. Because dishwashers are 24 in. wide, they fit neatly under a 24-in. counter. If the kitchen is tiny and there's no undercounter dishwasher, 18-in.-wide sink counters are minimal. Have a splashback behind the sink.

Cooktop counters should be at least 18 in. to 24 in. wide on both sides of the unit, and at least one side should be made of a heat-resistant material. Placing a stove on an exterior wall keeps exhaust-fan ducts short, but never place a gas stove in front of a window because a draft could blow out burners. The wall behind a stove should be washable.

By the refrigerator, next to the latch side, have a counter at least 15 in. wide so you can place things there as they go in and out of the fridge. If the refrigerator and the sink share a counter, the space should be 36 in. to 42 in. long. Because this counter is typically a food-prep area, you'll need a large surface to store countertop appliances.

Cabinet space has few rules. The best indicator of how much cabinet space you need is the number of appliances, bowls, and paraphernalia you own. Or use this rule of thumb: Figure 18 sq. ft. of basic storage plus 6 sq. ft. for each person in the household.

Counter OUTLETS

Kitchen counters 12 in. wide or wider must have at least one electrical receptacle to serve them. All points on a counter must be within 2 ft. from a receptacle, and all counter receptacles must have ground fault circuit interrupter (GFCI) protection. Chapter 11 addresses this.

LAYOUT CHOICES: WORK AREAS

The person preparing and cooking the meal moves primarily in a space bounded by the refrigerator, the stove, and the sink—the so-called work triangle. When laying out such work areas, designers try to keep the distance traveled between the three points within 12 ft. to 22 ft. Three of the layouts shown below feature a work triangle. The fourth is a single-line kitchen, but the distance traveled should be roughly the same.

U-shaped kitchens are the most practical because they isolate the work area from family traffic. Because the cook spends most of the time at the sink, position it at the base of the U, with the refrigerator on one side and the stove on the other. If one person preps food or washes while the other cooks, their paths won't cross too often. If possible, place the sink beneath a window so the eye and the mind can roam.

L-shaped kitchens are popular because they allow various arrangements. That is, you can put a dining table or a kitchen island in the imaginary fourth corner. However, this becomes a somewhat less efficient setup if one leg of the L is too long. Again, position the sink in the middle.

Galley kitchens create efficient work triangles, but they can become hectic if there's through traffic. If you close one end of the galley to stop traffic, the galley should be at least 4 ft. wide to accommodate two cooks. To avoid colliding doors, never place a refrigerator directly across from an oven in a tight galley kitchen.

Single-line kitchens, common to small apartments, are workable if they're not longer than

Kitchen Lighting Basics

Kitchen lighting should be a combination of natural light (windows), general lighting, and task lighting to illuminate specific work areas. For light that is both warm and efficient, combine incandescent and fluorescent bulbs. Warm fluorescent lights are another option.

General lighting can come from overhead fixtures, recessed ceiling lights, track lighting, or perimeter lighting. Mount ceiling lights 10 in. to 12 in. out from cabinet faces to illuminate kitchen surfaces evenly, while minimizing shadows cast by wall cabinets or by people using the counter. For an average-size kitchen (75 sq. ft. to 100 sq. ft.), ceiling-mounted general lighting should total about 200 watts incandescent or 80 watts fluorescent; if there's recessed ceiling lighting, four 100-watt incandescent bulbs should be enough. For larger kitchens, figure 2 watts of incandescent or 1 watt of fluorescent light per square foot of kitchen area.

Task lighting over sinks and cooktops should be at least two 75-watt incandescent bulbs or two 30-watt fluorescent bulbs. Ideally, task lighting should be placed behind a face trim board of some kind, so that the bulbs shine more on the work surface than in one's eyes. To illuminate countertops, task lighting is often installed under wall cabinets, hidden by face board or a cabinet rail. Low-voltage halogen "puck" lights or slim-line fluorescent bulbs can be shielded by a face board that's only 1¼ in. high. In general, under-cabinet lights should be two-thirds as long as the counter they illuminate.

Common Kitchen Layouts

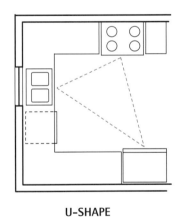

U-SHAPE

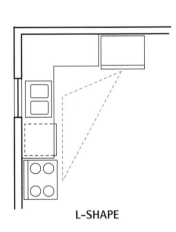

L-SHAPE

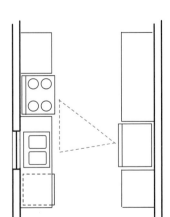

GALLEY

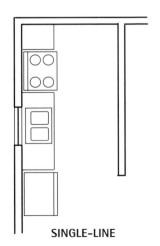

SINGLE-LINE

12 ft. and there's a minimum of 4 ft. to the opposite wall. Compact, space-saver appliances can maximize both floor and counter space.

Islands are great in multiple-use kitchens, for they can provide a buffer between cooking tasks. To make sure the island doesn't interfere with the work triangle, keep 4 ft. to 5 ft. of open space for nearby counters and appliances.

KITCHEN CABINET LAYOUTS

Once you've chosen a work layout that you like, make to-scale floor plans: A ¼ in. to 1 ft. scale provides a good amount of detail for a single room yet still fits on an 8½-in. by 11-in. sheet of graph paper. Include windows, doors, appliances,

and cabinets. You may find it helpful to cut to-scale rectangles to represent the refrigerator, sink, and cooktop. If you cut them from different colored paper or label each piece, you'll have an easier time trying out your layouts.

Basic layout. Refining the layout is a fluid process, but a few spatial arrangements are so common they're almost givens. Place the sink under a window. Don't put a refrigerator and a stove side by side because one likes it hot; the other, cold. In general, place the refrigerator toward the end of a cabinet run, so its big doors can swing free. When the appliances are comfortably situated, fill in the spaces between with cabinets.

Try not to fit cabinets too tightly to room dimensions. If you're fitting cabinets into an older house, it's safer to undersize cabinet runs slightly—allow 1½ in. of free space at the end of each bank of cabinets—so you have room to fine-tune the installation. You can cover gaps at walls or inside corners with scribed trim pieces. Speaking of inside corners, allow enough room for cabinet doors to open freely.

Cabinet dimensions. Basically, there are three types of stock cabinets: base cabinets, wall cabinets, and specialty cabinets.

▶ Base cabinets are typically 24 in. deep, and 34½ in. tall so that, when a countertop is added, the total height will be 36 in. Base cabinet widths increase in 3-in. increments, as do wall cabinet widths. Single-door base cabinets range from 12 in. to 24 in. wide; double-door base cabinets run 27 in. to 48 in. wide. Drawer cabinets vary from 15 in. to 24 in. wide. Tray units are generally 9 in. to 12 in. wide.

▶ Wall cabinets are 12 in. to 15 in. deep, with 12 in. being the most common depth. They vary from 12 in. to 33. in. high. Wall cabinet widths generally correspond to base cabinet widths, so cabinet joints line up.

▶ Specialty cabinets include tray cabinets, base corner units, corner units with rotating shelves, tall refrigerator or utility cabinets, and wall-oven cabinets. Specialty accessories include spice racks, sliding cutting boards, and tilt-out bins. Specialty cabinet dimensions vary, not always in predictable increments. Base sink cabinets range from 36 in. wide (no drawers on either side) to 84 in., typically in 6-in. increments.

ORDERING CABINETS

After numerous refinements, your kitchen layout should be tight enough to take it to a home center and get an estimate on the cabinets. Or you can go online, where numerous Web sites will walk you through measuring and ordering. If

Adding Cabinets, Refining the Layout

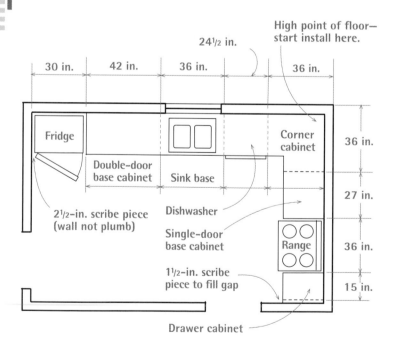

Once you choose a layout that works well, use base cabinets to tie appliances and work areas together. On your floor plan, note room irregularities that could affect layout and installation. Using light pencil lines, mark cabinet and appliance locations onto the walls.

you've never ordered cabinets before, it's smart to hire a finish carpenter to help figure out exactly what you need.

Before ordering cabinets, clean up floor plans and elevations, and survey the kitchen one last time, noting window, door, and appliance locations; electrical outlets, switches, and lights; and plumbing stub-outs (protruding pipe ends before hookup)—in short, every physical aspect of the space. Carefully remeasure the room and note potential problems such as sloping floors, walls that are wavy or out of plumb, and corners that aren't square or that have excessive joint com-

pound that could interfere with installation. Most of these irregularities can be corrected by shimming cabinets to level and scribing end panels to cover irregular surfaces, but you need to know about them beforehand.

Installing Cabinets

The key to a successful cabinet installation is leveling the base and wall cabinets and solidly securing them to wall studs and to the floor. As noted earlier, carefully measure and assess the kitchen walls, floor, and corners *before* you order

Cabinet Basics

Cabinets today are basically boxes of plywood, particleboard, or medium-density fiberboard (MDF) panels that are glued and screwed together. Side panels, bottoms, and partitions are typically ¾ in. thick; back panels are usually ¼ in. thick. Cabinet faces are either *frameless* (the edges of the panels are the frame, although they may be veneered or edge-banded) or *face frame* (a four-sided wood frame covers the edges of each box).

Factory-made cabinets are frameless (also called European style). Having fewer elements and a simpler design, they are easier to manufacture. (The cabinets shown in the installation photos are frameless.) Doors and drawers typically lie flush on the case and overlay the panel edges. Usually, there's ⅛ in. between the door and the drawer edges.

Face-frame cabinets are a bit more work, but offer more visual variety. You can expose more or less of the frame, vary the gaps between drawers and doors, use different hinge types, and so on. In general, designers who want a more ornamental, less severe, more traditional look often specify face-frame cabinets.

In addition to the elements above, cabinet cases have *nailers* (mounting rails) that you screw through to secure the cabinets to the studs. Base cabinets also have *stringers*—plywood webs across the top—to make boxes more rigid, keep partitions and sides in place, and provide something solid to screw the countertop to.

This frameless base cabinet will have a countertop or its substrate attached to the two plywood webs (stringers) running across its top. The two mounting rails on the back of the cabinet will be screwed to studs, securing the unit.

Kickspaces

The indentation at the bottom of a base cabinet that provides room for your toes, so you can belly up to the cabinet while prepping food or doing dishes, is called the *kickspace*. Without a kickspace, you'd need to lean forward to work at the counter—a sure recipe for backaches. Custom-made cabinets sit on a separate *rough toekick* (also called a plinth or sub-base), which is often assembled on site; whereas most (but not all) factory-made base cabinets arrive with *toekicks* built in. Toekicks are covered by a *kickface*, or finish toekick, a ⅛-in. plywood strip with the same finish as the cabinets or a vinyl strip; the kickface is better installed after the finish floor.

Scribes

Cabinet assemblies also include small but important filler strips called a *scribe pieces*. These typically have a rabbeted back so they can be easily be ripped down to fill gaps between cabinets or between a cabinet and a wall. On a frameless cabinet, a separate scribe piece may be attached to a side panel, near its face; whereas on face-frame cabinets, the frame stile (vertical piece) has a rabbeted back edge (for scribing). In addition, many cabinet side panels extend slightly beyond the back panels, so those side panels can be scribed to fit snugly to the wall, as shown in the top left photo on p. 311. Custom cabinet-makers often create a separate scribe panel to dress up the end cabinet in a run and cover any gaps along the wall.

When installing cabinets, start from a high point in the floor—in this case, at the upper right corner of the photo. As you work out from the high point, add shims as necessary to level the toekick (or the base of the cabinet) in two directions.

Cabinet-Mounting and Edge Details

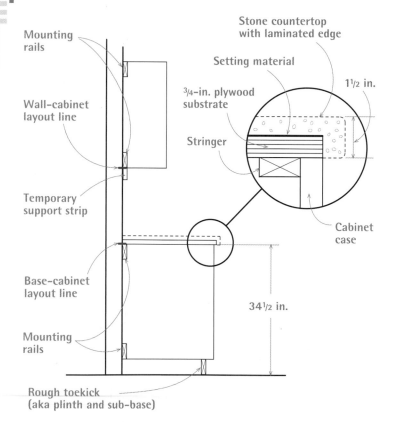

Mounting rails

Wall-cabinet layout line

Temporary support strip

Base-cabinet layout line

Mounting rails

Rough toekick (aka plinth and sub-base)

Stone countertop with laminated edge

Setting material

³/4-in. plywood substrate

1¹/2 in.

Stringer

Cabinet case

34¹/2 in.

Better-grade cabinets have mounting rails on the outside of back panels so the rails are not visible inside the cabinet case. The edge detail shown in the enlargment is typical. The countertop substrate—here, ³/4 in. plywood—screws to stringers at the top of the cabinet case. Screw the cabinet bottom to the rough toekick.

the cabinets—and review those measurements and conditions again after the cabinets arrive.

LAYING OUT CABINETS

Using a long level atop a straightedge, locate the high point of the floor. It's easier to set a base cabinet (or rough toekick) at the floor's high point and shim up the other cabinets to that level than it is to cut down cabinet bases and toekicks. From the floor's high point, measure up the height of a base cabinet (usually 34½ in. high) and mark the wall. Use a laser level, as shown in the top left photo on p. 45, to transfer the base cabinet mark to other walls, creating a level line around the room, which we'll call the base *cabinet layout line*.

Marking off elements. Along the base cabinet layout line, mark off fixed elements, such as the stove, range hood, and refrigerator. Often, a sink cabinet will center under a window. If upper cabinets are to frame a window evenly on both sides, mark the edges of those cabinets. Once the large elements are marked onto the walls, mark off the widths of the individual cabinets. For frameless cabinets, measure from the outside of the side panels. The frames of face-frame cabinets extend slightly beyond the side panels, creating slight gaps between the boxes. Much of the time, the sides of wall and base cabinet units will line up vertically because they are the same width.

Wall cabinets. Use the base cabinet layout line to establish the bottoms of wall cabinets, too. Because wall cabinets are normally placed 18 in. above the finish countertop, measure 19½ in. up from the base cabinet layout line to position the bottoms of the wall cabinets; shoot a laser level through that mark and lightly pencil a second level line around the room, which is the *wall cabinet layout line*. Over refrigerators and stoves, the bottoms of the wall cabinets will be higher. If you are also installing full-height pantry or broom cabinets, make sure their tops align with the tops of the wall cabinets; if they don't, raise or lower the wall cabinets till the tops line up. Next mark off the width of the wall cabinets along the wall cabinet layout line.

Scribe locations. Layout marks should also include *scribe locations*, where you must install a narrow scribe piece (filler strip) to cover a gap between cabinets and an appliance or a space between an end cabinet and an irregular wall. Where cabinets meet at inside corners, 1½-in.- or 2-in.-wide scribes are often needed to offset drawers or doors slightly, so they have room to pull past the cabinet knobs or appliance handles sticking out from the adjacent bank of cabinets.

Marking studs. Finally, find and mark stud centers, to which you'll screw the cabinets. To find studs, either use an electronic stud-finder, rap the walls with your knuckles, or drive small finish nails into wall areas that will be covered by cabinets. Whatever works! Use a spirit level to plumb light pencil lines that indicate the stud centers. It's desirable to screw into as many studs as you can to secure wall cabinets, but screwing into only one stud is acceptable for base cabinets and for narrow wall cabinets that don't reach two studs.

INSTALLING BASE CABINETS

Cabinet installers wrangle about whether it's easier to install base or wall cabinets first. If you hang the wall units first, you won't need to lean over the base cabinets as you work. Whereas if you install the bases first, you can brace the bottom of the wall cabinets off the bases and thereby install the uppers single-handedly. There isn't one right answer, but the photos on p. 318 make a convincing case for hanging the wall cabinets after installing stone countertops. Above all, be patient. Setting cabinets means endlessly checking and rechecking for level, fussing with shims, and so on. So don't begrudge the time it takes. You can't hurry love or cabinets.

Setting rough toekicks. If your cabinets have separate toekicks, install them first, starting at the highest point on the floor—as you did during layout. Make the toekicks as long as possible to minimize joints because joints tend to sag and separate under load. Level the toekicks side to side, front to back, and from section to section. Shimming is an inexact science: As a rule of thumb, shim under the corners and in the middle of a span—roughly every 18 in. to 24 in. A 24-in.-deep base cabinet is typically supported by a 20-in.-deep toekick.

Leveling cabinet bases and toekicks takes shims and several spirit levels, as well as patience. After leveling each unit in two directions, run a third level diagonally to the adjacent toekick to make sure all are at the same height.

PRO TIP

To make rough toekicks, rip down ¾-in. plywood, which is more durable and water resistant than particleboard should there be a leak. Don't use 2×4s because they are rarely straight enough to use as a sub-base for cabinets. Besides, rough toekicks must be 4 in. high, and a modern 2×4 placed on edge would be just 3½ in. high.

If floors are seriously out of level—say, 1 in. in 8 ft.—construct several *ell supports* such as the one shown in the top right photo on p. 308. Screw one leg of each ell to the subfloor, level the top of the toekick, and then screw the side of the toekick to the upright leg of each ell. Ells aren't hard to construct, and they're far more stable than a 1-in.-high stack of shims. Once you've leveled the toekicks, place the base cabinets atop them and see how everything fits together. If this dry run looks good, set aside the cabinets and screw the toekicks to the subfloor.

Because you'll be securing both base and wall cabinets to stud centers, use an electronic stud-finder to help locate them.

INSTALL THE Toekick FIRST

If finish floors aren't yet installed and you don't want the cabinets dinged up by the flooring installers, then install only the toekick initially, shimming it level and screwing it to the subfloor. This is especially recommended if you'll be laying tile floors because mortar and grout are messy. Then flooring installers can run the flooring snug to the toekick, covering the shims. When the flooring is complete, simply place the base cabinets atop the level toekick and screw them down. When constructing the toekick, increase its height by the thickness of the finish floor, so the top of the toekick will be 4 in. above the finish floor. If you're installing tile over a mortar bed (1 in. to 1½ in. thick), make the rough toekick 5 in. to 5½ in. high.

TWO WAYS TO SECURE A TOEKICK

PRO TIP

As you install each cabinet, first transfer the stud center marks to the mounting rails on the back of the cabinet. Then drill through the marks, using a bit that's thinner than the shanks of the mounting screws— or a countersink bit. Drill slowly to avoid splintering the plywood on the inside of the cabinet, or stop the countersink bit just as its point emerges. Then finish drilling from the other side.

||||

Once you've leveled all the toekicks in a cabinet run, screw them to the subfloor. If you use square-drive screws, the driver bit is less likely to slip out when the screw meets resistance.

If a floor is badly out of level, avoid using a stack of shims to level a unit because they wouldn't be stable. Instead, use plywood ell-supports: Screw one leg of the ell to the subfloor. Then screw the leveled toekick to the other leg.

Once you've leveled the toekicks along a wall, start setting the base cabinets on top, and check them for level as well. If the cabinets are in an L- or U-shaped layout, work outward from a corner.

Setting cabinets with integral toekicks. If your cabinets have integral (built-in) toekicks, be sure to review the preceding section on rough toekicks. Shimming units with integral kicks is similar, but more difficult. Basically, you'll shim each cabinet under its sidewalls, front, and back. The difficulty arises because you can't go back and adjust rear shims once you've installed the next cabinet. So take the time to level the top of each base cabinet perfectly. Otherwise, the order in which you install cabinets is the same for either type.

Setting base cabinets. If you're installing a single run of cabinets along one wall, it really doesn't matter where you start, except that if there's a sink cabinet centered under a window, start there. If your cabinet layout is L- or U-shaped, start in a corner because there, where cabinet runs converge in a corner, their tops will need to line up perfectly if the countertop is to be level in all directions. So take pains to be sure that first corner top is at the right height—in relation to the base cabinet layout line—and level in all directions. Once that corner cabinet is perfectly level,

When you're sure that base cabinets are at the correct height and leveled, align their front edges or face frames and use padded clamps to draw adjacent cabinets together. Then sink two wood screws through side panels to secure them.

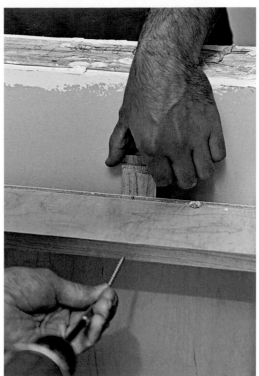

If the walls are irregular—and most are—shim behind the cabinet mounting rails before screwing them to the studs. Otherwise, back panels and rails could distort.

Screw through cabinet bottoms into toekicks. Predrill screw holes with a countersink bit so screw heads will be flush. Then cover them with wood plugs or stick-on screw covers.

you have a good shot at extending that level outward as you add cabinets.

When you've leveled the corner cabinet in all directions, you can screw it to the toekick and, through its mounting rails, to the studs behind it. But more often, carpenters prefer to "gang" cabinets together, lining up their tops so they're level and, using quick-release clamps with padded jaws, aligning and drawing the cabinet edges or face frames together. Once you've lined up the cabinet edges and frames, use two wood screws to join them. Drill pilot holes first with a countersink bit so the screw heads will be flush. If cabinet panels are ¾ in. thick, use 1¼-in. screws to join them, so the screw points don't pop through.

After securing the cabinet edges and frames, check the cabinet tops for level and height one last time. Then, depending on the type of cabinet, screw the cabinet bottoms to the toekicks, or screw integral toekicks to the subfloor. Finally, screw the cabinet backs to the studs, through the pilot holes you predrilled. If a wall is wavy, shim low spots behind the mounting rails; otherwise, screws could distort the mounting rails and possibly misalign the cabinet boxes. Screws should sink at least 1 in. into the studs, so use #8 screws that are 2½ in. or 3 in. long.

Bore slightly oversize holes in the sink cabinet so you'll have an easier time lining up pipe stub-outs. When the installation is complete, spray expanding foam to fill the gaps.

electrical outlets, if any. Perhaps the easiest way to transfer the locations of those utilities to the back of the cabinet is to position the cabinet as close as you can to layout marks on the wall, and then place a spirit level behind it. Holding the level vertically, place it next to each stub-out, plumb the level, and then mark that pipe's position on the wall and on the cabinet's back stringer. Pull the sink base away from the wall, measure how far each stub is below the layout line, and measure down an equal amount on the back of the cabinet. Use a slightly oversize hole saw to bore holes, stopping when the saw's center bit comes through the inside of the cabinet. Finish drilling from the inside of the back panel to avoid splintering it.

Setting islands. Kitchen islands are installed much the same as other base cabinets, except that they can't be screwed to studs. Therefore, the rough toekick must be sturdy and well attached to the subfloor. For that reason, use ell-supports to level rough toekicks or integral toekicks and anchor them to the subfloor. Here, glue and screw the ells to the subfloor after snapping chalklines to show you exactly where the island will sit. Place an ell at least every 18 in. to 24 in. and, to further bolster rough toekicks, add crosspieces at the same interval. You can't overbuild a kitchen island, especially if you've got kids who think cabinets are jungle gyms.

Don't use drywall screws because they don't have much shear strength. If your base cabinets have top and bottom mounting rails, drive two screws per stud to anchor the cabinets—in other words, sink a screw each time a mounting rail crosses a stud. Later, you can use wood-grained, stick-on screw covers to hide the screws.

Setting sink bases. Sink bases with back panels take a bit more work because you must bore or cut through the back panel for pipe stub-outs and

Scribing A BASE CABINET

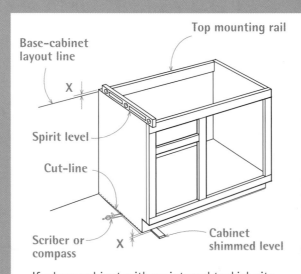

If a base cabinet with an integral toekick sits above the base-cabinet layout line once the unit has been leveled, scribe and trim its bottom to reduce its height. Set the scriber to the amount (X) that the cabinet sits above the layout line.

To cut down a base cabinet (with an integral toekick) whose top is too high, place the cabinet as close as possible to its final position and shim it level. Set a pencil compass to the distance the cabinet top projects above the base cabinet layout line, and scribe the base of the cabinet along the floor. By cutting along those scribed lines with a jigsaw, you'll reduce the height of the cabinet the correct amount. If either side panel is finished, place masking tape along the base of the panel before scribing and cutting. A pencil line drawn on the tape may be more visible, and the tape will keep the metal shoe of the jigsaw from scratching the panel.

INSTALLING WALL CABINETS

Wall cabinets must be leveled, plumbed, and solidly anchored, so transfer the locations of stud centers to the back of each wall cabinet, and predrill screw holes in the mounting rails, as you did for base cabinets. Remove the doors and shelves so the cabinets will be easier to lift and position next to the alignment marks you drew earlier along the wall cabinet layout line. Before lifting anything, however, use a 6-ft. spirit level to refresh your memory as to where the wall's surface is out of plumb and where it bulges or recedes. Make light pencil notations on the wall.

Supporting cabinets. It's better to have a helper hold wall cabinets in place as you mount them. But if you're working solo, the simplest support is a *temporary support strip*, a straight, predrilled ¾-in. by 1½-in. plywood strip placed immediately below the wall cabinet layout line and screwed to each stud with a #8 wood screw (see "Cabinet-Mounting and Edge Details," on p. 306). With the cabinet bottom sitting atop it, the strip will support the box's weight, freeing one of your hands to screw the top mounting rail to a stud. That first screw will hold the cabinet in place, but don't sink it so deep that it bends the mounting rail.

Plumbing and shimming. Once that first screw is in, the cabinet should stay put, so you'll have both hands free to shim the cabinet and check for plumb. A cabinet sitting on a leveled strip should have a level bottom and plumb sides—but check to be sure. The front of the cabinet must also be plumb. So if it's not, insert shims between the wall and the cabinet. Although you can easily shim behind the top mounting rail, the support strip will prevent shimming from underneath; instead, shim the bottom corners from the side. If the top of the cabinet needs to come forward, slightly back out the screw in the top mounting rail. Once all the cabinet faces are plumb, drive a second screw through the top mounting rail and a third screw through the bottom rail, near the shim point. You will add another screw to the bottom rail later, after you remove the support strip and shim behind the fourth corner of the cabinet box.

Ideally, each wall cabinet should be secured to at least two studs with two #8 wood screws through the top mounting rail and two screws through the bottom rail. However, many wall cabinets are too narrow to reach two studs. Screwing cabinet boxes to each other lends additional support and spreads the load. But if a cabinet will be heavily loaded or if you're uneasy

SCRIBING A PANEL TO AN IRREGULAR WALL

To scribe an end panel (here, a refrigerator panel), first level and plumb its edges. Put painter's masking tape on the panel and scribe directly onto the tape to make the line more visible. If the wall irregularity is slight, hold a pencil flat to the wall and slide it up and down.

A belt sander held 90° to a scribed line enables you to see how much wood you're removing. Use a 120-grit belt, back-bevel the edge slightly, keep the sander moving, and stop just shy of the line. Finish off with a sanding block or a handplane.

Hanging wall cabinets is easiest with four hands: Two hold and adjust, while two check level and drive screws.

If you plumb and level the corner units, it will be easier to level cabinet runs on both walls. The corner strip, held in place with a clamp, covers the gap between the two cabinets. Note: European-style hinges—seen here on the cabinet cases—allow you to remove the doors easily, so there's less weight to lift.

hanging it on only one stud, cut open the wall and *let in* (mortise) a piece of 1× blocking into at least two studs. You'll need to repair the wall—a rough patch is fine if it's hidden by cabinets—but you'll have plenty to screw to.

Tying cabinets together. Install the wall cabinets in roughly the same order you did base cabinets. If the cabinet layout is L- or U-shaped, start with a corner cabinet and work outward. As you set successive cabinets, place a straight-edge or a 6-ft. level held on-edge across several cabinet faces to make sure they're flush. You may need to back out screws or drive them deeper to make the cabinets flush. Once they're flush, clamp and screw them together as you did for the base cabinets. At that point, you can remove the support strip. With the strip gone, the space

behind the bottom mounting rail will be accessible, so add shims and screws as needed.

Finishing touches. Patch holes left by the support-strip screws or cover them with trim. Custom cabinetmakers often use a piece of trim with the same finish as the cabinets as a support strip and just leave it in place. Thus if the front of the cabinet has a 1¼-in.-wide trim piece running along the bottom to hide a lighting strip, use a piece of 1¼-in.-wide trim as a support strip. Cover the cabinet-mounting screws with wood plugs or stick-on screw covers. Finally, install the shelves, drawers, doors, and hardware such as pulls or knobs.

These days, most cabinets use European-style door hinges (shown at left), which are easy to remove, reattach, and adjust. Hinges are set into 35mm-diameter holes bored precisely into the door frames. The doors are attached to the cabinet box via baseplates; these hinges easily clip on and off the baseplates without the need to remove any screws. Once the cabinets are installed, clip on the doors and use the adjustment screws to raise the hinges up or down, in or out, until the *reveals* (gaps) between the doors are equal and the doors lie flat.

Countertops for Kitchens and Baths

Most materials in this section require special training and equipment for installation. In fact, solid-surface and stone-polymer countertop makers will sell counter stock only to certified fabricators. Some materials, such as plastic laminates, can be successfully installed if you're handy. But,

In this Eugene, Oregon, bungalow, you're more aware of individual elements because painted base cabinets offer a nice contrast to the red oak floors and maple butcher-block countertops. The traditional enameled cast-iron sink continues the contrast-and-enjoy scheme.

The dining area does double-duty. Both bench seats have built-in hanging file cabinets, so the owner can sit at the table and deal with household bills. And under the butcher-block top, a small end drawer holds flatware.

Countertop Choices

CHARACTERISTIC	PLASTIC LAMINATE	SOLID SURFACE	QUARTZ COMPOSITE	CERAMIC TILE	STONE	CONCRETE	WOOD
Durability, scratch resistance	Fair	Excellent*	Excellent	Good	Good†	Good	Fair‡
Ease of cleaning	Excellent	Excellent	Excellent	Fair§	Excellent	Good	Fair
Stain resistance	Good	Good	Excellent	Fair	Fair	Poor	Poor
Water resistance	Good	Excellent	Excellent	Fair	Good	Good	Poor
Heat resistance	Poor	Fair	Good	Excellent	Excellent	Excellent	Poor
Expense	$	$$$	$$ to $$$	$$	$$$	$ to $$	$$

* Material scratches, but scratches are easily sanded out.

‡ Durability depends on type of wood and finish; wood is generally a bad choice near sinks and water.

† Harder stones (granite) wear well; softer stones (soapstone) scratch and stain easily.

§ Glazed tiles resist stains, water, and heat; but grout joints deteriorate if not sealed and maintained.

as you'll see, desirable details, such as wrapped front edges and integral backsplashes (no seams to leak!), are best fabricated in a pro shop. All in all, it's smarter to choose a reputable installer than to try installing a countertop yourself. Tile countertops are discussed in Chapter 16.

CHOOSING COUNTERTOPS WISELY

The wide array of countertop colors, materials, and details (such as edges and backsplashes), give you tens of thousands of combinations to choose from. Here's help narrowing your choices.

Plastic laminate, a tried-and-true surface (often called Formica® after a popular brand), accounts for more than two-thirds of all countertop installations. Standard laminate is only $\frac{1}{16}$-in. thick, so it is typically glued to a ¾-in. particleboard substrate to lend rigidity and ensure adequate support. Plastic laminate remains so popular because it's tough, stain-resistant, quite economical, and available in a great range of colors and patterns. There are also extra-thick and fire-resistant laminates. One disadvantage is that the seams can degrade and admit water. And once the substrate is water damaged and the laminate is lifting, the countertop is beyond repair.

Solid-surface countertops began with DuPont's Corian®, which is still the best-seller in this category. Most brands are polyester or acrylic resins with a mineral filler. Solid-surface countertops have a lot going for them: They're water and stain resistant; nonporous and easy to clean and thus great for food prep; and

leakproof because they have seamless, chemically bonded backsplashes and integral sinks. Unlike laminates, solid-surface sheets are the same material top to bottom, so if you scratch them or put too hot a pot on them, you can sand out the blemishes. Most brands come with a 10-year warranty. Note that this material is generally expensive.

Quartz composites are a new and rapidly growing group that includes brands such as Zodiaq® and Silestone®; the blend is roughly 93 percent quartz and 7 percent polymers and pigments. Quartz composites have many of the virtues of stone countertops and few of the failings. Quartz composites are scratch, heat, and stain resistant; completely nonporous so they're easy to clean; and less likely to fracture during transit because mineral particles are uniformly dispersed and free from the imperfections of natural stone. Plus, a 10-year warranty is standard. However, these composites are expensive. And stone connoisseurs will know the countertop is not natural stone because of its uniformity.

Ceramic tile is beautiful and durable. Its great variety of colors, shapes, and sizes allows almost unlimited freedom to create your own patterns. Glazed tiles themselves are largely resistant to heat, water, stains, and scratches. Tile can be applied successively over a plywood substrate or a mortar bed, and a diligent novice can install it successfully. Tile prices vary widely, and thus can fit almost any budget. But its grout joints are relatively fragile, easily stained if they're not sealed and maintained, and tend to collect crud. Also,

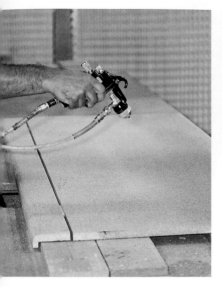

1. After rough-cutting the substrate and the laminate and touch-sanding them, spray both surfaces with a water-based contact cement. (Wear a respirator mask with organic vapor filters.) The curved piece at left, separated from the counter by a ¼-in. spacer, will become the backsplash. The gap will enable the laminate to bend in a gentle radius.

2. After allowing the contact cement to set for 15 minutes—surfaces are usually warmed to speed drying—place ½-in. sticks atop the particleboard, and then place the laminate on the sticks. The sticks allow you to accurately position the laminate over the substrate without allowing cemented faces to touch.

3. After measuring the laminate's overlap and correcting its position, pull a middle stick and hand-smooth the laminate to the particleboard. Once there's contact, you're committed. Working outward from the middle, pull out sticks and smooth the laminate by hand.

4. Once you've removed the sticks, use a hand-roller to apply greater pressure to bond the laminate to the particleboard.

irregular tile surfaces can be tricky to seal around sinks and splashbacks, so water can seep in and damage wood substrates.

Stone slabs include granite, marble, soapstone, limestone, and slate. Stone is naturally beautiful, but it's also heavy, hard to work, and very expensive. Yet for all its heft, stone is relatively fragile and must be supported by a substrate—usually ¾-in. plywood. Granite, the most popular stone, is available in slabs ¾ in. and 1¼ in. thick, up to 5 ft. wide and 10 ft. long. But because of its great weight, granite is usually installed in several sections 6 ft. long or less. Section seams are filled with a caulk that's color-matched to the granite, so seams are virtually invisible. To create a thicker edge, fabricators epoxy two layers of stone. When pattern matched and polished correctly, the seams are almost invisible. Harder stones such as granite are highly scratch resistant. Softer stones, such as soapstone, can be scratched, but their softness allows you to easily sand out scratches or buff them out with steel wool. Stone is generally water resistant, though most stones are somewhat porous and so will stain unless protected. Penetrating sealants such as Aqua Mix Stone Sealer's Choice® and Miracle Sealant's 511 Porous Plus™ are well regarded in

the stone trade. For more recommendations, visit www.stoneworld.com.

Because stone is a natural material with inherent flaws and irregularities, few installers offer a warranty once an installation is complete. In the trade, it's called "a tail-light warranty"; in other words, once the installer's truck leaves your driveway, the warranty expires.

Concrete has become *très chic* as a countertop material because it's tough, reasonably priced, and highly malleable. It can be stained and polished to look like exotic stone, factory-cast with colorful glass shards in the bottom of its mold. Or it can be cast directly atop a base cabinet. Concrete weighs roughly the same as stone. However, because a concrete slab needs to be fully 1½ in. thick, you need to overbuild base cabinets to support the additional weight. (Stone tops need to be 1½-in. thick only along their front edge.) Because the bottom of in-place form molds can sag between supports until the concrete sets, it's smart to add cross-counter webs to support the forms. Concrete is notorious for cracking and staining, but you can minimize those problems by reinforcing the slab adequately with steel or poly fibers and finishing the surface meticulously.

Concrete gurus praise Berylex®, an admixture that strengthens and internally waterproofs slabs

POST-FORMING A COUNTERTOP

1. At a custom-counter shop, the post-forming machine is a vacuum press that applies heat and pressure to wrap the laminate to the shaped edges of the countertop and splashboard. Note: The substrate is still in two pieces, so when moving the assembly, both pieces must be supported.

2. Plastic laminate can be brittle when it's cold, so the assembly is next moved to a bench with a heated edge. Inverted, the countertop is clamped to the bench and the backsplash is pulled to its final position—at a right angle to the countertop.

3. The ¼-in. spacers placed earlier are removed, and coved strips along the joint between the countertop and backsplash are hot-glued. Coved strips keep the top and back pieces in place and, because the cove has the same arc as the laminate, they support it as well.

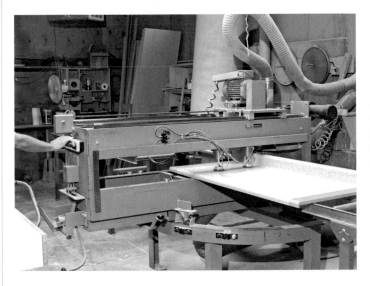

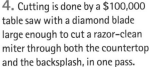

4. Cutting is done by a $100,000 table saw with a diamond blade large enough to cut a razor-clean miter through both the countertop and the backsplash, in one pass.

and, to a degree, stain-proofs them, too. Miracle Sealant's 511 Porous Plus, a penetrating sealer, is effective at stain-proofing cementitious materials from grout to concrete. One of the best books on casting your own countertop is Fu-Tung Cheng's *Concrete Countertops* (The Taunton Press).

Wood is a sentimental favorite because it's warm and beautiful, but it must be correctly finished and carefully sealed to prevent damage around sinks or along seams where water could collect. There are so many types of wood that it's tough to generalize about traits, but most types scorch, scratch, and stain easily, and water will swell and rot wood unless you keep it sealed. Thus a growing number of fabricators such as Spekva of Denmark, are producing oil-finished, butcher-block and laminated-wood countertops that will remain durable if you peri-

odically apply a food-safe oil recommended by the manufacturer. Such countertops are pricey but, in Spekva's case, the wood is harvested from sustainable, managed forests.

POST-FORMED PLASTIC LAMINATE TOPS

Roughly half of residential laminate countertops are *post-formed*—in which a shop or factory adheres and wraps a single, continuous sheet of laminate to a particleboard substrate, creating a seamless joint between the counter and backsplash. This leak-free joint is the principal reason why most contractors order post-formed laminate tops rather than adhering the laminate to the substrate themselves. However, if you want a different transition from countertop to wall, perhaps a tile backsplash, or simply want to save money, laminating a flat countertop is not that difficult.

PRO TIP

Once the laminated countertop is scribed and secured to the base cabinet(s), do the cutout for the kitchen sink. Kitchen-sink cutouts are best done on site because the remaining substrate front and back would likely break in transit if you did the cutout at the shop.

PRO TIP

If you choose a replacement sink the same size as the old one, you won't need to adjust the counter opening to install a larger sink. Moreover, if there's an under-counter dishwasher next to the sink cabinet, there may be no room for a longer sink.

Although the photos in "Adhering Laminate Yourself," on p. 314, were shot entirely in a custom counter shop, they depict the most critical steps for doing the job yourself. The photos in "Post-Forming a Countertop," on p. 315, show tasks that require specialized equipment and can be done only in a shop. A custom counter shop will also trim the counter to length, trim excess laminate, and cut miter joints if the counter is L- or U-shaped.

If you opt for a post-formed top, the installation becomes a good deal simpler. The counter installer's principal tasks will then be scribing the top of the backsplash so it fits flush to the wall, drawing mitered sections together with *draw-bolts,* and securing the counter substrate to the top of the base cabinet. However, as discussed in the next section, the first step in fitting countertops is taking careful measurements.

ORDERING COUNTERTOPS

Once you've identified several reputable countertop shops in your area, get bids. For your protection, develop detailed floor plans and, as you proceed, put everything in writing. That way, you'll be sure that quotes from different shops reflect similar details, deadlines, and so on. The following guidelines are adapted, with permission, from Sullivan Counter Tops, Inc. (visit www.sullivancountertops.com).

Visit suppliers in your area. Look at countertops in several different showrooms, and discuss your options with the salespeople. Share any information—samples of wall paint or cabinet finishes, magazine ads showing counter surfaces, photos of sinks or sink fixtures—that will clarify the style and look you're after. A salesperson's willingness to spend time and answer questions says a lot about a supplier.

Get bids. Provide a floor plan, drawing, or sketch to the countertop suppliers, and ask each to generate a written bid. The bid should also specify a completion date, terms of payment, and the scope of the installation. In most cases, quoted prices will not include plumbing, electrical work, or adjustments to the cabinets such as sink cutouts and leveling plywood substrates. Tearing out old countertops is usually extra, too. Based on bids and supplier reputations, choose a supplier.

Schedule the job. Most installations require two visits from the supplier: the "measure date" and the "install date." It's difficult to pinpoint a measure date until the cabinets are installed, but in general, 2 weeks' to 4 weeks' notice should be enough. Typically, solid-surface (such as Corian) and plastic-laminate countertops require about 1 week between the measure date and the install date. Quartz-composite countertops (such as Zodiaq) require about 2 weeks. Most countertop suppliers will allow you to change the installation time without penalty, provided you give them enough notice.

Be prepared for meetings. The measure date is your last chance to give input on details such as underlayment issues, color, edge treatment, and splash detail. Whatever you finally decide on, get it in writing. During this meeting, the supplier will review job site conditions, so the general contractor should be there, too.

Important prerequisites

▶ Cabinets must be set before the job can be measured. In other words, the cabinets must be screwed together and screwed to the walls, not just pushed into place. The cabinets cannot be moved even $\frac{1}{8}$ in. after the countertop supplier has measured because countertops are fabricated to close tolerances.

▶ Cabinets must be set level. As general rule, cabinets must be set on a level plane within $\frac{1}{8}$ in. over a 10-ft. length. Such stringent requirements are a concern not only to installers but also, in some cases, to manufacturers as a condition of warranty.

▶ All appliances and sinks should be on the job site at the time of the measure. The fitting of sinks and appliances is often critically close. Design or construction issues that could cause problems or delay the installation should be resolved on the measure date. If the sinks and appliances are on site, the supplier can inspect them. If there's a defect, damage, or, say, a sink rim that won't fit the countertop, you'll need time to replace the item before installation.

Kitchen Sinks

Because a kitchen is one the most-used rooms in the house, do a little research before choosing its most-used fixture.

CHOOSING A KITCHEN SINK

Keep four criteria in mind when considering sinks: size and number of bowls, sink-hole compatibility with faucets and accessories, materials, and mounting styles.

Size and number of bowls. Sinks are available in dozens of sizes and shapes. For the record, a 22-in. by 33-in. two-bowl unit is the most popular, perhaps because it fits neatly into "standard" sink cabinets 24 in. deep by 36 in. long. Two bowls allow you to prep food in one, and put used bowls and pots in the other, during the mad dash to dinner. Typically, there's a garbage disposer on one side. If you've got a dishwasher and don't need to wash dishes in the sink, a large single-bowl sink is best suited to washing pots and pans; 10 in. deep is optimal. If you've got plenty of counter space and two family members like to cook, install two separate sinks. By the way, three-bowl sinks (45 in. wide) are overkill for most home kitchens.

Most sinks have one to four holes. Typically the spout and faucet handles take up three of those holes, but some single-lever faucets require only one hole. Filling an extra hole is generally not a problem, what with soap dispensers, hot-water dispensers, spray units, filtered-water dispensers, and so on to choose from. Incompatibility more often occurs when a faucet assembly's valve stems have a different spacing than the holes in the sink. Always measure the sink and the faucet assembly to be sure. Likewise, if the sink is undermounted, an installer must drill holes into a countertop, making sure they have the same spacing as the faucet to be installed.

Materials. Sink materials include many of those used for countertops. You can use almost anything that will hold water, but ideally it should be light enough to install without breaking your back, easy to clean, durable, moderately priced, heat resistant, and stain resistant. Few materials fill the bill as well as stainless steel.

▶ Stainless-steel sinks represent roughly three-quarters of all kitchen installations. Typically, they have a brushed or polished finish; brushed finishes are easier to maintain

THE Beauty OF TEMPLATES

Templates are useful for transferring accurate measurements to any sheet material or flat surface, whether it's a piece of drywall that needs to be notched beneath an exposed stair or a new door that must be fit to an old, out-of-square door frame. When the going gets rough, the pros make templates. Nowhere is this truer than when those large sheets are granite slabs. Often, countertop suppliers create templates during the "measure date" described in "Ordering Countertops," on the facing page.

Templates are most often made by hot-gluing strips of ⅛-in.-thick plywood (also called doorskin), which is rigid enough to keep its shape yet light to transport and position on counter stock.

This enameled cast–iron farmhouse sink is big enough to rinse as large a turkey as you can lift. The faucet's spout swings out of the way for complete access to the sink. (Fixture available from www.bathsfromthepast.com.)

The more complex the site conditions or cutouts, the more information the template contains. This small section notes the type of granite, edge bevels, and thickness and the location of the sink cutout. The template's back edge registers to the window width.

because water spots don't show as conspicuously. A sink's gauge (thickness) is the real differentiator. Thicker gauges (16 gauge to 18 gauge) are harder to flex and dent and are quieter to use; whereas thinner gauges (20 gauge to 22 gauge) are less expensive, less durable, and more inclined to stain. *Cost:* This can range widely, from $40 for a 22-gauge single-bowl sink to hundreds for a custom-made, 16-gauge commercial-grade sink with multiple bowls.

▶ Enameled cast-iron or enameled-steel sinks are available in numerous colors and provide a classic look that works in modern and traditional kitchens. Enameled sinks have a hard finish; but the enamel can chip, making the metal substrate likely to rust. Abrasive

Installing a Granite Countertop

Once you've looked at granite samples and narrowed your choices to a few varieties, consult the fabricator—the company that will be cutting and installing your stone. For example, if you choose a granite with large crystals, joints between sections may be more obvious than those between finely grained stone. Besides, some richly figured stones are more likely to crack or spall when subjected to everyday use. A fabricator's practical concerns can be a good counterpoint to a kitchen designer's artier point of view. In any event, cabinets and the plywood substrate must be installed before measurements for a stone countertop can be made.

1. An experienced installer takes nothing for granted and will scrutinize substrates for high and low spots before anything else. However, it's a general contractor's responsibility to make the substrates flat—not the counter installer's.

2. After ensuring that the substrate is flat, installers typically lift the slabs, stand them on edge, and carefully lower them into position to test clearances, cutouts, overhangs, and so on.

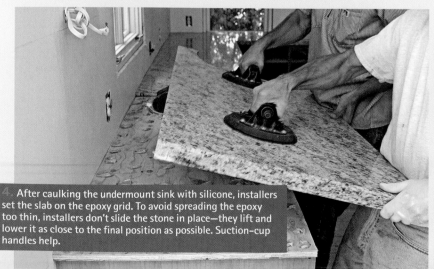

4. After caulking the undermount sink with silicone, installers set the slab on the epoxy grid. To avoid spreading the epoxy too thin, installers don't slide the stone in place—they lift and lower it as close to the final position as possible. Suction-cup handles help.

5. After leveling the slabs, pros ensure that the joints are flush by sliding a razor blade back and forth across them. If one side is higher, the razor blade clicks as it hits a high point or falls from a high point to a low one. More sensitive than a fingertip!

cleaners quickly dull enamel finishes. Cast iron is so heavy that it takes two people to install it and so hard that it's monstrously difficult to drill if you need an additional hole for a water filter or some other accessory. Delicate dishes or glasses dropped on it are doomed. *Cost:* $200 to $500+ for cast iron; slightly less for steel.

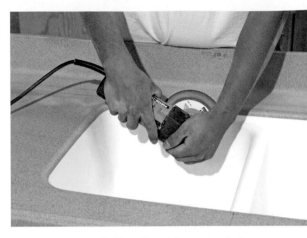

Solid-surface sinks are chemically bonded to a counter of the same material, creating a leak–free seam.

▶ Solid-surface sinks are usually manufactured from the same material as the counter and glued (chemically bonded) to the underside of the counter for a seamless, leakproof joint that won't catch food scraps. As with counters, solid-surface sinks are stain resistant, nonporous, and easy to clean. And you can sand them smooth if they get gouged or scorched. For aesthetic reasons, solid-surface sinks are rarely installed with dissimilar counters; although a near-cousin, quartz composite, looks enough like granite that it contrasts well with other counter materials. *Cost:* $200 to $750 for a solid-surface sink.

▶ Acrylic sinks have a lot going for them. They're lightweight, nonporous, and easy to keep clean. They're also stain and crack resistant, available in many colors, and reasonably priced. However, compared to solid-surface materials, acrylics are relatively soft, so they should be cleaned with nonabrasive cleaners. They can be damaged by extreme heat and may be incompatible with petroleum-based cleaners and caulks. *Cost:* $150 to $300.

Mounting style. There are a number of mounting styles, although almost all require a bead of sealant along their perimeter to keep water from getting under the sink rim. Mounting styles include self-rimming, undermount, integral, flush mount, and separate rim.

▶ Self-rimming sinks (see p. 320) are popular and easy to install because the sink rim sits on the countertop—after you've applied a bead of silicone sealant around the perimeter of the sink cutout. Heavier sinks, such as cast iron, are held in place by the adhesion of the sealant and the weight of the sink; whereas lighter sinks, such as stainless steel, require clips on the underside of the counter. When a self-rimming sink is set under a countertop, as shown at left, it may be called a counter-under sink.

▶ Undermount sinks are placed under a counter whose sink opening must be finished because it isn't covered by the sink rim. Counters with undermount sinks are easy to keep clean because there's no rim to block food scraps; just sweep them into the sink. Typically, clips attach the rim to the underside of the counter; many contractors also add framing inside the sink cabinet to support the sink when it's filled with water.

3. If the dry-fit is acceptable, installers set the slabs aside and apply a grid of epoxy blobs, which adhere the stone to the substrate and act as a support. Epoxy typically takes 48 hours to set fully. To keep the stone from moving while the epoxy grid cures, installers use a smaller amount of a different fast-acting epoxy.

6. To avoid transporting a slab weakened by cutouts or holes, installers usually bore faucet holes on site, using a diamond-tipped hole saw.

Sink-Mounting Details

SELF-RIMMING SINK

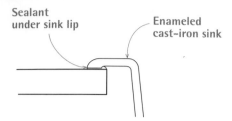

Weight of sink holds it in place.

UNDERMOUNT SINK

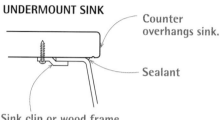

Sink clip or wood frame supports sink.

INTEGRAL SINK

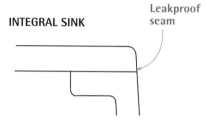

Counter and sink are same material, bonded chemically.

FLUSH-MOUNT OR TILE-EDGE SINK

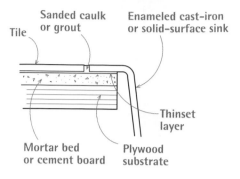

SEPARATE-RIM SINK

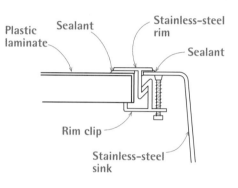

PRO TIP

Cutting sink openings is best left to a pro if your countertop is stone, solid-surface, quartz composite, or some other hard, exotic, or very expensive material. The plywood substrate beneath the countertop still needs a sink cutout, however.

PRO TIP

If you're cutting a finish surface such as plastic laminate, cover the metal shoe (base) of your jigsaw with masking tape to keep the shoe from scratching the countertop.

▶ Integral sinks are bonded to a counter of the same material, creating a seamless, leak-free joint. Integral sinks are common to solid-surface and quartz-composite counters.

▶ Flush-mount (tile-edge) sinks, have a rim the same thickness as the tile layer, when both rest atop a thin-set mortar bed. Such sinks are typically enameled steel or cast iron. You can fill the tile-sink rim joint with grout or silicone sealant, but acrylic latex sanded caulk has the best qualities of both and comes in several colors.

▶ Separate-rim sinks are usually stainless steel and employ a separate stainless-steel rim to cover the joint between the small sink rim and the edge of the counter. To prevent leaks, you must seal both the sink-side and the counter-side of the rim.

INSTALLING A KITCHEN SINK

Because self-rimming sinks are the most common, this section focuses on their installation. If your sink has another mounting device, follow the manufacturer's installation instructions.

Lay out the opening. Mark the sink cutout (opening) on the counter or the plywood substrate. Most sinks come with a paper template of the cutout; if yours doesn't, make one of cardboard. To do that, turn the sink upside-down onto the cardboard and, with a felt marker, trace its outline. Next, use a yardstick to draw a second outline, ¾ in. inside the first, on the cardboard. Sink rims are typically ¾ in. wide, so the inner line represents the size of the cutout, and the outer line shows how much clearance the sink rim needs. Position the cutout template on the counter so there's clearance on all sides; then use a felt marker to trace around the template.

Cut the opening. Drill a hole at each corner of the cutout for your jigsaw blade; if you use a hole saw to drill the corners, its arc should match the rounded corners of the sink body. As you cut each side of the sink opening, stop just short of the corner hole. Then drive a shim into the saw kerf—from the underside of the counter—to keep the cutout section from falling. (A wood shingle is a perfect shim.) With a few shims in place, finish cutting

Cutting Out a Sink Opening

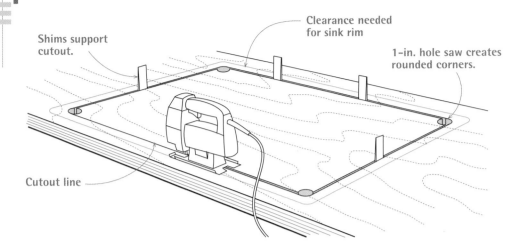

Shims support cutout.

Clearance needed for sink rim

1-in. hole saw creates rounded corners.

Cutout line

Because sink rims are typically 3/4 in. wide, create cardboard templates to show both the clearance needed for the rim and the cutout line needed for the sink body.

This self-rimming stainless-steel sink was installed as a counter-under sink. After routing the perimeter of the cutout so the sink rim would be flush to the plywood, the installer set the rim in epoxy. Just before installing the stone, he caulked the top of the rim with silicone.

to the corner holes and lift the cutout section, using the corner holes as finger holds. Use a wood rasp to smooth rough cut-lines or splinters.

Install the sink. Wearing heavy work gloves, put your fingers in the sink drain and faucet holes, lift the sink, and lower it into the cutout. Two people should lift and set the sink if it's cast iron; put wood scraps around the cutout to set the sink on so it doesn't crush your fingertips. Check the sink's fit in the cutout—look under the counter as well—before lifting the sink out. Trim the cutout as needed. Then mount the drain basket, faucet

assembly, and accessories to the sink; they're harder to attach once the sink is in place. To cushion the sink hardware and create a water-tight seal, use the flexible seals or plastic plates provided by the manufacturer. If the unit has a hollow body, put a bead of plumber's putty beneath its lip. *Don't do this if the countertop is stone;* the oil in the putty may stain the stone. Silicone will work, too, but it can make the faucet difficult to remove if you decide to replace it.

Just before installing the sink in its opening, apply a cushion of sealant for the sink rim to rest

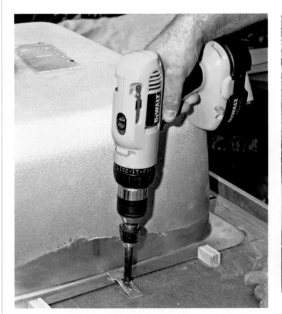

Here an undermount sink is being clip mounted to the underside of a solid-surface counter...

...and then lifted as a unit and placed atop a base cabinet. Supplemental plywood frames inside the cabinet will also support the sink rim.

Choosing a Range Hood

Cooktops and stoves should be vented by a range hood. In addition to sucking up the smoke of a charred steak, range hoods exhaust airborne grease that might otherwise migrate to a cool corner and feed mold or adhere to woodwork and discolor its finish, as shown in the photos on p. 454.

Range hoods are most often *wall-mounted* directly over a range. Alternatively, there are *downdraft* and *side-draft* vents that pop up from a counter area to suck away fumes. Over island and peninsula ranges, you can install *chimney-type* vents. In general, install the type of vent that will carry exhaust gases outdoors with the shortest and straightest duct run possible. Because heated air rises, wall-mounted and chimney types are inherently efficient, whereas downdraft and side-draft vents pull heated gases in directions they wouldn't go naturally and can even pull burner flames sideways.

Range hoods vary from low-powered and inexpensive (less than $50) to custom-designed units that cost thousands. A 100-cfm (cubic feet per minute) wall-mounted hood should be adequate to vent the average four-burner, 30-in.-wide range. But if that same range is located on a kitchen island, its range vent should draw 125 cfm to 150 cfm. More is *not* better when sizing range hoods. For one thing, larger hoods are noisier. Midsize range hoods average 3 sones to 3.5 sones (a measure of noise), which is too noisy to have a conversation near; monster hoods can reach 8 sones. (As a comparison, refrigerators register 1 sone.) Oversize hoods can also expel so much air that they create *back-drafting*, in which negative in-house air pressure draws furnace or fireplace exhaust gases back down the chimney (see Chapter 14 for more on back-drafting).

Ideally, a range hood should be slightly wider than the range, say, 3 in. wider on each end, and mounted 30 in. above the range. But follow the hood maker's suggested mounting height; more powerful hoods can be installed higher. Finally, buy a unit with a good-quality filter that can withstand regular washing with soap and water. Most filters are aluminum mesh, better ones are stainless steel; many can be popped into the dishwasher, which spares homeowners a very greasy and unpleasant task. In general, be skeptical of range hoods that recirculate air through a series of filters rather than venting it outside.

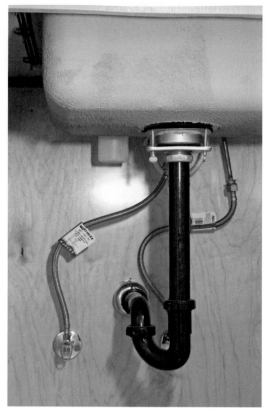

The stainless-steel supply connectors under this sink are strong, watertight, and, above all, flexible. They're easy to maneuver onto fittings and you can disconnect them easily if you replace the sink later on.

A nicely matched stainless-steel range hood and cooktop. Because cooktops are used far more often than ovens, the architect paired an oven and a microwave on an opposite wall, and put large drawers for pots and pans under the cooktop—so they'd be close at hand.

on. The sealant will be a layer of plumber's putty or, more likely, silicone caulk: Follow the sink manufacturer's recommendations. Make any final adjustments to the sink's position before applying a bead of silicone caulk along the edge of the sink rim, where it rests on the counter. With a moistened finger, compress this caulk line and remove the excess silicone. (If you will install a counter over the sink rim, apply the silicone on top of the sink rim just before the countertop is installed, as shown in the photo on p. 321.)

Fasten mounting clips, if any, and then attach the supply risers and the sink drain.

Bathroom Planning

If a bathroom is comfortable and its fixtures are in decent shape, you might want to add only light fixtures or a vanity. But if the bathroom is musty, add a bath fan (see Chapter 14). If fixtures are tired or chipped, you can minimize renovation costs by hooking new fixtures to existing pipes. But if a bathroom is drafty, cold, or uncomfortable, you may be wise to tear out finish surfaces, insulate it well, and position the fixtures more efficiently. But first, here are a few thoughts on what makes bathrooms pleasant.

Kitchen Lighting

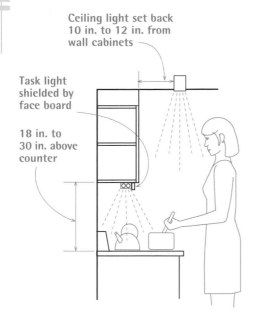

Ceiling light set back
10 in. to 12 in. from
wall cabinets

Task light
shielded by
face board

18 in. to
30 in. above
counter

To illuminate work areas without strong shadows, use a combination of task lighting and general lighting.

CREATING BATHROOMS THAT WORK

Here are 12 factors that help make a bathroom comfortable, functional, and easier to clean:

▶ **Enough room to use fixtures.** Bathroom space isn't efficient if there's not enough room to use the fixtures easily and safely. "Bath Fixture Clearances," on p. 324, shows minimums, which may be superseded by local building codes.

▶ **Keep it secure and intimate.** Although shared bathrooms should be accessible to the rooms they serve, bathroom users should feel secure once inside. Avoid multiple-door accesses. Keep the room's scale intimate as well: Warm, cozy spaces are best.

▶ **Put private fixtures far from the door.** The most-used and least private fixture, the lavatory, should be nearest the door, so people can pop in and wash their hands quickly. But toilets and tubs should be farther away. Insulate walls and install a tight-fitting door to suppress bathroom sounds. Cast-iron waste pipes are quieter than plastic ones.

▶ **Alcoves and half-walls.** Placing fixtures in alcoves and odd spaces around the perimeter of a room maximizes the floor space in the middle. Isolating toilets or tubs with

The Rutherfords' kitchen is well stocked with Mexican spices and colors. At left is a brushed-stainless-steel range hood. Sheet-copper counters are "not for the faint of heart," Marty Rutherford notes. "Everything stains copper. But each time you polish it, it just glows and becomes more mellow."

The tile on the tub surround and floors is Solnhofen limestone, which was formed 150 million years ago in the Mesozoic Era, when warm seas covered present-day Germany. Close up, you can see fossilized sea snails in the stone.

The understated beauty of nature continues in this cabinet's soft, beveled edges and muted finishes. Slip-matched "ropey" cherry doors and drawers are edged with solid wood. Note the fine-grained "absolute black" granite countertop and matte black metal pulls.

their own doors also makes it possible to share a bathroom during morning rush hours, yet still have privacy.

▶ Natural light. Windows and skylights allow rooms to be small without causing claustrophobia. To block the view of neighbors, install translucent or textured glass, or place windows high on the wall. Windows in showers are generally not a good idea because water sits on windowsills and rots them. Ideally, skylights should open.

Bath Fixture Clearances

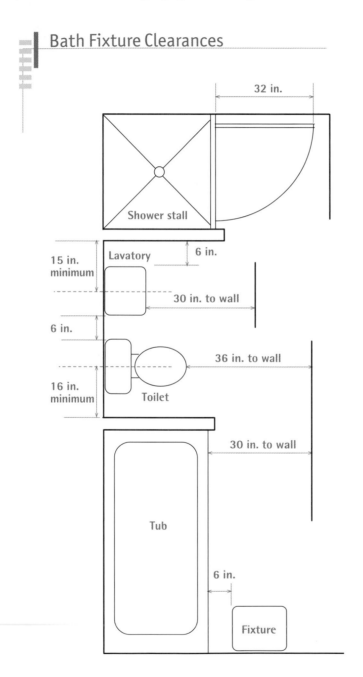

Bathrooms with minimal clearances are a tight fit. If you've got room to spare, by all means space fixtures farther than the prescribed minimums.

▶ Adequate artificial light. For general lighting, plan on 3 watts to 4 watts of incandescent or 1.5 watts to 2 watts of fluorescent lighting per square foot. For fixtures in alcoves, use a 75-watt or 100-watt recessed, vapor-proof ceiling fixture. To illuminate bathroom mirrors, however, install light fixtures on the walls: one over the mirror and one on each side. Ceiling fixtures alone will make that face in the mirror look ghoulish.

▶ Comfortable fixtures. "Standard Cabinet Dimensions," on p. 301, suggests counter heights. If they are too high or low for your family, change them so you don't need to stoop or stand on tiptoes. As for tubs, if you can't stretch out in a standard tub or squared tub as you'd like, look into oversize models or slope-back, cast-iron clawfoot tubs in a salvage yard. Shower stalls should be big enough to towel off in—36 in. by 36 in.

▶ Handsome hardware. Buy well-made shower valves, showerheads, and lavatory faucets with nickel- or chrome-plated finishes. They cost two or three times what bargain home-center accessories do, but they'll last. The same goes for towel bars, switch plates, mirrors, and other accessories—buy quality.

▶ Use appropriate materials. Water reigns in a bathroom, so use materials that can withstand it. Resilient flooring and tile are great on bathroom floors; wood isn't. Even when wood is face sealed with a tough modern finish, its end grain can absorb water. And in time, standing water will cloud most finishes. As explained in "Setting Beds," on pp. 383–384, don't use drywall as a substrate for tile around tubs and showers.

▶ Ventilate, ventilate. Even if there's a window in the bathroom, be sure there's an exhaust fan in the ceiling near the shower. If it's a light/fan combo, the fan switch should have an integral timer so the fan can keep running after the light is turned off. See "Controlling Moisture and Mold," on p. 332, for the whole story.

▶ GFCI protection. All electrical outlets, including fans, must be protected by ground fault circuit interrupters (GFCIs). Shocks could be fatal in such a moist environment, so the National Electrical Code requires GFCI protection on all bathroom and many kitchen outlets. See Chapter 11 for more information.

▶ Easy-to-clean details. Countertops with integral bowls are much easier to keep clean because there's no seam for crud to collect in. For the same reason, undermount sinks are preferable to sink rims or mounting clips that sit atop the counter. Nonporous baseboards or backsplashes allow you to swab corners with a mop or sponge without worrying about dousing walls or wood trim. Finally, you can mop bathroom floors in a flash if you have wall-hung toilets.

AN OVERVIEW OF BATHROOM FIXTURES

This short section provides an overview of what's available and a few buzzwords to use when you visit a fixture showroom. Start your search on the Internet, where most major fixture and faucet makers show their wares and offer design and installation downloads. One of the most elegant and informative sites is www.kohler.com.

Lavatories (bathroom sinks) are available in a blizzard of colors, materials, and styles. Styles include *pedestal* sinks, *wall-hung* units (including corner sinks), and *cabinet-mounted* lavatories. Wall-hung lavs use space and budgets economically, but their pipes are exposed, and there's no place to store supplies underneath. Pedestal sinks are typically screwed to wall framing and supported by a pedestal that hides the drainpipes. Counter-mounted lavatories are the most diverse, and they use many of mounting devices discussed earlier in this chapter for kitchen sinks. Less common are *vanity top* (vessel) basins, which sit wholly on top of the counter, as shown in the photo at right.

Lavatory materials should be easy to clean, stain resistant, and tough enough to withstand daily use and the occasional dropped brush or blow-dryer. The most durable lavs are *enameled cast iron*. Although lighter stainless-steel lavs are tough and stain resistant; their sleek, polished look is distinctively modern, so they may not look good when matched with traditional porcelain fixtures. *Vitreous china* (porcelain) lavs have a hard, glossy finish that's easy to clean and durable, but it's not as durable as enameled cast iron. Hard use can chip and crack vitreous fixtures. *Spun-glass* lavatories are made from soda lime glass, often vividly colored and irregularly textured. Finally, *solid-surface* lavatories are typically bonded to the underside of a countertop of a similar material (see "Countertops for Kitchens and Baths," earlier in this chapter).

Important: Make sure lavs and lav faucets are compatible. Most lavatories are predrilled, with faucet holes spaced 4 in. (centerset) apart, or 8 in. to 12 in. (widespread). There are single lavs for single-hole faucets. And undermounted lavs may have no faucet holes at all; you need to drill the holes in the counter itself.

Fetching as the rough granite lavatory bowl is, the showstopper in this Japanese-inspired bathroom is the band of loose river stones at the base of the cabinet. Barefoot, you can give your feet quite a massage with them.

Toilets and bidets are almost always vitreous china and are distinguished primarily by their types and their flushing mechanisms. Close to 99 percent of toilets sold are of these three types: traditional *two-piece* units, with a separate tank and bowl; *one-piece* toilets; and *wall-hung* toilets. The other 1 percent includes composting toilets, reproductions of Victorian-era toilets with pull-chain flushing mechanisms, and so on. As noted in Chapter 12, toilet-base lengths vary from 10 in. to 14 in. (12 in. is standard), which can come in handy in a renovation when the wall behind the toilet is too close or too far.

Choosing a toilet is a tradeoff among factors such as water consumption, loudness, resistance to clogging, ease of cleaning, and cost. *Washdown* toilets are cheap, inclined to clog, and

A classic: chrome over solid brass lavatory faucet.

banned by some codes. *Reverse-trap* toilets are quieter and less likely to clog than wash-downs. The quietest and most expensive models are typically *siphon-jet* or *siphon-vortex* (rim jet) toilets. Siphon toilets shoot jets of water from beneath the rim to accelerate water flow. Kohler® also offers a PowerLite™ model with an integral pump that accelerates wastes to save water and a Peacekeeper™ toilet that "solves the age-old dispute over leaving the seat up or down. . . . To flush the toilet, the user simply closes the lid." A Nobel Prize for that one!

Bathtubs and shower units are manufactured from a number of durable materials. And site-built tub/shower walls can be assembled from just about any water-resistant material. Bathtubs are typically enameled steel, enameled cast iron, acrylic, or fiberglass; preformed shower units are most often acrylic or fiberglass. *Steel tubs* are economical and fairly lightweight; set in a mortar bed, they retain heat better and aren't as noisy if you knock against them. *Cast iron* has a satisfying heft, retains heat, and is intermediate in price; but it's brutally heavy to move. For that reason, many remodelers choose enameled steel, acrylic, or fiberglass to replace an old cast-iron tub. *Acrylic and fiberglass* are relatively lightweight and are available in the greatest range of shapes and colors; their prices range widely, from moderate to expensive.

Standard tub sizes are 2 ft. 6 in. to 3 ft. wide; lengths are 4 ft. 6 in. to 5 ft. However, if space is tight, you can opt for a compact tub or replace a tub with a shower stall. Shower stalls come as compact as 32 in. sq., but that's a real elbow knocker. Stalls 36 in. sq. or 36 in. by 42 in. are more realistic. One-piece molded tub/shower units don't win beauty prizes, but if properly detailed and supported, they are virtually leakproof.

CHOOSING A LAVATORY FAUCET

If you're buying a new lav and new faucets, make sure they're compatible. As noted earlier, lavatories often have predrilled faucet holes spaced 4 in., 8 in., or 12 in. apart. Most inexpensive to moderately priced faucets with two handles have valve stems 4 in. on center. Beyond that, the biggest considerations are faucet bodies, finishes, handle configurations, and spout lengths.

Faucet bodies will last longest if they're brass, rather than zinc, steel, or plastic. Brass is less likely to leak because it resists corrosion and can be machined to close tolerances. Forged brass parts are smoother and less likely to leak than cast brass, which is more porous. If you spend 5 minutes operating an nonbrass faucet, it will likely feel looser than it did when you started.

This Moorish-inspired bath alcove has iridescent glass tiles.

Faucet finishes are applied over faucet bodies to make them harder, more attractive, and easier to clean. The most popular finish by far is polished chrome, which is electrochemically bonded to a nickel substrate; it doesn't corrode and won't scratch when you scrub it with cleanser. Manufacturers can apply chrome plating to brass, zinc, steel, and even plastic. But although chrome plating protects faucet surfaces, their inner workings will still corrode and leak, if they're inclined to.

By the way, brass-finish faucets consist of brass plating over chrome (over a solid-brass base). Brass finishes oxidize, so they should be protected with a clear epoxy coating. Alternatively, faucets finished with physical vapor deposition (PVD) coatings gleam like brass, but won't dull or corrode.

Faucet handles are an easy choice: one handle or two. Hot on the left, cold on the right—who'd have thought you could improve on that? But there's no denying that single-lever faucets are much easier to use. Also consider the valves inside the faucets. Ceramic-disk and brass ball-valves will outlast plastic and steel.

Spouts should have a little flare and be long and high enough to get your hands under them to lather up properly. If you're a hand scrubber, look for a spout at least 6 in. to 8 in. long that rises a similar amount above the sink.

Energy Conservation and Air Quality

14

Controlling the movement of air, moisture, and heat determines how comfortable, affordable, and durable a house will be. In the old days, houses were often drafty and cold, but because energy was cheap homeowners could compensate by throwing another log into the woodstove or by cranking up the thermostat. All that changed in the 1970s, when energy costs went through the roof. . .literally, in houses with uninsulated attics. In response, builders yanked fuel-guzzling furnaces and replaced leaky doors and windows with tight, factory-built ones. They also caulked gaps; installed weatherstripping; and insulated walls, floors, and ceilings to block drafts (*infiltration*) and slow the escape of conditioned air (*exfiltration*). This insulated layer between inside and outside air is called the *thermal envelope*.

Although tightening the thermal envelope saved energy, it spawned a whole new set of problems, including excessive interior moisture, peeling paint, moldy walls, rotted studs, and a buildup of pollutants that were never a problem when windows rattled and the wind blew free. In many houses, furnaces no longer had enough incoming air to burn fuel or vent exhausts efficiently. In some super-tight houses today, turning on a bathroom fan or a range hood can even create enough negative pressure to pull exhaust gases back down the chimney (*back–drafting*) and suck mold spores up from dank crawl spaces.

Fortunately, this chapter can help you control the flow of air, moisture, and heat while balancing comfort, costs, and health concerns. Because HVAC (heating, ventilation and air conditioning) systems have become incredibily sensitive and complex, installing and adjusting them is best left to HVAC specialists. If you want information on designing and constructing energy-efficient houses, consult Joe Lstiburek's *Builder's Guide to Mixed Climates* or *Builder's Guide to Cold Climates* (both The Taunton Press).

Sealing Air Leaks

Retaining conditioned air is tricky, even in well-insulated houses. As air is heated, it rises and expands, pushing against the inside of the thermal envelope. If it finds holes or gaps in the envelope, it escapes. Likewise, winter winds can drive cold air into a building. In new construction, airflow retarders such as housewrap are installed in large sheets on exterior walls before the siding is put on. Or inside walls are insulated and covered with polyethylene vapor barriers before the dry-

The explosion of new insulating materials includes these itch–free, environmentally friendly cotton batts created from mill wastes.

wall goes up. However, where siding and drywall are already in place, sealing air leaks is largely a piecemeal affair of locating and caulking leaks, one gap or hole at a time.

LOCATING AIR LEAKS

Professionals use powerful blower-doors to depressurize interiors and thereby draw-in huge volumes of air to help locate leaks. But during the heating season, you can find most leaks yourself with a wetted finger, a smoking incense stick, and common sense. Begin by running your hand around window and door frames and along room corners. If your house has leaks, you'll feel drafts, especially if it's cold and windy outside. The incense smoke will also show where warm air is leaving the building. But common sense is the best detector.

Heated air rises, so start your detective work in the attic. If it's uninsulated, you'll see plumbing ducts, electrical cables, recessed lighting cans, heating and fan ducts, chimneys, and a host of other penetrations in the attic floor through which heated air is escaping. If there's an old

How Air Moves through a House

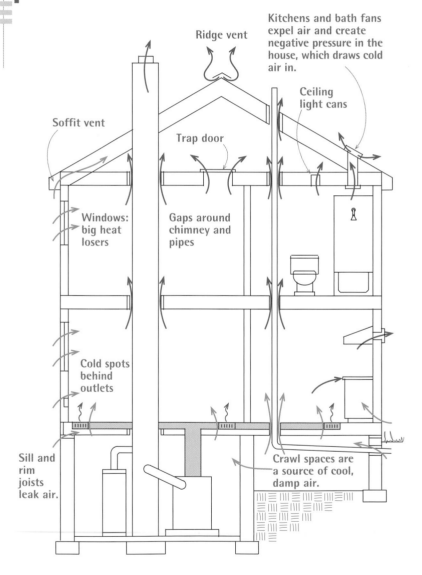

Ridge vent

Kitchens and bath fans expel air and create negative pressure in the house, which draws cold air in.

Ceiling light cans

Soffit vent

Trap door

Windows: big heat losers

Gaps around chimney and pipes

Cold spots behind outlets

Sill and rim joists leak air.

Crawl spaces are a source of cool, damp air.

By insulating living spaces, you create a boundary—a thermal envelope—between inside and outside air. Leaky walls and windows are obvious energy losers, but so are holes and gaps inside the envelope, which allow warm air to flow into unheated attics, creating negative pressure in living areas that draws in cold replacement air.

How Heat Moves

Heat is transferred by one of three mechanisms: radiation, conduction, or convection. *Radiation* is the movement of heat through space, in the form of infrared waves; heat and light waves radiate in all directions from a central source, such as the sun or a hot stove. *Conduction* is the passing of energy from particle to particle, usually between objects touching each other, as when a stovetop burner touches a tea kettle. *Convection* is the transfer of heat or cold by the movement of air, with warmer air rising and cooler air descending.

Heat transfer in houses is usually a combination of all three mechanisms. For example, sunlight radiates into a room and heats a dark tile floor. A cat lying on the floor receives radiant heat from the sun and conductive heat from the floor. And even in a room where the air seems still, there will be convective loops as warmed air rises from warmed floors and heat vents, and falls near cold windows. As likely, there will also be convective heat loss—that is, air moving through walls can account for 20 percent to 30 percent of the total heat loss of an insulated house.

Building materials conduct heat at different rates. The more resistance a material has to heat transference by conduction, the higher its resistivity value, or R-value. In general, the less dense the material, the better insulator it is and the higher its R-value. And the denser the material, the better it conducts heat or cold and the poorer it is as an insulator. Thus dense masonry materials tend to be poor insulators, wood intermediate, and fluffy cellulose fibers excellent. Glass, being very dense, is an excellent conductor but a poor insulator. Thus glass windows, even double- or triple-paned ones, lose a lot of heat, compared to other building materials.

plaster ceiling below, there may also be a lot of heat loss through cracks. Especially note bath- or kitchen-fan vents that terminate in the attic. They should be vented outside, rather than into the attic, because the moist air they pump into an attic can condense there, soaking insulation, framing, and drywall—creating a paradise for mold and rot (see the photo on p. 12).

After investigating the attic, go downstairs and examine ceilings for cracks, cold spots, and mold. Frequently, corners on exterior walls will be cold because insulation stops short of framing. Or insulation may have slumped at the tops of walls. Continue down the walls, noting drafts or gaps around windows and doors—especially under doors—and cold spots around electrical receptacles and switches on exterior walls. Common walls between houses and attached garages are frequently underinsulated, and openings there can allow car exhaust and volatile fumes to infiltrate living spaces. Check local building codes: Most require fire-resistant drywall and fire-stopping caulks on common walls with garages.

Finally, inspect basements and crawl spaces. Caulk gaps between framing and foundations, and use rigid-foam panels to insulate basement walls. Conventional wisdom long held that outside air should circulate freely through dirt-floored crawl spaces. But as house envelopes grew tighter, scientists determined that the normal pressurization of heated air and negative

pressures from exhaust fans routinely pull moist, often mold-laden crawl space air up into living areas. Consequently, engineers now recommend sealing, insulating, and conditioning crawl spaces, especially in hot, humid regions, as explained later in this chapter.

FIXING LEAKS

Polyurethane sealants are the best bet for filling gaps around door and window frames, electrical cable, water pipes, and plumbing vents. These sealants are typically expanding spray-in foams,

DIFFERENT JOBS, DIFFERENT FOAMS

To seal holes around pipes and ducts and prevent air leaks between floors, use an expanding spray-in foam. This foam-dispensing gun delivers a higher volume than a straw-type applicator can.

To fill gaps around window and door frames, use a mild-expanding latex foam; typical foams can bow frames. Because latex sealant stays flexible, frames can move slightly as doors and windows are operated—or are buffeted by wind—without breaking the seal.

To seal duct joints, apply a generous amount of water-based mastic sealant. Correctly applied, the sealant should ooze through gaps; when it hardens, those tiny mastic fingers will hold the seal in place.

available in 12-oz. to 33-oz. aerosol cans with straw-type applicators for incidental home use. Contractors often use screw-on cans designed for dispenser guns. High-volume pros attach 10-lb. to 16-lb. disposable cylinders to pneumatic dispensers.

Foams vary in many ways, including durability, temperature ranges, curing times, fire resistance and—most notably—expandability. Read the product literature carefully. As handy as foams with 700 percent expansion would be to fill large gaps, they could buckle door frames badly. To seal gaps around doors and windows, instead select a low-pressure or mild-expanding foam sealant. Expandable latex polymer foams are gaining popularity because, like latex caulk, they clean up with soap and water before they've cured.

Because gaps between foundations and framing can involve high humidity, great temperature shifts, and dissimilar materials, acrylic latex or silicone caulks may be more appropriate to seal air leaks in basements and crawl spaces. If gaps are wider than ½ in., stuff foam backer rod into the gaps before caulking. *Important:* If the house has mouse or rat problems, stuff larger holes or cracks with ¼-in. galvanized mesh before spraying foam into gaps. Rodents will chew through foam, so place the mesh toward the house exterior.

If you find holes too big for expandable foams, stuff plastic garbage bags full of insulation and jam the bags into the openings. Or cover the opening with a sheet of rigid-foam insulation or a piece of plywood, and seal the edges with spray-on foam. Don't forget uninsulated attic hatch covers: Use construction adhesive to glue a 3-in.-thick piece of Styrofoam® (or two 2-in.-thick panels) to the upper face of the hatch.

SEALING LEAKY DUCTWORK

Because ductwork usually runs through basements or unconditioned crawl spaces, sealing it will reduce heat loss and subfloor moisture being drawn into living areas. Leaky ducts can waste 25 percent to 30 percent of total heating/cooling costs. Supply ducts most often leak where they take off from the main supply trunk, at section joints, and where ducts join register boots. Ironically, many leaks are caused by fabric duct tape that has dried out and cracked after a few years. Even if it looks intact, remove fabric duct tape.

Sealing Ducts

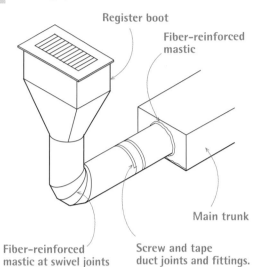

Living space

Register boot

Fiber-reinforced mastic

Main trunk

Fiber-reinforced mastic at swivel joints

Screw and tape duct joints and fittings.

Secure joints between duct sections and fittings with at least three sheet-metal screws. Then wrap the joints with aluminum duct tape—not fabric duct tape! Apply fiber-reinforced mastic to hand-snipped and swivel joints.

There are three ways to reduce duct heat loss. Apply aluminum duct tape to joints between sections and to the factory-formed joints where round ducts snap together. Along hand-snipped or swivel joints, which aren't as airtight, seal ducts with fiber-reinforced mastic, which you can apply generously to joints, using a brush or your hand (wearing disposable plastic gloves). Finally, to further reduce heat loss and condensation, insulate ducts in unconditioned spaces. Wrap 1-in.-thick, foil-backed batts around the outside of the ducts; avoid interior duct linings such as ductboard, which can reduce airflow, absorb moisture, and grow mold.

WEATHERSTRIPPING AND CAULKING

Weatherstripping can reduce air leaks around doors and windows. Door weatherstripping is discussed in Chapter 6; two of the more popular types, tubular and metal-leaf, are also appropriate for windows. Install tubular weatherstripping for casement or awning windows, which are hinged as doors are and thus will seat solidly against compressible stripping. Metal-leaf stripping offers a tighter seal for double-hung windows, but installing it requires removing interior stops and possibly planing down sashes.

Interior door and window casing may leak air if there's not a good paint seal to surrounding

Install sheet-metal stops to fill the cavities around metal and masonry chimneys and to limit heat loss between floors. Use a high-temperature silicone sealant to fill gaps between the metal stops and the chimney.

Vapor Barriers

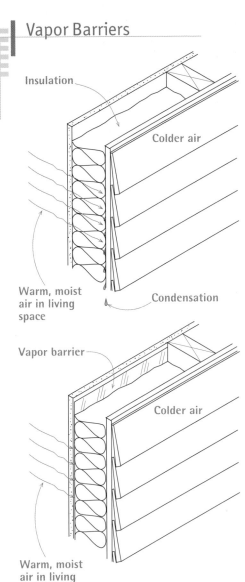

Insulation

Colder air

Warm, moist air in living space

Condensation

Vapor barrier

Colder air

Warm, moist air in living space

In cold and very cold climates, polyethylene vapor barriers on the living-space side of insulation may prevent water vapor from condensing inside walls, which can lead to peeling paint, mold, and, in extreme cases, rotted framing.

walls. If you notice gaps or cracks around the perimeters of the casing, caulk them with acrylic latex caulk, which you can tool smooth with an index finger. (Wash up with warm, soapy water.) Allow the caulk to cure before painting it.

Gaps around exterior casing are most common on south-facing walls, where the sun is strongest. Typically, wood trim shrinks across its width, creating gaps where siding abuts. Fill gaps with exterior acrylic latex or siliconized latex caulk. (Pure silicone caulks don't paint well, and many polyurethane caulks have poor UV resistance.) Because caulking alone is not terribly durable, paint it as soon as it has cured. To effectively block air and moisture infiltration, the edges of door and window *frames* should be caulked, flashed, recaulked (over flashing strips), and then recased, as shown on p. 129.

AIR AND MOISTURE RETARDERS

Any building material that is sufficiently impermeable to slow the flow of air and airborne moisture is considered an *air-flow retarder,* even if that's not its primary function. If a retarder is installed specifically to stop water vapor, it's called a *vapor barrier.* Most houses have both interior and exterior air-flow retarders: housewrap or building paper, flashing, sheathing and siding on the outside, and drywall or plaster

inside. (Housewraps such as Tyvek are semi-permeable: They keep rain out but allow water vapor trapped in walls to migrate outward.) Some insulation, such as high-density cellulose and polyurethane foams, can be considered air-flow retarders, as discussed later in this chapter.

In cold and very cold climates, there should be a polyethylene vapor barrier installed on the living-space side of the insulation to prevent warm, moist air from migrating into wall cavities and condensing there during cold weather. Several things to note about vapor barriers: To be effective, they must be continuous—no gaps or

PRO TIP

If windows rattle when the wind blows, remove and reset the interior stops snugly to the window sashes before weather-stripping windows. In moderate climates, tight-fitting sashes will cut air infiltration significantly.

Soffit-to-Ridge Ventilation

If sealing holes and insulating attic floors are the first steps in reducing excessive moisture and heat in an attic, increasing ventilation is the second. And nothing exhausts moisture or cools the area under a roof as effectively as passive soffit-to-ridge ventilation, as shown here and in Chapters 5 and 7. (Gable-end vents help but are usually 1 ft. to 2 ft. below the highest and hottest air; power vents require electricity to do a job that soffit-to-ridge vents do for free.) As a bonus, in winter, cool incoming air can prevent snowmelt and ice dams along eaves. Also, in summer, when unvented roofs can reach 150°F to 160°F, soffit-to-ridge ventilation can prolong shingle life and make upper-floor rooms appreciably cooler.

Keeping vent channels open from soffit to ridge is essential to keeping air flowing. Continuous soffit vents are typically screened to keep critters from blocking the vents with nests or food caches. In snow country, experts recommend *baffled ridge vents* because they're less likely to become clogged by wind-driven snow. (Wind passing over baffles creates a negative pressure that sucks air up from under the roof, clearing the vents.). And whenever there's insulation between rafters or attic floor joists, install *air chutes* (also called baffles) to hold insulation back from vent channels.

If the roof has no overhang (and thus no soffits), you can still ventilate its lower edges. Trim back the top 1 in. of fascia boards, as shown at right, and install *vented drip edges*, which have perforated or slotted undersides. Their upper flanges fit under shingle starter courses. Add a ridge vent and you're set to go.

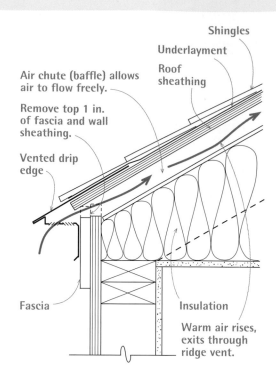

Drip-edge vents allow you to add ventilation to a roof that has no soffits. Carefully cut off the top 1 in. of the fascia, using a nail-cutting circular-saw blade (wearing eye protection). Slide the upper leg of the vent under the shingles and, if possible, under the underlayment.

---

tears. Vapor barriers must never be installed on ceilings, because water vapor should be allowed to rise into and be ventilated out of the attic. And vapor barriers should generally *not* be installed in moderate or hot climates because buildings in those regions tend to dry toward the interior, where the air is cooler.

Note: The only exception to putting a vapor barrier on the living-space side of the insulation is in the basement. Because moisture can wick through concrete or concrete block walls, apply polyethylene sheeting directly to the interior foundation and crawl space walls, affix furring strips (if needed), and then install rigid insulation panels *over* the vapor barrier. The barrier must be continuous, without tears or gaps, as explained in "Using Rigid-Foam Panels in Basements," later in this chapter.

Dissenting opinions. Some builders strongly advise against installing vapor barriers in any climate because, as the builders assert, moisture that enters wall cavities will be trapped there, without enough air circulation to allow drying or enough wall permeability to allow migration. Further, if insulation gets soaked by driving rains, mold and rotted framing are almost inevitable. Even if the dissenters overstate their case, it's smart to allow in-wall moisture a way out. If you do install a vapor barrier inside, create a more permeable exterior "skin" by using latex paint rather than oil-based paint on exterior walls. Latex breathes better. You can also increase exfiltration by installing rain-screen walls (see p. 141) or by driving plastic shims (see www.wedgevent.com, for example) under the siding to increase circulation.

Controlling Moisture and Mold

Moisture inside a house generally isn't a problem unless it's excessive and sustained. (Indoor relative humidity should be 35 percent to 40 percent during the heating season.) Signs of excessive moisture include condensation running down windows, moldy bathrooms or closets, soggy attic insulation, and exterior paint peeling off in large patches. Figure out where the water's coming from, and you're halfway to solving the problem.

SOURCES OF EXCESSIVE MOISTURE

Common sources of excessive interior moisture are (1) air infiltration; (2) faulty or poorly installed roofing, siding, windows, and doors; (3) improper surface drainage; (4) unsealed crawl spaces; (5) inadequately vented bathrooms, kitchens, laundry appliances, water heaters, and furnaces; and (6) leaking HVAC ducts.

Air infiltration, discussed earlier, is the primary way that moisture migrates through a house. Roofing, windows and doors, and siding are discussed in Chapters 5, 6, and 7, respectively. When looking for leaks outdoors, always inspect flashing first. Poorly installed, damaged, or missing flashing is by far the most common source of exterior leaks.

Because 90 percent of basement wetness is caused by improper surface drainage—especially clogged gutters and downspouts—examine those possibilities first. For additional strategies on how to reduce dampness caused by exterior water, see Chapter 10. Finally, if there's fibrous insulation (cellulose or fiberglass) on the inside of the basement or crawl space walls, remove it because it will retain moisture and foster mold. Below grade, install only rigid-foam panels.

Poorly supported, shedding insulation, and leaking air, this duct should be replaced. Low spots in sagging ducts can become reservoirs for condensation and mold.

SEALING CRAWL SPACES

Crawl spaces are well named: They tend to be dark, dank, dirt-floored areas only a few feet high. To disperse moisture, building codes prescribe 1 sq. ft. of ventilation for each 150 sq. ft. of dirt floor or 1 sq. ft. of vents for every 1,500 sq. ft. of floors covered with a moisture barrier. Problem is, open crawl spaces mean cold floors and heat loss in winter; and in summer, warm moist air entering through the vents invariably condenses on the cooler surfaces of the crawl space—leading to mold and worse. So it makes more sense to seal and condition crawl spaces. Otherwise, mold spores growing in the crawl space will be sucked into living spaces by bath and kitchen exhaust fans and carried all up to the attic by the *stack effect* of rising heated air.

You'll start by raking the crawl space to remove debris and sharp rocks, which could puncture plastic moisture barriers. But before stirring up crawl space dust and debris, please read the safety alert on p. 334. Heavy sheeting will last longer: 6-mil polyethylene is minimal, but commercial waterproofing firms, such as Basement Systems®, use 20-mil polyester cord–reinforced sheeting, which can withstand workers crawling and objects stored on it. Seal vent openings by gluing 2-in.-thick foam insulation over them, using a polyurethane sealant such as Vulkem 116, which is also appropriate for sealing moisture barriers to concrete walls.

In a rectangular crawl space without jogs, it typically takes five large sheets of polyethylene to

Poor ventilation and a damp dirt floor helped this gaudy fungus blossom on a crawl space joist. The same conditions encouraged mold to flourish behind the baseboards on the floor above.

PRO TIP

If you're unsure whether basement-wall wetness is caused by moist interior air condensing or ground water seeping through, try this: Wipe dry a section of wall, then duct tape a 1-ft. by 1-ft. piece of aluminum foil to the dried area. In a day or two, remove the tape and note which side of the foil is wet.

isolate the space: a single floor sheet which runs about 1 ft. up onto walls; and four wall pieces which overlap at the corners and the floor by 1 ft. and run up the walls to a height 2 in. to 3 in. below the mudsills. (Leave mudsills exposed so they can be inspected periodically.) Because the sheets are heavy, cut them outside on a well-swept driveway, roll them up, and then unroll them in the crawl space. Overlap seams roughly 1 ft., caulking each overlap with polyurethane sealant, and then taping the seams with a compatible peel-and-stick tape such as Tyvek tape. Use polyurethane caulk to attach the tops of sheets to the crawl space walls; if the walls are dirty, wire-brush them first to ensure a good seal.

Because the moisture barrier must be continuous to be effective, sealing the floor sections becomes more difficult if there are masonry piers or wood posts present. In that case, use two pieces of polyethylene to cover the floor, with each piece running roughly from the base of a post to the crawl space perimeter. Slit the plastic and run it up 6 in. to 8 in. onto each pier; caulk and tape the plastic to the pier. If there is metal flashing under the wood posts, wrap the posts with plastic, too. But if the posts rest directly on masonry pads, jack each post enough to slide a piece of metal flashing or heavy plastic underneath; otherwise, moisture will wick up through the post and eventually rot it.

The wall portions of the sheeting will be less likely to pull loose if you mechanically attach them toward the top of crawl space walls. If you use sheeting as heavy as a pool liner (20-mil), you can drill holes through it into the concrete and drive in nylon expansion fasteners. Lighter grades of polyethylene can be wrapped several times around furring strips and then attached to walls with a powder-actuated nailing system. (For this, wear eye and hearing protection.) If condensation persists in a sealed crawl space, insulate the walls with rigid-foam panels over the plastic wall sheeting. Finally, add a dehumidifier to condition damp air that gets into the crawl space.

Before screwing a bathroom fan box to a ceiling joist, apply several parallel beads of silicone caulk between the box and the joist to minimize vibration. The scrap of drywall to the right of the box ensures that fan-box flanges will be flush to the finish drywall ceiling.

INSTALLING A BATHROOM FAN

Bathrooms add a tremendous amount of moisture to interior spaces. Fortunately, bathroom fans are increasingly powerful and quiet running. And remote inline fans, typically installed in attics some distance above bathrooms, are quieter still. Place the fan near the shower, and vent the ductwork from the fan out the roof or through a gable-end wall. Soffit and sidewall vents aren't as desirable because expelled moisture could get drawn up into the attic by a soffit to ridge airflow. Keeping moisture out of attics and wall cavities is crucial, and you can achieve it by airtight connections—by caulking the fan housing to the ceiling and sealing each duct joint with aluminum foil tape, not fabric duct tape.

First create a cardboard template of the fan box (housing). Mark the approximate position of the fan by driving a screw or nail through the ceiling before going up into the space above the bathroom and finding the marker. If you have an insulated attic above, take along a dustpan to shovel loose insulation out of the way; wear a dust mask and gloves. After you've located the marker, place the fan template next to the nearest joist—most fan boxes mount to ceiling joists—and trace around it. (If the fan box has an adjustable mounting bar, you have more latitude in placing the fan.) Use a jigsaw or reciprocating saw to cut out the opening. To keep the drywall cutout from falling to the floor below, screw to the drywall a piece of scrap wood slightly longer than the cutout.

To mount the fan housing, you may need to remove the fan assembly first. If the housing

Bath-Fan BELLS AND WHISTLES

Removing moisture is the primary function of a bathroom fan—good to remember when considering all the extra features you could buy. First, get a quiet fan: 3 sones to 4 sones is tolerable, 1 sone is very quiet. Next, consider switches. Because fans usually need to continue venting after you leave the shower, get an electronic switch with an integral timer so the fan can keep running after the light has been turned off. Or put the light and the fan on separate switches. You can also connect the fan to a *humidistat,* which is a moisture sensor that will turn off the fan when a preset moisture level is reached.

flange mounts flush to the underside of the ceiling, as shown in the photo at left, use a piece of drywall scrap to gauge the depth of the unit relative to the finish ceiling. But whether the housing flange sits above or below the ceiling drywall, caulk the flange well with polyurethane sealant to create an airtight seal between the two materials. To further secure the fan and anchor the edges of the drywall opening, run blocking between the joists—along two sides of the opening—and screw the drywall to the blocking. In some cases, you'll be screwing through the fan's housing flanges as well.

Follow the wiring diagrams provided by the manufacturer. In general, it's easier to run electrical cable through a switch box first because junction boxes inside fan housings tend to be cramped. Bathroom fans should be protected by a GFCI (ground-fault circuit interrupter); see Chapter 11 for more information.

Keep duct runs as short as possible to reduce air resistance. After attaching the lower end of the flexible duct to the fan's exhaust port and sealing the joint with metal duct tape, hold the free end of the duct to the underside of the roof sheathing (or gable-end wall) and trace its outline onto the sheathing. Drive a screw through the middle of the circle. Then go outside and locate the screw, which represents the middle of the vent hole you need to cut. Sketch that circle onto the roof: If the circle would cut into the tabs of any shingle—roughly the bottom half of a shingle strip—use a shingle ripper (see the left photo on p. 121) to remove those shingles before cutting the vent hole in the sheathing. Be gentle when removing shingles so you can reuse them.

Use a utility knife to cut the circle into any remaining shingles and the roofing paper. Flash the fan's roof vent as you would any other roof vent: Feed its upper flange under the shingle courses above and over the courses below. Caulk or nail the flange edges per the installation instructions and renail the surrounding shingles. Once the roof vent is flashed, go back under the roof and attach the free end of the duct, also sealing that joint with metal duct tape. Enjoy your shower.

CLEANING UP MOLD

Mold can't grow without moisture, so first identify and correct the source(s) of the excess moisture before you start cleaning up. Otherwise, the mold can return.

Necessary precautions. Limit your exposure to mold spores by wearing a respirator mask with N95 (or higher) filters, rubber gloves, eye protec-

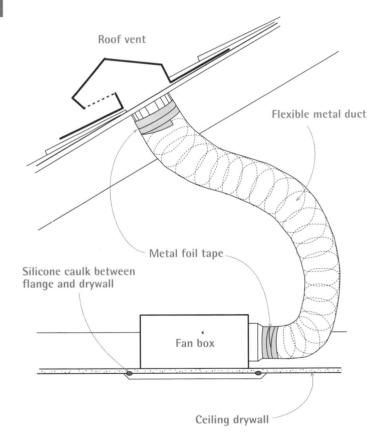

A Bathroom Fan

To keep moisture from leaking into the attic, apply silicone caulk between fan box flanges and mating surfaces, such as drywall. To ensure airtight joints, use metal foil tape to seal ducting to the fan's exhaust port and to the roof vent or sidewall vent.

After mounting the fan box, attach ducting to the fan box's exhaust port. Keep duct runs short and seal metal duct-fitting joints by wrapping them with self-adhering foil tape.

Whether they're removing asbestos or mold-contaminated drywall and framing, professionals dress up for work: A respirator mask with N95 filters, gloves, boot covers, and disposable Tyvek coveralls and hood. Duct tape seals the coveralls at the wrists and ankles.

PRO TIP

Moisture can condense in bathroom-fan ducts that run through unheated areas. To reduce in-duct condensation, insulate the ducts; keep the duct runs short; and if you're venting the duct through a wall, slope the duct downward toward the wall cap so the moisture will run out if it does condense.

▐▌▐▌

tion, and disposable coveralls, which you should discard at the end of each day. After assessing the mold's extent, determine the shortest way out of the house for contaminated materials—maybe out a window—to minimize spreading mold spores to clean areas. Use sheet plastic to seal doorways and heating registers in affected areas, and turn off central HVAC systems till the remedial work is complete. Seal damaged materials in plastic before transporting them from the site. Never sand moldy materials because that will spread spores. Finally, rent a commercial-grade vacuum with HEPA filters; if possible, vent it to the outside.

Assessing the extent. If mold is limited to small areas at the top of a bathroom or exterior wall, it may be surface mold caused by condensation or inadequate ventilation. However, if mold is widespread around windows or doors, bathroom drywall is crumbling, or tiles mounted on drywall are loose, there's probably mold growing in the walls. Start looking at the base of the walls. 🚫 Turn off the electrical power to the area, remove the baseboard, and use a utility knife or a hole saw to cut small holes in the drywall. If there's no mold, you can easily patch the holes and cover them with the baseboard. More likely, you'll find stained or rotted wall plates and extensive mold colonies.

Throw out moldy drywall or hardboard. On the other hand, moldy lumber and engineered wood products such as plywood, particleboard, and OSB (oriented strand board) may just have surface mold, so probe them with an ice pick or

pocketknife to see how sound they are. If they are spongy, replace them. Engineered wood products are particularly susceptible to rot because they contain adhesive binders that fungi feed on.

Remediation. Wash surface mold with soap and water and let it dry well. There's no need for caustic bleaches to kill mold spores (and irritate your lungs) because washing should remove mold. After the surface has dried, paint it with a stain killer such as B-I-N.® If mold has caused the drywall's paper facing to roughen or delaminate, cut back the drywall at least 1 ft. beyond the damaged area and replace it.

If your inspection revealed mold growing inside wall cavities, use sheet plastic to seal off the affected area, including the heating registers; then cut back damaged drywall to the nearest stud center on both sides, and cut out damaged framing, if any. If you must replace more than one stud, erect temporary shoring to support the loads above (see Chapter 10). To contain spore-laden dust, have a helper hold the hose of the commercial-grade vacuum near the materials being cut. Using soapy water, scrub the surface mold from the framing, and allow all materials to dry before installing new drywall—framing moisture content should be 15 percent to 20 percent

REMOTE INLINE Fans

Even a well-made bathroom fan will be relatively noisy if its motor is in the bathroom ceiling, 2 ft. from your head. But if you install the fan some distance from the bathroom, you'll reduce the noise considerably. That remote location may mean longer duct and wiring runs, but routing them is rarely a problem. In fact, with a large-enough fan motor and a duct wye-connector, you can vent two bathrooms with one fan. Because longer duct runs can mean greater air resistance, consider installing rigid-metal or PVC ducts, whose smooth surfaces offer less resistance, rather than flexible metal ducts. Alternatively, you could oversize the fan slightly. Better fan makers such as Fantech® and American Aldes™ offer acoustically insulated cases to deaden sound further.

or less. (Borrow or buy a moisture meter to check.) Wrap moldy debris in 6-mil plastic and have it carted away.

Insulation

Seal air leaks before installing insulation because insulation won't be an effective thermal barrier if air can move freely around and through it. As you'll see, stopping air is also a major consideration in choosing insulation that's right for the renovation.

CHOOSING INSULATION

There are dozens of insulating materials, which can be classified into four groups: batt (in precut lengths or continuous rolls), blown in, rigid foam, and sprayed on.

Batts are made of recyled cotton, mineral wool, and fiberglass; but fiberglass batts are the giant

Before disturbing mold–contaminated surfaces, contain them by sealing doorways with sheet plastic and taping heating registers. Blue painter's tape is less likely to mar metal and wood finishes than other kinds of tapes.

Insulation Values

TYPE OF INSULATION	R-VALUE PER INCH
Batts and blankets	
Fiberglass	3.2
High-density fiberglass	3.8
Cotton	3.2
Mineral wool	3.2
Loose fill (blown in)	
Cellulose	3.2
Fiberglass	3.2
Mineral wool	3.1
Cotton	3.2
Rigid board	
Expanded polystyrene (EPS)	4.0
Extruded polystyrene (XPS)	5.0
Polyisocyanurate	6.5
Spray on (contractor applied)	
Polyurethane	6.0
Open-cell polyurethane	3.6
Wet-spray cellulose	3.5
Magnesium silicate	3.9

R-Values of Common Building Materials

MATERIAL	R-VALUE
8-in. concrete (solid)	0.90
4-in. common brick	0.80
3½-in. wood stud (on edge)	4.5
½-in. plywood sheathing	0.63
¾-in. plaster or ½-in. drywall	0.40
Glass	
Single pane	0.89
Double pane	1.91
Triple pane	2.80

Precut fiberglass batts are by far the most commonly installed insulation. Always read labeling before opening to be sure the batts inside are of the correct length, width, thickness, and R-value for the task at hand.

of the group, accounting for three-quarters of all residential insulation. As a group, batts are easy to install; cost effective; and available in a variety of widths, thicknesses, and densities. Batts *faced* with kraft paper, foil, or plastic are installed by stapling facing flanges to framing edges; *unfaced* batts are friction fitted between studs, joists, or rafters. In attics, unfaced batts are instead laid perpendicularly atop existing batts to improve heat retention.

Batt insulation is an effective thermal barrier if it's installed correctly and fills cavities completely. Unfortunately, framing is often irregular in older houses, and batts with precut widths may not totally fill the cavities. Consequently, if installers don't fill gaps, cut batts a bit short, allow facing flanges to pucker, or don't take time to fit insulation behind pipes and electrical cables, air movement can dramatically reduce the insulation's R-value.

That caveat noted, batts are safer to work with and more insulative, thanks to numerous innovations. In response to eye, skin, and lung irritation caused by loose glass fibers, insulation makers now offer fiberglass batts encapsulated in perforated or woven plastic wrapping—particularly

helpful when you're insulating ceilings and don't want fiberglass fibers raining down on you. In some products, such as Miraflex®, the fiberglass has been reformulated so that it's soft, itchless, and formaldehyde free. And there is a slew of high-density fiberglass batts: 3½-in.-thick batts that are rated at R-11, R-13, and R-15 and 5½-in.-thick batts rated at R-21. *Note:* If you compress batts into the cavities, you'll decrease the insulation's loft and thus reduce its R-value slightly.

Cotton batts (usually unfaced) are formaldehyde-free, absorb sound well, block air infiltration, insulate well, and won't make you itch. Cotton batts are treated with a natural biostat (borate) to inhibit mold and make them fire resistant. Wear a disposable paper mask when installing cotton: Although its lint is more benign than airborne glass fibers, avoid breathing it anyway. Mineral wool (also called rock wool) is spun from natural stone such as basalt or from blast-furnace slag and is the most fire resistant of any insulation. Mineral wool batts are installed mainly in commercial buildings because they are costly, heavy, and raise health-related concerns similar to those of fiberglass.

Blown-in insulation is the best insulation for wall cavities when you don't want to rip out finish surfaces. It's also good for insulating attic floors for the first time and adding to insulation that's already there. Loose-fill fiberglass is occasionally blown in, but cellulose is by far the material most often blown in. At low densities (1.5 lb./cu. ft.) cellulose traps air and is an effective insulator (R-3.5). And when it's *dense packed* (3 lb. to 4 lb./cu. ft.), that increased density effectively seals air leaks. In fact, some New England contractors report that old houses retrofitted with dense-packed cellulose are as airtight as new houses with polyethylene vapor barriers under the drywall.

Blowing-in insulation is dusty work, so most contractors prefer to gain access to wall cavities by prying off small sections of exterior siding and drilling through exterior sheathing. You can work from the inside, drilling discrete holes in the plaster or drywall, but empty the room first. In either case, a successful insulation depends on filling all cavities completely—not so easy if walls contain nonstandard framing, diagonal bracing "let into" studs, or fire-stop blocking.

Most blown-in cellulose is environmentally friendly and reasonably pleasant to work with if you wear a dust mask. Made from recycled paper, cellulose doesn't itch, and is often treated with borates to make it more resistant to mold, insects, and fire. Treated cellulose will not rot if it becomes wet, but it will absorb water. If leaks or condensation are minor, moisture will migrate

Spray-on insulations are frequently ingenious. Airkrete®, here applied through a fine screen stapled across open studs, attains an R-value of 3.9 per inch. Once the lightweight foam cures, it can be cut with a handsaw. Because its principal ingredient is magnesium silicate, an inert mineral, Airkrete is petrochemical free and virtually fireproof.

out of the walls in time. But cellulose doesn't dry quickly, so if it gets soaked, remove it; otherwise, drywall installed over it could get moldy and deteriorate. For this reason, although cellulose can be wet-sprayed into open cavities, only an experienced installer should do so.

Rigid-foam panels are the best choice for insulating below-grade areas such as basement and crawl space walls, where there's sometimes seepage or condensation, and for retrofitting insulation to exterior sheathing or foundations. In other words, use panels wherever batt, blown-in, or sprayed-on insulation can't do the job. Conversely, don't use rigid foam where odd spaces and air infiltration require insulation that can be shaped. Rigid-foam panels boast some of the highest R-values per inch, but the poorest UV and fire resistance, so consult local codes to determine how to fireproof rigid panels.

Expanded polystyrene (EPS), extruded polystyrene (XPS), and polyisocyanurate (polyiso) are the panels most commonly installed in homes. Panels come in widths of 12 in., 16 in., 24 in., and 48 in.; lengths in multiples of 2 ft., up to 12 ft.; and thicknesses from ½ in. to 4 in. EPS is the least expensive and has the lowest R-value (R-4 per inch); it is usually unfaced. XPS is intermediate in price and R-value (R-5 per inch); often faced with foil or polyethylene film, it is the most water resistant of the panels discussed here and hence the best for insulating foundations. Polyiso is the most costly, has the highest R-value (R-6.5 per inch), and has the lowest compressive strength of the three materials—though its foil

facing improves its durability. Since the insulation industry switched from ozone-depleting blowing agents to pentane in manufacturing it, polyiso has been considered an environmentally friendly material.

Sprayed-on foams should be applied only by contractors with specialized training and equipment. Most foams are two-part compounds that mix at the applicator nozzle. If the components don't mix properly or the nozzle partially clogs, you can end up with a substance that won't cure completely or insulate well. But correctly applied, sprayed-on foams fill even the oddest-shaped cavities, achieve high R-values, and block air movement effectively.

Permeability—the ability of water to permeate and migrate through the foam—is another critical factor. Basically, permeability depends on the

HOW MUCH Insulation DO YOU NEED?

How much insulation you need depends on climate, the house's heating system, and which part of the house you're insulating, as shown in "Recommended Levels of Insulation," on p. 340. Or you can use the U.S. Department of Energy's interactive ZIP Code Insulation Program™ (which is free online). To get a detailed insulation plan, type in your ZIP code, and then check the boxes that best describe the house and its heating system. Major insulation manufacturers offer similar calculators. You should also consult your local building authority, which has the final say and, in many cases, can tell you about tax incentives or rebates that encourage homeowners to insulate and save energy.

amount the foam expands. Open-cell foams, which use water as a blowing agent, expand as much as 100 times and so are quite permeable (high-perm ratings). Use open-cell foams where you want moisture to migrate through wall or ceiling cavities or on the inside of foundation walls that haven't been damp proofed adequately on the exterior. Closed-cell foams, manufactured with pentane as a blowing agent, expand roughly 30 times, and thus are less permeable (low-perm ratings).

It's not always obvious what type of foam to install where. In warm regions, for example, high-perm, open-cell foam is typically sprayed under roof sheathing, to allow moisture to migrate freely. But in very cold regions, low-perm, closed-cell foam is sprayed to the underside of roof sheathing. So ask reputable local insulation contractors for their recommendations.

INSTALLING FIBERGLASS BATTS

All batts are installed in basically the same way, so the following tips for installing fiberglass batts also hold true for cotton and mineral-wool batts, unless otherwise noted.

Getting started. Carefully seal air leaks before insulating; air currents can dramatically reduce an installation's R-value. Then suit up with the appropriate safety gear to keep fiberglass off your skin and out of your lungs. Wear a respirator mask, eye protection, long-sleeved shirt, long pants tucked into your socks, and work gloves.

To determine how much insulation to buy, measure the square footage of walls, ceilings, and floors and then divide by the number of square feet in an insulation package. Also printed on the packaging is the insulation's R-value and the width of the batts. Because most joists, studs, and rafters are spaced 16 in. on center, 15-in.-wide batts are the most common size. The fewer cuts you make, the faster the job will go; thus many contractors buy precut 93-in. batts to insulate standard 8-ft. walls. (Although 8 ft. equals 96 in, the 3-in. shortfall in batt length anticipates the space occupied by the top and bottom plates.) Batts that long can be a bit unwieldy, though, so you might want to use precut 4-ft. batts in those stud bays where you must fit insulation around pipes and wiring.

When no vapor barrier is required or a separate vapor barrier will be installed later, most contractors prefer to install unfaced batts. They're quicker to install because there's no facing to cut through, and you can friction fit the batts. By contrast, kraft paper–faced or foil-faced batts,

Recommended Levels of Insulation*

IF YOU LIVE IN A CLIMATE THAT IS...	AND YOUR HEATING SYSTEM IS†...	...INSULATE TO THESE LEVELS			
		CEILING	WOOD-FRAME WALL	FLOOR	BASEMENT/CRAWL SPACE WALLS‡
Warm: cooling and minimal heating needs (FL, HI, coastal CA, U.S. southeast)	Gas/oil or heat pump	R-22 to R-38	R-11 to R-13	R-11 to R-13	R-11 to R-19
	Electric resistance	R-38 to R-49	R-13 to R-25	R-13 to R-19	R-11 to R-19
Mixed: moderate heating and cooling needs (U.S. southwest, southern midwest, northwest, mid-Atlantic)	Gas/oil or heat pump	R-38	R-11 to R-22§	R-13 to R-25	R-11 to R-19
	Electric resistance	R-49	R-11 to R-26§	R-25	R-11 to R-19
Cold: heating and moderate cooling needs (all of Canada except Pacific coast; mountainous regions, U.S. northern midwest, New England)	Gas/oil or heat pump	R-38 to R-49	R-11 to R-22§	R-25	R-11 to R-19
	Electric resistance	R-49	R-11 to R-28§	R-25	R-13 to R-19

* Table adapted from U.S. Department of Energy (DOE) Energy Star Program table "Cost-Effective Insulation R-Values for Existing Homes" (www.energystar.gov) and 1997 "Insulation Fact Sheet."

† Insulation is also effective at reducing cooling bills; levels assume you have electric air-conditioning.

‡ Do not insulate crawl space walls if the crawl space is wet or ventilated with outdoor air.

§ R-values are for insulation only, not the whole wall; R-values may be achieved with a combination of cavity insulation and rigid-board insulation.

If stud walls are exposed, always seal air leaks before you start insulating.

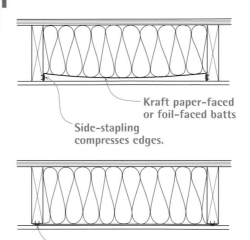

Kraft paper-faced or foil-faced batts

Side-stapling compresses edges.

Face-stapled insulation fills bay.

Always staple the insulation's kraft-paper or foil facing to the edges of the framing. Stapling facing to the sides of the studs or rafters compresses the insulation's edges and creates voids that air can flow through.

whose facing serves as a vapor barrier, must be cut carefully to avoid tears and face-stapled to the framing edges as shown in the drawing above. In general, place insulation facing toward the side of the building that's usually warmer—in cold climates, place the facing toward the inside of the building.

Cutting and placing insulation. Fiberglass insulation cuts easily with a utility knife, although its short blade requires several passes and should be changed as it gums up or gets dulled. Consequently, professional insulators use a long-bladed *insulation knife* or hone one edge of a putty knife till it's razor sharp. A common way to cut an insulation batt is to place it on the subfloor, measure off a cut-line, and press a 2×4 into the batt to compress the insulation and guide the knife. If you're cutting several pieces to the same length, you can save measuring time by marking the batt length on the subfloor with masking tape. To cut faced batts cleanly, place the facing side down on the subfloor.

However, most insulation contractors prefer to insert batts into stud bays and trim them in place. To trim a batt's width, for example, place one side of the batt into the bay and use the stud on the other side as a cutting guide. To get a tight fit, cut the batt about ¼ in. wider than the stud bay.

The pros trim insulation in place: It saves time, ensures a tight fit without measuring, and saves floor finishes from inadvertent knife marks. Here, an installer leaves the batt folded because his 3-in. knife blade is long enough to cut through a double thickness in one pass.

As you place batts, make sure they fill the bays fully. Fiberglass insulates best at "full loft," so before placing a batt between studs or joists, shake it gently to plump it up to its full thickness. Thus, if you use several batts to fill a bay, butt their ends together rather than overlapping and compressing them. To avoid compressing the edges of faced batts, always staple facing flanges to the edges—not the sides—of studs or rafters. Use a hammer tacker with ⅜-in staples.

Insulating the attic. Start insulating the attic by sealing air leaks (described earlier in this chapter). If attic floor joists are exposed, place planks across them so you can move safely. (Stepping from joist to joist is a good way to misstep and fall through the ceiling.) If there is a rough floor and you're not ready to finish the attic, it's easiest to remove floorboards every 6 ft. to 8 ft. and blow in loose-fill insulation. But batts are easy enough to install if you can pry up floorboards and insulate the floor in sections. Starting at one side of the attic, pry up and stack the floorboards, place batts, and renail the floorboards before moving to the next section.

To allow moisture to migrate, use unfaced batts when first insulating a floor in warm or mixed-climate zones. Use unfaced batts when *adding* insulation in any climate. When insulating an attic floor for the first time in very cold climates, use kraft paper–faced insulation because it's permeable; install with the facing down, toward the living spaces. *Never* use impermeable foil-faced batts or plastic vapor barriers when insulating an attic floor or ceiling because they'd trap moisture.

Fitting batts is straightforward: Cut them to length and place them so they fill the joist bays completely. If there's diagonal bridging, slit the insulation down the middle, 4 in. to 6 in. from the end, and fit the slit ends around the bridging. As with walls, split batts (see accompanying photos) to feed them over and under wires and pipes. *Note:* Keep insulation and other combustible materials back at least 3 in. from masonry or metal chimneys, and non-IC-rated recessed light fixtures, as noted in the Safety Alert on p. 330. When adding insulation, place new batts

Fiberglass achieves its highest R–value when it's not compressed. As you place batts in each stud bay, plump them up to full loft, and adjust them so they fill the space completely.

PRO TIP

Before insulating attic floors, locate electrical boxes and IC-rated recessed lights. Using coat hangers and bright scrap plastic—newspaper delivery sleeves are perfect—make little flags about 1 ft. high and staple them to the joists near each box or fixture. When the floor is covered with insulation, those little flags will show you where the electrical elements are, should you need to repair or replace them.

Preventing COLD SPOTS

To prevent cold spots behind pipes and wiring, split batts in two—sort of like pulling apart a sandwich—so that each piece is roughly half the batt thickness. Slide one half of the batt behind the wiring or pipes, and place the other half in front. Where it would be tedious to split and slide batt ends behind the obstruction in the middle of the stud bay, instead slice halfway through the batt as shown below; split the fiberglass at the cut-line, and fit the insulation behind the obstruction.

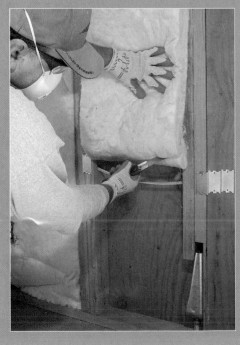

perpendicular atop old ones. Finally, install air chutes (baffles) between rafters, or block off insulation where rafters meet walls, so that air can flow freely from soffit vents to ridge or gable-end vents.

If you want to finish the attic with drywall, you can forego insulating the floor and instead insulate the kneewalls and rafters. But because an insulated floor deadens sound, you may want to insulate it anyhow. Before inserting batts into the rafter bays, staple lightweight rigid-foam air chutes to the underside of the roof sheathing. The chutes create a 1-in space between the sheathing and the insulation on the attic floor, so that air can keep flowing under the roof. If the rafters are spaced regularly on 16-in. centers, unfaced friction-fit batts will stay in place till the drywall goes up. But if the rafter spacing is wide (24-in. on center or greater) or irregular, friction-fit batts may sag or fall out. Instead, you might use any of these options: (1) staple paper-faced batts to the rafter edges, (2) have foam insulation sprayed to the underside of the roof sheathing after installing air chutes, or (3) trim rigid-foam panels to fit between the rafters and glue them to the underside of the roof sheathing. If there are gaps between the panels and rafters, shoot a compatible foam into the gaps.

INSULATING AROUND ELECTRICAL Outlets

Electrical outlet boxes in exterior walls can be big energy losers because builders often forget to insulate behind boxes. To stop air leaks, split insulation batts and slide portions behind the boxes. In very cold climates, you might also want to install airtight outlet boxes. Be careful not to knick cables around boxes.

⊘ Before insulating around any outlet, disconnect the electrical power to the area and use a voltage tester to be sure the power is off.

When installing batt insulation, be careful to leave an airspace of at least 1 in. between the top of the insulation and the underside of the roof sheathing. The holes in the unfilled bays at the right are fascia vents.

Insulating FLOORS ABOVE BASEMENTS AND CRAWL SPACES

When insulating a floor over an unconditioned crawl space or basement, you're fighting gravity and moisture.

First, let's deal with gravity. The easiest way to install fiberglass batts without needing three hands is to precut a number of thin wood slats—¼-in. fence lath is light and springy—¼-in. longer than the distance between the joists. As you hold the unfaced batts in the joist bays with one hand, use the other to wedge the slats into place, under the insulation. Being slightly long and springy, the slats will bow up and support the insulation; insert them every 16 in. to 24 in.

If the subfloor area is damp or if there's heavy condensation during warm months, rigid-foam panels are a better choice than fiberglass batts. (Mice are also less likely to tunnel through or nest in rigid foam.) Use a compatible construction adhesive to glue the foam panels to the underside of the subfloor. If floor joists are straight and regularly spaced, trim panels so they are ⅛ in. wider than the distance between the joists. But if the joists are irregular, trim the foam panels a bit smaller and use expanding foam to fill any gaps.

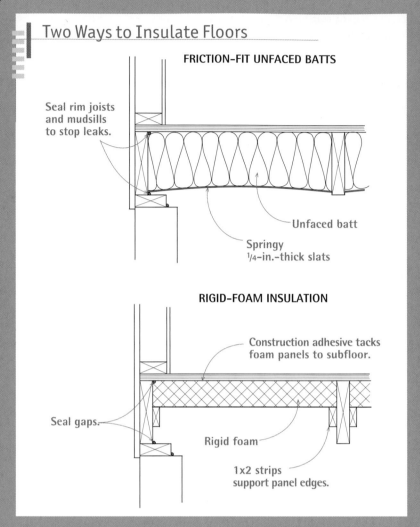

Two Ways to Insulate Floors

FRICTION-FIT UNFACED BATTS

Seal rim joists and mudsills to stop leaks.

Unfaced batt

Springy ¼-in.-thick slats

RIGID-FOAM INSULATION

Construction adhesive tacks foam panels to subfloor.

Seal gaps.

Rigid foam

1x2 strips support panel edges.

BLOWING-IN INSULATION

Loose-fill insulation—usually cellulose—can be blown in at low pressure to supplement existing attic insulation or pumped into wall cavities at high pressures to achieve a dense pack that's virtually airtight. Before insulating, be sure to review earlier sections of this chapter on sealing air leaks, correcting excess moisture, and blocking insulation to keep it away from potential ignition sources such as chimneys and unrated recessed lights. Also keep insulation away from knob-and-tube wiring that's still energized (see Chapter 11 for more information about this old wiring).

Equipment. You can rent insulation blowers and hoses. And some suppliers will loan the equipment free if you buy the insulation from them. If you're loose-filling an attic in a two- or three-story house or dense packing insulation in walls,

you'll need a more powerful machine, usually wired for 240 volts or 120/240 volts. Almost all pumping units require two workers, one to feed insulation into a hopper and the other to operate the hose. Consequently, most machines have a remote on/off switch so the hose operator can stop the blower as cavities fill up. A remote switch also allows you to shut off the blower at the first sign of a clogged hose. Most machines have adjustable gates or air inlets that control the air–insulation mixture. Have the equipment supplier explain safe operating procedures to both workers.

Units typically come with 3-in. corrugated plastic hoses whose sections join with steel couplings. If you're blowing-in attic insulation at low pressure, 3-in. hoses can blow a lot of insulation quickly. (When filling large, open places such as attic floors, pump a low-air, insulation-rich mix.) When filling wall cavities at low pressure, installers typically use a 3-in. by 1-in. reducer to minimize the size of the holes they'll need to patch later. However, when dense-packing cellulose into wall cavities, some professionals prefer to duct-tape a 5-ft. or 6-ft. length of 1-in. clear vinyl tubing to the end of the 3-in. hose. Narrower hoses are easy to snake into tight spaces—you can feed them into the far reaches of a cavity—and they deliver insulation at greater velocity. Clear vinyl tubing also allows you to see if the insulation is flowing freely. Because narrower hoses are more likely to clog, run an air-rich, low-insulation mix through them. To clear clogs, blow air alone through the hoses.

In addition to a tight-fitting dust mask and eye protection, you'll need a drill and drill bit (or hole saw) to drill into exterior sheathing, a flat bar to pry up siding, and a shingle ripper or a mini-hacksaw to cut through nail shanks if you've got wood siding. If there's vinyl or aluminum siding, you'll also need a *zip tool,* which has a hook on one end, to lift the tops of the courses you want to remove and get access to the nails holding the siding strip. If the exterior is stucco, you'll need a tungsten carbide hole saw to drill through it.

Hoses often clog near the reducer. To clear a clog, remove the reducing nozzle, insert the end of the hose in a trash bag, and turn on the blower. If that doesn't work, rap the sides of the hose and use a stick to dig out whatever you can.

Prep work. When insulating from inside the house, first seal off the heating registers to keep insulation out of the ducts, and rent a commercial shop vacuum with a fine filter for cleanup. Before insulating, clear the room of furniture or cover it with plastic tarps. *Important:* 🚫 Before drilling, turn off the electrical power to the affected areas, and use a voltage tester (see p. 235) to make sure the power's off.

Insulating open attics. You'll want to avoid blocking the airflow from soffit vents; so before blowing insulation, install blocking or air chutes to hold the insulation back. If the attic joists are exposed, run planks across them so you can move safely around the attic. If you staple location flags to the joists, they can double as rough depth gauges as you add insulation. If the attic has floorboards (rather than plywood), pry them up in the center of the attic to expose the joists. Then blow insulation into the joist bays. It's difficult to blow insulation much farther than 4 ft., so remove boards every 8 ft. or so and feed in about

Blown-in installation is typically fed through a 3-in. hose that is reduced into a 1-in. nozzle, which is inserted into holes drilled in the siding. The remote switch draped over the end of the hose enables the operator to shut off the blower quickly, should a clog develop.

Vermiculite: A POTENTIAL ASBESTOS RISK

Vermiculite is a small, pebble-like, gold or brown mineral fiber (colored rather like mica) that was widely used for insulation and soundproofing. A loose-fill material, it was often poured in attic floors. But vermiculite often contains asbestos. If you see it in your home, don't disturb it, for only an experienced asbestos-abatement contractor should remove it. Visit the U.S. Environmental Protection Agency's (EPA's) Web site for more information (www.epa.gov).

4 ft. of the blower hose under the floorboards on both sides of the opening, gradually withdrawing the hose as the bays fill.

Insulating closed walls. Blowing-in insulation is a dusty job, so do it from outside the building if possible. The task varies according to the siding you have. If you have wood, vinyl, or alu-minum siding, remove a course or two when you drill your exploratory holes toward the top of each wall cavity. It's possible to drill through wood siding and plug it later; but it's preferable to remove the wood siding, drill through the sheathing, and then replace the siding over the plugged sheathing. If there's vinyl or aluminum siding, insert a zip tool under the top of the course you want to remove, and slide a flat bar under nails holding the siding strip. Then replace the siding after plugging the insulation holes. If you have stucco siding, drill directly through it; stucco is tenacious and malleable so plugs will hold well and can be hidden easily by texturing patches to match the surrounding surface.

Ideally, the holes you drill should be slightly larger than the diameter of the insulation injector—the hose reducer or the vinyl tubing used to blow in insulation. If the injector is smaller than the hole, pressurized air escaping will roughly equalize the amount being blown in. If the holes and the injector are exactly sized, little air will escape and the wall cavity will quickly become so pressurized that you can't blow in insulation. Conversely, if the holes are too large, insulation will be blowing all over the place and you'll have larger holes to patch. So make the holes roughly ¼ in. larger than the diameter of the injector.

As you blow cellulose into each drilled hole, cover the hole (and the inserted tube) loosely with a rag or a scrap of fiberglass insulation. The rag will allow pressurized air to escape but will prevent the cellulose from blowing out.

As the insulation starts becoming densely packed, the insulation flowing through it will slow. When a cavity is almost full, it will become so airtight that it will block the flow of additional insulation, causing the blower to whine. (If you stick your index finger into the hole of a filled cavity, it will meet resistance similar to that of poking a middle-aged stomach.) After filling a few cavities, you'll get a sense of how much insulation you need to fill each one, and the blower's whine will become familiar. At that point, use the remote on/off to shut off the blower and allow the pressure in the hose to subside. Then pull out the injector and go on to the next cavity. *Note:* If you insert clear vinyl tubing all the way into cavities to dense-pack them, gradually pull back the tubing 8 in. to 12 in. as each starts to fill and the insulation flow slows.

Plugging the holes. After each cavity is filled, plug the holes in sheathing with precut beveled wood plugs or corks. (Your insulation supplier should have them in stock.) Smear exterior-grade polyurethane glue around the edges of each plug, and use a hammer and a scrap block to drive the

Exploring Exterior Walls

Before you order insulation and rent a blower, see if the exterior walls are already insulated. ⚡ You can explore them from inside the house by turning off the electrical power to a section of wall (use a voltage tester to be sure the power's off) and removing a section of baseboard. Use a utility knife to cut through a small section of plaster or drywall and look inside the wall. Or you can go outside and pry off a section of siding and drill a hole through the sheathing to see what's inside. If there's no insulation, you're good to go.

In houses built in the 1940s and later, you may find anything from multiple layers of crinkly, tar-impregnated insulation paper to 1-in. or 2-in. fiberglass or mineral-wool batts. If wall cavities are less than half filled, you can probably insert 1-in. vinyl tubing into them and blow-in cellulose to improve heat retention. But if you wad up old batts as you try to push in tubing, blowing in more insulation probably won't be cost-effective: You'll have cold spots. Focus instead on adding attic insulation and sealing air leaks.

If you find that the exterior walls are uninsulated, next explore to locate fire-stops (blocking between studs) and let-in braces running diagonally. A length of stiff insulated wire or flexible vinyl tubing makes a good probe. Typically, there will be one fire-stop per stud bay, thus dividing each bay into two cavities. You'll need to drill one hole in each cavity to fill it with insulation, so drill holes in the upper third of each cavity. Drilling toward the top of a cavity also minimizes the chances that you'll drill through electrical cables in exterior walls. Cables that run horizontally are usually 12 in.—the height to most receptacles—to 24 in. above finish interior floors. Finally, don't forget to drill into the stud bays above and below windows and above doors.

Before filling each wall, shut off the electrical power to the wall and drill test holes; then insert a stiff insulated wire to probe for obstructions in the stud bay.

plugs flush to the sheathing. Replace the siding sections, caulk the joints, prime, and paint.

If you drill holes in interior walls to blow in cellulose, plug the holes with manufactured styrene foam plugs that push in till they're slightly below the wall surface. To reduce dust and ensure clean edges, some installers hand-make a drywall punch by angle-cutting a short length of electrical metal conduit (EMT) at a sharp angle, so that one end looks like the point of an enlarged hypodermic needle. Use a hammer to rap the blunt end of the punch. Finally, cover the plug or the punched hole with self-adhering mesh tape (see Chapter 15), and one or two coats of setting-type joint compound; feather it out to make a smooth join.

USING RIGID-FOAM PANELS IN BASEMENTS

There are almost as many ways to insulate basement walls as there are builders. In this brief section you'll find two space-conserving assemblies that should prevent mold, while retaining conditioned air.

Suggestions. Here are six suggestions for insulating below grade:

▶ If a basement is chronically damp because of exterior water, correct that problem before insulating. See "Damp Basement Solutions," on p. 224.

▶ Plastic vapor barriers aren't usually needed on foundation walls insulated with foam panels, unless required by local codes—typically, in regions with severe winters. Once you've remedied exterior water sources, allow incidental moisture in the foundation walls to migrate outward or inward, so the walls can dry.

▶ Seal and insulate the tops of foundation walls because that's where basements most often leak air and lose heat. Caulk along the mudsill–foundation joint and apply expandable foam along the tops and bottoms

Transfer cut-lines quickly to rigid insulation by using your measuring tape as a marking gauge. Slide your hands in unison—one holding the tape in position along the panel edge, the other holding a utility knife next to the tape's free end.

Rigid insulation cuts easily with a crosscut saw. Cut the panel width ⅛ in. proud so that friction will hold it in place between the joists or the studs.

Space-Saving Walls

To conserve space, builders often attach 1×3 furring strips to basement walls. These strips help secure insulation and provide a base for attaching drywall. But furring strips are viable only if the foundation walls are dry and relatively plumb and flat. If foundation walls are lumpy and off-plumb, a stud wall erected inside the foundation is the only way to create a flat plane for finish materials.

Fortunately, not all stud walls guzzle space. Lightweight steel studs are only 1⅝ in. deep; but, as noted in Chapter 4, they can be quirky to work with. The third option, *flat-framing*, is a winner: Rotate 2×4 studs 90° so that their broad side faces the foundation wall and use 2×2 plates at top and bottom. Because modern 2×4s are actually 1½ in. by 3½ in., a flat-framed wall is only 1½ in. deep, and the 3½-in. faces give you plenty of surface for screwing on drywall. Besides, unlike skimpy furring strips, 2×4s won't split.

of the rim joists. Then insulate the rim joists with rigid insulation or encapsulated (poly-wrapped) fiberglass batts.

▶ Lumber in direct contact with masonry walls or floors should be pressure-treated; relatively benign biocides in pressure-treated wood include alkaline copper quat (**ACQ**) and copper boron azole (**CBA**). If you use non-treated furring strips, prevent rotted ends by keeping the bottoms of the vertical strips 1½ in. above concrete floors.

▶ Don't place fiberglass or cellulose next to masonry walls because fibrous materials will retain moisture and foster mold. In basements and crawl spaces, closed-cell XPS panels are a better choice because they are impermeable to and unaffected by moisture. Open-cell XPS is

Cold-Climate Basement Insulation

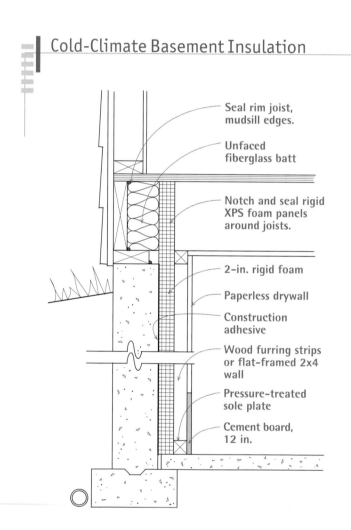

Seal rim joist, mudsill edges.

Unfaced fiberglass batt

Notch and seal rigid XPS foam panels around joists.

2-in. rigid foam

Paperless drywall

Construction adhesive

Wood furring strips or flat-framed 2x4 wall

Pressure-treated sole plate

Cement board, 12 in.

In cold climates, avoid thermal breaks by butting rigid-insulation panels together and sealing seams with builder's tape.

Moderate-Climate Basement Insulation

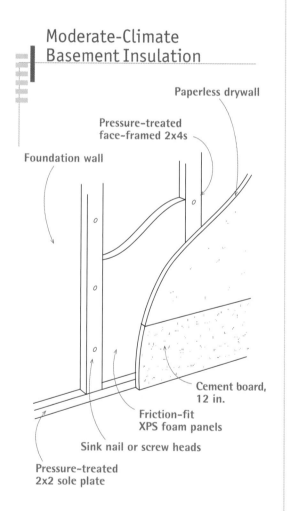

Paperless drywall

Pressure-treated face-framed 2x4s

Foundation wall

Cement board, 12 in.

Friction-fit XPS foam panels

Sink nail or screw heads

Pressure-treated 2x2 sole plate

Where winters are less severe, it's acceptable to have thermal breaks between insulation panels. Use power-actuated nails or concrete screws to attach furring strips directly to masonry walls. See the wall-top details shown in the drawing at left.

This old 1930-era forced-hot-air system has asbestos-insulated ducts and a gas burner that guzzled fuel in the dead of winter.

The induced-draft, condensing gas furnace that replaced the old one (above) is much smaller (note the duct holes of the old furnace) and achieved 95 percent fuel efficiency.

also acceptable in subfloor areas but, as noted earlier, open-cell foams are more permeable and will allow moisture to migrate.

▶ Mold grows on paper-faced drywall, so don't use it in basements. Instead, use paperless drywall such as Fiberock®, Humitek™, and DensArmor™. Cement board, such as WonderBoard® and HardiBacker®, is completely impervious to water, but it is expensive and requires more work to install. Consider running a 12-in. band of cement board along the bottom of the walls to prevent moisture absorption through the basement floors, and then use something less expensive above it, as shown in the drawings on the facing page.

Cold climates. In cold climates, basement wall insulation should be continuous; in other words, there should be no thermal breaks. To achieve this continuity, use construction adhesive to adhere XPS panels directly to the foundation or to a vapor barrier adhered to the walls, if required by code. To find an adhesive that's chemically compatible with rigid-foam panels, read the product literature for both materials. As you install the panels, butt their edges tightly together and cover the joints with builder's tape.

Rigid-metal duct (left) offers the least resistance to airflow; seal its joints and insulate the runs through unheated areas. Flexible insulated ducts, such as Wire Flex™ (center), and Aluma Flex™ (right) don't need fittings to make turns; but Wire Flex can be punctured. Aluma Flex offers a good balance of strength and flexibility.

If space is tight in the basement, flat-frame a 2×4 wall 16-in. on center, with 2×2 top and bottom plates. Use a powder-actuated nailer or concrete screws to secure the bottom plate to a concrete floor. (Wear ear and eye protection.) Use wood screws to attach the top plate to the first-floor joists or, where joists run parallel, to 2×4 nailers inserted between the floor joists and rim joists. (Predrill holes for the concrete screws.)

Installing 2-in. panels of XPS will yield an R-10 rating. In very cold climates, you might want add 1½-in. panels between the studs of the new 2×4 wall as well, creating a composite rating of R-17.5 for the two layers.

Moderate climates. In moderate climates, thermal breaks in the basement walls are acceptable. So you can attach vertical furring strips directly to the masonry walls, using powder-actuated nails or concrete screws, and then place foam panels between the strips. Use pressure-treated wood. Because conventional 1×3 furring strips are only ¾ in. thick, use 2×2s or 2×4s on-face instead, spacing them 16 in. on center. If there's a possibility that they could wick moisture from the basement floor, keep the furring strips 1½ in. above floors.

Three Things to Ask an HVAC Specialist

Upgrading the heating and cooling equipment in your house is a good way to improve interior air quality and conserve energy. Ask a reputable local HVAC contractor about the following:

▶ **Induced-draft gas furnaces.** Roughly two-thirds of North American homes have forced-hot-air (FHA) systems, so replacing an existing FHA furnace is a great way to increase efficiency without disturbing existing ducts and registers. Induced-draft furnaces can achieve annual fuel-use efficiencies of 90 percent to 97 percent because they extract heat from combustion gases. (Older well-maintained furnaces might have efficiencies closer to 70 percent, or less.) Because combustion gases are cooler, they're less buoyant, so the system uses a fan to expel them—hence the name *induced draft*.

▶ **Heat-recovery ventilators.** Tightly insulated houses conserve energy, but they may also recycle stale air endlessly. In response to the dilemma of introducing fresh air without expelling conditioned air, heat-recovery ventilators (HRVs) were developed. Typically, an HRV has two fans: one to bring in fresh air and one to expel stale air. It also has a heat exchanger that recovers 75 percent to 80 percent of the heat in the outgoing air and preheats incoming air. HRVs can filter pollen and dust from incoming air and, by

equalizing air pressure in tight houses, prevent potentially dangerous situations such as back-drafting (furnace combustion air, including carbon monoxide, being sucked back down a vent flue by negative air pressure). Some HRVs also remove excess humidity from incoming air.

▶ **Central air cleaners.** Most standard central heating/air-conditioning filters don't do a good job. If you're concerned about interior air quality and removing allergens (such as dust mites, mold, and pet dander), you have a variety of air cleaners to choose from, including pleated media, self-charging electrostatic filters, electronic air cleaners, and by-pass HEPA filters. In general, air cleaners vary by fineness of filtering (dust arrestance), ease of installing into existing ductwork, airflow impedance, and cost. To make sense of this and many other HVAC topics, visit www.dulley.com. On air filters, mechanical engineer Jim Dulley notes, "For do-it-yourself installation, self-charging electrostatic models are ideal because they require no sheet-metal ductwork to install."

▶ **Upgrading ducts.** Sealing ducts can prevent air leaks and, in many cases, reduce excess moisture. But if ducts are rusty and as tired as the one shown on p. 333, or are uninsulated as they traverse unheated areas, maybe it's time to replace them. Three popular types are shown above.

Finish Surfaces

People have used plaster in buildings since prehistoric times. Archaeologists have unearthed plaster walls and floors dating to 6000 B.C. in Mesopotamia. And the hieroglyphics of early Egypt were painted on plaster walls. In North America, plaster had been the preferred wall and ceiling surface until after World War II, when drywall entered the building boom. Although drywall represents a historic shift in building technology, the shift was more one of evolution than revolution because drywall's core material is gypsum rock—the same material used since ancient times to make plaster.

Drywall

Sometimes called Sheetrock® after a popular brand, drywall consists of 4-ft.-wide panels that are screwed or nailed to ceiling joists and wall studs. Sandwiched between layers of paper, drywall's gypsum core is almost as hard and durable as plaster, though it requires much less skill to install. Appropriately, the term *drywall* contrasts these dry panels with plaster, which is applied wet and may take weeks to dry thoroughly.

Panel joints are concealed with tape and usually three coats of successively wider layers of joint compound that render room surfaces smooth. Each panel's two long front edges are slightly beveled, providing a depression to be filled by joint tape and compound. *Note:* Each layer of joint compound should be allowed to dry thoroughly before sanding smooth and applying the next coat.

DRYWALL TYPES

Drywall's paper facing and core material can be manufactured for special purposes to make it more flexible, water resistant, fire resistant, sound isolating, scuff resistant, and so on. The upcoming pages will help you determine the size and type of drywall you choose.

▶ **Where it will be used.** Local building codes may require water-resistant (WR) drywall in high-humidity rooms or fire-resistant (type-X) panels elsewhere to retard fires.

▶ **Distances it must span.** Because gypsum is relatively brittle, the drywall must be thick enough to span the distance between ceiling joists without sagging and between wall studs without bowing (see "Drywall Types, Uses, and Specifications," on p. 352).

Sturdy scaffolding keeps you safe and allows you to focus on the task at hand. This lightweight setup is easily rolled from room to room.

▶ **Skill and strength of installers.** The longer the sheets, the heavier and more unwieldy they are to lug and lift, especially a concern if you're working alone or if ceilings are high.

▶ **Access to work areas.** Using sheets longer than the basic 8 ft. reduces the number of end joints that need taping. But these jumbo 14-ft. and 16-ft. panels are practical only if your doors and stairwells are large enough to admit them.

Regular drywall comes in four thickness: ¼ in., ⅜ in., ½ in. and ⅝ in; and in sheets 8 ft. to 16 ft. long, in 2-ft. increments. There are also 4-ft. by 9-ft. sheets. To minimize wall joints when installing drywall horizontally, regular drywall also comes in 54-in. widths.

The most commonly used thickness is ½ in., typically installed over wood or metal framing. A sheet that size weighs about 70 lb., still manageable for strong people working solo.

To increase fire resistance and deaden sound, you can double up ½ in. panels, but that may be overkill. More often, a single layer of ⅝-in. drywall is used for those purposes. Being stiffer, ⅝-in. panels are harder to damage, so they're a smart idea in hallways if you've got kids. And they're less likely to sag between ceiling joists and bow between studs.

Renovators commonly use ¼-in. and ⅜-in. sheets to cover damaged surfaces and thereby avoid the huge mess of demolishing and removing old plaster. For best results with this thin drywall, use both construction adhesive and screws to attach it. However, neither thickness is sturdy enough to attach directly to studs in a single layer.

Because they're thin and flexible, two layers of ¼-in. drywall are routinely bent to cover curving walls, arches, and the like. Attach the second layer with construction adhesive and screws. If the curved area has a short radius (3 ft. to 5 ft.), wet the drywall first (discussed in detail later in this chapter). There's also a ¼-in. *flexible* drywall with

Drywall Types, Uses, and Specifications

DRYWALL TYPE AND THICKNESS (in.)	COMMON USES	MAXIMUM FRAMING SPACING	AVAILABLE LENGTHS (ft.)
Regular			
▶ ¼	Renovation, over damaged surfaces; curved surfaces	16 in. o.c., as double layer over framing, single layer over existing plaster, and so on	8, 10
▶ ⅜	Renovation, mostly on walls	16 in. o.c.	8, 10, 12
▶ ½	Walls and ceilings; most popular thickness	24 in. o.c.; 16 in. o.c., if hung parallel to ceiling joists	8, 9, 10, 12, 14, 16
▶ ⅝	Walls and ceilings	24 in. o.c.; 16 in. o.c., if hung parallel to ceiling joists	8, 9, 10, 12, 14
Water-resistant (WR)			
▶ ½	Bathrooms; high-humidity rooms	16 in. o.c., on walls; 12 in. o.c., on ceilings	8, 10, 12 (other sizes with special order)
▶ ⅝	Bathroom ceilings	16 in. o.c., on walls and ceilings	8, 10, 12 (other sizes with special order)
Fire-resistant (type X)			
▶ ½ (45-minute fire rating)	When portion of wall does not require fire-rated surface and is covered with regular ½-in. panels	24 in. o.c.	8, 10, 12
▶ ⅝ (60-minute fire rating)	Walls and ceilings; most popular thickness; garages	24 in. o.c.	8, 10, 12 (other sizes with special order)
▶ ¾ (120-minute fire rating)	Where code requires it	24 in. o.c.	8, 9, 10., 12

heavier paper facings designed for curved surfaces, but this usually needs to be special-ordered.

Water-resistant drywall (WR board) is also called greenboard, after the color of its facing. Its water-resistant core and water-repellent face are designed to resist moisture in bathrooms, behind kitchen sinks, and in laundry rooms. In general, it is a good base for paint, plastic, or ceramic tiles affixed with adhesives, and for installation *behind* fiberglass tub surrounds.

Although WR board can cover most bathroom walls, it should *not* be used above tubs or in shower stalls. In particular, it's not recommended as a substrate for tile in those areas because sustained wetting and occasional bumps will cause the drywall to deteriorate, resulting in loose tiles, mold, and water migration to the framing behind. As a substrate for tile around tubs and showers, cementitious backboard is a far more durable and cost effective. Mortar is also durable there, but more expensive.

For the reasons just cited, don't install WR board over a vapor barrier, especially if this drywall will later be painted with oil-based paint, papered with vinyl wallpaper, or otherwise covered with a vapor-retarding membrane. Sandwiched between two impervious layers, the drywall will deteriorate.

Fire-resistant drywall (also called type X) is specified for furnace rooms, garages, common walls between garages and living spaces, shared walls in multifamily buildings, and so on. The thicker the type-X drywall, the higher the fire rating: 45 minutes for ½ in., 1 hour for ⅝ in., 2 hours for ¾ in. Fire-resistant drywall has a core reinforced with glass fibers, making it more durable and somewhat harder to cut.

Most codes specify ⅝-in. drywall for single-family residences—a thickness also adequate to span garage ceiling joists spaced 24 in. on center.

Other specialty drywalls are available. *Foil-backed* drywall is sometimes specified in the Cold Belt to radiate heat back into living spaces and prevent moisture from migrating to unheated areas. *Abuse-resistant* drywall, *sound-mitigating* drywall, and *vinyl-* and *fabric-covered* panels with prefinished edges are also manufactured.

Blueboard is a base for single- or two-coat veneer plastering and is now widely used instead of metal, wood, or gypsum lath. It is available in standard 4-ft.-wide panels.

Gypsum lath is specified as a substrate for traditional full-thickness, three-coat plastering. Its panels are typically 16 in. by 48 in.

Cementitious backerboard has a core of cement rather than gypsum. Used as a tile substrate, it is installed much like drywall (see Chapter 16 for details).

Basic drywall tools. Top: drywall hammer, utility saw, and rasp. Bottom, from left: 6-in. taping knife, spackling knife, utility knife, multibit screwdriver, chalk, and chalkline box.

TOOLS

You can install drywall with common carpentry tools—framing square, hammer, tape measure, utility knife, and chalkline. Still, a few specialized, moderately priced tools will make the job go faster and look better. If you've got high ceilings, rent scaffolding.

Layout tools include a 25-ft. *tape measure*, which will extend 8 ft. to 10 ft. without buckling; a 4-ft. *aluminum T-square* for marking and cutting panels; a *chalkline* box for marking cutlines longer than 4 ft.; a *compass* or a *scriber* to transfer out-of-plumb wall readings to intersecting panels; and a 2-ft. framing square to transfer the locations of outlet boxes, ducts, and such onto the panels.

Cutting and shaping tools may be simple, but must be sharp. Drywall can be cut with one pass of a sharp *utility knife*, a quick snap of the panel, and a second cut to sever the paper backing, as shown in the center photo on p. 362. Buy a lot of utility-knife blades and change them often; dull blades create ragged edges. Use a *Surform®* rasp to clean up cut drywall edges. The sharp point of a *drywall saw* enables you to plunge cut in the middle of a panel without first drilling, though the edges of the cut will be rough.

A *drywall router* or a *laminate router with a drywall bit* is the pro's tool of choice for quick, clean cuts around electrical outlet boxes, ducts, and the like. With a light touch and a little practice, you can use this tool to cut out boxes

For 8-ft. to 9-ft. ceilings, benches can support platform planks and enable workers to raise and attach panels easily.

Adjustable *drywall benches* should enable you to reach 8-ft. or 9-ft ceilings easily. Alternatively, you can lay planks across sturdy wooden sawhorses.

Ultimately, renting a *drywall lift* and/or *scaffolding* is the safest way to go, especially if ceilings are higher than 10 ft. If there's no danger of falling off your work platform, you can focus on attaching drywall. Scaffolding is also indispensable during the taping and sanding stages.

Attachment tools are typically a *corded screw gun* or a drill with screw bits to attach drywall. A cordless drill with screw bits is fine for a drywalling a room, but pros who have thousands of screws to drive use corded screw guns, which have clutches and depth settings that set the screws heads perfectly—just below the surface. The pros also use a *drywall hammer* for incidental nailing. A standard carpenter's hammer will do almost as well, but the convex-head of a drywall hammer is less likely to damage the paper facing of a panel, should you need to drive down a nail.

Adding a *self-feeding screw attachment* to the screw gun would probably speed up the job, but few pros use them. Finally, if you'll be installing double layers of drywall, use a *caulking gun* to apply construction adhesive to the outer face of the first layer.

Taping and finishing tools are used to apply joint compound through to sanding the joints. The workhorse of taping is the *6-in. taping knife,* perfect for filling screw holes, spreading a first layer of joint compound, and bedding tape.

To apply the successively wider and thinner second and third coats of joint compound, you'll need wider taping knives or *curved trowels.* Taping knives typically have straight handles and blades 10 in. to 24 in. wide; a 12-in.-wide knife will suffice for most jobs. Trowels have a handle roughly parallel to the blade and a slightly curved blade that "crowns" the compound slightly. Trowel blades run 8 in. to 14 in. long.

Applying "mud" (joint compound) takes finesse, so most pros use a *mud pan* or a *hawk* to

already covered by drywall panels, as shown in the photo on p. 363.

Similarly, you can use a *utility saw* to cut out the waste portion of a drywall panel that you've "run long" into a doorway or window opening.

Lifting tools will help get you or the drywall up into place. Two lifting tools can be handmade: A *panel lifter* is just a first-class lever inserted under the bottom of a panel to raise it an inch or so,

A panel lifter leaves your hands free to attach the drywall panel.

leaving your hands free to attach the drywall. Metal lifters are not expensive, but 1×2 scraps work almost as well.

The second homemade tool, a *T-support,* temporarily holds a panel against ceiling joists while you attach it. Cut a 2×4 T-support about ½ in. longer than the ceiling height so you can wedge it firmly against the panel. Or you can rent a hydraulic *stiff arm,* an adjustable metal version of a T-support.

Drywall router (bottom) and screw gun.

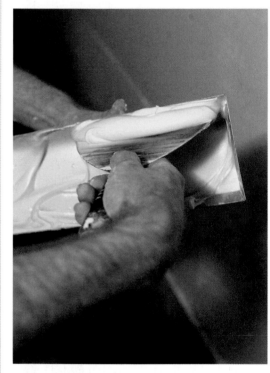

A mud pan holds enough joint compound to cover hundreds of screw holes or several long panel joints.

hold enough mud to tape several joints. As they work, drywallers are constantly in motion: scooping mud, centering it on the knife blade, scraping off the excess, and returning it to the pan or onto the hawk.

Corner knives enable you to apply mud to both sides of an inside corner simultaneously. To finish outside corners (those that project into a room) consider making your own tool. Boil a plastic flat knife, and once it's soft, bend into the shape you need, as shown in the photo at right.

For high-volume jobs, you can rent taping tools that dispense tape and compound simultaneously. See "Mechanical Taping Tools," on p. 369, for more information.

Sponges and a pail of water will keep tools clean as you go. Even tiny chunks of dried compound will drag and ruin freshly applied layers, so rinse tools often, and change water often. A *perfectly clean* 5-gal. joint compound container is a great rinse bucket. Use a second one to store and transport delicate trowels and knives.

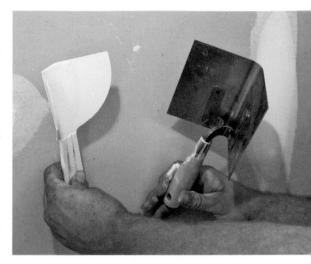

Left: a home-bent knife for shaping outside corners.
Right: an inside-corner knife.

Sanding equipment starts with special *black carbide–grit sandpaper,* which resists clogging by gypsum dust; it comes precut to fit the rubber-faced pads attached to poles and hand sanders. Sandpaper grit ranges from 80 (the coarsest) to 220 (fine); 120-grit paper is good to start sanding with. Finish-sand with 220-grit or a rigid *dry-sanding sponge* (a special sponge that is never wetted).

A sanding pole with a pivoting head enables you to sand higher—8 ft. ceilings are a snap—and with less fatigue because you use your whole upper body.

Sanding joint compound generates a prodigious amount of dust, so buy a package of good-quality paper *dust masks* that fit your face tightly; they're cheap enough to throw out after each sanding session. If you're sanding over your head, lightweight goggles and a cheap painter's hat will minimize dust in your eyes and hair.

A shop vacuum with a fine dust filter is a must; vacuum at each break so you don't track dust all over the house. Dust-free sanding attachments are available for shop vacuums (as shown in the top photo on p. 356). Although they virtually eliminate dust, they'll sand through soft topping coats and expose the joint tape in a flash if you're not careful. For best results, run them at low speed settings and use fine, 220-grit sandpaper.

A dust–free sander attached to a shop vacuum cuts dust dramatically, but in unskilled hands it will oversand soft topping coats.

PRO TIP

Tape dispensers hold paper or mesh tape and clip to your belt, so your tape is always ready to roll. Bigger dispensers hold a 500-ft. roll.

Adjust your screw gun so that it sets screws just below the surface of the drywall.

Finally, tape up sheet plastic to isolate the rooms you're sanding, especially if you're living in the house. Painter's tape will do the least damage to trim finishes and paint.

MATERIALS

This chapter began with sizes and types of drywall. Now let's look at screws, joint tape, corner beads, and joint compound before planning and estimating supplies.

Drywall screws have all but replaced nails. Here are the three principal types:

▶ Type-W screws have a coarse thread that grips wood well. They should be long enough to penetrate framing at least ⅝ in. In double-layer installations (two ½-in. panels), use type-W screws at least 1½ in. long.

▶ Type-S screws have fine threads and are designed to attach drywall panels to light-steel framing and steel-resilient channels. At least ⅜ in. of the screw should pass through metal studs, so 1-in. type-S screws are commonly used for single-ply ½-in. or ⅝-in. drywall installations. If you're attaching drywall to heavy-gauge (structural) steel, use self-tapping screws.

▶ Type-G screws are sometimes specified to attach the second panel of a fire-rated,

double-layer installation. That is, the first panel is the substrate to which the second panel is screwed and glued with construction adhesive. Ideally, screws should also penetrate framing, so ask building inspectors about installation requirements if your local code specifies type-G screws.

Nails are still used to attach corner bead and to tack panels in place. Ring-shank drywall nails hold the best in wood; don't bother with other nail types. Nails should sink ¾ in. into the wood.

Wet-SANDING

Using a large sponge to wet-sand drywall joints will definitely reduce dust, but wet-sanding isn't feasible for a project of any size because you must rinse the sponge and change the water continually. Also wet-sanding soaks the paper facing, sometimes dislodges the tape, and tends to round joint compound edges rather than taper them. That said, if you're drywalling a small room and don't like moving the furniture out of the room, wet-sanding is a cleaner way to go.

Joint tape is used to reinforce drywall seams and is available as 2-in.-wide *paper tape* and 1½-in.- or 2-in.-wide *fiberglass mesh tape*. Self-adhesive mesh tape is popular because it's quicker. You can apply it directly to drywall seams and then cover it with joint compound in one pass. Whereas, with paper tape, you must first apply a layer of joint compound, press the paper tape into it, and then apply a coat of compound over that. If there's not enough compound under paper tape, it may bubble or pull loose.

Still, many professionals swear by paper tape because it's cheaper than fiberglass mesh, it's stronger than mesh and less likely to be sliced by a taping knife, it won't stretch, and it is lightly creased up the middle, making it easier to install and align in an inside corner. Consequently, pros use mesh tape only with setting-type compounds, which cure harder and stronger than drying-type compounds, described on p. 358.

However, self-adhesive mesh is perfect for drywall repair. If you press the mesh over a crack or small hole, you may be able to hide the problem with a single layer of joint compound.

Cornerbeads and trim beads finish off and protect drywall edges. They're available in metal, vinyl, PVC plastic, and paper-covered variations. Most attach with nails or screws.

Cornerbeads are used on all outside corners to provide a clean finish and protect otherwise vulnerable drywall corners from knocks and bumps. (As noted earlier, inside corners are formed with just tape and compound.) Cornerbeads come in a number of different radii; larger bullnose varieties give you a dramatic curve. Whatever type you choose, though, install it in one piece.

J-beads keep exposed ends of drywall from abrading. These beads are typically used where panels abut tile or brick walls, shower stalls, or openings that won't be finished off with trim—in other words, where the edge of the drywall is the

Fiberglass-mesh joint tape isn't as strong as paper tape, but it sticks directly to the drywall—without needing a bed of joint compound—so it's fast to apply. Use mesh tape only with setting-type compound.

Corner and Edge Treatments

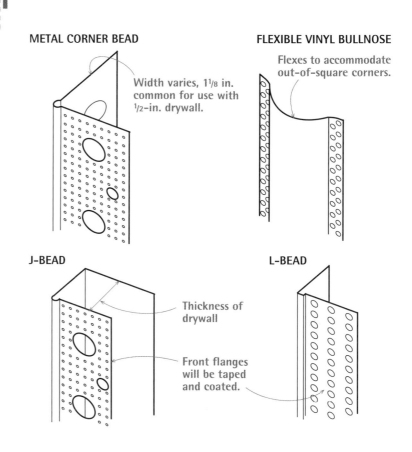

METAL CORNER BEAD

Width varies, 1⅛ in. common for use with ½-in. drywall.

FLEXIBLE VINYL BULLNOSE

Flexes to accommodate out-of-square corners.

J-BEAD

Thickness of drywall

Front flanges will be taped and coated.

L-BEAD

Drywall Fasteners

ATTACHING TO...	FASTENER USED	DRYWALL THICKNESS (in.)	MINIMUM FASTENER LENGTH (in.)
Wood studs, ceiling joists, rafters	Type-W drywall screws (coarse thread)	⅜, ½, ⅝	1, 1⅛, 1¼ (penetrate framing ⅝ in.)
Wood studs only	Ring-shank drywall nails	⅜, ½, ⅝	1⅛, 1¼, 1⅜ (penetrate framing ⅝ in.)
Light-gauge metal framing	Type-S drywall screws (fine thread)	⅜, ½, ⅝	¾, ⅞, 1

finished edge. L-beads are similar; they're used where panels abut windows, suspended ceilings, paneling and so on. In general, L-beads are easier to install on panels already in place. J- and L-beads are sized to drywall panel thickness; some types require joint compound, some don't.

Flexible arch beads often come in rolls that are presnipped, so as you unroll them, they assume the shape of the arch you're nailing or stapling them to. Apply joint compound and finish them as you would any drywall seam.

Joint compounds can be broadly divided into drying types and setting types. They differ in ease of use, setting (hardening) time, and strength.

Drying-type joint compounds are vinyl based and dry as water evaporates from them. They usually come premixed and are easy to apply and sand. Typically, you can apply a second coat 24 hours after the first, if you maintain a room temperature of 65°F. There's little waste with

drying-type compound. And, once opened, it will keep for a month if you seal the bucket tightly.

Setting-type joint compounds, which contain plaster of paris, are mixed from powders. They set quickly and so allow you to apply subsequent coats before the compound is completely dry. In general, they bond better, shrink less, and dry harder than drying types. They harden via a chemical reaction, hence their nickname, "hot mud." Depending on additives, they'll set in 30 minutes to 6 hours. However, setting-type compound sets up so quickly and so hard that it can be a monster to sand. Once it's mixed, you've got to use it up. It won't store.

So, unless you're a drywalling whiz, use a pre-mixed, all-purpose, drying-type joint compound. A 5-gal. bucket will cover 400 sq. ft., roughly, a 12-ft. by 12-ft. room. with 8-ft. ceilings. The compound is ready to use right out of the bucket. It's reasonably strong, and each application should dry in a day.

One further distinction: Drying-type and setting-type joint compounds are further formulated as either *taping compounds*—used for the first coat, in which you embed the tape—or *topping compounds*, used for the second and third coats because it feathers out (thins) better and dries faster. Again, all-purpose compound can be used for all three coats, but you might want to experiment with the two types once you've had some practice. Some pros use setting-type joint compound for the first and second coats and drying-type for the third (and last) coat.

Store premixed joint compound at room temperature (60°F to 70°F) so it's ready to apply. At lower temperatures, it doesn't spread as easily. Never allow it to freeze; throw it out if it does because it won't bond well after freezing. *Added tip:* Store self-adhering mesh tape in a plastic bag so its adhesive won't dry out.

Minimizing Drywall Joints

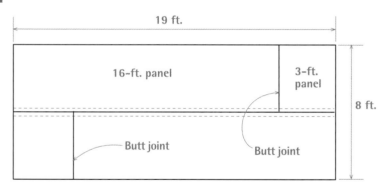

Joints = 25 lin. ft.

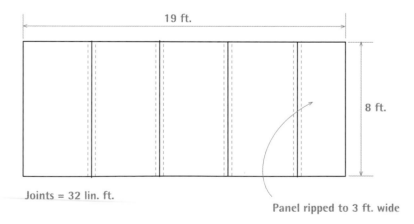

Joints = 32 lin. ft.

Panel ripped to 3 ft. wide

Hanging wall panels horizontally often reduces the number and length of the joints. With studs a standard 16 in. o.c., you could reduce the total lineal feet of taping by running panels horizontally instead of vertically. For the room dimensions shown, however, the upper layout also creates two butt joints, which can be tedious to feather out.

PLANNING THE JOB

Before estimating materials, walk each room and imagine how best to orient and install panels. These five rules, known to drywall pros, will save you a lot of pain.

Rule 1: Use the longest panels possible. This minimizes the number of joints. A 4-ft. by 14-ft. or 4-ft. by 16-ft. panel is heavier and less wieldy than a 4-ft. by 8-ft. panel. But hanging larger panels is relatively fast, compared to the time it takes to tape, coat, and sand the joints of the smaller panels.

Rule 2: Think spatially. Running panels horizontally—perpendicular to studs and ceiling joists—can reduce the number of joints and promote stronger attachments. For example, two 4-ft. by 12-ft. wall panels run horizontally will reach an 8-ft. ceiling and create only one horizontal seam to be filled. Two 54-in.-wide (4½-ft.) panels run horizontally will reach a 9-ft. ceiling. However, if ceilings are higher than 9 ft., you may be able reduce the number of joints by installing wall panels vertically (parallel to studs).

Rule 3: Minimize butt joints. Long edges of panels are beveled to receive tape joints, but the short edges (butt edges) are not. Consequently, butt joints are difficult to feather out, and they are likely to crack. So try to minimize the number of butt edges. Where you can't avoid them, position them away from the center of a wall or ceiling. Last, always stagger (offset) butt joints; never align them. Otherwise, you may need to feather joint compound out 3 ft. wide to get a barely acceptable joint.

Rule 4: Install drywall that's thick enough. Otherwise spans may sag between ceiling joists and bow between studs. For example, if you're running panels parallel to ceiling joists spaced 24 in. on center, ⅝-in. drywall is much stronger and less likely to sag than ½-in. panels. For this, be sure to comply with local codes.

Rule 5: Don't scrimp on panels. Expect a certain amount of waste, especially if you're installing around stairs or sloping ceilings. It's a mistake to try to piece together remnants, because that creates a lot of butt joints and looks awful. Likewise, scrimping on screws or joint compound results in weak joints and screw pops.

ESTIMATING MATERIALS

Start by consulting local building codes. They'll specify the type, thickness, and number of drywall layers you must install throughout the house.

It's possible to estimate drywall materials from a set of blueprints, but even the pros prefer to walk the job, measuring walls and ceilings and noting where using longer panels will minimize joints. That way, you get exactly the panel lengths you need.

As you walk through the rooms, record your findings on ¼-in. graph paper. Use one sheet of paper per room, letting each square equal 1 ft. Then, when your materials arrive, you'll know which room gets what.

1. Start by measuring the width and length of each room. In general, think in 2-ft. increments. That is, if a wall is 10 ft. 6 in. long, plan to buy 12-ft. panels and run them horizontally in order to get the fewest joints. If studs aren't spaced a standard 16 in. on center, note that on your graph paper. (If you're not sure of stud and joist spacing, use a stud finder.) Calculate the number of panels of each dimension you'll need for each room.

2. Note door and window locations and dimensions, but don't deduct their square footage from the room total. Portions of panels cut out for windows and doors will yield a high percentage of nonfactory edges and butt joints, so it's

Estimating Drywall Needs

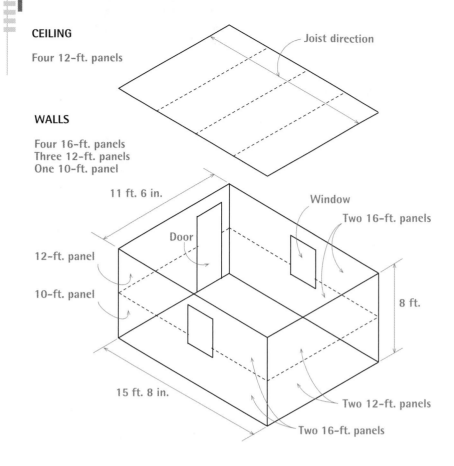

CEILING

Four 12-ft. panels

WALLS

Four 16-ft. panels
Three 12-ft. panels
One 10-ft. panel

Joist direction

11 ft. 6 in.

12-ft. panel

10-ft. panel

Door

Window

Two 16-ft. panels

8 ft.

15 ft. 8 in.

Two 12-ft. panels

Two 16-ft. panels

easiest to discard such scrap or piece it together in out-of-way places, such as closets.

3. Note the ceiling height. If the ceiling is 8 ft., two standard 4-ft. by 8-ft. wall panels run horizontally will reach it; if they're 9 ft. high, use two horizontal 54-in.-wide panels. If ceilings are higher than 9 ft., you may want to rent scaffolding and a drywall lift.

4. Note the direction and spacing of ceiling joists. Panels run perpendicular to ceiling joists (or rafters, if a cathedral ceiling) are less likely to sag.

5. Special rooms. Install WR (water-resistant) drywall in laundry rooms, behind kitchen sinks, and in bathrooms other than in tub/shower areas. Cover tub/shower areas with cementitious board if they'll be tiled. Install ⅝-in. type-X drywall on shared walls between the garage and living space. If existing plaster is in bad shape and you don't want to tear it out, cover it with ¼-in. or ⅜-in. drywall.

6. Special features include arches, curved stairwells, barrel ceilings, odd nooks, built-in bookcases or cabinets, and the like. For curves, you need flexible ¼-in. drywall. Expect a lot of waste around complex areas, such as stairways.

Calculating Drywall Square Footage

PANEL LENGTH (ft.)		SQUARE FEET PER PANEL*		NUMBER OF PANELS		TOTAL SQUARE FEET
8	▶	32	×	40	=	1,280
9	▶	36	×	35	=	1,260
10	▶	40	×	30	=	1,200
12	▶	48	×	25	=	1,200
14	▶	56	×	20	=	1,120
16	▶	64	×	20	=	1280
Total	▶					**7,340**

* Calculations assume that all panels are 4 ft. wide.

Chapter 4). Green or wet lumber will shrink as it dries, causing cracks and nail pops in a new drywall job, so don't use it.

▶ Sight along studs and ceiling joists to see if they are aligned in a flat plane. To be more precise, stretch a taut string or hold a straight-edge across the framing members. Running drywall panels perpendicular to framing will help conceal minor misalignments, as will textured finish surfaces. But it's better to adjust misaligned framing, especially if the drywall surface will be brightly lit or otherwise prominent. If a stud is misaligned more than ¼ in., your options include hammering it into line, power-planing it down, and shimming up low spots, as described in Chapter 8

▶ Use a framing square to determine if corners are square, and make sure there's blocking in the corners, so you'll have something to attach the panel edges to. Or you can use drywall clips to "float" the corners.

▶ Install steel nail guards to protect plumbing pipes and electrical cables within 1¼ in. of joist or stud edges. Few things are as frustrating as discovering a leak or an electrical short after the drywall is up. Then make a final check of the electrical outlet boxes. They should be securely attached to the framing with their edges flush with the drywall face (see Chapter 11).

▶ If appropriate to your climate, plastic vapor barriers or insulation should be in place now, as described in Chapter 14. If you're drywalling over rigid foam insulation—say, on a cathedral ceiling—first affix 1×2 furring strips so you'll have something to screw to. Do not attach drywall directly to the foam because the insulation expands, contracts, and compresses.

7. In older homes, especially those with narrow stairs, there may not be room to maneuver extra-long panels. If you're replacing windows, you may be able to have a boom truck deliver panels through window openings, but only if the truck can get close to the house without destroying your septic tank and field. In short, anticipate how you'll bring drywall into the house. In extreme cases, you may need to use shorter panels for some rooms. Inquire about options with your drywall supplier.

8. Once you've figured out how much drywall you need for each room, figure out where you'll store it. If possible, distribute drywall throughout the house, stacking panels on the floor rather than leaning them against walls, which can damage their edges. In each room, anticipate the sequence of installation—ceilings first!—so the panels you need first will be accessible.

9. Finally, make a master list of all the drywall you need for the complete renovation.

GETTING READY TO HANG DRYWALL

Here's a final checklist before installing drywall:

▶ The building should be dry and relatively warm (between 60°F and 70°F). Keep temperatures constant. If a room becomes too hot (80°F or above), joint compounds may dry too quickly and crack. If the heating system is inoperable, rent a portable heater. Ventilation is also important for drying: Drying-type joint compounds evaporate a lot of water.

▶ Framing lumber must be dry: 15 percent to 19 percent moisture content is optimal (see

Metal drywall clips can help secure drywall edges in corners where there's insufficient blocking. In conventional framing, blocking is nailed to top plates (and to wall ends) to create a solid base to screw or nail panels to.

HANDLING, MEASURING, AND CUTTING DRYWALL

Handling drywall is a bit like waltzing: You can do it by yourself, but it's not all that much fun. For starters, carrying an cumbersome 70-lb. panel around a work site is a two-person job. Both of you should be on the same side of the panel, same hand supporting the bottom edge, same hand balancing the top. (Imagine ballet dancers in a line.) As you walk, lean the upper part of the panel against your shoulder.

Hanging ceilings is definitely a two-person job, especially if you're hanging longer panels to minimize joints. Once the two (or three) of you tack up a ceiling panel, one of you can finish attaching it, while another measures or cuts the next piece.

Measuring isn't difficult, but you need to be aware of framing quirks. For example, if the walls aren't plumb where they meet in the corners, take at least two measurements so you'll know what angle to cut in the end of the panel you're installing. If the two readings vary only slightly—say, ¼ in.—there's no need to trim the end of the panel because taping and filling the joint will take care of the gap. But if readings vary more than ¾ in., trim the panel end at an angle, so there's no gap where it abuts the out-of-plumb wall.

Second, if you're running panels perpendicular to the framing, butt ends must meet over joist or stud centers. If framing members aren't evenly spaced, you may occasionally need to trim a butt end to make it coincide with a joist center.

Last, and most important, cut panels about ¼ in. short so you never need to force a panel into place. Forcing will crush an end that you'll need to repair later. If it's a ceiling panel, the gap will eventually be covered by wall panels fitted snugly against it.

Once you've cut a panel, snap parallel chalklines across its face, indicating stud or joist centers behind the drywall once it's in place. Guided by these lines, your screws or nails will always bed into framing.

Cutting drywall is literally a snap if the blades in your utility knife are sharp. Run the blade along a drywall T-square or a framing square, if that's all you have. In one pass, score the paper covering. Then grasp the smaller section and snap it sharply away from the cut, breaking the gypsum core along the scored line. Then cut through the paper on the backside, and set aside the waste section.

Cutting is usually easiest if you lean the panel against a wall so you don't need to bend over. But if you've already stacked panels on the floor, you

Guesstimating Materials

Measuring each room is the only accurate way to develop an estimate of drywall needs. But a rough estimate of square footage can help you figure about how much joint tape, joint compound, and fasteners you'll need.

Add up the square footage of all rooms to be drywalled. For rooms with 8-ft. ceilings, use a factor of 3.5 multiplied by the room length and room width. For example: 3.5×20 ft. $\times 30$ ft. = 2,100 sq. ft. of drywall. For rooms with 9-ft. ceilings, use a factor of 3.85.

For each 1,000 sq. ft. of drywall, you'll need approximately

▶ 1,000 screws or nails (using construction adhesive reduces this total)

▶ 375 ft. of joint tape

▶ 11 gal. of premixed, all-purpose, drying-type joint compound.

Note: If you use construction adhesive to reduce the number of fasteners, a standard 10.5-oz. tube of adhesive will yield 15 lineal ft. if you apply it in a ⅜-in.-wide bead.

Before hanging drywall, check to see if the studs are plumb, corners are square, and (as shown) if studs align in a flat plane. If not, they must be built up with shims or planed down.

Drywall over Plaster

Drywalling over plaster is a cost-effective way to deal with plaster that's too dingy and deteriorated to patch or too much trouble to tear out. But this requires some important prep work.

▶ If you see discoloration or water damage, repair the cause of the leak or excessive indoor moisture before attaching drywall.

▶ Locate ceiling joists or studs behind the plaster. Typically, framing is spaced 16 in. or 24 in. on center, but you never know with older houses. If ceiling joists are exposed in the attic above, your task is simple; otherwise, use a stud finder or drill exploratory holes. Once you've located the joists or studs, snap chalklines to indicate the centerlines you'll screw the drywall into.

▶ Use screws and plaster washers to reattach loose or sagging plaster sections before you install drywall. To minimize the number of such fasteners, apply adhesive to the back face of the drywall, and be sure the screws grab framing—not just lath. Plaster washers are shown on p. 373.

▶ For ceilings, use 2-in. type-W drywall screws, which should be long enough to penetrate ⅜-in. drywall, 1 in. of plaster and lath, and ⅝ in. into joists. On walls, ¼-in. drywall is a better choice because drywall sagging is not an issue, and thin drywall doesn't reduce the visible profile of existing trim as much. Otherwise, you may either need to build up existing trim or remove the trim and reinstall it over the drywall.

▶ If there's living space above the plaster ceiling, attaching resilient channel may be a good move. These channels bridge surface irregularities and deaden sound. Screw the channels perpendicular to the joists. Then screw drywall panels perpendicular to the channels (see the photo on p. 376).

Trim Considerations

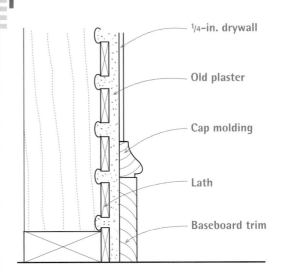

- ¼-in. drywall
- Old plaster
- Cap molding
- Lath
- Baseboard trim

New drywall over old plaster can reduce the visible profile of existing molding it abuts so much that the molding looks undersize. In this case, you have two alternatives: Use molding to build up (increase the thickness of) trim where drywall abuts it. Or remove the trim and reinstall it over the drywall.

CUTTING DRYWALL

1. In one pass, score the paper face of the panel using a utility knife guided by a drywall T-square.

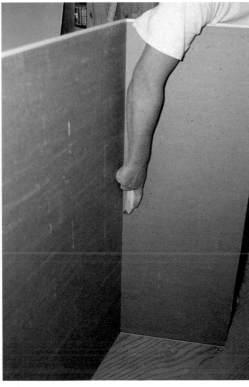

2. Snap the panel sharply away from the face cut (here hidden), to break the gypsum core along the scored line. Then cut through the paper backing along the break.

3. If the cut is rough, clean it up with a drywall rasp.

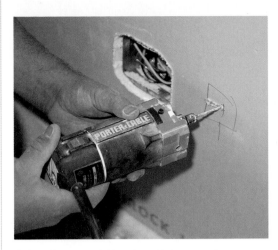

A drywall router quickly cuts out holes around outlet boxes. Beforehand, shut off the electricity to that circuit, and tuck wires well into the box so they can't get nicked.

can use them like a workbench, cutting them in place.

Start by tearing off the end papers that join pairs of panels face to face, allowing you to move panels individually. In this manner, you'll cut every other panel from the back.

Most professionals would rather score the front face first, but it doesn't truly matter which side you cut first, as long as your blade is sharp, your snap is clean, and you don't rip or snag the paper on the front face.

If the gypsum edge is a bit rough or the panel is a little long, clean up the edge with a drywall rasp. But be careful not to fray the face paper.

Outlet box, switch, and duct cutouts can be made before or after you hang the drywall. To make cuts *before*, measure from a fixed point nearby—from the floor or a stud, for example—and transfer those height and width measurements to the panel. A framing square resting on the floor is perfect for marking electrical receptacles. That done, use a drywall saw to punch through the face of the panel and cut out the opening, being careful not to rip the paper facing as you near the end of the cut.

That's one way to do it. Problem is, the cutout rarely lines up exactly to the box.

Using a drywall router is quicker and more accurate. 🚫 First *make sure the power is off* and push any electrical wires well down into the box so the router bit can't nick them. The router bit should extend only ¼ in. beyond the back of the drywall.

Next, measure from a nearby stud or the floor to the (approximate) center of the box, and transfer that mark to the drywall. Then tack up the panel with just a few nails or screws—well away from the lumber the box is attached to. Gently push the spinning bit through the drywall and move it slowly to one side till you hit an edge of the box. Pull out the bit, lift it over the edge of the box, and then guide the bit around the outside of the box, in a counterclockwise direction. This method takes a light touch—plastic boxes gouge easily—but it's fast and the opening will fit the box like a glove.

ATTACHING DRYWALL

Most professionals use drywall screws exclusively, although some use a few nails along the edges to tack up a panel temporarily. Corner bead is often nailed up, too.

When attaching drywall, push the panel firmly against the framing before driving in the screw. Fasteners must securely lodge in a framing member. If a screw misses the joist or stud, remove the screw, *dimple* (indent) the surface around the hole, and fill it later.

The screw (or nail) head should sink just below the surface of the panel, without crushing the gypsum core or breaking face paper. You will later fill the resulting dimple with joint compound.

A Ripping GOOD TIME

Cutting along the length of a drywall panel—*ripping* a panel—is fast and easy if you know how. Extend a tape measure the amount you want to cut from the panel. If you're right-handed, lightly pinch the tape between the index finger and thumb of your left hand to keep the tape from retracting. Your right hand holds the utility-knife blade against the tape's hook. Using your left index finger as a guide along the edge of the panel, pull both hands toward you evenly as you walk backward along the panel. Remember, the blade needs only to score the paper, not penetrate the core, so relax and keep moving.

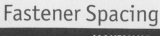

Fastener Spacing

FRAMING MEMBERS	FRAMING SPACING	MAXIMUM FASTENER FRAMING*
Ceiling joists	16 in. o.c.	12 in.
	24 in. o.c.	10 in.
Wall studs	16 in. o.c.	16 in.
	24 in. o.c.	16 in.

* Fasteners should not be closer than ⅜ in. to the panel's edge.

When sizing screws or nails, see "Drywall Fasteners," on p. 357. Fasteners that are too short won't support the panel adequately. On the other hand, fasteners that are too long are more likely to drive in cockeyed or pop the drywall if the framing shrinks.

PRO TIP

Screws are generally spaced every 12 in. along panel edges and "in the field," for ceiling joists or studs 16 in. on center. Drywall edges are a bit fragile, so place screws back at least ⅜ in. from the edges. Where butt edges meet over framing, space screws every 8 in. along both sides of the butt joint.

Screws driven in crooked don't hold as well, are more likely to tear the face paper, and can be tricky to fill with compound. That said, you sometimes need to angle screws slightly when securing both sides of a butt joint to a shared stud or joist. Just go easy.

Nails follow the spacing guidelines in "Fastener Spacing," except that you should double-nail in the field. Paired nails are 1½ in. to 2 in. apart, so the *center* of each pair of nails is spaced every 16 in. on wall panels. Along panel edges, do not double-nail. Instead, space single nails every 8 in. For best holding, use ring-shank nails.

Adhesives are most often used to affix drywall where nails or screws can't—say, over concrete—but it's sometimes used in tandem with them. Adhesive applied to wood studs allows you to bridge minor irregularities and to use about one-third the number of fasteners. And adhesive creates a stronger bond than screws or nails alone.

Because adhesive adds a step and requires 48 hours to dry before you can tape the joints, it's usually more practical to use adhesive only on butt joints. Apply two parallel ⅜-in. beads of adhesive down the middle of the joist or stud edge. Don't make wavy, serpentine beads because that allows adhesive to ooze out onto the drywall's back face, wasting adhesive. On such glued butt joints, space screws every 10 in. to 12 in. on both sides of the joint.

If you're applying a second sheet of drywall over a first, you can apply construction adhesive or roll-on thinned joint compound. Myron Ferguson's excellent book *Drywall* (The Taunton Press), discusses adhesives at greater length.

PRO TIP

Mark joist centers onto the top of the wall plates before you install the first ceiling panel. That will enable you to sink screws into the joist centers when they're covered by drywall. The pencil marks will also help you align screws across the panel, simply by eyeballing from those first screws to the uncovered joists on the other side.

With a helper and a set of drywall benches, you can safely raise long panels to the ceiling. Lift one end at a time. Whenever possible, run the panels perpendicular to the joists.

If the ceiling is higher than 9 ft., and especially if it's a cathedral ceiling, rent a drywall lift.

HANGING DRYWALL PANELS

Ceilings. Attach ceiling panels first. It's much easier to cut and adjust wall panels than ceiling panels, should there be small gaps along the wall–ceiling intersection. Also, wall panels can support the edges of ceiling panels.

First, ensure there's blocking in place to nail the panels' edges to. In most cases, you'll run panels perpendicular to the ceiling joists, thereby maximizing structural strength, minimizing panel sag, and making joists easier to see when fastening panels.

The trickiest thing about hanging ceiling panels is raising them into position. If your ceilings are less than 9 ft. high, drywall benches will elevate you enough to work. As you raise each panel end, keep its other end low. In other words, allow one worker to raise one end and establish footing before the second worker steps up onto the bench. Then, while both workers support the panel with heads and hands, they can tack the panel in place.

If the ceiling is higher than 9 ft., rent a drywall lift. Because the lift holds the panel snugly against ceiling joists, it allows you to have both hands free to drive screws.

Flying solo. If you can't find an adjustable lift or friends to help, you can hang ceiling panels solo by using two tees made from 2×4s. Lean one tee against a wall, with its top about 1 in. shy of the ceiling joists. (The tee should be ½ in. to 1 in. taller than the ceiling is high.) Raise one end of the panel up, onto that tee. Then, being careful not to dislodge the first end, position and raise the lower end of panel with the second tee until the entire panel is snug against the ceiling joists. Gradually shift the tees until the panel's edges are aligned with the joist centers. Be patient.

Walls. It's easier to hang drywall on the walls than on ceilings. Although one person can usually manage wall panels, the job is easier and goes faster with two. Be sure there's blocking in the corners to receiver fasteners before you begin. To help you locate studs once they're covered with drywall, mark stud centers on the top plates (or ceiling panels) and sole plates at the bottom.

When hanging wall panels, always start at the top, butting the first panel snugly to the drywall on the ceiling. That way, you'll minimize gaps and support ceiling edges better.

Important: If you're installing wall panels horizontally, the top panel edge must be level and the butt ends, plumb. Otherwise, subsequent panels may be cockeyed and butt ends may not be centered over the studs.

Once the upper wall panel is secured, raise the lower panel(s) snug against it. A homemade

Install the top wall panel first, butting it snugly against the ceiling panel. At the same time, level the bottom edge of wall panel so that subsequent panels butted to it will also be level and correctly aligned to the stud centers.

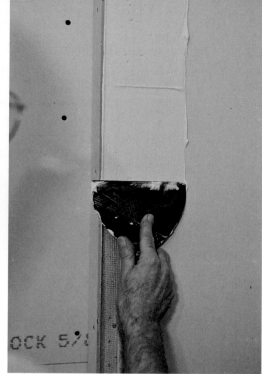

Cornerbead protects fragile drywall edges and ensures a clean finished edge.

To prevent cracking along an outside corner, this installer covers the edges of the cornerbead with mesh tape before applying a setting-type compound.

panel lifter is handy because it frees your hands to align the panels and sink the screws. A panel lifter is simply a first-class lever of scrap wood set on a fulcrum. Pressing down on one end of the lever with your foot, raises the other end, which lifts the panel, as shown in the bottom photo on p. 354.

Doors and windows. Joints around doors and windows will be weak and likely to crack if panel edges butt against the edges of the opening. That is, run the panel edges at least 8 in. past door or window jambs, and cut out the part of the panel that overlaps the opening. Pros do this because the wall framing twists and flexes slightly when doors or windows are opened and closed, which stresses the drywall joints.

Finally, expect to waste a lot of drywall when cutting paneling for doors and windows. Old houses are rife with nonstandard dimensions and odd angles, so don't fight it. You can use some of the larger cutoffs in inconspicuous places like closets, but remember that the more joints, the more taping and sanding. Anyway, drywall panel isn't expensive. So, when in doubt about reusing a piece, throw it out.

Curves. Curved walls are easy to cover with drywall. For the best results, use two layers of ¼-in. drywall, hung horizontally. Stagger their butt- and bevel-edged joints. For an 8-ft. panel run horizontally, an arc depth of 2 ft. to 3 ft. should be easy. Sharper curves may require back-cutting

panels (scoring slots into the back so that the panels bend more easily), wetting (wet-sponging the front and back of the sheet to soften the gypsum), or using special flexible drywall, which has heavier paper facings that are better suited for bending.

Corners. Cornerbead reinforces and protects outside corners, uncased openings, and the like. It's available in many materials. For best results, install it in a single piece. Cut the bead for outside corners about ½ in. short: Push it snugly to the corner and slide it up till it touches the ceiling. The ½-in. gap at the bottom will be hidden by baseboard trim.

Galvanized metal bead was at one time the only type available, and it's still widely used. To cut it, use aviation snips (also known as tin snips). The metal bead goes on the outside corners before the tape and joint compound are applied. Nail it up, spacing nails 8 in. apart, on both legs of the bead. Then cover it with compound.

Vinyl bead is less rigid than metal and able to accommodate outside corners that aren't exactly 90°. Attach vinyl bead either by stapling it directly to the drywall, spraying the drywall corner with vinyl adhesive before pressing the bead into the adhesive and then stapling, or using a taping knife to press the bead into a bed of joint compound.

Paper-faced beads are embedded in joint compound. One of the best is the Ultraflex structural corner, which comes in varying widths and has a plastic spine that flexes in or out so it can reinforce inside or outside corners. Because they're flexible, such tapes are great for corners of just about any angle.

TAPING AND FINISHING

To finish drywall, seal the panel joints with tape or cornerbead, then cover them with joint compound. Typically, three coats of compound are applied in successively wider coats and sanded after each application. The first coat, usually a high-strength taping compound, embeds the tape. The second coat should be a thin layer of topping compound or all-purpose compound that you feather out to hide the joints. With the third coat, you feather out the compound farther, creating a smooth, finished surface. (See "Joint Compounds," on p. 358, for more about these materials.)

First coat. Fill nail holes or screw dimples in an *X* pattern: One diagonal knife stroke applies the compound, and the other stroke removes the excess.

If you use paper tape on the joints, apply a swath of taping compound about 4 in. wide down the center of the joint. Press the tape into the center of the joint with a 6-in. taping knife. Then apply compound over the tape, bearing down so you remove the excess.

If you use self-sticking mesh tape, stick it directly over the joint and apply the bedding compound over it. In other words, don't apply a bed of compound first. Mesh tape must be bedded in setting-type compound, as explained earlier in this chapter.

AN ORDERLY Finish

All that raw drywall can seem a bit overwhelming, so here's a taping and mudding sequence that starts easy, so you can become comfortable with the tools and materials:

▶ Screw and nail holes

▶ Bevel-edge joints (the long edges of panels)

▶ Butt-edge joints

▶ Outside corners

▶ Inside corners.

Have a pail of clean water and a sponge handy so you can rinse your taping knives periodically. They glide better if they're clean. Keep the job site clean, too: If you drop a glob of compound on the floor, scrape it up and discard it so you don't track it around the house.

BEDDING THE TAPE

1. Before applying paper tape, cover the seam with an generous bed of joint compound.

2. After using your taping knife to center the tape on the seam, press the tape into the joint compound.

3. After applying a layer of compound over the tape, remove the excess. If the tape moves, you're pressing too hard or your taping knife needs to be cleaned. (Steps continue on next page.)

PRO TIP

Apply joint compound generously. Without enough mud, the tape won't stick. But as you feather out the wet mud, scrape off excess; sanding off dried globs later would be tedious and time consuming.

5. Applied correctly, the third coat should need only hand-sanding. A dry-sanding block is great for light sanding and corners.

4. Use a 10-in. knife to apply the second coat of compound.

Allow the first coat to dry thoroughly before sanding it. This will take about a day, if the room temperature is 65°F to 70°F and there's adequate ventilation. Sand lightly with 120-grit to 150-grit sandpaper. Because there are two more coats to come, this taping coat can be left a little rough.

Second coat. The second coat is also called the *filler coat*, and with this one you'll apply the most compound. At this stage, many professionals use a 10-in.-wide taping joint knife and feather out the seams roughly 8 in. to 10 in. wide. After applying the compound, smooth it out with an even wider blade—say, a 14-in. trowel.

As you'll learn when working with joint compound, the lower the angle of the blade and the less pressure, the easier it is to smooth and feather (spread out) the mud. The greater the angle and pressure, the more compound you'll remove. This is easier to do than explain. Because butt-end joints are not beveled, they'll mound slightly at the center of the seam. That's okay. Use a 10-in. taping knife to build up the compound on both sides of the joint, feather out the edges, and then smooth the center. Consequently, butt-end joints may need to be wider than bevel-edge joints. You may often need to feather butt-end joints 16 in. to 20 in. wide.

When this second coat is dry, sand with 150-grit to 220-grit paper. A pole sander will extend your reach and enable you to sand longer without tiring, but don't sand too aggressively or you'll abrade the paper face or expose the tape. Easy does it.

Third coat. The third coat is the last chance to feather out the edges, so use a premixed, all-purpose, drying-type compound, which is easy to thin out and sand because it has a fine consistency and dries quickly. Although premixed compound will be the right consistency, it's okay to add a little water to thin it even more.

Because the third coat is only slightly wider (2 in.) than the second coat, you'll be applying a relatively small amount of compound. Use a 12-in. trowel, with a light touch. Some pros thin this coat enough to apply it with a roller, and then smooth it with a trowel, so there are no trowel marks when they're done.

The Art of Inside Corners

Use paper tape for inside corners. After applying a bed of compound to both surfaces, crease the tape, and place it in the corner. Then use a double-edged corner knife to press the tape into the compound before spreading a second layer of compound over the tape.

Some pros snort at corner knives, preferring to use a flat 6-in. taping knife to press tape into compound, one edge at a time. When feathering-out joint compound, pros allow the compound to dry on one side of the corner before working on the adjacent surface. In other words, "Never run wet mud into wet mud."

Hand-sand the final coat, using fine, 220-grit sandpaper or a very fine sanding block. Shining a strong light on surfaces will highlight the imperfections you need to sand.

Wrap up. If you intend to texture the surfaces, the third coat doesn't need to be mirror smooth. Even so, don't scrimp on the second coat, or else the joints may be visible through the texture

To give yourself the greatest number of decorating options in the future, paint the finished drywall surface with a coat of flat, oil-based primer. It will seal the paper face of the drywall and provide an excellent base for any kind of paint or wall covering.

DRYWALL REPAIRS

To keep solutions concise, let's divide drywall repairs into four groups: nail pops and surface blemishes; fist-size holes through the drywall; larger holes; and discolored, crumbling, or moldy drywall. Any repair patches should be the same thickness as the damaged drywall.

Popped nails and screws are generally a quick fix: Drive another nail or screw 1½ in. away from the popped one to secure the drywall. If it's a popped screw, remove it and fill the hole. Cover both the old hole and the new screw with at least two coats of joint compound. If it's a popped nail, don't try to remove it; drive it slightly deeper to dimple the drywall.

When a piece of drywall tape lifts, pull gently until you reach a section that's still well stuck. Use a utility knife to cut free the loose tape, cover the exposed seams with self-sticking mesh tape, and apply two or three coats of compound—sanding lightly after each. Drywall repair kits with precut patches are available at most home centers.

To repair drywall cracks, cut back the edges of the crack slightly to remove crumbly gypsum and provide a good depression for a new filling of joint compound. Any time the paper face of drywall is damaged, cover the damaged area with self-adhering fiberglass mesh tape. Then apply three coats of joint compound. Because the repair area is small, it doesn't matter what type of compound you use, though setting-type compounds are preferred.

Small holes in drywall are often caused by doorknobs, furniture, or removed electrical outlet boxes. Clean up the edge of the hole so the surface is flat. Then cover the hole with self-adhering fiberglass mesh tape. (Better drywall repair kits have metal-and-fiberglass mesh tape.) Use a light touch when applying the first coat of joint compound, pushing the mud through the tape, but don't press so hard that you dislodge the mesh.

Mechanical TAPING TOOLS

Mechanical drywall taping tools are commonly referred to as Bazooka® tools, after a popular brand, and they can be rented, usually for 2 weeks at a stretch. The suite of tools includes a taper that applies tape and compound simultaneously, as well as finishing tools, various head attachments, and flat boxes for taping seams.

These tools are great for larger jobs, creating uniform, flat surfaces that need little sanding. "You can put tape and mud up almost as fast as you can run," notes one pro. Most rental companies supply a video on how to use these tools, but taking a class in addition isn't a bad idea.

Give the repair three coats of compound, feathering out the edges as you go. Take it easy when sanding. Especially after the first coat, the tape frays easily. By the way, there are precut drywall patches for electrical outlet boxes, which save time.

Large holes should be cut back till you reach solid drywall. Because mesh tape and compound will probably sag if the hole is much wider than 4 in., holes larger than that should be filled with a patch of drywall roughly the size of the damaged area. These patches need to be backed with something solid, so they'll stay put.

The easiest backing is a couple of furring strips cut about 8 in. longer than the width of the hole and placed on both sides of the hole. To install each furring strip, slide it into the hole and, while holding it in place with one hand, screw through the drywall into the wood. Screws will pull the furring strips tight to the back of the drywall. Then cut the drywall patch, place it in the cutout area, and screw it to the strapping.

Cover the edges of the drywall patch with self-adhering mesh tape, fill the screw holes, and apply joint compound—three coats in all. Here, a setting-type compound, such as Durabond® 90, is a good bet because it dries quickly and is unlikely to sag. The more skillfully you feather the compound, the less visible the patch will be.

For holes larger than 8 in., cut back to the centers of the nearest studs. Although you should have no problem screwing a replacement piece to the studs, be sure to back the top and the bottom of the new piece. The best way to install backing is to screw drywall gussets (supports) to the back of the existing drywall. Then position the replacement piece in the hole and screw it to the gussets, using drywall screws, of course.

Discolored, crumbling, or moldy drywall is caused by exterior leaks or excessive interior moisture. Be sure to attend to those causes before repairing the drywall. Excessive moisture is often due to inadequate ventilation, which is especially common in kitchens and baths. Leaks around windows and doors are often caused by inadequate flashing over openings.

If the drywall is discolored but solid, and if you've remedied the moisture source, wash the area with soap and water, allow it to dry thoroughly, and prime it with white pigmented shellac or some other stain-resistant primer. The same solution works for minor mold on sound drywall.

However, if there's widespread mold and the drywall's crumbling, there's probably extensive mold growing inside the walls. You'll need to rip

out the drywall and correct the moisture problems before replacing finish surfaces. In extreme cases, you'll need to replace the framing. Chapter 14 covers mold abatement at greater length.

Plastering

This section is limited to plaster repairs because applying plaster takes years to master. The tools needed for plaster repair are much the same as those needed for drywall repair: a screw gun or cordless drill; 6-in. and 12-in. taping knives; a mason's hawk; and a respirator mask, if you'll be removing or cutting into plaster. There's a lot of grit, so wear goggles, too. The tools and techniques for plaster are similar those needed for stucco, discussed in Chapter 7.

ANATOMY OF A PLASTER JOB

Traditional plastering has several steps:

1. Nail the lath to the framing.

2. Trowel a scratch coat of plaster onto the lath. The wet plaster of this coat oozes through

PRO TIP

Drywall seams that coincide with door or window openings are likely to crack, vertically. That's merely a cosmetic problem. But large cracks running diagonally from the corners of windows or doors (inside or out) may be caused by foundation settling—a problem worth a closer look, perhaps by a structural engineer. For more information, see Chapter 1.

Texturing Drywall and Plaster

Joint compound is a marvelous medium for texturing a drywall patch or matching the texture of existing plaster. All that's needed is a little ingenuity.

▶ For a stippled plaster look, place joint compound in a paint tray, thin it with water till it is the consistency of thick whipping cream, and roll it onto the wall or ceiling using a stippled roller. Don't over-roll the compound, or you'll flatten the stipples.

▶ Create an irregular "splatter" texture by thinning the compound to a heavy-cream consistency, sucking it into a turkey baster and squirting it onto the wall.

▶ For an open-pore, orange-peel look, use a stiff-bristle brush or whisk broom to jab compound that is just starting to dry. Jab lightly and keep the bristles clean.

▶ To achieve the flat but hand-tooled look of real plaster, apply the compound in short, intersecting arcs. Then knock down the high spots with a rubber-edged Magic Trowel®, as shown.

▶ If you're trying to duplicate a slightly grainy but highly finished plaster surface, trowel on the topping coat as smoothly as possible and allow it to dry. Then mist the surface slightly and rub it gently with a rubber-edged grout float.

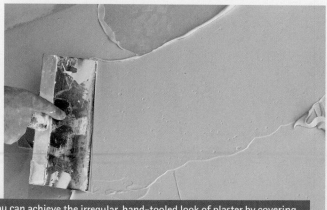

You can achieve the irregular, hand-tooled look of plaster by covering drywall with joint compound applied in tight, intersecting arcs. Because of its crack-resistance, use 90-minute or 120-minutes setting-type compound. It's okay if the drywall isn't completely covered.

Before the compound starts to set, use a rubber-faced Magic Trowel to knock down high spots and partially smooth out the knife marks. The trowel should glide. Unload excess compound into your mud tray after each pass, and sponge the rubber edge clean every four or five passes.

PLASTERING

1. If casing, baseboards, or floors are already installed, cover them with paper and tape to protect them from plaster splatters.

2. Mix the plaster to the consistency of soft-serve ice cream before ladling it onto a mason's hawk. For skim-coat plaster, follow the manufacturer's mixing instructions, which typically recommend adding 12 qt. to 15 qt. of water for each 50-lb. bag of plaster.

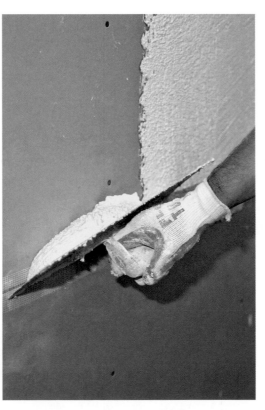

3. To prevent cracking, cover blueboard seams with self-adhering mesh tape. Load your trowel from the hawk and...

4. ...sweep the trowel in an upward arc to spread the plaster, then back down to embed it (make it adhere). As you apply plaster, the blade shouldn't lift off the surface. Sweep the blade back and forth, covering bald spots and erasing trowel marks. Use a double-bladed knife on the corners.

the gaps in the lath and becomes a mechanical key when it hardens.

3. Trowel on, then roughen the brown coat after it has set slightly.

4. Trowel on a finish, or white coat, which becomes the final, smooth surface.

In the old days, plasterers often mixed animal hair into scratch and brown coats to help them adhere. Thus old plaster that's being demolished is nasty stuff to breathe. The finish coat was usually a mixture of gauging plaster and lime, for uniformity. Scratch coats and brown coats were left rough and were often scratched with a plasterer's comb before they set completely, so the next coat would have grooves to adhere to. Finish coats were quite thin (1⁄16 in.) and very hard.

Lath can be a clue to a house's age. The earliest wood lath was split from a single board so that, when the board was pulled apart (side to side), it expanded like an accordion. Although metal lath was available by the late 1800s (it was patented in England a century earlier), split wood lath persisted because it could be fashioned on-site with little more than a hatchet. By 1900, however, most plasterers had switched from lime plaster to gypsum plaster, which dried much more quickly. And about the same time, plasterers began using small paper-coated panels of gypsum instead of wood or metal lath. Called *gypsum lath* or *rock lath*, the panels were so easy to install that they dominated the market by the 1930s. But time and techniques march on. As mentioned earlier, after World War II, drywall all but replaced plaster as a residential surface.

Repair or Replace Plaster?

To decide if plaster should be repaired or replaced, first assess how well it is attached to the lath. To do this, near stains, cracks, holes, or sagging sections, press the plaster with your hand. If the plaster is springy, it has probably separated from its lath and must be reattached before you try to repair it.

▶ If the plaster has a few surface cracks and isolated holes but is stable, it can be repaired.

▶ If there's widespread discoloration and there are cracks wider than ¼ in., but the plaster's basically stable, cover it with ¼-in. or ⅜-in. drywall or replace it.

▶ If you see water stains, crumbling plaster, and widespread cracking or sagging surfaces, remove the plaster and replace it with drywall. If there are water stains, of course, eliminate their source before doing any other work. Widespread sagging suggests that lath has pulled away from framing. Although lath can be reattached, concomitant plaster damage will usually be so extensive that you're better off tearing out the plaster.

Keying Plaster to Wood

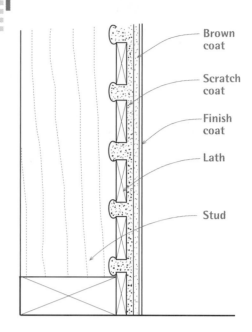

- Brown coat
- Scratch coat
- Finish coat
- Lath
- Stud

This plaster cross section shows how the scratch coat of plaster oozes through the lath and hardens to form keys, the mechanical connection of plaster to wood.

SMALL REPAIRS

Small cracks or holes in plaster can be filled with patching plaster or a setting-type joint compound such as Durabond 90, which sets in 90 minutes. Because joint compound is softer, sands easily, and sets slower than patching plaster, it's easier to work with. Setting-type joint compounds (also known as *hot mud*) are also better for patching than drying-type joint compounds, which just aren't as strong. *Note:* To ensure a good bond, strip paint from the surfaces you're patching and sand the adjacent areas lightly before applying compound.

Small cracks in plaster are repaired by stripping surface paint, cleaning loose plaster, and undercutting the cracks slightly with a knife or a small, sharp-pointed lever-type can opener (also called a "church key") Undercutting allows the patching material to harden and form a key that won't fall out. Before patching, wet the exposed plaster well and brush on a PVA (polyvinyl acetate) bonder such as Plasterweld® or Elmer's White Glue® to bond the patch to the old plaster.

Over the crack, stretch a length of self-adhering fiberglass mesh. Then use a taping knife to spread the patching material into the crack. Leave the first coat of joint compound a little rough so the second adheres better. After lightly sanding the first coat, apply the second, feathering it out to blend-in the patch's edges.

When the patch dries, sand it lightly with fine, 220-grit sandpaper, wipe it clean, allow it to dry thoroughly, and prime the patch with an oil-based primer.

Large cracks often accompany sections of bowed or sagging plaster, which have pulled free from the lath behind. If the plaster is sound—not crumbling—you can reattach it to the lath using type-W drywall screws and plaster washers, which fit under the heads of the screws. A screw gun is good for this operation.

However, before you attach the screws, mark their locations on the plaster, and use a spade bit to countersink a hole ⅛ in. deep for each washer.

Sunk below the surface of the plaster, the screw heads and washers will be easy to cover with patching compound.

Place screws and washers every 8 in. to 10 in. on both sides of the crack and anywhere else the plaster seems springy and disconnected from the lath. Once you've stabilized the crack in this manner, scrape, tape, and fill it, as described earlier.

Small holes the size of a removed electrical outlet are easy to fill if the lath is still in place. Remove any loose plaster, brush out the debris, wet the lath and the surrounding plaster well, brush on a PVA bonder, and trowel in patching material. Leave the first coat a little rough, let it dry well, and apply bonder again before troweling in a second, smooth coat.

Patching Cracked Plaster

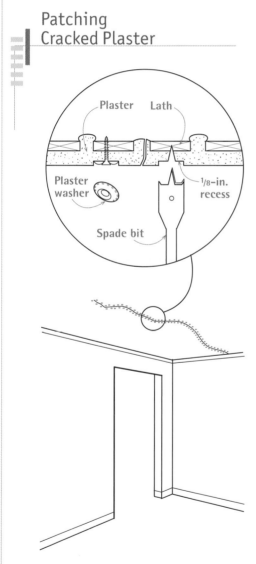

Cracked plaster often means that it has pulled free from its lath. Use screws and plaster washers to reattach it, countersinking them so they'll be easier to patch.

Patching Holes in Plaster

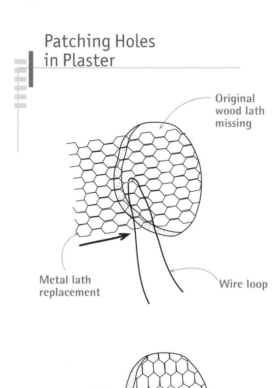

If plaster lath has been cut out, replace it before patching the hole. Insert and secure a small section of wire lath with a wire looped around a pencil, as shown. Twirl the pencil to draw the wire lath tight to the back of the plaster, then fill the hole with two coats of patching plaster. Unwind the wire and snip it when the first coat is hard.

If the hole has no lath behind it, you'll need to add some. Scrape the loose plaster from the edge of the hole. As shown in "Patching Holes in Plaster," on p. 373, cut a piece of metal lath larger than the hole and loop a short piece of wire through the middle of the lath. Then, holding the ends of the wire, slide the lath into the hole. To pull the lath tight against the back of the hole, insert a pencil into the front of the loop and turn the pencil like an airplane propeller until the wire is taut. The pencil spanning the hole holds the lath in place.

After wetting the lath and surrounding plaster, spread a rough coat of compound into the hole. When the coat has set, unwind the wire, remove the pencil, and push the wire into the wall cavity. The hardened plaster will hold the metal lath in place. Trowel on the finish coat.

Large holes with lath intact should be partially patched with a piece of drywall slightly smaller than the hole. Because a hole with square corners is easier to patch than an irregular one, square up the edges of plaster, using a chisel or a Dremel tool with an abrasive wheel. (Wear goggles.) Be careful not to cut through the lath. Use type-W drywall screws to attach the drywall to the lath behind, stretch self-adhering fiberglass mesh tape around the perimeter of the patch, and apply joint compound or patching plaster as described earlier. For best results, the drywall should be slightly thinner than the existing plaster, so you have some room to build up and feather out the patch.

As an alternative, pegboard is a dandy substrate for such patches because you can cut it easily with a jigsaw to fit irregular holes. Hold a sheet of ¼-in. pegboard over the plaster, eyeball and trace the shape of the patch through the holes in the pegboard, and screw the pegboard to the lath—textured side out. The patching plaster will ooze through the holes in the pegboard and harden in the same manner that plaster keys into the spaces between lath strips.

RESTORING PLASTERWORK

Think twice before trying to restore damaged crown molding, medallions, or other plaster ceiling ornaments. Plastic or composite reproductions of plaster elements are good-looking, lightweight, easy to install and—once painted—indistinguishable from plaster ornaments. Given the hourly rates of a skilled plasterer, replacing plaster with plastic repros is often more cost-effective.

However, if your plaster ornament has a repetitive pattern with only a few damaged sections, you can cast replacement sections by creating a mold from an original, undamaged section.

Removing an ornamental section. If you want to make a casting, you need to remove an undamaged ornamental section. First, support the section that you will remove. To do this, position a 2×4 tee, its head covered with rubberized floor padding, under the ornament to cushion and protect its delicate details. Then use a circular saw with a carborundum blade or a reciprocating saw with an 18-teeth-per-inch (TPI), bimetal demolition blade to cut around the section. The section should include a complete pattern repeat plus 2 in. on each end to allow for some damage when you remove the piece. This is dusty work and you're sure to hit nails, so wear a respirator mask and goggles.

⃠ *Note:* There may well be wires or pipes running through the ceiling, so explore beforehand after turning off the electricity to the area. In many cases, ceiling joists will be exposed in the attic above. Plan cuts so they miss wires and pipes. Replacing the section will be easier if you don't cut through the lath, but that's sometimes impossible to avoid. After cutting around the section, you can often slide a chisel behind it, and try to break off the plaster keyed into lath spaces.

Casting replacement sections. To reproduce replacement sections, you must first create a mold. After you've removed an original section in good condition, use a toothbrush to remove flaking paint; then repair any small damage with plaster of paris. Shellac the section so its surface will be slick. Then let it dry.

Casting Larger Replacement Molding

RTV-rubber-and-cheesecloth mold

Replacement casting

Sand bed to support mold

Box

When a repetitive plaster pattern is damaged, replace damaged sections with castings made from sections that are intact.

To make the mold, paint on a coat of RTV rubber and allow it to dry. Thereafter, alternate strips of cheesecloth and rubber, allowing each RTV-and-cloth layer to dry before applying the next coat. Three or four layers should give you a mold that's sturdy enough. When the final coat is dry, peel the RTV mold off the original plaster section, and pour a new casting into the mold.

Here are some thoughts on casting materials. Although plaster is a suitable casting material, it's heavy. If the original object is large—for example, a ceiling medallion—consider casting with a lightweight polymer like polyurethane or polystyrene, which won't shrink, paints well, and is available in different densities. Or you may need to support the mold in a bed of sand, so the new casting material doesn't distort the mold. For such larger casts, fill a large enough box with sand, and—before peeling the mold from the original plaster section—press the mold into the sand. Then lift out the mold, and peel the rubber carefully from the original plaster. Return the empty mold into the impression it made in the sand. Pour the new plaster (or polymer), and level it off to the top of the mold. When the casting is completely dry, lift it and the mold out of the box, and peel off the mold.

Installing new castings. Once you have cast replacement sections, measure both the damaged and replacement sections carefully so the repetitive pattern will match exactly when you install each replacement section. Then cut out the damaged ceiling sections, leaving the lath intact and being careful to cut the ends as cleanly and squarely as possible.

Before cutting the new casting to length, minimize fragmentation by first scoring the cutting line with a utility knife and then cutting with a fine-toothed hacksaw.

How you attach the replacement piece depends on its composition. If your casting is plaster, use Durabond 90 quick-setting compound to adhere the plaster ornament to the lath. Dampen the replacement piece so it doesn't leach moisture from the Durabond, and use the 2×4 tee to support it till the compound sets—about 90 minutes. For good measure, predrill holes at a slight angle, every 10 in. along the edge of the casting to receive drywall screws with plaster washers. But if your replacement casting is a lightweight polymer, you won't need screws. A few beads of construction adhesive or white glue will do the job. Before setting the replacement piece, dry-fit it to make sure it's the same thickness as the old plaster; you may need to build it up slightly. Last, fill the cracks or flaws where the new sections join old, before painting the restored ornaments.

Soundproofing

Most noise-related problems can be solved inexpensively, without major architectural remedies. Basically, you can install materials that absorb sound or try to reduce the sound's transmission by isolating it.

SOUND-ABSORBING MATERIALS

Within a room, use materials that absorb sound. Absorbent materials are often soft, porous, or bulky, such as carpet, cork, cloth drapes, furniture, or a shelf full of books. Conversely, avoid hard, highly finished surfaces that reflect soundwaves.

Fiberglass batts stapled between wall studs and ceiling joists are perhaps the most common means of absorbing sound. Two layers of ⅝-in. drywall, 3½ in. of fiberglass, and the air trapped in the wall will muffle sound effectively. You can also insulate between ceiling joists with fiberglass batts, nail up resilient channels, and then attach ⅝-in. drywall to the channels with 1¼-in. type-S drywall screws. Metal resilient channels are commonly used to hang ceilings and even walls. The resilient channel allows the surface to float, so it can move imperceptibly as soundwaves strike it.

A less common option is cellulose and mineral fibers troweled or sprayed onto walls and ceilings, somewhat like an acoustical plaster—the thicker the better. By using a special sprayer, you can apply these compounds up to 3 in. thick. Rigid-foam insulation panels are another option, but because the panels must be carefully fit and caulked to stud and joist bays, most installers opt for friction-fit fiberglass batts instead.

ISOLATING SOUND

Isolating sound, such as constructing double walls, generally takes more work and expense. In addition, wherever sound can be transmitted through the building structure, you should add resilient materials.

If you have a central hot-air heating system, fans can be annoying sources of noise, causing vibration along ductwork. In this case, try to

Options for Deadening Sound

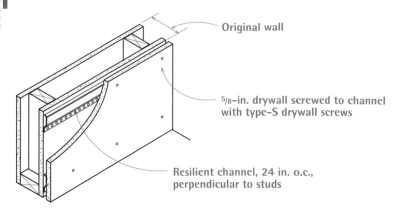

OPTION A

To reduce sound transmission through an existing wall, attach resilient channel and a layer of ⅝-in. drywall.

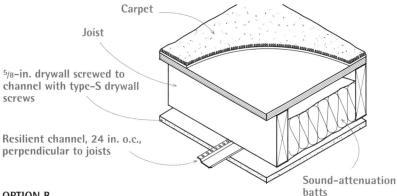

OPTION B

Deaden noise between floors by carpeting the floor, insulating between joists, and installing a ceiling of resilient channel and drywall underneath. For optimal sound deadening, insulate with special sound-attenuation batts.

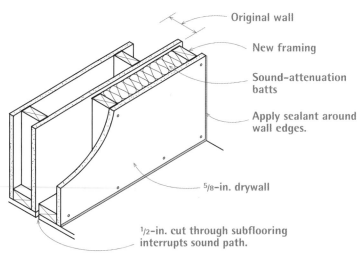

OPTION C

Double walls with discontinuous flooring is effective but eats up living space.

attach flexible collars (neoprene or canvas) to isolate ductwork vibration. Likewise, if your bedroom is plagued by a noisy fan in a heating system, you can reduce the noise either by remounting or replacing the fan or by packing insulation where the ductwork passes through a wall.

Double walls effectively isolate sound, but they require a lot of material and dramatically reduce room space. To further deaden (and literally cut off) the transmission of sound, say, between floors and walls, you can also cut a kerf through the flooring and subflooring between two walls. The kerf should stop short of the floor joists, however. 🚫 *Note:* If either of the double walls contains electrical outlets, turn off the electricity and check with a voltage tester before cutting such a kerf.

Resilient neoprene or foam-rubber pads above the stud-wall top plates and below the sole plates can further deaden sound transmission. Any opening in a wall will allow sound to enter. If you need an extremely quiet room, minimize the number of doors and windows, and weatherstrip them. Installing weatherstripping gaskets around interior doors also cuts sound. Finally, minimize the openings that run through walls, such as ducts, back-to-back electrical outlets, and so on.

To deaden sound between floors, install insulation between the ceiling joists, run resilient channel perpendicular to the joists, and attach drywall to the channel, using fine-thread, type-S drywall screws.

Tiling

Tile surfaces can be beautiful, durable, and—if you're patient—fairly easy to install. Yet although tile has a hard finish, the ultimate durability of the installation depends on the integrity of what lies beneath.

Choosing Tile

There's a riot of tiles to choose from, including slate, white porcelain hexagonals, ruddy Mexican pavers, tumbled marble, glass mosaic, brick veneer, cast cement, limestone quarry tile embedded with fossils, and so on. You can even paint your own designs on unglazed tiles and then have them kiln-fired. Although some types of tile are better suited to certain uses than others, finding a tile you like is rarely a problem.

SEVEN TIPS FOR SELECTING TILE

▶ Where will you use it? Does it need to be waterproof? Does it need to withstand kitchenware?

▶ Sketch the area to be tiled. Include dimensions, fixtures, corners, odd jogs, and adjoining surfaces such as wood flooring or carpet. This sketch is a systematic first step in assembling a materials list.

▶ Choose a tile store with knowledgeable staff that will take the time to answer your questions. Plan to visit the shop on a weekday, which is likely to be less busy and thus a good time to get extra help. High-end tile stores have room mockups and may also have a Web site showing a wide selection of tiled kitchens and baths. Stores will also display many types of tile in 2 ft. sq. or 3 ft. sq. panels. Such visual expanses of tile convey much more than single-tile samples.

▶ If you like a particular tile, have your salesperson determine the manufacturer's specs, which should tell you its suitability for various uses. For example, you wouldn't want to install a wall-rated tile on a floor.

▶ At some point, reconcile the tiles you like with your budget. Some tile is breathtakingly

Decorative and durable, tile can handle high humidity and heavy use—making it a great choice for kitchens and baths. A little Mexican, a little Moorish, this bathroom is always sunny.

These tumbled-marble sheets are attached to a paper backing, which is embedded into the adhesive.

expensive. Also check on availability. Will specially ordered tile arrive in time to meet your renovation schedule?

▶ Determine if trim tile is available for the pattern or type of field pattern you select. Trim tile is used to finish edges and corners and is especially important for counter installations.

▶ Test a tile sample at home. Here, you want to determine its suitability for your intended location by simulating actual use; for example, by scuffing it with shoes, banging it with pots, or dribbling it with water to check for absorption. Does the tile clean easily?

Color and size. In general, smaller tiles are better suited for small areas, such as counters. Larger tiles are more appropriate for larger areas, such as patio floors. Because light-colored tiles reflect more light, they make a room seem larger. Conversely, dark tiles make a room seem smaller. However, light colors tend to show dirt more readily. Vivid colors or busy designs can provide nice accents, but when used to cover large areas, they may seem overpowering.

Grout is a specialized mortar that seals the joints between tiles. Its color can make a big impact on the overall look. The closer the grout color matches the tile color, the more subdued and formal the surface. The more contrast between grout and tile, the busier, more festive, or more geometric the tile job will appear and the more it will highlight your tiling skill.

Manufactured vs. handmade. Mass-produced ceramic tile is popular because it has a clean classical look, and its uniform size makes it easy to install. Most smaller (½-in. to 2-in.) mass-produced tiles come evenly spaced and pre-mounted on paper sheets or fiberglass mesh, allowing you to simply to align the sheets' edges.

Field and Trim Tile

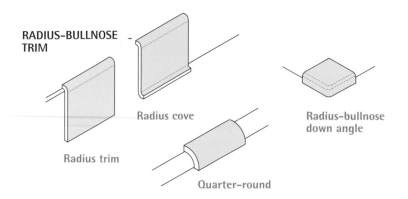

SURFACE-BULLNOSE TRIM

Field tile

Surface trim

Field cove

Right-hand cove stop

Left-hand cove stop

Surface-bullnose corner

V-cap trim

Surface-bullnose down angle

RADIUS-BULLNOSE TRIM

Radius trim

Radius cove

Quarter-round

Radius-bullnose down angle

Trim TILE

Trim tile is specially shaped to trim or finish off surface edges, corners, and the like and is thus distinguished from the main body of *common*, or *field*, tile. Trim tile is further classified as *surface* (or surface bullnose) and *radius* (or radius bullnose). Surface trim is essentially flat tile with one rounded edge. Radius trim, also known as quarter-round, curves dramatically to conceal the built-up bed on which it is set. Both types of trim include a range of specialty pieces that finish inside corners, outside corners, wall joints, and so on.

Handmade tiles offer unique color and a handsome, handcrafted look. But these irregular tiles take greater patience and skill to lay out and install. Often handmade tiles need thinset adhesive applied to each back, as well as a thinset layer-troweled onto a setting bed. Because they are irregular, handmade may also need to be arranged with plastic spacers to align their edges with the underlying layout lines.

Sheet-mounted tiles. Some tile comes either face mounted or back mounted, typically on 12-in. by 12-in. sheets. You install face-mounted tiles by leaving the paper facing on till the adhesive dries. Then dampen the paper and remove it. *Disadvantage:* Paper facing obscures tile joints, making them tougher to align. Back-mounted sheets are easier to align, but the bond between the tile and the adhesive may be compromised slightly because the backing remains stuck in the adhesive.

WATER RESISTANCE AND DURABILITY

There are almost as many physical distinctions among tiles as there are tile types, but the most important traits to consider are water resistance and durability.

Water resistance. Here, three of four official categories of tiles include the word *vitreous*, which means glasslike, and suggest how much the tile will resist or absorb water. The categories are *nonvitreous, semivitreous, vitreous,* and *impervious.* Nonvitreous is the most absorptive, and impervious the most water resistant.

Use nonvitreous tiles on dry areas, such as interior fireplace surrounds and hearths. Use semivitreous or better on shower walls, tub surrounds, backsplashes, and areas that are intermittently wet. Use vitreous and impervious tiles for wet installations like pools, hot tubs, and outdoor surfaces in rainy climates. In general, the less water a tile absorbs, the less hospitable it will be to bacteria and mold. That's why hospitals and laboratories usually use impervious tiles.

Durability. Tile durability ratings, based on structural strength and surface imperfections, typically assign softer, weaker tile to less demanding areas and harder, impervious tile to heavily trafficked, wet, and outdoor areas. In like manner, tiles are rated for walls, floors, and counters. A reputable tile supplier will give you good advice on appropriate uses and durability and will stand behind the tiles you buy.

Tools

Many tile suppliers sell or rent tiling tools and offer workshops on techniques and tool use.

Tools and safety. Tiling is deliberate, methodical work and is not as inherently dangerous as some remodeling tasks. Still, it poses hazards; so for starters, please note these minimal safety rules:

▶ 🚫 **Use a voltage tester to ensure that power has been shut off to outlets, fixtures, switches, and devices you'll work near. In addition, ensure that bathroom and kitchen receptacles have ground-fault circuit interrupter (GFCI) protection, as spelled out in Chapter 11. Corded power tools should be double insulated and grounded with a three-prong plug. Or use cordless tools instead.**

▶ **Rubber gloves reduce the risk of electrical shock and prevent skin poisoning from prolonged handling of mortar, adhesives, sealers, and the like.**

▶ **Wear goggles when cutting tiles, whether making full cuts with a wet saw or nibbling bites with a tile nipper. Tile shards can be as sharp as a scalpel.**

▶ **Wear a respirator mask when mixing masonry materials, applying adhesive, cutting cementitious backer board, and so on.**

▶ **Knee pads will spare you a lot of discomfort. Buy a pair that's comfortable and flexible enough to wear all day. Flimsy rubber knee pads won't protect your knees.**

▶ **Open windows and turn off pilot lights on gas appliances when using volatile adhesives or admixtures. Closely follow manufacturer's instructions.**

Classic vitreous porcelain tile is widely used in bathrooms because it resists stains and sheds water.

BASIC TOOLKIT FOR TILE

▶ Safety equipment: rubber gloves, goggles, respirator mask, voltage tester, and knee pads.

▶ Measuring and layout: straightedges, framing square, spirit level, pencil or felt-tipped pen, chalkline, tape measure, story pole, and scribe (or an inexpensive student's compass).

▶ Setting and grouting: notched trowel, margin trowel, plastic spacers and wedges, beater board, rubber mallet, grout float, round-cornered sponge, and clean rags.

▶ Cutting: snap cutter, tile nippers, utility knife with extra blades, and wet saw.

▶ Cleanup: sponges, rags, plastic buckets, plastic tarps, and shop vacuum.

▶ Miscellaney: hammer and wire cutters.

MEASURING AND LAYOUT

Substrates are never absolutely flat or perfectly plumb, so layout is a series of reasonable approximations. Clean tools give the most accurate readings, so wipe off mortar or stray adhesive before it dries.

▶ A 4-ft. spirit level is long enough to give you an accurate reading. It's indispensable for checking plumb and leveling courses of wall tiles. If a 4-ft. level proves unwieldy on the short end walls of a bathtub, use a 2-ft. level or a torpedo level instead.

▶ A tape measure lets you measure areas to be tiled, triangulate diagonals for square, and perform general layout.

▶ Snap a chalkline to mark tile layout lines before applying adhesive.

▶ Straightedges are useful for aligning tile courses, marking layout lines on substrate, and guiding cuts on backer board and plywood. Professional tilesetters have metal straightedges of different lengths, but wood's okay if it's straight and sealed to resist water.

▶ A framing square establishes perpendicular layout lines on floors, walls, and countertops.

▶ A story pole is a long straight board marked in increments representing the average width of a tile plus one grout joint (see "Storytelling," on p. 395). With it, you can quickly see how many tiles will fit in a given area, as well as where partial tiles will occur.

▶ Use a scribe to fit sheet materials (cementitious backer board, plywood) to a bowed wall or to transfer the arc of a toilet flange to a tile.

CUTTING

Always wear goggles when cutting or nipping tile, especially when using power tools.

A snap cutter works well on manufactured vitreous and impervious tile. This tool has a little cutting wheel—make sure it's not wobbly or

Straightedges are an indispensable part of tile layout and installation. They tell you whether surfaces are flat and help you align tile edges, as shown.

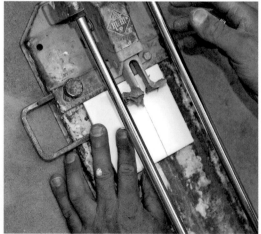

Snap cutters work great for straight cuts on vitreous tile. With this model, you score the tile in one pull and then push down on the tool's wings to snap the tile along the scored line. Here, blue painter's tape keeps the cutter's wings from scratching the tiles.

Wet saws are relatively cheap to rent, and they cut almost any type of tile cleanly. Wear safety glasses and hearing protectors when using one. To extend blade life, change the water often.

chipped—that should score the tile in one pull. Then reposition the handle so the "wings" of the tool rest on the scored tile, and press sharply to snap it. *Note:* When using a snap cutter, it's tough to get a clean break on nonvitreous tile, tiles with textured surfaces, and floor tiles. For those you'll need to rent a wet saw.

A wet saw, which you can rent, is especially useful when cutting nonvitreous or irregular tiles or trimming less than 1 in. off any tile. It cleanly cuts all tile types. To make U-shaped cuts around soap dishes and the like, make a series of parallel cuts with the wet saw before removing the waste with tile nippers.

Tile nippers allow you to cut out sections where tiles encounter faucet stems, toilet flanges, and the like. Nippers require some practice and lots of patience. Take small nibbles—use only part of the jaws—nibbling away from the sides of a cut into the center, gradually refining the cutout. As you approach your final cut-lines, go slowly.

A carbide-tipped hole saw is perfect for cutting holes for faucet stems and pipe stubs. To be safe around pipes and water, use a cordless drill with this saw.

A handheld grinder with a diamond blade can cut curved lines in tile (make a series of shallow passes) or plunge cuts for holes in the middle of a tile. Be sure to stop the cuts short of your cut-lines and remove the waste with a pair of

Using nippers is more like nibbling an ear of corn than chomping through a hamburger. Twist the nipper handles slightly as you break off little pieces of the tile's edge, and be patient.

nippers. Because a grinder is noisy and throws lots of dust, use it only outdoors, and wear a respirator mask and eye protection.

A utility knife scores cementitious backer board (which you snap like drywall), marks off tile joints in fresh mortar, cleans stray adhesive out of joints, and so on. However, if you've got much backer board to cut, instead use a handheld grinder with a diamond blade.

Keep tile from overheating and cracking as you drill by immersing it in a water-filled box just larger than the tile—build the box from scrap wood and caulk it so it won't leak. If countertop tile is already installed, build a dam of plumber's putty around it and add water before drilling. Mexican and other handmade tiles tend to crack when drilled without mortar support underneath, so install them before drilling. To avoid electrical shocks, use a cordless drill.

A small group of setting and grouting tools. Clockwise from upper left: grout floats, notched trowels, hand-drill mixing bit, and sponges (of which you'll need a variety).

Because handmade tiles are irregular, they often need to be moved slightly after they've been set in adhesive. Use plastic shims to raise tiles so they're level with others in the course.

SETTING AND GROUTING

Setting means positioning and adhering tile to a substrate. *Grouting* means sealing the joints between tiles with a special mortar.

A notched trowel spreads adhesive. Two edges of the tool are flat, designed to spread the adhesive initially. Then on subsequent passes, use the notched edges to comb a series of parallel ridges, which will spread evenly when the tile is pressed into it. Notch height should be about two-thirds the thickness of the tile.

A margin trowel is a utility tool that's great for mixing small batches of powdered adhesives, cleaning mortar off other trowels, buttering individual tiles with adhesive, and removing excess grout or adhesive that oozes up between tiles.

Plastic spacers and wedges enable you to shim individual tiles so their edges align to your layout lines.

A beater board is just a flat board placed over tile sections and rapped gently with a rubber mallet to seat the tiles in the adhesive. Not all tilesetters use a beater board. Many just press tiles in firmly or use a fist to seat them better.

A **grout float** (rubber-faced trowel) applies grout in a process that takes at least two passes. Holding the face of the grout float at about 30°, sweep the grout generously over the tile and pack it into the joints. Then, holding the float almost perpendicular to the surface, remove the excess grout, unloading it periodically into a bucket. To avoid pulling grout out of the joints, make your passes diagonally across the tile joints.

Round-cornered, tight-pored sponges are less likely to pull grout out of tile joints. After grout starts to haze over, wipe lightly with a dampened sponge, rinsing the sponge often. Get several types of sponges. Kitchen sponges with scrub pads on the back are useful for removing stubborn grout.

A mixing bit in an electric drill can mix large amounts of powdered adhesives or grout. Slow mixing speeds of 300 rpm to 400 rpm work best. And keep the bit immersed to minimize mixing in air, which weakens the batch. Wear a respirator mask.

Typical Wet Installation Floor

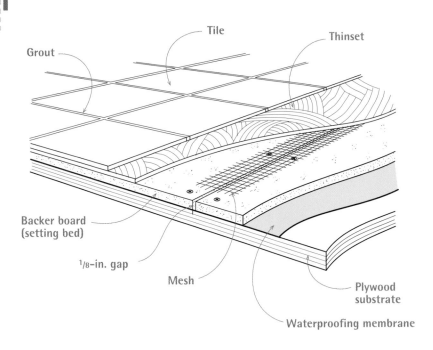

Tile

Thinset

Grout

Backer board
(setting bed)

¹/₈-in. gap

Mesh

Plywood
substrate

Waterproofing membrane

Materials

Here's a quick survey of materials you might use to create a durable tiling job.

Think of the job as if it were a layer cake. For example, in floor tiling, the bottom layer (conceptually the table under the cake) would be the floor joists. Nailed to the joists, in most cases, is a plywood *substrate*. For a wet installation such as a shower wall, next comes a *waterproofing membrane*, followed by a setting bed of cementitious backer board or a *mortar bed*. Troweled onto the setting bed is a *setting material*, typically *thinset adhesive* or *organic mastic*. Tiles are applied to the setting bed, and once the bed has hardened, tiles joints are grouted. Later, a *sealer* may be

applied to make tile and grout more water or stain resistant.

Methods and materials are rarely predictable in renovation, so it's a good idea to survey the back or underside of the surface you're about to tile, both to see how many layers there are and to check if they're in good condition. You can pull out a heating register to see a cross-section of the flooring, for example. Or test-drill a small hole in an inconspicuous spot to determine the thickness and composition of an existing wall, floor, or countertop.

SETTING BEDS

Tile can be set on a variety of setting beds. Keep in mind that the substrate below the setting bed must be securely attached to the framing members. That assembly must be thick and stable enough to support loads with minimal deflection (¹/₃₆₀ of the span). And when used in damp or wet areas, it needs to remain unaffected by sustained exposure to water.

Mortar beds. Where walls aren't plumb, floors aren't flat, and corners aren't square, mortar beds are usually the best setting bed. They can easily be screeded level or plumb to create a flat surface. In fact, a mortar bed is the *only* practical choice if you're tiling the sloping floors of a shower stall. But few novices have enough skill to float a mortar bed. If your surfaces are badly out

Applying mortar beds takes strength and a lot of skill. After installing a curing membrane and attaching wire mesh, you must carefully mix and trowel the mortar on, level or plumb float strips, and screed off excess mortar till the bed is uniformly flat. Then, after it has set a bit, use a wood float to roughen its surface slightly, which improves the adhesion for the thinset to follow

of whack and you're not experienced in floating mud, hire a pro for this job.

Backer board. If walls and floors are reasonably plumb and level, backer board is a durable setting bed for wet and dry installations. It's stable, unaffected by moisture, and easily cut and attached. Backer board is also called cementitious backer units (CBUs), HardiBacker®, Durock®, and WonderBoard—the last three being popular brands. These products feature a cement-based core, reinforced by fiberglass mesh or integral fibers. Because there's considerable variation among brands, always consult product literature for details on installation.

Glass-mat gypsum board. This board (one brand is DensShield®) has a water-resistant core and heat-cured acrylic coating. It's not as rugged as backer board, but it's an acceptable setting bed in tub surrounds and other light-duty wet areas. Don't confuse this product with drywall. Glass-mat gypsum board is specifically designed to be a tile backer.

Unpainted drywall. Drywall is an acceptable setting bed where walls stay dry. *Caution:* Never bond tile directly to drywall in damp or wet

installations. Water-resistant (WR) drywall (or greenboard) is an acceptable *substrate* in damp or wet installations only when it is covered with a waterproofing membrane and then a mortar bed or backer board.

Tile applied directly to drywall in wet installations invariably fails sooner or later, often because people showering bump the walls, compressing the drywall's gypsum core. No longer supported evenly by the core, the grout loosens, water enters and soaks the paper, and—all too often—the framing rots.

Exterior-grade plywood. It's usually a mistake to use plywood, even exterior grade, as a setting bed. Exposed to moisture, plywood tends to swell and delaminate. If you must use it as a setting bed for floor or countertop installations, be sure to cover it with a continuous waterproofing membrane; the base should be at least 1⅛-in. thick (for example, ½-in. plywood underlayment laminated to a ⅝-in. plywood subfloor). On walls, ⅝-in. plywood is the minimum. *Never* use particleboard, oriented strand board (OSB), or interior-grade plywood as setting beds.

Self-leveling compounds. Self-leveling compounds (SLCs), such as LevelQuik®, have many of the virtues of a mortar bed but require few of the skills needed to float one. Basically, SLCs are fortified mortar powders mixed thin and poured onto out-of-level floors. With a small amount of troweling, they spread across the floor and, within minutes, start to set. Just 2 hours later you've got a hard, almost perfectly level mortar-setting bed ready to tile.

That's the short list of common setting beds. For other materials see "Odd or Problematic Setting Beds," on p. 392.

ADHESIVES

Once you've chosen a suitable setting bed for your wet or dry installation, choose a compatible adhesive. Adhesives vary greatly from brand to brand, so again, always follow the manufacturer's mixing and application instructions exactly. There are three major groups of adhesives: *mastics,* which come ready mixed; *thinset adhesives,* which are cementitious powders generally mixed on-site just before setting the tile; and *epoxy thinsets* that, like most epoxies, require your mixing a hardener and a resin.

Organic mastics are the least expensive of the three adhesive options. Because they come premixed, they're the most convenient option, but they're also the weakest. They are okay for attaching tiles to dry counters or walls—over drywall, for example—but they're inappropriate where there's water, heavy use, or heat. Mastics just don't have the strength of thinsets.

Mastics require a nearly flat setting bed. That is, when they are applied thickly to fill voids, they neither cure completely nor bond thoroughly. Mastic cleans up well with water or solvent if you remove the excess material at once. Opened containers don't keep well, so throw away any leftover mastic after you've set the tiles.

Thinsets have great bonding and compressive strength. Being cement based, they bond best with mortar beds or backer board but are appropriate for virtually all setting-bed materials. Thinsets are also used to laminate rigid setting beds to substrates in order to create an inflexible substructure for tiling. (Construction adhesive is also used in such laminations, but it is flexible and so doesn't achieve the rigidity of a thinset lamination.)

Despite the cement ingredients they have in common, thinsets vary widely, depending on their additives. *Water-based* thinsets are the weakest of the group, although they are generally stronger than mastics. *Latex-* and *acrylic-based* thinsets (also known as polymer-modified thinsets) are strong and somewhat water resistant and are, all in all, the best choice for bonding tile to backer board, mortar beds, SLCs, drywall, and concrete slabs. And they're a close second for bonding almost everything else.

Most thinsets are mixed from powder. After mixing, they have a "bucket life" of about 2 hours. After being troweled onto a setting bed, they start to set in 15 minutes to 20 minutes.

Epoxy thinsets have excellent compressive and tensile strengths. They also bond well and yet retain flexibility when cured. After drying, they are unaffected by moisture and so are suitable for all situations and substrates. There's a catch, of course: Epoxies are four or five times more expensive than other thinsets and quite temperamental. You must mix the liquid resins and hardeners in exact proportions with the dry ingredients. Setting times are similarly exacting. If directions say 20 minutes, you can set your watch by them. Above all, clean up epoxy before it sets; some types sponge clean with water, others with solvents.

GROUT

Grout is a specialized mortar that seals the joints between tiles. Most grouts contain sand, cement, and a coloring agent. Grout may also contain additives to stabilize color, increase water and stain resistance and increase strength and flexibility. Most grouts and premixed additives are sold as a powder, which is subsequently mixed with liquid and allowed to stand (or slake) for

Here, a trimmed slate tile gets "buttered" with thinset. With the correct consistency, thinset spreads easily yet will adhere to a trowel turned on edge. Because polymer-modified thinsets have great bonding strength, you're safer wearing rubber gloves (unlike this pro). Also, be sure to clean tools immediately.

Waterproofing a Tub Surround

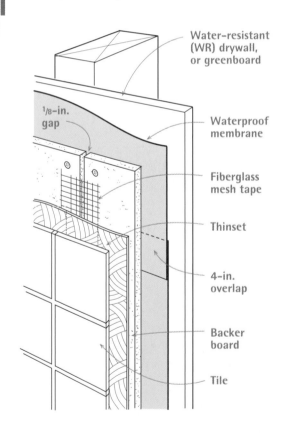

Water-resistant (WR) drywall, or greenboard

Waterproof membrane

Fiberglass mesh tape

Thinset

4-in. overlap

Backer board

Tile

⅛-in. gap

This tub surround would be sufficiently rigid without the WR drywall. But installers frequently add a drywall layer to build up the wall thickness when they'll be using bullnose edge trim.

10 minutes before final stirring to the correct consistency.

Use *sandless grout* for joints narrower than ⅛ in. Use *sanded grout* for joints ⅛ in. and wider.

Most tile suppliers carry grout in hundreds of colors. Whatever the color, remember that the greater the contrast between grout and tile, the more obvious the joints and workmanship.

MEMBRANES

Tile, grout, and many setting beds are unaffected by water. But they are porous, so water can migrate through them, potentially damaging plywood substrates or wood framing. To prevent such damage in damp or wet areas, install a *waterproofing membrane* first. Even areas that are normally dry, such as entryways, should have a modest building-paper membrane if the floors will be subject to wet mopping and dripping umbrellas.

For walls above the water line in wet areas and for countertops subjected to occasional water, a 15-lb. building-paper membrane is standard, but installing a 60-minute stucco paper

All wet installations need a waterproofing membrane. Here, a tub surround gets two layers of Fortifiber's Super Jumbo Tex 60 Minute stucco paper, which is a fiber-reinforced barrier that's tougher and more water resistant than regular building paper.

(which is impermeable for 60 minutes) makes sense. It's stronger, less likely to tear, and more water resistant. When installing such membranes, overlap the lower courses and vertical seams of paper by 4 in. Although some builders recommend 4-mil. polyethylene as a waterproofing membrane, stucco paper has one big advantage: Unlike plastic, it is semipermeable. Therefore, it allows water to escape should any get behind the barrier.

Below the water line, such as in a shower pan, you need to protect wood substructure with an *impervious* membrane. Thus most shower pans are lined with sheet rubber, such as 30-mil, fiber-reinforced chlorinated polyethylene (CPE), whose seams are overlapped and chemically bonded with a solvent. Of course, you don't want to puncture CPE shower-pan membranes with screws or nails. Instead, roll the membrane onto a fresh layer of latex thinset adhesive, and cover it with a mortar bed.

Note: The comments in this section are generalizations. Follow the manufacturer's installation instructions for specific adhesives, membranes, and setting-bed materials.

Getting Ready to Tile

If the substructure beneath the tile isn't sturdy and stable, the job won't last. Likewise, if walls aren't plumb or floors aren't level, tiles may adhere, but they may not look good. Start by assessing the existing surfaces. And that will inform your next steps, which can range from merely sanding finish surfaces to tearing out and reframing with studs and joists. The condition of existing floors, walls, and counters will also determine which setting bed you choose—and whether you should tile at all.

ASSESSING AREAS TO BE TILED

To check whether floors or countertops are level, use a long spirit level or a shorter level atop a perfectly straight board. Take several readings and use a pencil to mark individual high spots and dips. If variations from level exceed ⅛ in. in 10 ft., floating a mortar bed or pouring SLC may be your best bet for establishing a flat setting bed. If the surface irregularities are less than that or the substrate just needs stiffening, adding a single layer of backer board may be all you need.

If room corners aren't square or facing walls aren't parallel, you may need to angle-cut floor tiles around the room's perimeter. This is not ideal, especially in narrow alcoves or hallways, but baseboard trim will partially cover those angled cuts. Similarly, at the back of counters, blacksplashes will cover angle-cut tiles.

When assessing surfaces for plumb and level, take several readings with a spirit level, especially in corners. If they're out of plumb, tile joints won't align, and the mismatch will be glaringly obvious. Correct the condition or don't tile.

To check walls for plumb, use a long spirit level or a plumb bob; a taut string is also handy to detect high and low spots. Begin by surveying the entire wall. Unless the tiled corners are plumb, you'll have tapering cuts or mismatched grout lines where the planes converge, especially noticeable on outside corners. To correct out-of-plumb walls, your choices are floating a mortar bed, reframing the walls, or not tiling. *Note:* A wall that's plumb in the corner may have a twisted stud elsewhere that throws another section out of plumb.

Finally, survey surfaces for water damage, deflection, and other factors that could affect a tile job. Examine the bases of bathroom and kitchen fixtures for discoloration, delamination, and springiness, especially under toilets and tubs. Crumbling grout atop a tub often means that water has gotten behind the tile. Open kitchen and bath cabinets and examine the undersides of sinks and countertops. If you see discoloration, probe it with an awl to determine whether materials are solid. Particleboard countertops often deteriorate from sink leaks and dishwasher steam. If there's extensive rot or subfloor delamination, replace failed sections, as described in Chapter 8. To test for deflection, thump walls

with your fist, or jump on the floors. If you see or feel movement, there may be structural deterioration or, more likely, the substructure may be undersize for the span.

PREPPING THE ROOM

Tiling will go faster and look better if you first remove fixtures and other obstructions so that you can lay a continuous field of tile. This is a good time to upgrade or replace electrical boxes, install thresholds, and cut a little off the door bottoms so they don't scrape when tiling raises the floor level. For information on disconnecting and installing plumbing fixtures, see Chapter 12.

Removing the toilet lets you reinstall it on top of the new tile. Some people mistakenly leave the toilet in place and so need to make a lot of unsightly tile cuts around its base, which can also be troublesome to caulk and maintain.

Begin by turning off the shutoff valve to stop incoming water, disconnect the supply line, flush the toilet and remove the remaining water, and disconnect the anchor bolts holding the base to the floor.

Because toilets are heavy, find someone to help you move the toilet out of the way. To block septic gases and keep objects from falling through the closet flange into the closet bend, stuff a plastic bag filled with crumpled newspaper into the pipe; of course remember to remove it before reinstalling the toilet.

With the waste pipe temporarily sealed, consider the toilet's *closet flange* atop the closet bend. Ideally, the top of the flange should be the same height as the finish floor. If your tiling increases the height of the floor ½ in. or less, the height of the flange shouldn't be a problem. Just run tiles to within ⅛ in. of the flange. When you apply a new wax ring to the bottom of the toilet horn, the

PRO TIP

Weather-resistant barriers and flashing designed for exteriors often double as waterproof membranes indoors, beneath tile. After all, a shower's just indoor rain. Though sold primarily as stucco paper, Fortifiber's Super Jumbo Tex 60 Minute will also keep shower substrates dry even if you take hour-long showers. Polyken Foilastic, a peel-and-stick flashing, does a good job of sealing shampoo niches, pipe cutouts, and troublesome joints around kitchen counters (see the drawing on p. 399).

The Thick and Thin of Setting Beds

Each year the Tile Council of America (TCA) updates its handbook of tile-installation standards, which spell out acceptable materials and structural details for each type of setting bed, including framing and underlayment tolerances.

Thin-bed installations such as latex thinset adhesive over backer board are, well, thin. Because they offer little depth for adjustment, framing must be exact:

▶ Subfloors and countertops must be level and flat to within ⅛ in. in 10 ft. That is, no high or low points greater than ⅛ in. of level.

▶ Walls must be plumb and flat to within ⅛ in. in 8 ft.

As you might expect, standards are more tolerant for mortar-bed installations, which are thick enough to accommodate less-than-perfect framing. Mortar-bed tolerances are roughly double the thin-bed specs given here.

Corner out of Plumb

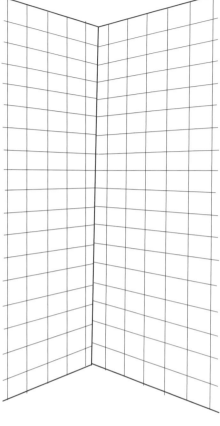

Corner walls too far out of plumb can't be tiled successfully. Their tile joints won't align, and the mismatch will be glaringly obvious.

PRO TIP

If the thicker new walls reduce the visible profile of existing valve stems, don't panic. Most major plumbing suppliers offer threaded *valve extensions* to make the stems longer. That's much cheaper than tearing out the walls to replace the valves.

||||

If you're replacing tub/shower walls or installing backer board, protect chrome gooseneck pipes or threaded spout stubs by replacing them with 6-in. pipe nipples. The nipples are place-holders for the originals, ensuring that pipe stubs line up to holes in the backer board. Here, Foilastic flashing reinforces the waterproofing membrane and later will serve as a dam for silicone caulking.

wax will compress and seal the joint adequately. In fact, you can buy extra-thick wax rings for such situations.

But if the tiled floor will be more than ½ in. higher than the closet flange (which may result if you install a mud bed or backer-board setting bed) replace the flange and set the new one higher. If waste pipes are plastic, cut off the existing bend-and-flange section and cement on new components to give you the flange height you need. This is easier said than done, however: If there's no room to maneuver new pipes, you may need to cut into flooring or framing. Thus many plumbers prefer to build up existing flanges by stacking ½-in. plastic *flange extenders* (the same diameter as the flange), caulking each with silicone, and using long closet bolts to resecure the toilet base. But check your local plumbing code to see if this method is allowed.

If drainpipes are cast iron, whose sections join with band clamps, you may want to hire a plumber to replace flanges that are too low or waste pipes that have deteriorated. Often, there's not enough room to attach band clamps adequately, or the substructure may need replacing as well.

Removing a sink may be a good idea, too. The method depends on the sink type: whether countertop, pedestal, or wall mounted. For each, shut off the water, and then disconnect supply lines and drainpipes.

Countertop sinks vary in their attachment. Most are held in place with clips on the underside of the counter and sealed with a bed of caulking or plumber's putty between the sink lip and the counter. After disconnecting the pipes, unscrew the clips and, if necessary, break the caulking seal by running a utility knife between the sink lip and the counter. If the new sink is smaller than the old one, you'll need to reframe the opening in the counter.

Remove in-counter faucet assemblies. Then tile within ¼ in. of the holes, and caulk the spaces with silicone or plumber's putty. If your installation will involve just thinset and tile, the old valve stems should be long enough to reuse. But if you're building up the setting bed with backer board or mud, buy new faucet assemblies with longer valve stems.

Shower and tub hardware can be masked off with plastic bags if you're not tearing out the shower walls or building up setting beds, but do remove chromework so it doesn't get discolored by mortar or adhesive.

To remove a showerhead assembly, gently pry the escutcheon from the wall (it may be seated in plumber's putty). Then wrap a rag around the chrome gooseneck pipe and use a pipe wrench to unscrew it. (The rag prevents the wrench's teeth from gouging the chrome finish.) Removing valve handles is slightly more complex because you must first unscrew valve handles from valve stems, and those screws are frequently hidden behind decorative caps. Once you've removed handles and escutcheons, wrap the exposed valve stems with plastic so their threads don't get fouled with mortar.

The last item on the shower wall, the tub spout, can often be unscrewed by hand. If not, you can usually gain some leverage by inserting a rubberized pliers handle into the spout opening.

Tile to within ¼ in. of the valve stems and pipe stubs, and caulk the gaps with silicone so water can't get behind the wall. Escutcheons will cover the cut tiles.

Build up electrical boxes so they're flush with new tiled surfaces. 🚫 After turning off electricity to the box—and using a voltage tester to make sure it's off—remove the outlet faceplate, unscrew the device from the box, and screw in a *box extender*. Run tiles to within ¹⁄₁₆ in. of the extender; the faceplate will cover tile cuts. *Note:* All bathroom receptacles and all those within 4 ft. of a kitchen sink must be GFCIs.

Move appliances so the floor they're sitting on can be tiled. Where those appliances are under-

Extending Electrical Boxes

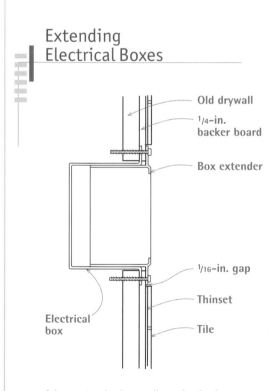

A box extender is usually a plastic sleeve that screws to an existing electrical outlet box, so that the box face is flush to a new tiled surface.

Tile Height at Toilet

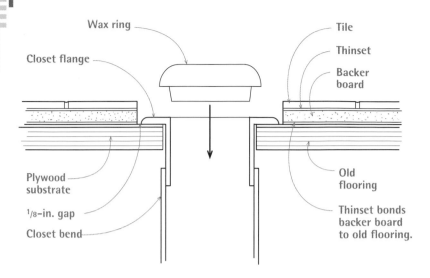

Ideally, the top of the toilet flange should be the same height as the finished floor. If not, consider the options outlined in the text.

counter, anticipate the additional height of the new flooring and raise or alter countertops accordingly so appliances can be returned to their nooks.

Cut door bottoms so there's about ¼-in. clearance between the bottom and the highest point of the tiled floor or the threshold. Do this after the tile and threshold are set because it's difficult to know beforehand exactly how thick the floor will be.

Choose a threshold that reconciles floor heights and materials on either side. For this, you'll need to think through its installation, such as scribing and cutting it to the door jambs and the adhesives or fasteners.

Installing Setting Beds

This section addresses mainly the most common setting beds and mentions only briefly those that are less common or problematic. Backer-board brands vary, so follow manufacturer-specific recommendations about waterproofing, connectors, installation procedures, and so on.

Expansion JOINTS

All tile substrates and setting beds need ¼-in.-wide expansion joints where they abut walls, fixtures, and cabinet bases. This keeps grout joints from compressing and cracking when materials expand. These joints are usually caulked with flexible sealants, such as silicone.

This worker wasn't able to score the WonderBoard enough to snap it after several passes with a utility knife, so he switched to a handheld grinder with a diamond blade. Faster, but dusty.

To install a backer–board setting bed over an existing substrate, drive 2–in. galvanized roofing nails into the framing. Instead, you could use 2–in. corrosion-resistant screws.

COMMON SETTING BEDS

Here you'll find additional details on backer board, mortar beds, SLCs, drywall, and concrete slabs. Setting tile directly on plywood is not recommended. But it's widely done, so that's addressed, too.

Installing backer board. Backer boards are cementitious backer units. They are strong, durable, and unaffected by moisture—and so are superb setting beds for wet and dry installations. However, because moisture will wick through CBUs, install a waterproofing membrane first in wet applications in order to protect wood substructures from damage.

Wear a respirator mask and eye protection when cutting and drilling backer-board panels, which can be scored and snapped much like drywall, though many installers score both sides. Although a utility knife can do the job, a dry-cutting diamond blade in a handheld grinder leaves other methods in the dust—literally. Wear a face mask when using this grinder, as well as hearing and eye protection. To drill holes for pipes, use a carbide-tipped hole saw.

For most backer-board installations, space galvanized roofing nails or corrosion-resistant screws every 6 in. to 8 in. Screws are more expensive and slower to install, but some tilesetters swear by them; Rock-On® cement-board screws cut their own countersink so the heads will be flush. Nail advocates argue that nails are less likely to crush panel edges and are easy to drive flush. To attach ½-in. backer-board panels directly to studs, use 1¼-in. screws or nails. If installing panels over drywall or plywood substrates, use 2-in. screws or nails.

Backer-board panels are available in a variety of widths (32 in. to 48 in.), lengths (3 ft. to 10 ft.) and thicknesses (¼ in., ⁵⁄₁₆ in., ⁷⁄₁₆ in., ½ in., and ⅝ in.). Thinner panels are typically installed over plywood or drywall. Use at least ½-in. backer board if you're attaching it to bare studs; otherwise it will flex too much and crack the tile joints. For a floor rigid enough to tile, install ½-in backer board over ¾-in. tongue-and-groove plywood, with joists spaced 16 in. on center. For all installations, leave a ⅛-in. gap between the backer-board panels. Cover those joints with 2-in.-wide, self-adhering fiberglass mesh tape before covering the tape with thinset adhesive—the same material used to set the tiles.

Feather out the thinset as flat as possible, but it doesn't have to be perfect because the joints will be covered by adhesive and tile. Finally, leave a ¼-in. expansion gap where the panels abut the base of walls, tubs, and plumbing fixtures; you'll fill those gaps later with flexible sealant. Keep the bottom edge of backer board ¼ in. above the tub so water doesn't wick into panels; caulk the gap later with silicone.

Installing the mortar bed. Mortar beds make a superb substrate but are complicated to install. First attach a *curing membrane* (a waterproofing membrane beneath the mortar) over the framing or drywall; then add *reinforcing wire mesh*. Next apply two or more parallel mortar columns, and place a wooden *float strip* atop each column. Checking frequently with a spirit level, tap the float strips into the mortar until the floor strips are level or the wall strips are plumb. Then fill between the strips: Dump mortar onto floors between the strips or trowel it onto walls. Flatten

PRO **TIP**

Don't use drywall screws to attach backer board. They're not strong, screw heads can shear off, and the dry-wall screws invariably rust out in damp and wet applications. Use only corrosion-resistant screws or nails. *Don't* use drywall joint tape either, for it's not up to the task.

Note how well self-leveling compound levels itself when accidentally dumped onto the ground of a work site. Even its thin tapered edge is strong. When used to level floors, its optimal thickness is about 1 in.

Stronger INSTALLATION, LESS WASTE

Construction adhesive is often used to join backer board to other substrate layers, but thinset adhesive (applied with a ¼-in. square-notched trowel) creates a far more rigid lamination. When installing backer board, cut pieces lengthwise if possible. For example, if you have 2-ft.-wide countertops, cut a single piece of backer board 2 ft. by 8 ft. rather than two 2-ft. by 4-ft. pieces. The panel will be slightly stronger, there will be no waste, and you'll have one fewer seam to tape and top.

Create a level mortar bed by drawing a metal screed board across two float strips pressed into mortar columns. After the mortar has been screeded, the wood float strips are removed and their voids filled with mortar.

the mortar by placing a *screed board* across the float strips and drawing it side to side in a sawing motion. Dump excess mortar into a bucket as the screed board accumulates it.

Once the mortar bed is more or less flat, remove the strips, and fill the float-strip voids with mortar. Then trowel out the irregularities. To help the thinset coat adhere, lightly roughen it by rubbing the surface with a wood float or a sponge float. Allow the mortar to set about an hour before using a margin trowel to clean up the mortar bed's edges. Some veteran tilesetters set tile immediately thereafter, but most mortals should allow the mortar to cure for 24 hours before tiling.

Mixing mortar in correct proportions is an art. Floor mud, or *deck mud,* is dry and rather crumbly: 1 part portland cement, 5 parts sand, and 1 part water. However, once screeded, compacted, and well cured, deck mud can support great loads. Wall mud is wetter and more like plaster because it must be spread onto vertical surfaces; it contains lime to improve its adhesion. Wall mud's proportions: 1 part portland cement, 4 parts sand, ¾ part lime, and 1+ parts water; use enough water so the mud trowels on easily. Add water slowly because mud won't stick if it's too wet.

Applying leveling compound. SLCs can level isolated low spots or even whole floors. Application requires few skills beyond opening 50-lb. sacks of SLC powder, mixing the powder with water, and pouring the mix onto a floor. You don't even need to spread it around much. It flows like water, levels itself, and starts to harden in about 15 minutes. Well, that's a bit oversimplified, but not much.

First, be sure the substructure is sturdy enough to bear the weight. Specs for one popular

SLC, LevelQuick, recommend at least a ¾-in. exterior-plywood subfloor over joists spaced up to 24 in. on center; use two ½-in.-thick pours to achieve a 1-in. optimal thickness. Wait 24 hours between pours. Whatever the substrate, it should be clean, dry, and free of chemicals—such as curing compounds in concrete slabs—that might prevent a good bond.

Before pouring, install a waterproof membrane and reinforcing mesh, which is usually wire, although a self-furring plastic lath called Mapelath® shows promise. One essential prep detail: *Completely* seal and dam off the section of floor you're leveling, or the free-flowing SLC mix will disappear down the smallest hole and form a heavy mortar pad where you least want one. Pay close attention to board joints, baseboards, and the like; caulk or seal joints with duct tape, pack them with fiberglass insulation—whatever it takes to contain the liquid till it hardens. SLCs are expensive but, in most cases, less expensive than floating a mortar bed. As important, they're great setting beds.

Preparing masonry surfaces. Concrete walls, slabs, and block are good setting beds as long as they've cured for at least a month and as long as they're clean (no chemical residues), dry, free from active cracks, and level or plumb within ⅛ in. in 10 ft. (If it's an out-of-level floor, see "Applying Leveling Compound," on p. 391.)

If you're tiling basement surfaces, the big issue is cracks. If masonry cracks expand and contract seasonally, it's unwise to tile over them because the tiles will crack. Likewise, if one side of a crack is higher than another, it's probably caused by soil movement. (If the crack is inactive and both sides of it are in the same plane, you can vacuum out the crack, dampen it, and fill it with a latex thinset adhesive before applying the thinset setting bed.)

Dry installations. Unpainted drywall is an acceptable setting bed for dry installations. (In damp or wet installations, never adhere tile directly to drywall.)

In dry installations, use at least ⅝-in. drywall if attaching it directly to studs 16 in. on center. Or sandwich two layers of drywall, with a layer of adhesive between, to create a more rigid lamination. But if you install a double layer of drywall, offset the panel edges by at least 16 in.

In either case, leave a ⅛-in. gap between panel edges, cover the joints with self-sticking fiberglass mesh tape, and then apply a layer of latex thinset adhesive over the tape. Drywall tools are fine for this application—but *not* drywall joint tape or compound. When installing drywall as a setting bed, you don't need to fill screw holes or feather out joints perfectly smooth because you'll be covering them with thinset and tile.

Plywood beds. Plywood is not recommended as a setting bed, but if you must use it, use only exterior grade and leave ⅛-in. gaps between the panel edges. Plywood substrates for floors and countertops must be at least 1⅛ in. thick—best achieved by laminating a ½-in.-thick plywood underlayment panel to a ⅝-in. plywood subfloor. To prevent squeaking and to stiffen the assembly, trowel construction adhesive between the panels. Offset the panels so their edges don't align. In addition to the adhesive, use 1-in. corrosion-resistant nails or screws spaced every 6 in. on center. To secure this laminated plywood to the joists, drive 16d galvanized nails into the joist centers. To avoid high spots that might crack the tiles, sink all screw or nail heads below the surface of the top layer. Sand and vacuum the plywood before notch-troweling on an epoxy thinset adhesive.

ODD OR PROBLEMATIC SETTING BEDS

The beds described next may require special techniques and materials.

Plastic laminate countertops are acceptable setting beds if they're solidly attached. Scuff the surface with 80-grit sandpaper, wipe with a rag dampened with solvent to remove grit and grease, and fill any voids. Then use an epoxy-based thinset to bond the tiles. Alternatively, you can cover the old laminate with ¼-in. backer board, adhering it with an application of epoxy thinset, and 1-in. corrosion-resistant screws spaced every 6 in. around the perimeter of the countertop and every 8 in. in the field. Sink screw heads flush, vacuum the backer board, and then use latex or epoxy thinset adhesive to bond tiles. *Note:* The recommended 1-inch screw assumes the combined thickness of the countertop materials is at least 1⅛ in.

Tiling over existing tile is a reasonable alternative to ripping it out, as long as the old tile isn't cracked and is well adhered and the substrate is solid. Scuff the tile with a carbide-grit sandpaper. Vacuum the surface well, and wipe with a damp rag. Because tile surfaces are not perfectly regular and grout joints are recessed, first use a flat trowel to spread a layer of epoxy thinset to build up grout joints and level the surface. Wait a day. Then use a notched trowel to apply a setting bed of epoxy thinset.

Two caveats: Because of the risk of leaks, don't tile over tiled shower-stall floors. Rather, tear out the old floor, replace the shower-pan membrane, and tile atop a newly floated mortar bed. Second,

To avoid cutting handmade tiles on the tub sidewall, the installer laid out tiles on the floor, using plastic spacers to simulate grout joints. She then floated the walls to the exact dimensions of the tile assembly. (Vacuum floors well before laying tile on them because dust can compromise a setting bond.)

don't install tiles 2-in.-sq. or smaller over existing tile because they will telegraph the old surface's irregularities. Instead, use large tiles.

Resilient flooring is acceptable if there's a single, uncushioned layer that's well adhered to a stable subfloor. Cushioned or multilayered flooring will flex too much to be a stable base for tile so, to be sure, use a utility knife with a hooked blade to cut out a cross-section of flooring in an inconspicuous spot.

Painted walls are okay as long as the paint is well attached and the wall doesn't flex. Drill a small exploratory hole to determine the composition and thickness of the wall. If it's drywall less than ⅝ in. thick, install a layer of ¼-in. or ⅜-in. drywall over it. If the wall is traditional plaster (hard to drill through), it's probably fine. Prep painted walls by sanding them with 100-grit sandpaper, and wipe with a damp rag. Use a latex thinset adhesive.

Other situations.

▶ Papered walls? Strip 'em! Vinyl wall coverings are supposedly tenacious enough to support tile, but it's risky.

▶ Veneer paneling? Not recommended. Typically ¼-in.- to ⅜-in.-thick, it will flex, cracking grout joints, and eventually dislodging tiles.

▶ Wainscoting or lumber flooring? Not recommended. Solid wood expands and contracts, and all those board seams would be a nightmare to fill.

Tile Estimation and Layout

At this point we'll assume that the substructure is sturdy and stable and the setting bed is in place. Careful layout is the key to a good-looking job, so don't begrudge the time it takes. The right layout will align tile joints correctly, create a pleasant symmetry, allow you to cut tiles to size beforehand and—most important—enable you to set tile accurately and quickly while the clock is ticking for that fast-drying adhesive.

ESTIMATING TILE

If you're installing a popular tile that a local supplier has in stock, wait till you've installed the setting bed before estimating tiles. If you order too many, most local suppliers will take back extras, as long as they aren't damaged or returned too long after purchase. Ordering tiles is not complicated unless surfaces to be tiled have a lot of jogs, recesses, odd angles, and obstacles. Using a tape measure and a pad of graph paper, calculate the square footage of the surface to be tiled and add 8 percent to 10 percent for waste, damage, and future repairs.

Handmade or exotic tiles are another story. Because they're expensive and must be ordered

Tile layouts impose a grid that's basically square in a room that often isn't. Start by recording the room's dimensions, use a framing square to see which corners are square, and note any obstacles to be tiled around.

FIRST CONTROL LINE

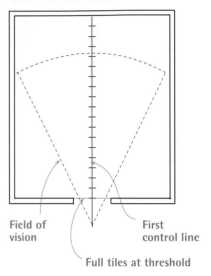

Field of vision   First control line

Full tiles at threshold

SECOND CONTROL LINE

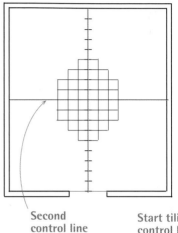

Second control line   Start tiling where control lines meet.

PARTIAL TILES

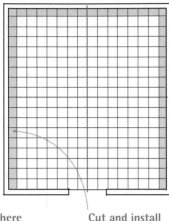

Cut and install partial tiles last.

If the doorway is the focal center of the room, use a story pole to find the tile-joint mark closest to the middle of the doorway. Ideally, the first control line will run through that mark, and there will be full tiles along the threshold.

The second control line is perpendicular to the first, intersecting it roughly midway along its length. Although you can start setting tiles anywhere, it's best to start where control lines meet in the highly visible middle of the room.

Place angle-cut and partial tiles away from the room's focal center. Because cutting tiles takes longer than installing full tiles, most installers cut tiles after the field of full tiles is in place.

well in advance, suppliers rarely accept returns. To save money, try to draw layouts that are accurate to an inch so you can count individual tiles. But you should still order extra tiles—say, 5 percent above your tile count—which is preferable to waiting 2 months for the next tile shipment from Italy. Besides, tile colors can vary greatly between batches. Your detailed drawings will also help you accurately frame out the area to be tiled.

Finally, when ordering tile, calculate the number of trim pieces separately from your calculations for field tiles. For each distinct piece of tile trim (such as surface cove, V-cap trim) add 15 percent to the lineal feet of trim indicated by the layout. Order at least *two* specialty trim pieces for any one-of-a-kind piece (such as *radius-bullnose down angle*). This is also the time to order compatible adhesives and color-matched grout and caulk.

TILE LAYOUT

Most tiles are square or rectangular. So the most common floor-layout dilemma is in imposing a grid that's basically square onto a room that isn't. Laying out walls and countertops is much the same, except that wall layouts are more affected by *plumb*. Wherever they occur, though, layout lines have the same purpose: They keep tile joints straight. When setting tile, it's easy to obsess about individual tiles and spacers, getting lost in close-up details. Thus layout lines help you keep the big picture in view and so keep tile joints from straying.

FOUR TIME-TESTED TIPS OF TILING

Though the following rules make sense most of the time, bend them when you must.

Use full tiles at focal centers. A focal center is any area that the eye is drawn to: the front edge

Tiles at the Sink

DON'T DO THIS!

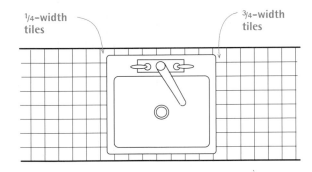

¼-width tiles

¾-width tiles

DO THIS!

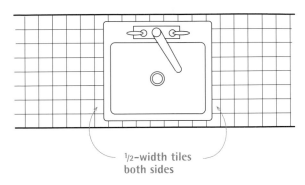

½-width tiles both sides

Symmetrical layouts look better. When a layout results in unequal tile widths along the sides of a kitchen sink—a very noticeable spot—either shift the layout or move the sink to create equal tile widths on both sides.

of a counter; a room's entryway; or a center of activity such as a sink, large window, or hearth. Common sense says full tiles look better than cut tiles, so put full tiles in conspicuous areas. Conversely, put cut tiles where they'll be least noticed.

Cut as few tiles as possible. Cut tiles are extra work, and they don't look as good as whole tiles. To avoid cutting tiles, you might be able to shift the layout a little to the right or left or *slightly* vary the width of tile joints.

Make layouts as symmetric as possible. This rule is both an extension and, occasionally, a contradiction of the two above. Imagine a kitchen-sink counter: The sink is certainly a focal center but may be smack dab in the middle of a tile field. There's often no way to avoid cutting tiles around the perimeter of a sink. In that case, try to shift the layout (or the sink) so that you can cut tiles an even amount on both sides of the sink. The result will look much better than almost-full tiles on one side and narrow tiles on the other.

This is also a good rule for small counters, which you can see from side to side without turning your head. If you must cut tiles, split the difference at each end.

Don't use tile pieces half size or smaller. They'll look terrible. It's better to adjust the width of tile joints. Or shift the layout so that you have large cut tiles on both ends rather than a row of narrow ones on one end alone.

StoryTELLING

A story pole (also called a jury stick) is like an oversize yardstick but is divided into units that represent the average width of one tile *plus* one grout joint. Story poles give you a quick read on the number of full-size tiles you'll need to get from point A to point B. For these homemade measuring devices, any straight board will do.

1. This installer is lightly snapping a chalked control line that will run roughly through the midpoint of the doorway to the room's opposite wall. In the background are dark full tiles he initially positioned outward from the wall to mark the eventual tile joint near the doorway's midpoint.

Installing a Floor

Using a framing square and a tape measure, check to be sure the room's corners are square and parallel. Make a quick sketch of the room, showing which way corners diverge. Or sketch this directly onto the setting bed.

FLOOR LAYOUT

Floor layout begins by identifying the focal point of the room, and snapping two chalklines (*control lines*) onto the setting bed, perpendicular to each other. In the photos on these two pages, the doorway is the focal point of the room. Thus, the first control line will run through the middle of that doorway and continue across the room till it hits the opposite wall at roughly a right angle.

Full tiles look best in a doorway. So the installers butted uncut tiles against the threshold and continued the course until it met a sidewall near the doorway. The installers then shifted the course slightly till an uncut tile butted into the sidewall, as well. They noted the tile joint closest to the middle of the doorway and marked it on the subfloor. Then they moved to the wall opposite the doorway, measured out from the same

Applying Thinset Adhesive

Once you've snapped layout lines and vacuumed the setting bed one last time, use the straight edge of a notched trowel to spread thinset adhesive. Then, using the notched edge of the trowel, comb ridges into the adhesive. As you apply and comb adhesive, try to stop just short of the layout lines, so you don't bury them under adhesive.

2.

In theory, you can start setting tiles anywhere, but it's usually best to start where the control lines meet and work out toward the walls. That way, you know that tile joints in the middle of the room—which are the most visible—will line up. Set several tiles; then pull up one and examine its back, which should be uniformly covered with adhesive. If it isn't, you may have applied too thin a layer of thinset, or used a notched trowel with teeth that are too small, or mixed the thinset too thin. If you are using large, handmade tiles like Mexican pavers, they are often irregular, so you may need to "butter" additional adhesive onto their back surfaces before setting. For buttering, use the straight edge of a trowel.

Conversely, if adhesive oozes up between tiles, the notched trowel's teeth are probably too large; try one with smaller teeth. Use a margin trowel to remove excess thinset between the tiles before it hardens. Left in place, the thinset between tiles would prevent grout from filling the joints and bonding properly.

3. When corners aren't square, start in the middle of the room—where control lines intersect—and work toward the walls. As you near out-of-square walls, cut tiles to fit. Avoid sliding tiles into place. Instead, align one edge to a control line or grout joint, "hinge" the tile down, and press it into the thinset.

4. As tile fills each quadrant, have a straightedge nearby to see if tiles edges line up, especially if thinset has obscured the chalklines. Note: Chalklines indicate the middle of the tile joints. An experienced installer uses both the chalkline and a straightedge to align tiles—whichever gives the better-looking result.

5. After setting the field of full tiles, attend to those that need cutting or special fitting. The installer used a wet saw to cut the two longer lines, then a nipper to finish off the rounded inner corner.

sidewall, and made a second mark that represented an extension of that middle tile joint. They lightly snapped a chalkline (as shown in photo 1) through the two marks to create a *first control line.* But they snapped the line lightly because they knew they might need to move it a bit before settling on its final location, as explained next.

Before photo 2 was taken, the installers used a framing square to mark a second control line perpendicular the first, thus dividing the bathroom roughly into quadrants. They wanted full tiles against the threshold, so they placed one end of the story pole there and measured away from it to find a tile-joint mark close to the midpoint of the first control line.

The rest of such a layout is mostly fine-tuning, with an eye to the four time-tested tips of tiling, as outlined earlier: using full tiles at focal points, cutting as few tiles as possible, making layouts as symmetrical as possible, and avoiding tiles less than half size. For this, a story pole is essential.

SETTING THE TILES

Set full tiles before partial tiles. To get a rhythm going, most tilesetters first set all the full tiles, and then attend to partial tiles, which take time to cut and set. However, you may want to make complex cuts beforehand, for example, where tiles meet obstacles in the middle of the field, such as a toilet closet flange. By cutting these tiles first, you can set them quickly and install other full tiles around them. Give the adhesive a day to harden, and you're ready to grout the surface.

Note: This description is much condensed. If you're a perfectionist, you'll fuss with the spacing between tiles or between tile sheets, and continue making little adjustments till the job is done. Be sure to stand back from time to time for an overview of the layout.

Countertops

The front edge of a counter is almost always the focal point. Thus the primary control line runs parallel to the front of the counter, and all other layout lines are secondary to it. If the counter will be subject to moisture, install a membrane before installing a setting bed.

STRAIGHT COUNTER, NO SINK

The simplest surface to lay out is a straight counter with no sink because it has only one control line. Begin by using a framing square and a story pole to survey the countertop.

"Counter Layout," on p. 398, assumes that the counter edges are finished with V-cap trim, a

"Counter Layout," on p. 398, assumes that the

PRO TIP

Thinset adhesive should be moist enough to stick to the tile, but not so wet that it slides off a trowel. If thinset skins over while you're setting tile, recomb it with a notched trowel. But if it gets stiff in the pan or it doesn't stick readily to the tiles, discard it and mix a fresh batch. Likewise, if you move a tile after the adhesive has started to set, scrape the thinset off the back of the tile and the setting bed, and apply fresh mortar to both surfaces.

Counter Layout

STRAIGHT COUNTER

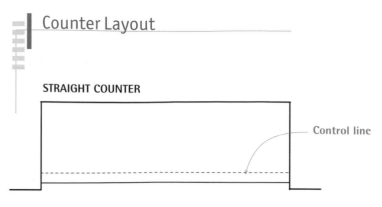

—— Control line

A straight counter needs only one layout control line to indicate the first tile joint back from the edge.

COUNTER WITH SINK OR COOKTOP

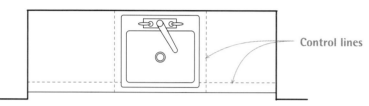

Control lines

If a sink or a cooktop in the counter interrupts the layout and requires tile cutting, mark secondary control lines on either side to indicate where full tiles resume.

L-SHAPED COUNTER

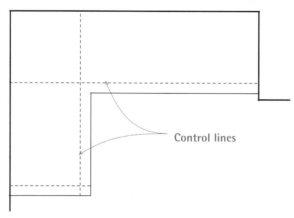

Control lines

An L-shaped counter will have two major control lines, running perpendicular to each other. Add lines as needed to indicate sink placement, open counter edges, and so on.

common choice, and tile joints are ⅛ in. wide. Place several V-caps along the counter edge; then measure back from the edge 1⁄16 in. from each cap to mark the middle of the first grout joint. Snap a chalkline through these marks to establish a control line. Because the front edge is the counter's focal point, you'll place full field tiles next to the row of V-caps.

Using your story pole, measure the length of the counter to see if you must cut tiles. If one end of the counter abuts a wall and the other is open, plan a row of full tiles along the open end, thus consigning cut tiles to the wall end where they'll be less conspicuous. If both ends of the counter are open, and you see that you'll need to cut tiles, move the story pole so that cut tiles will be the same dimension on both ends. That decided, mark positions for the tile units along the control line.

Last, measure to the back of the counter to determine whether the final row of tiles will need cutting. You can precut tiles; but on a counter so simple, you can just measure and cut partial tiles individually after all the full tiles are set, likely giving you more accurate measurements anyway.

FROM THE ARCHIVES

Because the front edge of a counter is the most visible, start layout and installation there. Place V-cap trim along the front edge to position successive courses of field tile. As you set each course of tile, use a straightedge to align them.

Waterproofing Counter Edges

Installers often mistakenly overlook countertop edges when installing the waterproof membrane. A membrane is especially important if you're floating a mortar bed because the moisture from curing mortar is enough to swell unprotected plywood edges and, in time, cause V-cap trim to fall off. At the very least, extend the membrane and wrap it down over the edge of the plywood substrate. However, because building paper folds unevenly and can create a welt that won't lie flat, a better solution is to cover counter edges with a self-sticking flashing such as Polyken Foilastic. It will lie flat, it's impervious to water, and most thinsets will stick to it—but check your thinset's specs to be sure.

The back edge of a counter, where it abuts a wall or backsplash, is also susceptible to water damage if not detailed correctly. Run the waterproof membrane all the way to the wall; then flash the countertop–wall joint using self-sticking flashing. Fold the flashing lengthwise (into an L), adhering one leg of the L to the membrane, and running the other leg up the wall, at least 1 in. above the finish-tile level.

MOSAIC TILE

After you've set paper-backed sheets of mosaic tile in adhesive, the paper will start to soften, allowing you to reposition the tiles slightly. To move a row of tiles, place the straight edge of a trowel against them, as shown, and tap the trowel lightly with a hammer handle.

Countertop Front and Back Edges

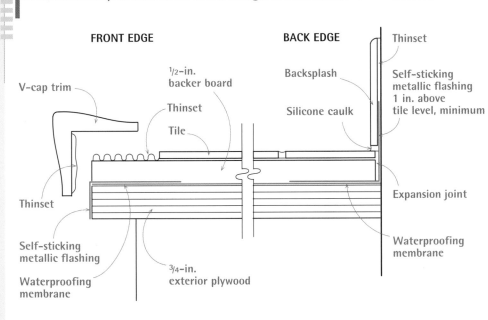

FRONT EDGE

- V-cap trim
- ½-in. backer board
- Thinset
- Tile
- Thinset
- Self-sticking metallic flashing
- Waterproofing membrane
- ¾-in. exterior plywood

BACK EDGE

- Backsplash
- Silicone caulk
- Thinset
- Self-sticking metallic flashing 1 in. above tile level, minimum
- Expansion joint
- Waterproofing membrane

Flash the front edge of a counter, as shown, to prevent the exposed edges of the plywood from wicking moisture from the thinset adhesives and then swelling. Because the back edges of the countertops are also vulnerable to water damage, caulk and flash them, too.

Use a grout float to seat mosaic tile in the thinset adhesive. Be sure to don knee pads that are comfortable enough to wear all the time.

STRAIGHT COUNTER, WITH SINK

To tile a straight counter with a sink, the layout is much the same as a counter without a sink, except that here, your main concern is making symmetrical tile cuts (if necessary) on either side of the sink. If you need to cut tiles, move the story pole side to side until the tile joints are equidistant on each side of the sink's rough opening. Then transfer those two marks to the control line. Finally, use a framing square to run lines through those marks, perpendicular to the control line, to the back of the counter.

L-SHAPED COUNTER

On an L-shaped counter you have, in effect, two counters at right angles to each other, so you will need two control lines, perpendicular to each other, running along the front edge of each section. Any other layout considerations are subordinate to these two control lines, for they determine how the two oncoming tile fields will align.

Use your framing square and a straightedge to establish control lines and to keep the tiles aligned once you've turned the corner. After setting V-cap trim tiles, start tiling where the two control lines intersect. As with straight counters, put full tiles along the front of the counters and work back, relegating cut tiles to the very back, to be covered by the backsplash. If you use the same tile for the backsplash, continue the tile joints up the wall so that the backsplash and counter joints line up.

Tub Surround

Never assume tub walls are plumb. Always check them with a 4-ft. level. If walls aren't plumb within ⅛ in. in 8 ft., correct them with a mortar bed or reframe them. Otherwise, tile joints from adjacent walls won't align. Moreover, never assume that a corner is a good place to start tiling, for it may not be plumb. Instead, establish level and plumb control lines on each wall to guide your layout.

Most tilesetters start by laying out the longest wall, which we'll call the *back wall*. Use your 4-ft. level to determine if the tub is level on all three sides of the surround. If tub shoulders are level, you can start measuring tile courses up from the tub; but in renovation, tub shoulders are rarely level. More likely, the tub will slope. So, *from the lowest point of the tub shoulder,* measure up one tiling unit and mark it onto a wall. (A tiling unit is a tile width plus one grout joint.) Through that mark, draw a horizontal control line, and extend that line to all three walls of the surround.

Now locate a vertical control line, roughly centered along the back wall. Holding your story pole horizontally, determine whether you need to cut tiles and, if so, where to place them. In most cases, back walls look best if there are symmetrical (equally wide) vertical columns of cut tiles at each end. That decided, chose the joint mark on your story pole closest to the middle of the wall, and run a plumbed line up, bisecting the back wall and the horizontal control line you drew

Laying Out a Tub Back Wall

Almost all tubs slope slightly, so use a spirit level to locate the lowest point. From that lowest point, measure up the height of one tile, plus ¼ in., and mark the wall. Draw a level control line through that mark, as shown in the illustration at right, and extend that level line to all three tub walls. Use a story pole to see if you'll need to cut tiles. If so, lay out tiles so cuts are symmetrical on both ends of the back wall. Draw a plumb line on each end of the wall to indicate where the cut tiles will begin. Finally, through a tile joint along the level control line, draw a plumb control line that roughly bisects the backwall. Start tiling where control lines meet.

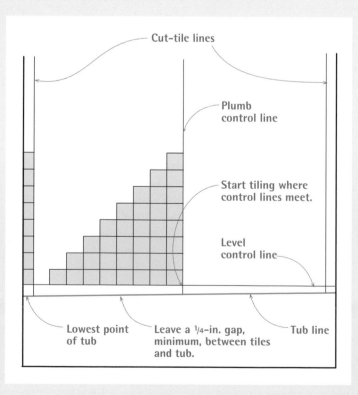

Cut-tile lines

Plumb control line

Start tiling where control lines meet.

Level control line

Lowest point of tub

Leave a ¼-in. gap, minimum, between tiles and tub.

Tub line

TILING A TUB SURROUND

1. After checking tub walls for plumb, use a spirit level to check whether the tub is level along all three sides. If the tub slopes, note the lowest point.

2. At the lowest point of the tub shoulder, measure up one tiling unit (tile width plus one grout–joint width) and mark that onto the wall. Through that mark, draw a level line that extends to all three walls of the surround. Next, nail narrow wooden strips to the underside of that line, as shown.

3. The first course of full, uncut tiles should rest on the wooden strips. After you've installed tiles on all three walls and the setting–bed has hardened, remove the wood strips and install cut tiles below.
(Steps continue on next page.)

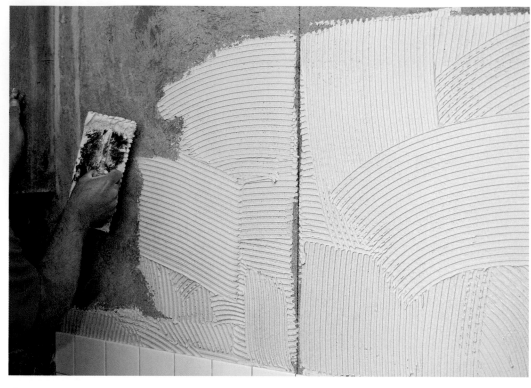

PRO TIP

About the same time you're sponge-wiping the tile, use a margin trowel or a utility knife to remove grout from the expansion joints and from the ¼-in. gap where tile meets the tub. Allow a day for the grout to cure; then seal these gaps with an acrylic or silicone caulk. Tile suppliers sell caulk that's either sandless or sanded, and color matched to your grout.

▐▐▐▐

4. Typically, tilesetters mark a vertical line to bisect the long, sidewall of a tub. As you trowel on thinset, try not to obscure the line with adhesive. Although this pro is setting a whole wall without interruption, most mortals should set tile a half or quarter wall at a time.

6. Use nippers for the curved cuts around pipes and the plastic protective covers over shower valves. Wear goggles when nipping.

5. Periodically check to see if tile courses are level, inserting plastic shims as needed. Leave them in place until the thinset cures. Note: Because walls aren't perfectly regular, you'll often need to use spacers as well as shims. Spacers are uniformly thick; shims are tapered.

7. If it's necessary to cut tiles, place them symmetrically on both ends of the sidewall. Though it's possible to cut all partial tiles at once, measuring each ensures a better fit.

earlier. (This is also a good time to draw plumbed lines at either end of the back wall, indicating where cut tiles begin.)

Next, use your story pole on the sidewalls, to see if it's necessary to cut tiles for them and, if so, where to place those tiles. In most layouts, a full column of tiles is placed along the outside edges of sidewalls because they are visually conspicuous; cut tiles are consigned to the corners. But if the back will have no cut tiles, consider putting full tiles in the inside corner of each sidewall. Also draw plumb lines to indicate the outside edges of sidewall tiles. Finally, you may want to draw additional layout lines to subdivide the back wall and anticipate tile cuts around the soap dishes, the tub spouts, the shower mixing valves, and so on.

As with floor-tile installations, pros often begin setting tub surrounds in the middle of a tile field, where control lines intersect, setting a quadrant of full tiles at a time, then going back later—often, the next day—to cut and set partial tiles and trim pieces. It's also advisable to leave plastic tile spacers in place till the thinset cures. After pulling out the spacers with needle-nose pliers, you're ready to grout.

Rejuvenating Grout Joints and Caulking

If your grout is moldy, use a soft-bristle plastic brush to scrub the joints either with household cleaner, a weak bleach solution, or a tile-specific cleaner like Homax® Grout and Tile Cleaner. Wear rubber gloves and goggles, and always brush such solutions away from your face. If the mold returns, try installing a ventilator fan to reduce the moisture in the room. If the grout is intact but dingy, scrub, rinse, and allow it to dry before applying a grout colorant, which will both color and seal the grout. Follow the manufacturer's instructions.

However, if tiles are loose; if surfaces flex; or if you see water damage around fixtures, at the base of a tub or shower, or along the backsplash of a counter, the substrate has probably deteriorated and should be replaced. In other words, you'll need to tear out tiles and substrate.

There's an interim condition, often caused by applying grout that was too thin or by over-sponging it, in which tile is intact but grout is worn or crumbling. In that case, use a grout saw to cut out the old grout, taking care not mar the tile edges. As you'll realize quickly, this is a tedious job. Vacuum out the debris, scrub the joints with a cleaning solution, rinse well, and then use a grout float to apply polymer-modified grout, which will adhere better. It's possible to regrout only part of a surface, but matching old and new grout color can be difficult, so it's better to regrout the entire surface. Wait 72 hours, before sealing the grout joints.

Removing hardened caulk along the tub can be a chore. Chiseling it out is perilous because tub enamel and tile chip easily. Fortunately, acetone dissolves caulk. To use the acetone, cut cotton clothesline to the length of the caulk seam, wet the clothesline with acetone, and place it next to the caulking before covering both with duct tape. Left overnight, the acetone will soften the caulk. *Caution:* Acetone is volatile and thus flammable, and nasty to handle and breathe. Don't use acetone around pilot lights, open flames, and the like. Wear rubber gloves and a respirator mask with cartridges.

Supporting TILES

It's smart to tape specialty tile pieces in place until their thinset has hardened. That's especially true for heavy pieces, such as the soap niche shown, and for pieces with a relatively small bonding surface, such as bullnose edge trim. *Caveat:* Wait until the field tiles have bonded securely before taping to them.

Getting Grout Right

Most grout is packaged as a powder containing sand, portland cement, colorants, and additives that improve strength and adhesion. Labels on grout bags offer good information, including the correct liquid-to-powder ratio and, on most bags, a chart showing how much grout to buy based on the square footage of the tile area and the width of the grout joint.

Using a margin trowel, mix powdered grout in a clean bucket, starting with three-quarters of the recommended liquid and gradually pouring in the rest. Let the grout stand (slake) for 10 minutes, and then stir it again to test its consistency. Grout should be wet enough to stick to the side of a tile, but not runny—a consistency rather like hummus or thick toothpaste. Depending on the wetness of the mixture and the temperature of the room, grout starts to set up in about 30 minutes, so mix as much as you can spread in 15 minutes—at which point you should start cleaning up the grout.

If you're grouting a floor or a countertop, just dump the bucket onto the surface. (Grout with the right consistency may need a little help out of the bucket.) Holding the face of the grout float at about 30 degrees to the surface, sweep grout generously over the tile and pack it into joints. After you've packed all joints, remove the excess grout. Holding the float almost perpendicular to the surface, sweep the float diagonally across the tile joints. Periodically unload excess material into a bucket. Diagonal passes are less likely to pull grout out of the joints.

In about 15 minutes, when the grout has begun to set, use a clean, damp (not wet) sponge to clean grout residue off tile faces. Rinse the sponge often. If the sponge pulls grout out of the joints, either wait a little longer, wring the sponge a little dryer, or don't press so hard. Sponge-wiping also smoothes out grout joints. So, for best results, use a round-shouldered, tight-cell sponge. Wide-cell sponges will pull grout out of the joints.

In another 15 minutes, use soft, dry rags to rub off any haze that's dried on the tile. Because it's porous, grout can stain. Let it cure for 72 hours before applying a liquid grout sealer or impregnator to the grout alone or to the whole tile surface. Two recommended sealants: TileLab® penetrating sealant and TEC™ sealants.

Holding the grout float about 30 degrees to the floor, pack grout into the tile joints.

GROUTING A FLOOR

In about 15 minutes, when the grout has begun to set, wipe the tile with a clean, damp sponge. Rinse and wring the sponge often. To avoid pulling grout out of joints, sweep the sponge diagonally across tile joints, using a sponge with tight pores.

Finish Carpentry

After framing walls, running pipes and wires, insulating, and hanging drywall, it's time to install interior trim. Somewhat like a picture frame, trim is decorative. But it's also functional, concealing gaps and rough edges where walls meet floors, ceilings, doors, and windows. Although finish carpentry is not as fundamental as structural framing or foundation work, it completes the picture, and often makes or breaks a renovation project.

Interior trim is often called *casing,* or *molding* if its face is shaped. Trim helps establish the character of a room, so it's wise to respect existing trim when replacing or supplementing it. Carefully remove and save existing molding if it's in decent condition. If that type is no longer available, try to locate new molding with a similar feeling. Or you might be able to combine and overlap stock moldings to create a more complex and interesting look. Another choice is using pre-fab, high-relief synthetics that duplicate large-scale moldings not available in wood today. Many woodworkers and carpenters can re-create old trims. A homeowner who's good with a router and can find the right bits may be able to do the same.

Finally, see Chapter 13, for concise advice on choosing and installing counters, cabinets, and fixtures appropriate to those rooms. For guidance on installing door and window hardware, read Chapter 6.

Tools

Most of the tools for finish carpentry are presented in the basic collection discussed in Chapter 3, though upcoming sections address a few specialty tools. Still, by and large, successful trimwork depends more on the hands behind the tools than on the tools themselves. Also, when working with power tools and striking tools, safety glasses are

Trim covers gaps between building materials and dresses up a room. Here, baseboards are shimmed ½ in. above a concrete basement subfloor so carpet can be tucked under it. Pneumatic nailers are much faster than hand nailing and far less likely to split or dent trim.

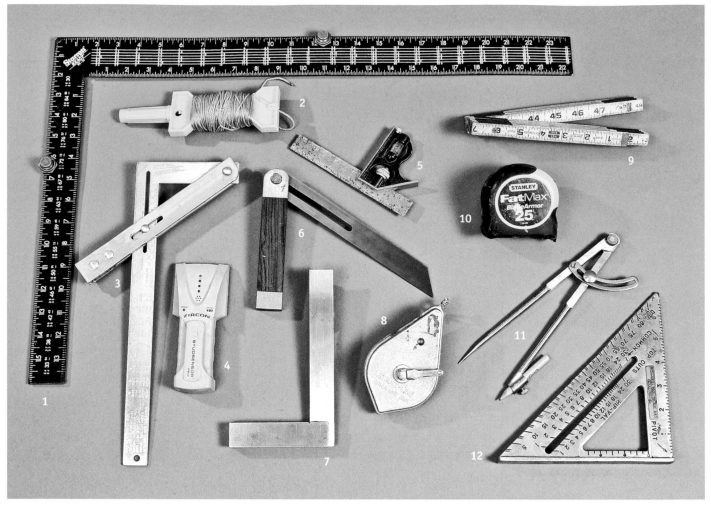

Measuring and layout tools. 1, Framing square; 2, string; 3, adjustable square; 4, stud-finder; 5, combination square; 6, adjustable bevel; 7, steel try square; 8, chalkline; 9, folding rule with sliding extension; 10, tape measure; 11, compass; 12, Swanson Speed Square.

a must, especially when joinery requires close work at eye level.

MEASURING AND LAYOUT

PRO TIP

Get organized. Before you begin, set up a workstation with all the tools and materials you'll need. Keep the area clean and your materials sorted: Clutter and chaos eventually lead to wasted time and costly mistakes.

||||

Whenever possible, hold a trim piece in place and use a pencil or a utility knife to mark the cut-line. This is usually more accurate than transferring tape-measure readings.

Tape measures are frequently used to measure trim longer than 6 ft. Check your tape measure to be sure that the hook at the tape end isn't bent and that the rivet slot hasn't become elongated from the hook's repeated slamming into the case—either of which will give inaccurate readings. However, for best accuracy, start measurements from the 1-in. mark, remembering to deduct 1 in. when taking readings.

A 6-ft. folding rule with a sliding-brass extension is best for readings less than 6 ft. because the rigid rule won't flop around as a tape measure will. Unfold the rule to its greatest length between two points and slide the extension the rest of the way. Then hold the extended rule next to the trim stock and mark the cut-line.

A framing square held against a door or window frame quickly tells if it's square or not—a good practice when sizing up a trim job.

A combination square is both a square and a 45° miter gauge, so it can be used to mark square and miter cuts. Because its ruler can be extended from the tool body and fixed with a screw, the square can double as a depth or marking gauge. The combo also has a bubble-level insert for leveling small surfaces such as windowsills.

An adjustable (sliding-T) bevel copies and transfers angles accurately. Because frame corners are rarely 90° exactly, use an adjustable bevel to record the angle needed and then make miter cuts that bisect the actual angle.

Levels, 2 ft., 4 ft., and torpedo, should be part of any finish carpenter's tool chest; use smaller levels in tight spaces.

Buy or borrow a laser level if you need to set cabinets at the same height or align different trim elements in a room.

CUTTING

Which tool you choose depends on how much trim you'll cut. Wear safety glasses and hearing protection when operating any of these tools.

A miter box with a backsaw will suffice if you are casing only a doorway or two. A backsaw has a reinforced back so its blade is rigid; it should have 12 teeth per inch (TPI) or 13 TPI, with minimal offset (splay), so it cuts a thin kerf. Also useful: a *dovetail saw* (a small backsaw with 20+ TPI) and a *slotting saw,* whose kerf is even finer because its teeth are not offset.

Buy a power miter saw if you'll trim at least one room or several casings. Well worth the cost, a power miter adjusts to any angle for *miters* (angles cut across the face of a board, with the blade perpendicular to the stock). A *sliding compound-miter* saw, though more expensive, is more versatile. In one stroke, this saw will cut a miter and a *bevel* (an angle cut across a board, in which the sawblade is tilted)—hence the name compound miter. It will also cut through wider stock such as wide baseboards or crown molding.

A table saw may be the only table tool you need if you are cutting only miter or butt joints. Table-saw guides are generally not as accurate or as easily to re-adjust as the guides on power miter saws, so recutting miter joints will be a bit more work. With a power miter saw, you clamp the stock steady and move the blade, whereas cutting a miter on a table saw requires feeding long pieces of trim at an odd angle to the blade.

Still, table saws be can a good choice for tight budgets because they can also cut stock to length (crosscut) and width (rip cut), prepare edges for joining, and cut dadoes (slots) easily.

A sliding miter trimmer (also known as a Lion Miter-Trimmer™) looks like a horizontal guillotine and bolts to a bench. Because its blade is razor sharp, it slices wood rather than sawing through it. Although it can shave off paper-thin amounts of wood till joints fit exactly, it's been eclipsed by power miter saws for on-site trim installations.

A quality power jigsaw (sometimes called a saber saw) is indispensable for fitting and notching wood, such as fitting thresholds around integral door stops.

Use a coping saw to cut along molding profile lines, ensuring a tight fit where molding meets in inside corners. For more, see p. 414.

A plate joiner (biscuit joiner) is a specialized saw with a small, horizontal circular blade that cuts slots into board edges. After slotting boards to be joined, inject glue and insert a football-shaped wooden wafer, called a *biscuit,* which will swell to create a strong joint with no need for nails or screws.

SHAPING AND SANDING

A block plane and a palm sander are probably all you'll need unless you plan to shape board edges to create complex molding, in which case, get a router.

Block planes are most often used to trim miter joints for a tight fit. If you slightly back-bevel

PRO TIP

For razor-smooth cuts and tight joints, buy an 80-tooth carbide-tipped blade for a 10-in. power miter saw or a 100-tooth blade for a 14-in. saw. If you save such blades for finish work only, they'll last a lifetime.

▌▌▌▌

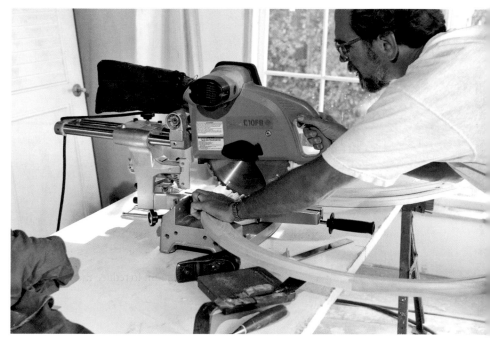

A power miter saw is a must if you're installing a houseful of trim. The 10-in. sliding compound–miter saw shown is big enough to make complicated beveled miter cuts in large crown molding.

Plate joiner (biscuit joiner) and biscuits. The fence on the front of the tool rests on the board being slotted to receive glue and biscuits.

Sanders. From left: palm sander, orbital sander, and belt sander.

upside-down, to the table's underside, so the router bit protrudes above the tabletop. A guide fence enables you to feed stock so that the router bit shapes its edges uniformly—much as a large shaper in a lumber mill would.

Before setting up a router table, however, read up. *Fine Woodworking* magazine's Web site (www.taunton.com/finewoodworking) has hundreds of references on routers and router tables. Above all, heed all safety warnings about routers: Their razor-sharp blades spin 10,000 rpm to 30,000 rpm.

Sanders are needed for a variety of jobs. A *palm sander* (or *block sander*), is useful for shaping contours and sanding in tight places and for light sanding between finish coats. *Orbital sanders* are intermediate in cost, weight, and power. *Random orbital sanders* sand back-and-forth and orbitally (the center of the sander's pad shifts constantly); they cut faster and leave fewer sanding marks. If you buy only one sander, this is the one to get. *Belt sanders* are great for preparing stock and stripping old finishes, but they are so powerful that they tend to obliterate details, so use them sparingly. A belt sander is particularly useful for fitting scribed cabinet panels, as shown in the top right photo on p. 311. Whatever the size of the sander, change the paper often; you shouldn't need to lean on a sander to make it cut.

NAILING AND DRILLING

Because most trim is light, it is usually nailed up with finish nails, which have slimmer shanks and smaller heads than other nails. *Trim-head screws* (shown in the photo on p. 90) are often specified when molding is heavy or complex or when trim pieces will be subject to twisting or flexing, as happens with door frames and stair treads.

A finish hammer has a smaller head than a framing hammer and so is easier to control when trying to avoid denting the trim. Stop when the nail head is almost flush with the wood surface; then use a *nail set* to drive the nail head below the surface. Always set nails before sanding or finishing.

Finish nailers have largely replaced hand nailing, because pressure settings can be adjusted so the nail goes just below the surface; thus you don't have to set the nails. Finish nailers won't dent trim, and you can nail with one hand while holding joints together with the other. Production carpenters favor pneumatic models with air hoses running to a compressor, but cordless models with spare batteries work well, too, for installing small amounts of trim.

Nailers are designed to shoot specific nail *gauges* (thicknesses). Standard finish nailers

miters, the edges of the face will make contact first. Block planes can also shave down a door or window jamb that is too *proud* (too high above the wall plane), thereby allowing the trim to lie flat. A *power plane* (see the photo on p. 167) can do everything a handplane can but more aggressively, so practice on a piece of scrap and check your progress after each pass. *Caution:* Before planing existing trim, first use a magnet to scan the wood for nails or screws, setting them well below the surface before planing.

Rat-tail files and 4-in-1 rasps (see the bottom photo on p. 40) remove small amounts of wood from curved surfaces, so that coped joints fit tightly.

Routers are reasonably priced and invaluable for edge-joining, template cutting, mortising, and flush trimming when used with a table. Router tables vary, but on most you mount the router

Handplaning TIPS

When handplaning, clamp the wood securely, and push the tool in the direction of the grain. While holding the shoe of the tool flat against the edge of the wood, angle the tool's body 20° to the line of the board, so that the plane seen from above looks like half of a *V*. At this angle, the plane blade encounters less resistance and clears shavings better.

shoot 15-gauge nails, whereas *brad nailers* (*pin tackers*) shoot 18-gauge to 20-gauge brads. (The higher the gauge number, the thinner the nail shank and the weaker the nail.) Most homeowners should stick with 15-gauge nailers, but brad nailers are great for tacking up trim: Brad holes are tiny, so you can easily pry off and reposition the trim if needed. Brads are also useful for attaching thin cabinet elements like finish toekicks or cabinet side panels. If you don't have many brads to drive, use a hand *brad pusher*.

Cordless drill drivers are the essential tool in most carpenters' belts. Although they range up to ½-in., 18-volt monsters, unless you've got forearms like Popeye get a ⅜-in., 12-volt cordless drill-driver, which has a keyless chuck for quick changing of bits. A 12-volt model accepts either drill bits or screw tips and has plenty of power for finish carpentry tasks. For production carpenters, the next step up in power (and price) is a 12-volt *impact driver,* which accepts only screw tips; some models can drive more than 250 two-inch screws on a single battery charge. (Whichever tool you buy, get a spare battery for recharging while you work with the other one.) You'll find more on drills, drivers, and bits in Chapter 3.

True Grit: Which Sandpaper for What

COMMON NAME	GRIT NUMBER ("teeth"/sq. in.)	USES
Coarse	40–60	Stripping finishes
Medium	80–120	Sanding down minor bumps
Fine	150–180	Final sanding before finishing
Very fine	220–240	Polish sanding (rarely used)

A SANDPAPER Primer

Sandpaper is coated with tiny abrasive particles (grit), which make tiny cuts in the material being sanded. Sandpaper is rated according to the concentration of grit per square inch. The lower the grit number, the larger, coarser, and more widely spaced the grit particles. Conversely, the higher the grit number, the finer and more closely spaced the grit is.

The abrasive on today's sandpaper will be either aluminum oxide, silicone carbide, ceramic particles, or garnet. Aluminum oxide is the most common abrasive for sanding wood because it's relatively long lasting; whereas silicone carbide, being harder, is better for sanding metal, fiberglass, paint, and such. If you're renting a big drum sander to strip wood floors, its belts will likely be low-grit ceramic sandpaper. Garnet, the softest of the bunch, is often the grit found on fine and very fine sandpapers.

If you're sanding wood, avoid *closed-coat* sandpaper, which will clog quickly because there's no place for wood dust to go. A better choice for woodworkers is *open-coat* sandpaper, in which only one-third to two-thirds of the surface is coated with grit. Closed-coat sandpaper is used to sand metal.

When it comes to finish nails and nailers, smaller is often better. This pin nailer weighs less than 5 lb. and shoots 1-in. to 2½-in. nails.

Interior Trim

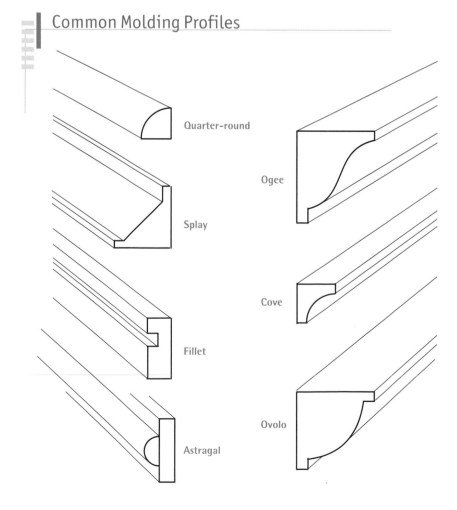

Crown molding

Window casing

Picture molding

Door casing

Baseboard

Chair rail

Common Molding Profiles

Quarter-round

Splay

Fillet

Astragal

Ogee

Cove

Ovolo

Materials

Trim materials include custom-milled hardwoods; softwood boards, molding, and stock caps; MDF (medium-density fiberboard); and polymer moldings that replicate detailed historical styles in lightweight, easy-to-install sections.

CHOOSING TRIM

Because trim is costly (especially hardwood trim), buy it from a local shop that mills its own. That way, you'll be more likely to get trim that is straight, knot-free, and stored in humidity- and temperature-controlled warehouses. If you're trying to match existing trim, a local milling shop is also your best bet. You may pay a setup fee but, all in all, the final cost of a room or two of custom trim may be more reasonable than you think.

Stock trim from a lumberyard or home center is often so warped that you must pick through the racks and eyeball each piece to see if it's straight. Discard any pieces that are obviously heavier than the rest—usually a sign of excessive moisture. (Trim is typically dried to 7 percent to 10 percent moisture content.) Examine each piece for splits and cupping across the width. Also sight down the length of each board for excessive twisting. You can force a twisted piece into position by toenailing and clamping it, but the extra stress is likely to open a joint or cause splitting down the road.

If you want the wood grain to show, be even more picky or pay more for a *select* grade. But if you plan to paint the trim, most surface blemishes can be sanded, filled, or sealed with white pigmented shellac (see Chapter 18) or a primer-sealer to suppress knot or tannin bleed-through. *Finger-jointed* molding, which joins short sections of clear softwood, is another option. Though usually painted to conceal its glued finger joints, finger-jointed molding is also available with a wood veneer, which can be stained and clear finished.

COMBINING STOCK ELEMENTS

Standard molding is often milled from 1-in. stock (actual size, ¾ in.). Thus you'll find it easy to create more complex trim by combining 1-in. boards with stock molding caps. For example, with baseboards, you might start with a 1×8, add a quarter-round shoe at the bottom and a cove-molding cap at the top.

However, if you want to dress up a room with complex crown moldings, consider installing polymer millwork instead—whose monolithic casting greatly simplifies installation. Likewise, though you can build them up by hand, mantels and fireplace surrounds also are sold as pre-

Specialty blocks cover saw cuts, allowing you to join sections of polymer molding without the need for fancy miter cuts.

PRO TIP

Don't bring trim stock to a job site till the drywall joints are dry and the building is heated. Otherwise, trim ends will absorb moisture, swell, and become difficult to install. Never store trim in unheated areas or garages.

IIII

PRO TIP

Most glues will bond MDF, but its edges tend to suck water out of the thinner ones. To minimize this tendency, *double-glue* joints (rub in a thin first layer to seal the edges, then a second to bond the joints) or apply *glue size* to seal the edges. Polyurethane glue is probably the best all-around choice.

IIII

assembled units and as kits requiring minimal assembly.

You can combine stock moldings with relatively inexpensive paneling to make wainscoting and frame-over-panel walls. By cutting a piece of paneling in half, you can use two sections, each 4 ft. by 4 ft., topped with a built-up combination of moldings to form a cap. Paneling with vertical, regularly spaced grooves gives the illusion of individual boards. To change the style and create Craftsman-style wainscoting, you could use ¼-in.-thick redwood plywood with the grain running vertically and install redwood strips every foot or two to create detail and cover the seams between sheets. For more, see "Wainscoting," on p. 430.

WORKING WITH MDF

If you want a cost-effective, easily worked material for plain-profile trim, MDF (medium-density fiberboard) is hard to beat. And you can add visual interest by installing cove, bullnose, quarter-round or other simple molding along MDF's plain edges.

Advantages. MDF cuts and shapes beautifully. For smooth edge cuts, use a 60-tooth 10-in. blade. Because it has no grain, MDF crosscuts and rips equally well, and its edges can be routed as well, although most MDF trim is simply butt joined. (No need for biscuits to hold the joints closed.) Use a pneumatic nailer to attach it; MDF won't split. Sand it with 150-grit sandpaper and prime with an oil-based primer (latex roughens the surface). However, MDF does have quirks you need to work around.

Disadvantages. MDF is heavy (a ¾-in. sheet weighs about 100 lb.); lighter versions cost more. It's dusty to cut and shape. As noted in the tip above right, its edges suck moisture. In fact, MDF can swell from ambient moisture, so seal it immediately after cutting or shaping it. Seal the edges with two coats of shellac-based primer. Then paint all six sides of the panels with an oil-based primer. Perhaps MDF's most annoying quirk is its tendency to mushroom around nail heads: MDF is so dense that it doesn't compress when you nail it; fiber near the nail just bulges up. After setting the nail heads, use a Sandvik *carbide scraper* to scrape down bumps, and then prime it.

Because of MDF's tendency to wick moisture, it's a poor choice for bathroom trim or window installations where condensation is common—no matter how well it's sealed. In those locations, go with wood instead.

POLYMER MOLDINGS

Though many old-house owners prefer wood molding, its supply and quality have been dwindling for decades, leading to a run on third-world forests—now being cut down at an alarming rate. Whereas polymer moldings (especially polyurethane) are available in most traditional architectural styles, from simple colonial to elaborate Victorian. Once installed and painted, polymer moldings are virtually indistinguishable from wood trim. The following sections note some of the unique features.

Stability. Unlike wood, polymer molding won't warp, split, rot, or get eaten by termites. Although it does expand slightly (⅜ in. for a 12-ft. piece) in a heated room, special corner pieces "float" over section ends, allowing them to slide freely as they expand. Polymer molding has no grain, so there is no built-in bias to twist one way or the other; there are no splits, cracks, or knots.

Many traditional cornice-molding types are available in high-density polyurethane. Once filled and painted, they're indistinguishable from wood molding.

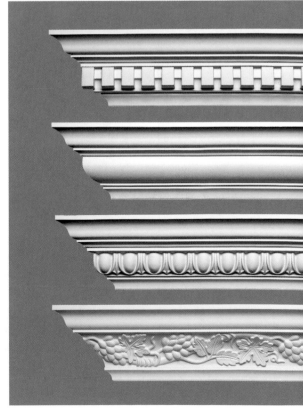

Quick installation. Synthetic moldings are less labor intensive. Whereas complex wood moldings are built up piece by piece and their joints painstakingly matched, synthetics come out of the box ready to install. Most polymer moldings are glued up with a compatible adhesive caulk, such as polyurethane or latex acrylic, and tacked up with finish nails or trim-head screws, which are needed for support only till the glue sets. Pieces are so light, in fact, that you can install them single-handedly.

Easy working and finishing. Most polymers can be trimmed like soft pine, using a 12-TPI (teeth per inch) to 13-TPI saw in a miter box. There's no need for fancy joinery because most systems have corner pieces that cover joints. Touch up holes with plastic wood filler, and caulk field joints on long runs. You also may need a bead of caulk where straight lengths of molding meet existing surfaces that are irregular.

Polymer molding is typically primed white in the factory and could be installed as is, but most homeowners paint it. You paint smooth-surfaced urethanes just like standard wood trim. Some products can be stained, but that gets into the iffy territory of making plastic look like wood.

Basic Skills

Using quality tools and materials matters but not as much as the skill and judgment of the renovator. This section of tips will help hone your skills in measuring, cutting, and attaching trim.

When mitering or coping corner joints, make sure a joint fits well before cutting the other end of the trim to final length. Whenever possible, mark the trim in place—that's easier and more accurate than transferring tape-measure readings.

Accurate measurements are crucial because trim is pricey, and even small discrepancies will stand out. In the following paragraphs you'll find a few new twists on the old chestnut "Measure twice and cut once."

Use a sharp point to mark stock. A stubby lumberyard pencil is fine for marking framing lumber. But because the margin of error is small on trim, use a sharp pencil to mark precisely. A utility knife leaves an even thinner line, though it's more difficult to see.

Mark trim in place, if possible. It's almost always more accurate than taking a tape reading and transferring it to stock, especially if your memory's bad.

Change directions. If you normally measure left to right, double-check your figures by changing direction and measuring right to left.

Use templates instead of remeasuring. When you need to cut many pieces the same length, carefully cut one, check it in position to make sure it's accurate, and use that piece to mark the cutline on others. You can also clamp a template to a bench or saw table, to act as a stop block. As you cut successive pieces, simply butt a square-cut end against the block, and the blade will cut each in exactly the same place.

When in doubt, go long. If you're not quite sure of the exact measurement and don't want to climb back up the ladder to recheck, cut the piece a little long. You can always make a long board shorter, but reversing the process is quite a trick.

***X* marks the scrap.** As you mark cut-lines, pencil a prominent *X* on the scrap ends of boards. This habit will sooner or later help you avoid wasting trim because you mistook the scrap end for the measured end.

GENERAL CUTTING

Tight trim joints require accurate layouts, sharp saws, and consistent methods.

Recuts are a fact of life. If you're filling and painting trim, slight gaps are acceptable. But if you're using a clear finish, joints must be tight. Before you start cutting trim, always check the accuracy of power-saw miter-stop settings by cutting a few joints from scrap. Then cut stock a hair long so that you can recut joints till they're right.

Cut lines consistently. It doesn't matter whether your sawblade cuts through the middle of a cut line or just past it. What matters is that your method is consistent. For example, moving the width of a saw kerf to one side of the line or the other can make the difference between tight and open joints. Some pros prefer to just "kiss" the inside of the cut-line with the saw kerf so that the line stays on the board.

Keep tools sharp. This applies to saws, chisels, planes, and utility knifes. Whenever a blade becomes fouled with resin or glue, wipe it clean immediately with solvent. A sharp tool is easier to push and thus less likely to move the stock you're cutting. Likewise, a clean power-saw blade is less likely to bind or scorch wood.

Handsaws usually cut on the push stroke. Start handsaw cuts with gentle pull strokes, but once the kerf is established along the cut-line, emphasize push strokes. (Western saw teeth are set so that they cut more on the push stroke, whereas Japanese saws cut more on the pull stroke.) As you continue the cut, keep your elbow behind the saw, which will help you push the saw straight and follow the cut-line.

Clamp that stock. If your hands are big enough, it's possible to hold stock against a miter-saw fence with one hand and operate the saw with the other, but it's far easier—and safer—to clamp the stock, using a *spring clamp* or a *quick-release clamp* (see the bottom photo on p. 42). Newer models of compound-miter saws have flip-up stops that hold molding against the fence. Finally,

Mitered casing joints look dressy and conceal the end grain of intersecting pieces.

use an *outfeed roller* or a sawhorse to support the far end of long pieces so they don't bow or flap as you try to cut them.

CUTTING MITER JOINTS

A miter splits a 90° corner in half, with a 45° cut on each board. With the sawblade set perpendicular to the stock (0° bevel), cut a 45° angle across the face of the trim. When the cut edges are closed together, the boards should form a right angle. Of course, if door or window frames aren't square, corners may be 89° or 91°, requiring that each miter be slightly more or less than 45°, though equal. That is, miter joints should bisect whatever angle is there.

If you'll be painting the joints and the trim stock is relatively narrow (3 in. wide), you can fudge the joints and fill any gaps with spackling. But if you're installing stain-grade molding, espe-

Back-Cutting Trim

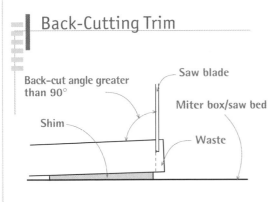

Back-cut angle greater than 90°
Saw blade
Shim
Miter box/saw bed
Waste

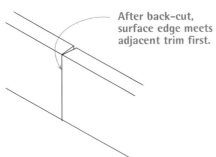

After back-cut, surface edge meets adjacent trim first.

By raising the board's end and keeping the sawblade plumb, you create a back-cut joint whose surface edges can easily be shaved to create tight joints.

Back-Cutting Miters

Ideally, miter cuts will meet perfectly, creating a tight joint. But *back-cutting* (also called undercutting) can improve the odds that joints will be tight even if corners aren't perfectly square and frame jambs aren't flush to the surrounding walls. In other words, the front faces of back-cut boards make contact before the backs, so the front edges can be finely shaved to fit. It's far less work to shave the leading edge of a back-cut board with a block plane than it is to recut the joint.

The easiest way to back-cut trim is to shim under it slightly in the miter box or on the saw bed, as shown in the drawings at left. The sawblade is still set at 90 degrees (0 degree bevel), but the shimmed boards receive a slight bevel because they aren't lying flat. Even a ¹⁄₁₆-in.-thick sliver under the board is enough to give you a decent back cut.

Fussing over a miter joint is probably not worthwhile if you plan to paint the trim because slight gaps can be filled with wood filler. But open joints are difficult to disguise when wood is to be stained and almost impossible when it is clear sealed.

Glued biscuit joints will keep butt joints or miter joints from spreading due to seasonal expansion and contraction. Here, a biscuit joins a mitered window-stool return. Biscuits can also join straight runs of crown molding or baseboard when a wall is too long for a single board.

cially if it's 5 in. or 6 in. wide, faking a miter joint will look terrible. So if a frame is out of square, take the time to cut and recut joints as necessary so that they bisect the frame's angle.

There are two good reasons to use miters. First, mitering aligns the profiles of moldings so that bead lines and other details join neatly along the joint and sweep uninterrupted around the corner. Second, although flat trim allows you to butt or miter joints at corners, with butt joints you would see the rough end grain of one of the adjoining boards. Even if you sand down the roughness, end grain soaks up extra paint or stain and so often looks noticeably different from adjacent surfaces.

SPLICING TRIM

When a wall is too long for a single piece of trim, you can splice pieces by beveling their ends at a 60° angle and overlapping them (called a *scarf joint*), or by butt joining them and using a biscuit to hold the joint together. If boards shrink, gaps will be less noticeable in a scarf joint because you'll see wood, rather than space, as the overlap separates. In general, scarf joints are better suited to flat stock, whereas shaped molding will display a shorter joint line if butted together. (Viewed head-on, the joint is a thin, straight line.)

Position splices over stud centers so you can nail board ends securely to prevent cupping. Where that's not possible, say, where a baseboard butts to door casing, nail the bottom of the baseboard to the wall sole plate, and angle-nail the top of the baseboard to the edge of the casing. Predrill the trim or snip the nail points to minimize splits.

COPING A JOINT

All wood trim shrinks somewhat. Where beveled boards overlap, gaps aren't as noticeable, but shrinkage on some joints—mitered inside corners, in particular—are glaringly obvious because you can see right into the joint. For this reason, carpenters cope such joints so that their meshing profiles disguise shrinkage. Basically, a coped joint is a butt joint, with the end of one board

Two Ways to Splice Trim

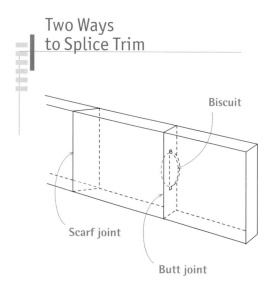

Biscuit

Scarf joint

Butt joint

Coping a Joint

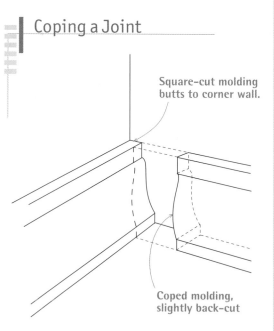

Square-cut molding butts to corner wall.

Coped molding, slightly back-cut

A coped joint is first mitered, then back-cut along the profile left by the miter so that the leading edge of the trim hits the adjacent trim first. That thinner, leading edge can be easily shaved to fit tightly.

carefully cut to fit the profile of the molding it butts against.

Cut the first piece of trim square, butt that end right into the adjacent wall, and tack-nail it up. Coping the second piece of trim is a two-step operation. First cut the end with a 45° miter, as if you were making an inside miter joint. Use a pencil to darken the profile of the edge. Clamp the trim face up. Then, using a coping saw, carefully cut along the profile created by the miter—while slightly back-cutting it. If precisely cut, this coped end will mesh perfectly with the profile of the first piece. If you're not happy with the fit, shave it with a utility knife or recut it from scratch.

Coping requires ingenuity. If the top of the trim curves like quarter-round molding, back-cutting would create a little spur that will probably break off before you can finish the cut, so don't back-cut it. Leave the rounded top as a 45° miter and chisel a corresponding 45° miter into the top of the piece of molding that you're coping to.

GLUING AND ATTACHING TRIM

To increase holding power and keep joints closed, apply yellow carpenter's glue to mating edges after the casing has been dry-fit and is ready to install. If you allow the glue to *tack* (set) slightly, the casing ends will slide around less as you nail

To cope a joint, first use a table saw or a miter saw to cut the trim at a 45° bevel. Use a power saw to cut the straight part of the trim profile, then use a coping saw to back-cut along the shaped part, as shown.

The Case for *Not* Leveling Trim

The older a house, the less likely its floors and ceilings will be level. So don't make yourself crazy trying to level baseboards and crown molding: You won't succeed, and trim that's level next to a surface that isn't will only emphasize the discrepancy. Interior trim, like politics, is an art of compromise. Trim edges should be roughly parallel to floors and ceilings. As master carpenter Joseph Beals puts it, "Baseboard is effectively floor trim, and the floor plane is the critical reference, level or not."

Midwall elements such as chair rails, picture rails, and wainscoting call for yet more fudging. Ideally, chair rails should be level and wainscoting stiles (vertical pieces) should be plumb, but those ideals may clash with existing trim that's neither. In that case, split the difference: Tack up a length of trim that's level. Then raise or lower one end till your eye accepts the compromise.

Trim can also help give the illusion of a level ceiling—helpful, when upper kitchen cabinets must be set level even if the ceiling isn't. So after leveling and securing upper cabinets, install a strip of molding to cover the gap above. (You may need to rip it down at an angle.) If you look for it, you'll see the uneven strip of molding between the cabinets and the ceiling. But if the cover trim matches the cabinet finish, chances are nobody else will notice the difference.

Finish Carpentry Fasteners

FASTENER	USES	COMMENTS
20-gauge brad	Attach small molding returns.	Glue returns first.
18-gauge brad	Tack-nail trim while adjusting; attach cabinet toekicks and side panels.	Tiny brad holes easily filled; easy to pry off tacked trim
4d (1½-in.) finish nail	Attach inside edge of casing to rough jambs (jambs of rough opening).	Snip nail point if worried about splitting casing.
6d (2-in.) finish nail	Attach outside edge of ½-in.-thick casing (through ½-in. drywall) to rough jambs.	Nail should sink at least ½ in. into framing.
8d (2½-in.) finish nail	Attach outside edge of ¾-in.-thick casing (through drywall) to rough jambs; attach baseboard; attach crown molding.	Place nails a minimum of ⅜ in. from edge; snip nail points to minimize splits.
2½-in. to 3-in. finish-head screw	Secure window- or door-frame jambs to rough openings.	Frame jambs twist or flex as doors and windows are operated, so use pairs of screws at each point.

Common Interior Glues

COMMON, CHEMICAL NAME(S)	PROS	CONS	BRANDS
White carpenter's, Polyvinyl acetate	Moderate strength; inexpensive	Runny; poor initial tack; clogs sandpaper	Elmer's® Glue-All®
Yellow carpenter's, polyvinyl acetate	Strong; good initial tack; sands well		Titebond® Original
Polyurethane	Bonds to most materials; sands well; takes stain; fills gaps; water resistant	Glue expansion can spread joints not tightly clamped; slow tacking time; stains skin	Gorilla Glue®; Titebond
Cyanocrylate	Instant bond; great for nonstructural joints; bonds many materials	Expensive; can't adjust pieces once placed, skin/eye hazards	Super Glue™; Hot Flash; Turbo Flash
Hot glue	Quick-tack glue to create thin plywood templates	Limited strength, but okay for temporary positioning; low-stress joints	Hotstik; Bostick HotMelt™
Contact cement	Instant bond; resists heat and water; best for attaching plastic laminate and veneers	Can't adjust once sheet and substrate make contact; volatile solvent; needs good ventilation	DAP® Weldwood™; 3M® Fastbond®

* Several Web sites offer interactive product selectors. Specify how and where you'll use the adhesive, and the selector will choose a product (www.titebond.com is particularly good).

Double-gluing creates strong joints. First use your finger to rub in a little glue to seal the end grain. When that's tacky, apply a second layer of glue to bond the trim pieces.

the trim. But splicing joints with biscuits is by far the better way to keep them from spreading. Use a biscuit joiner to cut slots into mating edges; then inject glue into the slots and spread it evenly on the casing ends. Place biscuits in the slots and reassemble the joints, drawing the joints tight with a single 4d or 6d finish nail angled into butt joints or end-nailed through miter joints. Use a damp cloth to wipe off excess glue.

Drive nails into framing whenever possible. If framing members are spaced 16 in. on center, nail trim to every stud or ceiling joist it crosses. Where trim runs parallel with the framing, as with side casing, nail the trim at the ends and roughly every 16 in. *in the field*. Equally important is using the right nail or screw to avoid splitting the wood trim. (The table on p. 415 recommends sizes for most trim applications.)

To attach narrow molding such as quarter-round, use a single row of finish nails. On wider molding, use two nails to prevent cupping: Set the nails at least ½ in. from the edge, and use a square to line up nail pairs.

It's usually not necessary to predrill softwood trim to prevent splits. If you use a pneumatic nailer, do not nail too close to the edge, and don't use to too big a nail. However, when nailing hard-

Door and Window Casings

MITERED

1/4-in. reveals (setbacks) from jamb edges

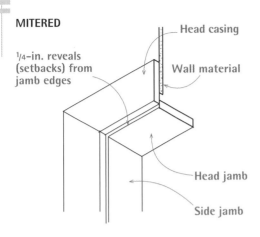

Head casing

Wall material

Head jamb

Side jamb

SQUARE-CUT OR BUTT

Thicker head casing projects slightly beyond side casing.

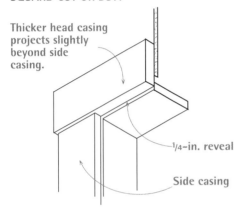

1/4-in. reveal

Side casing

CORNER-BLOCK

Thicker block extends beyond head and side casing.

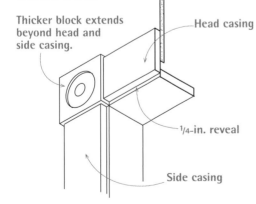

Head casing

1/4-in. reveal

Side casing

wood trim or nailing the ends of boards, predrilling is smart. Use a drill bit whose shank is thinner than the nail's. Alternatively, you can minimize splits by using nippers to snip off the nail points, as shown in the photo at right. It's a bit counterintuitive, but it works.

Before painting, caulk all gaps between the casing and the wall.

Casing a Door

Before casing doors and windows, review "Assessing and Prepping the Opening," on p. 92, particularly the remarks on *margining*, centering jambs in relation to a wall's thickness. Then survey the door and window frames to be cased; use a 4-ft. level and a square to see if the frame jambs are plumb, margined, and square.

CASING ELEMENTS

Door casing is trim that covers the gaps around a door frame. It thus goes on after a door has been hung. Most often casing consists of three pieces: two *side casings* (leg casings), which cover frame jambs, and one piece of *head casing*, which goes over the frame head. Six pieces, if you count both sides of a doorway.

There are three common casing joints: *mitered*, preferred for trim that is molded (shaped) because it enables you to match mold-

Use an end cutter (or nipper) to snip nail points. Nails with blunt points are less likely to split trim because they crush the wood rather than wedge it apart, as triangular points do.

Finishing Tips

Details on stripping trim, prep work, stains, clear finishes, and paints are given in Chapter 18. Here's a handful of additional tips:

▶ Most trim stock comes smooth enough to paint or stain. If you find rough spots, sand them with 120-grit to 180-grit sandpaper before finishing. If molding has only a few rough spots, wrap sandpaper around a block for flat trim or use a sanding sponge for shaped stock. Use a palm sander or an orbital sander on flat trim with a lot of rough spots.

▶ If you apply a first coat of finish or paint to the trim before installing it, you won't need to worry about getting finish on painted walls and ceilings. Cut and attach the trim, sand and fill joints as needed, sink nail heads, fill holes with crayon putty, and lightly final sand. Apply the final coat in place, using long brushstrokes to achieve a smooth finish.

▶ After cutting prefinished trim, wipe sawblades with solvent to clean them.

▶ If you decide to finish the trim in place, tape 12-in.-wide masking paper to the area around the trim. When the finish is dry, peel off the masking paper.

▶ Use wax crayon putty to fill holes in prefinished trim. Avoid wood fillers because their solvent can partially dissolve the finish. However, if the wood is unfinished, apply filler before staining it. Filler can be stained and sanded, but be sure to test the colors on scrap blocks first.

▶ Use the smallest possible brads or nails to attach the trim, and you'll have less to fill. On dark wood, brad holes are almost invisible.

ing profiles as they converge at a corner; *square cut*, made with basic butt joints; and *corner block*, a variation of square cut with discrete blocks at the top corners and sometimes bottom corners as well. (Bottom corner blocks are also called *plinths*. Top corner blocks are called *caps*.)

PREPPING THE FRAME

Frame edges should extend no more than ⅟₁₆ in. beyond finish surfaces. If they protrude more, sink any nails, and then plane down the frame. If frame edges are level or, say, ⅟₁₆ in. below the wall surfaces, leave them alone. If the edges are sunk more than that, build them up with shim strips ripped from stock of the same thickness. Scrape the old frame so that it's flat, glue on the strips, tack with brads if you like, and wipe up the excess glue at once. Also survey the walls around the frame, scraping down globs of joint compound or hammering down (compressing) high drywall spots that would make the trim cockeyed.

MARKING A REVEAL

Boards are rarely perfectly straight, and frame jambs and casing stock are no exception. So instead of trying to nail board edges flush, set the inside edge of casings back ¼ in. from the frame edges. This setback is called a *reveal:* It looks good and will spare you a lot of frustration. Use the rule of your combination square as a depth gauge. Set the rule to ¼ in., and slide along the edge of the frame, making pencil marks as you go. Where head reveals intersect with side reveals, mark the corners carefully.

INSTALLING SQUARE-CUT DOOR CASING

Few frames are perfectly square, so use a framing square to survey the corners. Note whether a corner is greater or less than 90°, and vary your cuts accordingly when you fine-tune the corner joints. Note, too, whether the floor is level, because side casing usually rests on the floor.

First, rough cut the casing. To determine the length(s) of side casings, measure down from the reveal line on the head frame to the finish floor. (If finish floors aren't installed yet, measure down to a scrap of flooring.) Cut the side casings about ½ in. long so you can fine-tune the joints; then tack the casings to the reveal lines on the side frames. (Use 18-gauge or 20-gauge brads.) Next measure from the outer edges of the side casings to determine the length of the head casing. If the ends of the head casing will be flush to the edges of the side casing, add only ½ in. to the head-casing measurement for adjustments. But if the head casing will overhang the side casing

slightly—a ¼-in. overhang is common if head casing is thicker than side casing—add overhangs to your head-casing measurement. Cut the head casing, place it atop the side casings, and tack it up.

Fine-tuning casing joints. Because you cut the side casings ½ in. long, the head casing will be that much higher than the head reveal line. But

Use a scraper with replaceable carbide blades to shave drywall high spots and hardened joint compound. Use a utility knife to cut back shims still protruding around frames.

To repair dings from doors or trim, hold a hot damp cloth over the spot, then apply a steam iron to the cloth till the wood swells slightly. Lightly sand the raised area until it's level. Then use a small artist's brush to apply thinned finish to already finished surfaces.

Square-cut casing needn't be plain. Here, square door casing is spiced up with a ¼-in.-thick beaded strip between the head and side casing and a beveled cap molding.

Using a combination square as a marking gauge, make light pencil marks on the jamb edges to indicate casing reveal (offset) lines. By offsetting casing and jamb edges, you avoid the frustrating and usually futile task of trying to keep the edges flush.

INSTALLING SQUARE-CUT DOOR CASING

Square-cut head casing can easily span ganged windows or, as shown, a double door with windows on both sides. Here, a carpenter tacked up the door side casings before eyeballing the head casing to be sure the joints were flush.

Use a pin-tacker (brad nailer) to tack the head casing till you're sure all joints are tight. When that's done, secure the casing with 6d finish nails.

Slightly back-cut the side casings to ensure a tight fit to the underside of the head casing.

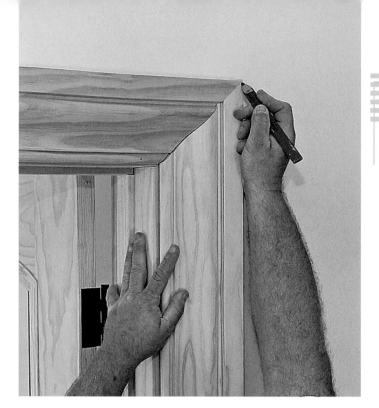

Recutting miters is a normal part of installing casing. To adjust for a slight gap at the bottom of the joint, this carpenter is marking the amount he needs to remove from the top of the side casing.

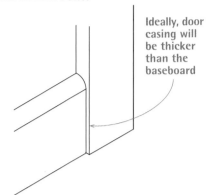

SIMPLE BUTT JOINT

Ideally, door casing will be thicker than the baseboard

PLINTH-BLOCK JOINT

Plinth block is thicker than door casing or baseboard.

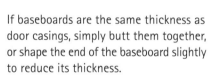

If baseboards are the same thickness as door casings, simply butt them together, or shape the end of the baseboard slightly to reduce its thickness.

with all casing elements in place, you can see if the head casing butts squarely to the side casings, or if they need to be angle trimmed slightly to make a tight fit. Use a utility knife to mark where the head reveal line hits each side casing, and then remove the side casings and recut them through those knife marks. Retack the side casings to the frame; then reposition the head casing so it sits atop the newly cut side casings. Finally, use a utility knife to indicate final cuts on both ends of the head casing, either flush to the side casing or overhanging slightly, as just discussed.

Gluing joints. Butt joints are particularly prone to spreading, so remove the tacked-up casing, and splice the joints with biscuits, as described earlier in this chapter. Spread glue on all joint surfaces, and nail up the side casing. (Insert biscuits, if used.) Draw the head casing tight to the side casing by angle-nailing a single 4d finish nail at each end. To avoid splits, predrill the two nail holes or snip the nails' points. Then remove excess glue with a damp cloth.

INSTALLING MITERED DOOR CASING

Before installing the casing, first use a framing square to see if the doorway corners are square. If they aren't, use an adjustable bevel to record the angles and a protractor to help bisect them. Then cut the miter joints out of scrap casing till their angles exactly match the door frame's. You

can install mitered casing by first cutting the side casing and then the head casing, as you would with square-cut casing. But some carpenters maintain that the best way to match mitered profiles is to work around the opening. That is, start with one side casing, cut the head casing ends exactly, and finish with the second side casing.

Mark the first piece of the side casing, and then cut it. After marking a ¼-in. reveal around the frame, align a piece of casing stock to a reveal line on a side frame. Where head and jamb reveals intersect in the corner, make a mark on the casing, using a utility knife. (Or make the utility-knife mark ¼ in. higher if you're not confident you can cut the correct angle on the first try.) Miter-cut the top of the side casing so it matches the bisecting angle you worked out earlier on the scrap. Square-cut the bottom of the casing, and tack it to the frame using 18-gauge or 20-gauge brads.

Cut one end of the head casing in the same bisecting angle, leaving the other end long for the time being. Fit the mitered casing ends together, and align the bottom edge of the head casing to the head reveal line. Then, using a utility knife, mark the head casing where side and head reveals intersect in the second corner. You'll cut through that mark, using the bisecting angle for the second corner (which may be different from the first corners). Again, there's no shame in recutting, so you may want that utility-knife mark to be ¼ in. proud. When its miter is correct, tack up the head casing, and then line up the inside edge of the second side casing to the side reveal line. Use a utility knife to locate its cutline. Back-cutting miters slightly can make fitting them easier.

Whether you simply glue mitered joints or biscuit join them, remove all three pieces of casing before securely nailing them. If biscuit joining, after slotting each piece, reinstall the leg jambs, apply glue and biscuits, and fit the head casing down onto the biscuits. You can use miter clamps or 18-gauge brads to draw the joint together till the glue dries. Be sure to wipe up the excess glue immediately.

Casing a Window

The casing of windows is essentially the same as the casing of doors, so review earlier sections about prepping frames and installing casing. The main difference is that the side casing of windows stands on a *window stool*, rather than on the floor. Consequently, most of this section

Corner-Block Casing

Casings with corner blocks are a variation of square-cut casing in which you have seven pieces of trim—two plinth (base) blocks, two cap blocks, two pieces of side casing, and one head casing—to measure, cut, and fit.

Start by installing the plinth blocks, which are thicker and wider than the side and head casing. Plinths and cap blocks may line up to reveal lines on door frames, or they may line up with the inside frame edges; be sure to match the detailing of the existing casing.

Tack up plinths, using 18-gauge brads. Then measure from the reveal line on the head frame to the top of the plinth blocks to determine the length of side casings. Tack up the side casings, aligning them to the reveal lines on the side frames. Depending on the detailing of the cap blocks, you may need to recut the tops of side casings. Recut the side casing as needed; then tack up the cap blocks and place a spirit level atop them to see if their top edges align and if they're level.

Finally, measure between the cap blocks to determine the length of the head casing. (Use a rigid folding rule with a slide-out extension for this task.) If the door frame is slightly out of square, cut the head casing ¹⁄₁₆ in. to ⅛ in. long, and back-cut both ends so you can shave them to fit. Once the tack-fit is tight, carefully pry off the tacked up pieces, cut biscuit slots, glue, insert biscuits, reassemble the pieces, and finish-nail the assembly. Glue all joints even if you don't use biscuits.

Window Trim

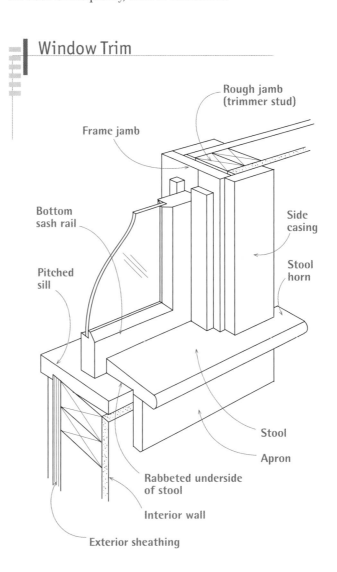

Rough jamb (trimmer stud)

Frame jamb

Bottom sash rail

Side casing

Stool horn

Pitched sill

Stool

Apron

Rabbeted underside of stool

Interior wall

Exterior sheathing

Use 6d or 8d finish nails to attach casing to rough jambs, 4d finish nails to attach the inside edge of casing to frame jambs, and 4d nails to tie the stool to the apron edge.

describes measuring and cutting the stool, which covers the inside of a windowsill, and the *apron* beneath the stool. Sills and stools vary, as described in "Windowsills, Stools, and Aprons," on the facing page. The following text focuses on installing replacement stools appropriate to older windows.

MARKING THE WINDOW STOOL

Before you start, decide how far the stool "horns" will extend beyond the side casings and how far the interior edge of the stool will protrude into the room. Typically, horns extend ¾ in. beyond 3½-in.-wide side casings, but use the existing casings as your guide.

Nail window casing to frame jambs and to the rough opening, spacing finish nails every 16 in. Use a combination square to line up each pair of nails.

To determine the overall length of the stool, mark ¼-in. reveals along both sides of the frame jambs. Then measure out from those reveals the width of side casings plus the amount that the stool horns will extend beyond that casing. Make light pencil marks on the drywall or plaster. Rough-cut a piece of stool stock slightly longer than the distance between the outermost pencil marks.

Next, hold the stool stock against the inside edge of the windowsill, centered left to right in the window opening. Using a combination square, transfer the width of the window frame, from the inside of one jamb to the other, to the stool stock. Use a jigsaw to cut along both squared lines, stopping when the sawblade reaches the square shoulder in the underside of the stool. So you'll know when you've reached that shoulder, lightly pencil the width of the shoulder onto the top of the stool, using a combination square as a marking gauge. Next, cut in from each end of the stock to create the stool horns. Carefully guide your saw along the shoulder lines, being careful to stay on the waste side of the line. Clean up cut-lines with a chisel, if needed.

The cutout section of the stool should now fit tightly between the frame jambs. Now, rip down the rabbeted edge of the stool so that it will be snug against the window sash, and the stool horns will be flush to the wall (and jamb edges). Push the stool in till it touches the bottom of the sash, and then pull the stool back ⅟₁₆ in. from the sash to allow for the thickness of paint to come. Finally, measure the distance between the stool horns and the wall, which is the amount to reduce the width of the stool, along the rabbeted edge.

Use a table saw to rip down the width of the stool, then test-fit it again. If it is parallel to (but ⅟₁₆ in. back from) the sash rail, you are ready to cut each horn to its final length. If your stool is flat stock, that's the last step. But if the stool is molded (has a shaped profile), miter returns to hide the end grain of the horns, as shown in the photo on p. 414.

ATTACHING THE STOOL AND APRON

Lightly sand and prime the stool, including its underside and ends to prevent its absorbing moisture from condensation or driving rains. After the paint is thoroughly dry, apply water-proof glue to the underside of the stool, level it, and nail it to the rough sill using two or three 6d galvanized finish nails. Try not to lean on the only partially supported stool till it's nailed to the top of the apron, which will steady the stool.

Next cut the apron, which is generally the same casing used for side and head casing, although here its thicker edge is butted to the underside of the stool. The apron should be as long as the head casing so that it lines up visually with the outside edges of the side casing. If the apron is molded, cope each end to accentuate its profile or miter-cut it and glue on a return. If you'll be painting the casing, caulk along the underside of the stool to prevent drafts. Then butt the apron to the underside of the stool. Nail up the apron, driving 6d finish nails into the rough opening beneath the sill. Finally, nail the

INSTALLING A WINDOW STOOL AND APRON

Start casing a window by installing its stool. Use a combination-square level or a torpedo level to level it, then 8d finish nails to secure it to the rough sill underneath. However, the stool won't be stable till it is also nailed and glued to an apron under its inside edge.

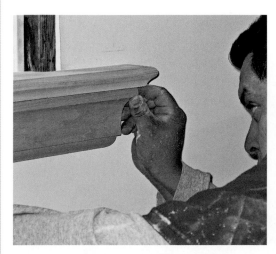

Typically, the apron is as wide as the casing above the window stool; the stool horns project ¾ in. beyond both.

Cutting a Window Stool

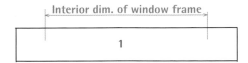

TOP VIEW

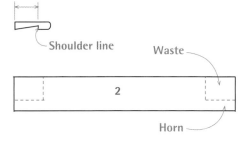

Interior dim. of window frame

1

SIDE VIEW

Shoulder line

1. After transferring the interior dimensions of the window frame to the stool stock, cut across the stock till the sawblade reaches the stool shoulder.

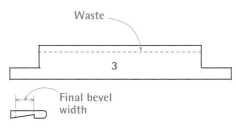

Waste

2

Horn

2. Following the shoulder line, cut in from the ends of the stock to create horns.

Waste

3

Final bevel width

3. Rip down the stock so its beveled portion butts the inner window sash, less ¹⁄₁₆ in.

Waste

4

4. Trim the horns of the stool so they protrude ¾ in. beyond the side casings.

Windowsills, STOOLS, AND APRONS

Windowsills have both an inner and outer life—one half is interior, and the other is exterior. It makes sense to pitch the outer portion of a sill so it can shed water. But in the old days, windowsills were pitched all the way, front to back, which created a uselessly pitched interior section that had to be covered with a stool piece, as shown in "Window Trim," on p. 421. To fit a pitched sill, usually set at 14° to 20°, the underside of a stool must be partially rabbeted at the same angle, so that when the stool is nailed on top of the sill, the top face of the stool will be level. It's an archaic design but, surprisingly, it survives in some new window designs.

Many modern windows, however, have a sill whose interior portion is flat on top and flush to the insides of the window frame. Consequently, there's no need for a stool or an apron. Such windows may be "picture framed." That is, the casing can be mitered around all four sides of the window frame.

If your windows have traditional stools and aprons, the trickiest part of casing the windows will be fitting the stools. Typically, a stool's outer edge *almost* abuts the inside of the lower window sash (allow a ¹⁄₁₆-in. space for the thickness of paint), and its interior edge overhangs the apron beneath it. And note that the stool's "horns" extend ¾ in. to 1¹⁄₂ in. beyond the width of the side casings. You can still buy replacement stools for window renovations in older houses.

1. After installing stop-strips inside the window frame and scribing reveal lines on all three jamb edges, cut and tack up the first piece of jamb casing, in this case, a miter cut.

2. Although many carpenters install both jamb casings before measuring the head casing, this carpenter chose to dry-fit the second jamb and head as a pair, so he could adjust the miter joint in place. An unglued biscuit held the pieces of casing together as he finessed the joint.

3. Set nails, fill holes, and touch-up sand all surfaces before finishing the wood casing. Generally, there won't be many nails to set if you've used a pneumatic nailer.

stool to the top of apron, using three or four 6d galvanized finish nails. Set and fill those nails.

Install the side and head casing in the same order that you would case a door: side casing, head casing, and second side casing. The main difference is that window side casing sits on the stool horns. If you're casing side-by-side windows with flat trim, you can run a single piece of head casing over both windows and butt the middle and side casings to the underside of the head casing, as shown, in in the top photo on p. 419.

Baseboard and Crown Molding

As noted in "The Case for *Not* Leveling Trim," on p. 415, baseboard and crown molding should follow floors and ceilings, rather than level lines projected across the walls. If floors and ceilings are level, fine. Otherwise, leveled trim next to out-of-level surfaces is glaringly obvious.

INSTALLING BASEBOARDS

Install the finish floors first, with a slight gap, typically ½ in., between the wood flooring and the walls so that wood strips or planks can expand and contract seasonally. Baseboards thus cover that gap along the base of the walls. You should also install door casing before baseboards, so that baseboards can butt to side casing or plinth blocks. Back-cutting the baseboard slightly yields a tight butt joint against plinth blocks or casing, even if the trim boards are not perfectly square to each other.

Locating studs beforehand will make installation easier. If walls have been newly drywalled, look along the base of the walls for screws or nails where panels are secured to stud centers. Otherwise, rap the base of walls with your knuckle till you think you've found a stud. Then drive in a 6d finish nail to locate the stud exactly. Studfinders work, but they are less reliable with plaster walls, whose lath nails meander all over the place.

Scribe the bottom of baseboards to follow the contour of the floor, especially if the floors are irregular. But first, shim the baseboard(s) up about 1 in. above the floor, butt one end of the board to a corner or a door casing, and tack the baseboard to a stud or two to keep it upright. Then run the scribe or compass along the bottom to transfer the floor contour to the baseboard. Cut the scribed line with a fairly rigid jigsaw blade that can cut with the grain; a Bosch T1001D™, with 6 TPI works like a charm.

Baseboard joinery employs basic techniques described earlier. Miter outside corners, cope inside ones, and glue all joints before nailing

Baseboard Strategies

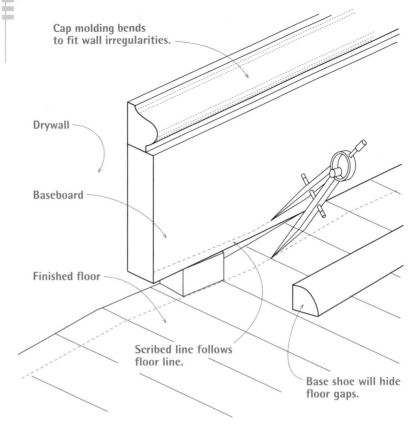

Cap molding bends to fit wall irregularities.

Drywall

Baseboard

Finished floor

Scribed line follows floor line.

Base shoe will hide floor gaps.

If you can't scribe and cut the bottom of the baseboard, use base shoe to cover gaps.

Arched Window Casing

There's something inspiring about arched windows. Restoration carpenter Jim Spaulding (shown on the following pages) offers this advice: "Order all the casing from the same shop so that the same knives cut the arches and the legs (side casing). That way, all the profiles will sweep continuously around the frame." Arched casings are different from casings for other windows, and so installing them takes some flexibility. After setting the stool and apron, for example, you install its head casing next. Side casings are last.

Although modern window makers offer a limited selection of prefab casing for the arched windows they sell, plan on custom-ordering casing for older arched windows. Correctly determining the radius of the arch is challenging: One method is to tack ⅛-in.-thick plywood (also called *doorskin*) to the inside edge of the arched frame head—run it about 1 ft. below the "spring line" of the arch, where the frame becomes straight. Go outside and trace the arch, tracing lightly so you don't bow the plywood. Make templates for each arched window, and take them to a local shop that mills trim.

Note: The inside edge of arched casing must be revealed (set back) from the arch you traced of the frame's inside edge.

Arched windows require complex framing around the arch so you have something solid to nail finish walls and casing to.

1. After scribing a reveal line along the edge of the arched head jamb, tack a finish nail at the apex of the line, and hang (balance) the arched head casing from it. Then level across the "spring lines" of the casing—the points at which the casing springs into its curve.

2. After cutting the arched casing at its spring lines, align the inner edge of the arched casing to the reveal line.

4. Work around the window, nailing the casing every 16 in. The thickness of the casing determines the nail size. In this case, the carpenter used 1-in. brads to nail the inside edge of casing to the frame edges, and 6d finish nails along the outside.

3. Next, install the straight side casing, cutting it a little long on the bottom and then trimming as needed till the casing fits tightly between the arched head casing and the window stool. After dry-fitting the side casing, apply glue, and tack it up.

5. If the casing is not wide or thick enough for biscuit joinery, angle 6d finish nails to draw the joint together. To avoid splitting the casing, you first need to snip off the nail points.

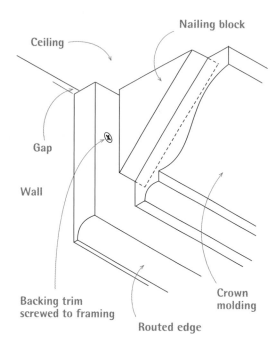

Ceiling

Nailing block

Gap

Wall

Backing trim
screwed to framing

Routed edge

Crown
molding

When installing nailing blocks without backing trim, nail the blocks directly to the wall plates. Keep a 1/16-in. space between the back of the molding and the face of the blocks to accommodate wall-ceiling irregularities.

Scribe baseboards so they follow the floor lines. Or, if you're installing the baseboard before the floors are in, shim the trim so it will be a consistent height above the subfloor. Use scrap to cushion the trim from hammer blows, as you tap the trim to align its edges.

them off. Use two 8d nails (aligned vertically) at every other stud center, and use a single 4d finish nail top and bottom to draw mitered corners tight. Used as baseboard caps, standard moldings, such as quarter-rounds, can hide irregularities between the top of the baseboard and the wall, and they dress up the top of the board. Where baseboards abut door casing and there's no stud directly behind the end of the baseboard, nail the bottom of the board to the wall plate, and angle-nail the top to the side of the casing or plinth block, using an 18-gauge brad to avoid splitting the trim. Finally, set the nails, fill the holes, and caulk all seams before painting.

INSTALLING CROWN MOLDING

Crown molding dresses up the wall–ceiling joint, as do its fancy cousins *cornices,* which are formed from several boards. Crown molding can be as simple as a single piece of shaped trim angled along the corners of the ceiling, or you can pair it with a *backing trim* to ensure a solid nailing surface, which is not always present in an old houses with irregular framing and springy plaster.

Start by locating and marking stud and joist centers on the walls and ceilings. Where joists run parallel to a wall or where you can't find framing on a regular nailing interval, install a row of triangular *nailing blocks* along the tops of walls, as shown above. Predrill these blocks to avoid splitting them, and nail them with 8d finish nails to the top plates or studs, spacing the blocks every 24 in. to 32 in. Cut nailing blocks at the same angle as the crown molding, when correctly seated to wall and ceiling.

To determine that angle, cut a short section of crown molding to use as a *seating gauge*. Hold the gauge so that trim edges seat solidly on both the ceiling and the wall. Using this gauge, make a light pencil mark every 3 ft. to 4 ft. so that when you nail up the molding you'll have reference marks for its bottom edge. (Because crown molding is relatively thin, it easily twists and misaligns.) Nail molding roughly every 3 ft., or to every other 16-in. on-center stud and joist. If walls are too long for a single piece of molding, splice boards over stud centers. Use a nailer to attach crown molding and cornices—hand-nailing is too erratic. If you're nailing molding to blocks, use 18-gauge brads to avoid splits; otherwise, use 6d finish nails. Nail the bottom edge first, then the top, keeping the nails back from edges by at least ⅜ in.

To install backing trim—basically, a flat board with a shaped bottom edge—snap a chalkline to line up the bottom edges of the trim. Backing trim is a godsend when you've got level upper cabinets but an unlevel ceiling. Install the backing trim level and the crown molding snug against the ceiling. The amount of backing trim revealed (exposed) will vary, but your eye won't notice it. Use screws to attach the backing trim because they hold better and are less likely to fracture plaster. Before nailing up crown molding, use a seating gauge to mark its position atop the backing trim.

As with baseboard molding, miter outside corners, cope inside ones, and glue all joints before nailing them off. If the first piece of crown molding is long enough to run from inside corner to inside corner, just cut both ends square, pop into place, and then cope the ends of adjacent pieces. Miter-cut the crown molding upside-down, with its bottom edge up—angled so that the molding's lower edge rests against the back fence of the miter box, and the molding's upper edge rests on the bottom of the miter box. (Inverting the molding in the miter box is the only way to support both of the molding's edges and re-create the same angle the crown molding will have when installed against the wall and ceiling. If you cut the molding right-side up in the miter box, the top edge of the molding would be unsupported.) Use the seating gauge you made earlier to establish this angle on your miter saw: Screw a piece

Cut or assemble a small section of crown molding to use as a seating gauge to tell you where the bottom of the molding will meet the wall. A pencil mark every 3 ft. to 4 ft. should do; don't use a chalkline because it could bleed through finish paint.

Outside corners are seldom square, requiring that miters be marked in place. Here, scrap was first positioned on both sides of the corner to guide a pencil line along its top edge. At that intersection, the top point of the miter was marked on both scrap pieces. The bottom point of the miter is the corner itself, here being marked.

PRO TIP

Crown molding must be solidly nailed. So, as you locate studs and ceiling joists, affix a small piece of blue painter's tape to indicate their centers. Place tape sufficiently back from the trim path, so you can still see the tape as you position the trim. Using painter's tape is easier than erasing pencil marks, and the tape won't pull off paint.

||||

PRO TIP

When installing crown molding, leave the last 2 ft. to 3 ft. unnailed till you've test-fitted all joints. Sometimes the molding needs to come up or down to make a coped joint fit exactly, and it's much easier to tweak the molding's position than to recut a joint.

||||

of scrap to the saw bed to hold the molding stock in place as you cut it. When in doubt, test the joints by cutting and joining pieces of scrap.

FALSE BEAMS

There are several ways to construct false beams. Two are shown here. The first is to make a ladder frame (imagine a ladder set horizontally) clad with finish boards. This type, shown below, runs perpendicular to ceiling joists so its top board can be screwed to them; end-nail "ladder rungs" to the top board before installing it. Once the top board is secured to joists, attach the bottom board and then the sides. A power nailer is a must because the assembly is shaky till all the boards are on.

The second type, shown in the photos on the facing page, is more correctly called a *box beam* because there's nothing false about the steel I-beam it's disguising. You can order I-beams with bolt holes predrilled, making it easy to bolt plywood nailing blocks to them. The plywood shown was faced with clear fir on three sides and stained to simulate redwood. Because the underside of the box was most visible at eye level, the carpenters took pains to create an even reveal along the bottom of the beam. The gaps along the top of the beam were later covered by the crown molding shown in the top photo on p. 429.

WAINSCOTING

In the old days, when raised-panel wainscoting was constructed from solid wood, fancy joinery was required to accommodate the expansion and contraction of the panels. Today, thanks to the stability of MDF panels and readily available stock molding, you can create good-looking wainscoting with simple joinery (see p. 432). Once painted, this new wainscoting will be almost indistinguishable from that built with traditional materials and methods.

Construct the frame rails (horizontal pieces) and stiles (vertical pieces) from clear, straight 1×4s; if you need more than one board to attain the length you need, use a biscuit joiner (see the

Scan left to right on the ceiling, and you'll see the evolution of a false beam. Preassemble the top board (which nails to the ceiling joists) and short nailer blocks. Install the bottom board, then the sides. Use a pneumatic nailer only, for hand nailing will loosen the assembly.

BOXING IN A STEEL I-BEAM

To provide nailing surfaces for the sides of the box beam, first bolt plywood strips to the predrilled I-beam. Attach the bottom panel of the box beam first, then the sides.

Because the underside is the most visible part of the box beam from eye level, measure to be sure the board reveals are consistent. Measuring also tells you exactly where the edge of the bottom board is—so nails don't miss it. Cover gaps along the ceiling with crown molding.

bottom photo on p. 407) to splice the board ends. Use this tool to strengthen the butt joints between rails and stiles, too. But first, snap chalklines onto the walls to indicate the position of rails and stiles; if any stiles coincide with electrical outlets, it may be easiest to relocate the outlets so that all the panels along a wall have a consistent width.

Assemble the frame on the floor. After allowing its glued and biscuited joints to cure, tilt the frame upright ,and screw it to wall studs, using 15-gauge finish nails. To avoid stressing the frame joints, have a helper tilt it up and hold it atop spacer blocks as you nail it. The ¾-in. MDF panels are best routed in several passes to avoid frying the router and scorching the panel edges. Once you're done routing, sand the panel edges lightly and nail them to the wall, leaving an even gap all around, between panel edges and frame elements.

Although you can use any type of stock molding to cover the gaps around the panels, a shaped molding adds visual interest and has a traditional feel—*bolection* molding has a nice profile and a rabbeted back edge that seats neatly against frame edges. Cap the top of the top rail with molding too, to cover the slight gap between the frame and the wall.

After screwing the preassembled frame to the studs, insert shaped MDF panels, nailing them directly to the wall with 2-in. brads. Leave a 1-in. gap around each panel, which you'll cover with stock molding.

Painting

Painting is probably the most popular renovation task because its effects are immediate and striking. For not much money or effort, you can get a complete change of scenery and heart. If you own a few basic tools, your costs will be limited to the few tools you'll need to rent and the paint you choose.

This chapter covers both exterior and interior painting, including trim, doors, windows, and cabinets. For information on stripping and finishing floors, refer to Chapter 20.

Sometimes art doesn't hang on a wall: It is the wall.

Essential Prep Work

If you want painted surfaces to look good and last long, the substrate—such as drywall, plaster, and wood—must be stable and dry before you start. Thus prep work (preparing surfaces) is crucial for a good paint job, vital advice that recurs in this chapter. Whether you'll be painting a building's interior or exterior, follow these guidelines:

▶ **Correct structural or moisture-related problems.**

▶ **Scrape or sand down paint that's poorly adhered or applied excessively.**

▶ **Sand surface irregularities.**

▶ **Choose primer that will adhere well and be compatible with the finish coats.**

▶ **Follow instructions on paint containers.**

▶ **Sand lightly between coats for better adhesion.**

Choosing Paint

Manufacturers frequently reformulate their primers, paints, and stains, so look for a reputable supplier who keeps up with changes. Before buying paint, examine the surfaces to be painted and think about the conditions it must endure. Then ask the following questions.

FOUR TELLING QUESTIONS

▶ **Interior or exterior paint?** Beware of any container labeled "interior/exterior." It's probably cheap. Quality exterior paints contain additives that repel moisture, block UV rays, and discourage mold. These additives are not substances you'd want to inhale indoors while the paint is curing. Thus never use exterior paints indoors and vice versa.

▶ **Has the surface been painted before?** Surfaces should be primed if they (1) have never been painted, (2) have been extensively scraped or sanded, or (3) are "chalky" or poorly prepped. However, if existing paint is

One big advantage of latex paint: You can easily clean brushes and your hands with soap and water.

well adhered, priming isn't necessary; just paint over the old coat.

▶ What type of finish (sheen) do you want? Top-coat finishes range from *flat* (also called dull or matte) to *semigloss* (a.k.a. eggshell, velvet, satin) to *gloss*. Glossier finishes tend to be more durable and easier to clean, so they're favored on doors and windows, on trim, and in high-use areas such as bathrooms and kitchens. Enamel, which dries to a hard, durable finish, is best for window sashes, doors, and casings.

▶ Is the surface unusual? There are specialty paints for masonry; for hard, nonporous surfaces such as tile and glass; for often-damp areas; and for nonslip surfaces. There are even paints for acoustical tile that don't reduce the tile's sound-deadening properties. Check with your supplier.

OIL-BASED VERSUS LATEX

Whether you're painting exterior or interior surfaces, latex paints are probably the best bet. The next sections explain why.

Two essential definitions.

▶ Oil-based paints and stains may contain linseed oil, tung oil, or synthetic resins called alkyds. Because alkyds are the most common "oil" in oil-based paints, professionals often use the term *alkyd* instead of oil-based. However, *oil-based* is the broader, more inclusive term for products that must be thinned and cleaned up with solvents. Today only about 10 percent of house-paint sales are oil based.

▶ Latex paints and stains are water based and thus can be thinned with water and cleaned up with warm, soapy water. In recent

Colorful LANGUAGE: PRIMERS, PAINTS, AND STAINS

▶ **PRIMER.** An important base coat, primer is applied to substrates such as raw wood, drywall, plaster, or previously painted surfaces. Above all, primers must stick to the substrate; they may also contain stain blockers, preservatives, pigments, or other additives to hide flaws and ensure more uniform top coats of paint.

▶ **PAINT.** If primer's job is adhesion, paint's is protection—protecting the primer and substrate from moisture, mild abuse, and (if it's exterior paint) UV rays. Paint must also hold color, dry smoothly, and withstand weather, so its pigments, solvents, and additives must be carefully blended and held together by a *binder*, or *resin*.

▶ **BINDER.** Binders determine a paint's penetration, adhesion, drying rate, flexibility, and durability. In relation to pigment, the more binder a paint has, the shinier and more durable its finish will be. Glossy paints tend to have high binder-to-pigment ratios.

▶ **PIGMENT.** Color is determined by pigment. The more pigment a paint has, the more intense its color and the better it hides what's beneath.

▶ **VEHICLE.** A paint's liquid component, the vehicle, is needed to suspend the pigments and binders. *Oil-based* vehicles (linseed oil, tung oil, or modified oils called alkyds) thin with mineral spirits, also known as paint thinner. *Latex paints* suspend polymer particles (plastic) in water.

▶ **STAIN.** Penetrating or semitransparent stains are most often pigmented oils that soak into wood and form a thin film on the wood's surface; there are also water-based stains. You can see wood grain through stain. Although stains may contain water repellants, preservatives, and some UV blocking, they don't protect wood as well as paint does and so must be reapplied periodically—say, every 2 years to 4 years.

▶ **SOLID-COLOR STAIN.** Despite the name, solid-color stain, a fast-growing group of exterior coatings, is more like thinned paint than stain. It's popular because wood texture (but not wood grain) remains visible. However, solid-color stains have only about half the life span of painted surfaces. Acrylic latex solid-color stains are the most durable.

decades, latex paints have improved so dramatically that they now account for about 90 percent of house-paint sales.

Oil-based: Advantages and disadvantages. Oil-based paints are durable and tenacious, adhering even to glossy or chalky surfaces. Thus many pros still insist on an oil-based exterior primer, even if they'll be applying latex top coats. Many old-school painters also favor oil-based paints for interior trim, because they dry slowly and level well, thus minimizing brush marks.

Problem is, oil-based paints never completely cure. Rather, they oxidize and, over the years, erode and crack. Any siding, especially wood, expands and contracts as temperatures fluctuate, so the inflexibility of oil-based paints leads to cracking and more commonly *chalking*, a powdery residue of oxidized oil and pigment. In addition, mold feeds on the organic compounds in oil-based paints. But the biggest problem is their solvents: noxious, volatile, polluting, and tedious to clean off tools and equipment.

Latex: Advantages and disadvantages. Acrylic latex has almost everything a painter or a substrate could want: As the paint or stain dries, its water base evaporates with minimal odor, leaving a thin coat of polymer particles (plastic) that remains flexible and so rarely cracks, as oil-based paints often do. Latex is also semipermeable, so moisture generated inside the house can migrate, through the paint, to the outdoors. Because latex is synthetic, it's inhospitable to mold. Finally, latex cleans up easily and dries quickly.

Inside, latex is the only paint to use on drywall, for it won't raise the paper surface of panels.

Clear FINISHES

Clear finishes include polyurethane, varnish, lacquer, and shellac. *Polyurethane*, also called poly, is the most durable of the clear finishes and thus the most suitable for heavy-traffic surfaces, such as trim and stair parts. Although poly and varnish resist moisture, they may become cloudy with sustained exposure to wet conditions. Shellac also clouds up near water. Spar varnish—originally used on boats—has a hard finish that stands up well to water, if well maintained. For more about clear floor finishes, see Chapter 20.

Exterior latex is colorfast, durable, and easy to apply. However, its quick drying characteristic can be a problem if you're painting an exterior in 90° heat, which causes the paint to dry on the brush. In that case, additives like Flood's Floetrol® will slow drying time and so extend latex's "brushability."

TIPS FOR THE PAINT STORE

Before heading for the paint store, calculate the square footage of surfaces to be painted. Then compare those figures with the coverage figures listed on the paint containers. Unless a wall is preponderantly glass, don't bother to subtract the square footage of windows and glass doors from your total. You'll eventually need the extra paint for touchups.

Although some artists can hand-tint 5-gal. quantities to match existing paint, the rest of us should rely on paint-store mixologists. They have color charts, recipes, and accurate measuring tools. The blue object at the lower right is a power-drill paint mixer.

Predicting the coverage of stains is more difficult, especially if the wood is untreated. Add 15 percent to 25 percent if you need to special-order the stain and must wait more than a day or two for delivery. That way, you'll be ensured of enough stain to finish the job.

If your paint job will be large, save money by buying 5-gal. rather than 1-gal. quantities. However, if it's more cost-effective to buy only a few 1-gal. cans, ensure uniform color by mixing their contents in a clean, empty 5-gal. bucket. This way, you'll avoid finishing one can in the middle of a wall and resuming with a noticeably different hue.

Protect your lungs whenever you sand, scrape, or strip paint—even if there's plenty of fresh air. While heating old paint for scraping, this worker is wearing a lightweight dust mask with P100 particulate filters.

Speaking of mixing, have your paint store mechanically shake the paint for you—unless, of course, the manufacturer's instructions indicate it shouldn't be shaken. For example, polyurethanes and varnishes trap air bubbles when shaken.

Tools and Equipment

Ladders and scaffolding are essential for many painting jobs. For more on them, see Chapter 3.

MASKS AND CARTRIDGES

Disposable paper masks will keep out sanding dust, but you need a filtered mask when spraying paints or applying chemical strippers. For any task involving leaded paint, wear a full-face respirator mask with replaceable HEPA (purple) cartridges. For most paint applications, a half-face mask with replaceable organic vapor cartridges will be adequate. Masks vary, so pick one that fits your face snugly. To test the fit, when you cover cartridge openings and inhale, no air should enter the mask.

Cartridge life varies according to the chemical you're using, the type of filter specified for that chemical, ventilation in your workspace, and the care you take to keep cartridges "alive" in storage. Change the cartridges whenever you smell fumes or whenever it becomes difficult to breath through the mask. Manufacturers suggest their own change schedules. For example, when filtering epoxy-based paints (very toxic) or urethanes, filters can become loaded in 8 hours. Whereas, filters for latex-based paints typically have a much longer change schedule—for example, 30 days or 40 working hours, whichever comes first.

BRUSHES

The bristles of high-quality brushes are *flagged*, meaning the bristle ends are split and of varying lengths, enabling them to hold more paint. As you shop for brushes, pull lightly on bristles. Are they well attached to the metal ferrule on the handle? Then, when you gently press the bristles as though painting, they should spread evenly and have a springy, resilient feel. Avoid brushes with stiff bristles.

Bristle types. Bristles are either natural (hog bristles, for example) or synthetic (usually nylon). Use natural bristles for oil-based paints, varnishes, shellacs, and solvent-thinned polyurethanes. Use synthetic bristles for latexes. Nylon bristles may dissolve in oil-based paints; whereas natural bristles tend to swell and clog when used with the water-base of latex. Although some synthetic bristles work with either painting

Quality bristles fan out as you apply paint. Here, the tapered bristles of a 2½-in. angled sash brush "cut" a straight edge where walls meet trim.

Heavy paper or cardboard covers help bristles keep their shape.

medium, once you've used a brush for a particular type of paint, continue using it for that type.

The width of the brush should depend on the amount of paint to be applied. Because rollers and spray guns are best for large surfaces, spend your brush money on smaller, better brushes. Many pros praise the 2½-in. angled sash brush as the most versatile brush in their arsenal; it's wide enough to smooth out paint on baseboard trim, yet slim enough to "cut an edge" at corners and along window casings. If you own only one brush, this should be it. But if you'll be painting many narrow window muntins, also buy a 1½-in. sash brush.

Brush care. Brush care begins with proper use. Don't stab bristles into tight spots. Instead, stroke the paint on. When you take a coffee break, leave a moderate amount of paint on the bristles so your bristles don't dry out.

Clean brushes immediately after you finish painting for the day. Remove excess paint from the bristles by drawing them over a straightedge, not over the edge of the paint can. Brush the remaining paint onto old newspapers. Clean the brush in an appropriate solution: paint thinner for oil-based paints, soap and water for latexes.

Wear disposable gloves during brush cleaning, and use your fingers to work the solution into bristles and all the way to the ferrule. After giving each brush a thorough initial wash, rinse it in a fresh batch of solution. When the brushes are clean, shake and brush out the excess solution. Rinse with *warm* water, shake out the excess, and comb the bristles. (Solvent-cleaned brushes require an intermediate cleaning with soap and warm water.) Don't use hot water when cleaning brushes because it splits the bristles.

ROLLERS, PANS, POLES, AND PADS

Rollers enable you to paint large areas quickly and evenly. In addition to the familiar 9-in. cylinder type, there are also 6-in. "hot-dog" rollers for tight spaces, such as inside cabinets, and beveled corner rollers that resemble a pointed wheel. There are also textured rollers, including stippled, faux finish, and distressed.

Choosing a roller cover. The surface and paint should determine the type of roller cover, also called a *sleeve*. For example, if you're painting smooth walls, use a short-nap cover (¼ in. to ½ in.). Whereas, concrete block and stucco need a long nap (1 in. to 1½ in.). Most covers are synthetic and work either with oil-based or latex paints. However, for fine finishes with glossy oil-based paints, use a fine-nap natural-fiber cover. For an ultra-smooth finish when rolling enamels, varnish, or polyurethane, use a fine-nap mohair cover.

Don't buy cheap cardboard-backed roller covers unless you intend to paint a single room with latex and throw the cover away. (Never use cheap roller covers with oil-based paint. The oil will pluck the fibers from the cylinders and leave them sticking to your wall.) Quality roller covers have plastic sleeves that survive repeated cleanings. As you do with brushes, use a roller cover for only one type of paint, whether oil-based or latex.

Roller pans. Ramped metal or plastic roller pans are routinely sold in packages that include a roller frame and a cover or two, but pros rarely use roller pans. Occasionally, pros may use a pan to hold a small amount of paint for decorative painting. But when pros roll multiple rooms, they prefer a ramp of *expanded-metal* inside a 5-gal.

paint bucket about half full. This ramp gives you room to load the roller and remove excess paint quickly—so you can keep painting, rather than repeatedly filling a roller pan.

Paint pads. Pads for paint are about the size of a small kitchen sponge and have a short nap. Generally, they are used to paint hard-to-reach spots such as insides of cabinets. They're also used for applying clear finishes such as polyurethanes to flat surfaces.

Extension poles. Whether sectioned or telescoping, extension poles are indispensable for reaching ceilings and upper parts of walls with rollers or pads. Because the poles tax mainly your shoulder and back, rather than your wrist and arm, they enable you to work longer with less fatigue. Another advantage: By painting with an extension pole, you don't need to stand immediately under the drizzle, known as "paint rain."

Roller-cover care. If you buy quality roller covers, clean them as soon as you finish a job. For this, wear disposable gloves. Before washing a cover, use a 5-in-1 painter's tool shown below to remove excess paint. Then slide the cover off the metal roller frame and wash the cover in the paint-appropriate cleaner, working out the paint with your gloved fingers. Repeat the procedure with fresh cleaner. Then wash with soap and water. Blot the excess moisture with a paper towel or a clean rag. Air-dry the cover by sliding it onto a hanger somewhere; don't let it lie on its nap while drying. Store the dried cover or pad in a paper bag or foil. If a cover or pad wasn't cleaned properly and has become crusty, throw it away.

Expanded metal ramps allow you to quickly load and roll excess paint into the bucket. Note the building paper protecting the flooring from paint spatters.

Before washing roller covers, use this painter's 5-in-1 tool to remove the excess paint.

SPRAY-PAINTING EQUIPMENT

In recent years, spray-painting equipment has become much easier to operate and maintain. Spraying is most appropriate where you've got a whole house to paint or where surfaces are ornate (gingerbread trim), multifaceted (shingles), textured (stucco), or otherwise difficult to cover with a brush or roller. Spraying is also smarter when you need to apply numerous thin, even applications, as on cabinet doors. The key to successful spray-painting, as with any painting, is thorough prep work. That is, begin by correcting moisture problems, removing loose paint and dirt, caulking and filling holes and gaps, and priming unfinished substrates.

Spray-painting safety begins with a respirator mask with two replaceable organic-vapor filters. If you'll be spraying exteriors, a half-face mask should be adequate. For interiors, where paint concentrations build up quickly, wear a full-face respirator mask, gloves, a spray sock to keep paint mist off your head, and coveralls taped at the wrists and ankles. The greater the concentration of paint mist, the sooner filters will clog and cease filtering. Review additional comments on mask safety on p. 436.

Spraying equipment typically consists of a pump to pull paint out of a bucket, a connecting hose, and a spray gun. At this writing, you can

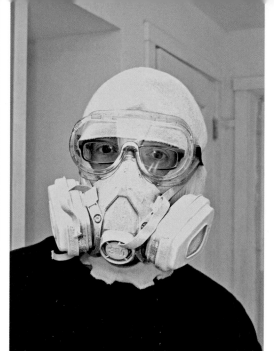

The right protective gear can keep paint mist off your skin and out of your lungs. This includes a respirator mask with replaceable vapor–filters, as well as a "spray sock" over your head, safety goggles, and disposable gloves.

rent contractor-grade equipment for $50 to $75 per day, or buy a quality setup for $1,200 to $1,500.

Compact, efficient airless sprayers have largely replaced the earlier units with their bulky com-pressors, pressurized paint pots, and two hoses. Today, single-hose, airless sprayers deliver paint at up to 2000 lb. of pressure, atomizing paint at the spray tip. High-volume airless sprayers can apply coatings of varying viscosity, from thin to extra-heavy.

High-volume, low-pressure (HVLP) sprayers are usually recommended for novices because the lower pressure makes spray patterns easier to control and less likely to overspray. The disadvantage of HVLP sprayers is the risk of applying insufficient paint, resulting in a uneven, "orange-peel" paint texture.

Spray tips control paint volume and pattern, or *fan*. Fixed-size tips are coded with three-digit numbers: The first digit (2–9) indicates in inches *half the width* of the paint fan when you hold the tip 1 ft. from the surface being painted. The next two digits (00–99) indicate the size of the tip opening in thousandths of an inch. So a no. 518 tip will spray a 10-in.-wide fan (at 1 ft. away) and has an 0.018-in. opening.

A few manufacturers make adjustable spray tips, but they're a specialty item. If, for example, you'll be at the top of a 20-ft. ladder, need several different spray patterns, and don't feel like climbing down the ladder to change tips, use an adjustable tip. But 99 percent of the time, fixed-size tips are the way to go: they cost less and maintain a precise aperture longer.

PRO TIP

Painting contractors overwhelmingly favor airless sprayers with reversible spray tips. Reversible tips allow you to clear clogs quickly—by turning the tip 180° and blowing out the obstruction—without needing to disassemble the spray gun. If you're concerned about applying too much paint with an airless sprayer, choose a smaller spray tip: say, a no. 511 or no. 611 tip for spraying cabinet doors and drawers.

Renting a Paint Sprayer

Don't rent spraying equipment that isn't well maintained. A first-rate rental company will size the pump to your job, recommend spray tips, and explain how everything works. For good measure, ask for an operator's manual, too.

Finally, get satisfactory answers to these questions: (1) Is the equipment clean? Rental companies charge extra if equipment is returned uncleaned. (2) Was the last paint used in the sprayer oil-based paint or latex? (3) Can you show me how to use this model?

The last question is especially helpful if you're a bit macho and don't want to admit that you've never operated *any* sprayer before. Another face-saver is, "Say, run a little water and show me how to pressurize this, would you?" Don't leave the rental yard without understanding how the equipment works.

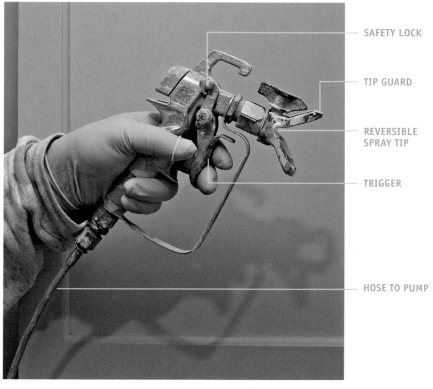

SAFETY LOCK

TIP GUARD

REVERSIBLE SPRAY TIP

TRIGGER

HOSE TO PUMP

Sprayer parts.

Painting Basics

A quality paint job takes preparation, patience, and experience. In addition, professionals also learn how to streamline their moves. As one pro put it, "Any time you eliminate a move in painting, you save time."

PAINTING SAFELY

Almost all paints, including latex, contain volatile organic compounds (VOCs), which are hazardous. So although latex is relatively benign, the following advice is pertinent for all kinds of paints and stains.

Read the label. There's valuable information on all paint containers: drying time, coverage, thinner data (what to use and how much), and safety instructions. Should an emergency arise—say, a child swallows some paint—the guidance you need may later be concealed under paint drippings. So read up before you open the can or, better, remove and save the label.

Don't breathe paint fumes. Breathing paint or solvent fumes can make you dizzy; impair your judgment; and, over a sustained period, damage your brain, lungs, and kidneys. Set up a fan to blow fumes away from your work area, and always wear a half-face mask with replaceable cartridges. Rule of thumb: *If you can smell fumes while wearing a snug mask, change the cartridge.*

Ventilation is a particular problem when chemically stripping paints because the chemicals are strong and because heat guns, sanders, and scrapers increase airborne particles. The now banned lead-based paints are especially dangerous when inhaled or ingested, so if you suspect that you will be stripping lead paint, always test it before disturbing it. See "Lead-Paint Safety," on p. 442, for more.

Avoid getting paint in eyes and on skin. Although most water-based paints are innocuous, oil-based paints can be extremely irritating. In most cases, flush your eyes with water if you get paint in them, and visit a doctor immediately.

There are few things you can do to protect your skin. Before you start, apply lotion to your skin to reduce irritation and speed cleanup. Also, wear gloves, even when using latex, because any paint will irritate skin over time. Gloves are a must for oil-based paints.

When it comes to cleanup, painters have traditionally used paint thinner or turpentine to clean their hands and then washed with hot soapy water. However, hot water opens skin pores, causing them to absorb more solvent than otherwise. Instead of volatile solvents and hot water, it may be safer to use waterless hand cleaner and wipe it off with paper towels.

Store paint safely. Store paint where children can't reach it. Solvents such as paint thinner, turpentine, and all paints—including latex—should be considered toxic and stored out of reach of children. (In fact, some "green" brands of latex such as Glidden's 2000™ and AMF Safecoat® contain no VOCs, but you still wouldn't want kids to drink them. So store these products safely, too.) Also, store paint where temperatures are moderate, because freezing ruins their bonding ability and heat increases their volatility. Close all containers completely so the paint doesn't dry out and contaminants can't get in. Never store rags or steel wool dirty with solvents, because of the danger of spontaneous combustion. Dispose of such articles safely: Most paint-can labels carry disposal suggestions, and many municipalities have annual curbside pickups of such materials.

BRUSH BASICS

The pros work steadily and methodically and note what works and what doesn't. The following tips will help you keep the job moving and get great results.

See "Lead-Paint Safety," on p. 442, for more.

PRO TIP

Amateurs mistakenly paint from a 1-gal. paint can instead of a painter's pail. Consequently, they dip into too much paint, which they then scrape off on the can lip. Better to dip into less paint and with two flicks of the wrist, *Dip-tap-tap* the brush on both sides of a pail. This removes excess paint that might drip, but leaves most of the paint on the brush, letting you paint farther.

Skin CARE

To minimize chemical contact with your skin, (1) wear goggles, especially when using chemical strippers; (2) use an extension pole so you don't need to stand immediately beneath a roller; (3) don't overload brushes and rollers; (4) brush or roll away from your face, especially on the first few strokes after loading up with paint.

PAINT FUMES AND OPEN FLAME: AN Explosive COMBINATION

Volatile paint fumes build up quickly, especially during spray painting. Minimize the risk of explosion by choosing latex paint, increasing ventilation, and using *electric heaters* to maintain a 60°F drying temperature. (Forced hot-air systems will kick up dust.) *Open-flame heaters are not acceptable* because they can ignite concentrated fumes. Likewise, appliances with pilot lights can cause an explosion, so turn off the fuel to such appliances until paint fumes have dispersed. And, of course, never smoke in such a situation. (Theoretically, even a light switch spark could cause an explosion, if fumes were concentrated enough.)

Acclimate a new brush. Stand a new brush in 1 in. of oil-based paint for 5 minutes. After absorbing a bit of paint, the new bristles will release paint more readily when you start to work. Whereas thirsty new brushes may drag at first. It's not necessary to acclimate brushes when using latex, which works into bristles within 20 seconds to 30 seconds.

Avoid overloading your brush. Most pros have only ½ in. to 1 in. of paint in the bottom of a paint pail when edging—and the same amount on the tip of the brush. With this small amount, you'll cut a cleaner paint line and keep paint off the brush handle and your hands. And, should the bucket tip over, you'll have less mess to clean up.

Retrieve loose bristles. If a bristle comes loose and sticks to the surface, pick it out by dabbing lightly with the tip of the brush. Quality brushes rarely lose bristles.

Paint with gravity. This is close to an absolute rule. Paint, as a liquid or mist, always falls or drips downward, so it's better if it lands on unpainted surfaces—rather than painted ones. Best sequence: ceilings, walls, trim, baseboards.

Paint with the grain. When painting trim, brush paint in the direction of the wood grain. Painting cross-grain doesn't help paint adhere better and will look terrible if brushstrokes dry quickly.

Steady hand, straight paint. Few pros use masking tape to achieve straight lines when brushing paint onto trim, window casing, and the like. Pros feel that tape takes too much time to apply and sometimes lets the paint seep under, leaving a ragged line. Besides, during removal, tape can pull off paint. Patience and a steady hand work better. With a little practice, it's easier than you might think.

ROLLER BASICS

Acclimate roller covers to paint. Before using a new roller cover, work paint into it well. Load the cover with paint. Then roll it up and down the paint ramp to work the paint down to the base of its nap, and remove the excess.

Pros prefer ramps for paint rollers in 5-gal. buckets. Unlike roller pans, 5-gal. buckets don't need frequent refilling, and there's plenty of room to load the roller cover and roll off the excess. The expanded metal ramp's open grid also allows excess paint to fall directly into the reservoir of paint, rather than coating the side of the bucket.

Roll upward, after loading a roller with paint. If you roll downward instead, you'll be more likely spray excess paint onto walls and floors. Instead,

As you load your brush, dip it only ½ in. to 1 in. into the paint before tapping the tip sharply against both sides of the pail to remove the excess.

Smart painters recycle brushes. This one began life as a finish–coat brush. Then, as it got tired and splayed, it was used for primer coats. When its bristles became too crusty and its handle separated from the ferrule, it became a duster.

with an initial upstroke, excess falls back onto the roller cover.

Roll paint in a zigzag. Roller covers contain the most paint during the first three to five passes, so first roll a *W* or an *N* to distribute "fat paint," which you can then reroll to spread the paint evenly.

Lighten up with the roller once the paint is spread on the wall. This is especially important for outside corners (corners that project into a room). Too much pressure can make the roller skid or leave roller-edge marks.

SPRAY-PAINTING BASICS

The information in this section is generally true for all spray applications. You'll find other suggestions later in this chapter.

Wear a respirator mask with two replaceable organic-vapor filters. If you're spray-painting exteriors, a half-face mask should be adequate. For interiors, where paint concentrations build up quickly, wear a full-face respirator mask.

Never touch a spray tip while it's spraying: It will inject paint into your skin (and bloodstream), which requires immediate medical attention, including removing the affected skin.

Carefully mask off everything you don't want painted—from ceilings to windows to shrubs. To protect large expanses, use 1½-in. painter's masking tape to attach high-density plastic sheeting. To cover baseboards, windowsills, and the like, apply 12-in.-wide masking paper. Careful masking takes time, but it's crucial to ensure crisp spray-painted edges.

Before turning on the pump, make sure the spray-gun trigger is locked, the pump's pressure control is turned to low, and the priming lever is turned off.

Test the sprayer on an inconspicuous area first, to make sure it's operating correctly and to familiarize yourself with its fan pattern and volume. If the pressure is correct, paint will stick when the spray tip is 12 in. from the wall. But if the paint bounces back at that distance (coating the sprayer and your gloved hand), reduce the pressure.

Moving with Spray Gun

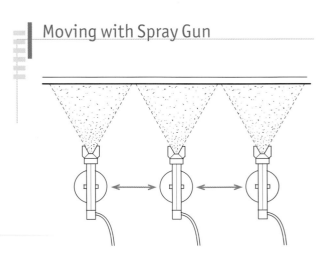

To achieve uniform spray applications, move with the tool, as shown, rather than remaining in one spot and swinging the spray gun in an arc.

If the sprayer clogs often, the paint may be contaminated and need straining. Buy strainer bags at a paint store or, in a pinch, strain paint through an old pair of panty hose or nylons.

Keep the sprayer moving in long, straight strokes. Hold the spray tip 12 in. away from the surface and overlap passes 30 percent to 50 percent. To prevent uneven paint buildup, move the spray tip parallel to the surface. If the surface you're painting has distinct edges, start spraying just before the edge and don't release the trigger until the paint fan is past the far edge. If you must start in the middle of a wall, begin moving your arm before pulling the trigger.

Use a hose that's long enough so you can move freely around the work site. For exterior jobs you'll need a 100-ft. hose; for most interior jobs, a 50-ft. one. As you spray, hold a loop of the hose in your free hand to keep it out of your foot path—and away from freshly painted surfaces. Sprayer hoses come in 50-ft. lengths with couplings on both ends.

Start at the top and work down as you spray. Because a fine paint rain falls when you spray, better that it falls on unpainted surfaces—which will be painted over for a uniform finish.

Use a cardboard painting shield to keep paint overspray off adjacent surfaces you have already painted or won't paint at all, as shown in the top photo on p. 462.

Keep spray tips clean because they are easily clogged. So when you're done painting for the day, soak them in the appropriate vehicle (solvent for oil-based paint, hot water for latex). If the tip is really gunky, soak it in lacquer thinner.

Replace the spray tip if, after cleaning it, its spray pattern is still blotchy or the spray unit seems to be guzzling paint. Solids in the paint actually abrade the inside of the tip, enlarging it over time.

Keep filters clean and replace them often. Using a paint-appropriate thinner, clean filters every time you change paint colors, at the end of each day, and if you're pumping a lot of paint—say, 40 gal. by lunchtime. A 100-mesh filter is minimum; coarser filters will admit debris that can clog the tip.

Lead-Paint Safety

The presence of lead paint in older houses is serious, but it's probably not a dire problem if your home is well maintained and old paint is well adhered. Lead is most dangerous when it becomes airborne, especially during sanding or heat stripping, for then it can be inhaled and easily absorbed into the bloodstream. So be methodical: Postpone any demolition or paint removal, test to see if lead paint is present, and develop a plan for dealing with it. Then wear proper safety equipment, confine lead-paint debris, and clean up thoroughly.

Lead: Some background. Lead-based paint adheres to almost any surface and weathers well, so it's not surprising that it can be found in 90 percent of houses built before 1940. However, as lead paint's health hazards became known in the 1950s, paint manufacturers began to phase it out. It was banned altogether in 1978 by the U.S. government.

Because lead is a neurological toxin, it is particularly damaging to children 6 and younger, who seem drawn to it because it's slightly sweet. Breathing or eating it can cause mental retardation in children. In people of all ages, lead can also cause headaches, anemia, lethargy, kidney damage, high blood pressure, and other ailments.

Because of its durability, lead paint was commonly used on exteriors, glossy kitchen and bathroom walls, in closets (where a single coat would last forever), and as an enamel on interior doors, windows, stair treads, and woodwork. So each time a swollen window or sticking door was forced open, it ground lead paint into flakes and dust. Roof leaks, drainage problems, and inadequate ventilation add to the problem because excessive moisture causes the paint to degrade and detach sooner.

Safe lead abatement is two-pronged. First, contain dust by attaching mechanical scrapers or sanders to industrial-strength vacuums with HEPA-rated filters. Second, wear disposable coveralls, booties, and gloves taped shut at all openings, as well as a respirator mask with replaceable HEPA filter cartridges. A half-face mask and eye protection should be adequate in most cases.

DEALING WITH LEAD: FIRST STEPS

If you suspect that your house has lead paint, test it to be sure. There are several options:

▶ To test a cut-out chip, buy an inexpensive lead-testing kit from a hardware store.

▶ Or order a lead-testing kit from an accredited testing lab; some of these kits test paint chips, whereas others test for dust wiped from floors; the EPA's National Lead Information Center (NLIC) lists testing labs at www.epa.gov/lead/nlic.htm.

▶ Or hire a certified lead-paint inspector to survey all the painted surfaces in your house. This will cost several hundred dollars, but you'll get a written report.

If the home has lead paint, here's an alternative set of options:

▶ If the paint is intact and you don't have small children, either leave the lead paint alone or paint over it to seal it in place.

▶ If you have construction experience, your renovation isn't extensive, and you're fastidious about cleanup, remove the affected materials yourself—or cover them with ¼-in. drywall.

▶ Hire an experienced lead-abatement contractor. This makes sense if your renovation is extensive, there are small children at home, you can afford to hire someone, and local codes require it.

Finally, think through the project carefully even if you plan on hiring a contractor. Lead abatement will be very disruptive. During abatement, where will you live? (It's unwise to stay in a house with airborne lead dust.) Where will you store your possessions? How will debris be contained and disposed? Start by consulting local building codes and visiting the EPA's excellent NLIC site mentioned earlier in this section.

LEAD ABATEMENT: AN OVERVIEW

Although comprehensive guidance for removing lead is beyond the scope of this book, these suggestions will start you in the right direction.

Dress for the job. Wear a half-face respirator mask with replaceable HEPA filter cartridges and snug-fitting goggles; a full-face mask with HEPA filters is also appropriate but may be hot to work in. Workers occasionally exposed to lead dust should wear at least an N100 disposable respirator. Disposable coveralls, gloves, and booties are also a must; tape shut neck, wrist and ankle openings. Finally, change out of lead-dust-contaminated work clothes at work because wearing them home can endanger your family.

Minimize on-site dust. Use a spray bottle to wet areas before hand-scraping or wet-sanding them. A shop vacuum with a HEPA filter can capture fine lead dust and prevent it from recirculating into the room; standard vacuum filters aren't fine enough for the job. Stripping doors and window

sashes off-site or in an on-site "stripping room" will isolate a major source of lead dust. Old trim can be relatively brittle and tedious to remove and reattach, so strip it in place. Finally, shut off the central heating system during demolition and lead-abatement so it won't recirculate lead dust throughout the house

Contain and clean up the mess. Use sheet plastic to isolate and contain the mess. Duct tape it across door openings to seal off work areas from living space, and cover floors with a double layer of 6-mil plastic duct taped to baseboards to keep it in place. If two layers of plastic prove too slippery, protect the floor with rosin paper or heavy cardboard instead, and cover that with plastic. The top layer of plastic will catch the debris and dust, so roll it up and discard it when demolition is done.

Outdoors, sheet plastic is also indispensable for lead abatement: Run a drop cloth of 6-mil plastic at least 8 ft. out from the building, to catch paint chips and the like. Duct-tape it to the foundation so it will stay put. Because it's not feasible to physically isolate the outside of a building, you'll need power tools with vacuum attachments to capture lead dust generated by a sander or power scraper. A HEPA-filtered vacuum will capture about 95 percent of the dust; the plastic drop cloth needs to catch the rest.

After stripping and vacuuming interior or exterior surfaces, hand wash contaminated areas to remove any residual lead dust. Don't use a power washer, which can soak the walls and scatter the debris you've worked so hard to contain. Rather, use a three-bucket clean-up: (1) Spray on detergent, using either a spray bottle or a gardener's pump sprayer before scrubbing the surface with a dampened sponge or a sponge mop. (2) Squeeze out the dirty water into the first bucket before dipping the sponge in a second rinse bucket and squeezing it again. (3) Dip a mop into a third bucket of clean water, squeeze, and you're ready to repeat the process. Change the water in all three buckets often. Follow the NEPA's NLIC suggestions for disposing of waste water.

Painting the Interior

If you see water stains, widespread peeling, mold, or large cracks that suggest structural movement, attend to the underlying causes first.

GETTING READY TO PAINT

When painting interiors, it's best to move the furniture out. If that's not possible, group it in the center of the room and cover it with a plastic tarp. Remove drapes, wall hangings, and mount-

---

On Priming Painted Surfaces

Primers bond to substrates and provide a stable base for finish coats. Thus it's wise to prime previously painted surfaces in the following situations:

▶ You're switching paint types—say, applying latex over oil-based.

▶ The old paint is flaking, chalking, stained, or otherwise in bad shape.

▶ The old paint is glossy and thus would prevent the new paint from adhering well.

Before applying primer, scrape, fill, sand, wash, and rinse the surface and allow it to dry thoroughly.

In general, *like* bonds best to *like*. That is, latex paint bonds best to latex primer, oil-based to oil-based. But a quality acrylic latex primer is a good all-purpose choice because it bonds well and suppresses water stains, crayon marks, smoke, rust, and creosote. However, if you get severe bleed-through, switch to an oil-based sealer-primer instead.

Stickability test

Here's how to test old paint before selecting a new paint, to ensure that the new paint will stick:

▶ Bend a paint chip that's coming off. If it cracks, it's oil-based; if it flexes, it's latex.

▶ Duct-tape a wet sponge to the wall; then wait 15 minutes. If there's paint on the sponge or you can rub any off the wall, it's latex.

▶ Put a few drops of latex solvent such as Goof-Off® on a painted windowsill; if the paint bubbles, it's latex.

---

ing hardware, and fill holes. 🚫 Turn off electric power to the room—use a voltage tester to be sure it's off—and remove the cover plates of electrical outlets and switches. Light fixtures or hardware left in place should be masked off or wrapped in plastic. Finally, cover the floor with canvas drop cloths—plastic is too slippery to work on.

Previously painted surfaces don't need much preparation if they are intact: Sand lightly with 150-grit sandpaper or a sanding block. If paint's flaking or loose, remove it with a paint scraper or spackling knife. Then sand rough paint edges with 120-grit to 150-grit sandpaper. Use spackling compound to fill holes, and sand it when dry. Apply a bead of paintable caulk (acrylic latex) to fill gaps where the trim meets walls, smoothing it with a moist finger. Caulking makes the finished paint look much better.

Before you apply paint, lightly sand all painted surfaces so successive coats will adhere better. After sanding, dry mop or vacuum surfaces to remove dust. Then sponge wash them with a mild detergent solution and rinse with clear water. If the walls are especially greasy (kitchen walls, for example), use a more aggressive cleaner like TSP (trisodium phosphate). After rinsing, allow walls to dry thoroughly before painting.

LINGERING PAINT Smells

As paint dries, it outgasses (gives off gases), releasing water vapor or mineral spirits and additives into the air. The warmer the room and the better the ventilation, the sooner the smells will dissipate. Labels on paint cans indicate drying times. Typically, in a room that is 60°F or warmer, acrylic latexes will be dry enough to recoat in 2 hours to 4 hours. Oil-based paints can be recoated in 24 hours. However, odors may linger because the paints need longer to cure: 8 days to 10 days for latex, 28 days to 30 days for oil-based paints.

A good test of dryness is to check whether a piece of transparent tape will stick or not.

Unpainted drywall and plaster must always be primed. You can prime drywall as soon as the final, top coat of joint compound has dried and has been sanded. Some pros still prefer an oil-based primer for drywall, but today's acrylic latexes seal as well and are far easier to clean up.

Plaster surfaces must be cured thoroughly before painting. Although latex primers can be applied as soon as the plaster is dry to the touch, it's better to wait 3 weeks to 4 weeks. Latex paint allows some migration of moisture, so plaster can continue to "breathe off" water vapor. Restorationists familiar with plaster recommend

Highlight all blemishes for filling later, by circling them with a pencil or attaching scraps of painter's tape near them, as shown.

Use a sanding block or fine sandpaper to lightly sand all fills and patches before priming.

diluting latex primer 15 percent with water so its coating is thinner and even more permeable.

Oil-based paints are another story. Because the alkali in plaster can remain "hot" for up to 3 months, *wait that long* before using oil-based paints. Otherwise, free alkali in the plaster will attack the paint. Akaline-resistant primers formulated for new plaster may shorten your wait somewhat, but they must be special ordered. But before ordering, make sure that primer will be compatible with your final-coat paint.

PAINTING CEILINGS AND WALLS

Before painting, read this chapter's earlier sections on equipment (especially respirator masks), safety concerns, and painting basics. All offer tips that can save you hours and keep you safe.

As you paint, be methodical so you won't need to touch up missed areas. *Paint top to bottom:* Do ceilings, walls, trim and baseboards before doing doors and windows. *Paint back to front:* Many painters go to the deepest recess of a room—often, a closet—and work methodically toward a

Primers and Paints*

SURFACE	PRIMER AND PAINT	COMMENTS
Drywall		
Unpainted	Acrylic latex primer and paint	Don't sand between coats
Painted with oil-based semigloss or gloss	Oil-based (alkyd) or latex	To switch to latex: sand oil-based paint, vacuum, prime with acrylic latex primer
Painted with latex	Acrylic latex	Sand lightly before first new coat; not needed thereafter
Plaster		
Unpainted	Acrylic latex primer and paint	Plaster must be cured before painting; dilute primer coat
Painted with oil-based semigloss or gloss	Oil-based or latex	To switch to latex: sand oil-based paint, vacuum, prime with acrylic latex primer
Painted with latex	Acrylic latex	Lightly sand before painting
Interior trim		
Doors, unpainted	Oil-based primer and paint; semigloss finish	Oil-based paint soaks into wood, dries harder, resists abrasion; sand between coats
Unpainted	Clear finishes, such as polyurethane and varnish	Always seal bare wood or it will become grimy and dull
Painted with oil-based semigloss or gloss	Oil-based paint	Sand between coats
Painted with latex	Acrylic latex	Not as durable as oil-based paint
Exterior		
Siding and trim, unpainted	Acrylic latex primer and paint	Latex stays flexible, allows some moisture migration
Painted with oil-based semigloss or gloss	Oil-based paint	Unless you strip siding, stick with oil-based paint
Painted with latex	Acrylic latex	

* Oil-based *here is synonymous with alkyd, now mentioned on most containers of paint and stain. Alkyds are synthetic resins that have largely replaced the traditional petroleum-oil base.*

Use a brush to cut in a 2-in. to 3-in. border; then follow up with a roller. You can quickly paint the vast expanse of wall—and cover brush marks—without getting wall paint on the crown molding.

PRO TIP

When cutting corners or trim, slightly overlap the paint on the adjacent surface: ⅛ in. to ¼ in. Overlapping prevents unpainted spots, fills minor irregularities, and ultimately produces a cleaner line. It's also faster. Remember: You don't need to paint a perfectly straight cut-line till you apply the finish coat to the trim.

run the roller up and down the bucket ramp several times when loading. But don't fret about small, stray spots on walls because you'll cover them later when you roll the walls.

Painting the walls is nearly the same as painting ceilings—cutting in with a brush and rolling larger areas—except that you can load more paint on the roller. To reduce spatter, roll up on the first stroke; the excess will fall back to the roller. Continue rolling in a zigzag pattern to unload the roller before rolling out the paint. A 6-in. hot-dog roller can paint the areas over doors and windows that are too narrow for a standard 9-in. roller. Rolling is always faster than brushing because you don't need to dip a roller in paint continually. If you're careful around electrical outlets, you can also use a hot-dog roller there.

door. *Paint inside to out:* If you start painting in the backs of built-ins and cabinets, your final brushstrokes on the outermost edges will be clean and crisp.

Once you've prepped the surfaces, masked off baseboards, and spread your drop cloths, it's time to paint.

Painting the ceiling begins by using a brush to *cut in* a 2-in. to 3-in. border where the ceiling meets the walls and near all moldings. This cut-in border reaches where a roller can't and thus allows you to roll out the rest of the ceiling without getting paint on the walls. Later, as you roll within ½ in. to 1 in. of the ceiling–wall intersection, you'll cover the brush marks, so the paint texture will look uniform. This operation goes much faster if one painter on a step bench cuts in, while the second painter rolls on paint, using an extension pole to reach the ceiling.

To avoid obvious lap marks, paint the ceiling in one session, working across the narrowest dimension of the room. Roll out paint in 3-ft. by 3-ft. sections—about one roller-load of paint. First roll the paint in a zigzag pattern, which distributes most of the paint (*fat paint*) in three or fours strokes; then go back and roll the paint evenly. When the roller is almost unloaded, slightly overlap adjacent areas already painted. Keep roller passes light, and don't overwork an area. Once the paint is spread evenly and starting to dry, leave it alone so its nap marks can level out.

For a smooth finish, use a standard 9-in. roller cover with ⅜-in. to ½-in. nap. Thanks to the extension pole, you can reach the ceiling easily, without needing to stand directly under the roller and its fine paint rain. To minimize mist and drips,

Use a hot-dog roller to fill those tight spaces over doors, around windows, inside cabinets, and the like.

After unloading most of the paint on the roller in a zigzig pattern, spread it out evenly, top to bottom.

PRO TIP

Most amateurs fold sheets of sandpaper in half, then in quarters. But sheets will last longer if you fold them in thirds. Folding sandpaper in fourths places abrasive surfaces face to face, causing premature wear.

With more paint on your roller, you can cover slightly larger expanses of wall, say, 3 ft. by 4 ft. If you start at the top of the wall and work down, you'll roll over any drips from above. Cover brush marks by rolling within ½ in. to 1 in. of the ceiling; this is important when applying darker hues because rolled-on paint reflects light differently from brushed-on. Slightly overlap adjacent sections. To avoid unloading excess paint along outside corners, lighten up as you roll.

Finally, sand lightly between coats when you apply oil-based paint, especially enamels on cabinets or trim. On walls, use 220-grit sandpaper or a dry sanding block. It's not necessary to sand latex paint, unless you've waited several weeks between coats; until latex is 100% dry, new coats adhere easily.

Painting the interior trim begins with the preparation tasks. Prepare the trim, window sashes, and doors by filling nail holes with nonshrinking wood filler, priming bare wood, caulking gaps with acrylic latex caulk (letting it dry overnight), lightly sanding all trim with 180-grit sandpaper, and vacuuming dust and debris. Enamel paint—which dries to a hard, glossy finish—is best for trim, window sashes, and doors because it's the most durable. By the way, there are both oil-based and latex enamels.

Painting straight edges requires a quality brush and a steady hand. If you can develop a steady hand, you won't need to apply and remove masking tape, which takes a lot of time. In most cases, all you need is a 2½-in. or 3-in. angled sash brush, unless your baseboards are exceptionally wide. Start with crown (ceiling) molding, proceed to door and window trim, and finish with the baseboards. Always paint with the grain, cutting trim edges first, then filling in the field with steady back-and-forth strokes. To avoid lap marks, paint about 3 ft. of trim at a time, overlapping adjacent sections while they're still wet. If the paint is drying too fast, add Flood's Floetrol to latex paint or its Penetrol to oil-based paint.

PRO TIP

Too often, amateurs dab paint on, which leaves crooked lines and uneven paint thickness. As you cut-in or paint trim, use long brush-strokes. Apply paint generously to the surface, and then smooth it out. For best brush control, hold the handle, not the ferrule, as if you were throwing a dart.

Rather than masking window panes or attempting to cut-in clean paint lines, paint slightly (¹⁄₁₆ in.) onto the glass. After the paint dries, use a razor to cut a clean line.

If trim edges are thinner than ³⁄₁₆ in., they'll be difficult to cut-in without spreading trim paint on the wall. In that case, overlap the wall paint onto the trim edge so that it covers the edge completely, producing a clean, straight line. In other words, the thin edge of the trim will be covered with wall paint, not enamel, but your eye won't notice.

Windows sashes vary greatly in design. But as a general rule, paint them from the inside of the sash out. That is, if sashes are divided into multiple panes by *muntins* (narrow wood sections between panes of glass), paint the muntins first. Then paint along the insides of sash rails and stiles where they meet glass. Finally, paint the faces of sashes. To develop a rhythm, paint all the

Faux-Painted Walls

Faux (pronounced *foe*) is French, meaning "false" or "imitation." It's used here to describe various advanced painting techniques that create layered finishes, sometimes to imitate stone or wood or simply to allow underlying layers of paint to show through. Typically, two accent colors are applied to already painted walls and ceilings. If the surfaces are irregular—say, rough plaster—all the better, for colors will look more varied and unpredictable. In general, thin coats of paint allow you to see layers underneath. The photos here show a few faux-painting basics; if this whets your appetite for more, there are lots of good books on the subject.

2. You'll apply the second accent color with a sponge, while the first coat is still wet. Tip: Because dipping a sponge will load too much paint onto it, instead brush the paint onto one side of the sponge, as shown.

FAUX TEXTURING

In this sequence, the painter was trying to achieve an old look, as if an imperfectly plastered wall had been painted many times. There's no single right way to apply a faux finish, so you can experiment with methods and materials till you get a look you like. Then just try to re-create that look consistently throughout the room.

1. After pouring a small amount of the first accent color into a shallow container, load your stippling brush lightly. Then quickly jab the bristles at the wall to create a stippled effect. Follow with a dry rag, lightly patting the just-applied paint to flatten the stipple points. Just flatten the points, don't remove the paint itself.

3. Pat the second accent color on. Then flip the sponge to its dry side and gently move the color around, spreading paint, not removing it; the wet side of this sponge would have streaked the paint. Stand back periodically to check whether the faux effect looks consistent from wall to wall.

vertical muntins—one side at a time—then the horizontal muntins. By painting similar windows elements at the same time, rather than jumping around, you'll be less likely to miss elements and the work will go faster.

Don't worry about cutting in clean edges at the glass. Instead, paint slightly onto the glass (1⁄16 in.), even if unevenly, thus creating a tight seal. After the paint dries, use a razor to cut a clean line on the glazing.

Painting a Double-Hung Window (Interior View)

1. Before painting, make sure both sashes are operable. Raise the inner sash, as shown, so you can paint it completely, including the tops and bottoms of its rails (horizontals).

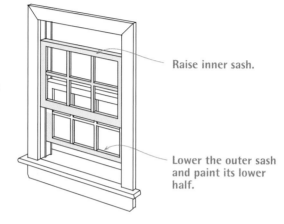

Raise inner sash.

Lower the outer sash and paint its lower half.

2. Reverse the position of the sashes and paint the rest of the upper sash.

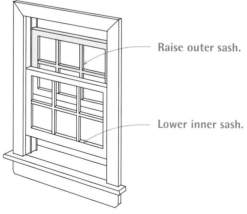

Raise outer sash.

Lower inner sash.

3. Once the paint is dry enough to handle, lower both sashes completely and paint the upper half of the jambs. When that's dry, raise both sashes, and paint the lower half, and then the window trim.

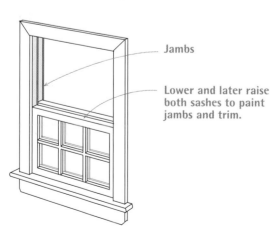

Jambs

Lower and later raise both sashes to paint jambs and trim.

Open windows to paint their edges. When painting double-hung windows, follow the steps at left. If you are repainting the exterior of the house at the same time, go outside and paint the accessible parts of the window. Slide the window sashes back to their original position, and finish painting. To prevent binding, move the sashes as soon as the paint is dry.

Painting a door is easiest if you pull its hinge pins and lay it across a pair of sawhorses. (If that's not possible, shim beneath the door so it can't move.) For the best-looking results, remove all door hardware except hinge leaves, especially if you're spray-painting. Cover the hinges with masking tape. If you prefer not to remove the old latch mechanism and escutcheons, carefully mask them too.

If you're brush-painting a flush door (flat surface), divide it into several imaginary rectangles, each half the width of the door. Apply paint with the grain and overlap the edges of adjacent sections. Work from top to bottom. Painting panel doors is similar, but work from the inside out: Paint the insides of the panels first, next the rails (horizontal pieces) top to bottom, and finally the vertical stiles.

Painting cabinets is faster if you remove and spray-paint drawers and doors, and brush-paint cabinet frames. You'll need a spray room isolated from the house (a clean garage is ideal); a drying rack for doors; and a sprayer, which you can rent.

Be sure to read the earlier sections on painting safety and spray-painting, which emphasize ventilation, using electric heat in spray and drying rooms, and wearing a respirator mask.

Start by washing doors and drawer fronts, especially those near the kitchen stove. If your cleaner isn't cutting the grease, try TSP or denatured alcohol, wearing goggles and gloves. That done, examine the cabinet parts and their hardware, and plan to replace the doors or drawer fronts that are warped or not repairable, as well as hardware that's broken or outdated. Before disassembling cabinet parts for spraying, assign each door and drawer a number. Write these numbers just inside the cabinet frame, where they won't be covered by paint. Number the doors on bottom edges (least visible) or behind the hinges.

If you're reusing the hinges, use a utility knife to score the hinge locations into each door. *Note:* Tape over door-hinge mortises if you'll reuse the hinges. Otherwise, paint buildup in the mortise may misalign the hinges and thus the doors. Either cover the mortises with tape or leave the hinges on the doors and mask off the hinges.

Remove hardware before prepping the doors. If existing paint is flaking or the doors are dented, start with 100-grit sandpaper in a random-orbit

To spray-paint a door, first place it across sawhorses at a comfortable working height. Mask hinges to keep paint off and ensure that the doors will hang correctly when reinstalled. Then move the sprayer smoothly and continuously, maintaining a constant distance from the surface. Overlap preceding passes by about a third. On each pass, begin spraying before the spray tip is over the door, and don't release the trigger till the paint fan is past the far edge. Use your free hand, as shown, to keep the hose out of the way.

sander, wipe off dust with a damp rag, and then fill cracks and holes with nonshrinking wood filler. Repeat the sequence as needed, ending with a 220-grit sanding by hand. However, if the old paint is in good condition, a single pass with 220-grit paper and a damp rag is all you'll need to prep before painting.

For the most durable surface, apply a coat of primer-sealer, followed by three coats of enamel, which will hide well, even if you're applying light paint over dark. Use acrylic-latex paint for the primer and finish coats, even if the cabinets are presently covered with oil-based enamel. Top-quality latex enamel is almost as tough as any oil-based enamel, it dries faster, and it's much easier to clean up. To minimize runs, keep the doors horizontal during spraying and drying. Between coats, sand lightly with 320-grit garnet sandpaper. Painting drawer faces is essentially the same, except that you should mask off the drawer sides. Paint cabinet frames from the inside out, finishing with long, vertical strokes on the frame faces.

When spray-painting only the face of a drawer, mask off the rest.

Homemade Drying Rack

This freestanding drying rack is constructed from 8-ft. lengths of ½-in. galvanized-steel electrical conduit, 2×2 frames lag-screwed together, and two pieces of ¾-in. plywood. The plywood base is roughly 30 in. by 30 in.; the plywood top can be smaller, say, 18 in. by 18 in. Drilling the holes slightly larger than the conduit diameter allows quick disassembly. To keep the conduit from getting dinged during transport, store it in 3-in. plastic DWV (drain, waste, and vent) pipe with capped ends; wrapping blue tape around the conduit prevents the metal's marring newly painted cabinet doors. To avoid tipping, load the rack from the bottom, unload it from the top, and balance the weight carefully side to side.

PRO TIP

To paint both sides of a door without waiting for the first painted side to dry, drive a pair of nails into the top and bottom of the door; then rest those nails on a pair of sawhorses. You and a helper can grab the nails and flip the door over. When both sides are dry, pull the nails; then fill and paint the holes.

▐▐▐▐

PRO TIP

For some old-house purists, spray-painted finishes are *too* perfect. So, after spraying two finish coats, they use a 6-in. roller to apply a thinned (10 percent to 15 percent) final coat. They then *tip off* the surface with light strokes of a brush tip. Use a ⅜-in. mohair roller cover, which will not shed. Easy does it: Brush marks should be faint—barely visible, in fact.

▐▐▐▐

Stripping and Refinishing Interior Trim

Natural wood can be handsome, but stripping layers of old paint or dulled finish is an enormously tedious, messy job. The following questions and tests may give you easier options.

SIX QUESTIONS BEFORE STRIPPING

▶ **What kind of wood?** Builders often used plain or inferior-grade softwood for trim they intended to paint. Test-strip a small section to see if the wood is worth stripping. Common pine or spruce and badly gouged wood probably aren't.

▶ **How thick is the wood?** If wood paneling is a ⅟₁₆-in. veneer, it may be too thin to sand, let alone scrape and strip. 🚫 After turning off the electrical power, move panel battens (vertical pieces) or electrical outlet covers to see the edge of a panel.

▶ **What kind of paint?** Trim paint in houses built before 1960 likely contains lead, which becomes hazardous if you sand it or heat-strip it. Yet it may be perfectly safe if it's intact and well maintained. Analyze a paint sample, as explained on p. 443. Also, the more paint layers, the bigger the mess.

▶ Clear finishes that have become dull and grimy may just need a good washing. Using a damp rag, rub Murphy's® Oil Soap onto a small section and wipe it dry quickly. If that clouds the surface, stop; but if it brightens the woodwork, keep going.

▶ If a clear finish remains dull after a test-wash or is worn looking, scuff-sanding and a new application of the old finish may do the trick.

▶ If painted or clear finishes are cracking, peeling, or otherwise coming off, new coatings won't stick. To test adherence, use a utility knife to lightly score a 1-in. by 1-in. area into nine smaller squares (like a tic-tac-toe array). Press a piece of duct tape onto the area and pull up sharply: If two or more little squares pull off, you should strip the paint or finish.

STRIPPING SAFELY

Before stripping woodwork, read "Painting Safely," on p. 440, and "Lead-Paint Safety," on p. 442. Many of the concerns when stripping are the same as those when painting. Most important, wear a respirator mask with replaceable filters. Also wear rubber gloves, goggles, and a long-sleeved shirt. Lay down plastic tarps (or layers of newspaper) to protect floors and capture paint debris, mask off areas you're not stripping, and ensure adequate ventilation. Even if a chemical stripper is relatively odorless and claims to be eco-friendly—keep it off your skin and out of your lungs! Read instructions for all stripping chemicals before using them, and if you're using a heat gun, have a fire extinguisher close by.

STRIPPING METHODS

Test-strip small sections of woodwork to see which method—or combination of methods—works best for you.

Stains and clear finishes are thinner than paint and more inclined to run, so mask off adjacent areas before starting prep work.

Metal scrapers with straight edges work well on flat surfaces without too many layers of paint or clear finish. A scraper with changeable heads enables you to scrape varying contours. For best results, hold the scraper head roughly perpendicular to the surface and pull the tool toward you. *Caution:* Sharp scraper heads can easily gouge wood, especially softwoods like fir and pine, whose contours may obscured by thick paint.

Heat guns soften paint so you can scrape it off. Heat guns can remove many layers of paint, but stay alert when using them. Maintain a constant distance from the surface you're stripping, and keep the gun moving so you don't scorch one spot. Using a heat gun on shellac and varnish gets tricky because they have low kindling temperatures and tend to burn when heated; first, try stripping them with metal scrapers.

Never use a heat gun next to glass—for example, on window muntins—because you could crack the glass. Heat guns can also ignite dry materials within walls, so stop using guns well before the end of the workday so woodwork can cool. Before you leave for the day, sniff around for smoke or "hot smells."

For chemical strippers, a rule of thumb is the stronger and smellier the chemical, the faster it

PRO TIP

Never use ammoniated cleaners to wash old woodwork with a clear finish. If the finish is shellac, ammonia, which is strongly akaline, will dissolve it.

IIII

What's That Finish?

To identify your woodwork's finish, rub on a small amount of the test-solvents in this list, starting at the top of the list (the most benign) and working down till you've got your answer. When applying solvents, wear rubber gloves, open the windows, and wear a respirator mask.

▶ **Oil.** If a few drops of boiled linseed oil soak into the woodwork, you have an oil finish: tung oil, linseed, Watco® or the like. If the oil beads up on the surface, the woodwork has a hard finish, such as lacquer, varnish, or shellac. Keep investigating.

▶ **Denatured alcohol.** If the finish quickly gets gummy, congratulations! It's shellac, which will readily accept a new coat of shellac after a modest sanding with an abrasive nylon pad or 220-grit sandpaper. Older woodwork with an orange tinge is often shellac-coated.

▶ **Mineral spirits (paint thinner).** This will dissolve wax immediately. Dampen a rag and wipe once. If there's a yellowish or light brown residue on the rag, it's definitely wax. If your woodwork finish has an unevenly shiny, runny appearance, suspect spray-on wax.

▶ **Lacquer thinner.** This solvent dissolves both varnish and shellac, so try denatured alcohol first. If alcohol doesn't dissolve the finish but lacquer thinner does, it's varnish.

▶ **Acetone.** This one will dissolve varnish, too, in about 30 seconds. But if acetone doesn't affect the finish, it's probably polyurethane.

In this 1920s house, the homeowner wanted an older look for the cabinets. So after spraying three coats of oil–based enamel, the painters rehung the doors and rolled on a final coat . . .

. . . which they then lightly tipped off with a dry brush, intentionally leaving very faint brush marks.

COMMON CLEAR-FINISH PROBLEMS

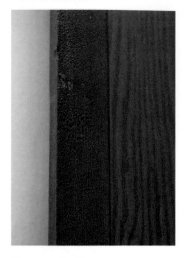

Orange peel, often seen near kitchens, is caused by airborne cooking oils.

Weeping is wood sap excreted over decades.

Wax buildup is characterized by uneven, shiny sections where sprayed-on wax has run.

will strip paint or finish. For example, methylene chloride will soften multiple layers in 10 minutes to 15 minutes; whereas "safe" DBE (dibasic ester) based strippers may need 24 hours. Given enough time to work, a stripper should soften *all* layers of paint or finish. Follow the stripping-time recommendations on the container label. By the way, *semipaste* strippers are best for vertical surfaces. Even when brushed on thickly, they won't run.

Chemical strippers require patience and care. Use a rag to cover the cap before opening the container, so stripper won't splash on you. Pour stripper slowly into a work pail, and close the container immediately so it won't spill if the container is bumped or knocked over. As you apply stripper, brush away from yourself. To avoid tracking stripper throughout the site, replace plastic tarps as they become fouled with softened paint. Or lay down newspaper, which is cheap and easy to roll up before stuffing it into a garbage bag.

Once your tarps or newspaper are in place, brush on stripper liberally. A ⅛-in. to ¼-in. coating of stripper should stay wet long enough to soften all the layers of paint or finish. To make sure that slower strippers stay moist, press a sheet of light-weight plastic (polyethylene) right onto the stripper-coated woodwork; the stripper won't dissolve the plastic. Periodically lift an edge of the plastic and try scraping off the paint. Be patient: Remove the plastic only when the softened paint scoops off easily. Till then, leave the plastic on.

Although renovators usually use a wide spackling knife or a putty knife to scoop off softened paint, a wooden spatula with a beveled edge is a near-perfect tool because it won't gouge the chemically softened wood. Whatever tool you use, unload sludge from your scraper after each pass. Use a toothbrush, a nylon potato brush, or a handful of wood shavings to dislodge softened paint from detailed or hard-to-reach areas. Only occasional spots should need additional stripper.

When the woodwork is bare, scrub off the stripper residue with a solvent recommended by the manufacturer—typically, mineral spirits applied with a nylon abrasive pad, then blotted dry with paper towels. Follow that with a dilute solution (5 percent to 10 percent) of household cleaner in warm water and wipe that off with paper towels. Allow the wood to dry thoroughly—at least a day or two—before filling holes or sanding. *Note:* Don't use steel wool to scrub stripper or remove paint. Otherwise, steel particles can stick in the wood and then rust, marring the new finish.

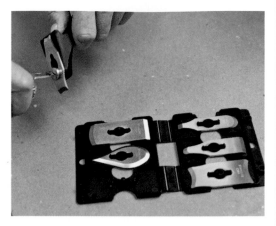

This hand scraper comes with six interchangeable stainless-steel blades, which will fit most contours you're likely to encounter.

REFINISHING WOODWORK

Once your stripped woodwork has dried, patch it with wood putty that dries to the same color as the unfinished wood. (Putty lightens as it dries.) Test a number of putty colors, allowing each to dry well before test-staining or finishing. When a patch is so hard that your thumbnail can't gouge it, the putty's dry enough to sand.

Sanding. If the woodwork is in good shape and doesn't need filling, just scuff-sand it (sand it lightly) with 220- or 320-grit sandpaper before applying a clear finish. More likely, you'll need to use several grades of sandpaper, starting with 80-grit or 100-grit to sand down tool marks or dings, moving on to 150-grit, and ending with 180-grit or 220-grit.

Sand sections completely with one grit before switching to another, even if you think an area is smooth enough. If you switch from 120-grit to 150-grit while sanding a baseboard, for example, it may have two different shades when you stain or finish it.

If there's a lot of woodwork to sand, use a palm-size power sander (also called a block sander) for the first three sandings, and finish up by hand sanding with the wood grain, using 180-grit or 220-grit garnet paper. Wrap sandpaper around a standard blackboard eraser or a scrap of 2×4 to hand-sand flat areas; sandpaper wrapped around a dowel works well on concave areas. After sanding, wipe or vacuum the surfaces to remove the dust.

APPLYING A CLEAR FINISH

Clear finishes can be brushed on like paint or wiped on and off with a rag or pad—or some combination thereof. Brushed-on finishes tend to be thicker and shinier, whereas wiped-on finishes are thinner and less shiny. As with oil-based paints, use natural-bristle brushes to apply oil-based clear finishes. Use synthetic bristles for water-based polyurethanes and such.

Don't shake containers of clear finish. If you do, you'll entrap air bubbles. Instead, stir them well by hand till the thick, flattening agent at the bottom of the can is evenly distributed. Clear finishes tend to "skin over," so pour out small amounts into a painter's pail and replace the can lid promptly. If finish builds up around the rim, the lid won't seat well. To prevent buildup, use an old slotted screwdriver to punch slots around the rim's recess. These slots will let excess finish

Staining and Sealing: A Sampler

There should be a Ph.D. in stains. There are all-pigment stains that won't fade (a good choice for window trim), water- and oil-based stains, liquid stains, penetrating stains that both stain and seal, and gel stains that won't run on vertical surfaces. Plus, there are wood conditioners, sanding sealers, presealers, and a plethora of putties and wood fillers. If you want to learn more, excellent resources are Michael Dresdner's *Painting and Finishing* and *Finishes and Finishing Techniques* (both The Taunton Press).

▶ To achieve an even stain on softwoods such as fir, preseal them with a thinned coat of whatever the clear finish will be, say, 1 part oil-based polyurethane to 4 parts mineral spirits. Presealer soaks into the softer parts of the wood and seals them slightly. But once dry, the surface should still feel like wood.

▶ Oil-based polyurethane over water-based stains is okay, but do not use water-based polyurethane over oil-based stains. The polyurethane won't stick.

You can usually apply oil-based penetrating stains over previously varnished surfaces, but they can be tricky to work with. Test-stain an inconspicuous section. If the penetrating stain is compatible with the old finish, it should dry hard overnight.

After brushing stain on, use a clean, dry rag to remove any excess. You may need to apply several coats—over several days—to match existing stains. So be patient.

PRO TIP

If you're using water-based finishes, use damp rags to wipe dust off surfaces, rather than tack rags. Because tack rags are typically a piece of cheesecloth treated with varnish to make it sticky, tack rags leave a faint, oily film that water-based coatings may have trouble adhering to. Tack rags are fine, however, if followed by oil- or solvent-based finishes.

PRO TIP

After stripping with hand scrapers and a heat gun, if you decide that your old trim is too beat up or too plain to look good under a clear finish, don't bother with chemicals. Sand down the remaining paint edges, prime the trim, paint it, and call it a day. It'll look great.

||||

Sheet-peeling is caused by excessive moisture migrating through a wall—in this case, an unvented bathroom wall.

drain into the can, allowing the lid to seat tightly into the recess. If the finish skins over, strain the finish or discard it.

Polyurethanes are favored for wood in kitchens, bathrooms, hallways, and other busy areas. Once cured, they're tough and water resistant. And they're easy to apply. Oil-based and water-based polyurethanes are equally durable but require slightly different application methods. For both types, apply at least two coats, preferably three.

▶ Water-based polyurethanes: Because water-based polyurethanes dry clear, use them if you want light-colored wood to stay light. Seal woodwork before application. Thereafter, brush on full strength. Although water-based poly dries quickly, tempting you to apply two coats in a day, wait a full day between coats so it can harden. There's no need to sand between coats unless a week passes, in which case, use a fine nylon abrasive pad. If you want to add a wax finish, wait a month after application, mindful of the several-week curing time.

▶ Oil-based polyurethanes: Oil-based polyurethanes impart a rich, amber color to wood. So use them if you favor dark wood or an historic look. They don't need a preliminary sealer coat, but they will flow on better if you thin each coat with 10 percent mineral spirits.

Oil-based polyurethanes dry slowly, so apply only one coat per day, unless the manufacturer recommends otherwise. Here again, sanding between coats is not imperative unless you wait a week between coats—or you need to sand down imperfections. Before waxing an oil-based poly, be sure to wait a week after the last coat dries.

Shellac doesn't have the water-resistance of polyurethane, but it dries fast; has a wonderful old-fashioned sheen; and, as noted earlier, adheres well to earlier shellac coats and can be touched up repeatedly. If wood is new or recently stripped, apply a sealer coat of thinned-down shellac: If you'll be staining the wood, brush on a 1 part shellac to 4 parts denatured alcohol sealer first, allowing it to dry. Otherwise, brush or wipe on a coat of 1 part shellac to 2 parts alcohol, wiping off the excess and allowing the coat to dry 2 hours before sanding lightly with 320-grit sandpaper. Thereafter, apply two or three shellac coatings, thinned with 10 percent denatured alcohol. If the surface is smooth, there's no need to sand between coats. Wait 1 day between coats and 3 days before waxing. Because shellac dries so quickly, don't attempt to rebrush it.

Oil finishes include boiled linseed oil, tung oil, and the so-called Danish oils like Watco. Using a nylon pad or a rag, rub a generous amount of oil onto the wood. Let that soak in for 10 minutes or 15 minutes before rubbing off the excess with a clean, dry cloth. With each coat, the wood will darken slightly. Allow each coat to dry 24 hours and reapply the oil till you get the look you like; usually, two or three coats do the trick. Oil finishes offer the least protection but are easiest to reapply.

Painting the Exterior

Exterior paint jobs can last 10 years or more if you're fastidious about prep work and attentive to water-related building details. Key factors include proper flashing of windows, doors, and roof junctures; maintaining gutter systems; caulking gaps in exterior siding; and adequately venting excess moisture from interior spaces.

WHY PAINT FAILS

Before you sand or scrape anything, figure out why the paint is failing . . . and where.

Blistering is usually caused by painting over damp wood or an earlier coat of paint that isn't dry. Blisters often contain water vapor, although "temperature blisters" are largely hot air, caused by painting a surface that was too hot. Scrape and sand blisters, allow the wood siding to dry thoroughly; then spot prime.

Peeling off in sheets, is blistering on a grand scale—sometimes an entire wall. Such peeling is most common on older homes lacking vapor barriers and occurs especially on siding outside bathrooms or kitchens, when excessive moisture migrates through the wall. If your old house has been retrofitted with insulation and a vapor barrier, peeling may indicate moisture trapped inside the walls and, possibly, rotted framing. At the very least, add ventilator fans to exhaust water vapor. And on outside walls, drive thin plastic wedges behind the lap siding to help moisture escape.

Intercoat peeling, a new coat of paint separating from the old, is a classic case of poor prep work. Typically, chalky old paint was not scrubbed or sanded, and thus new paint could not adhere. Or, less often, the painter waited too long between the prime and finish coats. Scrape failed paint, sand, and wash the surface well, letting it dry before repainting.

Wrinkling is caused by applying paint too thickly, painting an exterior that is too cold, failing to thin paint sufficiently, applying paint before earlier coats are dry, or letting the paint get rained on before it cured adequately. Use a power sander to even out the surface before repainting.

Alligatoring or cross-grain cracking, is caused by too many layers of paint, usually old, oil-based paint. The thicker the paint, the less it can flex as siding expands and contracts. So the paint cracks—sometimes, all the way down to bare wood. Alligatoring may also be caused by painting over an undercoat that didn't dry completely. In either case, it's big trouble, because you'll need to strip the paint down to bare wood and seal it with a primer-sealer before repainting. It may be easier to replace the siding

Chalking is a normal occurrence and isn't a problem unless it's excessive, usually the result of cheap paint. Because new paint won't adhere well to a powdery residue, you must scrub and rinse the old surface and allow it to dry before repainting.

Rusty nail stains are common where siding nails were not galvanized. The fastest fix is sanding each stain lightly and priming with a rust-inhibiting primer like Kilz® stain blocker. For a longer-lasting repair, sand till you expose each nail head, use a nail set to sink each one $\frac{1}{8}$ in. below the surface, prime with stain blocker, and fill with wood filler. Then sand and spot-prime before painting.

Tannin bleed through, a widespread brown staining, occurs when waterborne resins in woods, such as cedar and redwood, bleed through porous latex primers. Scrub the surface well and prime it with one or two coats of an oil-based (alkyd) primer like Kilz or Benjamin Moore Fresh-Start®. Paint what you like—latex

PRO TIP

Although white pigmented shellacs like B-I-N® are terrific for blocking stains on interior surfaces, they're not advisable for priming exteriors. Hot sun softens and degrades shellac.

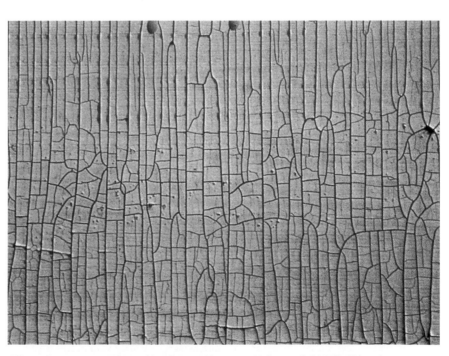

Alligatoring, or cross-grain cracking, is caused by too many layers of old, inflexible paint.

or oil-based—over that. At this writing, stain-blocking acrylic latex primers show promise but don't yet have the track record of oil-based stain-blocking primers. Get a second opinion from an up-to-date paint supplier.

Graying wood is a natural response to sunlight when siding is left unfinished or has been sealed with a clear finish that degrades. Never leave wood siding exposed to the elements—both because bare wood quickly degrades and because paint or clear finishes don't adhere well to degraded wood. Sand and wash the surface, and reapply a clear finish with a UV-blocking agent. Clear finishes need to be reapplied every 2 years to 4 years. If that sounds like too much maintenance, prime the siding with an oil-based primer, and then switch to paint.

Mold and moss are common in damp climates, on north-facing and foliage-shaded walls and where lawn sprinklers hit the house. Siding that's constantly damp can lead to structural rot. For starters, cut back foliage and the adjust sprinklers. Scrub moss off by hand, using a wire brush. Remove mold by applying a cleaner/mildewcide such as Zinsser Jomax® before scrubbing or power washing the surface (but see the cautions later in this section). After the exterior has dried for about a week, prime as needed, and repaint with a paint containing a mildewcide.

PREPARING THE EXTERIOR

Before you start prep work, be sure to review this chapter's earlier sections on equipment and lead-paint safety. Even though you're working outside, wear a respirator mask when sanding or scraping paint and when working with solvents or paints of any kind. Likewise, when applying cleaning solutions (which can be caustic), wear rubber gloves and eye protection.

Prep work is prodigiously messy, so spread dropcloths out 8 ft. from your house to protect your lawn and shrubs. Otherwise, you'll be picking paint scraps out of your grass for years or—even worse—exposing kids and pets to old lead-based paint. If it's hot and sunny don't cover your plants with plastic drop cloths; the plants will cook. Instead use fabric drop cloths, which shade plants, won't tear, and are far less slippery to walk on. But if tests indicate lead paint, capture the debris in heavy 6-mil plastic tarps, which you can roll up and discard at the end of each day.

Washing surfaces. Before installing new wood siding, apply primer-sealer to front and back faces and to all edges. When that coat is dry, scuff-sand it with 100-grit sandpaper, and dust it

off with a whisk broom. Then install the siding before applying the top coats.

However, if the siding is already painted—even if the paint is in good shape—first wash it. Start by applying a house-cleaning solution, using a garden pump-sprayer. A dilute solution of TSP is often recommended, but urban houses may need a cleaning agent with a degreaser that will cut soot, automobile exhaust, and the like. As noted earlier, if there's mold present, use a cleaner with a mildewcide. Once the cleaner has had time to work, rinse it off with a garden hose and allow it to dry thoroughly for a week or so before painting. That's a minimal wash.

To thoroughly wash and rinse an exterior, rent a *pressure washer,* which has a small boiler and a high-pressure electric pump. The rental company will recommend a detergent suitable for the unit and explain how to use it safely. For most cleaning jobs, 1,800 psi to 2500 psi (pounds per square inch) is specified—for softwoods like cedar or redwood, 1,000 psi to 1,500 psi. Tip sizes range from 0° (concentrated pressure that can easily damage siding) to 40° (a wider *fan* of water favored for light cleaning). In general, start with a low-pressure setting till you are familiar with the machine, and keep the spray wand moving. *Note:* Always spray downward if you're cleaning lapped siding. Otherwise, you'll force water underneath.

Scraping, sanding, spot-priming, caulking. Once the siding has dried, hand-scrape the loose paint. For this, use a large scraper with 3-in.-wide blade, preferably one with a forward grip over

PRO TIP

Although power washing is widely used to clean stucco, brick, aluminum, and vinyl siding, it's not appropriate for wood siding. It can gouge and even shred wood, force water into gaps around doors and windows, soak insulation inside walls, and inject water into wood that will take weeks to dry. Certainly, *never use power washers to strip paint:* They'll scar wood and scatter paint flecks to the ends of the earth.

Ladder SAFETY

If you're painting a whole house, the job will go much faster if you rent scaffolding. However, if you decide to use an extension ladder or two, follow these safety rules:

▶ Don't place ladders near incoming electric service lines. When the air is moist, electricity can arc to nearby objects or people; so keep your distance.

▶ Securely position the ladder feet. Never ascend a ladder that lists to one side. On uneven ground, use a ladder with adjustable leveling feet, as shown on p. 36.

▶ Place the ladder bottom out from a building no more than one-quarter the ladder's height.

▶ Wear hard-soled shoes so your feet won't tire quickly on the ladder rungs.

Hand-scrape nooks and crannies that power tools can't reach or could damage. Here, heat guns and chemical scrapers also make sense.

Where a random-orbit sander won't fit, use a palm sander, as shown, with 60-grit or 80-grit sandpaper. A palm sander is also handy for scuff-sanding old paint in good condition so new paint will adhere better.

To maximize adhesion, spot-prime seams and gaps before caulking them with an exterior-grade, paintable acrylic or multipolymer caulk. Paint won't stick to pure silicone caulk.

the blade. Be sure to scrape the lower edges of the clapboards and beneath the windowsills. For hard-to-reach areas when siding abuts trim or where trim is curved or intricate, use a hand scraper with interchangeable blades. If paint doesn't come off easily, that's a good sign—it's well adhered. However, if isolated areas of paint are too thick or obscure ornamental details, use a chemical stripper or a heat gun to remove more paint.

After scraping loose paint, use 80-grit sandpaper to feather out the edges of the remaining paint, smooth uneven surfaces, and scuff up surfaces so new paint will adhere well. For this work, an electric palm sander or random-orbit sander is a good tool, powerful yet light enough to use all day. If you're prepping painted stucco, brick, or concrete, instead use a wire brush. When you're done, brush off the dust with a hand broom.

If the paint is largely intact, you may not need to prime it, but you should spot-prime all areas you've scraped down to bare wood; exposed nail heads; and cracks, gaps, and holes you intend to fill or caulk. Spot-priming blocks nail stains, seals wood from moisture, and provides a better surface for filler or caulk to adhere to. Use either an exterior-grade polyurethane, a paintable

acrylic, or a multipolymer caulk; don't use silicone caulk because paint won't stick to it.

This is also a good time to set and fill nail heads. Because wood filler shrinks as it dries, slightly overfill the holes. When the filler's dry, sand it flush.

Where wood is badly deteriorated, you should replace it. If the trim has only localized rot and would be difficult to replace, scrape the loose matter away and impregnate the remaining area with an epoxy filler, such as the one shown in the photos on p. 134.

Stripping exterior paint. Stripping exterior paint is a nasty job. Fortunately, only a few paint conditions require stripping. One of those conditions is *alligatoring,* in which many layers of old, cracked, oil-based paint resemble the skin of an alligator (see the photo on p. 457). In that case, before stripping to bare wood, get a bid to replace the siding. Labor costs should be less, to say nothing of the cost, mess, and health concerns of stripping lead-based paint. But if you decide to strip, wear a respirator mask, eye protection, and other apparel related to lead safety

Basically, stripping exterior paint becomes a choice between mechanical scrapers and chemicals. Sandblasting is too dirty, damaging, and dangerous to be done by anyone but an expert. Sanding and hand scraping a whole house is impossibly slow. And whereas heat guns are okay for small areas, the snail's pace of stripping a house and the real risk of starting a fire make it a distant third option. So, in the end, some combination of mechanical scraping, chemicals, and limited hand scraping will probably serve best.

Mechanical scrapers such as AIT's Paint Shaver® are serious, two-handed tools. Mechanical scrapers look somewhat like angle grinders, but have carbide-tipped rotary cutterheads that shave paint from the clapboard faces and edges. The better models have vacuum attachments that collect most of the debris. Nonetheless, have tarps in place before starting; and to prevent cutter damage, set siding nails well below the surface. Thus, as you strip, you'll need a hammer and a nail set to set the nails you missed. Also, be sure to install scaffolding so you can focus on the tool and not your footing.

To minimize damage to the siding, first set the tool's depth adjustment so you need several passes to strip a surface. Finding the right cutting depth is largely a matter of trial and error, so first test the tool on an inconspicuous section. Beyond that, the real trick to mechanical scraping is keeping the steel shoe/guard flat to the surface so the tools strips evenly. Where a Paint Shaver won't reach, use hand scrapers, a chemical stripper, or small mechanical scrapers like the Metabo™ Lf714S. When finished stripping, use a palm sander or a random-orbit sander with 50-grit to 80-grit sandpaper to smooth out the rough spots before washing, caulking, dusting, and priming.

Chemical strippers are most appropriate where trim is intricate or where you want to remove lead paint without dispersing particles into the air and soil. Strippers vary in strength, environmental impact, working time (4 hours to 48 hours), and method of application. Most often, chemicals are brushed on ⅛ in. to ¼ in. thick, but it's possible to apply some strippers with modified paint-spraying equipment. (If you spray, wear a full-face mask, gloves, and disposable coveralls.)

A mechanical scraper with a vacuum attachment is the tool of choice when you've got to strip exterior paint. But set the nail heads first, or you'll chew up expensive scraper blades. Eye protection is a must.

Given enough time to work, chemical strippers should remove all paint layers in one application. To keep its stripper from drying out while working, Dumond Chemical's Peel-Away® system comes with plasticized paper that's pressed directly onto stripper-coated surfaces. Peel-Away's active agent is lye, which is extremely caustic, so after stripping surfaces, you need to apply a special neutralizing solution before priming or painting. Another product, Back to Nature's Multi-Strip™, is biodegradable, non-caustic, and water soluble. Thus it doesn't need a neutralizing agent.

APPLYING EXTERIOR PAINT

Prep work done, it's almost time to paint. Even if you've read this entire chapter, you might want to scan it one last time for tips about paint quality, tools, basic techniques, spray-painting, and so on.

Here's a quick review of factors mentioned in greater detail earlier in this chapter: Regarding exterior coatings, the more opaque the finish, the better it will protect wood siding. *Clear, oil-based sealers* help siding shed water without obscuring the wood grain, but they must to be reapplied every 2 years to 4 years because they offer relatively little protection from UV rays. A second option, *semitransparent stains* resemble thinned down-paints and represent a compromise that adds UV protection but reduces siding visibility, That is, you can see wood texture but not its grain. Third, there's paint that completely hides and so protects wood the best, if correctly applied. Which brings us to acrylic latex.

Acrylic latex is king. What's not to like? Simply called latex, it's durable, flexible, virtually odorless, and cleans up with soap and water. Use good-quality latex primer-sealer and paint on all exteriors, whether covering existing paint or unfinished siding. Oil-based primers are justified only if your siding is raw redwood or cedar, or if you've had problems with tannin bleed-through and so need to block stains before repainting. Latex is also best for masonry, stucco, aluminum, and vinyl siding because it's the only coating flexible enough to expand and contract as siding heats and cools.

Optimal conditions. Check the weather before you start painting. Ideally, wait until several dry days are forecast. If possible, wait a week after a rain. Also allow morning mists to evaporate before painting. Humidity near 90 is risky, because it doesn't allow the paint to cure. The best temperatures for curing range between 60°F and 85°F. Don't paint when temperatures are 90°F or above, because surfaces that are too hot can cause paint to blister. Finally, stop painting 2 hours before sundown if nighttime temperatures could drop below 40°F.

If possible, don't paint in strong sun. Paint the west and south faces of the house early in the morning; the north face at noon; and the east face and any part of the south face still remaining in the afternoon.

Latex paint should flow on easily and dry slowly enough that brush marks level (disappear). To slow the rate of drying, add a dash of Flood's Floetrol to latex, as indicated on the container. To slow the rate of drying of oil-based paint, add Flood's Penetrol.

A painting sequence. Paint the house from top to bottom. To minimize overlap marks on clapboards, paint horizontal sections all the way across, till they end at window or door trim or at the end of a wall. After painting large sections, go back and paint the trim, windows, and doors, top to bottom. Last, paint gutters, porches, and decks. If you can remove shutters, doors, screens, and the like, do so; they are much easier to paint if placed across sawhorses. Don't bother to mask trim or windows unless you're spray-painting. Again, you can later scrap stray paint from window glass with a razor tool.

Using a brush, paint the bottom edges of horizontal siding before applying paint to the flat face of each board. To distribute paint evenly along siding, after loading the brush with fresh paint, partially unload the brush by dabbing every foot or so; then spread out the dabs, brushing the paint in and smoothing it with the wood grain. For exteriors, a 4-in. brush is the workhorse for the big spaces. A 3-in. angled sash brush is handy for cutting in trim edges and corners. For a sequence of painting window parts, see p. 450.

If the house has a stucco exterior or some other flat expanse, roll the paint on—after using a brush to cut in the edges—or spray it. Exterior rolling is much the same as interior rolling: Roll on fat paint in a zigzag pattern, before rolling it out evenly. To minimize spatter, roll the first stroke up. In general, the smoother the exterior surface, the shorter the roller cover nap.

Apply primers and top coats full strength, except when the paint seems to be drying too quickly. Latex dries quickly and adheres well, so you don't need to sand between coats unless you wait several days or more. Consult the label on the paint container for drying times and maximum intervals between coats. For a lasting paint job, apply one coat of primer and at least two top coats. Though it's probably not imperative to

For a sequence of painting window parts, see p. 450.

PRO TIP

It's impossible to tell from a manufacturer's small sample swatch how a paint color will look on a house. Instead, prime and paint a sheet of plywood—and repaint it till you find a color you love. By the way, paint stores often are willing to tint primer to match your eventual top coat, which helps top coats cover better and look truer.

Avoiding Direct Sun

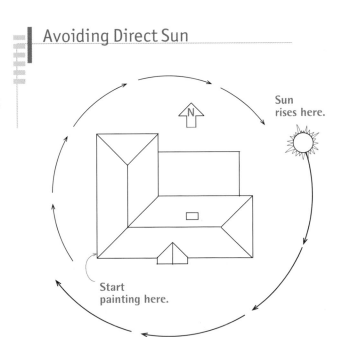

Sun rises here.

Start painting here.

Avoid the sun around the house as you paint, so that you apply paint in the shade if possible. Paint applied in full sunlight is more likely to blister later.

prime existing paint that's in good shape and well prepped, it's advisable. However, prime all siding that has been sanded or begun weathering down to bare wood.

Oil-based stains and semitransparent stains do not need thinning. Apply them full strength to bare wood. If you've stripped the house of its original paint and want to switch to stain, test a small section first. Because a clear stain will probably look uneven, a semitransparent stain is likely the better bet. To apply stain, a paint pad will hold more stain than a brush but requires a little practice to avoid runs.

As with paint, apply stain to the undersides of the shingle or clapboard courses first. To avoid getting stain on your skin, wear a long-sleeved shirt, rubber gloves, a hat, and safety glasses.

A Spray OF TIPS

Use a cardboard shield to prevent overspray onto adjacent areas.

▶ Spray exterior trim first. Mask the siding, spray the trim, and let it dry before removing the first masking. Then mask over (cover) the trim so you can paint the siding.

▶ To mask-off windows, apply double-sided masking tape around the perimeter of the window. Press sheet plastic to the tape and trim off the excess plastic.

▶ To keep paint off features such as chimneys and roofing, use a cardboard shield to block the spray, as shown at left.

▶ Don't spray when it's windy. Even if the air is calm, move cars and lawn furniture away from the house, or cover them. If your house is close to a neighbor's—ask the neighbors to do the same or, better, do it for them.

▶ After you spray a section, immediately brush the paint into the surface. Back-brushing helps sprayed paint adhere better, look great, and last longer. But because latex dries so quickly, back-brush before spraying the next section.

After spraying a section of siding, immediately brush the paint into the wood—and into the building seams—using a 4-in. brush.

Wallpapering

Wallpaper has been popular for centuries, particularly in formal rooms where there's less danger from little ones' grimy fingers and rowdy ways. Paint has long been favored for rooms that get the most use and abuse because it's durable and easy to clean and apply.

Today "wallpapers" are available in so many materials—including grasses, bamboo, rice paper, foil, and cork—that they are collectively called *wallcoverings,* and some of them are stronger, more durable, and easier to maintain than wallpapers and some paints. Many are backed with paper or cloth, with cloth being stronger. But by far the most popular are vinyl-coated wallcoverings, which are washable and grease resistant.

Today, most wallcoverings come prepasted. This makes them easier to apply and—years later—to strip from the wall. Because the manufacturer has already pasted the covering, all you need do is unroll it, and soak it briefly in a water tray. But, as you'll see in this chapter, many pros avoid the drips and mess of a water tray by rolling a prepaste activator onto the backing.

Selecting Materials

Choose a wallcovering whose pattern and color are appropriate for the room. There are no hard and fast rules on what works. But in general, lighter colors make rooms look larger, and darker colors make rooms look smaller. Smaller, subdued patterns are better for quiet rooms. Splashy floral prints tend to serve better in places such as front halls that bustle with activity. Delicate textiles or grasses are best reserved for rooms with little traffic and little risk of bruising. Also, consider the age and energy level of the people in the room. For example, vinyl-coated murals of rock stars or sports themes will appeal to kids and endure abuse.

Washable wallcoverings can be sponged clean occasionally with a mild soap or cleaning solution. Scrubbable coverings can take a vigorous scouring with a nylon-bristled brush or a pad, as well as stronger cleaning agents. There are also strippable and peelable wallcoverings, discussed

To hang wallcovering, first unfold the top half of a pasted strip and carefully align it to a plumbed line, or to the plumbed edge of the preceding strip.

Papering OVER DIFFERENCES

Almost everybody still refers to *wallcovering* as "wallpaper." But in this chapter *wallcovering*, the noun, will be the general term for both paper and nonpaper coverings. However, when used as a verb, *wallpaper* refers to the act of hanging either type of covering. Last, you can assume that advice on papering or prepping walls also holds true for ceilings.

at greater length in "Stripping Wallpaper," on p. 470.

For do-it-yourselfers, it's smart to choose a covering that's easy to hang. That is, textured coverings can be fragile and difficult to handle. The condition of existing walls should also affect your decision. For example, heavy coverings can conceal minor wall flaws; whereas lightweight papers will accentuate flaws and won't conceal underlying bold paints or vivid patterns. If walls or trim are badly out of square, avoid coverings with large, bold patterns because slight mismatches along their edges will be more obvious than if patterns are subdued.

Choosing the Right Adhesive

Most of the adhesives described here come premixed, unless otherwise noted.

▶ **Clay-based adhesives** dry quickly and grip well. Use them to install heavy vinyls, Mylars, foils, or canvas-backed coverings or to adhere wall liners to difficult surfaces like block or paneling. *Caution:* Clays stain delicate materials. They may attack paint substrates, and they probably dry too quickly for amateurs to use successfully.

▶ **Clear adhesives** may be the best all-around pastes. They're strippable, grip almost as well as clays, and won't stain. Clear adhesives are frequently classified either as *standard mix* (good for most lightweight coverings) or as *heavy duty* (for weightier coverings).

▶ **Cellulose** has the least grip of any adhesive in this listing, but it's strong enough for delicate papers—especially for fine English wallpapers and unbacked murals. It won't stain but is somewhat less convenient because it comes as a powder to be mixed with water.

▶ **Vinyl-to-vinyl adhesive** is recommended for adhering vinyl borders over vinyl wallcoverings or new vinyl wallcovering over old. It's so tenacious that it can't be stripped without destroying the substrates, so wipe up stray adhesive immediately. It's also used to adhere wall liners, Mylar, and foil.

▶ **Prepaste activator** makes prepasted wallcoverings easier to install. It improves adhesion, while letting you avoid the mess of water trays. Instead, you roll-on prepaste activator, which conveniently increases *slip time*, the time in which you can adjust wallcovering after hanging it.

▶ **Seam adhesive** typically comes in a tube, reattaches lifted seams and tears, and is compatible with all wallcoverings. After applying seam adhesive, roll the seam.

Wallpaper, actual paper, is most appropriate for historically accurate restoration and wherever you want fine detail. Although vinyl coverings are increasingly hard to distinguish from paper, vinyls tend to look glossier. Although paper may have an aesthetically pleasing flat finish, it is more vulnerable to grime and abuse.

Vinyl is today's workhorse, available in a dizzying range of patterns and in finishes ranging from flat to glossy. Vinyl is especially suitable for areas with traffic and moisture. Most vinyls are washable, and cloth-backed vinyls are usually strippable—that is, they are easily removable when you want to change them. Although no wallcovering is intended to conceal major cracks and irregularities, heavier vinyls can conceal minor ones.

Fabric coverings include cotton, linen, silk, stringcloth, and wool. They're often chosen to match or coordinate with colors and textures in drapes and fabric-covered furniture. They come paper-backed, acrylic-backed, or unbacked (raw). And the backing largely determines the method of installation. Avoid slopping adhesive or water onto the fabric facing because some fabrics stain easily; delicate fabrics are usually *dry hung*, in which paste is applied to the wall and the dry wallcovering is smoothed onto it, as explained on p. 477.

Natural textures such as rice paper, grasses, and bamboo tend to be expensive, temperamental, and delicate. And because the thinner coverings reveal even minor flaws in wall surfaces, you first need to cover the walls with a lining paper. Still, natural textures are evolving, with vinyl-coated versions that are relatively durable and easy to install. Besides their beauty, most natural textures have no pattern that needs matching.

Foils and Mylars also vary greatly in appearance and ease of handling. For example, heavier, vinyl-laminated foils are durable and easy to

A Wall OF YOUR OWN

Thanks to technology, you can have wall coverings fabricated with virtually any pattern or image you want, including historical documents or wall-size photos of family members. The cost has come down a lot. Make sure that such coverings are treated with a protective coating, so they will wear well.

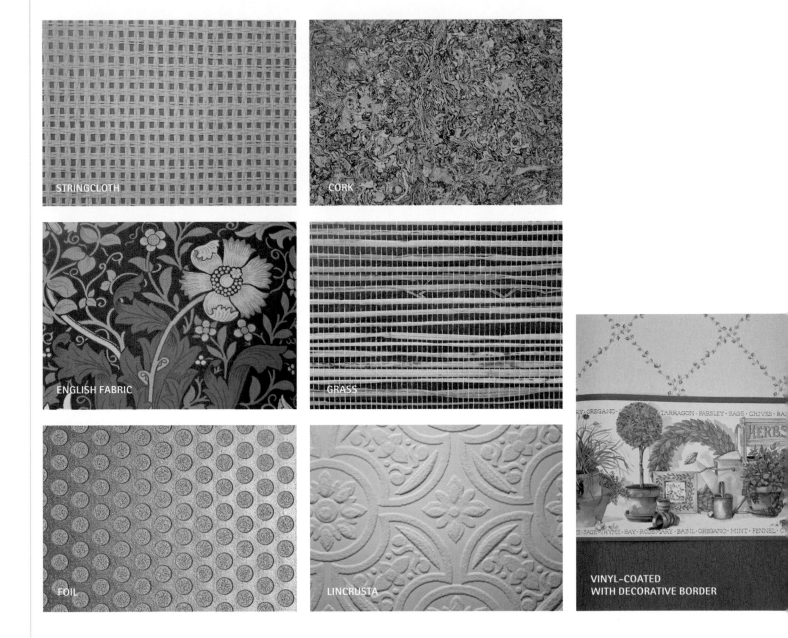

STRINGCLOTH

CORK

ENGLISH FABRIC

GRASS

FOIL

LINCRUSTA

VINYL-COATED
WITH DECORATIVE BORDER

install. However, some uncoated metallic coverings retain fingerprints, so you should wear gloves when hanging them, or perhaps avoid them altogether. That said, foils are well suited to small rooms because they reflect light, thus making the space appear larger.

Lincrusta, an embossed wallpaper similar to a fine cardboard, is making a comeback. The modern version of Victorian lincrusta is called *anaglypta*.

Cork and wood-veneer wallcoverings are finely milled and manufactured to use cork and rare woods efficiently. Typical veneer dimensions: ¹⁄₆₄ in. thick, 1 ft. to 4 ft. wide, 12 ft. long. Such specialty coverings may be available through suppliers of professional paperhangers.

Borders are thin strips of wallcovering that run along the edges of walls where they meet ceilings, wainscoting, and trim. They can be installed over wallcovering or directly to drywall or plaster. The surface determines the adhesive.

PASTES

Like wallcoverings, pastes have evolved. Probably the best advice is to follow the manufacturer's paste specifications, usually printed on the wallcovering label, along with the code and run numbers. If the paste isn't specified, ask your supplier to get that information from the manufacturer.

Wheat pastes were the standard for centuries, but that changed in the 1960s and 1970s, with the introduction of vinyl wallcoverings. Trapped behind an impervious skin of vinyl, wheat paste was an ideal medium for mold. Moreover, wheat paste wasn't strong enough to adhere many of the newer, thicker materials. Wheat pastes are occasionally specified for delicate wallpaper, but mostly they've been supplanted by clay- or starch-based adhesives with additives that increase grip and discourage mold.

Pastes come premixed or as powders to be mixed with water. Premixed pastes are generally stronger, more consistent and more convenient. Once opened, however, such adhesives have a relatively short life. In general, the thicker the paste, the quicker it dries and the greater the weight it can support.

Wall Coverings, Adhesives, and Application

WALL COVERING	ADHESIVES AND APPLICATION	COMMENTS
Prepasted	Paste already on backing; soak in water tray or machine according to manufacturer's recommendations.	To avoid mess of water tray, roll prepaste activator onto backing, which allows longer work time.
Lightweight vinyl	Standard clear adhesive; kitchen and bath adhesive with mildewcide in high-humidity areas	To avoid stretching vinyl when smoothing, use rubber squeegee or plastic wallcovering smoother.
Heavy vinyl	Heavy-duty clear adhesive; clay-based adhesive	If surface to be covered is rough or textured, install liner first.
Vinyl border over vinyl covering; new vinyl covering over old vinyl	Vinyl-over-vinyl adhesive	If adhesive gets on facing, sponge off immediately.
Vinyl border over flat paint	Standard clear adhesive; vinyl-over-vinyl adhesive	Sponge paste off walls quickly.
Wallpaper (including delicate English papers)	Cellulose adhesive; standard clear adhesive	Smooth with soft-bristle brush; if paste gets on facing, blot off with damp sponge.
Natural fibers (grasses, rice paper, bamboo)	Follow manufacturer's recommendation, usually clear adhesive.	Fibers vary greatly; some are vinyl coated and durable; dry-hang delicate types.
Paper-backed fabrics	Cellulose adhesive; standard clear adhesive	Dry-hanging usually best, test-hang small sample to be sure; avoid getting adhesive on fabric face.
Paper-backed upholstery, drapery, or other heavy fabric	Heavy-duty clear adhesive	Requires stronger bond; roll adhesive onto backing, but test-hang small sample to be sure.
Raw (unbacked) fabric	Cellulose adhesive; standard clear adhesive	Dry-hang; avoid getting adhesive on fabric face; test-hang sample to be sure.
Foils; Mylar	Clay-based adhesive; vinyl-over-vinyl adhesive	Not strippable; often dry-hung
Paper-backed murals	Follow manufacturer's recommendation; cellulose adhesive; standard clear adhesive.	Follow manufacturer's recommendations; may require liner and/or dry-hanging.
Canvas backed	Clay-based adhesive	Prime wall first or adhesive and covering may not be strippable.
Lincrusta, anaglypta coverings (embossed, often of heavy paper)	Clay-based adhesive	Roll adhesive onto back of covering; smooth with brush; don't roll seams.
Cork, thin wood veneer	Clay-based adhesive	Run liner perpendicular to finish covering; wipe paste off face at once.
Wall liner; lining paper	Clay-based adhesive; vinyl-over-vinyl adhesive	Prime walls first; smooth coat or fill textured walls, block, and paneling.

Ordering Wallcovering

Before ordering wallcovering, calculate the square footage of your walls and ceilings. Once you've determined the overall square footage, subtract 12 sq. ft. for each average-size door and window. To determine the total number of rolls you'll need, divide each room's square footage by the square footage listed on the wallcovering rolls. If you're using American single rolls (see "How Much on a Roll?," below left), you could instead divide by 36 (the number of square feet on each roll). But dividing by 30 gives you an allowance for waste.

If the room has numerous recesses, difficult corners, or a lot of trim to cut around, order an extra roll or two. Also, if the pattern is large, you'll waste more because you'll need to match patterns along seams. On the back of most wallcovering, you'll find the pattern repeat, usually stated in inches: The larger the pattern repeat, the greater the waste. Also, order an extra roll or two for repairs. You never know when a roof will leak or a child will bruise a wall.

The wallcovering type determines which paste you need. Pastes come premixed, as shown, or as powders you mix with water. Many wallcoverings are prepasted and require that you either roll prepaste activator onto their backing or soak them in water trays.

Equipment

You'll need some special tools and work surfaces to apply your wallcovering.

▶ A spirit level will tell you whether walls and wallcovering edges are plumb. Be sure to plumb the leading edge of the first strip of wallcovering. A 4-ft. level with metal edges can double as a straightedge when trimming selvage (manufactured edges).

▶ Your pasting table should have a washable top about 3 ft. by 6 ft. Avoid covering it with newspaper because newsprint may bleed. To protect the top from scarring during cutting, cover the tabletop with hardboard or use a zinc cutting-strip. (If you don't have a suitable table, lay a sheet of smooth, void-free plywood over sawhorses.)

▶ Have a 16-ft. retractable tape measure for measuring and marking.

▶ A razor knife with replaceable blades gives the cleanest cuts. Don't be stingy about replacing blades during use because dull

How Much on a Roll?

Wallcovering rolls (also called *bolts*) are available in American single rolls, Euro rolls (metric), and commercial widths. At this writing, Euro rolls dominate the market.

▶ American single rolls are 18 in. to 36 in. wide. (A 27-in. width is comfortable for most people.) The wider rolls generate fewer seams but are much more difficult to handle. Whatever the width of an American single roll, it will contain 36 sq. ft. of material.

▶ Euro rolls are 20½ in. to 28 in. wide, and are generally sold as double rolls (twice as long). Typically, there are 56 sq. ft. to 60 sq. ft. on a Euro roll.

▶ Commercial coverings are typically 48 in. to 54 in. wide, a width usually beyond the skills of nonprofessionals.

LIFE ON THE Edge

The edges of most wallcoverings are pretrimmed at the factory, allowing you simply to butt them after matching the patterns. If the edges aren't pretrimmed, do it yourself with a razor knife and long straightedge. Untrimmed edges are called *selvage*.

If the edges of a pretrimmed roll are frayed, refuse that roll. Similarly, refuse vinyls with edges that have become crimped in shipping or storage, for they cannot be rolled flat. To avoid damaging the edges yourself, always store the rolls flat—rather than on end.

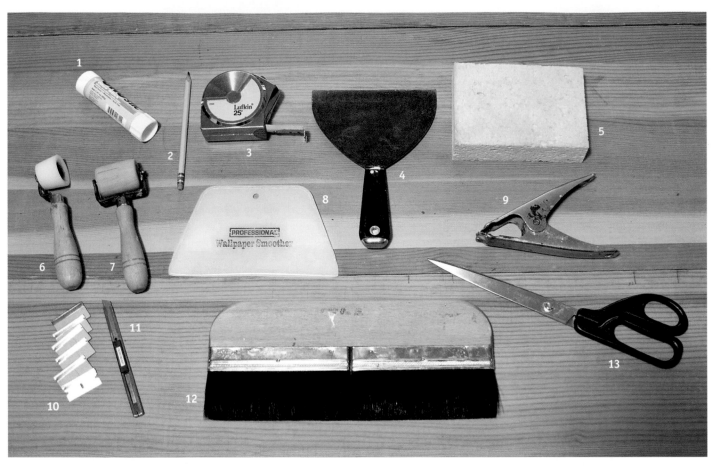

Wallpapering tools. 1, Glue stick for touchups; 2, pencil; 3, tape measure; 4, 6-in. taping knife; 5, sponge; 6, beveled seam roller, used close to trim and in interior corners; 7, standard seam roller; 8, smoother-scraper; 9, spring clamp, to hold wallpaper while pasting; 10, single-edge razor blades; 11, razor knife with snap-off blades; 12, smoothing brush; 13, shears for rough-cutting strips.

blades can rip wallpaper. A professional may use 200 or 300 blades on a big job. Some pros prefer single-edge razor blades, though knives with snap-off blades are popular, too.

▶ Shears help you rough-cut from a roll.

▶ Paste brushes spread wheat paste on backing—or on walls, in some cases.

▶ A roller and pan are needed to spread vinyl paste, which is too heavy to brush on. Ask your supplier how long the nap of the roller cover should be.

▶ A smoothing brush, with soft bristles, will smooth out the wallcovering paste.

▶ A wallpaper smoother smooths vinyls, liners, and other heavy materials. It is also handy for flattening the occasional paste lump.

▶ A seam roller spreads glue along the edges of the strips to ensure that seams will stick well. *Caution:* Seam rollers are not generally recommended for delicate or finely textured papers or grasses.

▶ A 6-in. taping knife, also called a joint knife, is useful for filling low spots and scraping off high spots in a wall. Also use this knife to press the wallcovering snugly against the trim before cutting away excess paper.

▶ A sponge and water pail are handy for wiping excess paste off the pasting table, trim, and most wallcovering surfaces. In general, the sponge should be just damp. Change the water in your pail often. To avoid creating a sheen along the seams, wipe the entire strips rather than just their edges.

▶ Other useful equipment includes a sturdy fiberglass stepladder; a long, straight board for detecting irregularities in walls and ceilings; and a plenty of clean, soft rags. If you use a prepasted wallcovering, you'll also need a water tray in which to soak the strips to activate their adhesives.

Preparing Surfaces

Surface prep determines how well coverings adhere, hence how good the job looks and how long it lasts. Ideally, surfaces should be clean, dry, flat, and stable. Before hanging wallcoverings, assess existing surfaces; remove, replace, or repair them as necessary; and then prime and seal them. Sealing surfaces improves adhesion and, just as important, allows you to remove coverings later without destroying the underlying drywall or plaster.

In the old days, a wall was *sized,* or brushed with a glutinous mixture to improve the adherence of the wallpaper. But sizing is rarely done today because it's chemically incompatible with many pastes, causing them to crystallize, lump, and bubble, creating voids where the covering is unattached. Instead, professionals use one of the primer-sealers described in "Primer-Sealers for Wallcoverings," below.

Before you start prep work, move furniture from the room or move it to the room's center and cover it with a tarp. That will allow you to work faster and be safer. 🚫 Speaking of safety, always use a voltage tester to be sure electrical power is off where you're working. Also set up ladders and scaffolds so they don't wobble. Wear a respirator mask when applying chemicals, and clean up waste as you go.

PREPPING PAINTED SURFACES

Before you wallpaper painted surfaces, figure out what kind of paint you've got and what shape it's in. In general, oil-based paints are stable surfaces for wallcovering because they aren't water soluble. Yet some primer-sealers can stabilize even latex paint. You could scrape off a small patch of paint and have a paint store analyze it, but two simple tests should suffice.

Hot towel test. Soak a hand towel in hot water, wring it well, and then rub the paint vigorously for 20 seconds to 30 seconds. If paint comes off on the towel, you've probably got latex. Alternatively, you can use duct tape to hold a moist sponge next to a painted surface for 15 minutes before removing the sponge. If you see paint on the sponge, it's latex.

X-tape test. If paint didn't come off on your towel or sponge, it's probably oil based. To see how well it's adhered, use a razor blade to lightly score a 1-in. *X* in the paint surface (don't cut into the drywall or plaster). Press masking tape over the *X*, and then pull it off quickly: If there's no paint on the tape, the paint is well adhered. If paint does come off, scrape and sand it well before proceeding.

If the existing paint is well-adhered glossy or semigloss oil-based, sand it lightly with fine sandpaper, using a sanding block or an orbital sander. Then use a sponge mop, dampened with water, to remove the sanding dust. Or, instead of sanding, you can spray or wipe on paint deglosser to dull glossy and semigloss paint surfaces.

If the paint is well-adhered flat oil-based paint, you can begin hanging wallcovering. Simply rinse the surface with a mild detergent solution to remove grime, rinse with clear water, and allow to dry.

Latex paint should be prepared by scraping lightly and sanding. You needn't remove the entire coat of paint; just sand it enough so the primer-sealer can bond. Avoid gouging or ripping the surface underneath, especially if it's drywall. When you're done sanding, wipe the wall clean and apply a coat of pigmented acrylic primer-sealer.

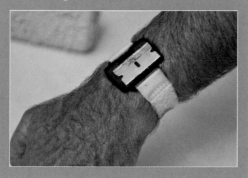

LOOKING Sharp

This clever magnetic bracelet keeps a single-edge razor blade handy. A sharp blade is essential, especially if you're working with prepasted wallcoverings soaked in water. Wetted paper will snag a dull blade and rip easily. Blades are far cheaper than wasted wallcovering.

Primer-Sealers for Wallcoverings

PRIMER-SEALER TYPE	USES	COMMENTS
Pigmented acrylic	Seals all surfaces, including existing wallpaper, vinyl covering, and latex paint; suitable base for all wall coverings.	Also known as universal primer-sealer; cleans up with water; protects drywall when coverings are stripped; add pigment to hide existing wallpaper patterns.
Clear acrylic	Same uses as for pigmented acrylic; but can't bond latex paint; suitable base for all wall coverings.	Cleans with water; won't protect drywall; can't hide patterns.
Heavy-duty acrylic	Mostly for weighty vinyl coverings used for commercial installations.	Soaks into raw drywall, so won't protect it when covering is stripped away.
Alkyd/oil-based	Seals all surfaces except existing wallpaper or vinyl coverings; fast drying (2 hours to 4 hours); suitable base for all wall coverings.	Thin with paint thinner to improve bond with existing paint; protects drywall; can be tinted.
Stain sealer; pigmented shellac	Hides or contains stains from water and smoke, wallpaper inks, grease, crayons, and more.	Not a primer-sealer; when dry, apply acrylic primer-sealer top coat.

NEW WALLPAPER OVER OLD

You can wallpaper over an existing covering if:

▶ It is not highly textured, as lincrusta, stringcloth, and bamboo are.

▶ There are no prominent seams.

▶ There's no more than one or two layers already on the wall.

▶ The old wallpaper is well adhered.

Check edges and seams first: If they're peeling or poorly adhered, strip the walllcovering. But if there are only a few isolated unadhered spots, use seam adhesive to reattach them. Or use a razor blade to cut out the loose seams. Then fill voids with spackling compound, allow it to dry, and sand it lightly with 180-grit or 220-grit sandpaper.

Another potential problem is bleed-through from metallic wallpaper inks. To test, dampen a cloth with diluted ammonia (1 part ammonia to 4 parts water) and rub the old wallpaper. If inks change color (usually, they turn blue-green), they'll bleed. To prevent this, seal the old wallpaper with pigmented shellac or a similar stain killer. Allow the sealer to dry thoroughly before painting surfaces with a universal primer-sealer.

Otherwise, if existing wallpaper is well adhered, wipe it with a damp sponge, let it dry, and then paint surfaces with pigmented acrylic primer-sealer. Tint the primer-sealer to match the background color of the new wallcovering.

STRIPPING WALLCOVERING

1. Stripping takes patience. Start at one end of a strip, pulling slowly and steadily so that the strip comes off in a single piece, if possible. This covering was peelable, meaning that its facing peeled off, but its paper backing stayed stuck to the substrate.

STRIPPING WALLPAPER

Strip existing wallcovering if it is tired or grimy and can't be washed, poorly adhered or damaged, puckered or lumpy because there are too many layers, water stained or damaged, moldy, strongly textured, or you want to paint the walls instead. Before you apply new wallcovering, repair and prime the finish surfaces.

Before stripping, reconnoiter. Peel up a corner of the wallpaper in an out-of-the-way place. Then determine whether the walls are plaster or drywall. Plaster is harder and can survive a lot more steaming and scraping than drywall. Next, test how easily the wallpaper strips. Peelable and strippable types should be relatively easy to remove if the wall was properly sealed before it was papered. But if surfaces were not sized or primed first, you're in for some work. Moreover, if the unsealed substrate is drywall, stripping the wallpaper may destroy the paper face of the drywall. In theory, you can patch and then seal damaged drywall with products like Allpro Seal 'n Bond®; but removing the damaged drywall, or covering it with ¼-in. drywall will yield far better results.

Scarifying TOOL

Some pros recommend using a scarifying tool, such as Paper Tiger®, to perforate wallpaper so steam can penetrate. But such tools can also perforate drywall and scar its surface. Damage can also occur if you use metal-edged scrapers. So use such tools only as a last resort when the paste is especially tenacious, and use them with great care. Instead, try steaming the wallpaper, before scarifying or scraping it.

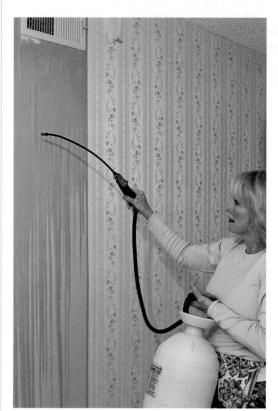

2. To remove the paper backing, spray it with a solution of hot water and a wallpaper-stripper such as DIF, which breaks down the paste. Allow the solution to soak in 3 minutes to 5 minutes. Because spraying is messy, place old towels or a tarp at the base of the wall.

3. Applying steam will hasten the penetration of the stripper solution and soften the paste, making removal easier. On this wall, heat from a nearby register had baked the paste hard.

4. A plastic wallpaper smoother-scraper will scrape off steamed paper backing without damaging drywall beneath. When all paper is off, use a soft-bristle nylon scrub brush to gently remove paste residue.

Stripping wallpaper is messy, no matter what method you use. You'll need painters' tarps or old towels to protect floors from stripping solutions, condensed steam, and sticky wallpaper. Canvas tarps, or even old towels, are better than plastic tarps, which tend to be slippery. Have trash bags handy for stripped paper. 🚫 As noted earlier, turn off the electricity to areas you're stripping, and use a voltage tester to be sure the power's off.

Use the least disruptive stripping method. Start stripping at the top or bottom of a strip. Use a putty knife or a plastic scraper to lift an edge. Then gently pull off the wallpaper, in the largest strips possible. This takes patience.

If you can't pull off the covering or if it begins tearing into small pieces, try spraying a small area with a wallpaper-removing solution like Zinsser's DIF®, which is also available as a gel, that you brush on. A time-tested alternative is 1 cup vinegar per gallon of hot water; sponge on or apply with a spray bottle. Allow either solution to soak in 5 minutes to 10 minutes, before trying to pull off the paper. If this method doesn't work, chances are the paper is vinyl coated and the solution is not penetrating. In this case, instead

try a wallpaper steamer. Hold the steamer pan against the wallcovering long enough for the paste to soften—usually a minute or two—then pull or scrape the covering free.

If your wallcovering is peelable, chances are its facing layer will strip off, leaving its paper backing adhered to the wall. If you wish to strip it, either spray on or sponge on wallpaper-removing solution, and then apply steam. The backing should release easily; otherwise, use a plastic scraper or smoother to remove the backing. When the walls are stripped, wash them with a mild cleaning solution. Then rinse and let them

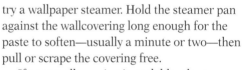

Strippable VS. PEELABLE

Strippable wallcovering can be dry stripped (no spraying or steaming needed); both the facing and the backing material come off easily, with only a faint paste residue left on the wall. *Peelable* coverings usually require spraying with a wallpaper-removing solution or steaming to remove the wallpaper facing. If the paper backing is in good shape, it can stay on the wall as a wall liner for the new wallpaper. Otherwise, remove it, too.

dry thoroughly before applying a primer-sealer. If paste lumps remain, remove them with a nylon-bristle scrub brush.

PREPPING RAW DRYWALL OR PLASTER

Newly installed drywall must be sealed before you hang wallcoverings. Otherwise, the drywall's paper face will absorb paste, making it impossible to remove the covering at a future date without damaging the drywall face. To seal drywall, apply a coat of universal primer-sealer, which is an excellent base coat for papering and painting.

Plaster must be well cured before you apply either wallcovering or paint. Uncured plaster contains alkali that is still warm, causing the paint and paste to bubble. "Hot plaster" has a dull appearance, whereas cured plaster has a slight sheen. Curing time varies, but keeping the house warm will hasten it. Cured plaster can also be coated with universal primer-sealer.

Starting and Finishing Points

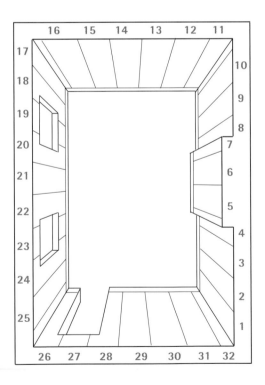

Because a room's final strip of wallcovering usually needs to be trimmed narrower to fit, try to end a job where the final strip is inconspicuous. Here the job begins and ends in a corner.

Laying Out the Work

Before ordering materials, walk the room and determine if the walls are plumb and if the woodwork is plumb and level. Also, use a long, straight board or a 4-ft. spirit level to determine if the walls have mounds and dips. Use a pencil to circle irregularities so you can spot them easily later. You can hang almost any wallcovering type or pattern, but if door or window casing is markedly out of plumb, small patterns make plumb problems less noticeable than large, loud patterns.

Mold and Mildew

Mold is a discoloration caused by fungi growing on organic matter such as wood, paper, or paste. *Mildew* is essentially the same, but usually refers to fungi on paper or cloth. *Note:* Without sufficient moisture and something to eat, mold (and mildew) can't grow. Mold can grow on the paper and adhesives in drywall; but, technically, mold can't grow on plaster because plaster is inorganic. If your plaster walls are moldy, the fungi are growing on grease, soap, dirt, or some other organic film on the plaster.

Anyhow, if your walls or ceilings are moldy, first alleviate the moisture. To determine its source, duct-tape a 1-ft.-sq. piece of aluminum foil to a wall. Leave this up for a week. Upon removal, if there's moisture on the back of the foil, the source is behind the walls. However, if the foil front is damp, there's excessive moisture in the living space, which you might reduce by installing ventilator fans, for starters.

If the drywall or plaster is in good condition, clean off the mold by sponging on a mild detergent solution. (Though widely recommended, diluted bleach isn't any more effective than a household cleaner.) The sponge should be damp, not wet. Rinse with clean water, and allow the surface to dry thoroughly. Then paint on a universal primer-sealer. If you'll be wallpapering the room, use a mildew-resistant, kitchen-and-bath adhesive.

If mold or water stains are widespread and the drywall has deteriorated, there may be mold in the walls. Remove a section of drywall to be sure. If the framing is moldy, it may need to be replaced—a big job and one worth discussing with a mold-abatement specialist, especially if family members have asthma or chronic respiratory problems (for more, see Chapter 14).

Starting and finishing points. To decide where to hang the first strip, figure out where you want to end. The last strip of wall covering almost always needs to be cut narrower to fit, disrupting the strip's full-width pattern. Thus avoid hanging the last strip where it will be conspicuous.

A common place to begin is one side of a main doorway. There, you won't notice a narrower strip when you enter the room. And when you leave the room, you'll usually be looking through the doorway. The last piece is normally a small one placed over the doorway.

Another common starting point is an inconspicuous corner. To determine exactly where wallcovering seams will occur, mark off intervals the same width as your wallcovering. Go around the room, using a ruler or a wrapped roll of wallcovering as your gauge. Try to avoid trimming and pasting very narrow strips of wallcovering in corners; this usually looks terrible, and the pieces don't adhere well. You may want to move your starting point an inch or two to avoid that inconvenience.

Before hanging wallcovering, check the trim for plumb and level. For example, if the crown molding isn't level, you may need to raise or lower the wallpaper strips so that the tilting trim doesn't chop off the head of a prominent pattern.

To determine exactly where seams will occur, mark off intervals the same width as your wallpaper.

After determining your starting point, draw a plumb line to align the first strip of wallcovering.

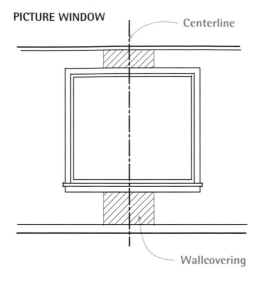

PICTURE WINDOW

Centerline

Wallcovering

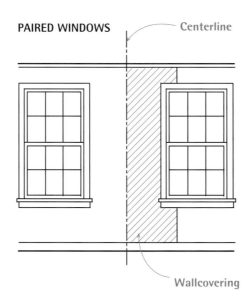

PAIRED WINDOWS

Centerline

Wallcovering

Where windows are the focal point of a room, position the wallcovering accordingly. If the window is a large picture window, center the middle of the strip on the middle of the window. If the focal point is two windows, center the edges of the two strips as shown.

However, if the pattern is conspicuous, you might start layout with a strip centered in a conspicuous part of a wall—over a mantel, over a sofa, or in the middle of a large wall. Determine such a visual center and mark off roll-widths from each side of the starting strip, until you have determined where the papering will terminate, again preferably in an inconspicuous place.

You may want to center the pattern at a window, if that's indisputably the visual center of the room. In the case of a picture window, the middle of the strip should align with the middle of the window, as shown at left. If there are two windows, the edges of two strips should meet along a centered, plumbed line between the two windows, as shown, unless the distance between the windows is less than the width of a strip. If the distance is less, center a strip between the windows.

Basic Papering Techniques

🚫 Before you start hanging wallcovering, turn off the electricity to affected outlets, switches, and fixtures, and check with a voltage tester to be sure the power's off.

Measure out from the door casing, if that's where you'll begin, and draw a plumb line that will become the leading edge of the first strip. If the casing is out of plumb, allow the trailing edge of the strip to overlap the casing enough to be trimmed with a razor knife without creating a space along the casing. If the casing is plumb, simply butt the trailing edge to the casing. As you progress, however, continually check for plumb.

CUTTING STRIPS TO LENGTH

Measure the height of the wall and cut several strips to length, leaving extra at each end for trimming and vertically matching patterns. Cut the first two strips extra long. Slide the first strip up and down the wall until most (or all) of its pattern shows near the ceiling line. Don't show less than half the pattern. The pattern along the baseboard will be less visible and thus less important.

Place the second strip next to the first, and align the patterns along their edges. From the first two strips, you'll have a sense of how much waste to allow for pattern matching. (A pattern-repeat interval is often printed on the label packaged with the wallpaper.) Depending on the size of the patterns, each succeeding strip can usually be rough-cut with an inch or two extra at each end and then trimmed after being pasted.

Do the rough-cutting at the table using shears. Do the trimming on the wall using a razor knife. Patterns that run horizontally across the face of a

Use shears to rough-cut strips, leaving extra at each end for trimming and pattern matching. This pasting and layout table is a professional model, strong yet light, easily transported from job to job.

Gently pull cut strips over the edge of the table to counteract the tendency of wallpaper to curl.

Three Types of Seams

You can join strip edges in three ways: butt seam, overlap seam, or double-cut seams.

▶ The butt seam is the most common, its edges are simply butted together and rolled with a seam roller.

▶ An overlap seam is better where corners are out of square or when a butt seam might occur in a corner and not cover well. Keep the overlap as narrow as possible, thereby avoiding a noticeable welt and patterns that are grossly mismatched.

▶ Double-cut seams (also called through-cut seams) are the most complex of the three. They are used primarily where patterns are tough to match or surfaces are irregular; for example, where the walls of an alcove aren't square.

How to Cut Seams

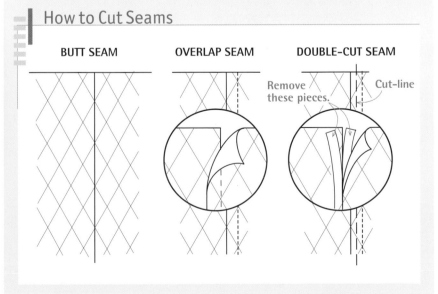

BUTT SEAM   OVERLAP SEAM   DOUBLE-CUT SEAM

Remove these pieces.   Cut-line

covering are called *straight match*. Patterns that run diagonally are called *drop match* and waste somewhat more material during alignment.

Unless you are working with a delicate covering, cut several strips at a time. But be careful not to crease them. Flop the entire pile of strips face down on the table so the piece cut first will be the first pasted and hung. The table must be perfectly clean; otherwise, the face of the bottom strip could become soiled.

PASTING

Unless you're experienced, buy a premixed adhesive. But if mix you must, try to achieve a mixture that's slightly tacky to the touch. Add paste powder or water slowly: Even small increments can change the consistency radically. Finally, mix thoroughly to remove lumps.

As you work, keep the pasting table clean, quickly sponging up stray paste so it won't get on strip faces. Some coverings, such as vinyl, are not marred by stray paste on their face, but many others could be. Although the batch of paste you mix should last a working day, keep an eye on its consistency. Paste should glide on, never drag. Rinse the paste brush or roller when you break for lunch and when you quit for the day.

Until you become familiar with papering, apply paste to only one strip at a time. Using a roller, apply paste in the middle of the strip, toward the top. Spread the paste to the far edge and then to the near edge. For good measure, run the roller over strip edges twice because it's often hard to see if the paste along the edges is evenly spread.

As you apply paste, roll it out from the center toward the edges. Hold down the wallcovering with one hand to keep it from sliding as you roll.

BOOKING STRIPS

For convenient handling, create folds of pasted covering that you can to carry to the wall, unfold without mess, hang, and smooth. The most practical folding method is known as *booking*, perhaps because the folds resemble the folds of a book dust jacket. When folding strips, do so loosely; avoid creasing them.

Booking a strip (typically, for 5 minutes) also allows it to absorb the moisture in the paste, expand, and contract slightly to its final width. If you do not allow the wallcovering time to expand and contract before hanging it, it will do so on the wall, either buckling or gapping at the seams. Booking times vary: Pros who know their pastes and papers will sometimes cut, paste, and book several strips at once, placing them into a plastic trash bag so the paste doesn't dry out.

However, if you paste several strips at once, keep track of the order in which you pasted them. And hang them in the same order.

HANGING PASTED STRIPS

To hang a strip of wallcovering, unfold the booked upper fold (leaving the lower one folded) and align the edge of the strip to your plumb line.

Prepasted Papers and Water Trays

Most wallcoverings come prepasted. Typically, manufacturers specify that individual strips be soaked for 30 seconds in a water tray filled with lukewarm water. But follow the directions printed on the back or supplied by the retailer. After soaking, pull each strip out of the tray and onto the work table, book (fold) it, and allow it to expand before hanging it on the wall. Precut the pieces before placing them in the water tray. Otherwise, if you try to trim soaked strips, they'll snag or tear.

Many professional paperhangers will hang prepasted wallcoverings but hate water trays because (1) water and diluted paste drips everywhere; (2) the water in the tray must be changed often; (3) a thin film of paste also ends up on the *front* of the wallcovering; and (4) if the strips are soaked too long, they may not adhere well. Instead, these pros roll prepaste activator onto the backing of strips, just as you'd apply standard paste. Rolling on an activator reduces mess and ensures good adherence to the wall.

Last, pros sometimes roll thinned-down paste instead of activator. That may be okay, but first ask the wallcovering supplier if the two pastes will be compatible.

Position the upper end of the strip an inch or so above the ceiling line. Smooth the upper end of the strip first, by running a smoothing brush down the middle of the strip and out toward the edges. Working from the center outward, brush air bubbles, wrinkles, and excess paste from the middle to the edges. Align subsequent pieces to the leading edge of each preceding strip, checking periodically to make sure the strips are plumb.

If the upper half of the strip is adhering well, simply unfold the lower fold and smooth the paper down, again brushing down the center and out toward the edges with small strokes.

If a butt seam doesn't meet exactly, you have three choices:

▶ Move a strip slightly by raising one of its edges, and—palm on paper—using your other hand to slide the strip toward or away from the seam. Raising one edge of the strip reduces the grip between paper and wall.

▶ Pull the strip off the wall, realign its patterns along the seam, and brush it down. But you've got to move quickly: Don't wait much more than a minute to pull the strip off.

▶ Pull off the strip, quickly sponge clean the wall, and hang a new strip.

Don't try pulling just one edge of the strip, however. At best, it will stretch, draw back when it dries, and open the seam. At worst, you'll pucker or rip the strip.

SPONGING

It's impossible to overstate the importance of gently wiping paste off the wallcovering and adjacent surfaces. Left on the wallcovering, paste can shrink and pull the ink off. If paste dries on a painted ceiling, it will pull the paint off. (If you see a brown crust along a ceiling-wall intersec-

Dry-HANGING

If handled too much, many fabrics, foils, Mylars, and grasses will separate from their backing once they absorb the paste. For that reason, pros often dry-hang them. Here's how: They roll paste onto the wall and smooth the dry covering onto it. However, leave this job to a pro because the paste must be applied impeccably even, and the strips placed exactly—there's little chance to adjust them. Likewise, these materials can't tolerate sponging, rubbing, or seam rolling. Pros sweep them on with a soft-bristle smoothing brush and let them be.

HANGING WALLCOVERING

1. After pasting the back of the strip, fold both ends in, as shown, so they meet in the middle. Be careful not to crease the folded ends. This folding is called booking the paper.

2. To hang the first strip, unfold the top half and carefully align it to the plumbed line you marked earlier, leaving an inch or so extra at the top. Gently slide the strip into place. Align each subsequent strip to the leading edge of the preceding one.

3. Once the strip is correctly positioned, smooth it onto the wall, smoothing the upper end first, brushing out from the center toward the edges. (Continued on next page.)

4. With a taping knife pressed against the woodwork, trim the joint with a single-edge razor blade or razor knife. After trimming excess paper and smoothing out the strip one last time, sponge away any paste smeared on the woodwork.

5. Join the seam with a roller, removing emerging paste with a sponge. Rinse the sponge and change the water in your pail often.

6. Use a plastic wallpaper smoother to flatten any lumps of paste. This tool is also useful for smoothing out heavier vinyls and the like.

tion, that's dried paste.) Paste will even pull the finish off wood trim. Vinyl-on-vinyl and clay adhesives are especially tenacious, so sponge off the excess immediately.

Equally important: Change your sponge water often so diluted paste doesn't accumulate. Warm water is best. And wring the sponge almost dry before wiping. When you've wiped the surfaces

clean, come back with a soft, dry rag. But apply only light pressure so you don't move the wallcovering, disturbing its seams.

Note: Don't rub delicate wallpapers. Instead, blot them clean with a just-damp sponge. Before you commit to any wallcovering, ask your supplier if it can be wiped (or blotted clean) with a sponge. If not, consider other materials.

TRIMMING AND ROLLING

Where a strip of wallcovering meets borders such as woodwork, a ceiling line, or a baseboard, use a 6-in. taping knife to press the edges of the covering snug. Cut off the excess by running a razor knife along the blade of the taping knife. Because strips may cover door or window casing, you may want to rough-cut the ends of strips first so you don't cut them too short. Then, using your taping knife to tuck the wallcovering snugly against the casing, trim it more precisely. For clean cuts, razor blades must be sharp.

Conventional wisdom suggests rolling wallcovering seams 10 minutes or 15 minutes after the strips are in place—that is, after the paste has set somewhat. But the master craftsman shown hanging wallpaper in photos here prefers to the roll seams before he brushes out the paper. If you position the strips correctly, roll the seams, and then smooth the covering, he asserts, you're less likely to stretch the wallpaper. Also, if seams don't align correctly, you want to know that sooner, rather than later, so you can adjust or remove the strip before the paste sets up.

In any case, rolling may cause paste to ooze from the seams. So, be sure to sponge wallcovering clean as you work, unless you're installing delicate or embossed wallcovering, which shouldn't be rolled or wiped at all. Finally, use a moderate pressure when rolling. After all, you're trying to embed the wallcovering in the paste, not crush it.

Complex and Special-Care Areas

Installing wallcovering would be a snap if there were no corners, doors, windows, and electrical outlets, where you need to use extra care.

TILTING TRIM AND COCKEYED CORNERS

In renovation, trim and corners are rarely perfectly plumb, but strips of wallcovering must be, regardless of tilting trim and corner walls out of plumb. If your first strip begins next to an out-of-plumb jamb casing, overlap it by the amount the casing is off plumb. After brushing

To avoid a noticeable welt of overlapped paper in an inside corner seam, pull back one strip and trim off the excess paper. If corners are out of square, plumb the leading edge of each wall's first strip.

out the wallpaper, trim the overlapping edge. Thus the leading edge of that strip will be plumb, as will the next strip's. But always double-check for plumb before hanging subsequent strips.

Inside corners. If an inside corner is cock-eyed, a strip of wallcovering wrapping the corner will be out of plumb when it emerges on the second wall. First use your spirit level to determine which way the walls are leaning. Then trim down the width of the strip so it is just wide enough to reach the second wall—plus a ⅛-in. to ¼-in. overlap. (Save the portion you trim off: If it's wide enough, you may be able to paste it onto the second wall, thus attaining a closer pattern match in the corner.)

Now hang a strip of wallcovering on the second wall, plumbing its leading edge to a plumbed line you've marked on the wall first. Tuck the trailing edge of the strip into the corner so that it overlaps the first strip. There will be a slight mismatch of patterns, but in the corner, it won't be noticeable. If you don't like the small welt that results from the overlap, use a razor knife to double-cut the seam. However, if your walls are old and undulating, they'll make it tough to cut a straight line. Ignoring a slight welt may spare you

a lot of frustration. In any event, don't butt-join strips at corners because such seams almost always separate.

Outside corners. Outside corners project into a room and so are very visible. So when laying out the job, never align the edge of a strip to the edge of an outside corner. Such edges look terrible initially and then usually fray. If the edge of a strip would occur precisely at a corner, cut it back ½ in. and wrap the corner with the edge of a full strip from the adjacent wall. Relief cut the top of the wallcovering where it turns the corner, as shown in the photo below, so the top of strip can lie flat. Remember to plumb the leading edge of the new strip.

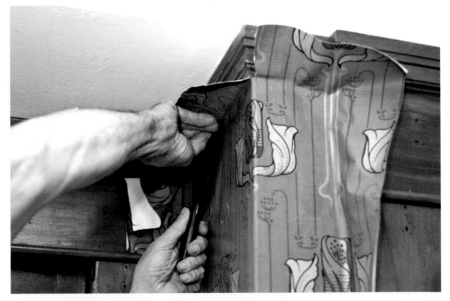

As you wrap an outside corner with wallpaper, relief-cut the top of the strip at the corner, as shown. Otherwise, the paper won't lie flat on both walls.

FITTING OVER OUTLETS AND FIXTURES

🚫 Before hanging paper over an electrical outlet, switch, or fixture, turn off power to that outlet and check that it's off by using a voltage tester.

Cutting option 1: Loosely hang the paper, locate the outlet, and cut a small X over the center of the outlet, extending the X until the paper lies flat.

Cutting option 2: Loosely hang the paper and cut around the outside of the outlet box. When the cutout is complete, brush the paper flat.

PAPERING AROUND ELECTRICAL OUTLETS AND FIXTURES

🚫 Turn off electricity to the affected outlets and fixtures, and confirm that it's off by using a voltage tester, as shown on p. 235. Remove the cover plates and other hardware from the outlets so the hardware protrudes as little as possible.

For an outlet relatively flush with the surface, simply position the strip over it. Then, over the center of the outlet, cut a small X in the strip. Gradually extend the legs of the X until the strip lies flat. Even though the outlet's cover plate will cover small imperfections in cutting, cut as close as you can to the edges of protruding hardware or the electrical box. Smooth the strip with a smoothing brush, and trim any excess paper. If the edges of the cutout aren't adhering well, roll them with a seam roller.

It's preferable to remove fixtures such as wall sconces, but that's not always possible. For example, sometimes mounting screws will have rusted so badly that you would damage the fixture trying to remove them. In that case, after matching the wallcovering patterns, cut the strip to the approx-imate length. Then measure on the wall from the center of the fixture in two directions—say, from the baseboard and from the edge of the nearest strip of wallcovering. Transfer those dimensions to the strip you will hang. If you apply paste after cutting a small X, avoid fraying the edges of the cut with your paste brush or roller.

Hang the strip, and gradually enlarge the X until it fits over the base of the fixture. Smooth down the entire strip, trim closely around the fixture, and wipe away any paste that smeared onto the fixture.

PAPERING CEILINGS

In papered rooms, ceilings are usually painted. Even professionals find papering them challenging and time-consuming because you must fight gravity and neck cramps. So get a helper if possible, and paste only one strip at a time until you get the knack of it. Cover ceilings before walls, because it's easier to conceal discrepancies with wall strips.

Because shorter strips are easier to handle, always hang across the ceiling's shorter dimension. Snap a line down the middle of the ceiling and work out from it. Cut strips for the ceiling in the same manner described for walls, leaving an inch or two extra at each end for trimming. However, folding the covering is slightly different. It's best to use an accordion fold every 1½ ft. or so, which you unfold as you smooth the strips across the ceiling. (Be careful not to crease the folds.)

With your smoothing brush, sweep from the center of the strip outward. Once you have unfolded the entire strip, make final adjustments to match seams, and smooth well. Roll seams after the strips have been in place for about 10 minutes.

ARCHES AND ALCOVES

Papering curved sections isn't difficult, provided you allow enough extra wallcovering for overlaps and trimming, and for making pattern adjustments.

Before papering an arch, position wall strips so their edges don't coincide with the vertical (side) edges of the arch. Just as it's undesirable to have wallpaper seams coincide with an outside corner, seams that line up with an archway corner will wear poorly and look tacky. When hanging strips over an arch, let each strip drape over the opening; then use scissors to rough-cut the paper so it overhangs the opening by about 2 in. Make a series of small wedge-shaped relief cuts in the ends of those strips, and fold the remaining flaps into the arch. Then cover the flaps with two strips of wallpaper as wide as the arch wall is thick. Typically, these two strips meet at the top of the arch, in a double-cut seam. If possible, match patterns where they meet.

Double-cutting is also useful around alcoves or window recesses, where it's often necessary to wrap wall strips into the recessed area. Problem is, when you cut and wrap a wall strip into a recess, you interrupt the pattern on the wall. The best solution is to hang a new strip that slightly overlaps the first, match patterns, and double-cut through both strips. Peel away the waste pieces, smooth out the wallpaper, and roll the seams flat.

Papering an Arch

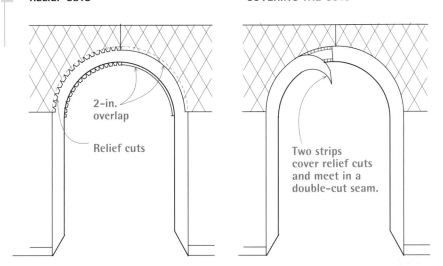

RELIEF CUTS

2-in. overlap

Relief cuts

COVERING THE CUTS

Two strips cover relief cuts and meet in a double-cut seam.

Overlap the edge of the arch by 2 in. Then cut the overlapping wallcovering with a series of small relief cuts, as shown. Fold the flaps back into the arch and smooth them down. Finally, paper the inside of the arch with two strips that meet in a double-cut seam at the top of the arch, as shown.

Ceiling Folds

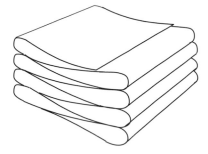

An accordion fold is easiest to unfold as you paper a ceiling and helps keep paste off the face of the wallcovering.

Touch-Ups AND REPAIRS

▶ **SMUDGES AND STAINS.** Clean washable wallcoverings by gently rubbing them with soap and water. A commercial cleaning dough removes stains when rubbed lightly over a soiled spot. As the dough gathers grime, fold the dough in on itself, creating cleaner dough surfaces for rubbing. You can blot (not rub) most nonwashable coverings with commercial, stain-removing solvents. Your wallcovering supplier can suggest one.

▶ **GASHES.** First try to repaste the torn flap. If that doesn't look good, rip—don't cut—a patch from a spare roll of the same covering. The ragged edge of a ripped piece will be less obvious than straight edges cut with shears or a razor knife.

▶ **DENTS AND CRACKS.** Repair dents and cracks in the wall behind, and gently tear free any unpasted paper around the gash. Paste the back of the ragged-edge replacement, carefully aligning its pattern with that of the existing covering before smoothing down the patch.

20 Flooring

In the old days, flooring was the last building material to be installed and the first to show its age, as it was crushed by footsteps, swollen by moisture, and abraded by dirt. Foot traffic is as heavy and gritty as ever, but today's crop of engineered flooring and floor finishes is far more durable—and varied.

However, flooring is only the top layer of a system that usually includes underlayment and subflooring, as well as structural members such as joists and girders. If finish floors are to be solid and long lasting, all parts of the flooring system must be sized and spaced correctly for the loads they will carry. Also, although some flooring materials can withstand moisture better than others, all will degrade in time if installed in chronically damp locations. In other words, correct underlying problems before installing new flooring.

This chapter begins by introducing some of the more exciting flooring choices. Then it explains how to strip and refinish wood flooring and how to install wood flooring, resilient flooring, and carpeting. Tile floors are covered in Chapter 16.

Flooring Choices

These days, choosing flooring is almost as complicated as buying a car. The old standbys such as solid wood, tile, and linoleum have been joined by hundreds of ingenious hybrids, from snaptogether laminates that mimic wood or tile to

You can rent many of the specialized tools needed to refinish or install flooring. Before you leave the rental company, have a salesperson explain how to operate the equipment safely and, in the case of sanders, how to change the paper.

bamboo planks to prefinished maple the color of plums. To make them tougher, floor finishes may include ceramics, aluminum oxides, or titanium.

Basically, you should try to choose flooring that's right for the room. Some factors to consider:

▶ **Compatibility with the house's style or historical period**

▶ **Ease of installation**

▶ **Ease of cleaning and maintenance**

▶ **Scratch and water resistance**

▶ **Durability**

▶ **Comfort underfoot**

▶ **Sound absorption**

▶ **Anti-allergenic qualities**

▶ **"Green" practices for wood flooring, such as sustainable-forest harvesting**

▶ **Cost.**

WOOD FLOORING

The revolution that produced engineered lumber has also transformed wood flooring. In addition to solid-wood strips and planks, there are laminated floorings, some of which can be sanded and refinished several times. There's also a wide range of prefinished flooring.

Solid-wood flooring is solid wood, top to bottom. The most common type is tongue-and-groove (T&G) *strip flooring,* typically ¾ in. thick by 2¼ in. wide, although it's also available in ½-in.-thick strips and widths that range from 1½ in. to 3¼ in. Hardwood *plank flooring* is most often installed as boards of varying widths (3 in. to 8 in.), random lengths, and ⅜ in. to ¾ in. thickness. *Parquet flooring* comes in standard ⅜-in. by 6-in. by 6-in. squares, though some specialty patterns range up to 36-in. squares.

Because red and white oak look good and wear well, they account for roughly 90 percent of hardwood installations. Ash, maple, cherry, and walnut are also handsome and durable, if somewhat more expensive than oak. In older homes, softwood strip-flooring is most often fir, and wide-plank floors are usually pine. If you know where to search, you can find virtually any wood—old or new—which is a boon if you're restoring an older home and want to maintain a certain look. On the Internet, you can find specialty mills, such as Carlisle Restoration Lumber™, that carry recycled wood that's often rare or extinct, such as chestnut salvaged from barns or pecky cypress pulled from lake beds. There's also new lumber made to look old, such as the hand-scraped cherry shown in the photo at right.

It's not surprising that wood flooring is a sentimental favorite. It's beautifully figured, warm hued, easy to work, and durable. *Disadvantages:* Wood scratches, dents, stains, and expands and contracts as temperatures vary. And, when exposed to water for sustained periods, it swells, splits, and eventually rots. Thus wood flooring needs a fair amount of maintenance, especially in high-use areas. In general, solid wood is a poor choice for rooms that tend to be chronically damp or occasionally wet.

Here's a typical cross section of solid-wood tongue-and-groove strip flooring.

These HomerWood® hand-scraped planks have a cinnamon cherry finish. Prefinished flooring, such as this, spares you the effort of sanding, the stink of noxious fumes, and a week of waiting for the floors to dry.

Prefinished wood flooring is stained and sealed with at least four coats at the factory, where it's possible to apply finishes so precisely—to all sides of the wood—that manufacturers routinely offer 15-year to 25-year warranties on select finishes. Finishes are typically polyurethane, acrylic, or resin based, with additives that help flooring resist abrasion, moisture, UV rays, and so on. To its prefinished flooring, Lauzon® says it applies "a polymerized titanium coating [that is] solvent-free, VOC [volatile organic compound] and formaldehyde-free." Harris Tarkett® coats its wood floors with an aluminum oxide–enhanced urethane. Another big selling point: These floors can be used as soon they're installed. There's no need to sand them or wait days for noxious coatings to dry.

The solid-wood wear layer of this engineered flooring can be sanded and refinished several times. The finishes shown are (left to right) white ash, vintage chestnut, and cherry.

This array of Natural Cork™ flooring is sealed with a UV-cured acrylic finish that keeps out moisture. The cork wear layer is bonded to a high-density fiberboard.

Tough as prefinished floors are, however, manufacturers have very specific requirements for installing and maintaining them, so read their warranties closely. In many cases, you must use proprietary cleaners or "refreshers" to clean the floors and preserve the finish. Also, board ends cut during installation must be sealed with a finish compatible with that applied at the factory.

Engineered wood flooring is basically an upscale plywood, with a top layer of solid hardwood laminated to a three- to five-layer plywood base. Most types are prefinished, with tongue-and-groove edges and ends. This flooring is typically sold in boxes containing 20 sq. ft. of 2½-in. or 3¼-in. widths, and assorted lengths. Engineered wood flooring may be stapled to a plywood subfloor or glued to a concrete slab. Because it's more dimensionally stable than solid wood, engineered wood is better suited to occasionally damp areas such as kitchens or finished basement rooms. And acrylic-impregnated varieties are even more moisture resistant.

There are many price points and quality levels of engineered wood flooring, and you get what you pay for. Better-quality flooring has a thicker hardwood layer—Mirage® engineered wood flooring touts its ⁵⁄₃₂-in. hardwood layer on a five-ply board whose total thickness is ⅜ in. In general, a hardwood layer that is *dry sawn* will have richer, more varied grain patterns than wood that is rotary peeled or sliced.

Disadvantages: The thin top layer of engineered wood flooring can be refinished only a time or two. Mirage maintains that its ⁵⁄₃₂-in. top layer can be sanded three to five times, but that seems optimistic, given the condition of most rental sanding equipment.

OTHER NATURAL FLOORINGS

The materials in this group—bamboo, coconut palm, and cork—are engineered to make them easier to install and more durable. And their beauty is 100 percent natural.

Bamboo flooring sounds implausible to people who visualize a floor as bumpy as corduroy. However, bamboo flooring is perfectly smooth. It is first milled into strips and then reassembled as multi-ply, tongue-in-groove boards. Available in the same widths and lengths as conventional hardwood, bamboo boards are commonly ⅜ in. to ⅝ in. thick. Bamboo flooring can be nailed or glued. But if you glue it, allow the adhesive to become tacky first so the bamboo doesn't absorb moisture from it.

Bamboo flooring comes prefinished or unfinished, and can be sanded and refinished as often as hardwood floors. It's a warm, beautiful surface, with distinctive peppered patterns where shoots were attached. Bamboo is hard and durable, with roughly the same maintenance profile as any natural wood product, so you must vacuum or mop it regularly to reduce abrasion. Avoid installing it in chronically moist areas.

Coconut palm flooring, like bamboo, is plentiful and can be sustainably harvested. Its texture is fine pored, reminiscent of mahogany. Because coconut palm is a dark wood, its color range is limited, from a rich, mahogany red to a deep brown. And it is tough stuff: Smith & Fong™ offers a ¾-in.-thick, three-ply, tongue-and-groove strip flooring, called Durapalm®, which it claims to be 25 percent harder than red oak. Durapalm is available unfinished or prefinished. One of the finish options contains space-age ceramic particles for an even tougher surface. So if you're thinking of installing a ballroom floor in your bungalow, this is definitely a material to consider.

Cork flooring is on the soft end of the hard-soft continuum. Soft underfoot, sound deadening, nonallergenic, and long lasting, cork is the ultimate "green" building material. Cork is the bark of the cork oak, which can be harvested every 10 years or 12 years without harming the tree (some cork trees live to be 500 years old). Traditionally sold as ³⁄₁₆-in. by 12-in. by 12-in. tiles, which are glued to a substrate, cork flooring now includes colorfully stained and prefinished squares and planks that interlock for less visible seams. Cork flexes, so many manufacturers use a flexible coating such as UV-cured acrylic to protect the surfaces and edges from water. Cork's resilience comes from its 100 million air-filled cells per cubic inch; so it's a naturally thirsty material. Wipe up spills immediately and avoid soaking a cork floor when mopping it: Damp mop instead and periodically refresh its finish.

Disadvantages: Avoid dragging heavy or sharp-edged objects across it, because it will abrade. Chair and table legs can leave permanent depressions.

Typically, engineered cork flooring has a three-ply, tongue-in-groove configuration. The surface layer is high-density cork, the middle layer is high-density fiberboard with precut edges that snap together, and the underlayment layer is low-density cork that cushions footsteps and absorbs sound. First developed in Europe, snap-together panels float above the substrate, so owners can easily replace damaged planks or, when it's time to move, pack up the floor and take it with them. Many snap-together floors are glueless, but floors requiring glue usually need it to bond planks together, not to glue them to a substrate.

LAMINATE FLOORING

Most engineered flooring is laminated to some degree, so here the term applies to a group of floorings whose surface layers are usually photographic images covered and protected by a clear *melamine* (plastic) layer. The photographic images often show wood grain, tile, or stone. Although plastic-laminate "wood" flooring may be a hard sell to traditionalists, the stuff wears like iron and every year captures a larger share of residential flooring. Moreover, as this category increases in popularity, manufacturers offer more and more colors and textures, including many that don't mimic natural materials and are quite handsome on their own.

Amber horizontal Plyboo® flooring. Laminated bamboo is about as hard as oak; and thanks to its extensive root system, bamboo can be harvested repeatedly without replanting.

This array of colors is a small sample of the hundreds available from Marmoleum, one of the oldest makers of linoleum.

However, linoleum has proven resilient in more ways than one by bouncing back from near-extinction, thanks to new presealed linoleums that don't need waxing. In addition, linoleum (sometimes called Marmoleum®, after the longest continuously manufactured brand) has antistatic and antimicrobial qualities. It's also possible to custom-design linoleum borders and such, which are then precisely cut with a water jet. Flooring suppliers can tell you more.

Vinyl has similar attributes to linoleum, though it is a child of chemistry. Its name is short for polyvinyl chloride (PVC). Vinyl flooring is also resilient, tough to damage, stain resistant, and easy to clean. It comes in many grades, principally differentiated by the thickness of its top layer—also known as its *wear layer*. The thicker the wear layer, the more durable the product. The more economical grades have designs only in the wear layer; whereas *inlaid* designs are as deep as the vinyl is thick. If you're thinking of installing vinyl yourself, tiles are generally easier, though their many joints can compromise the flooring's water resistance to a degree.

STONE AND TILE

If stone and tile are properly bonded to a durable substrate, nothing outlasts them. However, handmade tiles or stones of irregular thickness should usually be installed in a mortar bed to adequately support them. And leveling a mortar bed is best done by a professional. Tile or stone that's not adequately supported can crack, and its grout joints will break and dislodge. Chapter 16 has the full story.

Tiles are rated by hardness: Group III and higher are suitable for floors. Slip resistance is also important. In general, unglazed tiles are less

Developed and first adopted in Europe, laminate flooring is most commonly snap-together planks that float above a substrate, speeding installation, repairs, and removal. Of all flooring materials, laminate is probably the most affordable; and as noted, it's almost indestructible. Because it resists scratches, chemicals, burns, and water, it's a good choice for high-use or high-moisture areas. It's also colorfast, dimensionally stable, and easy to clean—though many manufacturers insist that you use proprietary cleaning solutions. For a good overview of installing laminates, see www.armstrong.com.

Disadvantages: Laminate flooring dents, exposing a fiberboard core, and you can't refinish it, although damaged planks can be replaced.

RESILIENT FLOORING

Vinyl and linoleum are the two principal resilient materials, available in sheets 6 ft. to 12 ft. wide, or as tiles, typically 13 in. or 12 in. square. Linoleum is the older of the two materials, patented in 1863. It may surprise you to learn that linoleum is made from raw natural materials, including linseed oil (*oleum lino,* in Latin), powdered wood or cork, ground limestone, and resins; it's backed with jute fiber. (Tiles may have polyester backing.) Because linoleum is comfortable underfoot, water resistant, and durable, it was a favorite in kitchens and baths from the beginning; but it fell into disfavor in the 1960s, when it was supplanted by vinyl flooring, which doesn't need to be waxed.

Top: Porcelain 12-in. by 12-in. tile from BJCeramic®.
Bottom: Natural cleft slate from Mohawk®.

slippery than glazed ones, but all tile and stone—and their joints—must be sealed to resist staining and absorbing water. (Soapstone is the only exception. Leave it unsealed because most stone sealers won't penetrate soapstone and the few that will make it look as if it had been oiled.) Tile and stone suppliers can recommend sealants, and you'll find a handful of good ones in "Countertop Choices," on p. 313. If stone and tile floors are correctly sealed, they're relatively easy to clean with hot water and a mild household cleaner.

CARPETING

Carpeting is favored in bedrooms, living rooms, and hallways because it's soft and warm underfoot, and deadens sound. In general, the denser the *pile* (yarn), the better the carpet quality. Always install carpeting over padding; the denser or heavier the pad, the loftier the carpet will feel and the longer it will last. Wool tends to be the most luxurious and most expensive carpeting, but it's more likely to stain than synthetics. Good-quality polyester carpeting is plush, stain resistant, and colorfast. Nylon is not quite as plush or as colorfast, though it wears well. Olefin and acrylic are generally not as soft or durable as other synthetics, although some acrylics look deceptively like wool.

Disadvantages: Carpeting can be hard to keep clean, and it harbors dust mites and pet dander, which can be a problem for people with allergies. In general, wall-to-wall carpet is a poor choice for below-grade installations that are not completely dry, because mold will grow on its underside. Far better to use throw rugs in finished basement rooms.

Refinishing Wood Floors

Wood floor refinishing can be as simple as lightly sanding an existing finish and applying another coat of the same finish or as extensive as stripping the floor finish completely and sanding it several times before applying a new finish. If the floor is just grimy and dull from too many coats of wax, it may just need a thorough washing. If washing doesn't do the trick, try to determine what the existing finish is before you rent a sander.

THREE TESTS TO DETERMINE A FLOOR FINISH

Wood floors installed in the 1960s or earlier were usually finished with some combination of wax, shellac, and varnish. After that, they were most likely finished with a penetrating oil, or oil- or water-based polyurethane. (For more on finishes,

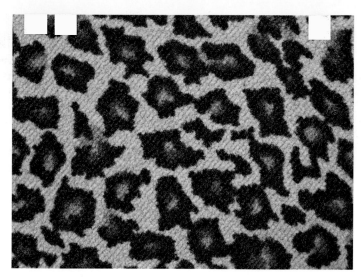

Not grandma's wall-to-wall carpet, unless she lived in Hollywood. This faux-leopard, cut-pile carpet is part of Shaw™ Carpet's Wildebeest series.

see p. 494.) Here are a few tests to help figure out what's there, and what to do next.

Test 1: Wax. Place several drops of water on the floor: If the surface turns white in 10 minutes or 15 minutes, there's wax on the floor. *If the water doesn't leave a white spot,* try Test 2. If the finish is dull, try cleaning it with a wax cleaner. If scratches and scuffs are limited, wax will be reasonably easy to remove by applying wax stripper or mineral spirits and wiping up the residue. Then apply a new coat of wax. However, if floors are badly abraded and can't be buffed out, sand the floors, refinish them with a penetrating stain, and then wax them. Even if you sand wax-sealed floors down to bare wood, wax clinging to board edges may prevent a nonwax finish from adhering properly. (Get a second opinion from a professional floor refinisher.)

Test 2: Shellac or varnish. Find an area where the finish is poor shape and scrap it with your thumbnail or a penny. If the finish flakes off, it's shellac or varnish, which were good in their day but should now be sanded off completely and replaced with polyurethane. *If the finish doesn't flake,* try Test 3. If the abraded areas are small, try restoring damaged areas by lightly sanding them, vacuuming and dust-mopping them well, then applying a new coat of finish. If there's not too much sanding to do, you may not need to rent a sander: A random orbital sander with 100-grit or 120-grit sandpaper should do the job. Use a natural-bristle brush or a lamb's wool pad to apply shellac or varnish.

Test 3: Polyurethane. In an inconspicuous place, brush on a small amount of paint stripper. If the finish bubbles, it's polyurethane. If it doesn't

PRO TIP

If you're not sure what finish was used on floors, first examine old paint and finish cans in the basement, garage, or workshop. The contents of the cans will almost certainly be useless, but their labels may tell you what's on your floors.

||||

Most rental companies offer drum sanders because their paper clamping–slots make changing sandpaper easy. Before accepting a rental drum sander, inspect slot lips for nicks or metal spurs, which could damage wood floors. Before leaving the rental company, learn how to insert sandpaper so it's tight to the drum.

bubble, the floors were probably sealed with a penetrating oil finish. If floor damage is limited, you may be able to touch up the penetrating oil with a similar substance, testing small areas till you find a good color match. If the finish is polyurethane, which is a surface finish, sand the floor lightly if it is in good shape, to help the new coating adhere. Fortunately, polyurethane will stick to other polyurethane even if one is oil based and the other is water based. As long as the base coat is dry, it doesn't matter whether you apply oil-based urethane over water-based urethane or vice-versa. Of course, if the finish is in bad shape, you should sand down the whole floor to bare wood and then refinish it.

RECAP: WHEN TO REMOVE FLOOR FINISHES

Sand floors to bare wood when

▶ Floor finishes are gouged, pitted, or showing bare spots.

▶ Stains go below the surface, such as mold stains beneath potted plants.

▶ Floorboards are irregular or uneven.

▶ New finishes won't adhere to the flooring.

▶ You need to patch repair rotted or split boards.

▶ The floor is thick enough to withstand a sanding.

How Deep Can You Sand?

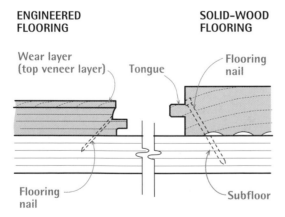

ENGINEERED FLOORING

SOLID-WOOD FLOORING

Wear layer (top veneer layer)

Tongue

Flooring nail

Flooring nail

Subfloor

You can sand only the top veneer layer of engineered flooring. Solid-wood, tongue-and-groove (T&G) flooring is a lot thicker, but you can sand only to the top of its tongue. If you sand lower, you'll hit flooring nails. T&G nail heads should be just flush, as shown.

IS IT THICK ENOUGH TO SAND?

To avoid splintering wood floors when sanding them, keep at least ⅛ in. of solid wood above the tongue of T&G flooring. The easiest way to assess the floor's thickness is to remove a forced-hot-air floor register and look at the exposed cross section of flooring. If that's not possible, pull up a threshold or a piece of trim and bore a small hole to expose a cross section. Or drill in a closet, where no one will see the hole. If you've got engineered flooring, its wear layer (top veneer layer) won't be very thick to start with—3/32 in. is typical—so start sanding with a less aggressive sandpaper, as suggested in "Floor-Sanding Materials," on p. 490. In most cases, you can sand an engineered floor at least one or two times. But even if you have solid-wood flooring, avoid sanding into board tongues: T&G flooring is nailed through its tongues, and if you hit nails, the sandpaper will shred quickly.

EQUIPMENT

Most sanding equipment can be rented. Be sure to have a knowledgeable person at the rental company explain how to operate the machines safely, how to change sandpaper and adjust wheels and drive belts, and what size circuit breaker or fuse each tool requires. Finally, inspect each piece of equipment. Sander drums and edger disks should be smooth and free of nicks or metal spurs that could scar floors. Check to see that sander wheels roll freely and that electrical cords aren't frayed or swathed in tape because they're been run over by the sander.

A large floor sander does most of the heavy sanding. Most professional refinishers favor large belt sanders, as shown in the photo on p. 482, because their belts are continuous; whereas rental companies usually rent *drum* sanders, because the paper is somewhat easier to change. Typically, a special wrench or *key* turns a nut at the end of the drum, which opens a paper-clamping slot on the face of the drum. Drum sandpaper must be tight or it will flap and tear: Use old pieces as templates for new ones.

Caution: A drum sander is a powerful machine that can gouge even the hardest wood, so always keep the machine moving when the sanding drum is down. A lever on the handle lowers or raises the drum. Start the machine only when the drum is up. Then, as you walk, gradually lower the drum.

Worth a look: The Trio Floor Sander, a new triple-headed random orbital sander, won't gouge floors as drum sanders can and doesn't need to sand with wood grain, so it's great for parquet floors.

When renting sanders, be sure to get any specialized tools they require, such as the T-wrench needed to change sandpaper on this edger.

An edger (disk sander) goes where drum or belt sanders can't—along the perimeter of floors and into tight nooks. (Large floor sanders should not be used within 6 in. of walls.) Edgers may be smaller than floor sanders, but they can still gouge flooring quickly. So first practice on plywood. The edger's paper is held in place against a rubber disk by a washered nut. To prevent gouging the floor with the edger, many professionals leave three or four used disks beneath the new one, which cushions the cutting edge of the sandpaper somewhat.

A buffer is a versatile tool. With abrasive *buffer screens,* it can lightly sand floor finishes you want to restore or fine-sand a floor that you've stripped down to bare wood. Its slow, oscillating movement is perfect to scuff-sand between finish coats. Or, when the final coat is down, you can

PRO TIP

Empty sander bags when they become about one-third full. As bags fill up, they become less efficient filters, and more dust will stay in the air or on the floor.

Refinishing Floors Safely

As the Safety Maven of Wingdale notes, "The nice thing about working on floors is that you don't have far to fall." Nonetheless, there are safety issues to consider when refinishing.

Electrical. Before renting sanders, examine their electrical cords and plugs, rejecting any that are frayed or appear to have been sanded over. If you don't have a heavy-duty extension cord, rent or buy one; lightweight household cords could overheat and start a fire. User's manuals or labels on big sanders indicate minimum cord spec's. Household circuits must be adequately sized for the equipment: 220-volt drum sanders often require 30-amp circuits; 110-volt sanders typically require 20-amp circuits. In most cases, a drum sander's 30-amp plug will fit a home's 30-amp dryer receptacle.

Volatile chemicals. Finish manufacturers have reduced the volatility and strong odors of their products, but you should always limit your exposure to them by wearing an organic-vapor respirator mask, long sleeves, and gloves when sanding old finishes or applying new ones. Even water-based polyurethane is unhealthful to breathe, so as soon as finishes are dry to the touch, open windows to let vapors disperse. And sleep elsewhere till they're completely dry.

Fire and explosion hazards. Sparks or open flames can ignite chemical fumes or dust. So before you start sanding or applying finish, turn off pilot lights for water heaters, ranges, and furnace. Also tape light switches down so they can't generate a spark. Trash bags of moist sawdust or covered garbage cans full of oily rags can generate enough heat to combust spontaneously, so don't allow debris to collect on site. Empty sander bags often into a metal container safely away from the house and other combustibles.

Lead paint and asbestos. Floors painted before 1978 may contain lead-based paints, so don't sand them till you've had the paint tested, as suggested in Chapter 18. Lead paint is generally not a problem till it becomes airborne, unless it's flaking in an area where small children might eat it. Old linoleum floors may have been adhered with asbestos adhesive, which wasn't banned till 1977. Here again, asbestos is usually harmless if undisturbed, so first consult a local health department to get the name of a test lab.

put a lamb's wool *buffing pad* on the buffer to bring up the sheen of a finish; thus it's often used to buff out a new wax coat.

Hand scrapers and sanding blocks reach corners, flooring under cabinet toekicks, and other places edgers can't reach. Hand scraping is tedious, but it goes more quickly if you periodically use a fine metal file known as a *mill file* (bastard file) to sharpen the scraper blade.

Other hand tools you'll need include a *nail set* to sink nail heads below the surface of the wood before you begin sanding, a hammer, and wide-blade spackling knives or metal squeegees to apply wood filler. If you cut your own edger disks, you'll need a pair of heavy scissors. Brushes and applicators should be matched to specific finish types. You'll find those tools discussed and paired with finishes in "Finishes, Cleaning Solvents, and Applicators," on p. 494.

Personal safety equipment is not optional. Get a close-fitting respirator mask with organic vapor filters. During the sanding phases, wear eye goggles with side vents; vented goggles admit a bit of sanding dust, but they won't cloud up with water vapor. Drum sanders and edgers are noisy and tiresome; wearing hearing protection will keep you alert longer, so you'll be less likely to gouge the floor because you're punchy with fatigue. Wear disposable plastic gloves when applying finishes or wood filler. If you can, buy latex-free nitrile plastic gloves, which auto mechanics, gardeners, and postal workers swear by. Nitrile gloves are tough enough to withstand automotive

PRO TIP

When sanding floors, follow the physician's creed, "First, do no harm." It can take hours to repair a trough cut by paper that's too coarse. In fact, you may have to replace the damaged section. So start with the least aggressive sandpaper grit that will do the job, whether it's removing old finish or leveling uneven boards. If that proves too gentle, you can easily switch to a more aggressive grit.

Buffer screens are held on with friction. Use them to fine sand a floor that's been stripped or to sand between finish coats.

Backpack vacuums are less likely to gouge flooring or bash woodwork, but their capacity is generally less than that of floor models. Empty vacuums when they're one-third full because the fuller they get, the less efficient they become.

Floor-Sanding Materials*

TYPE OF MATERIAL	GRIT SIZE	WHEN TO USE
Sandpaper belts for large floor sander; disks for edger	36	Aggressive; use on first pass if boards cupped, uneven
	36 open coat	Use on first pass if floors coated with wax, paint
	60	Try for first pass; switch to 36 if not enough cut
	100	Second or third pass
Buffer screen (use with backer pad)	100	Final screen before applying finish
	220	Smooth between coats of finish
Sandpaper strips (attach to buffer backer pad)	180	Smooth between coats of oil-based finish
	220	Smooth between coats of water-based finish

* Consult finish manufacturer's specs for sanding requirements.

solvents and garden grit, yet thin enough to sort mail with. You can easily find nitrile gloves at auto parts stores, typically sold in boxes of 50 to 100 in sizes ranging from small to extra large.

Edging and hand scraping are hard on your knees, so get a pair of kneepads comfortable enough to wear all day.

Rent a heavy-duty vacuum, since there's no point in frying a home vac that's really not up to the task. Ideally, the vacuum should have a HEPA (high-efficiency particulate air) filter to capture dust rather than recirculate it into the room, but not all rental companies carry them. A backpack vac, shown in the bottom photo on the facing page, is less likely to bash woodwork and has no wheels to compact sawdust, but most rental companies offer only wheeled canister types.

SANDPAPER AND BUFFER SCREENS

Sandpaper and buffer screens are rated according the concentration of grit per square inch. The lower the grit number, the larger, coarser, and more widely spaced the grit particles. Lower-grit papers cut more aggressively. Whereas, the higher the grit number, the finer and more closely spaced the grit. Consequently, as you sand floors, each grit should be slightly finer than the preceding one, smoothing out scratches of the previous grits, till you arrive at the grit level specified on the label of your floor finish. *Always read the finish manufacturer's sanding requirements before renting equipment and buying sanding material.*

If you're sanding floors to bare wood, you'll typically need to make two or three passes with a large floor sander and an edger and one pass with a buffer with abrasive screen, before floors are smooth enough to apply finish. (Vacuum after each pass.) Get 36-grit, 60-grit, and 100-grit paper for the floor sander and the edger; both use the same grit on each pass. To screen the floor before finishing, buff with 100-grit screens backed by a nylon backing pad. To smooth between coats, use a 220-grit screen, or hook-and-loop sandpaper strips that attach to the buffer pad.

Note: If floors are coated with paint or wax—which gum up sandpaper quickly—*use open-coat sandpaper* for the first sanding pass. You can use regular closed-coat sandpaper (most sandpaper is closed coat) for subsequent passes.

If you're simply recoating a finished floor, you probably won't need a drum sander and an edger; a buffer with a nylon pad and two grades of screen (100 grit and 220 grit) should do the job. Again, check your floor finish's label to see what grit sandpaper to use between coats. Finally, sandpaper wears out quickly, so get more than

you think you'll need. Most rental companies will credit you for unused paper when you return the equipment.

PREPARING FOR SANDING

After testing floors to determine their finish, empty rooms of all movable items (don't forget window blinds and shades). Then use 3-mil polyethylene sheeting to cover the cabinets, radiators, smoke detectors, doorways, and heating or air-conditioning openings, using painter's tape to avoid pulling paint off the walls and trim. Dust migrates through the smallest openings, so use painter's tape to seal the perimeters of closed doors and keyholes. Because baseboards will get bumped by edgers, remove them if possible—though often that's not possible. Alternatively, you can use a metal shield to protect such trim, as shown in the top photo on p. 493.

Before you start sanding floors, cover cabinets, air registers, and other fixed elements with plastic sheeting. To seal edges, use blue painter's tape to avoid lifting off paint or cabinet finishes, but remove the tape as soon as possible.

To prevent sanding over the cord, keep the excess looped over your shoulders. Drum sanders sand whether you're going forward or backing up, so as you back up, continually pull the cord away from the path of the sander.

Vacuum the floor so you can survey it closely for nails sticking up, and floorboards that are split or uneven. Use a nail set to sink nails below the floor surface. If boards are uneven or cupping, you may be able to sand them down evenly if they are solid wood. If any boards are split or splintered, replace them now.

SANDING FLOORS

A quick review: Shut off all pilot lights, seal off doorways, open windows for ventilation, wear a respirator mask and ear protection, start with the least aggressive sandpaper, and lower the sander drum only when the machine is moving.

Start sanding with the drum sander. Sanding with the direction of the wood grain cuts less aggressively and minimizes scratches that must be sanded out later. However, if there are high spots that need to be sanded down or if the floor is painted, sand diagonally to the wood grain on the first pass, then with the grain on all subsequent passes. (The diagonal angle should be 15° to 30° from the direction of the floorboards.) If you must sand the first pass diagonally, use the same grit on the second pass, as you sand with the grain. Because a parquet floor has grain running in various directions, sand it diagonally on the first pass, too.

When sanding with the grain, start along a wall and sand about two-thirds the length of the

Replacing a Floorboard

To remove a damaged board, drill holes across it so you can pry it out in splinters, using a hand chisel. Or you could cut into the damaged board by using a circular saw set to the depth of the flooring and then pry out pieces with a flat bar. To make this *pocket cut*, rest the heel of the saw on the floor, pull back the saw guard, and slowly lower the front of the saw sole until the turning blade engages the wood. *Be careful:* Holding a blade guard back is never advisable if you can avoid it, and the saw may jump when it engages the wood. Let the blade stop before you lift the saw.

Find a replacement board that's similar in color and grain: Try to pull a board from a nearby closet or from floor section that's usually covered by an appliance. Hold the board next to the hole and use a utility knife to mark off the appropriate length. To make the replacement fit more easily, slightly back-bevel its lower edges on a table saw. If the stock is tongue-and-groove, use a table saw to cut off the lower leg of the groove. Apply construction adhesive to the underside of the new board, and then drive it into the opening using a piece of scrap to cushion the hammer blows. It's not possible to nail the board through its tongue, so predrill and face-nail two 6d finish nails at either end. Use a nail set to drive the nails below the surface. Fill the holes with wood putty.

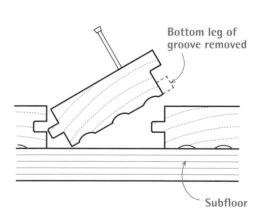

To insert a replacement board into an existing tongue-and-groove floor, use a table saw to remove the bottom of the groove. Slightly back-cut the ends of the new board so it will slide in easier.

Edgers sand right up to the base of a wall, but they are aggressive sanders with plenty of torque. To avoid scuffing baseboards and casing, cover the edger bumper with masking tape or, if possible, have a helper shield the woodwork, as shown.

Overlap Sanding Passes

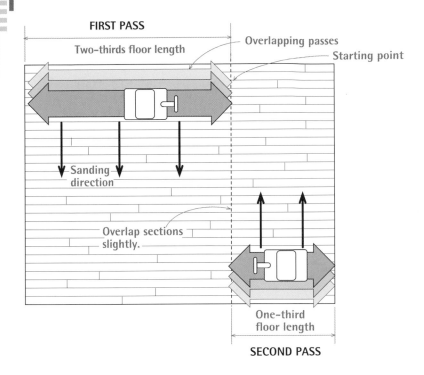

FIRST PASS

Two-thirds floor length

Overlapping passes

Starting point

Sanding direction

Overlap sections slightly.

One-third floor length

SECOND PASS

Start along a wall and sand about two-thirds the floor length. Sand up and back. Then raise the drum, and roll the sander over so the next pass overlaps by roughly half a drum-width. Sand till you reach the opposite wall. Then turn the sander 180° and sand the remaining third of the floor.

floor. Then, with the drum lowered and sanding, pull the machine backward over the strip just sanded. Raise the sander's drum toward the end of each backward pass and wheel the machine over about 6 in., so the next pass will overlap the first by roughly half the width of the drum. Again, sand down about two-thirds the length of the room, and then pull the sander backward, as shown in "Overlap Sanding Passes," above.

Continue sanding until you have reached the opposite wall (you will have sanded two-thirds of the room by then). Turn the machine 180° and start sanding the other end of the room (the third you haven't yet sanded). Again, sand one pass up and one back. When you reach the edge of the portion already sanded, overlap it by 1 ft. or 2 ft. before starting the next pass. In this manner you can blend the sanding of the two sections of the room.

Using an edger. After completing each sanding pass with the drum sander, use the edger to sand along the perimeter of the room, as close to the base of the walls as you can get. Use the same grit sandpaper that you just used on the drum. When it's upright, the sander disc moves in a

clockwise direction, so work from left to right, keeping the edger moving constantly to avoid scour marks. You don't need to press down on the edger to make it work. If the edger is sanding too aggressively, switch to the next finer grit. If it's not sanding aggressively enough, change its sanding disks more often. Again, try to sand with the wood grain as much as possible.

Finish up by hand. Hand scraping and sanding take care of the areas the edger can't reach, such as in corners and under cabinet toekicks. It's hard, tedious work, but fortunately there's not much of it. A sharp scraper will speed the job, scraping with the grain to remove the old finish. Then use a sanding block to smooth out the semicircular edger marks. (*Note:* If there are a lot of edger marks, use a random-orbital sander to feather them out.) Once you've drum-sanded, edged, and hand-scraped the room, vacuum it well before switching to the next-finer grit

Hand-scrape the areas the edger can't reach. Scrape with the wood grain, before sanding lightly with a sanding block.

Finishes, Cleaning Solvents, and Applicators

FINISH	CLEANS WITH	APPLICATOR	COMMENTS
Water-based polyurethane	Soap and water	Synthetic brush; pad; round applicator	Probably best all-around finish for nonpro; tough, water-resistant finish; easy cleanup, low smell; work fast, overlapping edged areas before they dry
Oil-based polyurethane	Mineral spirits	Natural-bristle brush; round solvent-resistant applicator	Tough, durable finish; favored by pros because dries slower than water-based; slightly stronger smell while drying
Penetrating sealers (tung and modified linseed oils)	Mineral spirits	Lamb's wool applicator, natural-bristle brush	Slow to dry; strong odor; scratches easily but can be touched up with new finish over old; usually waxed
Stain-sealers	Mineral spirits	Varies: natural-bristle brush to clean rags	Same profile as penetrating sealer; finish must be waxed to protect wood
Varnish	Turpentine or paint thinner	Natural-bristle brush; lamb's wool pads	Volatile; strong smelling; slow to dry; hard, amber finish gives historical appearance; often used to match older finish
Shellac	Denatured alcohol	Natural-bristle brush; lamb's wool applicator	Poor water resistance; flammable; chips; rarely used for floors anymore
Various (acrylic-impregnated; acrylic-urethane; UV cured)	Proprietary solvents	Computer-monitored sprayer	Factory applied in highly controlled environment; durable; water resistant coatings on prefinished wood flooring

and sanding the floor a second time. If you need to fill holes or gaps in the floor, do it before the second sanding.

SCREENING FLOORS

After you've drum-sanded and edged the floor with 100-grit sandpaper and vacuumed it well, use a buffer with an abrasive screen to smooth out any remaining marks. Use a 100-grit or 120-grit buffer screen, which is held onto the buffer pad by friction. Because the buffer rotates slowly and the screen is flexible, you can buff right next to the base of the wall. Start along a wall, moving the buffer from side to side (it rotates in a counterclockwise direction). As you did with the drum sander, overlap passes about one-half the width of the buffer pad. Buffer screens wear out quickly, so replace them when you've screened one-third to one-half the floor. Save at least one used screen, so you can fold it and use it to hand-screen the corners where the buffer couldn't reach.

To achieve an even smoother finish, vacuum the floor and wet-sponge it with clear water the night before screening it (the moisture will raise the grain slightly). The next day, when the wood flooring is dry, screen it smooth. Wetting the wood and then screening it is called *popping the grain*. Popping is optional, but strongly recommended if you'll be applying a water-based finish. After screening the floor and touching up corners by hand, vacuum the room thoroughly and use clean tack rags to remove dust from any horizontal surface. (A tack rag is a slightly sticky cheesecloth pad that adheres dust.) Finally, dry-mop the floor, wrapping the mop in a clean cloth lightly dampened with the same solvent you used to thin the floor finish.

Filling HOLES AND GAPS

Flooring stores carry color-matched *spot fillers* and *trowel fillers*. Spot filler is basically woodworker's putty, applied with a spackling knife to fill nail holes and obvious cracks. Trowel filler, which is thinner, is pored onto the floor in small amounts and worked into the narrow gaps between floorboards, using a large squeegee or a smooth-edge trowel. Done on your knees, applying trowel filler is hard work, requiring pressure to force the filler into gaps and to scrape off excess. Consequently, though spot-filling is common, trowel-filling is not. *Note:* If you've got wide pine planks, which expand and contract seasonally, *don't* fill the gaps between them. Brag about their rustic charm instead.

SELECTING A FLOOR FINISH

Floor finishes are often divided into two categories: *penetrating sealers* (*penetrants*) and *surface finishes*. Penetrating sealers usually contain plant-based oils, such as tung oil or modified linseed oil, and soak into wood fiber. In time, they harden to seal and protect the wood. Because penetrating sealers form a hard outer shell, they can be easier to touch up by sanding lightly and adding more sealer if wood becomes scuffed or scratches—touched-up areas won't be obvious. Wood stains penetrate and don't really seal. When they have dried, penetrating sealers are often waxed to make them more durable. But waxed floors are durable only if they're regularly maintained, which takes time. Thus most floors today are sealed with surface finishes, which don't require waxing.

Surface finishes, as their name implies, form a tough exterior shell to resist scuffs, scratches, and moisture. The earliest surface finishes were shellac and varnish, which have been largely replaced by oil-based and water-based polyurethanes. Shellac has poor water resistance and chips easily, and varnishes tend to be strong smelling and slow to dry. Besides, both are extremely flammable. Although surface finishes require less maintenance, their disadvantage is that they can't be touched up when they become worn, so you must refinish the whole floor. Surface-finish sheens range from matte (little shine) to satin to semigloss to gloss. In general, glossier finishes are harder, more durable, and more water resistant.

As you'll see, polyurethanes vary greatly in ease of installation, drying time, and durability. *Water-based polyurethanes* are the stars of the show these days: tough, nonyellowing, relatively mild smelling, and fast drying (2 hours to 6 hours). And brush cleanup is easy with soap and water. Because they contain lower levels of volatile organic compounds (VOCs), water based polyurethanes are also safer to use. Despite their volatility, *oil-based polyurethanes* are often applied by professional refinishers because they're slower to dry and thus allow more time to even out coats. Though solvent based and stronger smelling, oil-based polys are more durable and water resistant, and they turn a handsome amber with age. Let them dry for 24 hours before recoating or walking on them. *Moisture-cure polyurethanes* are the most durable of the lot; but because they must absorb moisture from the air, they're temperamental to apply, slow to dry, and best left to professionals.

Finally, there are surface finishes that require highly controlled environments and thus are factory applied to prefinished flooring. This group of finishes may include aluminum-oxide, titanium, or ceramic additives to resist abrasion and may require UV curing, rather than heat cur-

Between finish coats, screen the floor to improve adhesion, using a 100-grit or 120-grit screen. Before applying the next coat, vacuum and dry-mop the floor well with a tack rag.

Start each coat by cutting an edge around the floor's perimeter and along cabinet bases, using a brush or a paint pad. Then use a T-bar applicator to overlap the edged borders while they're still wet.

For newer, water-based polyurethanes, use a round synthetic T-bar applicator like this one. Pour the finish onto the floor, and then spread it in broad sweeps—like window washing with a squeegee.

Use a lamb's wool applicator to apply penetrating-oil finishes.

ing. Some of the toughest of these finishes infuse acrylic into the wood cells in a modern version of a penetrating sealer.

APPLYING A WATER-BASED FLOOR FINISH

Applying a water-based polyurethane does not differ much from applying an oil-based finish and, as noted in the preceding section, water-based finishes are more benign. Although "Finishes, Cleaning Solvents, and Applicators," on p. 494, offers general guidance, consider the can label as the last word on drying times, recommended applicators, and so on.

Cutting the edge is the first step when applying any type of floor finish. Use a brush or paint pad to apply a 6-in. swath of finish around the perimeter of the room, along cabinet bases—in short, any place that would be difficult to edge with a large applicator. Pour finish into a sloping paint tray with a replaceable liner, so you can easily reload the paint pad, brush, or large applicator.

If you're applying a slow-drying finish, you can edge the whole room before switching to a large applicator. However, because water-based finishes dry quickly, it's best to edge one section of a wall at a time, so you can use a T-bar applicator to overlap edged borders while they're still wet. Maintaining a wet edge is the key when applying water-based finishes: Edges that dry before they're overlapped have a distinct lap mark.

Working the floor with a T-bar applicator is like a ballet with chemicals. After cutting the edge, pour a thin puddle of finish along one wall, parallel to the floorboards, but stop the puddle 3 ft. to 4 ft. shy of the far wall. Holding the applicator pad at a slight angle—somewhat like a snowplow blade—pull the applicator through the finish. Angle the applicator so that excess finish flows toward the inside of the room so you can spread it out on the return pass. The ballet comes at the end of each turn, as you sweep the applicator pad 180°, spread the finish evenly, and set up for the next pass. It's easier to do than to describe.

Periodically pour more finish in a long puddle to maintain a wet edge. Having a second person to pour the finish and touch up missed spots is helpful but not essential. If you see a missed spot after the finish has started to set, let it dry and be sure to coat that area the following day, when you apply the next coat. Once each coat is dry, screensand it lightly, vacuum, and dry-mop it with a tack rag over the mop. Then apply the next coat.

Square-edge wood strip flooring is face-nailed, so use a straightedge to line up the nails for a neat, professional appearance. Because tongue-and-groove flooring is nailed through the tongues, those nails are hidden.

In general, don't walk on the floor till the final coat has cured at least 3 days, and—because this finish is water based—do not damp-mop it for a month.

Installing Strip Flooring

T&G strip flooring, ¾-in. thick and 2¼-in. to 3¼-in. wide, is by far the most commonly installed wood flooring. Installing it requires few specialized tools and, with a modest amount of prep work, it goes down fast and lasts long.

PREP STEPS

Wood absorbs water and swells, so don't bring hardwood flooring on site till the building is closed-in and "wet work" (such as plumbing, tiling, drywalling, plastering, and painting) are complete. Allow paint, plaster, or joint compound several days to dry. If necessary, turn on the heat-

Subflooring AND UNDERLAYMENT

Subflooring is usually CDX plywood or OSB (oriented strand board) panels whose long edges run perpendicular to the joists—although in older houses, subflooring may be 1-in. boards run diagonally. For joists spaced 16 in. on center, ¾-in.-thick panels give floor fasteners plenty to grip; ⅝ in. is minimal. To allow for expansion and to minimize squeaks, leave ⅛-in. gaps between square-edged panels, nailing the panels to joists every 6 in.; ring-shank or spiral nails hold best. (T&G panels have integral expansion gaps, so butt their edges tight.) Undersize subflooring often sags between joists, creating high spots over the joists and floors that are springy and squeaky. Adding blocking between the joists may stiffen and quiet floors.

Underlayment is a layer—over the subflooring—to level out and add rigidity to the subflooring and the finish flooring that follows. Underlayment is especially important if the flooring is thin and would telegraph gaps or irregularities underneath. So most resilient-flooring and carpet makers specify underlayment beneath their products. Particleboard, fiberboard, and hardboard are often used for underlayment, but they should *never* be used for subflooring. Lacking the cross-grain construction of plywood, these materials just aren't as strong, and they tend to delaminate when wet.

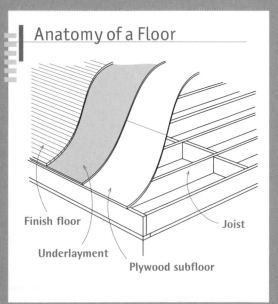

Anatomy of a Floor

Finish floor

Underlayment

Joist

Plywood subfloor

Floor Nailing Schedule*

SIZE AND TYPE FLOORING	SIZE NAIL TO USE	SPACING
T&G strips† (¾ in. × 1½ in., 2¼ in., 3¼ in.)	2-in. barbed flooring cleat,‡ 7d or 8d flooring nail, or 2-in. 15-gauge staples with ½-in. crowns‡	10 in. to 12 in. apart; 8 in. to 10 in. preferred
T&G† strips (½ in. × 1½ in., 2 in.)	1½-in. barbed flooring cleat or 5d cut-steel or wire-casing nail	10 in. apart
T&G strips (⅜ in. × 1½ in., 2 in.)	1¼-in. barbed flooring cleat or 4d bright wire casing nail	8 in. apart
Square-edge strips§ (⁵⁄₁₆ in. × 1½ in., 2 in.)	1-in. 15-gauge barbed flooring brad	2 nails every 7 in.
Square-edge strips§ (⁵⁄₁₆ in. × 1⅓ in.)	1-in. 15-gauge barbed flooring brad	1 nail every 5 in. on alternate sides of strip
Planks (4 in. to 8 in.)	2-in. barbed flooring cleat,‡ 7d or 8d flooring nail, or 2-in. 15-gauge staples with ½-in. crowns‡	8 in. apart

* Adapted, with permission, from NOFMA: The Wood Flooring Manufacturers Association, all rights reserved, © 2004. To see the chart in its entirety go to www.nofma.org/installation3.htm.

† Tongue-and-groove (T&G) flooring is blind-nailed on the tongue edge, with face-nailing required on the starting and finishing runs.

‡ NOFMA Hardwood Flooring™ must be installed over a proper subfloor.
Use 1 1/2-in. fasteners with a 3/4-in. plywood subfloor on a concrete slab.
A concrete slab with sleepers every 12 in. on center does not always require a subfloor.

§ Square-edge flooring is face-nailed.

ing or air-conditioning so indoor conditions will be close to normal (60°F to 70°F) for a week before installing flooring. Open the bundles of wood flooring and allow them to acclimate indoors for 72 hours before installing them.

Use a moisture meter to check interiors if your region has high humidity. Home centers and electronics stores carry reliable, inexpensive meters. Ambient humidity indoors should be 35 percent to 55 percent; if readings are higher, consider installing a dehumidifier. Also check the moisture content (MC) of wood subfloors and flooring, using a moisture meter with probes. Typically, wood flooring's MC is 6 percent to 10 percent. The subfloor's MC should not vary more than 4 percent from that of the flooring's.

If you're installing floors over a basement or crawl space, check the humidity of that area, too. If it's too high, correct any contributing factors before installing wood floors; high humidity also encourages mold. Crawl spaces with dirt floors

should be covered with plastic and sealed to limit moisture and air infiltration, as described in Chapter 14.

Survey subfloors to make sure they're solid, flat, and clean. If floors are excessively springy, stiffen them by adding blocking between the joists, adding plywood or OSB (oriented strand board) panels over existing subfloors, or sistering new joists to old ones, as described in Chapter 8. In older houses, floors are rarely level; so if they're solid, it's more important that they be flat—within ½ in. per 10 ft. Use a rental edging sander or a woodworker's belt sander with coarse sandpaper to lower high spots; use strips of building paper (15-lb. felt paper rather than rosin paper) or wood shims to build up low spots. In general, masonry floor-leveling compound is too inflexible to use beneath wood flooring because flooring nails will fragment it and board flexion will fracture it.

If you notice protruding nail heads, not enough nails, or squeaky spots, correct these conditions now. Squeaks can usually be silenced by screwing down subflooring to joists near the squeak or by nailing it down with ring-shank or spiral nails. Vacuum and sweep the floor well. If the floor is over an occasionally damp basement or crawl space, staple 15-lb. building paper to the subfloor, overlapping roll seams by 6 in. However, don't bother with building paper if the subfloor areas are dry or if the floor is on an upper story.

Finally, remove the baseboard molding if you can do so without damaging it. Baseboards hide the expansion gap between the perimeter of the flooring and the base of the wall. At the very least, install a piece of quarter-round shoe molding to cover the gap if you can't remove the baseboards. If door casings are already installed, undercut (trim the bottoms of) each side jamb, by the thickness of the flooring; an *undercut saw* is specially designed for this task. Remove doorway thresholds if they're nailed down. But if they're glued down or set in mortar, simply butt the flooring to them.

EQUIPMENT

Sawdust or debris trapped under a board can mean uneven, loose, or squeaky floors later on, so be obsessive about keeping subfloors clean as you install flooring.

Installation tools include safety glasses, hearing protection, kneepads, radial-arm saw or small table saw, hammer, nail set, tape measure, chalkline, flat pry bar to remove trim, large flat-bladed screwdriver to draw board edges tight to each other, flooring mallet, and a manual or pneumatic flooring nailer. For the little bit of face-nailing to be done, use a pneumatic finish nailer; if you haven't got one, use a ⅟₁₆-in. bit to predrill holes for the face nails. You'll need white glue to secure floorboards under toekicks and in other odd spaces where it's difficult to reach with any nailer. Finally, rent a shop vacuum if you don't own one. And be sure to have a good-quality broom and a dustpan.

Pneumatic flooring nailers are more expensive than manual nailers, but they don't depend on your strength to drive flooring nails to the correct depth. Nailers aren't foolproof, though. Take a sample of the flooring to the rental company to ensure that the pneumatic nailer will correctly engage the flooring edge profile. That is, the tool may need an adapter-fitting or -plate to avoid damaging the boards' tongues. On-site at the start of the job, calibrate the nailer's pressure by nailing a "practice row" of flooring to the subfloor. Typically, pneumatic nailers are set at 70 psi (pounds per square inch); adjust the pressure up or down till the tool sets nails correctly, as shown in "How Deep Can You Sand?," on p. 488. Once the setting is correct, pull up the practice row.

LAYOUT, STARTER ROWS, AND BEYOND

There are two places to install a starter row. The first and most obvious place is along a long wall. The second place is down the center of the room, which is recommended when rooms are wider than 15 ft., when rooms are complex, when several rooms converge, and when walls are out of parallel by 1 in. or more.

Flooring usually runs parallel to the length of a room, so start by measuring the width of the room at several points to see if the walls are parallel. If the walls aren't parallel, split the difference eventually by ripping down the final row of boards on both sides of the room.

Use baseboards to conceal the expansion gaps. If baseboards aren't thick enough to conceal the gaps, you may need to cut back the drywall as shown in "Concealing Floorboard Edges," below.

Installing the starter row along a long wall. At both ends of the room, measure out from the wall the width of a floorboard plus ¾ in. for expansion. Snap a chalkline through those two points so you'll have a straight line to align the starter row to. Place the groove edges of the first

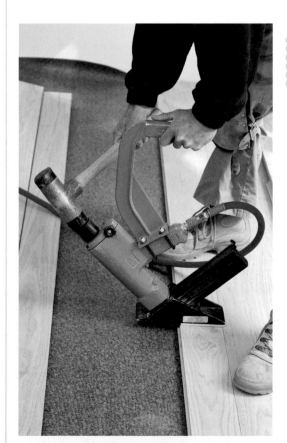

A pneumatic floor nailer will drive nails or staples at the correct depth all day long, once you've calibrated its pressure. You don't need to hit the rubber strike cap hard to make the nailer fire.

Concealing Floorboard Edges

Framing

Baseboard

Drywall cut 1 in. above subfloor

Flooring

Subfloor

¾-in. expansion gap

When walls are out of square, baseboards or shoe molding may not be wide enough to cover the ¾-in. gap wood floors require. In that case, trim the bottom of the drywall about 1 in. to gain additional space.

row toward the wall, so the boards' tongues face into the room. If you pick straight boards for the starter row, successive rows will be more likely to stay straight. Face-nail the boards in the starter row, driving pairs of 6d or 8d nails every 10 in. to 12 in., and placing them in 1 in. from the boards' edges.

If you use a pneumatic finish nailer to face-nail the boards, you'll be unlikely to split them.

Adding a spline, as shown on the left, creates a tongue–and–groove board with two tongues, so you can nail outward from that board in two directions. Use a spline when you want to start an installation in the middle of a room.

If you hand-drive the face nails, use a ¹⁄₁₆-in. bit to predrill for 6d spiral nails. In either case, sink the nail heads below the surface of the wood, and eventually fill holes with wood putty. Next, use the pneumatic flooring nailer to *blind-nail* (nail through tongues) boards every 10 in. to 12 in. To further avoid splits, don't nail within 2 in. to 3 in. of a board's end. Once the starter row is secured, blind-nail subsequent floorboards till you reach the opposite wall and run out of room to use the pneumatic nailer.

Installing the starter row in the middle of the room. Measure out from both long walls to find the approximate center of the room. If walls aren't parallel, the centerline should split the difference of the measurements between the two walls. Snap a chalkline to indicate the centerline; line up the starter row to it. Because you *don't* face-nail a starter course in the middle of a room, screw temporary blocks—scrap flooring is fine—along the chalkline to keep starter-row boards in place. Otherwise, they could drift as you drive nails through the tongues. Nail down five or six rows, before removing the temporary blocks.

Next, add wood *splines* (also called slip tongues) to the grooves of starter-row boards, which most flooring stores carry. Adding splines allows you to blind-nail toward the opposite wall as well. Glue splines to board's grooves, using scrap flooring to drive the splines snug without damaging them.

Installing the rest is straightforward. To speed the installation and ensure that board ends are staggered at least 6 in. between rows, have a helper *rack* (spread out) floorboards so you can quickly tap boards into position with the flooring mallet and nail them down. Floorboards come in regular lengths from 12 in. to 36 in. So to create a random joint pattern, use board remnants with irregular lengths to start rows.

Continue blind-nailing boards every 10 in. to 12 in., checking periodically to make sure the

rows are straight. If milling irregularities or warping prevents boards from seating correctly, use a large flat screwdriver to lever the boards snug, as shown in the top left photo on the facing page. Set aside boards that are too irregular to use; professional installers typically order 5 percent extra to allow for warped or poorly milled boards and waste.

As you approach within a foot or two of the opposite wall or next to a base cabinet, you won't have room to use the pneumatic flooring nailer, so switch to a pneumatic finish nailer. Nor will you have room to swing your flooring mallet, so use a pry bar to draw the boards' edges snug. As you get within 6 in. to 8 in. of the wall, measure the distance remaining, including ¾ in. for an expansion joint. In most cases, you'll need to rip down the last row of floorboards. If they are less than 1 in. wide, first glue them to the next-to-the-last row and install the two rows as a unit. Or, if you're installing floorboards of varying widths, rip down a wider board. The last row of boards should be face-nailed and glued to the subfloor as well. Finally, install prefinished transition pieces such as thresholds, reducer strips (strips that taper to accommodate differing floor heights) and so on. When you've sanded and finished the flooring, reinstall the baseboards.

Store extra flooring in a dry location. If the flooring has a warranty, file it in a safe place, along with the flooring's code number and floor care information.

Using a piece of scrap to avoid damaging the tongues, drive the boards snug before nailing them. The friction between the tongues and the grooves will usually hold them during nailing.

If boards are slightly warped or tongues and grooves are a bit swollen, use a thick screwdriver as a lever to draw them together. Hammer the screwdriver point into the subfloor to get some traction.

Glue the last row of boards, especially those at the base of a cabinet. Only one edge will engage the board next to it, and there's often not enough room to drive nails.

The first and last rows of tongue-and-groove floorboards are usually face-nailed, here with a pneumatic finish nailer. Draw boards tight with a flat board.

Whenever there's a tricky transition or a complex shape to cut, either scribe the shape or, as here, create a template to transfer the shape to the floorboards.

Wood Flooring over Concrete

Before purchasing wood flooring for installation over concrete slabs or in sub-grade areas, check the flooring warranty to see if subgrade installations are allowed. If so, be sure to correct excess moisture conditions beforehand. In general, engineered wood is a better choice than solid-wood flooring in such locations because engineered wood's cross-ply construction is more dimensionally stable. And thanks to impregnated acrylics and other factory finishes, it's also more water resistant.

Solid-wood flooring is typically installed by first covering the concrete slab with a 6-mil polyethylene vapor barrier, spacing 2×4 *sleepers* on-face every 12 in. to 16 in. over the plastic, and then using power-actuated fasteners to attach the sleepers to the slab. Although it's possible to nail ¾-in. T&G flooring directly to sleepers, it is likely to deflect. Most flooring manufacturers specify a ¾-in. plywood subfloor, with panels run perpendicular to the 2×4s, a ⅛-in. gap between panel edges, and a ½-in. expansion space around the perimeter of the subfloor.

Engineered wood and plastic-laminated flooring can be nailed or stapled to wood subflooring, glued directly to a slab, or "floated" over it. Floating systems typically call for the planks to be glued or attached to each other, rather than to the subfloor or slab. Many systems feature proprietary underlayments that block moisture and cold and cushion the flooring so you feel less like you're walking on concrete. Cosella-Dörken's DELTA®-FL underlayment is a dimpled plastic membrane, and other systems employ foam or felt pads. Floating systems can be used over slabs with radiant heating, as well.

Resilient Flooring

Resilient flooring surfaces, such as vinyl and linoleum, bounce back from use and abuse that would gouge or crush harder, less flexible materials. However, vinyl and linoleum are relatively thin, so their durability depends on a sufloor that's thick enough and an underlayment layer that's smooth, stiff, and flat.

Resilient flooring is installed either as tiles or as sheets; both require underlayment. Tiles are generally easier to install—their layout is similar to that for ceramic floor tiles, as described in Chapter 16, but are poorly suited to high-moisture areas because of their many seams. Resilient sheets are better for kitchens and bathrooms, as suggested in the kitchen installation shown here.

Creating a Paper Template

- 1-in. gap not covered by paper
- Alignment notch
- Overlap paper seams at least 2 in. and tape together.
- "Boats" cut out and covered with duct tape
- 15-lb. building paper
- Cutout for toilet flange
- Alignment notch
- Perimeter of room

By scribing the perimeter of a room onto felt building paper, you create a full-size template that you can transfer to the resilient flooring. Taping over boat-shaped cutouts keeps the template from moving.

LOW-MAINTENANCE Beauty

Resilient flooring seems to last forever, but it quickly dulls if you don't mop it regularly to remove grit. Sponge mopping with warm water is usually enough. If water doesn't clean the floor, use a mild, nonabrasive cleaner recommended by the flooring maker. Avoid scrub brushes and abrasive cleansers, which do more harm than good.

CHOOSING AN UNDERLAYMENT

Because resilient materials are thin—between 1/16 in. and 3/16 in. thick—they will telegraph subsurface irregularities, such as board joints, holes, and flooring patterns. So underlayment materials must be uniformly flat (no holes or voids), smooth, stiff, and dimensionally stable. Few materials fit the bill. *Note:* It's possible to adhere resilient flooring directly to concrete slabs, old resilient flooring, and wood flooring, but that often requires a lot of prep work to make such surfaces perfectly smooth. So in addition to creating a more durable, smoother resilient floor, underlayment speeds up its installation.

Plywood. Plywood is universally acceptable if it's correctly installed and is exterior-grade APA-rated CDX underlayment. It will be stamped "underlayment" or "plugged crossbands." Also, it should be at least 1/4 in. thick and have a *fully sanded* face (FSF)—not plugged and touch sanded (PTS). Type 1 lauan plywood, which has an exterior glue, is also specified by many resilient flooring makers; panels should be at least 1/4 in. thick. Three face-grades of lauan are acceptable as underlayment: BB, CC, and OVL. Type 2 lauan is not acceptable. APA Sturd-I-Floor® plywood is another option: It's a structural plywood that serves both as subfloor and underlayment. Sturdi-I-Floor panels range from 19/32 in. to 1 1/8 in. thick; span distances and loads dictate the thickness.

Hardboard, particleboard, and OSB. Hardboard, a very dense fiberboard, is generally an acceptable underlayment for resilient flooring in dry locations, but it should not be used in kitchens and bathrooms because its joints tend to swell when they get wet. *Particleboard* also swells along its edges when it absorbs moisture. OSB underlayment panels are more stable, but surface roughness can telegraph through resilient flooring. In dry locations, most of these materials are acceptable underlayments, but check your flooring manufacturer's recommendations to be safe. Those specs will also include nail lengths and spacing, as well as acceptable filler materials.

INSTALLING UNDERLAYMENT PANELS

Follow panel and flooring manufacturer specifications for the length and spacing of fasteners, and acceptable filler materials. In the installation shown here, the installer attached 5/16-in. underlayment panels, using 1 1/8-in. staples spaced every 4 in. to 6 in. in the field and every 1 in. to 1 1/2 in. along the panels' edges. Stagger underlayment joints so they don't align with subfloor joints.

Before filling panel joints and irregularities with a patching compound, use a wide spackling knife or drywall-taping knife to scrape off splinters. If the blade clicks against a nail or staple, use a nail set to sink the fastener below the surface.

Most resilient flooring makers specify a portland cement–based patching compound, which may contain a latex binder. If you use any underlayment other than hardboard, fill and level the panel joints and surface imperfections. But don't fill nail holes because if nails work loose, they'll raise the patching compound as well, creating a bump in the flooring. Apply one or two coats of compound, feathering it out along the edges of the seam. If you're careful, you won't need to sand the compound.

CREATING A TEMPLATE

Bring resilient flooring sheets onto the job site at least 24 hours before working with it, so it has time to acclimate to room temperatures (at least 68°F) Resilient materials are more pliable when they have warmed and less likely to crimp or crease. As you roll and unroll resilient sheets, be careful not to crimp the material, which could crease its surface and be visible forever after.

There are several ways to transfer a room's dimensions to resilient flooring sheets, but none so accurate as creating a template, especially if there are refrigerator alcoves or base cabinets to work around. Create the template with 15-lb. felt paper, which is inexpensive and, being stiffer than rosin paper, is not likely to tear as you transfer the room's outline to the resilient flooring. Using a utility knife, rough-cut pieces of the paper so they approach within 1 in. of all walls, cabinet bases and the like. Beyond that, don't agonize about fitting the paper too accurately. That is, the paper doesn't need to butt against walls and cabinets because the scribing tools will span small gaps between the edge of the paper and the perimeter of the room. If the jaws of the scribing tool are 1½ in. wide , they will scribe a guideline onto the paper that is uniformly 1½ in. away from the base of walls, cabinets, etc.

As you roll out individual pieces of paper, overlap their edges about 2 in. and use duct tape to join them. Once you've covered the floor with felt paper, use a utility knife to cut small (2-in. by 5-in.) boat-shaped holes in the paper every 3 ft. to 4 ft., as shown in the top right photo on p. 504. As you cut each boat-shaped hole, cover it with duct tape, which adheres through the holes to the subfloor. This will keep the paper from moving as you scribe the perimeter of the room.

Many installers use a scribing tool or a compass set at about 1½ in. to trace the shape of the

Because resilient flooring is flexible and easy to cut, you can fit it after the cabinets are installed, no matter how complex or curving they are. Given their wide range of colors and textures, linoleum and vinyl flooring can complement almost any decor.

room and cabinets onto the paper to create a template that they will later transfer. But the installer shown on the following pages preferred a *small framing square* and a *pin scribe*. The 1½-in. width of a framing square's blades (legs) ensured a uniform scribing distance, and the square fit easily under the cabinet toekicks. Holding one edge of the square flush to the wall, he ran the point of the pin scribe along the other edge— scribing a light line in the felt paper 1½ in. away from the wall. Because the square's blades are straight, along curved surfaces he moved the square often, making a number of scribe marks to indicate the arc of the curve.

PAPER TEMPLATE FOR RESILIENT FLOORING

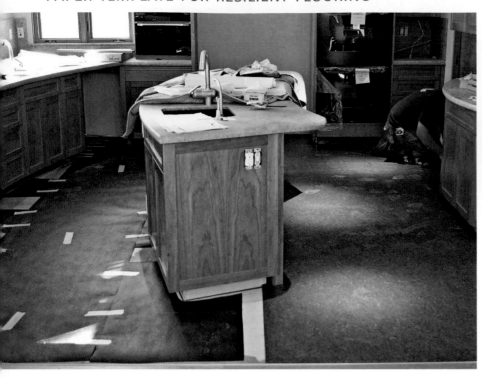

1. In this installation overview, a felt-paper template, to the left of the island, is about to be scribed to record the room and cabinet outlines. To the right, newly cut linoleum is dry-fit to see what adjustments need to be made before gluing it down.

2. Cut boat-shaped openings in the felt-paper template; then cover the holes with tape to anchor the template to the underlayment. To record the perimeter accurately and ensure precise cuts on the flooring material, it's vital that the template stays put.

3. You can use an adjustable compass or, as shown here, a pin scribe and a small framing square to trace the room's perimeter onto the template. By holding one edge of the square against walls and cabinets and scribing along the other edge, you ensure a scribed line that is a uniform distance from the perimeter.

It's okay to use several sections of felt paper if a room is large or unusually complex. In this case, be fastidious about marking section edges so you can reassemble and tape them to the resilient sheeting before transcribing the room outline. On a room of any size, you'll probably need to use several sheets of resilient flooring as well. (Sheet widths vary from 6 ft. to 12 ft.) *Important:* When you're done scribing, gently lift the template—but leave the duct tape stuck to the paper. Loosely roll up the template and carry it to the room where the resilient sheet has lain unrolled on the floor, face up, to warm and flatten. Line up template edges to trimmed flooring edges. Then carefully unroll the template so it lies flat atop the resilient material (Step 4). Press down the "boats" so the duct tape sticks to the resilient flooring, anchoring the template.

CUTTING AND FITTING RESILIENT SHEETS

To transfer the outline of the room to the resilient flooring, place a blade of the framing square on the scribed line and run a utility knife along the *outside* edge of the blade, as shown in the photo on the facing page. The mark made by the utility knife—1½ in. beyond the scribed line—represents the cut-line you'll make in the resilient flooring. But the utility knife should score the flooring

only about one-third deep. After you've scored with the utility knife, use a hooked knife to cut all the way through, with the scored line guiding the hooked knife. Hold the hooked knife at a slight angle, so it undercuts the edge. At some point, you'll also trim off the flooring's factory edge, which protects the material in transit.

Once you've cut the outline, remove the paper template and loosely roll the flooring with its back facing out. Carry it to the room to test its fit. If you need to retrim the flooring to make it fit exactly, you're in good company. Professional installers always assume they'll trim because no template measurement is ever 100 percent accu-

PRO TIP

Except for butt edges where two flooring sheets meet, linoleum edges are usually cut slightly *shy* because slight gaps can be concealed by baseboard trim, a finish toekick, or a threshold—or hidden by an appliance. Never force the material. In general, pros avoid cutting linoleum edges *proud* (too generously) because the material doesn't compress.

4. After scribing the template, carefully lift it off the underlayment, roll it loosely, and unroll it onto the resilient flooring. Press the taped "boats" onto the flooring so the template won't move.

5. To transfer the outline of the room and the shape of the cabinets to the flooring, align one edge of the framing square to the scribed line. Then use a utility knife to score along the other (outer) edge of the square. But score only one-third the thickness of the flooring.

6. Using the scored line as a guide, use a hook-blade knife to cut all the way through the flooring. (Continued on next page.)

rate. When you're satisfied with the flooring's fit and final position, use a pencil to draw *set marks* on the underlayment, so you'll know exactly where the sheet edge should be when you *lap the sheet* (roll it back on itself) to apply adhesive.

ADHERING AND SEAMING THE FLOORING

Some flooring materials are adhered only along the edges *(perimeter bond),* whereas others are completely glued down *(full-spread adhesion).* Flooring secured by full-spread adhesion is less likely to migrate or stretch and hence is more durable. Follow the installation instructions that come with your flooring. Be sure your supplier provides the manufacturer's instructions on adhesion and seaming methods that may be unique to your resilient flooring.

Full-spread adhesion. After the resilient flooring is final-trimmed in place, it is typically lapped back halfway, exposing roughly half the area underneath. Using a square-notched trowel, spread a compatible adhesive on about half the floor. Unroll the lapped portion down into the adhesive, and immediately use a 100-lb. roller on the material to spread the adhesive and drive out bubbles. Roll across the material's width first, then along its length. Next to the walls, use a

7. After cutting the flooring, carefully roll it with its backing out so it will lie flat when you unroll it onto the underlayment.

8. If the perimeter of the floor or the cabinets is complex, have a helper help unroll the flooring to avoid crimping it as you fit it into odd nooks and crannies.

hand seam-roller to seat the material in the adhesive. Repeat the process with the second half of the sheet. If you get adhesive on the face of the flooring, clean it off at once, using a cleaner recommended by the manufacturer. (Most glues clean up with water.)

Seaming edges. If one sheet of flooring doesn't cover the entire floor, you'll have at least one seam edge. Here, be sure to follow the manufacturer's instructions on seam spacing and adhesive applications between individual sections, called *drops.* For example, manufacturers indicate how far back from the edges to apply adhesive and whether the seams should be butted together or overlapped and double-cut through both layers.

Although manufacturers tell you to butt *vinyl* seams tightly, you'll need to leave a hairline gap between the sections of Marmoleum, which contracts along its length and expands across its width. Also, linoleums tend to expand slightly because of the moisture in the adhesive.

Wall-to-Wall Carpeting

Basically, there are two types of wall-to-wall carpeting. Conventional carpeting is laid over a separate rubber or foam padding and must be stretched and attached to *tackless strips* around the perimeter of the room. *Cushion-backed carpeting,* which has foam bonded to its backing, doesn't need to be stretched—it's usually glued down—so it's generally easier to install. However, it must be destroyed to remove it. Consequently, better-quality carpeting is almost always conventional, and that's the focus here.

Carpeting doesn't ask much of subflooring, which can be slightly irregular as long as it is dry, solid, and adequately sized (⅝-in. plywood is typical). Carpeting can be installed over existing wood, tile, resilient flooring, or concrete floors; but check the manufacturer's recommendations regarding subgrade installations, acceptable gaps in the substrate, padding thickness and type, and so on. Don't scrimp on padding; buy the densest foam or heaviest rubber padding you can.

CARPETING TOOLS

You can rent most of the specialized tools. To install conventional carpeting you'll need the following:

▶ A power stretcher stretches carpeting taut across a room, so it can be secured to tackless strips along opposite walls. Cross-room stretching eliminates sags in the middle of a room. You simply add and adjust stretcher sections to extend the tool.

▶ A knee-kicker is used in tandem with the power stretcher to lift the carpet edges onto strips, to stretch the carpet in a closet, or to draw the seams closer together before you hot-glue them.

▶ The stair tool drives carpeting into the spaces between tackless strips and walls and between stair risers and treads.

▶ A seam iron heats the hot-melt carpet seam tape that joins the carpet sections.

▶ The row runner, or row-running knife, cuts between the rows of loop-pile carpeting. Many installers use a large, flat-bladed screwdriver to separate the rows first.

▶ An edge trimmer trims the carpet edges so they can be tucked behind tackless strips; under baseboards; or under transition pieces such as metal carpet doors, which are used in doorways or where dissimilar flooring materials meet.

▶ Seam rollers can be either star wheeled (spiked) or smooth; they press the carpet edges onto the hot-melt seam tape to ensure a strong bond. Use a smooth roller for cut-pile carpets and a star roller for loop-pile carpets.

▶ Miscellaneous tools include a utility knife with extra blades, aviation snips to cut tackless strips, a hammer, a stapler if you're applying padding over plywood, a notched trowel if you're installing padding over concrete, heavy shears, a chalkline, a tape measure, and a metal straightedge to guide utility-knife cuts.

ESTIMATING CARPET

Carpeting comes on factory rolls whose standard width is 12 ft.; a handful of carpet manufacturers offer widths of 13 ft. 6 in. or 15-ft. Plan on covering most of the room with a large piece of carpet 12 ft. wide, then covering the remaining spaces with smaller pieces joined to the large piece with hot-melt seam tape. Professional installers call the full-width piece of carpet the *drop;* the smaller pieces are called the *fill.* Joining carpet seams is time consuming so choose a layout that minimizes seams.

Start by measuring the room's width and length at several points; then make a sketch of the room on a piece of graph paper. A ¼ in. to 1 ft. scale is a good size to work with. On the sketch, include closets, alcoves, base cabinets, floor registers or radiators, stairs, doorways, and so on. Also note the location of doors and windows, particularly the main entrance into the room. Carpet pile should slant toward the main entrance, so that a person entering the room looks into the carpet pile.

Carpet seams and edges must be trimmed, so factor that into your estimate. Add 3 in. for seamed edges, and allow 6 in. extra for each carpet edge that runs along a wall. Stair carpet pile should slant toward a person ascending the stairs. Try to carpet stairs with a single piece 3 in. wider than the stair treads, to allow for tucking along both sides of the tread. If the carpet has a repeating pattern, determine how often it repeats and add that amount plus 2 in. to the lengths of smaller pieces that must be seam-matched to the large piece of carpet covering most of the room. Given a detailed layout sketch, a flooring supplier can refine the estimate and order the correct amount of padding, tackless strips, and so on.

INSTALLING TACKLESS STRIPS

Wear heavy gloves when handling tackless strips. Nail the strips around the perimeter of the room, leaving ¼-in. gaps between the strips and the base of walls so you can tuck the carpet edges into those gaps. As you nail down each strip, try not to hit the angled tack points sticking out of the strip. (The tacks should always slant toward walls, away from the center of the room, so the carpet will stay impaled on the tacks.) Because it's difficult to grasp the strips without pricking a finger, use aviation snips to shorten them.

Each strip must be nailed down with at least two nails. Nail the strips *in front* of radiators or built-in cabinets, because it would be difficult to

Carpet Layout

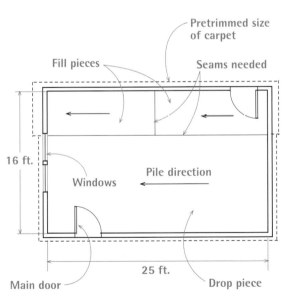

An ideal layout minimizes waste and seams, positions seams away from traffic, and orients carpet pile so that someone entering through the main entrance looks into the pile. Carpet comes in 12 ft.-wide rolls (also called bolts), so 41 RF (running feet) of carpet would allow enough extra for trimming edges in this 16 ft. by 25 ft. room.

nail the strips or to stretch carpeting behind or under such obstacles. To anchor carpet edges in doorways, you can use a *metal carpet bar,* which has angled barbs like a tackless strip, as shown in "Carpet Transitions," on the facing page. Or you can install a *hardwood threshold* to provide a clean edge to butt the carpet to, after first anchoring it to a tackless strip, or folding the carpet under about 1 in. and nailing down that hem.

INSTALLING PADDING

Padding, which is usually 6 ft. wide, should run perpendicular to the carpet to prevent padding and carpet seams from lining up. If the padding has a slippery side, face it up so carpet can slide over it as you position it. Once you've rough-cut the padding, carefully position the pieces so they butt to each other. *Do not overlap padding* sections, which could create a raised welt under the carpet; likewise, padding should not overlap tackless strips. Trim the padding so it butts to the edge of the strips. Then use duct tape, or something as strong, to tape the padding seams together so they can't drift.

If there's a plywood subfloor, staple the padding every 6 in. around the perimeter of the

In the old days, installers tacked the perimeter of a carpet every inch and hand-sewed sections together. Today, carpet seams are joined with hot-melt tape (above right) and stretched onto tackless strips that hold the edges securely. The tool in the foreground is a knee-kicker, used to move carpet.

Tackless strips come in 4-ft. lengths, with nails suitable for the substrate. This strip has short, case-hardened masonry nails for attaching strips to a concrete slab. Wear goggles driving such nails down.

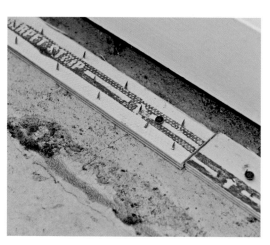

When installing padding over a concrete floor (which is somewhat slippery) tape the padding edges to the edges of tackless strips to keep the padding from riding up onto the strips. Tape just the edges of the strips, so the tack points remain exposed.

A Tackless TASK

You may wonder why strips with dozens of tack points sticking up are called *tackless.* In the old days, carpet installers had to hem (fold over) and tack down carpet edges every inch or so, which took thousands of tacks. When someone finally realized that it would be much quicker to hook carpeting onto strips containing slanted, inverted tacks, a generation of installers gave thanks. By and large, the strips did away with edge tacking, hence the name *tackless strips.*

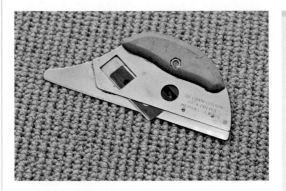

Adjust the row-runner blade so it cuts just through the carpet backing and not into the padding. Change blades often so they cut cleanly.

This row runner is cutting a looped-pile carpet. Note that the padding seams run perpendicular to the carpet seams, to prevent their ever lining up.

floor, and every 12 in. in the field, using ⅜-in. staples. If the substrate is concrete, sprinkle a latex-based carpet adhesive such as Parabond® M-4259 Solv-Free around the perimeter of the room and spread it out with a notched trowel; it's not necessary to adhere the entire padding. Finally, because concrete is slippery, tape the padding edges so they can't ride up onto tackless strips.

ROUGH-CUTTING CARPET

When rough-cutting carpet, it's helpful if you can unroll it completely. If you don't have enough room to do so indoors, unroll it on a clean, dry sidewalk or driveway. Sweep the area beforehand, and make sure there are no oil stains on the ground.

Cut the carpet to the overall room dimensions on your sketch—plus the extra you included for seams and trimming along walls. At this stage, don't cut out carpet jogs, such as along cabinets and around doorways, because you'll cut those later, when the carpet is spread out in the floor you're carpeting. *Important: Before making any cuts,* note the direction of the carpet pile, especially if you have more than one piece of carpeting to cut.

Carpet Pile and Layout

MOST carpeting consists of yarn loops stitched through a backing material. The upper face of the carpet is called the *pile*. When those yarn loops are uncut, the carpeting is called *loop pile*. When the loops are cut, it is called *cut pile*. *Sculpted pile* usually is a mixture of looped and cut, which frequently creates a pattern.

Because carpeting is stored and transported on a roll, its pile gets pressed down in a direction that it retains thereafter. By stroking a carpet's pile, you can determine its *pile direction*. When you look into the pile, the carpet color looks richer and when the pile direction points away from you, the carpet appears lighter. Thus when you install carpet, the main entryway of the room should look into the carpet pile, so that it appears as rich and luxuriant as possible.

Also, where it's necessary to join two pieces of carpet, the pile of at least one piece should lean into the seam, thus overlapping and concealing it to some degree. Finally, if you have to use more than one piece of carpet in a room, all pile should point in the same direction. Otherwise, the sections will appear to have different hues.

Carpet Transitions

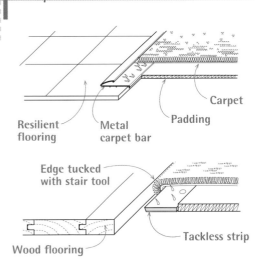

Tape the edge of the padding to keep it from riding up onto the tackless strips when stretching the carpet.

Transfer the room dimensions to the carpet. Use a felt-tip marker on the edge of the carpet to indicate the cut-line across its width, or use a utility knife to notch the carpet's edges at each end of the proposed cut.

In general, cut loop-pile carpet from its pile side (its face), and cut cut-pile carpet from its backing side. To cut carpet with *cut pile,* flop the edge of the carpet over so its backing is up, and snap a chalkline between the two notches you made in the carpet's edges. Cut along the chalk-line with a utility knife or a double-edged floor-

1. After unrolling the carpet, use the side of your foot, in a kicking motion, to adjust its position, as shown.

2. Many pros prefer to measure from the leading edge of the drop piece before cutting fill pieces. If you find that walls are not parallel, rough-cut the edges of the fill pieces at a slight angle so you'll have enough extra to trim.

3. Before hot-taping carpet seams, help the carpet lie flat by notching carpet edges where they abut doorways, cabinets, and so on.

ing knife, using a long metal straightedge to guide the blade. If the carpet is *loop pile,* cut it with the carpet facing up: Locate a pile row near the cut-line and run the blade of a large flat screwdriver between them, to separate the rows. Then push a *row runner,* as shown in the bottom photo on p. 509, steadily down the row to cut through the backing. The carpet pile will guide the cut.

POSITIONING THE CARPET

Carpet is heavy. So get help rolling it up and carrying it. Unroll it in the room where you'll install it. If you measured and cut properly, the edges of the carpet should curl up about 3 in. at the base of the walls. To adjust the carpet slightly once you've unrolled it, lift a corner about waist high. Then, as you stand with one foot on the carpet and one behind it, raise the foot that was on the carpet and, with the side of that foot, kick the carpet sharply. *Note:* By using the side of your foot, rather than your heel or toe, you'll be less likely to stretch or tear the carpet.

Many installers don't cut fill pieces of carpet till they've positioned the drop piece and measured from the drop piece to the wall. This allows them to double-check the size of the fill piece(s) needed. As with finish carpentry, "measure twice, cut once" is good advice, especially if the walls aren't parallel. Once you've cut the fill pieces and positioned them next to the edge of the drop piece, go around the perimeter of the floor and loosely notch the carpet where it butts against door jambs and corners, so the carpet will lie flat—but don't trim the carpet edges yet. First you need to join the carpet sections, using hot-melt seam tape.

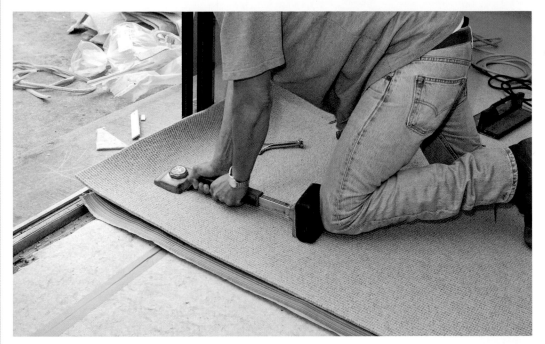

4. Straighten carpet seams before hot-taping them. Using just a knee-kicker, lift the carpet edges onto the tackless strips to create a slight tension. After the hot-melt tape seams have cooled, you can use a power stretcher to reposition the edges more securely to the strips.

5. Once the seam iron is hot enough, place it onto the tape and flop the carpet edges onto the tool so that only its handle is exposed.

6. As you heat sections of hot-melt tape, move the iron forward and roll the seam with a star roller. The spikes of a star roller penetrate the loop-pile carpet and press its backing into the tape adhesive at many points.

7. After seam rolling each section, weight it down till the tape has cooled. (Continued on the next page.)

HOT-MELT SEAMS

Join carpet seams before stretching and trimming the carpet. Correctly installed, hot-melt seams are strong enough to withstand stretching without separating.

Use the knee-kicker to draw the seam edges together. After lining up the carpet sections, roll back one section slightly and slip a piece of hot-melt seam tape under the carpet edge so that the tape will run exactly down the middle of the seam. The tape's adhesive-coated side should face up. Plug in the seam iron, and let it heat up. Once it's hot, place the iron on top of the seam tape at the start of the seam and let the carpet flop down on both sides, covering all but the handle of the iron. Most irons take about 30 seconds to heat the tape at a given point.

Once the adhesive has melted, move the iron farther along the tape. Then use a seam roller to embed the carpet backing in the melted adhesive. This operation isn't difficult, but you must make sure that carpet edges butt together over the tape, rather than overlap each other. (Back-cutting the

8. Once the hot-taped seams have cooled, they'll be strong enough to be stretched with a power stretcher and won't pull apart. When extended between opposite walls, the power stretcher's head typically moves the carpet about 2 in. as the lever is depressed.

PRO TIP

Before joining carpet seams, apply a bead of seam sealer to the edge of each section of carpet. Seam sealer fills any voids created when you trimmed carpet edges and keeps the pile from unraveling. Seam sealer looks like white glue and is usually latex based.

carpet's edges slightly with the row runner helps.) If it's a cut-pile carpet, use a smooth roller to press the carpet backing into the seam tape; if it's loop-pile carpet, use a star roller. After you roll a section of seam, weight it down as shown in the bottom right photo on p. 511. Continue along the seam—in roughly 12-in. increments—till the whole seam is bonded. Allow the adhesive to cool for 20 minutes to 30 minutes before stretching the carpet.

STRETCHING CARPET

Once the carpet seams have cooled, stretch and attach the carpet to the tackless strips around the perimeter of the room, using the knee-kicker, power stretcher, and stair tool. Actually, if you must join carpet seams, you already will have used the knee-kicker to draw the carpet edges taut so the glued seam will be a straight.

Typically, stretching begins in a corner, using a knee-kicker. Place the knee-kicker about 1 in. from the wall and rap the cushion of the tool

9. After stretching a carpet, use an edge trimmer to cut off the excess around the perimeter of the room. Then use a stair tool to tuck carpet edges behind tackless strips or under baseboards.

That's pretty much it. Once the second corner is attached, alternate using the knee-kicker and the power stretcher, somewhat as shown in "A Carpet-Stretching Sequence," below. There's no one always-best sequence. Keep an eye on what the carpet is doing, and use the tool that seems right. Seen from above, your carpet-stretching movements would resemble something between a tennis match and icing a cake. Back and forth, fine tuning as you go.

TRIMMING CARPET

Once the carpet is secured to the tackless strips and the transition pieces in the doorways, use an edge trimmer to remove the excess; trimmers also tuck the edge of the carpet to a degree. After trimming the edge, go around the perimeter with a hammer and a stair tool, tamping the carpet between the tackless strips and the wall, or under the baseboard trim. It's important that the trimmer's blade be sharp, so change razors whenever the tool drags, rather than cuts.

quickly with your knee. When done properly, this maneuver carries the carpet forward and onto the points of the tackless strips. Then use the stair tool to pack the carpet into the small gap between the strips and the wall, also to securely lodge the carpet on the tack point. Knee-kicking takes a little practice. But, as more of the carpet is attached, and there is some tension on it, the task becomes easier. As you work along an edge of the carpet, rest your hand on the section just attached. The extra weight will prevent the section from being dislodged by successive knee-kicks.

After securing a corner 2 ft. to 3 ft along each wall, assemble the power stretcher to stretch the carpet to an adjacent corner across the room. To do this, place the tail end of the power stretcher on a 2×4 block resting along a baseboard of the corner you just attached; the 2×4 prevents the tail end of the stretcher from damaging the finish wall. Unlike the knee-kicker, which rebounds, the stretcher has a lever that extends the tool and holds it there until the lever is released. Before you engage the stretcher's lever, place the stretcher head 5 in. or 6 in. from the wall you're pushing the carpet toward. Once you push down on the lever, the stretcher head should move the carpet about 2 in. forward, leaving you plenty of room to use the stair tool and secure the carpet to the tackless strip.

A Carpet-Stretching Sequence

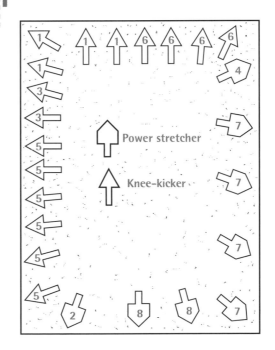

To stretch carpeting, alternate using a knee-kicker and a power stretcher. Typically, use a knee-kicker to secure a short section of carpet to tackless strips nearby, before using a power stretcher to stretch carpet across the room and secure it to strips along an opposite wall.

CARPETING STAIRS

If possible, use a single strip of carpet on stairs, eliminating seams. Stair padding can be many pieces because it will be covered by carpet. For the best-looking job, carpet pile on treads should slant toward you as you ascend the stairs. On risers, the pile should, therefore, point down. If you use several pieces of carpet on the stairs, for durability and appearance, carpet seams should always meet in riser–tread joints.

Estimating and ordering. First, determine the width of the runner. On closed stairs (which have walls on both sides), carpeting usually runs from wall to wall. On open stairs (with balusters on one or both sides), carpeting should run to the base of the balusters. In either case, each side of the carpet should be tucked under 1¼ in. to hide the cut edge and prevent its unraveling. Thus measure the width of the stairs and add 2½ in. to that width. So if your stairs are 36 in. wide, you'll be able to cut only three runners from each 12-ft. width of carpeting, allowing for tuck-unders and waste.

To determine the overall length of the stair runner, measure from the edge of the tread nosing to the riser, and from there up the riser to the nosing of the step above. Add 1 in. to this measurement to accommodate the padding over the step and multiply this by the number of steps. Add 6 in. to that total for adjustments at the top and bottom of the stairs.

That's a formula for straight-run stairs. If yours have bends and turns, create a paper template for each step that turns. Each template should cover a tread and the riser below. As noted above, add 1 in. for the distance the padding sticks out around the nosing. However, some old hands at laying carpet feel that stairs should be covered only with continuous pieces, with extra carpet tucked behind riser sections.

Installing carpet on stairs. Nail tackless strips on the stair risers and stair treads so that tack points on risers point down, and those on the treads point in, toward the risers. The tackless strip on each tread should be about ⅜ in. away from the riser, so there's a gap to tuck the carpet into. The tackless strip on each riser should be about 1 in. above the tread. Tackless strips should be 2½ in. shorter than the width of carpet with tucked-under edges. That is, each edge is 1¼ in. wide and does not attach to the tackless strip. So the strips must stop short by that amount. Instead, tucked-under edges of carpet will be tacked with a 1¼-in. tack on each side, driven into the riser–tread joint.

Padding pieces are as wide as the tackless strips are long. Butt the padding to the edge of the strips. To keep the pad from being seen from the open side of a stairway, cut the riser portion of the padding at an angle, as shown below left. Staple the padding every 3 in. to 4 in. To tuck the carpet edges, snap chalklines on the backing, 1¼ in. from the edges. Use an awl (not a utility knife) to score lightly along the lines, fold the edges under, and then weight them down for a few minutes to establish a slight crease.

Secure the bottom of the stair runner first, overlapping the carpet about ¼ in. onto the floor; push the carpet into the tackless strip at the base of the first riser. (The tackless strip on the first riser should be ¼ in. above the floor.) Press the carpet onto the strip points with a stair tool. Tack the bottom of the rolled edges onto the riser with a 1¼-in. tack at each end. Then pack the extra end of the carpet into the ¼-in. gap between the tackless strip and the floor.

To cover the first step, stretch the carpet with a knee-kicker, starting at the center of the tread. As you push the knee-kicker, use a stair tool to tamp the carpet into the riser–tread joint. Work out from the center of the step, until the carpet is attached to tackless strips along the entire joint. At the end of each side, secure the tucked-under edge with a single 1¼-in. tack. Continue up the stairs, using the knee-kicker and stair tool. If the width of the carpet varies (sometimes a tucked-under hem slips), insert an awl point in the hem and jimmy the tool to move the hem in or out.

Stair-Carpeting Details

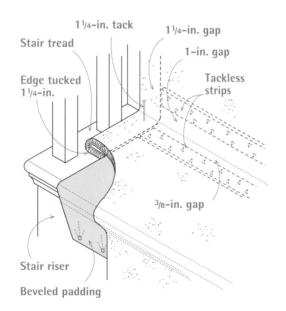

1 ¼-in. tack

1 ¼-in. gap

1-in. gap

Stair tread

Tackless strips

Edge tucked 1 ¼-in.

³/8-in. gap

Stair riser

Beveled padding

Along open stairs, allow an extra 1³/4-in. to tuck under the carpet. Angle-cut padding so it won't be visible from an open side of the stairs.

Glossary of Building Terms

This glossary contains many commonly encountered building terms. You'll find somewhat more specialized terms defined in contex in their respective chapters. For a comprehensive resource, get a copy of Francis D. K. Ching's *A Visual Dictionary of Architecture* (John Wiley & Sons).

AFCI. Arc-fault circuit interrupter. An electrical device that detects minute current fluctuations associated with arcing and instantaneously cuts power to circuits, thus preventing fires caused by loose or corroded connections, punctured cables, and so on.

Anchor bolts. Bolts used to secure a wood sill or plate to concrete or to masonry flooring or walls.

Apron. The inside trim of a window, installed against the wall immediately beneath the stool.

ASHRAE. American Society of Heating, Refrigeration, and Air-Conditioning Engineers.

Back-cut. To cut a board or a piece of molding at a slight angle so that more material is removed on the back face of the stock. Allows joints to fit tightly, (see "Back-Cutting Trim," on p. 413).

Backfill. The replacement of excavated earth in a trench around and against a basement foundation.

Balusters. Usually, small vertical members in a railing between a top rail and bottom rail or stair treads.

Balustrade. An assembly of balusters, top rail, and sometimes bottom rail. Used on the edge of stairs, balconies, decks, and porches.

Base (baseboard). A board that finishes (or trims) the joint between the bottom of the wall and the floor.

Base molding. Molding used to trim the upper edge of a baseboard.

Base shoe. On interior baseboard, molding abutting the floor. Also the bottom plate of a frame wall.

Batter board. At each corner of an excavation, one of a pair of horizontal boards forming an *L*, fastened to stakes driven into the ground. Stringlines stretched between batter-board assemblies may indicate elevation or the outlines of foundation walls.

Bay. The space between any pair of rafters, studs, or joists.

Bay window. Any window structure projecting outward from the walls of a building, either rectangular or polygonal in plan.

Beam. A structural member, usually horizontal, that supports a load.

Bearing wall. A wall that supports a vertical load in addition to its own weight.

Below grade. Below the surface of the ground, such as a basement floor.

Blind-nail. To fasten a board through its edge so the nail head isn't visible on the face of the work. For example, wood strip-flooring is usually blind-nailed through the tongue of tongue-and-groove boards.

Blocking. Dimension lumber installed to bolster framing and, in the case of floor framing, stiffen joists and reduce flexion. Also see BRIDGING.

Blueboard. Specialized drywall panel used as a base for single- or two-coat veneer plaster.

Brace. An inclined piece of framing lumber that stiffens a wall or floor. Also a temporary wall support removed after framing and sheathing are complete.

Brad nailer. A pneumatic nailer often referred to as a pin tacker.

Brick veneer. A facing of brick laid against and fastened to sheathing of a frame-wall or tile-wall construction.

Bridging (cross-bridging). Small wood or steel members installed diagonally between the top and the bottom edges of the floor joists to brace the joists and spread the action of loads. By contast, solid bridging (blocking) consists of short lengths of dimension lumber (at least 2×6s) butted perpendicularly between joists for similar effect.

Building paper. A general term for asphalt-impregnated felt paper as well as rosin papers. This term does not include plasticized materials such as Tyvek, usually referred to as housewrap.

Built-up roof (BUR). Low-pitch roofing composed of several layers—today, typically modified bitumen (MB) and fiberglass-reinforced interplies. In the old days, three to five layers of asphalt felt were laminated with coal tar, pitch, or asphalt.

Butt joint. The junction where square-cut ends of two boards meet, or where a square-cut end abuts the face or edge of another board.

Cant strip. A triangular piece of lumber used at the junction of a flat deck and a wall to prevent cracking of the roofing applied over it and to aid water runoff.

Cap. The topmost member of a column, pilaster, door, or window molding, and so on.

Cap flashing. Metal or vinyl flashing over the cap (head casing) of a window or door; crucial to divert water around the unit. Also called head flashing. (shown on p. 89).

Carriage. See STAIR CARRIAGE.

Casing. Molding of various widths and thicknesses, used to trim door and window installations.

Caulk (Caulking). Various flexible sealants intended to stop air or water penetration along building seams. *Sealant* is the term preferred by manufacturers to distinguish better-quality, more durable materials from *caulk*, a term for older, cheaper, less durable materials.

CDX. The grade of plywood most often used for roof and wall sheathing and subflooring; the *X* in CDX indicates that is has exterior-grade glues.

Checking. Cracks that appear with age in many exterior materials and paint coatings.

Chop saw. Jargon for a radial-arm saw, which makes only square crosscuts.

Collar tie. Member connecting opposite roof rafters, stiffening the roof structure and keeping rafters from spreading. Also called collar beams (see "Reinforcing a Roof," on p. 12).

Column. See POST.

Condensation. In a building, water beads or frost that accumulates on the inside of the exterior covering of a building when warm, moisture-laden air from the interior reaches the point at which it can no longer hold moisture.

Control lines. Especially useful in tiling, these are the primary layout lines that divide space into quadrants or smaller workable areas. They help in aligning joints and creating visual symmetry. Sometimes called layout axes.

Coped joint. In finish carpentry, a joint that allows two pieces of shaped molding to meet in an interior corner (see "Coping a Joint," on p. 414).

Corbel-out. To build out one or more courses of brick or stone from the face of a wall, either for decorative effect or to support elements above.

Corner bead. A strip of formed sheet metal installed on drywall or plaster corners to act as reinforcement.

Corner boards. Vertical trim along the exterior corners of a house. The ends of the siding often abut corner boards.

Corner braces. Diagonal braces at the corners of a frame structure, installed to stiffen and strengthen a wall.

Counterflashing. Two-piece flashing, consisting of base and overlapping cap pieces that keep water from entering joints around chimneys and skylights.

Cove molding. A molding with a concave face, used as trim to finish interior corners.

Crawl space. A shallow space below the living quarters of a house without a basement, normally enclosed by foundation walls and frequently dirt floored.

Cricket. A small drainage-diverting roof structure of single or double slope, placed at the junction of larger surfaces that meet at an angle, such as above a chimney. Sometimes called a saddle (see "Chimney Flashing," on p.74).

Crosscut. A saw cut across the grain of a board.

Crown molding. A usually complex molding at the top of an interior or exterior wall.

Cut-in brace. A diagonal brace notched into studs. See also LET-IN BRACE.

d. Indicates nail size. See PENNY.

Dado. A rectangular groove, usually across the width of a board or plank.

Dew point. The temperature at which a vapor begins to condense as a liquid.

Dimension lumber. Usually 2-in.-thick lumber such as 2×4s, 2×6s, and 2×8s, but not thicker than 5 in. (Wood thicker than 5 in. is called timber.) Most joists, rafters, studs, and planks are dimension lumber.

Door jamb, interior. The surrounding frame of a door, consisting of two vertical pieces called side jambs and a horizontal head (head jamb).

Dormer. A roofed structure that projects from a sloping roof, offering a vertical front wall suitable for windows.

Downspout. Vertical pipe that carries rainwater from roof gutters.

Drip cap. A molding placed on the exterior topside of a door or window frame, causing water to drip beyond the frame.

Drip-edge. A metal edge projecting along the edge of a roof that causes water to drip free of the building, rather than travel, by capillary motion, behind the siding or exterior trim (shown on p. 84).

Drip kerf. A groove under a sill that causes water to drip free from the sill rather than cling to and run down the face of a house.

Drywall. Wall and ceiling interior covering material, usually gypsum panels. Commonly called Sheetrock, after a major brand.

Ducts. Round or rectangular pipes that deliver air to and from a heating plant or air-conditioning device. Also channels that vent exhaust air driven by a kitchen or bathroom fan.

Eaves. The lowest parts of a sloped roof, overhanging a wall.

Edgebanding. A solid-wood band on the edge of a laminated panel, such as plywood.

End-wall studs. Partition studs that abut the studs in an exterior wall or another partition.

Elastomeric. A material that stays pliable during the life of its installation and is thus able to expand and contract with temperature changes.

Enamel. Any paint that dries to a hard, usually glossy finish. Because enamels are quite durable, they are often specified for trim, bathrooms, kitchens, and other high-use areas.

Face-nail. To nail into the face of a board. Also called direct nailing.

Fascia. A flat board fastened along the eaves ends of roof rafters (shown on pp. 130–133).

Female end. The receiving end of a pipe or socket.

Field. Any relatively flat, unobstructed expanse of building material.

Finish, natural. A transparent finish that largely maintains the original color or grain of wood.

Fire-stop. Located in a frame wall, usually 2×4 or 2×6 horizontal blocking between studs intended to impede the spread of fire and smoke in the event of a house fire.

Flashing. Sheet metal or other material used in roof and wall construction to shed water and protect a building from water seepage.

Flat paint. An interior paint that contains a high proportion of pigment and dries to a flat, lusterless finish.

Flue. A fire-clay (terra-cotta) or stainless-steel liner in a chimney through which smoke, gas, and fumes ascend. A chimney may have multiple flues, each dedicated to a different combustion source.

Footing. A masonry section, usually concrete, in a rectangular form wider than the bottom of the foundation wall or pier it supports.

Foundation. The supporting portion of a structure below the first-floor construction, or below grade (ground level), including footings.

Frieze. On a building exterior, a traditional trim board between the top of the siding and the soffit.

Frost line. The depth of frost penetration in soil.

Furring. Strips of wood or metal applied to a wall or another surface to even it and, normally, to serve as a fastening base for finish material.

Gable. The peaked portion of the roof above the eaves line of a double-sloped roof.

Gable end. An end wall that has a gable.

GFCI. A ground-fault circuit interrupter is a highly sensitive electrical device that detects minuscule current leaks and shuts off power instantaneously, thus greatly reducing the likelihood of fatal shocks.

Girder. A large, or the principal, beam of wood or steel used to support concentrated loads, such as joist ends, along its length.

Gloss. A paint that contains a relatively low proportion of pigment and dries to a sheen or luster. Most enamels are glossy.

Grain. The direction, size, arrangement, appearance, and quality of the fibers in wood.

Greenboard. Nickname for water-resistant drywall, named for the green coloring of its paper facing. It has a water-resistant core and water-repellent face. Also called WR board.

Grout. In masonry, a specialized mortar that seals the joints between tiles. The term is also applied to a watery mortar that is thin enough to flow into the joints and cavities of masonry work, filling them.

Gutter (rain gutter). A shallow channel of metal or wood installed below and along the eaves of a house to catch and carry rainwater to a downspout.

Hardibacker. A cementitious panel used as a substrate for tiling. Hardibacker and WonderBoard are brand names often used to refer to cement-based backer boards in general.

Header. A beam placed perpendicular to joists, to which joists are nailed, whether in framing for chimneys, stairways, or other openings. Or a beam above a door or window opening.

HEPA filter. High-efficiency particulate air filter specified for respirator-mask and vacuum filters when working with hazardous materials such as asbestos, lead paint, extreme cases of mold infestation, and the like. There are also HEPA furnace filters.

Hinge gain. A shallow slot cut into a door stile or jamb to receive a hinge plate.

Hole saw. A cylindrical saw blade that mounts to a power drill. Capable of drilling large-diameter holes such as those needed for doorknobs,

I-beam. A steel beam with a cross section resembling the letter I.

Insulation, thermal. Any material high in resistance to heat transmission that reduces the rate of heat loss when placed in the walls, ceilings, or floors.

Interior finish. Material used to cover the framing of walls and ceilings or other interior areas. Drywall and plaster are the most common interior finishes.

Jack rafter. A rafter that runs less than the distance from the ridge to a wall plate. For example, a rafter that spans the distance from the wall plate to a hip, or from a valley to a ridge.

Jamb. The elements of a door or window frame, excluding the sill; typically two side jambs and a head jamb.

Jigsaw. A portable electric saw with a thin saberlike blade that can make curved or detailed cuts in boards or panels 1 in. thick or less. Also called a saber saw.

Joint. The juncture of adjacent surfaces, whether sheet materials or framing members.

Joint compound. Generally, a ready-to-apply compound spread onto joints between drywall panels to bed joint tape, fill recessed areas, and—after several applications—hide joints so that the wall appears monolithic.

Joist. One of a series of parallel beams, such as 2×6s or 2×8s, placed on edge to support floor and ceiling loads and supported, in turn, by larger beams, girders, or bearing walls.

Kerf. A slot. A saw kerf is the thickness of its blade. A drip kerf is cut into the underside of a sill to cause water to drip free.

Laminating. Applying a plastic laminate to a core material. In framing, laminating is the nailing or bolting of two or more pieces of lumber together to increase load-carrying ability.

Lath. A thin building material of wood, metal, gypsum, or insulating board fastened to the frame of a building to serve as a plaster base.

Lav. Abbreviation for *lavatory*, a bathroom sink.

Ledger strip. A strip of lumber nailed along the side of a girder for joist ends to rest on. In deck construction, a critical horizontal frame member bolted to the house.

Let-in brace. Metal or wood braces notched into studs. Also called a cut-in brace. To stiffen wall framing, let-in braces run diagonally. By contrast, *let-in boards*, which support wall-hung sinks, run perpendicular to studs.

Light. The space in a window sash for a single pane of glass. Also a pane of glass.

Lintel. A horizontal structural member that supports the load over an opening such as a door or window. Also called a header.

Louver. An opening with a series of horizontal slats pitched to permit ventilation but exclude rain, sunlight, and unwanted viewing from outside.

Lumber, dressed size. The dimensions of lumber after it has dried and been milled. A 2×4's dressed size is actually 1½ in. by 3½ in. Also see NOMINAL DIMENSION.

Male end. The inserted end of a pipe, duct, or fitting.

Mantel. The shelf above a fireplace.

Margin. To center a window or door frame within the thickness of a wall so that frame edges are flush with finish surfaces on both sides or so that frame edges protrude equally. Centering a door or window frame in an opening is called margining the frame.

Masonry. Stone, brick, concrete, hollow tile, concrete block, gypsum block, or a combination of these materials bonded together with mortar.

MDF. Medium-density fiberboard.

Mfr. Abbreviation for *manufacturer*.

Mid-run. Midway through a pipe run, duct run, and so on.

Migration. In engineering, the unwanted movement of a jack or structural member due to the loads on it. Dangerous migration can occur if a jack is not plumb.

Millwork. Generally, any building material made of finished wood and manufactured in millwork plants and planing mills. This term applies to molding, trim, doors, window and door frames, blinds, porch-work, mantels, and so on—but normally not flooring or siding.

Mineral spirits. Solvents used to thin solvent-based paints, clean up solvent-based adhesives, and so on.

Miter joint. The joint of two pieces set at an angle that bisects the joining angle. For example, the 90° miter joint at the side and head casing of a door opening is composed of two 45° angles.

Mold. A fungal growth that feeds on organic materials such as wood and paper—as distinguished from mildew, black stains caused by mold.

Molding. Shaped wood or polymer strips used to finish a room, whether to cover gaps or add visual interest. Also called trim. (See "Common Molding Profiles" on p. 410.)

Mortise. A rectangular cavity or slot cut into the face or edge of a wood member. In wood joinery, a projecting tenon of the same size fits into the mortise. When installing door hardware, a door edge is often mortised to receive a lock case.

Mudsill. See SILL.

Mullion. A vertical bar or divider in the frame between windows, doors, or other openings.

Muntin. A small member that divides the glass or openings of a window sash or door.

Nail-protection plate. A metal plate at least ¹⁄₁₆-in. thick, nailed to a stud or joist edge to prevent screws or nails from puncturing cables or pipes running within 1¼ in. of the edge. Also called a nail plate; required by code in many instances.

NEC. The *National Electrical Code*, a book of periodically updated standards adopted by most local code authorities (published by the National Fire Protection Association).

Newel. A post to which the end of a stair railing or balustrade is fastened.

Nominal dimension. The stated size of a piece of lumber before it was dressed (milled) and shipped to the lumberyard. Thus a nominal 2×4 or 2×6 has actual dimensions less than its nominal dimensions: a 2×4 is actually 1½ in. by 3½ in.

Nonbearing wall. A wall supporting no load other than its own weight, also called a curtain wall.

Nosing. The projecting edge of a stair tread.

On center (o.c.). The measurement of spacing for studs, rafters, joists, and so on in a building from the center of one member to the center of the next one.

OSB. Oriented-strand board.

Outrigger. The extension of a rafter beyond the wall line. Usually a smaller rafter nailed to a larger one, forming a roof overhang.

Paint. A combination of pigments with suitable thinners or oils. Used as a decorative and protective coating.

Paint roller. A paint-rolling hand tool whose cylindrical rotating arm receives a napped roller cover.

Parting bead. A small wood piece in the middle of both side jambs of double-hung window frames. The beads separate upper and lower sashes and guide the sashes as they are raised and lowered. Also called a parting stop or strip.

Partition. A wall that subdivides spaces within any story of a house.

Penny. As applied to nails, originally indicated the price per hundred. Term is now a measure of nail length and is abbreviated as the letter *d*.

Pier. *A* column of masonry used to support other structural members.

Pin tacker. Nickname for a pneumatic brad nailer.

Pitch. The slope of a roof, or the ratio of the total rise to the total width of a house. Roof slope is expressed in inches of rise per 12 in. of run. A roof that rises 8 in. per 12 in. of run has an 8:12 (or 8/12) pitch.

Plaster grounds. Strips of wood used as guides or strike-off edges around window and door openings and around the base of walls.

Plate. *Sill plate:* a horizontal member anchored to a masonry wall. *Sole plate* or *shoe:* the lowest horizontal member of a frame wall. *Top plate:* the topmost horizontal member of a frame wall, which supports ceiling joists, rafters, or other members. Also see NAIL-PROTECTION PLATE.

Plow. To cut a lengthwise groove in a board or a plank.

Plumb. Perfectly vertical.

Pointing. In masonry, using a jointer or striking iron to shape and compress fresh mortar. Also called striking a joint.

Post. In engineering, a vertical structural compression member that supports loads acting in the direction of its longitudinal axis. Also called a column.

Prehung door. A door that comes prefitted to a frame, with hinges mortised to a jamb.

Preservative. Any substance that prevents the action of wood-destroying fungi or insects.

Primer. The base coat of paint, which seals the surface and minimizes absorption of subsequent coats. *Back-priming* denotes applying primer to the back sides of siding and exterior trim.

Proud. To cut a building material slightly long (or wide), for the purpose of fitting it tightly or trimming it later. The opposite of cutting a material shy. Also, material that protrudes or bows outward and needs to be trimmed back.

PVA. Polyvinyl acetate (glue).

PVC. Polyvinyl chloride is the basic compound in numerous building materials, ranging from plastic pipes to resilient (vinyl) flooring.

Quarter-round. A small molding that has the cross section of a quarter circle.

Rabbet. A rectangular, longitudinal groove cut in the edge of a board or a plank.

Rafter. One of a series of structural members of a roof designed to support roof loads.

Rafter, valley. A rafter that forms the intersection of an internal roof angle. Valley rafters are usually doubled 2-in.-thick members.

Rail. Horizontal structural members of panel doors, window sashes, cabinet frames, or wainscoting. Also the sloping or horizontal members of a balustrade or staircase extending from one vertical support (such as a post) to another.

Rake. On a sloping roof, trim or framing members that run parallel to the slope and define the outer edges. Rake boards usually project beyond end walls (see "Building Terms," on p. 6).

Repointing. In masonry, repairing deteriorated mortar joints by cutting back old mortar and then packing and pointing (shaping) new mortar into the joint. Also called tuck-pointing.

Respirator mask. A nose-and-mouth mask with replaceable cartridge filters capable of filtering out noxious fumes, harmful chemicals, and so on. As distinguished from a mere paper dust mask.

Reveal. In finish carpentry, the amount (usually, ¼ in.) that a casing edge is set back from a jamb edge. In addition to creating visual interest, reveals spare carpenters the frustrating task aligning board edges that are rarely perfectly straight.

Ridge. The horizontal line, usually at the top of the roof, where sloping roof planes meet.

Ridgeboard. The board placed on edge at the ridge of the roof, to which the upper ends of rafters are fastened.

Rim joist. Outermost joists, which create a kind of box around the joist grid. Rim joists sit on a mudsill.

Rip. To cut with the grain of a board, thereby reducing the board's width. Reducing the width of any board is called ripping it down.

Rise. In stairs, the vertical height of a step or flight of stairs.

Riser. Each of several vertical boards used to close spaces between stair treads.

Roll roofing. Roofing material composed of asphalt-saturated fiber, supplied in 36-in.-wide rolls, with 108 sq. ft. of material.

Roofover. Applying a new layer of roofing over an existing one.

Roof sheathing. Fastened atop rafters, boards or panels on which shingles or other roof coverings are laid.

Rough opening (RO). A framed opening in a wall, roof, or floor platform.

Run. In stairs, the front-to-back depth of an individual stair or the horizontal distance covered by a flight of stairs.

Saddle. See CRICKET.

Sash. A frame containing one or more lights of glass.

Sash balance. A device, usually operated by a spring or a weight, designed to counter-balance the weight of a window sash so it doesn't come crashing down.

Screed. A straight wood or metal strip drawn across concrete, plaster, or a mortar bed to create a flat surface. Also strips embedded in those materials and acting as thickness gauges.

Scribing. Using a compass or scribing tool to transfer the outline of irregular shapes onto woodwork or onto sheet materials such as drywall or resilient flooring.

Sealer. A finishing material, clear or pigmented, usually applied directly over uncoated wood to seal the surface. Distinct from *sealant*, which is the term manufacturers use for their better grades of seam and crack sealants, commonly called caulk.

Semigloss paint. A paint that has some luster but that isn't particularly glossy.

Set. To sink a nail below a surface.

Shake. A thick, hand-split shingle.

Shear wall. A wall reinforced to withstand sideways (shear) forces from wind, soil loads, or earthquakes.

Sheathing. Structural panels such as plywood or boards, attached to framing members to strengthen the structure, and provide a base for roofing, siding, and flooring.

Shy. To cut something slightly short.

Siding. The exterior cladding of a house, whether made of wood clapboards or shingles, stucco, metal, or vinyl lap siding, and so on.

Sill. In framing (here, a mudsill), the lowest member of the frame of a structure, which rests on the foundation and supports floor joists and frame walls. Also, the bottom of a door or window opening or unit. The exterior portion of a doorsill or windowsill is often pitched to shed water.

Sleeper. Usually, a wood member embedded in or placed on concrete, to which subflooring or flooring is attached.

Soffit. The underside of an overhang, especially at the eaves of a roof (shown on p. 130).

Soil stack. In plumbing, the vertical main of a system of soil, waste, or vent piping.

Sole (sole plate). See PLATE.

Span. The distance between structural supports, such as walls, columns, piers, beams, girders, and trusses.

Speed Square. Another one of those brand names—this one owned by the Swanson Company—that must be driving its trademark lawyers crazy. That is, virtually everybody who uses Swanson's tool or a lookalike calls their tool a *speed square*. This small framing square with reinforced edges is in every carpenter's tool belt—or should be. A great tool.

Splash block. A small masonry block placed beneath a downspout to carry water away from the building.

Square. A standard unit of measure—100 sq. ft.—usually applied to roofing materials. In measurement, two adjacent pieces that join in a 90° angle.

Stair carriage. Supporting member for stair treads. Usually of dimension lumber run diagonally, on-edge, and notched to receive the treads.

Step-flashing. L-shaped pieces of metal flashing, typically interwoven with shingle courses, to deflect water from roof dormers, chimneys, skylights, and the like (shown on p. 75).

Stile. A vertical structural member in a panel door, sash, cabinet frame, or wainscoting.

Stock. The basic materials from which a building element is fashioned. For example, stair carriages may be cut from 2×12 stock, or window cap flashing may be cut from 26-gauge aluminum stock.

Stool. A flat, horizontal molding at the bottom of a finished window, the part often adorned with small flower pots. Usually rabbeted on the underside and fitted over the inside edge of a windowsill.

Story pole (story board). A straight board marked off in uniform increments, to aid in layout. Story poles are used to mark siding intervals (see drawing on p. 136) and to help establish tile and joint intervals (see photo on p. 395).

Striking a joint. See POINTING.

Strip flooring. Solid wood flooring that is typically ¾ in. thick by 2¼ in. wide, with matched tongue-and-groove edges.

Stringers. In stairs, the supports on which stair treads rest. More or less synonymous with *carriage.*

Strong. To cut something a bit long. Also see PROUD.

Strong-Ties. Various steel lumber-connectors such as reinforcing plates, straps, clips, hangers, brackets, and so on. Pioneered by the Simpson Company, Strong-Tie Connectors have become the generic name for the category.

Stub-outs. Plumbing pipes that protrude into an unfinished room.

Stucco. An exterior plaster made with portland cement as its base.

Stud. One of a series of wood or metal, vertical structural members in walls and partitions. Wood studs are usually 2×4s, though 2×6s are also used.

Subfloor. Plywood panels or 1-in. boards installed over joists to support a finish floor. A subfloor may also be covered with underlayment.

Suspended ceiling. A ceiling system hung from overhead structural framing.

Tack rag. A slightly sticky cheesecloth pad that adheres dust and is used between sandings.

Taillight warranty. Any warranty that expires when the contractor's truck leaves your driveway.

Tail pieces. Pipe ends.

Termite shield. A shield, usually of corrosion-resistant metal, placed in or on a foundation wall or other mass of masonry or around pipes to prevent termite migration.

Thinset mortar. A thin, cement-based setting material (adhesive) troweled onto a mortar setting bed or substrate, to adhere tiles. Thinset formulations vary.

Threshold. A strip of wood or metal with beveled edges, installed over the sill of an exterior door or over the gap between finish flooring and the doorsill.

Tie-down. A metal connector used to keep lumber joints from separating during hurricanes, high winds, or other conditions of excessive stress. Also called hurricane tie. Also see STRONG-TIES.

Toenail. To drive a nail at an angle other than 90°, thereby increasing its resistance to pull out.

Tread. A horizontal board in a stairway that receives foot traffic.

Trim. Essentially the same as molding. Also, to install door and window casing, baseboards, crown molding, and so on.

Trimmer. In a rough opening, any structural member fastened side by side to a like member, thus doubling it for added strength. Hence trimmer studs, trimmer joists, and trimmer rafters.

Truss. A frame or jointed structure of smaller elements designed to span long distances. Roof trusses, for example, can be engineered to support great loads.

Tuck-pointing. See REPOINTING.

UBC. Uniform Building Code.

UPC. Uniform Plumbing Code.

Underlayment panels. Specified for resilient flooring, a layer—over the subflooring—designed to add rigidity to the subflooring and provide a smooth surface for the thin finish layer that follows.

Utility knife. A knife with sturdy, razor-sharp retractable, replaceable blades and a hollow handle for storing them.

Valley. The internal angle formed by the junction of two sloping sides of a roof.

Vapor barrier. Impermeable material such as polyethylene sheeting used to retard the movement of water vapor into walls and thus prevent condensation within them.

Vent. A pipe or duct that allows air to flow in or out.

VOC. Volatile organic compound; typically, a noxious solvent in solvent-based finishes or adhesives. You should wear a respirator mask with VOC-rated filters when working with VOCs.

VSR. Variable-speed reversible (drill).

Wallcovering. Formerly *wallpaper*, the collective term for any decorative sheet material adhered to walls, including paper, vinyl, foil, cloth, cork, and bamboo.

Weatherstripping. Narrow lengths of spring metal, vinyl tubing, or other materials designed to prevent air and moisture infiltration around windows and doors.

Wick. To draw moisture by capillary action.

Wythe. The width of a brick and one mortar joint.

Index

Credits

Unless noted below, all photos appearing in *Renovation* are by Michael W. Litchfield and Ken Gutmaker; all drawings are by Vincent Babak.

Chapter 1

p. 4: Photo by Michael W. Litchfield.

p. 7–8, 10–14, 16 : Photos by Roger Robinson.

Chapter 2

p. 29: Photo by Dean Rutherford.

p. 31: Remodel by Gary Earl Parsons, Architect.

p. 32: (left top to bottom and inset) Photos by Steve Rynerson.

Chapter 4

p. 61: Illustration courtesy Simpson Storng-Tie.

Chapter 5

p. 70: Photo by Roe A. Osborn, courtesy of *Fine Homebuilding*, © The Taunton Press, Inc.

Chapter 6

p. 125: Drawing adapted from an original by Velux.

Chapter 7

p. 131: Photo by Roe A. Osborn, courtesy of *Fine Homebuilding*, © The Taunton Press, Inc.

p. 139: Photo by Charles Miller, courtesy of *Fine Homebuilding*, © The Taunton Press, Inc.

Chapter 8

p. 131: Photo courtesy of Simpson Strong-Tie Co., Inc.

p. 176: Photo by Roe A. Osborn, courtesy of *Fine Homebuilding*, © The Taunton Press, Inc.

p. 181: Photo by Tom O'Brien, courtesy of *Fine Homebuilding*, © The Taunton Press, Inc.

Chapter 9

p. 183: Photo courtesy Bon Tool Co., www.bontool.com.

p. 189: Photos by Rosmarie Hausherr.

p. 190 (left): Photo courtesy Bon Tool Company.

p. 193: Photo courtesy Roger Robinson, Star Inspection Group.

Chapter 10

p. 202 (top): Photo courtesy David Peterson Construction.

p. 205 (right): Photo courtesy Simpson Strong®-Tie Company, Inc.

p. 213: (bottom left) Drawing adapted from Rob Thallon's *Graphic Guide to Frame Construction*, The Taunton Press.

Chapter 12

p. 265: Drawing adapted from Architectural Graphic Standards, Ramsey/Sleeper, 6th edition, ©1986, Reprinted with permission of John Wiley & Sons, Inc.

p. 279: Photos courtesy Watts-Radiant, www.waterpex.com.

p. 288: Photo courtesy Simpson Strong-Tie Co., Inc.

Chapter 13

p. 300: Kitchen designed by John Malick, Malick & Associates, Architect.

p. 312: (bottom) Photos courtesy David Edrington, Architect.

p. 322: (left) Photo courtesy David Edrington, Architect

p. 323: (top) Design and tile work by Dean Rutherford; (bottom left) Steve Rynerson, architect; Riley Doty, tile and stone work.

p. 325: John Larson, Jarvis Architects.

p. 326: (top right) John Larson, Jarvis Architects.

Chapter 14

p. 333: Photos by Roger Robinson.

Chapter 15

p. 365: (top) Photo by Mark Kozlowski, courtesy Myron Ferguson's *Drywall,* The Taunton Press.

p. 376: Photo courtesy Myron Ferguson's *Drywall,* The Taunton Press.

Chapter 16

p. 377: Dean Rutherford, design and tile work.

p. 398: Photo by Rosmarie Hausherr.

Chapter 17

p. 411: (bottom right) Photos courtesy Style Solutions/ Balmer Architectural Molding.

p. 429: (bottom) Photo by Charles Bickford, courtesy of *Fine Homebuilding,* © The Taunton Press, Inc.

p. 432: Photo by James Kidd, courtesy of *Fine Homebuilding,* © The Taunton Press, Inc.

Chapter 18

p. 443: Photo by Tom O'Brien, courtesy of *Fine Homebuilding,* © The Taunton Press, Inc.

p. 457: Photo courtesy Behr/Rohm & Haas.

p. 460: Photo courtesy American International Tool, Inc.

p. 462: (bottom) Photo by Tom O'Brien, courtesy of *Fine Homebuilding,* © The Taunton Press, Inc.

Chapter 20

p. 485: Photo by Albert Lewis, courtesy Smith & Fong Plyboo®.

p. 496: (top right) Photo by Charles Bickford, courtesy of *Fine Homebuilding,* © The Taunton Press, Inc.